San Francisco

© Robert Holmes

"What is this mysterious amalgam that keeps on working?
There is no plan, certainly, and never was.
It is almost in the realm of the metaphysical:
a brew of gold rushes and silver bonanzas,
sailing ships and shrouded dawns, overnight fortunes
and brilliant disasters, bootleg gin, champagne suppers,
minestrone and Peking Duck, new-old, beautiful-ugly
—a city like no other, sea-girt, Bay-blocked
and wide open to the winds and the wildest ideas,
none so wild that an audience can't be found.
Sometimes tacky, sometimes tawdry, often dirty and too
often heedless—and yet, even in the current explosion
of Plastic Inevitable, strong enough in personality
to anthropomorphize: San Francisco lives!"

San Francisco Chronicle columnist Herb Caen (1967)

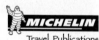

Travel Publications

Michelin North America
One Parkway South, Greenville SC 29615, U.S.A.
☎ 1-800-423-0485
www.michelin-travel.com
TheGreenGuide-us@us.michelin.com

Manufacture française des pneumatiques Michelin
Société en commandite par actions au capital de 2 000 000 000 de francs
Place des Carmes-Déchaux – 63 Clermont-Ferrand (France)
R.C.S. Clermont-Fd B 855 200 507

Dépôt légal Mai 2001 – ISBN 2-06-000880-8 – ISSN 0763-1383
Printed in France 05-01/3.1

Typesetting: NORD COMPO, Villeneuve-d'Ascq
Printing: LE SANGLIER, Charleville-Mézières
Binding: S.I.R.C., Marigny-le-Châtel

Cover design: Carré Noir, Paris 17ᵉ arr.

THE GREEN GUIDE:
The Spirit of Discovery

*The exhilaration of new horizons,
the fun of seeing the world,
the excitement of discovery:
this is what we seek to share with you.
To help you make the most of your
travel experience, we offer first-hand
knowledge and turn a discerning eye
on places to visit.
This wealth of information
gives you the expertise to plan
your own enriching adventure.
With THE GREEN GUIDE
showing you the way, you can explore
new destinations with confidence
or rediscover old ones.
Leisure time spent with THE GREEN
GUIDE is also a time for refreshing
your spirit, enjoying yourself,
and taking advantage
of our selection of fine restaurants,
hotels and other places for relaxing.
So turn the page and open a window
on the world. Join THE GREEN GUIDE
in the spirit of discovery.*

Contents

Stick Style Architecture

© Robert Holmes

Chinatown

City Lights Bookstore

Maps and plans

COMPANION PUBLICATIONS

Map 493 Western USA and Canada

Large-format map providing detailed road systems; includes driving distances, interstate rest stops, border crossings and interchanges.

– Comprehensive city and town index

– Scale 1:2,400,000 (1in = approx. 38mi)

Map 930 USA Road Map

Covers principal US road network while also presenting shaded relief detail of overall physiography of the land.

– State flags with statistical data and state tourism office telephone numbers

– Scale: 1:3,450,000

Map 933 USA Recreational

Descriptive section with color photos and profiles of 51 national parks complements a fold-out map of the US designating 500 parks, monuments, historic sites, scenic rivers and other recreational points of interest.

San Francisco (1868)

LIST OF MAPS AND PLANS

Using this guide

The guide is organized into five areas, San Francisco's Downtown, Bayshore, Central Neighborhood, Southern Neighborhoods and Oceanfront. Excursions from the city include East Bay, Marin County, the Wine Country and South Bay and Peninsula. Within these sections, each **Entry Heading** is followed by public transportation information, a map reference; tourist information phone number and web site when available; and population figure (where applicable).

● Following the names of sights mentioned in this guide you will find useful information in *italics*: sight location addresses, recommended visiting times, opening hours, admission charges, telephone numbers and web addresses. Symbols used in sight, descriptions include: ⚬ wheelchair access, ✗ on-site eating facilities, ⚠ camping facilities, ⓟ on-site parking and ⒦⒤⒟ sights of special interest to children. There are also symbols which indicate cable car ☐, Muni ⓜⓤⓝⓘ, and BART ⓑⓐ lines that access the area.

● Many entries contain **digressions**, entertaining breaks from sightseeing, that are marked by a purple bar. Those digressions that appear on a map within the guide are indicated by a purple dot ❶ with the number identifying it on the map.

● The Address Book Section, edged with a marbleized band, at the front of the guide features detailed information about hotels, restaurants, entertainment, shopping, sightseeing, sports and recreational opportunities.

At the back of the guide, the section of blue pages offers **Practical Information** on planning your trip, getting there and getting around and tips for international visitors. You will also find more **Practical Information** blue pages throughout the guide offering more information on visiting that certain area.

We welcome corrections and suggestions that may assist us in preparing the next edition. Please send your comments to:

Michelin Travel Publications
Editorial Department
P. O. Box 19001
Greenville, SC 29602-9001
Email: TheGreenGuide-us@us.michelin.com
Web site: www.michelin-travel.com

Nikolay Zurek/Tony Stone Images

Legend

Sight Symbols

Walking tour with departure point and direction

	Cable car terminus, line		Building described – Other
	Mission	▪	Small building
	Church, chapel		Lighthouse
B	Letter locating a sight	⊚	Fountain
▪ ▲	Other points of interest		Park described – Other
▪	Statue, monument		Wooded park described – Other
	Panorama – View		Cemetery described – Other

All maps are oriented north, unless otherwise indicated by a directional arrow.

Other Symbols

	Interstate Highway		US Highway		Other Route
	Highway, interchange				Visitor information
	Toll road, bridge				Gift shop
	Tunnel with ramp				Restrooms
	One way street				Elevator
	Pedestrian street – Steps	P			Parking
	Shopping street				Post office
	Airport – Bus station				Gate
	Passenger ferry – Cruise				Golf course – Stadium
●	Subway station	❶			Digressions *(see text opposite)*

Principal Sights

CITY OF SAN FRANCISCO

4 ★★ NOB HILL Principal section in guide
★★★ Highly recommended
★★ Recommended
★ Interesting

★★★ ALCATRAZ

★ Treasure Island

0   1 mi
0   2 km

10 ★★★ FISHERMAN'S WHARF

★★★ LOMBARD STREET

★★★ COIT TOWER

5 ★★ NORTH BEACH

6 ★ RUSSIAN HILL

★★ Transamerica Pyramid

9 ★ THE EMBARCADERO

4 ★★ NOB HILL

3 ★★ FINANCIAL DISTRICT

1 ★★★ CHINATOWN

16 JAPANTOWN

7 ★ UNION SQUARE AREA

★★ San Francisco Museum of Modern Art

2 ★ CIVIC CENTER

22 ★★ YERBA BUENA GARDENS

★★ PACIFIC BELL PARK

21 SOUTH OF MARKET

SAN FRANCISCO BAY

China Basin

Central Basin

★ BASIC BROWN BEAR FACTORY

■ Anchor Brewing

20 ★ MISSION DISTRICT

CASTRO DISTRICT & NOE VALLEY

India Basin

South Basin

■ 3Com Park

Candlestick Point

Cloverdale

Lake Sonoma

Healdsburg

Calistoga

Guerneville

35 ★ **UPPER SONOMA-RUSSIAN RIVER REGION**

St. Helena

Santa Rosa

33 ★★ **NAPA VALLEY**

Rutherford

Oakville

Sebastopol

Yountville

Vacaville

Bodega Bay

34 ★★ **SONOMA VALLEY**

Sonoma

Napa

Fairfield

★ **Petaluma**

Point Reyes Station

30 ★★ **POINT REYES NATIONAL SEASHORE**

Novato

San Pablo Bay

Six Flags Marine World ★

Vallejo

Grizzly Bay

Vallejo Naval & Historical Museum

Benicia

Martinez

Concord

★ **John Muir NHS**

29 ★★ **MOUNT TAMALPAIS**

Bolinas

2571

32 ★★ **TIBURON & ANGEL ISLAND**

Lindsay Mus. ■

Walnut Creek

27 ★ **AROUND THE EAST BA**

3849

★ **Mt. Diab SP**

31 ★ **SAUSALITO**

25 ★★ **BERKELEY**

Alamo

Danville

28 ★★ **MARIN HEADLANDS**

★ **Eugene O'Neill NHS**

26 ★ **OAKLAND**

Oakland Zoo

Blackhawk Automotive Museum ★

SAN FRANCISCO

Alameda

Western Aerospace Museum

★ **Dunsmuir House**

Hayward

San Francisco Bay

Pacifica

Point San Pedro

Coyote Point Museum

Ardenwood Historic Farm

Fremont

Santa José

★ **James V. Fitzgerald Marine Reserve**

Moss Beach

Hiller Aviation Museum

★ **Don Edwards SF Bay NWR**

Point Montara Lighthouse

Princeton

Pillar Point Harbor

Filoli

36 ★ **PALO ALTO**

★ **Intel Museum**

Half Moon Bay

Woodside

Francis State Beach

Stanford University

Triton Museum of Art

38 **SAN MATEO COUNTY COAST**

San Gregorio

37 ★ **SAN JOS**

San Gregorio State Beach

Pescadero State Beach

Pescadero Marsh Natural Preserve

Pescadero

Los Gatos

Pebble Beach

★ **Pigeon Point Lighthouse**

Boulder Creek

★ **Año Nuevo State Reserve**

Davenport

PACIFIC OCEAN

Principal Sights
SAN FRANCISCO BAY AREA

Santa Cruz

Monterey Bay

25 ★★ **BERKELEY**   Principal section in guide

★★★   Highly recommended

★★   Recommended

★   Interesting

0   10 mi
0   20 km

How to Spend Your Days in the City by the Bay

If you have just **one day** free in San Francisco:

The **Barbary Coast Trail** is a great introduction to the city, a 3.8mi urban hike that leads through five distinctive neighborhoods and 150 years of history. Grab an espresso at **Union Square*** and walk up Grant Avenue to bustling **Chinatown*****. Local Chinese throng to its markets early. Bronze medallions embedded in the sidewalks guide you into the skyscraping **Financial District****, whose fine architecture tops out in the **Transamerica Pyramid****. The city's tallest structure looms over **Jackson Square****, preserving the last remnants of San Francisco's bawdy Gold Rush-era Barbary Coast. Proceed down Columbus Avenue through the heart of **North Beach****, the "little Italy" that was the heart and soul of the 1950s' Beat Generation.

After lunch, climb Telegraph Hill to **Coit Tower*****, an Art Deco-era landmark with memorable views: Directly to the west, **Lombard Street*****, "the crookedest street in the world," winds down **Russian Hill***. Take the **Filbert Steps**** downhill to **The Embarcadero***, and follow the bayshore byway north to **Fisherman's Wharf*****. No longer mainly a commercial fishing terminal, the Wharf deserves exploration for its shopping centers and the historic ships docked here, including the three-masted **Balclutha**** and the **USS Pampanito****. If you've booked ahead, you can take a tour boat to the former prison island of **Alcatraz*****. As time allows, return to Union Square via cable car over **Nob Hill****, pausing en route to visit the **Cable Car Museum**** and the historic **Fairmont Hotel****.

If you have a **second day** in San Francisco:

Make tracks west to **Golden Gate Park*****, where the new M.H. de Young Memorial Museum is under construction. Until October 2001, the world-class **Asian Art Museum***** is a priority. (It soon will move to the Civic Center.) Also recommended are the **Japanese Tea Garden****, **California Academy of Sciences**** and **Strybing Arboretum****. If it's sunny and warm, you may want to pick up a takeaway lunch in nearby **Haight-Ashbury**, which still bears the flavor of its late-60s hippie denizens, and dine on the park's vast lawns. Then head north up Arguello Boulevard to **The Presidio****, a lush and historic former military base now administered by the National Park Service. Exit east into the **Marina District***, whose **Palace of Fine Arts**** holds the **Exploratorium**** science museum.

If you have a **third day** in San Francisco:

Yerba Buena Gardens** is a short walk south of Union Square. Between the Gardens' Center for the Arts and the impressive **San Francisco Museum of Modern Art****, this is "museum central." Don't miss **The Friends of Photography at the Ansel Adams Center*** or the **Metreon*** complex. After lunch, take a cab to the **Civic Center***, a First World War-era Beaux-Art complex that includes the magnificent **City Hall**** and a major performing-arts complex. Nearby neighborhoods of interest include **Japantown**, with its temples and shopping center, and **Pacific Heights****, whose hillside estates include the **Haas-Lilienthal House****.

If you have **a week** in San Francisco:

Spend a day in **Marin County**, crossing the famous **Golden Gate Bridge***** in the morning to the **Marin Headlands**** for incomparable city-skyline views before fog sets in. Meander downhill to the charming bayside town of **Sausalito***, finding lunch at a quaint cafe. Then follow Highway 1 to **Muir Woods National Monument***** and its majestic redwood grove. After a walk in the woods, drive to the summit of **Mount Tamalpais State Park**** for another remarkable Bay Area view. With an extra day, you could continue up Highway 1 to **Point Reyes National Seashore****, its wind-whipped lighthouse a beacon for generations of sailors.

Devote another day to the East Bay. Cross the **San Francisco-Oakland Bay Bridge**** and head first to **Berkeley****, home of the **University of California****. Center to the Free Speech Movement of the 1960s, the campus has several fine museums and **The Campanile**** bell tower. Then visit **Oakland***, whose historic highlights include the Art-Moderne **Paramount Theatre****. The **Oakland Museum of California**** has outstanding collections of history, natural history and especially art.

Don't miss an excursion to the **Napa Valley**** and **Sonoma Valley**** Wine Country. Besides myriad world-famous wineries in these valleys, within a 2hr drive of San Francisco, are numerous cultural and historical attractions. The town of **Sonoma**** itself fomented the spark of California freedom from Mexico.

Travel down the San Francisco Peninsula to the home of high technology, the Silicon Valley. Visit **Stanford University**** in Palo Alto, the **Intel Museum**** in Santa Clara, **The Tech Museum of Innovation**** and other sites in San Jose. En route, stop at the marvelous estate and gardens of **Filoli****, near Woodside.

More time to kill? There are neighborhoods of San Francisco that you haven't touched yet. **Mission Dolores***, the city's birthplace, is the heart of the vibrant Latino cultural neighborhood known as the **Mission District***. The city's highly respected gay population calls the **Castro District** home. Near Land's End sits the **California Palace of the Legion of Honor**** with its fine collection of European art.

View of San Francisco from Mount Tamalpais

Introduction

Landscapes

San Francisco boasts an incomparable setting of mountains, hills and water at the tip of a long peninsula forming the western boundary of a 496sq mi bay. Its dramatic topography, its agreeable climate and the pervasive presence of the sea have invited exploration and provided enjoyment for centuries. San Francisco Bay itself was immensely important in the city's early development as the commercial and cultural hub of the western United States.

Topography

The hills and valleys that characterize San Francisco and the Bay Area (as the surrounding region is known) form part of the **Coast Ranges**, a low but rugged belt of mountains extending from Santa Barbara County north to Oregon. Prominent Bay Area

SPOT Satellite Image, July 8, 1985, 10:30am — Nigel Press/Tony Stone Images

summits include **Mt. Tamalpais** (2,571ft), which looms over Marin County to the north; **Mt. Diablo** (3,849ft), which backdrops the hills of Oakland to the east; and **Mt. Hamilton** (4,213ft), which lies southeast of the city near San Jose. Heights within the city include Mt. Davidson (929ft), Twin Peaks (922ft and 904ft) and Mt. Sutro (908ft). San Francisco's famed steep streets came of an early planner's unwillingness to depart from the strict, perpendicular street grids that were the standard of the day. In 1847, on the bare hills of the infant city, surveyor Jasper O'Farrell imposed a resolutely rectangular grid. The result: a host of streets that abruptly ascend a hill, crest, then plummet vertiginously down the other side. Several commanding hilltops remained squatter settlements and goat pastures until the invention of the cable car made it possible for the well-to-do to get up and down. Later development in the city's environs took topography into account, so that in the hills of Berkeley, Oakland and other Bay Area towns, most streets sensibly follow the natural contours of the land.

Not all of San Francisco's original hills exist today, nor does much of its natural bay shoreline. Beginning in the 1850s, small prominences were leveled or terraced to

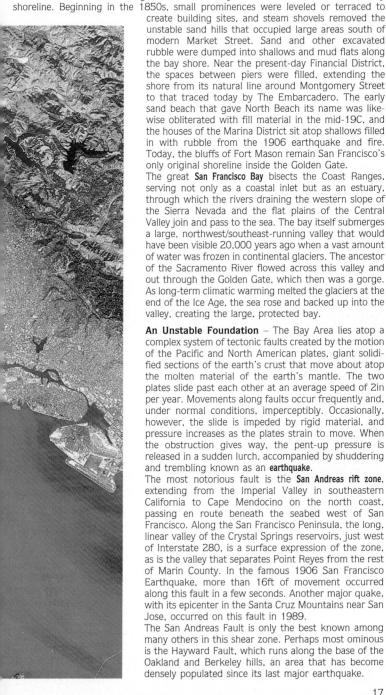

create building sites, and steam shovels removed the unstable sand hills that occupied large areas south of modern Market Street. Sand and other excavated rubble were dumped into shallows and mud flats along the bay shore. Near the present-day Financial District, the spaces between piers were filled, extending the shore from its natural line around Montgomery Street to that traced today by The Embarcadero. The early sand beach that gave North Beach its name was likewise obliterated with fill material in the mid-19C, and the houses of the Marina District sit atop shallows filled in with rubble from the 1906 earthquake and fire. Today, the bluffs of Fort Mason remain San Francisco's only original shoreline inside the Golden Gate.

The great **San Francisco Bay** bisects the Coast Ranges, serving not only as a coastal inlet but as an estuary, through which the rivers draining the western slope of the Sierra Nevada and the flat plains of the Central Valley join and pass to the sea. The bay itself submerges a large, northwest/southeast-running valley that would have been visible 20,000 years ago when a vast amount of water was frozen in continental glaciers. The ancestor of the Sacramento River flowed across this valley and out through the Golden Gate, which then was a gorge. As long-term climatic warming melted the glaciers at the end of the Ice Age, the sea rose and backed up into the valley, creating the large, protected bay.

An Unstable Foundation – The Bay Area lies atop a complex system of tectonic faults created by the motion of the Pacific and North American plates, giant solidified sections of the earth's crust that move about atop the molten material of the earth's mantle. The two plates slide past each other at an average speed of 2in per year. Movements along faults occur frequently and, under normal conditions, imperceptibly. Occasionally, however, the slide is impeded by rigid material, and pressure increases as the plates strain to move. When the obstruction gives way, the pent-up pressure is released in a sudden lurch, accompanied by shuddering and trembling known as an **earthquake**.

The most notorious fault is the **San Andreas rift zone**, extending from the Imperial Valley in southeastern California to Cape Mendocino on the north coast, passing en route beneath the seabed west of San Francisco. Along the San Francisco Peninsula, the long, linear valley of the Crystal Springs reservoirs, just west of Interstate 280, is a surface expression of the zone, as is the valley that separates Point Reyes from the rest of Marin County. In the famous 1906 San Francisco Earthquake, more than 16ft of movement occurred along this fault in a few seconds. Another major quake, with its epicenter in the Santa Cruz Mountains near San Jose, occurred on this fault in 1989.

The San Andreas Fault is only the best known among many others in this shear zone. Perhaps most ominous is the Hayward Fault, which runs along the base of the Oakland and Berkeley hills, an area that has become densely populated since its last major earthquake.

Climate

San Francisco's cool, dry summers and its mild, wet winters are characteristic of a Mediterranean climate—accentuated by the peculiarities of the city's location. The high mountains of the Sierra Nevada, to the east, block the frigid air masses that sweep across the rest of the United States. The Pacific Ocean, to the west, has a regulating effect on temperature extremes: San Francisco registers the lowest mean summer temperature of any city in the US outside of Alaska, and rarely sees a winter frost. Snow has accumulated in the downtown area only twice in the city's recorded history, both in the 1880s (although there have been flurries as recently as 1999).

Although seasonal temperature variation is remarkably slight, weather within the city—and throughout the Bay Area—is greatly affected by microclimates that result from the hilly topography. The dip of a mountain ridge or change in proximity to the ocean can create pronounced variations in weather between neighborhoods; temperatures may vary as much as 35°F between coast and inland areas. The staggered ridges of the Coast Ranges confine the chilling effect of the Pacific to a rather narrow frontage along the coast, and on the East Bay shore directly opposite the Golden Gate. A short distance east across the hills or south along the peninsula, towns broil under a brilliant sun.

One of the principal factors in San Francisco's cool summers is the city's renowned **fog**, created as westerly winds, laden with moisture from the Pacific, cross the cold California Current. The moisture condenses, creating dramatic rivers and banks of fog that flow suddenly over the city from the west, turning a brilliant day into a gloomy one within minutes. Such "advection fog" often forms a dense but shallow layer that hugs the ground and leaves higher elevations clear. In summer, fog typically builds during the day over the coast, then pours over the hills and through the Golden Gate, shrouding the Sunset District and other coastal neighborhoods in a dense gray mist while leaving other precincts with blue skies.

Most rain falls between November and April. In summer, atmospheric circulation causes a cell of high pressure to settle towards the earth's surface, suppressing upward convection that might form rain clouds and deflecting fronts and storms into the Pacific Northwest. In winter, this high-pressure cell moves south and allows storms in, bringing rain, sometimes for days on end.

Morning Fog Over San Fancisco Bay

Vegetation

As with the human population, much of the Bay Area's plant life originated elsewhere. The vast expanses of grass that shroud the "golden hills" are mostly European wild oats, seeds of which stowed away in bags of wheat sent to Spanish missions; once rooted, they crowded out the indigenous bunch grasses. The eucalyptus trees that perfume many a park, campus and backyard were imported from Australia in the 1860s as a potential new source of construction timber, although the experiment proved a failure. California's one native species of palm is found only in the southern part of the state; most palms now visible in the Bay Area come from the Canary Islands and other places.

Indigenous features of the plant landscape include stately **live oaks**, which grow widely spaced on grassy hillsides in the warmer and drier parts of the Bay Area. Coast redwoods, which live more than 2,000 years and grow to heights above 300ft, thrive in cooler and moister sites nearer the ocean.

Also typical of Bay Area landscapes are dense thickets of **chaparral**, formed not of a single plant but of an association of native species (including poison oak). The shrubby plants grow during wet winters, then survive the dry summers by minimizing water loss through leathery leaves and concentrated sap. As the chaparral dries in late summer, it becomes highly flammable, a perfect fuel for brush fires that periodically sweep over the hills, destroying houses and sometimes entire neighborhoods. The plants themselves are adapted to grow back quickly after a fire from burls below ground level.

■ San Francisco on Camera

San Francisco's quirky film history began in 1872 when Eadweard Muybridge, a Bay Area photographer, put together (at the request of Leland Stanford) a rapid succession of still photographs to prove that a running horse at one period of his stride has all four feet off the ground. Since then, directors from Erich von Stroheim to John Huston to Alfred Hitchcock to Francis Ford Coppola have used San Francisco's glorious cityscapes as the backdrop for numerous productions, from big-budget Hollywood blockbusters to smaller, independent films.

A selection of movies starring San Francisco:

Barbary Coast (1935)

After the Thin Man (1936)

San Francisco (1936)

The Sisters (1938)

The Maltese Falcon (1941)

Dark Passage (1947)

I Remember Mama (1948)

The Glenn Miller Story (1954)

Vertigo (1958)

The Birdman of Alcatraz (1962)

Guess Who's Coming to Dinner (1967)

The Graduate (1967)

Bullitt (1968)

They Call Me Mister Tibbs (1970)

Dirty Harry (1971)

Butterflies are Free (1972)

The Streets of San Francisco (1972)

What's Up, Doc? (1972)

The Towering Inferno (1974)

High Anxiety (1977)

Foul Play (1978)

Invasion of the Body Snatchers (1978)

Escape from Alcatraz (1979)

Time After Time (1979)

Serial (1980)

9 to 5 (1980)

Chan is Missing (1982)

48 Hrs (1982)

Times of Harvey Milk (1983)

Jagged Edge (1985)

Star Trek 4: The Voyage Home (1986)

The Presidio (1988)

Pacific Heights (1990)

Dogfight (1991)

Basic Instinct (1992)

The Joy Luck Club (1993)

Mrs. Doubtfire (1993)

When a Man Loves a Woman (1994)

The Rock (1996)

History

Native Americans began settling the Bay Area around the 11C BC, building small villages of brush and tule bulrush. They enjoyed a rich and varied diet of seeds, ground acorn meal, shellfish, deer and other game. Although regional residents spoke various dialects and distinguished themselves by different tribal names, historians group them into three distinct peoples. The **Coast Miwok** dwelt north of the city, in present-day Marin and western Sonoma counties. The **Wintun** lived north of the Carquinez Straits in modern Solano, Napa and eastern Sonoma counties. The **Ohlone**, or Costanoans, inhabited areas east of the bay, on the San Francisco Peninsula and south to Big Sur. Though discussion of death was taboo among the Ohlone, they believed their dead souls transmigrated westward across the sea to the Farallon Islands, which they called the Islands of the Dead.

Despite small-scale but merciless feuds between some villages, trade and intermarriage promoted a generally peaceful and prosperous existence, as did the region's remoteness from the more bellicose cultures of Mexico and the Great Plains, and from the sea lanes of Europe and Asia. By the time the Spanish arrived in the 18C, the Bay Area supported between 7,000 and 10,000 people, and was North America's most densely populated region north of Mexico.

After conquering Mexico in 1521, the Spanish Crown was eager to expand its influence in the New World, especially over territories that could supply gold and other transportable treasure to subsidize the costs of colonization and war. In 1542 Spain dispatched a sea expedition, commanded by **Juan Rodríguez Cabrillo**, up the coast of Alta California in search of a passage connecting the Pacific Ocean to the Atlantic. Although he made the first documented visit by a European to California, Cabrillo failed to find either the fabled Northwest Passage or the very real passage into San Francisco Bay that John C. Frémont—almost three centuries later—would christen the Golden Gate.

In 1579 English privateer **Francis Drake** put in for repairs at a sheltered bay in northern California—possibly present—day Drakes Bay, in the lee of Point Reyes. He claimed the land for Queen Elizabeth I as Nova Albion, but the English did not follow up on their claims, leaving California to gradual conquest by Spain.

In 1602, **Sebastián Vizcaíno** dropped anchor in Monterey Bay, 85mi south of the Golden Gate. Although he traveled no further north, his glowing but inaccurate description of the cove inspired the Sacred Expedition and the first European sighting of San Francisco Bay 167 years later.

Hispanic Enclave

Mexico dispatched stalwart soldier **Gaspar de Portolá** in 1769 with orders to plant colonies in Alta California, with a provincial capital at the acclaimed Monterey Bay. He was accompanied by a religious contingent, headed by Franciscan friar **Junípero Serra**, charged with founding a chain of coastal missions. While searching for Monterey Bay, but having overshot their mark, a scouting party led by **Sgt. José Ortega** stumbled upon San Francisco Bay in November of that year. Mistaking it for Drakes Bay, which the Spanish had renamed for St. Francis, the great inlet was incorrectly—but permanently—called San Francisco.

Commissioned by the colonial government in Mexico, an expedition led by **Juan Bautista de Anza** arrived at San Francisco Bay in 1776 and formally established The Presidio on a hill overlooking the entrance to the bay. De Anza also selected a site for a mission church near a small lagoon in the sheltered valley to the south, naming the lagoon for Our Lady of Sorrows (*Nuestra Señora de los Dolores* in Spanish). On October 9, 1776, Padre Serra officially dedicated the new mission to St. Francis of Assisi, although it wasn't completed until 1791. Today it is known as Mission Dolores.

The Spanish mandate was to colonize the land and pacify the natives, converting them to Catholicism and teaching agriculture. Overawed by Spanish bravado and firepower, and initially believing the newcomers to be ancestors returned from the Islands of the Dead, the native Ohlone and Wintun allowed themselves to be pressed into mission society. They labored in the fields, lived in barracks segregated by sex, and received religious instruction. Resistors fled to the remote hills and the marshes of the Solano Delta, from where they mounted raids against mission herds and were in turn hunted by Spanish and native soldiery. The old ways of life quickly disappeared as the Church seized tracts of land around the bay for grazing, eventually establishing three missions in Ohlone territory, and one each in the Miwok (at San Rafael) and Wintun (at Sonoma) homelands. Thousands of natives died of European diseases, especially after smallpox was contracted from a trading expedition to the Russian settlement at Fort Ross in 1837.

After Mexico declared independence from Spain in 1821, the missions were secularized. The government decreed that half of their lands go to indigenous peoples, the remainder to be sold or doled out to soldiers and civilians as private land grants in lieu of pensions or payments. The demoralized and undercapitalized natives, however, failed to work their lands, which were readily absorbed by the private landholders; the natives either went to work for them or drifted into vagabondage.

View of Mission Dolores (1856)

Among the largest landholders around the bay were the ranching families of **Noe, De Haro** and **Bernal** on the tip of the San Francisco Peninsula; **Peralta** and **Martinez** in the East Bay and—most powerful of all—**Mariano Vallejo** to the north of the bay. Another ambitious settler was **John Sutter**, a Swiss adventurer who built extensive workshops and a fort on his land grant in the Sacramento Valley. With virtually no interference from the Mexican government, the Californios, as they called themselves, lived autonomous, self-sufficient lives. Served by small armies of cheap, native labor, they prospered by selling hides and tallow to visiting ships, many of them Yankee traders who carried glowing reports of the harbor's size and excellence to the East Coast of the US.

Yankee Village

Until 1835, most of the San Francisco Peninsula's residents lived near the mission. In June of that year, an English sailor named **William Richardson**, who had married the daughter of the Presidio *comandante*, erected a tent dwelling and trading post on a hill overlooking Yerba Buena Cove. This inlet on the northeastern shore of the peninsula had long been a favorite anchorage for visiting ships, for it provided both sheltering hills and deep-water mooring close to shore.

The Richardsons improved their homestead with adobe buildings and drew up simple plans for a village called **Yerba Buena** (Spanish for "good herb"). Attracted by the prospect of trade with US whalers and other vessels, more American settlers set up trading posts, hotels, shops and other services. Hides and tallow were the biggest commodities, but the Yankees also began stocking a wider supply of ships' provisions, including sailors' grog. Among the most prominent settlers were Ohio trapper-turned-shopkeeper Jacob Leese; Hawaiian traders Nathan Spear and William Heath; **Sam Brannan**, a business leader and renegade agent of Brigham Young's Church of Latter-day Saints; and **William Leidesdorff**, a mulatto entrepreneur from the West Indies, who served as the first US vice consul and was the town's largest landowner at the time of his death in 1848. The focus of the settlement was the sleepy town plaza, where goats were tethered and sailors and vaqueros from the neighboring ranches slept off their binges.

Covetous of the fine bay and goaded by impending war with Mexico, politicians in Washington sent adventurer **John C. Frémont**, guided by Kit Carson, to assess (and encourage) local interest in joining the Union. Frémont's efforts bore fruit in 1846 when a party of Yankees in Sonoma declared California's independence from Mexico, establishing it as the **Bear Flag Republic**. Less than one month later, Commodore John Sloat claimed California as American territory at Monterey. On July 9, 1846, 70 US marines and sailors, commanded by Captain John Montgomery, raised the Stars and Stripes above Yerba Buena plaza, renaming it Portsmouth Square.

> "We sailed down the magnificent bay with a light wind, the tide, which was running out, carrying us at the rate of four or five knots... We passed directly under the high cliff on which the presidio is built, and stood into the middle of the bay, from whence we could see small bays, making up into the interior, on every side; large and beautifully wooded islands; and the mouths of several small rivers. If California ever becomes a prosperous country, this bay will be the centre of its prosperity. The abundance of wood and water, the extreme fertility of its shores, the excellence of its climate, which is as near to being perfect as any in the world, and its facilities for navigation, affording the best anchoring-grounds in the whole west coast of America, all fit it for a place of great importance ..."
> Richard Henry Dana,
> *Two Years Before the Mast* (1835)

As real-estate speculation boomed, other amenities quickly followed, including the town's first school and its first newspaper. **Washington A. Bartlett,** the town's first American *alcalde* (mayor), changed Yerba Buena's name to San Francisco in 1847, a decision he rightly believed would associate the little town with the growing fame of this huge port. Bartlett also hired Irish engineer **Jasper O'Farrell** to draw up a new town plan. O'Farrell laid out rectangular street grids, cut diagonally by the broad thoroughfare of Market Street.

Gold Rush Boomtown

Boosters celebrated San Francisco's promising future, but none could have predicted the extraordinary kismet that was shortly to befall it. This fate was unwittingly set in motion by good-natured John Sutter, whose prospering empire in the Sacramento Valley required timber. Dispatched to build a sawmill on the American River in the Sierra Nevada foothills, Sutter's foreman, James Marshall, noticed a glitter of metal in the mill's tailrace on January 24, 1848: It was gold! Sutter tried to keep a tight lid on the discovery, fearful that a frantic rush of prospectors might overwhelm his well-planned enterprise. Rumors did leak out, but San Franciscans remained skeptical until May, when Sam Brannan displayed a bottle full of gold dust and nuggets in Portsmouth Square. "Gold!" he cried. "Gold from the American River!" Much of the city emptied as gold-seekers headed for the mines, and in 1849, the first wave of gold-seekers from the outside world—the **Forty-niners**—hit San Francisco.

As thousands of treasure-hungry prospectors stormed ashore, the town exploded within months from a population of 800 into a boomtown serving 90,000 anxious transients. New American shopkeepers and old-time Californios rubbed shoulders with a floating population of men from Mexico, Hawaii, Australia, China, Chile and all countries of Europe. Tents crowded the slopes of Telegraph and Rincon Hills, and abandoned ships were winched ashore to serve as hotels and warehouses. New buildings rose daily and burned down with alarming frequency; the city center was virtually destroyed by fire six times in four years. After the great fire of May 1851 (the most destructive before 1906), the business district was rebuilt of masonry.

By 1852, San Francisco had 30,000 permanent residents, a lending library, restaurants, hotels, churches and hundreds of saloons and gambling halls, and was the fourth-largest harbor city in the US. Enthusiastic audiences filled new theaters to cheer stage companies and acts from thousands of miles away. New piers extending into the bay rapidly became obsolete as Yerba Buena Cove was filled to create a flat, new business district. A few speculators, Brannan among them, became millionaires by selling provisions to miners.

Crime bred furiously in the manic society as gangs robbed and extorted from the general public. Brannan mobilized vigilante action, prodding frustrated citizens to dole out exile and even lynching to brazen criminals. From their makeshift stronghold popularly known as Fort Gunnybags, a Committee of Vigilance lynched corrupt city councilman James Casey and seized control of the city, staging torchlight parades, secret trials and summary executions. Though the crime rate declined, the governor, mayor, legislature, responsible citizens and newspapers spoke out against the militia tactics, and the committee disbanded after two months.

Silver Metropolis

As placer gold deposits were depleted, lone prospectors were increasingly displaced by hydraulic and hard-rock mining corporations and engineers. San Francisco rose to meet new demands, becoming the financial and manufacturing center of the Far West. The 1859 discovery of the **Comstock Lode,** a fabulously rich vein of silver at what would soon become Virginia City, Nevada, brought a new boom as investors' profits flooded San Francisco. Ostentatious and high-living new millionaires capitalized a wide range of civic improvements and private construction, including factories, offices, theaters, wharves, hotels and transport systems. The nouveau riche pushed for a city park to rival that of New York. Millionaires vied to build spectacular mansions on Nob Hill. To provide service to the precipitous slopes, engineer **Andrew Hallidie** developed the **cable car,** which took the city by storm, opening new tracts of steep or remote land for development. (By 1890 San Francisco was crisscrossed by eight different cable car lines and more than 100 miles of track.) The city expanded south to the slopes of Potrero Hill and west over Russian Hill to Pacific Heights and the Western Addition.

Foremost among city boosters was **William Ralston**, founder and president of the Bank of California. Ralston had resurrected the profitability of the Comstock mines at a point when their fortunes seemed to be failing. With the help of his ambitious agent in Virginia City, William Sharon, Ralston earned millions and used his boundless capital to elevate San Francisco into a world-class city of economic dynamism and cultural refinement. Among the projects that Ralston helped capitalize were Golden Gate Park; the Spring Valley Water Company; the Palace Hotel, largest in the world in its day; and **Adolph Sutro**'s famous tunnel in the Comstock.

San Francisco investors were almost universally convinced that a plan to link the city to the Eastern seaboard by a transcontinental railway would enrich California. In 1861 an ambitious route was plotted across the treacherous Sierra Nevada by engineer **Theodore Judah** and heroically constructed under arduous conditions by an army of laborers, including thousands of Chinese men.

Driving eastward to meet the Union Pacific Railway at Promontory Point, Utah, the Central Pacific Railway was financed by a quartet of ambitious and cunning small businessmen in Sacramento: **Leland Stanford, Mark Hopkins, Collis P. Huntington** and **Charles Crocker.** Known as "the Big Four," they leveraged federal railroad right-of-way grants into a vast empire of real-estate holdings under the auspices of the Southern Pacific Corporation. Reaping vast personal fortunes, the Big Four turned Southern Pacific into the most powerful political and economic force in the West. Their power and reach, likened to the inexorable tentacles of an octopus, excited popular, passionate hatred and inspired the well-known proletarian novel by Frank Norris, *The Octopus.*

Crocker

On the Wrong Track

But rather than a boon to the state, the transcontinental railway, completed in 1869, proved a bust. Cheap goods from eastern factories flooded California, causing factory closures, unemployment and widespread financial ruin in the 1870s. Overextended by $5 million, William Ralston was forced to close the Bank of California; he was found dead the same day, a probable suicide.

Factory owners cut production costs by hiring Chinese workers at reduced wages, bestowing upon them the brunt of resentment from unemployed workers. As militant labor grew stronger, strikes became a common occurrence. Anti-Chinese riots spread across the West, bringing violence to San Francisco's Chinatown. Political pressure resulted in the federal Chinese Exclusion Act of 1882, which severely limited Chinese immigration until the act was repealed in 1943. Closed off from protection by the broader society, Chinatown fell prey to the **Tong Wars,** violent power struggles between criminal gangs.

Huntington

Despite an undercurrent of unrest, San Francisco's restaurants, hotels and mansions set the style to which other Western towns of the Victorian period aspired, and fed its reputation as the Paris of the West. Ostentation gilded the lives of the wealthy and infiltrated the flamboyant character of a city that cultivated notoriety as well as distinction. Arts and entertainment flourished in this prosperous and stimulating climate. While the **Barbary Coast,** a rough and licentious neighborhood of gambling clubs, saloons and brothels, thrived at the southern foot of Telegraph Hill, great European opera companies and world-famous stage performers routinely played in the glittering footlights of downtown theaters.

Hopkins

Distinguished writers like Mark Twain, Rudyard Kipling, Robert Louis Stevenson and Oscar Wilde celebrated its unique and rambunctious character in novel and essay. A fledgling bohemian movement, nurtured by Ina Coolbrith, Charles Stoddard, Gellet Burgess and Joaquin Miller, cultivated artistic tastes from ramshackle cottages on Telegraph and Russian hills, and at Miller's retreat in the Oakland hills. Architects A. Page Brown, Bernard Maybeck and Willis Polk cut their teeth on Bay Area projects. Photographer Arnold Genthe set up his studio in the city and began taking pictures of old Chinatown. Home from the mountains, John Muir scribbled the essays that would spark the early American conservation movement.

Rampant corruption crept into San Francisco politics, climaxing under Mayor **Eugene Schmitz,** candidate of the Union Labor party in 1901. Under the pernicious influence of his advisor, **"Boss" Abe Ruef,** the administration exchanged favors for bribes. Led by the *San Francisco Chronicle,* a reform party called for change.

Stanford

Earthquake and Fire

On the morning of April 18, 1906, San Franciscans were jolted awake by a massive earthquake on the San Andreas Fault. Residents of most neighborhoods were relieved and even bemused to find the most extensive damage to be fallen chimneys, broken water and gas mains, shattered windows, cracked plaster and smashed crockery. Downtown, however, and in the shoddily built neighborhood south of Market Street, the devastation was frightening. Although the modern skyscrapers had withstood the tremor with flying colors, fissures gaped in the streets and wooden tenement row

California Street West to Nob Hill and Fairmont Hotel after 1906 Earthquake and Fire

houses listed dangerously, or lay in ruins. The colonnaded walls of City Hall had fallen away, leaving its magnificent dome hovering on a weakened steel frame, the most prominent victim of Abe Ruef's reckless fund-siphoning. The Central Emergency Hospital had collapsed, crushing medical staff and patients. Scores of people were hurt or killed by falling bricks.

By noon, 52 fires were burning with impunity around the city. Unable to restore the water supply, firefighters watched helplessly as the conflagration spread alarmingly through the tenements south of Market Street. Hundreds evacuated by ferry to Oakland, which had survived relatively unscathed. By night, the flames of the burning city lit up the skies around the Bay Area.

Mayor Schmitz hastened to the newly finished Fairmont Hotel atop Nob Hill to form disaster plans. Coordinating with Brigadier General **Frederick Funston**, army troops from The Presidio began patrolling the city to remain (seven of whom were indeed shot) and dynamiting broad fire lines along Van Ness Avenue. By dawn on April 19, the fire crested Nob Hill, destroying the "hill of palaces" and gutting the Fairmont. Prisoners were moved from the city jail to Alcatraz, and thousands of refugees streamed westward to makeshift tent camps on the Presidio grounds and in Golden Gate Park.

By the third day, the fire had burned south into the Mission District and clear to the northern wharves. Then the wind changed, pushing the flames back onto themselves. The holocaust was stopped at Van Ness Avenue, sparing the western half of the city. Some 250,000 people were left homeless and 674 were dead or missing. Virtually the entire city center was destroyed, some 514 blocks of offices, homes, warehouses, factories, saloons, churches and public buildings. Yet a plucky holiday atmosphere prevailed in the refugee camps.

A Phoenix From the Ashes

Relief funds poured in from around the world and reconstruction proceeded with phenomenal speed. By 1915, the city was ready to celebrate its miraculous recovery. Building an enchanting "city" lit by electrical lights on newly filled land

PROCLAMATION
BY THE MAYOR

The Federal Troops, the members of the Regular Police Force, and all Special Police Officers have been authorized to KILL any and all persons found engaged in looting or in the commission of any other crime.

I have directed all the Gas and Electric Lighting Companies not to turn on Gas or Electricity until I order them to do so; you may therefor expect the city to remain in darkness for an indefinite time.

I request all citizens to remain at home from darkness until daylight of every night until order is restored.

I Warn all citizens of the danger of fire from damaged or destroyed chimneys, broken or leaking gas pipes or fixtures, or any like cause.

E. E. SCHMITZ, Mayor.
Dated, April 18, 1906.
ALTVATER PRINT MASON AND ZENO STS.

Handbill (1906)

in what is now the Marina District, San Francisco hosted the **Panama-Pacific International Exposition**, the most highly regarded of the city's three world fairs.

The momentum of reconstruction culminated in an era of epic civil-engineering projects. The Civic Center was rebuilt on a grand scale in the Beaux-Arts style. Mayor **James "Sunny Jim" Rolph** cleared the way for residential development of the Richmond District by ordering the city's many cemeteries closed and all human remains removed to Colma, south of the city limits. The electric streetcar began replacing the cable car as the premier form of public transport. San Francisco's financial institutions—particularly A.P. Giannini's Bank of Italy—regained the central role in a new California "rush" that outstripped the gold and silver bonanzas of the previous century by capitalizing new farms and agricultural towns and building the state's role as the nation's fruit and vegetable garden.

To secure a dependable source of good water, the city dammed the Tuolumne River at Hetch Hetchy Canyon, 150mi east in Yosemite National Park, carrying the river water by aqueduct to the Crystal Springs reservoirs on the peninsula. Most spectacularly, in spite of the Great Depression, the city simultaneously built two of the largest bridges in the world, connecting the long-isolated peninsula eastward across the bay to Oakland and north across the Golden Gate to Marin County. To again celebrate its vigor in flamboyant San Francisco style, the city threw another world's fair, the **Golden Gate International Exposition**, which rose on newly completed Treasure Island, largest artificial island in the world.

Labor problems beset the city throughout these decades. Springing from resentment against the "robber barons" of the 19C, the 20C labor movement reorganized into an effective, if sometimes corrupt, political force, winning an eight-hour work day and turning San Francisco into a "union town." Labor strikes became a fixture in local politics. Longshoremen staged the largest strike in American history in 1930, eventually winning better pay after strikebreakers stormed their lines, sparking riots that injured scores and left two dead. The century's most notorious unionist court case, however, was the **Mooney Trial**. A rabble-rousing socialist named Tom Mooney was railroaded through court for a bombing that left 10 dead at a parade on the eve of World War I. Mooney was found guilty but was pardoned in 1939 after witnesses admitted they lied under oath.

War and Uneasy Peace – World War II brought another boom to the Bay Area as shipyards at Hunters Point and Sausalito tooled up for wartime production. Many of the workers were women and black newcomers from Southern states. Thousands of Japanese-American citizens were rounded up from Bay Area cities and expelled to internment camps. While the army built bunkers and batteries in the Marin Headlands to fend off a Japanese invasion that never came, 1.5 million soldiers, sailors and marines embarked for the Pacific theater from San Francisco, most of them from piers at Fort Mason.

The population continued to grow after the war, but with most of the new residents settling in Bay Area suburbs, the city began to lose its luster as a commercial hub. As Los Angeles grew to become the premier manufacturing center of the West Coast, tourism became San Francisco's most important business. The city never surrendered its grand flamboyance and eccentric character. North Beach became the national focus of a bohemian movement, the Beat Generation, during the 1950s, when nonconformist writers like Jack Kerouac, Allen Ginsberg and Lawrence Ferlinghetti, encouraged by modest rents, cheap food and drink, and a society tolerant of unconventional behavior, frequented the Italian coffee houses, wrote poetry and "dug the scene." Curious tourists eventually drove the Beats from North Beach but the city generated another internationally celebrated bohemian movement in the 1960s, this time in the Haight-Ashbury: Thousands of young people—hippies and "flower children"—gathered to experiment with drugs, music and libertine society. By the 1970s, however, that neighborhood was degenerating into a haven of drug pushers. (It has rebounded as a middle-class enclave today.)

Partly because of these widely renowned social movements, the Bay Area acquired a national reputation for what some might call political and social idealism, others left-wing radicalism. Huey Newton founded the Black Panther Party in Oakland, as neighboring Berkeley, home of the University of California, became a national center of student protest against the Vietnam War and other issues. When thousands of gay men and women moved to San Francisco, the Castro District became the "capital" of the American gay community. Relaxed immigration laws permitted an influx of larger numbers of Asian and Hispanic immigrants, greatly changing the ethnic makeup of the city.

Urban problems like homelessness, crime and blight compounded in San Francisco during the 1980s, yet single-issue politics constricted the government's ability to form a consensus for dealing with them. The 1990s witnessed a welcome renaissance in many city institutions, most spectacularly in the building of the new San Francisco Museum of Modern Art and a new main library, the birth and growth of an arts center at Yerba Buena Gardens, and the refurbishment of City Hall, the opera house, the Geary Theater and the California Palace of the Legion of Honor. Urban renewal is continuing at the start of the 21C with the opening of a new Asian Art Museum at Civic Center, the redevelopment of the De Young Museum in Golden Gate Park, further cultural development by Yerba Buena Gardens, and construction of a 100-acre shoreline park at the foot of The Presidio.

Although San Francisco has acquired many of the trappings that serve its important role as one of the world's foremost tourist destinations, it remains a lively, creative city, true to its unconventional and radiant past.

Time Line

c.10,000 BC	Native Americans first settle in the Bay Area.
1579	Explorer Francis Drake anchors near Point Reyes to repair his ship and claims Alta California for England.
1769	Expedition led by **Gaspar de Portolá** and **Junípero Serra** sets out from Mexico to establish the mission chain in Alta California. Sgt. **José Ortega** and his scouting party first sight San Francisco Bay.
1775	**Lt. Juan Manuel de Ayala** and his crew are the first Europeans to explore and map the bay.
1776	First mass is celebrated near the site of Mission Dolores. The first building on The Presidio is completed on September 17.
1791	Mission San Francisco de Asís (Mission Dolores) is completed.
1833	Following Mexican independence from Spain (1821), the mission chain is secularized.
1834	First town council is organized near Mission Dolores, with **Francisco de Haro** appointed as *alcalde*, or mayor.
1835	William Richardson and his wife build the first structure in Yerba Buena. Richard Henry Dana visits San Francisco Bay as a sailor—later described in *Two Years Before the Mast.*
1846	American settlers in Sonoma declare the Bear Flag Republic; less than a month later, the US flag is raised in San Francisco.
1847	California's first newspaper, *The California Star*, is published by **Sam Brannan**. Yerba Buena is renamed San Francisco.
1848	First commercial bank and first American public school begin operating.
1849	California **Gold Rush** begins.
1852	**Wells Fargo** begins stage service for passengers and freight.
1857	California's first commercial winery, Buena Vista, is founded in Sonoma by Hungarian **Agoston Haraszthy**.
1859	The **Comstock Lode** silver deposits are discovered in Nevada.
1860	Pony Express begins carrying letters between San Francisco and St. Joseph, Missouri, ending with completion of first **transcontinental telegraph** line in 1861.
1865	Charles and Michael de Young found the *San Francisco Dramatic Chronicle*, later dropping the word *dramatic*.
1868	The College of California in Oakland is taken over by the state, chartered and renamed the **University of California**. The campus is moved to Berkeley in 1873.
1869	The Central Pacific and Union Pacific railroads are joined at Promontory Point, Utah, creating the first **transcontinental railway** link between San Francisco and the East Coast.
1873	Andrew Hallidie successfully tests the first **cable car** on Clay Street. **Levi Strauss** patents riveted blue jeans. Pacific Coast Stock Exchange is founded.
1882	Enactment of the federal **Chinese Exclusion Act** restricts immigration of Asians to the US. It is not repealed until 1943.
1891	**Stanford University** is established in Palo Alto.
1892	**Sierra Club** is founded with John Muir as president.
1895	World's first three-reel slot machine is invented by Charles August Fey at his Market Street workshop.
1904	Produce wholesaler A.P. Giannini, an Italian immigrant, founds the Bank of Italy, later renamed **Bank of America**, thus pioneering branch banking in California.
1906	Great Earthquake and Fire devastate San Francisco; the quake is estimated at 8.3 on the Richter Scale.
1915	**Panama-Pacific International Exposition** in San Francisco celebrates the city's recovery from the 1906 earthquake.
1917	Architect Willis Polk completes **Hallidie Building**, the world's first skyscraper clad in a glass curtain wall.
1919	Ina Coolbrith becomes California's first Poet Laureate.
1927	Philo Taylor Farnsworth invents first all-electronic television in San Francisco.
1936	Pan Am begins scheduled passenger air service between San Francisco and Honolulu on the "China Clipper."
1936-37	The **San Francisco-Oakland Bay Bridge** and the **Golden Gate Bridge** link San Francisco to the East Bay and Marin County.
1945	United Nations charter is drafted at the Fairmont Hotel and signed at the Civic Center.

1958	The New York Giants move to San Francisco, establishing the first major league baseball team in the Bay Area.
1964	Free Speech Movement sit-ins at the University of California, Berkeley, lead to mass arrests of student protesters.
1965	Promoter **Bill Graham** opens the Fillmore Auditorium, staging legendary rock-and-roll concerts.
1967	Haight-Ashbury's "Summer of Love" establishes San Francisco as the hippie capital of the world.
1971	Alice Waters opens Chez Panisse restaurant in Berkeley, beginning the rage for **California Cuisine**.
1973	First BART train travels through the transbay tube from the East Bay to the Montgomery Street station.
1978	San Francisco Mayor **George Moscone** and gay supervisor **Harvey Milk** are assassinated by ex-supervisor Dan White, whose sentence of just five years' imprisonment touches off massive riots.
1989	Loma Prieta earthquake, measuring 7.1 on the Richter Scale, rocks the entire Bay Area from an epicenter near Santa Cruz.
1993	When Bay Area politicians **Dianne Feinstein** and **Barbara Boxer** are elected to the US Senate, California is the first state to have two women senators simultaneously in office.
1995	San Francisco 49ers win an unprecedented fifth Super Bowl.
1998	Controversial state law bans smoking from public areas, including restaurants and bars. Bank of America merges with North Carolina-based NationsBank to become the largest US bank.

Economy

San Francisco's early economy was shaped by its location. Isolated on the western edge of the continent, without easy access to other US cities until the transcontinental railroad was completed in 1869, mid-19C San Franciscans built their own economy from scratch. The discovery of gold on the American River in 1848 transformed the settlement from the sleepy center of an active trade in cattle hides and tallow to a boomtown of commerce and manufacturing. Guarding the mouth of its great bay, San Francisco also became the premier West Coast shipping hub, a bustling outpost that benefited greatly from the millions of dollars worth of gold, silver and grain ("green gold") that flowed down two inland rivers and out through the Golden Gate.

In more than 150 years that have passed since the Gold Rush, San Francisco has made the slow, sometimes painful transition from small working-class boomtown to large international business center. In recent decades Oakland has assumed most of San Francisco's port activity, and heavy industry and factories have relocated to the East Bay's Alameda and Contra Costa Counties, while San Francisco has fashioned itself as a business-and-finance headquarters.

Voted "the No. 1 Best City for Business in the US" by *Fortune* magazine in 1995, the San Francisco Bay Area now boasts one of the strongest urban economies in the nation, with retailing, banking, tourism, biomedical research, legal services, real estate and high technology heading the list of local industries. Home to more than 60 foreign consulates and trade offices, San Francisco is also the center of global marketing for the Bay Area, which has enjoyed a rise of 13 percent in international trade since 1993.

Business and Finance – Magnate and dynamo of corporate headquarters, financial institutions and businesses of every stripe, San Francisco's Financial District has been called the "Wall Street of the West" since the mid-19C. Although its ability to generate capital remains as dynamic as ever, the city's ranking as the nation's third-largest financial market was challenged in the late 1990s as mergers and acquisitions forced three of its largest banks (Bank of America, Montgomery Securities and Robertson Stephens) to move their headquarters to other cities. The Pacific Exchange, founded here in 1882, was the nation's fastest growing stock exchange–and a key player in the booming US-Asia trade–until it merged with the Chicago Board Options Exchange in 1998.

Today San Francisco has the headquarters of Wells Fargo, a bank with deep roots in the American West; Charles Schwab & Co., the nation's largest discount brokerage firm; Bechtel engineering, Chevron Oil, and apparel makers such as The Gap, Esprit and Levi Strauss & Co. These and other downtown businesses employ more than 300,000 people—about 40 percent of the population of San Francisco. South of the city, Silicon Valley raised $3.66 billion in venture capital in 1997, fueling the continuing growth of its high-tech industries and boosting Bay Area merchandise exports to the highest level of any region in the US.

Conventions and Tourism – In 1997, San Francisco attracted more than 16 million tourists, business travelers and conventioneers, who together spent more than $5 billion on goods and services. Those dollars sustain more than 66,000 local jobs—

Pacific Exchange

about one in nine in the city. In 1998 San Francisco also hosted 84 major conventions of more than 1,000 attendees in such venues as the Civic Auditorium near Civic Center and Moscone Convention Center in South Of Market. The largest local facility, the Moscone Center contains 442,000sq ft of exhibit space and 160,000sq ft of meeting rooms, with plans for more in the works.

Retail and Restaurants – More than 10,000 retail establishments, employing upward of 76,000 workers, vie for San Franciscans' and visitors' dollars. Shoppers spend some $5.2 billion a year here, both in neighborhood shops and in Union Square Area department stores. San Francisco's world-renowned restaurant industry, which employs 50,000 workers in 6,000 establishments, caters to foodies of every stripe.

Computers and Electronics – Silicon Valley, situated near the Bay Area city of San Jose, represents the epicenter of US high-tech growth. With about 7,000 electronics and software firms, exports of computers and related hardware from Silicon Valley grew by 81 percent from 1994 to 1997, hitting $29.3 billion in 1996. Some of the biggest names in computers, such as Apple, Hewlett-Packard, Intel and Sun Microsystems, got their starts here, while Bay Area start-ups such as Oracle, Adobe and Autodesk have become big players on the international software scene. As a region, the Bay Area ranks fourth in the world (after the US as a whole, Japan and Germany) for obtaining patents on new technologies and inventions.

In San Francisco, Multimedia Gulch, centered around South Park in the South of Market area, has grown into something of a technology hot spot in recent years, drawing firms such as Macromedia, which designs authoring tools for the Internet, and the magazines Wired and MacWeek, which chronicle trends in new technology.

Shipping and Transportation – Most of the shipping that goes on in San Francisco today consists of bits and bytes flowing over fiber-optic cables, but from the Gold Rush until well into the 20C, San Francisco's waterfront thrived. In its 1880s heyday, the San Francisco port, which employed thousands of longshoremen and sailors, handled 99 percent of all West Coast imports and 83 percent of all exports. Through the 19C the city was the whaling headquarters of the Pacific coast, but shipping declined with completion of the transcontinental railroad. Although the shipyards came alive briefly during World War II, in the 1960s San Francisco quietly ceded the bulk of its industrial shipping business to Oakland, which had made a sizable investment in up-to-date loading equipment and dredged its harbor to accommodate the latest generation of deep-draft ships.

Today San Francisco Bay maintains three major international ports: San Francisco, Oakland and Richmond, located north of Oakland in the East Bay. Asia accounts for two-thirds of the Bay Area's shipping trade, with the remainder split between Latin America; New Zealand and the South Pacific; British Columbia (Canada); and Europe. The Port of Oakland, third-largest in California (behind Los Angeles and Long Beach), handles 90 percent of the containerized cargo that passes through the Golden Gate. The Port of San Francisco is the nation's third coffee futures exchange port, handling more than 90,000 metric tons of coffee annually. Automobiles and newsprint are other major imports. The Port of Richmond primarily handles liquid petroleum and chemicals for East Bay refineries and factories.

Owned by the city and county of San Francisco, San Francisco International Airport (SFO) contributes $15 million per year to the city's General Fund. It hosts more than 39 million passengers every year, making it the fifth busiest nationwide. SFO also handles all of the Bay Area's international air-cargo trade, which now exceeds (in dollar volume) the combined total of all Bay Area ports by 16 percent. A recently completed $2.5 billion expansion has made SFO one of the nation's largest international air terminals.

Biotechnology – Home to some 500 bioscience companies generating $5 billion in annual revenues, the Bay Area is the world capital of biotech, a growing industry that concerns itself with finding marketplace applications for scientific innovations— from genetically engineering plants to provide higher crop yields, to manufacturing human insulin for diabetics. Beginning in 1976, when Genentech was founded just south of the city, biotech companies began flooding the region, complemented by some of the top health education and medical research facilities in the nation at UC San Francisco, UC Berkeley and Stanford University.

Services – As in most densely populated cities, the service industry accounts for the lion's share of jobs in San Francisco. Government agencies employ more than 56,000 workers (125,000 in the three west Bay Area counties). Some 16,000 are employed at the University of California at San Francisco and San Francisco State University, including many of the nearly 35,000 health-care workers in the city. Real-estate, finance, and insurance firms provide 77,500 San Francisco jobs, and development projects such as Mission Bay promise to swell the ranks of local construction companies, which now support 14,000 workers.

People

With a population of 746,777 (1999 estimate) inhabiting an area of only 46.38sq mi confined on the tip of a peninsula, San Francisco has the second highest population density (16,101 persons/sq mi) in the US after New York. Surprisingly small, it ranks as the fourth largest city in California after Los Angeles (3,633,591), San Diego (1,238,974) and San Jose (867,675). The city forms the cultural and financial hub of the San Francisco Bay Area, a nine-county region of more than 6.6 million people. Though eclipsed in size in the mid-20C by Los Angeles and other cities with room to expand, San Francisco led the state in population, culture and economic influence throughout the 19C and early 20C. Within months of the discovery of gold in 1848, the town's population of about 800 doubled, quadrupled and septupled with young men (who outnumbered women by 10 to 1) from every American state and European country, especially England and Ireland, France, the German states and Scandinavia. Great numbers came from China and Mexico, sizable minorities from Hawaii, Australia, Chile and other Latin American countries. The population rocketed to 34,776 within four years and exploded between 1860 and 1870 from 56,802 to 149,473.
Though the rate of growth slowed in the financial depression of the 1870s, by the turn of the century San Francisco was still the largest city west of St. Louis, with a population of 342,782. Population peaked at 775,357 in the mid-20C, after which a slow decline mirrored the city's loss of industry and port facilities to Oakland and other Bay Area cities. The region's population is nothing if not diverse, harboring a rich array of immigrants from Europe, the Americas and Asia. Currently, about 34 percent of San Franciscans are foreign-born.

Latinos – People of Spanish and Mexican ancestry have formed an important segment of the Bay Area's population since the arrival of Europeans in 1776. Politically dominant until the American conquest of 1846, the established Californio families contributed greatly to the founding and development of the village of Yerba Buena, though their political and economic power dwindled considerably with the influx of newcomers from the US. Even as generations of Hispanic families acculturate to American society, the continuing arrival of new immigrants, legal and illegal, keep Latino cultures robust over much of California. People of Hispanic ancestry today comprise about 13 percent of San Francisco's population.

Chinese – Forming about 18 percent of the city's population, the largest of any single ethnic group, the Chinese have constituted a substantial minority since the Gold Rush. Though historically persecuted, the Chinese were instrumental in countless enterprises that developed the West, not least in construction, agriculture and the fishing industry. The numbers of Chinese in San Francisco dwindled after passage of the Chinese Exclusion Act of 1882, reaching a low of 1.5 percent, or 7,744 people, in the 1920 census. Repeal of the act during World War II heralded a second wave of immigrants, greatly diversifying the Chinese community with wealthy families from Hong Kong and Taiwan, poorer families from China, refugees from Southeast Asia, and students. Although Chinatown has prospered from this influx, most Chinese Americans dwell in widely scattered and well-integrated neighborhoods of San Francisco (especially North Beach, Russian Hill, the Richmond District and the Sunset District) and the Bay Area.

Schoolchildren at Play

Italians – People of Italian ancestry today constitute about 15 percent of the city's population. After the Chinese were expelled from the fishing wharves in the 1870s, Fisherman's Wharf became known as a Genoese harbor, although currently Sicilians hold sway. The heart of North Beach has been known as Little Italy since the first decade of the 20C. With declining immigration rates, rapid acculturation and movement to the suburbs, the numbers of immigrants have since retrenched, but the influence of Italian Americans is still keenly felt in many aspects of city life.

Others – Many of the city's most prominent movers and shakers of the 19C and early 20C were of English, German and Scandinavian stock. Large numbers of working-class Irish families settled in the Mission District from the 1870s, becoming more than 23 percent of the population by 1910. Other ethnic enclaves around the turn of the century included the Maltese and the Japanese, who settled after the 1906 earthquake in the present neighborhood of Japantown. The African American population burgeoned during World War II, when thousands of Southern blacks came to work in Bay Area shipyards. Many settled along Fillmore Street (vacated by the incarcerated Japanese) in the Western Addition. Thousands of Filipinos have settled in the Bay Area since World War II, particularly in Daly City on San Francisco's southern border, and in the East Bay. The old Russian community in the Richmond District, which burgeoned after the 1917 Revolution, then dwindled through acculturation, is once again thriving under a new wave of immigrants.

An Eccentric, Enchanting Place – With much of its economy dependent on tourism and finance, San Francisco attracts and nurtures a diverse, largely well-educated population with strong interests in the arts, social experimentation and good living. Two fifths of the city's residents are single, while nearly 60 percent have attended college. The arts thrive at all levels of society, from grand opera productions to neighborhood cultural centers. Eating well is a passion for San Franciscans, who are forever on a quest for new cuisines and creative restaurants, yet well-disposed toward traditional regional specialties. They enjoy working off their calories with outdoor exercise; weekends find them by the thousands jogging, hiking, biking and sailing, taking advantage of the waters and parklands surrounding their city.

San Franciscans actively guard their architectural heritage, willingly subsidizing the archaic cable car system and fiercely supporting zoning restrictions and retrofitting projects that preserve vintage buildings. They are also strong supporters of the conservation movement, and have preserved an unparalleled system of parklands in and around the city. Though a reputation for tolerance holds sway, San Franciscans value individualism over universality, and residents are notorious throughout the Bay Area for their stubborn political coalitions, special-interest groups that make consensus difficult, and neighborhoods that trenchantly guard their ethnic or cultural flavor.

Despite their preservationist attitudes, city denizens pride themselves for being at the forefront—though others might call it a sideline—of American social experimentation. Set in motion perhaps by its eccentric birth and history, the city's penchant for flamboyant eccentricity attracts an eclectic mix of people and ideas. Free-thinkers, poets, artists, counterculture gurus and revolutionaries have always thrived here. Following the same impulse, though on more established footing, are the many idealistic civic organizations that have taken root, such as the Sierra Club and Glide Memorial Church in the downtrodden Tenderloin district.

Architecture

The oldest major US city west of the Rockies, San Francisco revels in examples of many eras and styles of buildings. The city's built environment has been shaped by various entrepreneurial, artistic and political forces, all of which have contributed to its distinctive architectural legacy. San Francisco's role as a commercial and financial nexus continues to attract new and innovative forms of expression to its architectural landscape.

Native Americans and the Mission Period – Before the arrival of Europeans, many small Ohlone and Miwok communities dotted the shores of San Francisco Bay. The natives lived in cone-shaped structures made of reeds and trees lashed together. As these natural building materials had a limited life span, no constructions remain from this era, although archaeologists have recorded scores of shell mounds marking village sites around the bay shore, as well as acorn-grinding rocks in oak woodlands where the native peoples made seasonal camps.

Italianate Style

The earliest extant structures in the Bay Area date from the mission period. The center of each mission community was a simple church and monastery, built of thick walls of whitewashed adobe capped by gabled red-tile roofs, supported upon heavy rough-hewn timbers. Spanish friars designed the missions along classical lines, using elements such as pilasters, niches and arcades to embellish the exteriors, and ornate reredos, tiled floors and colorful frescoes to ornament the interior spaces. Much of the interest in mission decoration comes from the folk-art flavors imparted by the Native American laborers who did the construction work. San Francisco's oldest building, the chapel at Mission Dolores, remains the finest example of the architecture of this period, while the surrounding Bay Area holds a variety of others, most notably the well-preserved mission and town plaza of Sonoma. Mexican influence on California's architectural style ended following the American takeover of California in 1848. By the early 1850s, the immense wealth generated by the gold mines began to be channeled into increasingly substantial buildings, some of which still stand at the heart of the Jackson Square quarter of the Financial District.

The Victorian Era – From 1860 to 1900, as wealth poured into the city from the gold mines and the silver deposits of Nevada's Comstock Lode, San Francisco's downtown commercial district grew in stature. Grand hotels were constructed to house visitors to the burgeoning metropolis, the most opulent of which was the Palace Hotel, completed in 1875. The US Mint, now called the Old Mint, was built nearby around the same time. By the 1890s, Chicago School office towers such as the Mills Building and the Chronicle Building had begun to rise along the bustling streets. The landmark Ferry Building was begun in 1894, and the Victorian era also saw the construction of elaborate resorts, most notably the second Cliff House and the now-ruined Sutro Baths complex near Seal Rocks on the city's Pacific shoreline.

Stick Style

The best-known and most enduring legacies of the Victorian era remain the many blocks of homes erected in the distinctive sub-styles of this romantic period. Throughout Pacific Heights, Haight-Ashbury, the Castro District and other residential neighborhoods, streets are lined with abundantly decorated wooden houses, most of them built between 1870 and 1906. Using redwood, fir and pine lumber from the dense forests of the northern California coast, contractors could produce homes quickly and inexpensively for San Francisco's burgeoning middle class. Closely crowded on narrow lots and built to standardized floor plans, these houses were adorned with an almost endless catalog of decorative sidings, elaborately milled moldings and bay windows with carved frames. Some were accented with fanciful turrets, false gables and intricate art-glass windows. Most Victorian homes were designed not by architects but by home owners, builders and property developers. They often followed general principles laid down by "pattern books" that outlined design precepts of each of the main Victorian "styles." Most prevalent in San Francisco were **Italianate** (1860-80), marked by Neoclassical ornament and pedimented false gables; **Stick** or Eastlake (1870-90), epitomized by comparatively flat wall surfaces and more angular, geometric forms; and **Queen Anne** (1870-1906), the most free-form and asymmetrical of the Victorian styles, often incorporating corner towers, turrets and a sometimes-frenzied variety of wall sidings, all on the same facade.

The free spirit of these "painted ladies"—so called because, though once mainly gray, they had flamboyant color schemes applied—has captured the fancy of visitors and locals alike. Thousands of Victorian homes march up and down San Francisco's streets, imposing a distinctive and colorful stamp on the city's architectural signature. One of them has been preserved for public viewing: the imposing Queen Anne-style Haas-Lilienthal House in eastern Pacific Heights.

Queen Anne

The latter part of the Victorian era saw the emergence of the **Arts and Crafts** movement, which in San Francisco brought together a loose grouping of artists and architects interested in the bohemian, "back-to-nature" teachings of local preacher Joseph Worcester. The Swedenborgian Church epitomizes the movement's rustic approach to architecture, adapted by such diverse and prolific architects as A. Page Brown, Willis Polk, Ernest Coxhead and Bernard Maybeck, all of whom built numerous residences around the Bay Area. Using dark-stained shingles of redwood lumber and creating innovative spatial arrangements that took advantage of the picturesque topography and mild climate, these architects satisfied a Bay Area taste for cultivated rusticity.

The City Beautiful – At the turn of the 20C, San Francisco's civic government considered altering the city's layout along the lines of an ambitious plan proposed by Chicago architect Daniel Burnham. **The Burnham Plan** called for wide boulevards and Baroque public spaces like those of Paris or Washington DC, ideals at the forefront of the Beaux-Arts-inspired "City Beautiful" movement. The earthquake and fire of 1906 left a clean canvas upon which to implement Burnham's ideas, but urgency propelled the rebuilding of the city according to its previous layout. The only aspect of the Burnham Plan to be constructed after the earthquake was the new Civic Center. This monumental rectangle of libraries, theaters and other public buildings, centered upon the landmark Baroque-style dome of City Hall, forms a grand, dignified public space.

Some of San Francisco's most impressive commercial buildings, including the Bank of California and the grand Fairmont Hotel, date from the post-earthquake period, as do many of the mansions of Pacific Heights. The city's main architectural gesture of recovery was the **Panama-Pacific International Exposition of 1915**, which filled the reclaimed lands of the modern Marina District with a celebratory fairground of eclectic architecture. The sole survivor is Bernard Maybeck's stately Palace of Fine Arts. Across the bay, the Neoclassical campus buildings of the University of California, Berkeley, were erected by John Galen Howard and others, including Julia Morgan.

The growing economy of the 1920s supported another building boom in the Financial District. The city's first skyscrapers sprouted at the end of that decade, including Timothy Pflueger's Art-Deco Pacific Telephone Building, the Mayan-style tower at Four Fifty Sutter, and George Kelham's 31-story, Gothic-style Russ Building, then the tallest on the West Coast.

Depression and Postwar Era – Commercial construction slowed considerably during the Great Depression. Following World War II, San Francisco underwent a long period of suburbanization, with freeways constructed to reach new tract-housing suburbs of the outlying Bay Area. Through the late 1950s and early 60s, urban renewal caused the demolition of vast tracts of older buildings, in turn inspiring a movement to preserve the city's historic architecture.

Though by the 60s some 30 years had passed with little change to the San Francisco skyline, that decade and the one that followed saw it altered beyond recognition. The first distinctive new project was the 1959 Crown Zellerbach Building, now One Bush Street, an International-style glass box supported on piers above a paved plaza. More skyscrapers continued to be built, culminating in the city's two tallest—Skidmore, Owings & Merrill's monolithic Bank of America, in 1971, and William Pereira's unique Transamerica Pyramid, in 1972.

Public outcry against the pace of growth, which critics claimed had "Manhattanized" the previously attractive city skyline, resulted in stringent planning controls encoded in the **Downtown Plan** of 1985. This put a cap on the amount of square footage of new construction permitted in the Financial District and effectively shifted future growth to the less densely developed area South of Market.

© N. Kerby

Clos Pegase Winery

Contemporary Architecture – Recent years have brought a number of internationally renowned architects to design projects in San Francisco and the Bay Area, among them Philip Johnson, Mario Botta, James Ingo Freed and Michael Graves, whose signature contemporary take on the Classical style may be seen at Clos Pegase Winery in the Napa Valley. San Francisco has witnessed a renaissance in public architecture through major projects like the expanded Moscone Convention Center and the adjacent Yerba Buena Gardens. In 1995, Botta's new home for the San Francisco Museum of Modern Art opened, followed in 1996 by Freed's striking new San Francisco Public Library at Civic Center.

Visual Arts

The visual arts of San Francisco reflect the history, diversity and excitement of the entire Bay Area, making it one of the art capitals of the American West.

Early Artistic Landscape – San Francisco's rich, multilayered art history began with the Ohlone, Wintun and Coast Miwok Indians, who maintained a beautiful material and ceremonial culture. Today, baskets produced by native Californians are treasured for their dazzling geometric designs and precise weaving; many are on view at the Oakland Museum of California and other public collections.

Mission Dolores stands as the primary reminder of the city's Mexican period: Walls and ceilings of the old chapel reveal replicas of beautiful geometric patterns designed by native artisans. The population explosion during and after the Gold Rush introduced European values and aesthetics. Important pioneer artists began visiting San Francisco, including landscape painters Albert Bierstadt and William Keith. Early photographers Carleton Watkins and Eadweard Muybridge (who helped settle a bet about horse racing with his groundbreaking photographic studies of animal locomotion) paved the way for one of the area's most enduring obsessions. The San Francisco Art Association, precursor of today's San Francisco Museum of Modern Art, was founded in 1871 by members Bierstadt, Keith, Muybridge and others to display art publicly and offer classes. Railroad magnates Leland Stanford and Mark Hopkins assembled major collections of European art in the late 19C.

In the early 20C, important developments in the arts took root in San Francisco, including the California **Arts and Crafts** movement in painting, furniture and decorative arts, led by Arthur and Lucia Matthews. **Tonalist** painting, incorporating the colors of the city's distinctive foggy palette, was exemplified by Gottardo Piazonni and Xavier Martinez. Following the influential Panama-Pacific International Exhibition of 1915, where works by European and New York modernists were displayed at the Palace of Fine Arts, an explosion of color appeared in the work of Bay Area painters Clayton S. Price and Selden Gile. The latter was a member of the **Society of Six**, an informal association of artists who practiced a painterly, figurative style during the 1920s. In the 20s and 30s, several artists of Japanese and Chinese ancestry, including Chiura Obata and Dong Kingman, blended aspects of Asian art traditions with Western practices to create innovative Asian-American styles.

Photographers Ansel Adams, Edward Weston, Imogen Cunningham and others founded the **Group f.64** in 1932 and exhibited together the following year. Reacting against the blurred-focus work of their "pictorialist" contemporaries, they embraced a

Chinatown by Dong Kingman

sharp-focus, "precisionist" depiction of forms and textures. Social themes characteristic of the Great Depression are movingly rendered in the works of painter Maynard Dixon and his wife, photographer Dorothea Lange, as well as in pieces by African-American sculptor Sargent Johnson. Diego Rivera made repeated visits to the city with his wife, Frida Kahlo, during the 1930s; the Mexican muralist executed several works here, engendering mural projects by other artists in public locations throughout the city.

Abstract and Figurative – After World War II, visiting faculty Clyfford Still and Mark Rothko of the San Francisco Art Institute inspired an explosion of abstract expressionist painting by their students, including Sam Francis and Robert Motherwell. Painters Elmer Bischoff, Richard Diebenkorn and David Park responded with a representational movement known as **Bay Area Figurative**, a motif that Berkeley-based painter Joan Brown and sculptor Manuel Neri later personalized. Beat culture and Zen philosophy helped inspire the work of individualists like Bruce Conner, William Wiley and Jay de Feo. Popular culture of the 1960s is recorded in the work of painters Wayne Thiebaud and Robert Bechtle. The latter counterculture movement also saw unique developments in poster art around Haight-Ashbury, as the cartoon art of R. Crumb and others gained worldwide exposure.

Artists working in craft media have continued to challenge the boundaries of their materials—ceramists Robert Arneson, Viola Frey and Peter Voulkos are known internationally, and textile-based sculptors Kay Sekimachi and Ruth Asawa have helped redefine their medium. Asawa is also the creator of some of San Francisco's most popular public works, including fountains at Ghirardelli Square and at the Grand Hyatt Hotel near Union Square. Sculptor Beniamino Bufano created a menagerie of rounded and evocative animal forms and symbolic human figures that continue to populate city parks and public squares.

Street Arrow (1974-76) by Wayne Thiebaud

The Contemporary Scene – Today, the San Francisco Museum of Modern Art, at home in its new South of Market building, honors its commitment to displaying pieces by Bay Area artists along with cutting-edge works by international artists. Opposite, the Yerba Buena Center for the Arts maintains an ambitious program of temporary exhibitions that keep a continual flow of new art before the public eye. San Francisco's public and private galleries increase visitors' opportunities to see all kinds of visual art, most conveniently during the thrice-yearly Open Studios days when galleries and artists' studios across the city hold open houses. College galleries at San Francisco State University and the San Francisco Art Institute mount exhibitions of national and international work. The city remains the capital of the nation's alternative art centers with its concentration of nonprofit spaces and artist cooperatives, including S.F. Camerawork, New Langton Arts, Hunters Point Studios, Galeria de la Raza and the Headlands Center for the Arts in Marin County. Commercial galleries, many of them clustered in near Union Square, present a range of exciting contemporary and historical art. Well worth looking into are Gallery Paule Anglim, Hang, John Berggruen and Bomani Gallery, located within a few blocks of one another. The work of performance and conceptual artists Guillermo Gomez-Pena, Karen Finley and the SRL collective; painters Enrique Chagoya and Oliver Jackson; muralists Juana Alicia and Danel Galvez; and photographers Richard Misrach and Linda Connor, continue to infuse San Francisco arts with new ideas and vitality.

Performing Arts

Famed for its cultural diversity, San Francisco has always been a hotbed for the performing arts. A city of immigrants, it has nurtured the European traditions of opera, symphony and ballet while making room for Chinese opera, Latin jazz and ethnic dance. A haven for nonconformists, it has been the birthplace of new strains of rock-and-roll music and postmodern dance.

Opera – Of all the musical arts, opera is the one that has most enduringly won a place in San Francisco's heart. Even when the city was but a small, gritty mining outpost, luxuriant operas were staged on a regular basis in some of the most sumptuous theaters in the nation. Beginning with Bellini's *La Somnabula* in 1851, some 5,000 operatic performances were given by more than 20 companies prior to the 1906 earthquake. In 1923 pianist-producer Gaetano Merola founded the **San Francisco Opera** with a production of *La Bohème*, but not until 1934 did the company christen the War Memorial Opera House, its permanent home, with a performance of Puccini's *Tosca*. Widely recognized as the preeminent operatic institution in the western US, the company has presented such greats as Luciano Pavarotti, Elisabeth Schwarzkopf and Birgit Nilsson. Smaller companies such as the Lamplighters, a Gilbert and Sullivan company formed in 1952, and Pocket Opera, a troupe that has performed classic works in English since 1968, illustrate opera's mass appeal with their inventive, accessible productions.

Classical Music – San Francisco's taste for orchestral music is well established. Founded in 1911, the **San Francisco Symphony Orchestra** hosted the adolescent debuts of violinists Yehudi Menuhin (1926) and Isaac Stern (1936) and developed a repertory rooted in the classical and romantic traditions. However, with the 1995 installation of Leonard Bernstein protégé Michael Tilson Thomas as its director, the symphony has undergone a renaissance. Tilson Thomas has challenged his musicians and his audiences with an array of difficult, under-recognized 20C masterpieces by Copland, Debussy, Varese and onetime Bay Area composers Lou Harrison and Darius Milhaud. Among chamber-music groups, the **Kronos Quartet**, founded in San Francisco in 1977, stands out for crystallizing the city's ethos of experimentation and fun with its original, often-playful arrangements of contemporary works. The male choir **Chanticleer**, the nation's only full-time classical a cappella group, has performed and recorded an eclectic array of new and ancient music since its inception in 1978, including rare Renaissance choral pieces, vocal jazz and gospel.

Jazz and Rock – San Francisco and Oakland enjoyed a brief flowering as jazz hubs in the 1940s and 50s. Breaking from the Dixieland tradition parlayed locally by Crescent City musicians, Bay Area native Dave Brubeck pioneered a new sound, characterized by syncopated rhythms, percussive piano playing and classical song structures. Brubeck's runaway success with his albums for Fantasy, a then-fledgling local label, made San Francisco one of the world centers for jazz recording. Today a critically acclaimed "new jazz" style, grounded in bebop but inflected by rock and funk, has been developed by a younger generation of San Franciscans, most notably guitarist Charlie Hunter.

San Francisco's place in the rock-and-roll canon was clinched in the 60s when local bands the Grateful Dead, Jefferson Airplane and Big Brother and the Holding Company (featuring Janis Joplin) wrote the soundtrack for a decade of political protest and cultural revolution. Free concerts in Golden Gate Park and all-night jam sessions at the Family Dog, Fillmore, and Avalon ballrooms drew thousands to hear what became known as the **San Francisco Sound**. In the 1970s political folk singers like Joan Baez (from Carmel) and bands like Country Joe and the Fish emerged. Crooner Chris Isaak, whose stylish music has been described as rhythm-and-blues with roots in country and folk, burst onto the scene in the late 1980s. Around the same time, a hardcore punk scene coalesced around Jello Biafra's Dead Kennedys, preparing the way for a punk-pop explosion in the East Bay that hurtled the band Green Day from obscurity to platinum status in the 90s. Perhaps the most popular Bay Area band at the end of the 20C was the mellow-toned R&B quartet Boys II Men.

Theater – Demonstrating its flair for the dramatic, San Francisco has always supported the theater. In the 1850s, 22 of Shakespeare's 38 plays were staged, but circus acts and minstrel shows were equally popular. In the 1860s some of the most sumptuous playhouses in the nation were built here—just as Barbary Coast melodeons were gaining a toehold. Audacious local stars like Lola Montez, Adah Isaacs Menken and Lotta Crabtree achieved near-mythic status in this crude yet sublime environment.

Once the transcontinental railroad was completed in 1869, San Francisco became a must-stop on the national touring circuit. It was not until the mid-20C, however, that the city regained a strong local theater community. In 1951 San Francisco State University professors Jules Irving and Herbert Blau founded the **Actors' Workshop**, introducing the work of Harold Pinter, Samuel Beckett and Edward Albee to local audiences. The **San Francisco Mime Troupe,** founded in 1959, today travels the world with its canny, self-styled political satires. In 1967 actor and director William Ball established the **American Conservatory Theater** (ACT), today considered one of the best regional theaters and drama schools in the US. In addition, a theater community of more than 100 professional companies mounts everything from the local camp classic *Beach Blanket Babylon* to masterpieces by Shakespeare and Chekhov.

Dance – Second only to New York in the diversity, innovation and quality of its troupes, San Francisco stands at the forefront of classical and modern dance in the US. Founded in 1933, the **San Francisco Ballet** is the oldest resident classical ballet company in the country. The ballet presented the first full-length American productions of such 19C classics as Tchaikovsky's *Swan Lake* and *The Nutcracker*, in addition to building a large repertoire of 20C works by George Balanchine, Jerome Robbins and such resident choreographers as Lew Christensen and Michael Smuin. In the East Bay, the small but energetic Oakland Ballet has made its name by reviving classic ballets of the 20C, including the work of Vaslav Nijinsky.

Modern dance of every type is also well established in San Francisco. One of its foremothers, Isadora Duncan, was born here in 1877, though she spent most of her life abroad and performed in the city only twice. Anna Halprin emerged in the late 1950s as an influential teacher and choreographer; her explorations of ritual, physicality and the creative process sparked groundbreaking postmodern work in New York in the 1960s. Today, the Joe Goode Performance Group and Contraband have achieved stunning results by combining dance with theater and live music, and a wide array of ethnic dance companies explore and expand on everything from butoh and belly dancing to flamenco and capoeira.

Literature

Born in the wake of the Gold Rush, San Francisco's literary tradition began as a torrent of local magazines and newspapers that has since broadened and expanded into every genre and style. Today a host of renowned and up-and-coming journalists, novelists and poets make the city their home and source of inspiration.

The Golden Fifties and Silver Sixties – Legendary Mormon entrepreneur Sam Brannan founded San Francisco's first major newspaper, the *California Star*, in 1847. Soon the *Star* teamed up with *The Californian*, a Monterey-based publication, to form the *Alta California*, first daily newspaper in the West. By the mid-1850s San Francisco boasted a dozen dailies and nearly 40 weeklies—more publications than were produced in London at the time. While most of these were political organs or advertisers, they also encouraged some of the city's fresh young literary voices. Nearly every paper carved out room for a "poet's corner" on the front page, thereby nurturing the talents of miner-bards such as Alonzo Delano and John Rollin Ridge, who wrote under the noms-de-plume Old Block and Yellow Bird, respectively.

Through the 1860s, literary journals such as *The Pioneer*, the *Golden Era*, *The Californian* and the *Overland Monthly* flourished, as did the unconventional culture that aided and abetted them. Bret Harte *(The Luck of Roaring Camp and Other Sketches)* and Joaquin Miller *(Songs of the Sierras)* drew from their experiences working in mining towns for their early essays, short stories and poems. Others, like Ina Coolbrith and Charles Stoddard, found inspiration in nature and the emotions. Ambrose Bierce *(Occurrence at Owl Creek Bridge, The Devil's Dictionary)* and Mark Twain *(Roughing It, The Adventures of Huckleberry Finn)* made their reputations writing irreverent satires and burlesques. As the decade wore on, Bierce grew increasingly misanthropic and cynical, earning himself the nickname "Bitter Bierce" by becoming a vociferous champion of suicide and attacking progressive issues such as women's suffrage and the eight-hour workday. Twain, on the other hand, sharpened his skills and applied them to the picaresque fiction that would later assure his place in the American literary canon.

During the financial depression of the 1870s, many publications foundered and talents such as Harte, Miller, Twain, Bierce and Stoddard relocated elsewhere. A steady stream of writers came through the city in the next couple of decades, however. Poet Robert Frost was born in 1874 near the Embarcadero and lived there 11 years; Robert Louis Stevenson wrote in a flat near Union Square in 1879 and 1880; and in the late 1880s British Indian writer Rudyard Kipling tried, unsuccessfully, to publish his stories in the city's major journals. Across the bay Gertrude Stein lived in Oakland from 1880 to 1891 before going east to Radcliffe College and subsequently founding her salon in Paris. Of the 1860s bohemians, only Ina Coolbrith remained in San Francisco, hosting literary salons and encouraging the next generation of writers in their pursuits.

Social Realism – One of Coolbrith's many acolytes, Jack London *(Call of the Wild, The Sea Wolf)*, wrote in the tradition of Twain and Harte, using his adventures to fuel his fiction. And like many writers of his time, London addressed larger social and philosophical issues in his work. His story "South of the Slot" contains a sharp critique of class differences in San Francisco (the title refers to Market Street, which once sharply divided the rich from the poor). London's contemporary, Frank Norris, also saw contradictions in San Francisco society; his acclaimed naturalistic novel *McTeague* (1899), set in the Polk Gulch neighborhood, explores such themes as greed and social Darwinism from the point of view of a beleaguered dentist.

Taking a different tack, poet George Sterling wrote torrid romantic poems and famously described the city as a "cool, grey city of love." Other writers and artists of the era belonged to the fun-loving group Les Jeunes (the Young Ones), which published its work in *The Lark* (1895-97), "a magazine of humorous anarchy." Most members of Les Jeunes did their best-known work after the group's breakup, although founder Gelett Burgess remains famous for his frivolous poem "The Purple Cow," which appeared in *The Lark*.

From 1920 to 1929 crime writer Dashiell Hammett made San Francisco his home; the fog-cloaked slopes of Nob Hill provided a noir backdrop for the nighttime ramblings of Sam Spade, Hammett's hard-boiled detective hero of *The Maltese Falcon*. John Steinbeck also lived in the city in the late 1920s, although he drew from the environs of nearby Salinas and Monterey for his acclaimed novels *East of Eden* and *Cannery Row*.

Beat Happening – In the 1950s San Francisco underwent a literary renaissance as the Beat Generation came of age in North Beach. From the early to mid-1950s, Jack Kerouac churned out more than a dozen books about wanderlust, love and longing. Kerouac typed *On the Road* as one very long paragraph in 20 days of April 1951; upon publication in 1957, the book catapulted him and his Beat Generation cohorts to fame. According to poet and City Lights bookstore founder Lawrence Ferlinghetti: "The emergence of the Beat Generation made North Beach *the* literary center of SF—and it nurtured a new vision that would spread far beyond its bounds." Poet Allen Ginsberg, one of that vision's most articulate proponents, gave birth to the San Francisco poetry renaissance in 1955 when he read his poem "Howl" (first published by City Lights) to a standing-room-only audience in the Marina District.

Jack London

In 1960 and 1961 Ken Kesey wrote *One Flew Over the Cuckoo's Nest*, his best-selling novel about a mental institution, from his home in Palo Alto. Journalist Tom Wolfe vividly captured the psychedelic counterculture in his 1969 book *The Electric Kool-Aid Acid Test*. In the 1970s Armistead Maupin followed the lives of young drifters in his long-running *San Francisco Chronicle* column, later published as the book *Tales of the City*. Before he died of AIDS in 1994, *Chronicle* journalist Randy Shilts *(And the Band Played On)*, gained renown in writing about city politics, gay liberation and the AIDS epidemic. For six decades until his death in 1997, Pulitzer Prize-winning *Chronicle* columnist Herb Caen entertained a huge and faithful following of avid readers with his witty blend of gossip and news about the city he loved. Today the city boasts a wide range of resident writers, including novelists Amy Tan *(The Joy Luck Club)* and Alice Walker *(The Color Purple)*, and British-born poet Thom Gunn—as well as a lively "spoken word" scene of public readings of new work by local novelists, essayists and poets.

Cuisine

San Franciscans are curious and demanding diners. Their adventurous willingness to experiment with new cuisines and with innovative interpretations of traditional favorites has earned the city a well-deserved reputation for fine dining. Fueled and sated by a dedicated legion of celebrity chefs, this passion has elevated Bay Area dining to the level of high art. The region's multiethnic heritage has created an environment in which international gourmet specialties happily coexist.

Locally Grown – Thanks to California's mild climate and fertile soil, a year-round abundance of locally grown fruits, vegetables, meats and dairy products flows into the city daily. This produce stocks not only grocery stores and restaurant kitchens but also farmers markets at locations throughout the Bay Area. A stroll through one of these markets enables food-loving visitors to behold, taste or purchase exotic seasonal delights such as juicy white peaches, sweet fresh apricots, fragrant herbs, young garlic and many varieties of tomatoes. Much of this produce is organically grown. Shoppers will also find fresh eggs, local cheeses, and nuts from the Central Valley agricultural region.

Local waters no longer provide most of the city's seafood, but an enormous variety is flown or trucked in daily. Diners can select from a wide array—salmon and oysters from Washington state, sea bass from Chile, mussels from New Zealand, halibut from Canada—all absolutely fresh thanks to modern shipping techniques. From November through April, **Dungeness crab** appears on menus and in fish markets; this famed San Francisco treat is best consumed with sourdough bread and a glass of crisp white wine.

San Francisco's renowned **sourdough bread** remains a beloved local treasure. True devotees swear it cannot be produced anywhere but in the city. Dating from the 19C gold-mining days, the recipe for this tangy loaf calls for a yeast-like starter, no sugar, and microbes that apparently float only in San Francisco air.

California's phenomenally successful **wine** industry produces an array of vintages to suit any palate or budget, from good, hearty table wines to world-class award-winners. Most San Francisco wine lists prominently feature vintages from the Wine Country of the Napa and Sonoma valleys to the northeast, though fine wines also come from Mendocino County, to the north, and from Monterey and the Central Coast, to the south. Many restaurants also stock high-quality selections from Europe.

Locally brewed beers experienced a popular resurgence in the late 20C. Well worth sampling are brews from the San Francisco-based Anchor Brewing Company, whose Steam Beer traces its recipe from the Gold Rush era, and such respected microbreweries as Sierra Nevada, Mendocino Brewing and Anderson Valley Brewing Company, whose Boont Amber is a rich, creamy ale.

Bay Area **mineral waters** tickle many a local palate. The most famous brand is Calistoga, bottled at the source near the eponymous Wine Country town.

International Flavors – As in many port cities, San Francisco's abundant restaurants proffer cuisine from around the globe. In North Beach, a fragrant array of bakeries, trattorias, delicatessens and cafes dish up glorious **Italian** treats. Besides pasta, pizza and other Italian fare, look for the local specialty *cioppino*, a tomato-based seafood stew. **Chinese** restaurants are so plentiful, there seems to be one on every street corner. A Cantonese specialty, favored at lunch or brunch, is *dim sum*, a selection of sweet or savory dumplings filled with meat, seafood or vegetables. Lovers of other Asian cuisines can as easily sample sushi, coconut-milk curries, peanut noodles or teriyaki dishes.

Crabs on Ice

Open Kitchen, Kuleto's

© Robert Holmes

Mexican food may be found all over the city but particularly in the Mission District, where abundant Latino restaurants serve up large portions of tacos, burritos, enchiladas, tamales and *carne asada*. Other Central and South American specialties include *seviche*, a citrusy seafood soup.

California Cuisine – Drawing on California's polyglot heritage, and taking advantage of high-quality, readily available ingredients, a new approach to eating was introduced in 1971 when Alice Waters opened her Chez Panisse restaurant in Berkeley. Reacting to the prepackaged, mass-marketed food that had come to dominate American menus, and drawing on her experiences in France's Provence region, Waters developed a method of cooking based on fresh, seasonally varying, wild and locally grown produce. Presented in a visually appealing manner, **California Cuisine**, as it was called, transformed American gastronomy and reawakened the American palate.

Despite its popularity, California Cuisine also gained a reputation for small portions at high prices. In the late 1980s, a "New American" spin-off took San Francisco by storm. Featuring hearty platefuls of traditional foods, prepared with the California Cuisine emphasis on fresh, locally grown produce, restaurants like the Fog City Diner drew packed houses for their deliciously unpretentious food and lighthearted, retro-Americana ambience. Since the late 1980s, Bay Area chefs have pioneered a New American approach to Asian cooking, resulting in what is often called "Asian fusion" cuisine.

Restaurants with Attitude – San Francisco's restaurant culture thrives on residents' fascination with the experience of dining out. Local newspapers exhaustively cover the restaurant scene. Chefs of trendy, successful eateries are feted as celebrities, their comings and goings altering the fates of their establishments almost overnight. In keeping with this heightened sense of importance, restaurateurs pay close attention to style and design. Interiors, table settings, waitstaff attire and music are carefully choreographed to complement cuisine. Some restaurants feature "open kitchens" deliberately exposed to the dining rooms so that customers can keep an eye on proceedings. Bold colors and soaring spaces are the order of the day. Diners generally dress the part, though dress codes are rare and casual clothing is welcomed in many places.

Grand Café, Hotel Monaco, San Francisco

Address Book

Where to Eat

Choosing a restaurant in San Francisco can be an overwhelming task. So great are the number and variety of eateries here (the city has more restaurants per capita than any other in the US), so outstanding is their quality (readers of *Bon Appetit* magazine annually vote San Francisco their "favorite American city for dining out"), that dining has become a recreation in itself. A substantial segment of the population, dubbed "foodies," beats visitors to the punch in procuring reservations at hot new establishments. Let them: There are plenty of restaurants to go around, and locals will steer you to exactly the kind of place you're looking for.

The venues listed below were selected for their ambience, location and/or value for money. Rates indicate the average cost of an appetizer, an entrée and dessert for one person (not including tax, gratuity or beverages). Most restaurants are open daily for lunch and dinner—except where noted—and accept major credit cards. Call for information regarding reservations and opening hours.

Additional restaurants are listed throughout this guide in the form of Digressions. See Index for a complete listing of eateries described in the text.

$$$$	over $50	**$$**	$15-$30
$$$	$30-$50	**$**	less than $15

Luxury

Boulevard – *1 Mission St. at Steuart St., Embarcadero.* ♿ ☎ *415-543-6084.* **$$$$ New American.** Belle Epoque accents—mosaic tile, steel girders, a pressed-tin ceiling—have transformed the 1889 Audiffred Building, whose windows frame the Bay Bridge. Chef Nancy Oakes melds Asian and Mediterranean elements with classic French techniques. Dishes include grilled swordfish on artichoke hearts with a lemon beurre blanc, and a wild-mushroom sampler with balsamic-vinegar-roasted squash.

Farallon – *450 Post St., Union Sq.* ♿ ☎ *415-956-6969.* **$$$$ Seafood.** Whimsical blown-glass jellyfish chandeliers hang over tables, octopus stools rest beside kelp columns—these and other flamboyant undersea fantasies complement the seafood menu here. Chef Mark Franz prepares such entrees as seared walleye pike (with braised fennel, baby artichoke confit and salmon caviar) and a "hot pot" of lobster, shrimp, salmon, scallops, oysters, mushrooms, bok choy and lotus root. Menu choices change daily, but normally include at least one meat and one poultry dish.

Fifth Floor – *12 Fourth St. in the Palomar Hotel, near Yerba Buena Gardens. Dinner only. Closed Sun.* ♿ ☎ *415-348-1555.* **$$$$ French.** As in a sophisticated, Art Deco-inspired supper club in 1930s Paris, subtle lighting plays across red leather-and-velvet banquettes. Chef George Morrone may suggest a starter of tuna tartare with diced apples, mint and vinaigrette, followed by panchetta-crusted ostrich with white asparagus and morel mushrooms or suckling pig a l'orange with savoy cabbage and pig trotters terrine.

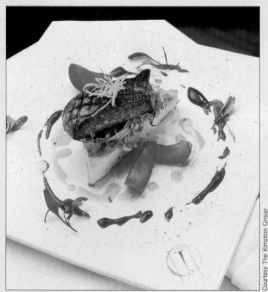

Courtesy The Kimpton Group

Fleur de Lys – *777 Sutter St., Union Sq. Closed Sun.* ♿ ☏ *415-673-7779.* **$$$$ French.** Chef-owner Hubert Keller adds a California flair and Pacific Rim accents to classic continental recipes at his elegant, top-of-the-line restaurant. Diners can't go wrong with venison, lamb, swordfish, prix-fixe tasting menus or special vegetarian selections. The classy décor features colorful draped fabric and wall mirrors.

Gary Danko – *800 North Point St., Fisherman's Wharf. Dinner only.* ♿ ☏ *415-749-2060.* **$$$$ Creative Continental.** Elegant but understated décor allows chef-owner Danko's culinary creations to take center stage at his intimate restaurant. Diners choose from among five-course tasting menus; one such offered Dungeness crab cake with bell-pepper and wasabi sauces; sauteed snapper fillet on fennel puree; seared filet of beef with Stilton cheese and potato gratin; domestic and imported cheeses; and a passion fruit and mango Napoleon. Service is impeccable.

Jardinière – *300 Grove St., Civic Center. Dinner only.* ♿ ☏ *415-861-5555.* **$$$$ California-French.** Hundreds of bubbles sparkle on the domed ceiling of the Champagne Rotunda in this elegant two-story restaurant, favored for pre- or post-theater dining. Chef-owner Traci Des Jardins may start diners with a duck confit salad or a tart of chanterelles and asparagus, then offer herb-crusted loin of lamb with potato gnocchi, followed by blueberry cake with lemon sabayon and apricots.

La Folie – *2316 Polk St., Russian Hill. Closed Sun.* ♿ ☏ *415-776-5577.* **$$$$ California-French.** Fresh produce like avocados and huckleberries enhances classic dishes at this family-run bistro. Whimsical white clouds on a sky-blue ceiling add to a dreamy and intimate ambience. The seasonal menu may include roast quail leg stuffed with foie gras or fricasseed lobster with a spicy mango-citrus vinaigrette.

Mid-Range

B44 – *44 Belden Pl., Financial District.* ♿ ☏ *415-986-6287.* **$$$ Spanish.** Chef Daniel Olivella, of Barcelona, may start diners with boquerones (white anchovies with pears and cheese). Try hearty seafood paella or roasted rabbit with hazelnut picada; conclude with a dish of cheese, honey and walnuts. At lunch, tables are wall-to-wall in the street. Within the bistro, the décor recalls 14C Catalonia.

Beach Chalet Brewery – *1000 Great Hwy., Ocean Beach, west end of Golden Gate Park.* ♿ ☏ *415-386-8439.* **$$$ California.** Built by Willis Polk in 1925 as a tea house, this building was restored and reopened in 1997 as a restaurant and brewery upstairs, a Golden Gate Park visitor center (with WPA frescoes) downstairs. The menu features steamed black mussels in coconut-lemongrass broth, herb-crusted rotisserie chicken and steak Delmonico.

Betelnut – *2030 Union St., Cow Hollow.* ♿ ☏ *415-929-8855.* **$$$ Pan-Asian.** Upscale Southeast Asian "street food" is served in red-lacquered, bamboo-accented British-colonial atmosphere, with overhead fans swirling beside sensuous paintings of Asian women. The delicious food is full of surprises—like Singapore chili crab and coconut chicken—complemented by imported beers.

Empress of China – *838 Grant Ave., Chinatown.* ♿ ☏ *415-434-1345.* **$$$ Chinese.** A central pagoda is the focal point of this sixth-floor pavilion whose windows overlook the bustling Chinatown street scene. Tasty seafood and other traditional Cantonese fare, including dim sum, is served.

EOS Restaurant and Wine Bar – *901 Cole St., Haight-Ashbury. Dinner only.* ♿ ☏ *415-566-3063.* **$$$ Asian fusion.** Artfully arranged experimental cuisine is presented in a modern but minimalist setting with high ceilings and black granite tables. The crowd is lively and fun. Dishes include green-papaya spring rolls, shiitake mushroom dumplings and five-pepper calamari.

Flying Saucer – *1000 Guerrero St., Mission District. Dinner only. Closed Sun.* ♿ ☏ *415-641-9955.* **$$$ California.** This quirky restaurant's eclectic, folk-artsy decor and cross-cultural cuisine could be from another world. Chef Albert Tordjman calls his menu "world-beat cuisine," with big portions of prawn-shiitake pot stickers or rack of lamb coated in pecans with wild rice.

Hawthorne Lane – *22 Hawthorne St., off Howard St. near Yerba Buena Gardens.* ♿ ☏ *415-777-9779.* **$$$ Asian fusion.** Bright, busy, innovative—and huge—describe this skylit restaurant on a small alley behind the Museum of Modern Art. Former Wolfgang Puck chefs David and Ann Gingrass make a duck schnitzel with crème-fraiche risotto and Sonoma lamb with tomato tarragon sauce.

McCormick & Kuleto's – *Ghirardelli Sq., Fisherman's Wharf.* ♿ ☏ *415-929-1730.* **$$$ Seafood.** Some of the best seafood in the Wharf area is served not on the water but in this spacious and attractive restaurant with views toward Alcatraz and rich wood and glass appointments. There's a full oyster bar and a wide-ranging menu of fresh fish, prepared to order.

MoMo's – *760 Second St., Embarcadero (China Basin).* ♿ ☎ *415-227-8660.* **$$$ New American.** Opposite Pacific Bell Park, this favorite of baseball fans offers roasted artichokes, pizzas, steaks, chops, chicken. Especially popular is the Peekytoe crab cake with a summer corn and tomato salad.

Moose's – *1652 Stockton St. at Washington Sq., North Beach.* ♿ ☎ *415-989-7800.* **$$$ California-Mediterranean.** Moose's lures a legion of actors and athletes, politicians and business people to its bar and grill. Diners might start with fried green tomatoes with a crawfish-remoulade, then move on to a potato and wild mushroom lasagna or an oven-roasted chicken breast with house-made gnocchi.

Plouf – *40 Belden Pl., Financial District. Closed Sun.* ♿ ☎ *415-986-6491.* **$$$ French.** A *très français* establishment, this brasserie offers wonderful steamed mussels in many styles, served streetside by day, indoors by night. Other dishes include a goat cheese-and-walnut croquette; roasted monkfish with cabbage, bacon and lemon; and fine desserts.

Postrio – *545 Post St., Union Sq.* ♿ ☎ *415-776-7825.* **$$$ California.** Wolfgang Puck's spacious and elegant Prescott Hotel eatery serves a hybrid of American, Mediterranean and Asian dishes. Splashy modern Pat Kuleto décor complements the great people-watching.

Shanghai 1930 – *133 Steuart St., Embarcadero. Closed Sun.* ♿ ☎ *415-896-5600.* **$$$ Chinese.** Amid a décor that evokes pre-communist-era Shanghai, dim sum and noodle lunches give way to gourmet dinners. They include red chili prawns, Peking duck, and Buddha Jumps Over the Wall—a special-occasion dish of abalone, sharks fin, scallops, oysters and blackened chicken.

Tommy Toy's – *655 Montgomery St., Financial District. Closed Sun.* ♿ ☎ *415-397-4888.* **$$$ Chinese-French.** Luxuriously decorated in 19C imperial Chinese antiques, this celebrity haunt bills its food as "haute cuisine Chinoise." Seafood bisque is served in a coconut shell and topped with puff pastry. Signature dishes include foie gras with sliced pear and watercress in ginger sauce, and breast of duckling smoked with camphorwood and tea leaves, served with plum wine sauce.

Zuni Café – *1658 Market St., Civic Center. Closed Mon.* ♿ ☎ *415-552-2522.* **$$$ Mediterranean.** First opened as a Southwestern restaurant (thus the name), Zuni now offers hearty French and Italian dishes infused with California flavor. An eclectic clientele crowds around the copper oyster-and-champagne bar, while a central brick oven dominates the décor.

Ace Wasabi's Rock & Roll Sushi – *3339 Steiner St., Marina District. Dinner only.* ♿ ☎ *415-567-4903.* **$$ Japanese.** Cameras in this bright and loud Generation X hangout are wired to the internet. Godzilla movies show on a screen behind the bar; nonstop rock and reggae music complete the experience. This is not your typical sushi bar, despite two dozen inventive varieties of rolls.

Alioto's – *8 Fisherman's Wharf at foot of Taylor St.* ♿ ☎ *415-673-0183.* **$$ Seafood.** Founded as a fresh-fish stall in 1925, Alioto's remains a Sicilian family venture. The "fastest crab-cracker on the bay" lures tourists inside, where diners enjoy views of the Golden Gate Bridge. Fresh fish are broiled, baked, grilled, sautéed, poached or steamed, in various styles.

Angkor Wat – *4217 Geary Blvd., Richmond District.* ♿ ☎ *415-221-7887.* **$$ Cambodian.** Classical Asian ballet is performed weekends amid exotic temple décor at what—20 years ago—may have been the first Cambodian restaurant in the US. Like Cambodia itself, the restaurant's cuisine falls between delicate Vietnamese and spicy Thai. Duck curry with tropical fruit is a favorite. Pope John Paul II ate here.

Anjou – *44 Campton Pl., Union Sq. Closed Sun–Mon.* ♿ ☎ *415-392-5373.* **$$ French.** Hidden in a small lane, this two-level restaurant offers traditional and creative cuisine. Favorites include a mushroom quiche with duck foie gras, and a ravioli of three mushrooms with black peppercorn and cognac sauce.

Café de la Presse – *352 Grant Ave., Union Sq.* ♿ ☎ *415-398-2680.* **$$ French.** Casual brasserie-style meals are prepared early and late at this international newsstand beside Chinatown Gate. A favorite of foreign residents and visitors alike is the espresso bar, with its wide selection of pastries.

Chez Nous – *1911 Fillmore St., Pacific Heights. Closed Mon.* ♿ ☎ *415-441-8044.* **$$ California.** Despite the name (French for "our place"), this is not a Gallic establishment. A fine list of wines by the glass complements dishes such as salmon steak with corn and red pepper relish, and a tomato-mozarella-basil salad.

Clémentine – *126 Clement St., Richmond District. Closed Mon.* ♿ ☎ *415-387-0408.* **$$ French.** This serene café blends California and continental elements with good value. Starters include mussels marinières and escargots de Bourgogne; entrées range from fish to poultry to meats and include veal kidneys and a filet of lamb with thyme. Desserts are superb; Sunday brunch is especially popular.

© Edward Thomas

Fina Estampa – *2374 Mission St., Mission District. Closed Mon.* ♿ ☎ *415-824-4437. Also 1100 Van Ness Ave., north of Civic Center.* ♿ ☎ *415-440-6343.* **$$ Peruvian.** Paellas, tapas and spicy South American specialties entice adventurous diners looking for out-of-the-ordinary cuisine. Try shrimp in garlic sauce from the Pacific coast, chicken with marinated onions and tomatoes from the Andes.

Fior d'Italia – *601 Union St. at Washington Sq., North Beach.* ♿ ☎ *415-986-1886.* **$$ Northern Italian.** America's oldest Italian restaurant, this institution opened in 1886 and has been at this location since 1954. Historical photos line the walls; the Tony Bennett Room honors San Francisco's favorite crooner. Cuisine remains tradition-bound: calamari, gnocci, osso buco and Caesar salad draw raves.

Fog City Diner – *1300 Battery St., Embarcadero.* ♿ ☎ *415-982-2000.* **$$ American.** Part rural 1930s diner, part urban 40s bar-and-grill, this chrome-and-neon landmark at the foot of Telegraph Hill draws kudos for its upscale cheeseburgers with fries, as well as gourmet seafood. Some diners opt for the eclectic small plates: chili dogs, mu shu pork burritos, cioppino, chicken satay.

Fringale – *570 Fourth St., near Yerba Buena Gardens. Closed Sun.* ♿ ☎ *415-543-0573.* **$$ California-Basque.** A stylish, intimate corner bistro in "multimedia gulch," Fringale is noted for mussels and pork dishes. Try the pork tenderloin confit with cabbage, onion and apple marmalade. Chef Gerald Hirigoyen also owns **Pastis** *(1015 Battery St., Embarcadero; closed Sun;* ♿ ☎ *415-431-7210)*, with a similar menu but a larger room.

Gordon's House of Fine Eats – *500 Florida St., Potrero Hill.* ♿ ☎ *415-861-8900.* **$$ American.** This hip techno-industrial café serves hearty fare with a trendy twist: The menu is divided by Comfort, Health, Luxury and Local Showcase. Try asparagus spring rolls or Angus rib-eye steak with skinny French fries.

John's Grill – *63 Ellis St., Union Sq.* ♿ ☎ *415-986-3274.* **$$ American.** The true Maltese Falcon, made famous by author-patron Dashiell Hammett and actor Humphrey Bogart, has been at home behind the bar here since 1908. The dark, moody interior is straight out of film noir. The shrimp Louis and chicken Jerusalem are classics.

Kabuto Sushi – *5116 Geary Blvd., Richmond Dist. Dinner only. Closed Mon.* ♿ ☎ *415-752-5652.* **$$ Japanese.** Often rated the city's best sushi bar, little Kabuto does swimmingly on the grace and showmanship of chef-owner Sachio Kojima. Fresh fish dishes include barbecued eel and flaming conch.

Katia's, A Russian Tea Room – *600 Fifth Ave., Richmond District. Closed Mon.* ♿ ☎ *415-668-9292.* **$$ Russian.** This casual, friendly cafe offers piroshki, stroganoff and blini with salmon caviar to homesick eastern Europeans. Fresh flowers grace every table, and in warm weather full windows open onto the sidewalk.

Kuleto's – *6221 Powell St., Union Sq.* ♿ ☎ *415-397-7720.* **$$ Italian.** Shoppers pack this flagship café for restaurant designer-entrepreneur Pat Kuleto. Salamis and garlics hang above the mahogany bar facing an open kitchen. Wonderful focaccia sandwiches are served amid classic Florentine ambience.

Le Soleil – *133 Clement St., Richmond District.* ♿ ☎ *415-668-4848.* **$$ Vietnamese.** French influence pervades Saigon cuisine at this thoughtfully decorated Asian eatery. The menu features squid salad, flaming beef and prawns, sautéed eggplant with coconut and curry sauce, and fried bananas with coconut ice cream.

Lhasa Moon – *2420 Lombard St., Marina District.* ♿ ☏ *415-674-9898.* $$ **Tibetan.** Rarely sampled, Indian-influenced cuisine offers a true adventure in dining. Tibet's national dish is steamed momo: savory dumplings of chicken, beef and/or vegetables. A popular dessert is bhatsa mahku: roasted barley, brown sugar and cheese-flavored bread with cream sauce.

Ma Tante Sumi – *4243 18th St., Castro District. Dinner only.* ♿ ☏ *415-626-7864.* $$ **Japanese-French.** The menu changes seasonally at this East-West eatery, whose chef and decorator deftly match contrasting cultures. Try wasabi-cured salmon or pan-roasted duck in a plum sauce.

Max's Opera Cafe – *601 Van Ness Ave., Civic Center.* ♿ ☏ *415-771-7300.* $$ **American.** The highlight of this New York-style deli is a cast of singing waiters and waitresses, who perform from 7pm until late night. If you're not in the mood for a giant pastrami sandwich, opt for a blue-plate special or a big salad.

Mifune – *1737 Post St., Japantown.* ♿ ☏ *415-922-0337.* $$ **Japanese.** This acclaimed noodle house serves 55 hot and cold varieties of udon and soba in a stark red-and-black minimalist ambience.

Millennium – *246 McAllister St., Civic Center. Dinner only.* ♿ ☏ *415-487-9800.* $$ **Vegetarian.** Neither meat nor dairy products are employed at this gourmet eatery, located in the basement of a 1920s carriage house. Wild mushrooms, polenta, tofu and bean medleys are staples. The "Full Moon Aphrodisiac" package includes a night at the parent Abigail Hotel.

PlumpJack Cafe – *3127 Fillmore St., Cow Hollow. Closed Sun.* ♿ ☏ *415-563-4755.* $$ **California.** This popular Mediterranean-style bistro, strong in herbs and vegetables, features an intimate stage-set ambience. The wine list offers especially excellent value.

Restaurant LuLu – *816 Folsom St., South of Market.* ♿ ☏ *415-495-5775.* $$ **Mediterranean.** This bright and noisy converted warehouse specializes in rotisserie grills. Try fried artichokes or skillet-roasted mussels before entrées of chicken or rib-eye steak. A popular wine bar makes evenings very noisy.

Rose Pistola – *532 Columbus Ave., North Beach.* ♿ ☏ *415-399-0499.* $$ **Italian.** There's live jazz most evenings at this busy family-style restaurant, which won the 1997 James Beard award as the best new restaurant in the US. A wood-burning oven dominates the open kitchen, which also prepares cioppino and baked fish in the sophisticated Ligurian-Genoese style.

Sam's Grill – *374 Bush St., Financial District. Closed Sat–Sun.* ♿ ☏ *415-421-0594.* $$ **Seafood.** Founded in 1867 as an open-air market, Sam's is today a no-nonsense cafe serving fresh fish and two-martini lunches to busy business people. Gruff veteran waiters add to the masculine atmosphere.

The Slanted Door – *584 Valencia St., Mission District.* ♿ ☏ *415-861-8032.* $$ **Vietnamese.** This trendy café offers Viet-inspired cuisine in a bustling atmosphere. Crowds arrive early for exotic dishes on a changing menu: crispy shrimp and pork spring rolls, "shaking beef" with garlic, grilled Muscovy duck with plum sauce.

South Park Cafe – *108 South Park Ave., near Yerba Buena Gardens. Closed Sun.* ♿ ☏ *415-495-7275.* $$ **French.** Latin Quarter ambience pervades this casual sidewalk café facing a pretty park. A blackboard menu may feature a sautéed pear and roquefort salad, a chicken liver-and-cognac terrine, couscous with braised vegetables and coriander mint yogurt, or a housemade boudin noir.

The Stinking Rose – *325 Columbus Ave., North Beach.* ♿ ☏ *415-781-7673.* $$ **Italian.** Tourists flock here for garlic-laden dishes guaranteed to repel vampires. Start with roasted garlic to spread on bread, and end your meal with garlic ice cream. If you don't want to reek from your pores, the lasagna is safe.

Tarantino's – *206 Jefferson St., Fisherman's Wharf.* ♿ ☏ *415-775-5600.* $$ **Seafood.** Tiered seating has assured diners' view of the boat basin since 1946. Steamed clams and abalone are specialties; there also are excellent sole and homemade pastas.

Thep Phanom – *400 Waller St., Haight-Ashbury. Dinner only.* ♿ ☏ *415-431-2526.* $$ **Thai.** Dishes like *ped sawan* (boneless duck in honey sauce on spinach) and "Siamese twins" (seafood curry on banana leaves) result in lines out the door. The gourmet and out-of-the-ordinary dishes appeal to Thai-food lovers looking for something different.

Thirsty Bear Brewing Company – *661 Howard St., near Yerba Buena Gardens.* ♿ ☏ *415-974-0905.* $$ **Spanish.** Dozens of cold and hot tapas, such as sautéed fish cheeks with garlic and sherry, grilled fennel sausage with white beans, and duck confit with lentils and cranberries, highlight a menu that complements 10 different house-made brews—including Polar Bear, a lightly hopped pilsner.

© Robert Holmes

Ton Kiang – *5821 Geary Blvd., Richmond District.* ♿ ☎ *415-386-8530.* **$$ Chinese-Hakka.** Clay-pot casseroles (rock cod with tofu, duck with bean thread) and flavorful steamed dim sum speak highly for Asian regional cuisines at this Hong Kong-style eatery. For something different, try sautéed geoduck clams or frogs' legs with ginger and asparagus.

Zarzuela – *2000 Hyde St., Russian Hill. Dinner only. Closed Sun.* ♿ ☎ *415-346-0800.* **$$ Spanish.** Flamenco-style guitar music accents tapas and paellas served on hand-painted plates at this bustling, friendly Madrid-style bar. Memorable dishes include chicken or ham croquettes, poached octopus and *zarzuela*, a seafood stew.

Budget

The Ramp – *855 China Basin St. at Pier 64, Embarcadero.* ♿ ☎ *415-621-2378.* **$$ American.** Locals congregate on Saturday afternoons for live music and salsa dancing at this waterfront burger-and-sandwich shack.

Brain Wash Cafe & Laundromat – *1122 Folsom St., South of Market.* ☎ *415-861-3663.* **$ American.** This whacky diner boasts live bands, a dance floor and, yes, a laundromat. The menu features burgers and daily specials.

Dottie's True Blue Cafe – *522 Jones St., Union Sq. Closed Tue. Breakfast daily, lunch weekdays.* ♿ ☎ *415-885-2767.* **$ American.** A classic 1950s-style diner, Dottie's doles out generous portions of eggs and pancakes for breakfast, vegetarian and other sandwiches for lunch.

Hamburger Mary's – *269 12th St. at Folsom St., South of Market. Closed Mon.* ♿ ☎ *415-626-5767.* **$ American.** This classic burger joint (with a cocktail bar) attracts many of the tattooed and pierced set.

La Méditerranée – *288 Noe St., Castro District. Closed Mon.* ♿ ☎ *415-431-7210. Also at 2210 Fillmore St., Pacific Heights. Closed Sun.* ♿ ☎ *415-921-2956.* **$ Eastern Mediterranean.** North African falafel and Greek spanikopita are favorites; the 10-item *meza* offers greatest value at these quiet and friendly cafés.

La Taqueria – *2889 Mission St., Mission District.* ☎ *415-285-7117.* **$ Mexican.** Fresh, basic tacos and burritos are dished up with healthy fruit drinks at this tiny neighborhood eatery. The grills are good, the salsa memorable.

Minh's Garden – *208 Clement St., Richmond District.* ♿ ☎ *415-751-8211.* **$ Vietnamese.** Excellent and authentic Southeast Asian food is served at this simple storefront café. Multi-course banquet meals are priced under $9 per person.

Rassellas – *2801 California St., Pacific Heights. Dinner only.* ♿ ☎ *415-567-5010.* **$ Ethiopian.** Spicy African food is served in a dark, exotic atmosphere that doubles as a jazz club after dark.

Sears Fine Foods – *439 Powell St., Union Sq. Closed Mon–Tue. Breakfast & lunch only.* ♿ ☎ *415-986-1160.* **$ American.** This campy diner in the Chancellor Hotel is known for its frumpy waitresses and delicate Swedish pancakes.

Ti Couz – *3108 16th St., Mission District.* ♿ ☎ *415-252-7373.* **$ French-Breton.** Patrons queue up for dozens of savory and sweet crepes, whose fillings range from ratatouille to caramel apples. Within this hideaway, designed like a village scene in Brittany, is a popular wine- and hard-cider bar.

Where to Stay

San Francisco is a treasure trove for aficionados of small, European-style "boutique" hotels, whose prices range from moderate to deluxe. But there is something for everyone here, with more than 31,000 hotel rooms in the city. There are small private hotels for the impecunious, hostels for the backpack crowd, and large luxury hotels, at which rates for standard rooms may start as high as $500. *For general information about hotel chains in San Francisco, see Accommodations section in the back of this guide.*

The properties listed below were selected for their character, location and/or value for money. Prices reflect average cost for a standard double room (two people) in high season (not including any applicable city or state taxes). Room prices may be considerably lower in off-season, and many hotels offer discounted weekend rates. The presence of a swimming pool is indicated by the ⌇ *symbol.*

$$$$$	over $300	$$	$75-$125
$$$$	$200-$300	$	less than $75
$$$	$125-$200		

Luxury

Mandarin Oriental, San Francisco – *222 Sansome St., Financial District.* ✗ & 🅿 ✆ *415-276-9888 or 800-622-0404. www.mandarin-oriental.com. 158 rooms.* $$$$$ Beautifully decorated guest rooms and suites, extending between the 38th and 48th stories atop 345 California Center, offer spectacular picture-window views across the City by the Bay. From the ground-floor entry, high-speed elevators whisk guests to their aeries. After dining in style at **Silks**, guests may relax in marble baths with top-end amenities.

The Palace Hotel – *2 New Montgomery St., Financial District.* ✗ & 🅿 ⌇ ✆ *415-512-1111 or 800-325-3535. www.sfpalace.com. 553 rooms.* $$$$$ A Market Street landmark since 1875, The Palace (p 83)—now a Sheraton hotel—bridges the gap between the 19C and the 21C. Renovated from head to toe in 1991, it has three restaurants and bars, a fitness center and conference center. Rooms are classically appointed, balancing antiques with modern amenities.

Hotel Palomar – *12 Fourth St.., Union Sq./Yerba Buena Gardens.* ✗ & ✆ *415-348-1111 or 877-294-9711. www.hotelpalomar.com. 198 rooms.* $$$$$ The Kimpton Group's top-of-the-line venture embraces the fifth through ninth floors of a post-quake, 1908 landmark building at the corner of Market Street. Tailored lines, rich textures and dramatic lighting offer elegance and sophistication throughout. **The Fifth Floor** restaurant is one of the city's best.

The Argent Hotel – *50 Third St., near Yerba Buena Gardens.* ✗ & 🅿 ✆ *415-974-6400 or 877-222-6699. www.argenthotel.com. 667 rooms.* $$$$ Towering 36 stories above Yerba Buena Gardens at the heart of the city's dynamic new cultural district, this stylish, contemporary hotel boasts marble floors, rich woodwork, golf-leaf trim and a world-class art collection.

Campton Place Hotel – *340 Stockton St., Union Sq.* ✗ & ✆ *415-781-5555 or 800-235-4300. www.camptonplace.com. 110 rooms.* $$$$ An intimate hotel once popular with the white-gloved "carriage trade" set, Campton Place is the epitome of elegance and service. In guest rooms, fluffy duvets top the beds and bathrooms feature limestone floors. Asian-inspired décor squares off with a French restaurant to provide a rarefied experience in a discreet location just off Union Square.

The Fairmont – *950 Mason St., Nob Hill.* ✗ & 🅿 ✆ *415-772-5000 or 800-527-4727. www.fairmont.com. 591 rooms.* $$$$ This famous grand hotel (p 85) has a rich history that includes the 1906 earthquake and creation of the United Nations in 1945. Handsomely appointed rooms are in the original main building and a 1961 tower that offers extensive views across the city. Within the hotel are four restaurants, three with lounges.

Hotel Monaco – *501 Geary St., Union Sq.* ✗ & ✆ *415-292-0100 or 800-214-4220. www.hotelmonaco.com. 201 rooms.* $$$$ This Theater District boutique hotel, a remodeled 1910 Beaux Arts classic, offers the warmth and comfort of home in a much grander setting. Baroque-style fireplaces and sumptuous striped armchairs invite conversation in the lobby; Provençal fabrics drape over canopy beds in the guest rooms. The **Grand Café** offers a bistro-style lunch and dinner.

Hotel Triton – *342 Grant Ave. Chinatown.* & ✆ *415-394-0500 or 800-433-6611. www.hotel-tritonsf.com. 140 rooms.* $$$$ A colorful avant-garde boutique hotel facing Chinatown Gate, this property was labeled "exceedingly groovy" by *Harper's Bazaar* magazine. Designers and artists created cutting-edge accoutrements for the Eco Floor, Zen Dens and suites dedicated to the likes of rock musicians Jerry Garcia and Carlos Santana.

The Huntington Hotel – *1075 California St., Nob Hill.* ✗ ♿ 🅿 ☎ *415-345-2888 or 800-227-4683. www.huntingtonhotel.com. 140 rooms.* **$$$$** Overlooking Huntington Park on the California Street cable-car line, this 1924 classic entered the 21C by opening its Nob Hill Spa, a state-of-the-art facility with the flavor of Asian tradition. Guest rooms are posh and oversized, as the hotel once housed a luxury apartment complex.

Hyatt Regency San Francisco – *5 Embarcadero Center, Financial District.* ✗ ♿ 🅿 🛝 ☎ *415-788-1234 or 800-233-1234. www.hyatt.com. 805 rooms.* **$$$$** An architecturally acclaimed hotel with a 17-story central atrium at the foot of Market Street, the Hyatt is tied to the Embarcadero Center by a pedestrian bridge. Every tastefully decorated room has a city or bay view.

Prescott Hotel – *545 Post St., Union Sq.* ✗ ♿ ☎ *415-563-0303 or 800-283-7322. www.prescotthotel.com. 164 rooms.* **$$$$** A richly upholstered lobby with a blazing fireplace welcomes guests to this elegant boutique hotel. Room furnishings reflect a European influence with custom-made cherry-wood stylings. Wolfgang Puck's **Postrio** restaurant adjoins the hotel.

Serrano Hotel – *405 Taylor St., Union Sq.* ✗ ♿ 🅿 ☎ *415-922-3200 or 800-333-3333. www.serranohotel.com. 236 rooms.* **$$$$** Don Quixote rides again at this ode to the Spanish renaissance. Rooms are colorful and sophisticated. Fine Asian fusion cuisine is served in **Ponzu** restaurant.

Washington Square Inn – *1660 Stockton St., North Beach.* ♿ ☎ *415-981-4220 or 800-388-0220. www.wsisf.com. 15 rooms.* **$$$$** A charming and intimate European-style inn at the foot of Telegraph Hill in the heart of bohemian North Beach, this charming bed-and-breakfast offers antique furnishings, afternoon tea, evening wine and highly personalized service.

Westin St. Francis – *335 Powell St., Union Sq.* ✗ ♿ 🅿 ☎ *415-397-7000 or 800-937-8461. www.westin.com. 1,189 rooms.* **$$$$** The most visible hotel in the city from its location facing Union Square, Westin's flagship hostelry *(p 102)* is a Renaissance- and Baroque-revival structure built in 1904. A historic charm still pervades the rooms in this main building; more contemporary rooms with notable city views occupy a 32-story tower built in 1972.

Mid-Range

Commodore Hotel – *825 Sutter St., Union Sq.* ✗ ♿ 🅿 ☎ *415-923-6800 or 800-338-6848. www.sftrips.com. 113 rooms.* **$$$** Hippest of the hip Joie de Vivre group, the Commodore is an offbeat urban oasis of neo-Deco styling. Whimsical custom furnishings, 1920s luxury-liner detailing and dramatic murals create an air of the unexpected. The diner-like **Titanic Café** serves breakfast and lunch; the hypnotic **Red Room** stays open late for martini lovers.

Dockside Boat & Bed – *Pier 39, Fisherman's Wharf.* ☎ *415-392-5526 or 800-436-2574. www.boatandbed.com. 8 vessels.* **$$$** From a 36ft Catalina sailboat to a 52ft Bluewater motor yacht, these private craft offer novelty and privacy in the bustling heart of the Wharf district. The largest have three luxury staterooms to accommodate multiple couples.

The Handlery Union Square Hotel – *351 Geary St., Union Sq.* ✗ ♿ 🅿 🛝 ☎ *415-781-7800 or 800-843-4343. www.handlery.com. 377 rooms.* **$$$** A three-generation family operation that opened in 1948 (on the site of a 1907 hotel), The Handlery is a gracious, centrally located inn with unpretentious rooms and a mid-city rarity: a swimming pool.

Hotel Bohème – *444 Columbus Ave., North Beach.* ♿ ☎ *415-433-9111. www.hotelboheme.com. 15 rooms.* **$$$** Reflecting the bohemian tastes of the Beat Generation in 1950s San Francisco, this quaint boutique hotel at the foot of Telegraph Hill is dedicated to the spirit of Jack Kerouac, Lawrence Ferlinghetti and their cohorts. Colorful rooms occupy a three-story building erected in the 1880s.

Hotel Diva – *440 Geary St., Union Sq.* ✗ ♿ ☎ *415-885-0200 or 800-553-1900. www.personalityhotels.com. 111 rooms.* **$$$** The glitziest of several moderately priced San Francisco hotels in the Personality Hotels group, the trend-setting Diva is a polished Euro-tech inn, dramatically renovated in 1999 in the manner of an Art Deco-era ocean liner. Located in the Theater District, popular with the film industry, it offers rooms heavy in black granite and stainless steel.

The Hotel Juliana – *590 Bush St., Union Sq./Nob Hill.* ♿ ☎ *415-392-2540 or 800-328-3880. www.julianahotel.com. 107 rooms.* **$$$** Bold, bright and stylish in its décor, this nine-story boutique hotel at the foot of Nob Hill retains an intimate atmosphere in its historic 1903 building.

Hotel Rex – *562 Sutter St., Union Sq.* ♿ ☎ *415-433-4434 or 800-433-4434. www.sftrips.com. 94 rooms.* **$$$** The redesign of this intriguing, historic boutique hotel follows the theme of the literary and arts salons rife in San Francisco in the 1920s and 30s. Quotes from regional authors adorn the walls of different floors, and photos and books can be found in the rooms. Appropriately, an antiquarian bookstore adjoins the lobby.

Hotel Vintage Court – *650 Bush St., Union Sq.* ✗ ♿ 🅿 ☎ *415-392-4666 or 800-853-1750. www.vintagecourt.com. 107 rooms.* **$$$** This Euro-style property creates a cozy atmosphere in its lobby, where guest gather around the fireplace each evening to sample Napa Valley wines. Rooms continue the wine country theme with a palette of deep jade and rose. Adjacent to the hotel, **Masa's** serves acclaimed French cuisine.

The Inn at the Opera – *333 Fulton St., Civic Center.* ✗ ♿ ☎ *415-863-8400 or 800-325-2708. http://innattheopera.citysearch.com. 48 rooms.* **$$$.** An elegant small hotel popular among musicians and stage performers, the stars among whom often choose the Symphony or Opera Suites. Intimate and romantic, the hotel includes the delightful **Ovation** restaurant.

The Mansions Hotel and Restaurant – *2220 Sacramento St., Pacific Heights.* ✗ ♿ 🅿 ☎ *415-929-9444 or 800-826-9398. www.themansions.com. 21 rooms.* **$$$** If you don't mind a haunting by the resident specter, Claudia, this hilltop manor guarantees an unusual stay. Décor is equally eclectic in guest rooms and public rooms, which house no fewer than five museums (of art, scupture, history, magic and—wait for it—pigs). Illusionists perform nightly in an after-dinner magic show, which like breakfast is included in the rate.

The Maxwell Hotel – *386 Geary St., Union Sq.* ✗ ♿ 🅿 ☎ *415-986-2000 or 888-734-6299. www.maxwellhotel.com. 153 rooms.* **$$$** Guest rooms in this chic boutique hotel, built in 1908 but restored in Art Deco fashion, reflect its Theater District location in their stylish furnishings. **Gracie's** restaurant serves American brasserie cuisine with a 1940s twist.

Radisson Miyako Hotel – *1625 Post St., Japan Center.* ✗ ♿ 🅿 ☎ *415-922-3200 or 800-333-3333. www.radisson.com. 218 rooms.* **$$$** Japanese visitors enjoy this lodging, where they can request to sleep upon futons on tatami-matted floors, and soak in deep Japanese-style baths. Outside is a Zen-like garden.

Sir Francis Drake Hotel – *450 Powell St., Union Sq.* ✗ ♿ ☎ *415-392-7755 or 800-227-5480. www.sirfrancisdrake.com. 417 rooms.* **$$$** A renovated 1928 classic whose 21st-floor penthouse holds one of San Francisco's most popular nightclubs, **Harry Denton's Starlight Room,** the Drake rests on the cable-car line one block from Union Square. Chandeliers hanging from the gold-leaf lobby ceiling lend an atmosphere of grandeur.

Budget

Hotel Bijou – *111 Mason St., Union Sq.* ✗ ♿ ☎ *415-771-1200. www.sftrips.com/hotels/bijou.html. 65 rooms.* **$$** Recalling a 1920s movie palace, this Art Deco building is adorned with deep-gold walls and black-and-white photos of San Francisco's old movie houses. Every jewel-toned guest room is named for a film shot in the city. Visit the small theater in the lobby to see nightly double-features—and don't forget the popcorn.

Andrews Hotel – *624 Post St., Union Sq.* ✗ ♿ ☎ *415-563-6877 or 800-926-3739. www.andrewshotel.com. 48 rooms.* **$$** This bright and cozy Victorian inn offers intimacy and personal service in the European style, three blocks off Union Square. An Italian restaurant—**Fino**—is connected to the intimate lobby.

Hotel Beresford – *635 Sutter St., Union Sq.* ✗ ♿ 🅿 ☎ *415-673-9900 or 800-533-6533. http://beresford.citysearch.com. 114 rooms.* **$$** This pleasant, small Victorian hotel attracts British visitors with its English pub, the **White Horse Tavern.** A similarly priced sister hotel, the **Hotel Beresford Arms** *(701 Post St., ☎ 415-673-2600; 102 rooms),* is three blocks distant.

Chancellor Hotel – *433 Powell St., Union Sq.* ✗ ♿ ☎ *415-362-2004 or 800-428-4748. www.chancellorhotel.com. 137 rooms.* **$$** Location is everything at this stately 15-story inn, opened in 1914 on the Powell-Hyde and Powell-Mason cable-car lines, one-half block from the St. Francis. A non-smoking hotel decorated in classic European motif, it is one of the central city's best bargains.

Grant Plaza Hotel – *465 Grant Ave., Chinatown.* ♿ ☎ *415-434-3883 or 800-472-6899. www.grantplaza.com. 72 rooms.* **$$** A remarkable value in the heart of Chinatown, this clean, bright inn may be simple, but it offers such modern conveniences as data ports, hair dryers and electronic key cards.

The Nob Hill Hotel – *835 Hyde St., Nob Hill.* ✗ ♿ ☎ *415-885-2987 or 877-662-4455. www.nobhillhotel.com. 50 rooms.* **$$** Restored in 1998, this neighborhood gem—which dates from 1906—has reclaimed its original marble flooring, alabaster chandeliers and stained-glass windows. Cozy rooms have Victorian furnishings and objets d'art; a charming Italian café is attached.

Phoenix Hotel – *601 Eddy St., Civic Center/Tenderloin.* ✗ ♿ ☇ ☎ *415-776-1380 or 800-248-9466. www.sftrips.com. 41 rooms.* **$$** Joie de Vivre's funkiest hotel is a rockers' paradise with its swimming pool fringed by palm trees. Jimmy Buffett would feel right at home amid the tropical island décor of the guest rooms. **Backflip** is a playful restaurant-lounge immersed in blue.

Renoir Hotel – *45 McAllister St., Civic Center.* ✗ ♿ ☎ *415-626-5200, 800-576-3388. www.renoirhotel.com. 135 rooms.* **$$** This ornate, triangular-shaped, historic landmark hotel—built in 1909 at the corner of Market Street—is very popular among European and Latin American visitors. It has seven stories of simple but comfortable rooms, and a ground-floor Brazilian restaurant.

24 Henry Guesthouse and Village House – *24 Henry St., Castro Dist.* ♿ ☎ *415-864-5686 or 800-900-5686. www.24henry.com. 10 rooms.* **$$** A largely gay and lesbian clientele frequent these two colorful, bed-and-breakfast inns that occupy classic Victorian houses a few blocks from one another in the heart of the Castro. Rates include a complimentary breakfast buffet served in the spacious parlor.

Central YMCA – *220 Golden Gate Ave., Tenderloin.* ♿ ☇ ☎ *415-885-0460. 108 rooms.* **$** Private rooms with shared baths, or dormitories with bunk beds offer security and value (including a light breakfast) in a sometimes-seedy neighborhood near United Nations Plaza.

Green Tortoise Guest House – *494 Broadway, North Beach.* ♿ ☎ *415-834-1000 or 800-867-8647. www.greentortoise.com. 40 rooms (110 beds).* **$** Operated by a long-distance budget bus service for backpack travelers, this clean, spacious hostel has private rooms and dorms (some co-ed) with up to nine bunks.

Hostel at Union Square – *312 Mason St., Union Sq.* ♿ ☎ *415-788-5604 or 800-909-4776. 230 beds.* **$** Five floors of dormitory rooms, none with more than four beds, draw international students to the Theater District. The pleasant hostel's amenities include a kitchen, library, TV room and smoking room.

San Francisco International Hostel – *Bldg. 240, Fort Mason.* ♿ ▢ ☎ *415-771-7277 or 800-444-6111. 160 rooms.* **$** Few youth hostels offer the views afforded by this one, perched on a bluff over San Francisco Bay with the Golden Gate Bridge in the distance. Guests are expected to perform a daily chore to help keep the dorm rooms neat and clean.

San Remo Hotel – *2237 Mason St., Fisherman's Wharf/North Beach.* ☎ *415-776-8688 or 800-352-7366. www.sanremohotel.com. 62 rooms.* **$** Like a European pension, all rooms in the San Remo share baths, and none have phones or TVs. Accommodations are simple and cozy, but charming and neatly kept with late-19C antiques. The staff is friendly and helpful.

Out on the Town

PERFORMING ARTS

Bay Area visitors may pick from among the region's abundant and diverse per-forming-arts offerings. Nearly 100 live-performance theaters mount a variety of stage productions performed by traveling Broadway companies and respected regional and local groups. Acclaimed dance, symphony and opera companies perform at Civic Center venues. The main theater district is centered just west of Union Square, while stages at Yerba Buena Gardens and Fort Mason Center host a variety of music, film, theater and dance events. Popular rock and alternative music performers play at intimate and large-scale nightclubs as well as at stadiums and arenas throughout the Bay Area. A variety of public readings by both established and up-and-coming authors are held at book-stores, coffeehouses and other locations (check *The San Francisco Bay Guardian* or *SF Weekly* for current listings). *For a detailed listing of events in five lan-guages, call the SFCVB's information line (☎ 415-391-2001) or consult the arts and entertainment sections of publications listed on p 276.*

Kathleen Mitchell in Balanchine's *Rubies*

Music and Dance

Classical Music	Venue	Season	☏
Philharmonia Baroque	Various locations	Sept–Apr	415-252-1288
Pocket Opera	Various locations	Feb–Jun	415-575-1100
San Francisco Contemporary Music Players	701 Mission St. Center for the Arts	Sept–Apr	415-252-6235
San Francisco Opera	War Memorial Opera House 301 Van Ness Ave.	Jun, Sept –Dec	415-864-3330
San Francisco Performances	Various locations	Sept–May	415-398-6449
San Francisco Symphony	Davies Symphony Hall 201 Van Ness Ave.	Sept–Jul	415-552-8000

Dance			
San Francisco Ballet	War Memorial Opera House 301 Van Ness Ave.	Feb–May	415-861-5600
Oakland Ballet	Paramount Theatre 2025 Broadway, Oakland	Sept–Dec	510-452-9288

Rock/Pop			
Bill Graham Civic Auditorium	50 Grove St.		415-974-4000
Cow Palace	Geneva & Santos Sts., Daly City		415-469-6065
Chronicle Pavilion	2000 Kirker Pass Rd., Concord		925-671-3123
The Fillmore	1805 Geary Blvd. at Fillmore St.		415-346-6000
Shoreline Amphitheatre	1 Amphitheatre Pkwy., Mountain View		650-967-3000
The Warfield	982 Market St.		415-775-7722

Theaters, Companies and Performances

Theaters	Address	☏
Actors Theatre SF	533 Sutter St.	415-296-9179
American Conservatory Theater Company	Geary Theater 415 Geary St.	415-749-2228
Asian American Theatre	1840 Sutter St.	415-440-5545
Aurora Theater	2315 Durant Ave., Berkeley	510-843-4822
Bannam Place Theater	50 Bannam Pl.	415-986-4607

Bayfront Theatre	Bldg. B, Fort Mason Center	415-474-8935
Berkeley Repertory Theater	2025 Addison St.	510-845-4700
Climate Theatre	252 Ninth St.	415-978-2345
Center for the Arts Theater	Yerba Buena Ctr., 700 Howard St.	415-978-2787
Cowell Theater	Pier 2, Fort Mason Center	415-441-3687
Curran Theatre	445 Geary Blvd.	415-551-2000
Davies Symphony Hall	201 Van Ness Ave.	415-552-8000
Exit Theatre/Exit Stage Left	156 Eddy St.	415-986-9194
42nd Street Moon	Eureka Theatre, 215 Jackson St.	415-281-5868
Geary Theater	415 Geary Blvd.	415-749-2228
Golden Gate Theatre	1 Taylor St.	415-551-2000
Herbst Pavilion	Pier 2, Fort Mason Center	415-441-3400
Il Teatro 450	449 Powell St.	415-433-1172
Julia Morgan Theatre	2640 College Ave., Berkeley	888-326-6906
Lorraine Hansberry Theatre	620 Sutter St.	415-474-8800
Luna Sea	2940 16th St.	415-863-2388
Magic Theatre	Bldg. D, Fort Mason Center	415-441-8822
Marines Memorial Theatre	609 Sutter St.	415-771-6900
New Conservatory Theater	25 Van Ness Ave.	415-861-8972
New Langton Arts	1246 Folsom St.	415-621-7797
Next Stage Theater	1620 Bush St.	415-778-4050
Orpheum Theater	1192 Market St.	415-551-2000
Paramount Theatre	2025 Broadway St., Oakland	510-465-6400
Shelton Theatre	533 Sutter St.	415-441-3687
SomArts	933 Brannan St.	415-453-2507
Theater Artaud	450 Florida St.	415-621-7797
Theatre on the Square	450 Post St.	415-433-9500
Theatre Rhinoceros	2926 16th St.	415-861-5079
Victoria Theatre	2961 16th St.	415-267-0642
War Memorial Opera House	301 Van Ness Ave.	415-864-3330
Zellerbach Hall	University of California, Berkeley	510-642-9988

Long-Running Performances

Beach Blanket Babylon	Club Fugazi, 678 Green St.	415-421-4222
Shear Madness	Mason St. Theatre, 340 Mason St.	415-982-5463
Teatro ZinZanni	Le Palais Nostalgique, Pier 29	415-438-2668
Tony 'n' Tina's Wedding	Cable Car Theatre, 430 Mason St.	800-660-8462

Theater Festivals

Shakespeare in the Park	Golden Gate Park	Labor Day–Oct	415-422-2222
California Shakespeare Festival	100 Gateway Rd., Orinda	Jun–Oct	510-548-3422
Mountain Theatre	Mt. Tamalpais SP	May–Jun	415-383-1100

Tickets

As some of the more popular events sell out months in advance, it is wise to buy tickets early. Full-price tickets can be purchased directly from the venue's box office or from one of the brokers listed below; major credit cards are accepted (a service charge of $1-$7 may be added to the ticket price). Ticket brokers sometimes have tickets available when the box office is sold out, but expect to pay a substantial service fee (up to 25%). Hotel concierges may also be able to help secure tickets.

San Francisco Performing Arts Websites
www.sfballet.org
www.philharmonia.org
www.bestofbroadway-sf.org
www.magictheatre.org
www.beachblanketbabylon.com
www.shearmadness.com
www.killingmylobster.com

TIX Bay Area offers half-price tickets for selected events on the day of the show. Purchases must be made in person from the box office in Union Square on Stockton St. between Post and Geary (cash or travelers checks only, open year-round Tue–Thu 11am–6pm, Fri–Sat 11am–7pm), or by phone (full price advance sale tickets only, VISA and MasterCard accepted; ☎ 415-433-7827; www.theatrebayarea.org). **Bass Ticketmaster** (☎ 510-762-2277) outlets are operated at most locations of Tower Records and The Wherehouse. **City Box Office** offers tickets for classical performances and lectures held at smaller venues (152 Kearny St.; ☎ 415-392-4400).

NIGHTLIFE

San Francisco's nightlife is as diverse as its population, and ranges from elegant Nob Hill piano bars to North Beach coffeehouses to clubs offering alternative music and jazz in the Haight-Ashbury or South of Market areas. Consult the arts and entertainment sections of the publications listed on p 276 for detailed listings of events. Some establishments have a cover charge. Some clubs and coffeehouses serve food (menu may be scaled down to light appetizers after 10 or 11pm). Proof of age (21) is required to enter most clubs that serve alcoholic beverages.

Bay Area Nightclubs

BLUES	Address	☎
Biscuits & Blues	401 Mason St. (Union Sq.)	415-292-2583
Boom Boom Boom	1601 Fillmore St. (Pacific Hts.)	415-673-8053
Eli's Mile High Club	3629 Martin Luther King Way (Oakland)	510-655-6661
Harry Denton's	161 Steuart St. (Embarcadero)	415-882-1333
The Saloon	1232 Grant Ave. (North Beach)	415-989-7666

COCKTAIL DANCING		
H. Denton's Starlight Room	Sir Francis Drake Hotel, 450 Powell St. (Union Sq.)	415-395-8595
Hi-Ball Lounge	473 Broadway (North Beach)	415-397-9464
Julie's Supper Club	1123 Folsom St. (SoMa)	415-861-0707
Plush Room	York Hotel, 940 Sutter St. (Union Sq.)	415-885-2800
Tonga Room	Fairmont Hotel 950 Mason St. (Nob Hill)	415-772-5278
Top of the Mark	Mark Hopkins Hotel 999 California St. (Nob Hill)	415-616-6916

COMEDY		
Cobb's Comedy Club	2801 Leavenworth St. (Fisherman's Wharf)	415-928-4320
The Marsh	1074 Valencia St. (Mission Dist.)	415-826-5750
Punch Line	444 Battery St. (Financial Dist.)	415-397-4337

DANCE CLUBS		
Cat Club	1190 Folsom St. (SoMa)	415-431-3332
DNA Lounge	375 11th St. (SoMa)	415-626-1409
The Endup	401 Sixth St. (SoMa)	415-357-0827
Nickie's	460 Haight St. (Haight-Ashbury)	415-621-6508
Polly Esther's	181 Eddy St. (Tenderloin)	415-885-1977
Ruby Skye	420 Mason St. (Union Sq.)	415-693-0777
Sound Factory	525 Harrison St. (SoMa)	415-979-8686
Ten 15 Folsom	1015 Folsom St. (SoMa)	415-431-0700
Townsend	177 Townsend St. (SoMa)	415-974-1156

JAZZ		
Bimbo's 365 Club	1025 Columbus Ave. (North Beach)	415-474-0365
Bruno's	2389 Mission St. (Mission Dist.)	415-550-7455
Cafe du Nord	2170 Market St. (Castro Dist.)	415-861-5016
Cypress Club	500 Jackson St. (Jackson Sq.)	415-296-8555
Elbo Room	647 Valencia St. (Mission Dist.)	415-552-7788
Enrico's	504 Broadway (North Beach)	415-982-6223
Jazz at Pearl's	256 Columbus Ave. (N. Beach)	415-291-8255
Kimball's East	5800 Shellmound St. (Emeryville)	510-658-2555
Storyville	1751 Fulton St. (Haight-Ashbury)	415-441-1751
Up & Down Club	1151 Folsom St. (SoMa)	415-626-2388
Yoshi's	Jack London Square, 510 Embarcadero West (Oakland)	510-238-9200

LATIN		
El Rio	3158 Mission St. (Mission Dist.).	415-282-3325
Mr. E's Spotlight	2203 Mariner Sq. Loop (Alameda)	510-523-8368
Roccapulco	3140 Mission St. (Mission Dist.)	415-648-6611

ROCK/FOLK

Bottom of the Hill	1233 17th St. (Potrero Hill)	415-621-4455
Freight & Salvage	1111 Addison St. (Berkeley)	510-548-1761
Great American Music Hall	859 O'Farrell St. (Tenderloin)	415-885-0750
The Last Day Saloon	406 Clement St. (Richmond Dist.)	415-387-6343
Lost & Found Saloon	1353 Grant Ave. (North Beach)	415-675-5996
Maritime Hall	450 Harrison St. (SoMa.)	415-974-0634
Paradise Lounge	1501 Folsom St. (SoMa)	415-861-6906
Slim's	333 11th St. (SoMa)	415-522-0333
The Stork Club	380 12th St. (Oakland)	510-444-6174

Shopping

From large complexes incorporating national chains, restaurants and entertainment venues, to intimate rows of boutiques scattered throughout the city, San Francisco satisfies the most ardent shopper. Most stores accept major credit cards and travelers checks, but not out-of-state checks. Many shops extend their hours during the holiday season *(mid-Nov–Dec)*. *The San Francisco Book (p 56)* offers detailed information on types of shops, locations and hours of operation.

MAIN SHOPPING AREAS

Union Square Area – *p 100*. San Francisco's leading shopping district, this area is home to major city department stores. **Nordstrom** *(☎ 415-243-8500)* is in the **San Francisco Shopping Centre** *(865 Market St.; ☎ 415-495-5656)*, an enormous complex of more than 100 shops and restaurants. Other major stores include **Macy's** *(corner of Stockton & O'Farrell Sts.; ☎ 415-397-3333)*, **Neiman Marcus** *(150 Stockton St.; ☎ 415-362-3900)*, **Gump's** *(135 Post St.; ☎ 415-982-1616)*, and **Saks Fifth Avenue** *(384 Post St., The Men's Store at 220 Post St.; ☎ 415-986-4300)*. Designer boutiques and specialty shops like **Emporio Armani** *(1 Grant Ave.; ☎ 415-677-9400)* and **Burberry's** *(225 Post St.; ☎ 415-392-2200)* are found along and around Grant Avenue, Post Street, Sutter Street and Maiden Lane.

Financial District – *p 75*. The major business district boasts the **Embarcadero Center** *(next to Justin Herman Plaza; ☎ 415-772-0550)*, a 10-acre office-and-retail complex incorporating more than 125 shops and restaurants. The **Crocker Galleria** *(50 Post St.; ☎ 415-393-1505)* contains nearly 50 designer and specialty shops. More than 25 fine **antique** shops are located in the Jackson Square Historic District near Jackson & Montgomery Streets *(Jackson Square Art & Antiques Dealers Association; ☎ 415-397-6999)*.

Chinatown – *p 64*. Haggle at an open-air market along Stockton Street, or admire luxurious silks and jades at Grant Avenue shops, in this colorful, bustling micro-city. Pharmacies sell traditional Asian herbal remedies and a plenitude of restaurants offer *dim sum* and other Chinese delicacies.

Ghirardelli Square

Fisherman's Wharf – *p 111*. Four major retail centers punctuate this festive strip of souvenir shops and novelty museums—**The Anchorage**, with more than 50 shops and restaurants *(☎ 415-775-6000)*; **The Cannery**, housing nearly 40 specialty shops and restaurants *(☎ 415-771-3112)*; **Ghirardelli Square**, featuring more than 70 shops including major retail chains *(☎ 415-775-5500)*; and **Pier 39**, boasting more than 100 specialty and gift shops *(☎ 415-981-7437)*.

Mission District – *p 163*. This lively area abounds with shops selling Latin American imports, including jewelry and clothing; alternative art galleries; small grocery stores, and restaurants. **Valencia Street** is the hub of the shopping district.

South of Market – *p 167*. A bargain hunter's dream, this area boasts dozens of outlet centers, resale shops and design showrooms. The factory outlet for **Esprit** *(499 Illinois St. at 16th St.; ☎ 415-957-2500)*, in Potrero Hill, offers great bargains in women's and children's clothing. The **San Francisco Antique & Design Mall** *(701 Bayshore Blvd.; ☎ 415-656-3530; www.sfantiquer.com)* and **Baker Hamilton Square** *(700 7th St.; ☎ 415-861-3500)* incorporate hundreds of antique stores.

Other Shopping Areas

In addition to the areas described above, charming neighborhood shopping areas can be found throughout San Francisco. Most harbor a pleasant mix of small boutiques, specialty shops, bookstores, restaurants and cafes.

Union Street (Cow Hollow)	*Van Ness Ave. to Steiner St.*
Chestnut Street (Marina District)	*Divisadero to Fillmore Sts.*
Fillmore Street (Pacific Heights)	*Jackson to Bush Sts. & Union to Greenwich Sts.*
Haight Street (Haight-Ashbury)	*Stanyan St. to Central Ave.*
Hayes Street (Civic Center)	*Franklin to Octavia Sts.*
24th Street (Noe Valley)	*Church to Douglass Sts.*
Castro Street (Castro District)	*16th to 19th Sts.*
Sacramento Street (Richmond District)	*Spruce to Baker Sts.*

ART GALLERIES

San Francisco's largest concentration of art galleries is located along Geary, Sutter, Post and Powell Streets. The *San Francisco Gallery Guide*, published bimonthly, provides a comprehensive listing of exhibits and their locations *(available from SF Bay Area Gallery Guide, 1369 Fulton St.; ☎ 415-921-1600)*. Commercial galleries' hours vary widely, with many of them closing Sundays and/or Mondays. Most open between 10am and 11am and close between 5pm and 6pm, though exceptions to that rule are commonplace.

San Francisco's greatest concentration of galleries can be found along Sutter, Post and Geary Streets in the blocks north and immediately south of Union Square. Particularly rich in galleries is Sutter between Stockton and Mason Streets. Jackson Square, Cow Hollow, Fisherman's Wharf, SoMa and other precincts have smaller concentrations of fine art.

Sightseeing

VISITOR INFORMATION

Two free publications, *Key This Week* and *Where San Francisco*, offer information on events, attractions, shopping and dining. Both are available at hotels and visitor kiosks. In addition, the **San Francisco Convention and Visitors Bureau** publishes *The San Francisco Book*. The SFCVB **Information Center** is located on the lower level of Hallidie Plaza *(Market & Powell Sts.; open year-round Mon–Fri 9am–5:30pm, Sat 9am–3pm, Sun 10am–2pm; ☎ 415-391-2000; www. sfvisitor.org)*. A multilingual staff is well equipped to assist visitors. The center stocks brochures for restaurants, hotels, clubs and attractions, and sells Muni maps and passes.

TOURS

City and Bay Area Tours

Several operators tour the main attractions of San Francisco and the surrounding Bay Area by mid-size coach. Packages may include a bay cruise or excursion to Muir Woods National Monument, Sausalito, the Wine Country or other sights. Pickup and foreign-language tours are available; reservations may be required.

Gray Line Deluxe City Tour: *year-round daily 9am, 11am, 2pm. 4hrs. $37.* 🚹 ☎ *415-558-7373. www.graylinesanfrancisco.com.*

Great Pacific Tour Co.: *year-round daily 9am, 11am, 2pm. 3hrs 30min. $33.* 🚹 ☎ *415-626-4499. www.greatpacifictour.com.*

Tower Tours: *depart from Pier 43 1/2. year-round daily 9:15am, 11am, 2pm. 3hrs 30min. $31.* 🚹 ☎ *415-434-8687. http:// towertours.citysearch.com.*

San Francisco Fire Engine Tours & Adventures: Novelty tour aboard 1955 Mack fire engine departs Beach Street at The Cannery and crosses the Golden Gate Bridge to Sausalito. *Year-round daily, schedule varies. 1hr 15min. $24.* 🚹 ☎ *415-333-7077. www.fireenginetours.com.*

Blue & Gold Fleet (🚹 ☎ *415-705-5555; www.blueandgoldfleet.com*) and **Red & White Fleet** (🚹 ☎ *415-673-2900; www.redandwhite.com*) also book bus tours.

Historical & Architectural Tours

City Guides of San Francisco, organized by the San Francisco Public Library, offers 25 different free walking tours; quality may vary depending upon the proficiency of the volunteer docent. *(Tours operate year-round daily, starting between 10am & 2pm; no tours Jan 1, Thanksgiving Day, Dec 25; 1hr 30min–2hrs; call for schedule & departure points.* 🚹 ☎ *415-557-4266; www.sfcityguides.org.)*

The **San Francisco Historical Society** offers free walking tours of many city neighborhoods, including the Financial District, Golden Gate Park, Haight-Ashbury and the Mission District. Most popular is the Barbary Coast Trail, led by historian Daniel Bacon. *(Tours operate year-round Sat 10am, weather permitting; 2hrs; call for schedule and departure points.* 🚹 ☎ *415-775-1111; www. sfhistory.org.)*

The **Victorian Home Walk** unveils the city's past through its treasured "painted lady" architecture. Depart from Westin St. Francis hotel lobby, Union Square *(year-round daily 11am; 2hrs 30min; $20.* ☎ *415-252-9485; www.victorian walk.com).*

The **Dashiell Hammett Tour** revisits Sam Spade's era on this popular literary walk, departing 100 Larkin St., at the northwest corner of the San Francisco Public Library *(May–Jun Sat noon, or by appointment; 4hrs; $10;* ☎ *510-287-9540).*

Neighborhood Tours

Several agencies offer in-depth walking tours examining the history, traditions and cuisine of fascinating **Chinatown**. Most offer lunch for an additional fee.

All About Chinatown Walking Tours depart from Jeanette's Travel Services *(812 Clay St.),* year-round daily 10am. *2hrs. reservations required. $25 tour, $37 including dim sum lunch noon–1pm.* 🚹 ☎ *415-982-8839. www.allabout chinatown.com.*

Wok Wiz Chinatown Tours depart from Wok Wiz Cooking Center *(654 Commercial St.),* year-round daily 10am. *3hrs 15min. $27 tour, $39 including lunch. reservations required.* ☎ *415-981-8989. www.wokwiz.com.*

Chinese Heritage Walk depart from the Chinese Cultural Center *(750 Kearny St., 3rd floor),* year-round Sat 2pm. *1hr. reservations required. $15 (luncheon walks also available for groups of six or more, $30).* ☎ *415-986-1822. www.c-c-c.org.*

Cruisin' the Castro highlights the fascinating past and lively present of the Castro District and San Francisco's gay and lesbian community. Trevor Hailey has offered the tour since 1989. Departs from Harvey Milk Plaza at Castro & Market Sts. *(year-round Tue–Sat & holidays 10am; 4hrs; reservations required; $40, brunch included.* 🚹 ☎ *415-550-8110; www.webcastro.com/castrotour).*

A **Haight-Ashbury Neighborhood Walking Tour** departs from Stanyan & Waller Sts. *(year-round Tue & Sat 9:30am; 2hrs; $15;* ☎ *415-221-8442).*

The **Pacific Heights Walking Tour** is offered by San Francisco Architectural Heritage. It depart from Haas-Lilienthal House, 2007 Franklin St. *(year-round Sun 12:30pm; 2hrs; $5;* ☎ *415-441-3000; www.sfheritage.org).*

Scenic Cruises & Ferries

Bay cruises offer panoramic views of the skyline, Golden Gate Bridge, Alcatraz, and the hills of Marin County and the East Bay. Some companies offer evening and dinner/dance cruises. Following are some popular cruises and ferries.

Blue & Gold Fleet Bay Cruise: frequent departures from Pier 39 *(May–Sept daily 10am–6:45pm; rest of the year 10am–4pm; 1hr; $17;* ✗ 🚹 🅿 ☎ *415-773-1188; www.blueandgoldfleet.com).*

Red & White Fleet Golden Gate Bridge Cruise: departs from Pier 43 1/2 *(Memorial Day–Sept daily 10am–6pm; early Mar–Memorial Day daily 10am–5pm; rest of the year daily 10am–4:15pm; round-trip 1hr; commentary; $18;* ✗ 🚹 🅿 ☎ *415-673-2900; www.redandwhite.com).*

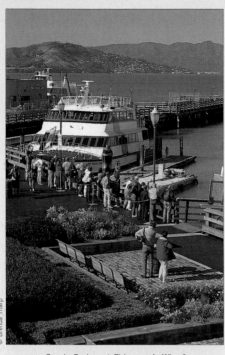

Alameda/Oakland Ferry: runs between Jack London Square (Oakland), Alameda, Pier 39 and the Ferry Building as well as to Angel Island *(depart year-round Mon–Fri 6am–8:55pm; weekends & holidays May–Sept 9:30am –10:30pm, rest of the year 9am–7:10pm; no service Jan 1, Thanksgiving Day, Dec 25; 30min one-way; $4.75; ✕ ♿ 🅿 ☎ 510-522-3300; 415-705-5555; www.blueand goldfleet.com).*

Golden Gate Ferry: access to Sausalito and Larkspur *(depart from the Ferry Building in San Francisco year-round; Larkspur Mon–Fri 6:35am–10:50am, $2.95; & weekends 10:45am–6:45pm, $5; Sausalito Mon–Fri 7:40am–8pm & weekends 11:30am–6:55pm (May–Sept til 8:05pm), $5; no service Jan 1, Thanksgiving Day,*

Scenic Cruises at Fisherman's Wharf

Dec 25; 30–45min; ✕ ♿ 🅿 ☎ 415-923-2000; www.goldengate.org).

Specialty Tours

Culinary Tours – Visitors may explore local history while savoring some of San Francisco's legendary cuisine. **Mangia North Beach** tours depart from the Bank of America at Stockton & Columbus Sts. *(year-round Sat 10am; 4hrs; reservations required; $45; ♿ ☎ 415-397-8530; www.graceannwalden.com).* **Glorious Food Culinary Walktours** visit Chinatown and North Beach. *(Chinatown year-round daily 9am, 4hrs, $35. North Beach year-round daily 9:30am; 3hrs; $30. Combined tour daily 9am; 6hrs; reservations required; $55; ☎ 415-441-5637.)*

Mural Tours – *p 166* . Several organizations offer tours of the Mission District's powerful works of public art. **City Guides** *(see above; meets at Precita & Harrison Sts., behind Flynn Elementary School, year-round Sat 11am).* **Precita Eyes Mural Arts Center** *(depart from 348 Precita Ave., year-round Sat 1:30pm; 1hr 30min; $5; ☎ 415-285-2287; www.precitaeyes.org). Note that use of public transportation to this area is not recommended.*

Nightlife Tour – For those who want to drink but not drive, **3 Babes and a Bus** offer an adventurous tour of four unique San Francisco dance clubs *(depart from The Blue Lamp, 561 Geary St., year-round Sat nights; reservations required, must be 21 or older; $35 includes cover charges; ☎ 415-552-2582; www.threebabes.com).*

Sports and Recreation

A mild climate promotes recreational opportunities year-round, most in the city or within an hour's drive of its limits. Hikers, bikers and equestrians avail themselves of trails throughout Marin County, the East Bay and San Francisco Peninsula. Lovers of water sports take to the waves for surfing, windsurfing and sea kayaking, though swimming in most places is unsafe. Jogging, roller-blading, hang-gliding, kite-flying and sportfishing are other recreational possibilities.

Golden Gate Park, Marin County and units of the Golden Gate National Recreation Area (GGNRA) are good places to start when seeking outdoor recreation information. Trail maps, facility hours and other information are available at the **San Francisco Recreation & Park Department** *(McLaren Lodge, Golden Gate Park; ☎ 415-831-2700)* and the **GGNRA** *(Fort Mason, Building 201; ☎ 415-556-0560).* The **Marin County Convention & Visitors Bureau** *(1013 Larkspur Landing Circle, Larkspur, CA 94939; ☎ 415-499-5000)* also provides maps and information.

Roller skating in Golden Gate Park

Hiking – The Bay Area is a hiker's paradise, with extensive trails exploring its valleys, scaling its peaks, tracing its coastlines and penetrating its forests. Contact the GGNRA or the San Francisco Recreation & Park Department *(above)* for trail maps and information. Within the city, the **Golden Gate Promenade** (4mi) from Aquatic Park to the Golden Gate Bridge, and the **Coastal Trail** (9mi) from the Golden Gate Bridge to Fort Funston, afford lovely ocean and cityscape views.

Biking – Mountain biking is an especially popular sport among the hills and valleys of Marin County and in The Presidio and Land's End areas of San Francisco. Most trails are accessible to both hikers and bikers, though some are restricted to hikers only. Routes within San Francisco include the Golden Gate Promenade and the Coastal Trail *(above)*. In addition, many streets have designated bike lanes. Shops offering rentals and trail information include:

Adventure Bike Company 968 Columbus Ave., ☎ 415-771-8735	bikes, tandems
Blazing Saddles Bike Rentals 1095 Columbus Ave., ☎ 415-202-8888	bikes, tandems
Park Cyclery 1749 Waller St., ☎ 415-221-3777	bikes, tandems, skates
Golden Gate Park Skate & Bike 3038 Fulton St., ☎ 415-668-1117	bikes, tandems, skates

Fishing – The most common fishes found in the bay are striped bass, halibut and rock cod. Sport-fishing charters, specializing in salmon (Jun–Oct) and giant sturgeon, depart for the ocean from Fisherman's Wharf. Public fishing piers include Aquatic Park Municipal Pier, Fort Mason Piers, Fort Point/Crissy Field Pier, Baker Beach, and Pier 7 at the Embarcadero. A fishing license is required to take fish and crustaceans (except for persons angling from a public pier); one-day nonresident licenses are available in fishing supply stores.

Swimming and Beachwalking – Waters of the Pacific shore and Golden Gate can be dangerous. Tides sweep in suddenly and powerfully and "sneaker waves" may appear without warning. Never turn your back to the ocean. Avoid walking along coastal cliffs; keep to established trails. Riptides (strong, narrow seaward flows), sudden dropoffs and strong currents make most areas dangerous for swimming and even wading. Besides, water temperatures average a chilly 55°F (13°C) year-round. Exercise caution when swimming at all times, and obey posted warnings.

Selected Bay Area Beaches	$	🏊	✚	⚠	♿	🏃
Aquatic Park Beach		●			●	
Baker Beach						●
Bean Hollow State Beach						
Bolinas Beach		●				●
China Beach		●	●	●		●
Crissy Field						
Drakes Beach		●			●	
Fort Funston		●				●

Selected Bay Area Beaches	$	☲	✚	△	♿	⚏
Francis State Beach	●	●		●	●	●
Kehoe Beach		●				●
Land's End		●				
Lighthouse Field State Beach					●	●
Limantour Beach		●			●	
McClures Beach		●				
Montara State Beach		●				
Muir Beach		●			●	
North Beach & South Beach	●		●			
Ocean Beach					●	●
Pebble Beach						
Pescadero State Beach						●
Rodeo Beach					●	●
San Gregorio State Beach	●				●	
Stinson Beach		●	●		●	●
Tomales Bay State Park	●	●		●	●	

Symbols on the above chart indicate: $ admission/parking fee; ☲ swimming; ✚ lifeguard; △ camping; ♿ disabled facilities; ⚏ surfing.

Golf – There are three public courses within the city limits of San Francisco; all rent out clubs and other equipment. Many others are throughout the Bay Area.

> **Lincoln Park** *open daily dawn–dusk*
> 34th Ave. & Clement St., ☎ 415-221-9911
>
> **Golden Gate Golf Course** *open daily dawn–dusk*
> 47th Ave. & Fulton St., ☎ 415-751-8987
>
> **Presidio Golf Course** *open daily 7am–7pm*
> W. Pacific Ave., Presidio, ☎ 415-561-4653

Windsurfing – Consistent westerly winds from March to October make San Francisco Bay a prime spot for windsurfing, particularly at Crissy Field, Candlestick Point and Lake Merced. Many organizations offer instruction and rental equipment, including **San Francisco School of Windsurfing** *(Candlestick Point & Lake Merced;* ☎ *415-753-3235)* and **City Fun Sailboards** *(Crissy Field;* ☎ *415-929-7873)*. Note that certification is required to rent windsurfing equipment; contact the **San Francisco Boardsailing Association** *(1592 Union St., P.O. Box 301, San Francisco CA 94123; www.sfba.org)* for additional information.

Hang-gliding – The cliffs of Fort Funston rank among the finest hang-gliding sites in the US *(main season Mar–Oct)*. Several hang-gliding shops, located near the fort, offer rentals and instruction. Contact the **San Francisco Bay Area Paragliding Association** for a list of shops, current conditions and hang-gliding events *(SFBAPA, P.O. Box 1809, Pacifica, CA 94044;* ☎ *415-864-6359; www.sfbapa.org)*.

Working Out – Many clubs allow non-members to utilize their facilities for a daily fee *($10-$15)*.

Club One	☎
Two Embarcadero Center *(Financial District)*	415-398-1111
950 California St. *(Nob Hill)*	415-398-1111
24-Hour Fitness	
350 Bay St. (North Beach)	415-395-9595
100 California St. *(Financial District)*	415-434-5080
1200 Van Ness Ave. *(Japantown)*	415-776-2200
303 2nd St. at Folsom St. *(SoMa)*	415-543-7808
Pinnacle Fitness Club	
345 Spear St. (SoMa)	415-495-1939
61 New Montgomery St. *(Union Square)*	415-543-1110
465 California St. *(Financial District)*	415-982-9800

Some hotels offer guest access to private fitness centers; check with the concierge.

YMCA memberships are valid worldwide; call for closest recreation center and available facilities ☎ 415-391-9622.

Spectator Sports

Tickets for professional sporting events can be purchased at the venue, or through Ticketmaster *(p 53)*. It's best to buy tickets well in advance.

Sport/Team	Season	Home Stadium	☎ Information
Major League Baseball	Apr–Oct	(81 home games)	
San Francisco Giants **(NL)**		Pacific Bell Park	415-972-2000
Oakland Athletics **(AL)**		Network Assoc. Coliseum	510-568-5600
National Football League	Sept–Dec	(8 home games)	
San Francisco 49ers		3Com (Candlestick) Park	415-656-4949
Oakland Raiders		Network Assoc. Coliseum	510-615-1888
National Basketball Assn.	Nov–Apr	(41 home games)	
Golden State Warriors		The Arena in Oakland	510-986-2200
National Hockey League	Oct-Apr	(41 home games)	
San Jose Sharks		San Jose Arena	408-287-9200

Pacific Bell Park is located on China Basin, at the south end of The Embarcadero within walking distance of Union Square. **3Com Park** (formerly Candlestick Park) is located south of San Francisco in the Candlestick Point State Recreation Area. By **car** take US-101 south to park exit. The "Ballpark Express" **bus** offers service between San Francisco and the stadium *($5 round-trip,* 🚌 *bus 9X, 28X & 47X,* ☎ *415-673-6864). Note: the park is windy and chilly; bring a jacket or sweater.* **Network Associates Coliseum** and **The Arena in Oakland** are located near Oakland International Airport. By **car** from San Francisco cross the Oakland Bay Bridge and take I-580 to I-980 to I-880 south to 66th Ave. exit. By rail, take the 🚈 Fremont line to the Coliseum stop, where a walkway leads to the stadium. **San Jose Arena** is located in downtown San Jose. From San Francisco, take I-280 or US-101 south.

Baseball Game in Pacific Bell Park

Yerba Buena Gardens and San Francisco Museum of Modern Art

Sights

1 • CHINATOWN★★★

all lines. bus 30–Stockton.
Map p 67

A teeming, colorful fusion of Cantonese market town and American Main Street, San Francisco's Chinatown spreads along the lower slope of Nob Hill overlooking the Financial District. One of the four largest Chinese settlements outside Asia (the others are in New York City, Toronto and Vancouver), Chinatown ranks among North America's most densely populated neighborhoods. About 30,000 people live in the 24-block core bounded by Broadway and Montgomery, California and Powell Streets. Most residents are immigrants who maintain their native dialects, customs, foods, festivals and religions. Chinatown is unique in that it also absorbs and refashions diverse American influences.

Historical Notes

Among the thousands who flocked to California during the 1849 Gold Rush were Cantonese treasure-seekers, men intent on striking bonanzas and returning to China. These expectations inspired few of them to learn English or assimilate Western culture, reinforcing their separation from American society. As China's ruling Manchu dynasty decayed through the 19C, however, and social and political conditions worsened in the homeland, ever-greater numbers of Chinese chose to remain and make their fortunes in the emerging American West.

By 1870 more than 63,000 Chinese, mostly men, were living in the US. In demand as laborers for large construction projects, they built much of the western half of the first transcontinental railroad, pioneered the fishing industry on San Francisco Bay, and planted crops on California's new farmlands. In many Western towns, Chinese entrepreneurs opened small businesses such as laundries, retail shops and grocery stores.

As the premier point of entry for Asian immigrants, San Francisco harbored North America's oldest and largest Chinese community. Several Chinese settlements formed around the city and its bay, but by the late 1860s, most Chinese immigrants had consolidated their homes and businesses along Sacramento Street a block south of Portsmouth Square.

Surviving Troubled Times – Violent waves of anti-Chinese sentiment swept the West after the economic depression of 1872. As bankruptcies put thousands out of work, tycoons bolstered their profits by hiring Chinese workers at low wages. Riotous mobs of unemployed men stormed Chinese communities, including San Francisco's Chinatown in 1877, beating (and sometimes killing) people and destroying property. Labor organizers pushed politicians to pass the Chinese Exclusion Act of 1882, barring Chinese laborers (but not merchants nor their families) from entering the US. The act effectively prevented thousands of men already in the US from sending for brides, thus preserving Chinatown's rough-and-tumble, male-dominated society well into the 20C. Chinese immigrants sought security in *tongs* ("associations" or "companies") whose memberships were usually based upon clan name or members' province of origin. These organizations often paid new arrivals' passage to San Francisco, assuming the roles of labor guild, insurance company, social club, legal advisor, protection agent and undertaker, in return for dues. A few tongs were little more than criminal gangs. By the late 19C, Chinatown had a villainous reputation as a haven for opium dens, gambling halls and brothels. Violent episodes—tong wars—erupted between factions seeking to control profits. In an effort to restore order to Chinatown and to represent Chinese interests outside the neighborhood, men from the six most powerful tongs in 1882 agreed to form a confederation. Known as the **Chinese Six Companies**, the organization remains an active, if gradually diminishing, force in modern Chinatown. The repeal in 1943 of the Chinese Exclusion Act and a further relaxation of immigration laws in the 1960s heralded a new influx of immigrants from Hong Kong, China and Southeast Asia. As families became Americanized, many moved to other areas of the city. So many have settled in adjacent North Beach since the 1960s that sections of that neighborhood between Broadway and Washington Square, long known as "Little Italy," are now culturally an extension of Chinatown. Parts of the Richmond District and the Sunset District in the western half of the city have also been transformed into "new" Chinatowns inhabited by wealthier, younger and better-educated Chinese.

Old Chinatown, however, remains the heart and soul of the far-flung Chinese community. Chinese from around the Bay Area flock here to shop, eat and socialize in the lively markets, restaurants, bookstores and cultural centers. Tourists come by the thousands to wander Grant Avenue, Stockton Street and the warren of side streets between them, visiting temples and herb shops, dining in the many restaurants, and shopping for Chinese groceries, embroidered linens, artwork, jewelry and souvenirs.

Visiting Chinatown – *www.sfchinatown.com*. To fully experience Chinatown's vibrant, intense character, visit the neighborhood on foot. Steep hills may present a challenge, but Grant Avenue and Stockton Street, the main thoroughfares, are relatively level. It's best to get to and from Chinatown by cable car or other public transportation, or by foot, as street parking is very difficult. Underground garages are located at St. Mary's Square, Portsmouth Square and the Holiday Inn at Kearny and Washington Streets. Temples and businesses typically open after 10am, but a visit to Chinatown can be interesting at any time of day. Arrive at Portsmouth Square before 8am to see neighborhood denizens practicing their morning t'ai chi. In the early evening, local residents throng the streets for evening shopping, and delicious cooking aromas waft through the air. Saturday morning is probably the most crowded time of the week, particularly along Stockton Street; Sundays are barely less hectic. Note that temples may close for certain periods during the day; if one is closed when you arrive, try again later. During Chinese New Year, which occurs between late January and late February depending on the lunar calendar, shops decorate with red and gold good-luck symbols and a festive air prevails. The popular **Chinese New Year Parade** typically takes place on the fringe of Chinatown, ending near Portsmouth Square on Kearny Street at Columbus Avenue; check with the San Francisco Convention & Visitors Bureau for the annual parade route.

WALKING TOUR *distance: .7mi.*

Begin at the intersection of Bush St. & Grant Ave. and walk north.

★★**Grant Avenue** – The eight blocks of Grant Avenue between Bush Street and Broadway comprise Chinatown's principal thoroughfare for visitors. The street abounds in architectural chinoiserie—painted balconies, curved tile rooflines, staggered towers and predominantly red, green and yellow color schemes—applied during the 1920s and 30s to otherwise-unremarkable buildings to give the neighborhood an exotic cachet. Ceramic carp and dragons on the roof of the **Chinatown Gate** *(Grant Ave. at Bush St.)* symbolize auspicious fortunes. Taiwan's government donated materials for construction of the gateway, which was designed in 1970 by Clayton Lee based upon ceremonial entrances of Chinese villages. North of the gate, shops selling curios, souvenirs, jewelry, artwork, furniture, cameras and electronics draw visitors in droves, while hardware stores, banks, poultry and fish markets, tea stores and small cafes cater to a mostly local clientele.

Numerous authentic Taoist, Buddhist and Confucianist temples are tucked away on upper floors behind unassuming doors throughout the neighborhood. Visitors are welcomed at the **Ching Chung Temple**★ *(615 Grant Ave., 4th floor; open year-round daily 11am–6pm; 20min guided tour available;* ☎ *415-433-2623)*, where portraits of the founders of three Taoist sects distinguish the main altar, overlooking a host of ancillary gods.

★**Old St. Mary's Cathedral** – *660 California St., at Grant Ave. Open year-round Mon–Fri 7am–7pm, Sat 10am–7pm, Sun 7:30am–5pm.* ᴋ ☎ *415-288-3800. www.oldstmarys.org.* The largest building in the state at the time of its dedication in 1854, this handsome Catholic church began as a cathedral, the first seat of the Archdiocese of San Francisco. The Gothic Revival structure was redesignated a

Shop Window, Chinatown

church following construction of a new St. Mary's Cathedral on Van Ness Avenue in 1891. Made of brick and iron on a foundation of granite quarried in China, the church was entirely gutted by the great conflagration of 1906, which melted its bell and marble statuary but left its stout walls intact. The somber inscription from Ecclesiastes on the exterior bell tower, "Son, observe the time and fly from evil," was reputedly aimed at the brothels that once flourished in the neighborhood. Historic photographs displayed in the vestibule offer fascinating views of 19C Chinatown.

Chinatown Temples

Among the most illuminating and evocative manifestations of Chinatown life are its many religious temples. Conventional Western scholarship may categorize Chinese religion as Confucianism, Taoism or Buddhism, but the truth is complex. Most Chinese adhere to elements of all three philosophies:

Confucianism is more an ancient state doctrine than a religion. Its prescribed rites constitute a symbolic pact upholding an ideal of harmonious social order and stability. Its hierarchy traditionally was headed by the emperor, with each member of society happily ensconced in his or her appropriate niche.

Taoism, a mystical religion, might be characterized as a way of organizing the enormous array of Chinese gods and natural forces into a formal system. Among the most popular Taoist deities worshipped in Chinatown temples are the god of warriors and poets, Guan Di, and the Queen of Heaven, Tin How, also known as Ma-Tsu.

Buddhism, carried into China from India more than 1,700 years ago, has been shaped over the centuries into a distinctively Chinese belief system, markedly different from traditional south Asian Buddhism. In China, a pantheon of different Buddhas and faithful disciples is worshiped. A less materialistic form of Chinese Buddhism is Ch'an, better known in the West by its Japanese name of Zen.

Since ancient times, the Chinese have paid reverence to their ancestors and propitiated the forces of nature through sacrifice and prayer. In every temple, worshipers can be seen offering sacrifices of fruit, rice wine, roast meats and flowers, burning incense to resident deities or to tablets inscribed with names of recently deceased relatives. After the spirits are thought to have consumed the essence of the sacrifice, the worshiper will remove the now-sanctified offering and freely partake of it at mealtime. Symbolic offerings of paper cars and houses, "cash" and even paper servants are sometimes burned in a temple furnace, by which means they are sent to deceased loved ones believed to be residing in the spirit world. The person sending the offering will often hit a drum announcing his or her sacrifice to the spirit.

Although Buddhist temples normally house only Buddha images, many Taoist temples freely mix Buddhist statues among figures of several deities. As long as beliefs do not interfere with social harmony—as long as the Confucian doctrine is upheld—the Chinese are very tolerant in matters of religion.

Visitors are welcome in most temples, though it may be necessary to ring a doorbell to gain admittance. Courtesy is expected; photography is not permitted. Contributions left in marked donation boxes are appreciated.

Ma-Tsu Temple, Interior

The church serves as the venue for popular noontime concerts of classical music, featuring a variety of local and touring professional artists *(year-round Tue & Thu 12:30; for schedule ☎ 415-288-3861)*.

Across California Street from the cathedral lies St. Mary's Square, a small, serene park anchored by a steel and granite statue of **Sun Yat-sen (1)** (1938) by sculptor Beniamino Bufano. Sun visited San Francisco's Chinese community several times around the turn of the century to raise money and support to overthrow China's Manchu Dynasty and establish the Republic of China. The successful revolution took place in 1911.

Return to Grant Ave. and continue north, turning right on Clay St.

★**Portsmouth Square** – Formerly the central plaza of the Anglo-Mexican settlement of Yerba Buena, this broad square is today Chinatown's most important outdoor gathering point. In 1846 Captain John Montgomery officially claimed Yerba Buena for the US by raising the American flag above the plaza, later renamed for his ship. California's first public school opened here in April 1848, and the square was the site of Sam Brannan's momentous announcement that gold had been discovered some 100mi east of San Francisco. During the ensuing Gold Rush, Portsmouth Square served as center of the rambunctious new boomtown and scene of many civic dramas. As commercial activity shifted to the landfill flatlands around Montgomery Street in the 1860s, however, Portsmouth Square was left on the periphery.

Today elderly men congregate in the square to socialize and play cards or Chinese chess. In the center of the square stands a **statue (2)** of the Goddess of Democracy, a somber memorial to the 1989 Tiananmen Square massacre in Beijing. On the north side stands a sailing-ship **monument (3)** to Robert Louis Stevenson, who enjoyed sitting here watching the crowds during his extended visit of 1879-80. To the east, a pedestrian bridge leads across Kearny Street to the **Chinese Culture Center** *(Holiday Inn, 750 Kearny St., 3rd floor; open year-round Tue–Sun 10am–4pm; ☎ 415-986-1822; www.c-c-c.org)*, featuring temporary exhibitions of Chinese and Chinese-American art and a permanent display of Chinese musical instruments. Many programs on Chinese culture and heritage are staged here.

Leave the square and walk uphill on Washington St.

Old Chinese Telephone Exchange – *743 Washington St.* The neighborhood's most exuberant example of chinoiserie rises in three graceful pagoda-like tiers above a glossy, red-pillared pediment. Now a branch of the Bank of Canton, the one-story building was opened as the Chinatown Telephone Exchange in 1909 to serve the community's 800 telephones. Female operators working the switchboards had to know how to speak Cantonese, Sze Yup and three other Chinese dialects, as well as English.

1 Ten Ren Tea Co.
949 Grant Ave. ☎ 415-362-0656. www.tenren.com. The oldest and largest American outlet of a Taiwan-based tea empire, this purveyor of Chinatown's traditional beverage sells tea by the metal canister or painted box, and samples by the hot, steaming cup. It costs from $6 to $200 (for high-quality ginseng root) a pound—a pricey product, but it takes 70,000 young leaves to make a pound of top-grade leaf tea.

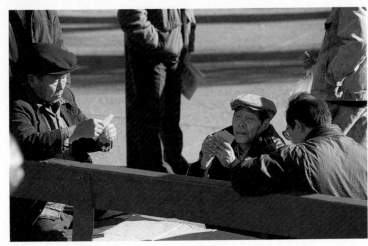

Game-playing, Portsmouth Square

Turn right on Grant Ave., walk one block and turn right on Jackson St. Walk half a block down the hill and turn left on Beckett St.

★**Ma-Tsu Temple of USA** – *30 Beckett St. Open Oct–Apr daily 9:30am–5:30pm, rest of year daily 10am–6pm. Donation requested.* & ☎ *415-986-8818.* This brightly attractive and very accessible temple honors the Queen of Heaven, using her title as known in China's coastal Fujian and Guangdong provinces and Taiwan. The central statue is guarded by figures of two ferocious warriors—the blue-faced Shun Feng Er ("Ear of Favorable Wind") on the left and the red-faced Chien Li Yen ("Eye of 1,000 Li") on the right—noted respectively for their prodigious powers of hearing and sight. (A *li* is a unit of distance; hence the guards can detect evil from 1,000 *li*.). Giant puppets of the pair can be seen striding the streets, arms swinging widely and rhythmically, in the annual Chinese New Year Parade.

Return to Jackson St. Turn right up the hill, across Grant Ave., to Ross Alley; turn left and continue to Washington St.

Jackson Street, Ross Alley and Washington Street traverse a densely populated enclave of herbalists, jewelers, restaurants, small groceries and fragrant bakeries. Suspended between Grant Avenue and Stockton Street, these side streets retain the dark, intriguing ambience of old Chinatown. Many late-19C tong war clashes occurred here, and **Ross Alley** is still known among old Chinatown residents as "Lu Song Hang" or "Spanish Lane," a reference to Hispanic prostitutes in the alley's 19C brothels. Today the narrow lane supports a shop purveying shrines, lanterns and religious statuary, and several clothing factories hum behind closed doors.

Popular with some visitors is the **Golden Gate Fortune Cookie Company**★ *(56 Ross Alley; open year-round daily 10am–midnight; ☎ 415-781-3956),* where passersby may step inside to see cookies being baked and stuffed with "fortunes" by workers seated at slowly rotating griddle-ovens. (A note of caution: Some visitors have been offended by "French adult" fortunes, inappropriate for children, that may be inserted in cookies.)

Cross Washington St., walk a few steps downhill; turn right on Waverly Pl.

★**Waverly Place** – This two-block alley is dubbed "the Street of Painted Balconies" for the handsome chinoiserie gracing otherwise plain three- and four-story Edwardian brick buildings. The colors are symbolic—red stands for happiness, green for longevity, black for money, yellow for good fortune. Among older Chinatown residents, Waverly Place is known as "Tin How Miu Gai" or "Queen of Heaven Temple Street." It is home to a cluster of temples and benevolent associations. From the street, pedestrians may hear drums booming from upper floors as youth groups practice lion-dance drills and other festival activities. Classes in Chinese calligraphy and brush painting are offered at the **Chin Fung Tong Art Gallery (V)** *(38 Waverly Pl.; ☎ 415-398-2286).*

Tin How Temple – *125 Waverly Pl., 4th floor. Open year-round daily 9am–4pm. ☎ 415-421-3628.* Chinatown's oldest temple has operated since 1852; the present building dates from 1911. It is devoted to Tin How, a Chinese woman of Fujian Province (AD 960-987) now revered as the Queen of Heaven and protector of seafarers. Credited with the miraculous rescues of many sailors, Tin How inspired a cult following after her death. The worship came to the US with Chinese immigrants who, of course, fell under Tin How's care when they crossed the Pacific

Chinatown Herb Shops

Along Stockton Street and the side streets leading down to Grant, visitors can find many traditional Chinese herb shops. These shops are usually recognizable for the curious collections prominently displayed in the front windows: bottled snakes, preserved ginseng roots that parody an almost human shape, medical charts of the human body, pieces of tree bark, elk horn, dried seahorse and other sundries. These are the stuff of an ancient Chinese system of pharmacology, a lore gathered by early Taoist monks and herbalists, chronicled, tested and refined over thousands of years.

Entering any shop, visitors will find a counter backed by wooden cabinets with drawers containing hundreds of dried herbs and other medicinals. Most by far are vegetable in origin: ginkgo for tuberculosis, mulberry leaves for cold and headache, sumac for laryngitis, loquat leaf for cough, climbing dogbane for rheumatoid arthritis, winter cherry leaf for diabetes, Job's tears for lobar pneumonia. Among the items most exotic to Western medicine might be dried centipedes, a remedy for infantile convulsions, spasms, cramps, and lockjaw; dead silkworm for sore throat and headache; snakeskin for abscesses; and decoction of silkworm cocoon to relieve exhaustion.

The herb most familiar to Westerners is ginseng, a root sliced and steeped to make a tea celebrated for its curative virtues. The finest examples of ginseng root grow wild in the mountains of north China and Korea, but these can be quite expensive and probably will not be casually displayed in the herbalist's shop. Less expensive grades of ginseng powders and teas, including a variety of American ginseng from Wisconsin, make popular gifts.

Clarion Music Center
816 Sacramento St. at Waverly Pl. ☎ *415-391-1317. www.clarionmusic.com.* A mecca for growing legions of world-music lovers, this living museum displays and sells such folk instruments as the Chinese *yangqin* and *gu zheng,* Australian didgeridoo, Indian tabla, Japanese koto and Bolivian panpipes—and arranges expert instruction in how to play any of them. Concerts are offered Friday nights, sometimes by the resident Jumping Buddha Ensemble.

Ocean. Gold and red electric lanterns glimmer in the incense-smoked interior, above a wooden statue of Tin How carried to California from Guangdong during the Gold Rush.

★**Norras Temple** – *109 Waverly Pl., 3rd floor. Open year-round daily 9am–4pm.* ☎ *415-362-1993.* A large, gilded statue of the Buddha surrounded by smaller, similar figures dominates this friendly hall of worship, the first purely Buddhist temple in the mainland US when it opened in 1960. As in most Chinese temples, visitors can cast their fortunes by shaking a tube of bamboo slips until one jogs loose, falling to the floor. Take the slip to a temple attendant, who will either interpret your fortune according to the number or hand you a printed interpretation to have translated.

Turn right on Sacramento St., walk uphill to Stockton St. and turn right.

Chinese Six Companies – *843 Stockton St. Open year-round Mon–Fri 2–5pm; closed holidays.* ☎ *415-982-6000.* Though its original function has changed, the Chinese Six Companies still wields influence among Chinatown's business establishments. The building's colorful, eye-catching facade, best viewed from the east side of Stockton Street is one of the most elaborate in Chinatown. Inside is a reception hall evocative of an imperial throne room.

★**Kong Chow Temple** – *855 Stockton St., 4th floor (elevator entrance to left of post office). Open year-round Mon–Fri 9am–4pm.* ☎ *415-434-2513.* The Kong Chow temple first opened on Pine Street in 1857. Among the original furnishings transferred to the present building (1977) are excellent examples of Chinese wood carving; the altar closest to the balcony depicts in sharp relief a social gathering hosted by the mythical lord of the sea. At the main altar, the swarthy-faced statue with a black beard represents Guan Di. Typically depicted with a sword in one hand, a book in the other, the figure is seen all over Chinatown in shrines and shop windows. A general in the Three Kingdoms period (AD 220-280), Guan Di fought ferociously and loyally for his lord, a contender for the imperial throne. Killed by treachery, he was elevated into the Taoist pantheon, becoming patron saint of a host of amazingly disparate professions, including soldiers, poets, prostitutes, police and gangsters. The figure of Guan Di is flanked by his bushy-bearded warrior "brother" Zhang Fei and his gentler son, in courtly clothing, holding an imperial chop (stamp) with both hands. Together they symbolize Guan Di's balanced devotion to both the civil government and the military.

Turn left on Clay St. for one block.

The National Chinese American Museum (R) – *965 Clay St. Scheduled opening mid-April 2001. Hours and admission to be determined.* ☎ *415-391-1188.* The new home of the Chinese Historical Society of America is a 1932 red-brick YWCA building designed by famed architect Julia Morgan. A pair of pagoda-like towers rise above a roofline crenellated with imported Chinese tiles, and a cast-stone arch with leaded glazing surmounts the double entrance doors. Six galleries of permanent and rotating exhibits are planned, four of them in the former gymnasium. Of unique interest is the Daniel Ching Collection of stereotypical late-19C and early-20C advertising images of Asian Americans. A learning center will be in the basement.

Return to Stockton St. and continue north to Broadway.

❸ **Imperial Tea Court**
1411 Powell St., just north of Broadway. Open daily 11am–6:30pm. ☎ *415-788-6080. www.imperialtea.com.* After plunging through bustling Chinatown, step into this tranquil teahouse, an oasis of dark woods and glowing lanterns. Beneath the soothing twitter of elegantly caged birds, a wide variety of rare teas is prepared and served in traditional fashion. Teapots, cups, canisters and kettles are offered for sale along with the tea.

★**Stockton Street** – The four blocks of Stockton Street between Clay Street and Broadway feature Chinatown's greatest concentration of produce, poultry and fresh fish markets. The street draws enormous crowds of mostly Chinese-American shoppers from all over the city, especially on weekend mornings. Savory Chinese specialties like pressed or roast duck, barbecued pork and soy-sauce chickens hang in the windows of food shops. Mounds of vegetables and fruits (including the aromatic durian), displayed on sidewalk stands, vie for space with vendors peddling live poultry or fresh-picked produce from curbside truck beds. Throngs of shoppers, market cries and vigorous bargaining contribute to the colorful but amiable havoc so characteristic of Chinatown.

Chinese Historical Society of America – *644 Broadway, Suite 402. Open year-round Mon–Fri 10:30am–4pm. Closed major holidays. Contribution requested.* ☎ *415-391-1188. www.chsa.org.* A small, yet fascinating, collection of photographs and artifacts documents the role played by Chinese immigrants and their descendants in such national ventures as the 1849 Gold Rush, the transcontinental railroad, the development of agriculture and the commercial fishing industry. The collection will move to the new National Chinese American Museum in 2001.

ADDITIONAL SIGHT

Pacific Heritage Museum – *Description p 80.*

2 • CIVIC CENTER★

bus 5–Fulton, 19–Polk, 42–Downtown Loop or 47–Van Ness;
all streetcars Civic Center station. Civic Center station.
Map p 74

Contained within the triangle of Market Street, Van Ness Avenue and Golden Gate Avenue, San Francisco's center of government occupies one of the finest groups of Beaux-Arts-style buildings in the US. Though today the area suffers from its proximity to the downtrodden Tenderloin district, the grandly designed complex still reflects the tenets of the turn-of-the-century "City Beautiful" urban planning movement, updated with sympathetic contemporary constructions.

Historical Notes

San Francisco's present-day Civic Center did not materialize until the early 20C, fairly late in the city's life. In order to provide a proper home for the city's government, which through the mid-19C had occupied a series of buildings around Portsmouth Square, a new city hall was planned in the vicinity of contemporary Civic Center in 1872. Endemic corruption, within both the construction industry and the city government, delayed completion of the building for more than 25 years and vastly inflated the cost of the structure. When the great earthquake struck in April 1906, this shoddy boondoggle of a building was damaged beyond repair.

■ **The City Beautiful**

Around the turn of the 20C, civic leaders across the country joined forces to improve the quality of life in American cities. This concerted effort, known as the City Beautiful movement, brought together business leaders, politicians and architects who worked to make urban areas better places to live and work. Their efforts included such seemingly mundane projects as widening streets, installing street lights and building sewer systems, but also encompassed more singularly aesthetic goals.

The most prominent designer associated with the City Beautiful movement was Chicago architect Daniel Burnham, who was hired by a group of San Francisco businessmen to develop a plan that would improve the image and efficiency of the city. Over the course of two years Burnham made many trips to the city, spending untold hours in a cabin on the slope of Twin Peaks, sketching and studying the topography and character of the city below. With help from local architect Willis Polk, in 1905 he presented what became known as the **Burnham Plan**, an ambitious proposal for wide boulevards, traffic circles with streets radiating outward, and public monuments much like those of Washington DC or Paris.

The Burnham Plan was adopted with strong support, and the leveling of the city by the great earthquake and fire of 1906 seemed to offer a clean slate on which to implement it. However, concerns for private property rights and the urgency of rebuilding homes and businesses outweighed civic altruism, and reconstruction of the city in the aftermath of the disaster occurred along the old street grid. Construction of Civic Center proceeded more slowly, and today the ensemble stands as San Francisco's only realization of Burnham's grand plan.

In the aftermath of the fire, an idealistic group of businessmen and politicians embarked upon an ambitious scheme to create a suitable new center for the city's cultural and political life. Following the design guidelines recommended by the Burnham Plan, the group of buildings that now form the core of Civic Center was erected over the course of 20 years, beginning in 1913. First completed was the Civic Auditorium, which opened in time for the Panama-Pacific International Exposition of 1915. The new City Hall opened to the public at the end of 1915, while a stately main library and federal office buildings followed soon after. The historic portion of the complex was effectively completed with the opening of the Veterans Building and the War Memorial Opera House in 1932.

United Nations Birthplace – In April–June 1945, the United Nations Conference on International Organization convened in the War Memorial Opera House, focusing international attention on the area. The United Nations Charter was signed in the Veterans Building's Herbst Theatre on June 26. Throughout subsequent decades, Civic Center remained a locus of federal, state and civic administration, as well as home to such cultural institutions as the modern art museum, ballet and opera.

Completion of Davies Symphony Hall in 1980 as home base for the city's esteemed symphony orchestra expanded the Civic Center's position as a cultural center. Although the San Francisco Museum of Modern Art moved to Yerba Buena Gardens in 1995, the area was boosted by the opening of the new Main Library in 1996, the four-year renovation of City Hall in 1995-99, and the scheduled relocation of the Asian Art Museum to the Old Main Library in 2002. Further plans for renovating buildings and public open spaces continue. As new hotels and dot-com companies move into once-blighted areas along Market Street, hopes are high for reducing some of the urban tarnish that has afflicted the neighborhood.

Visiting Civic Center – Civic Center is well served by BART and Muni subway trains, by the historic F-Market streetcar line, and by many bus lines. A large public parking garage lies beneath Civic Center Plaza, and street parking may be found along the plaza's perimeter. Office workers throng the streets at midday, the most cheerful time to visit, and performances at War Memorial Opera House and Davies Symphony Hall draw ballet, opera and symphony devotees by night. Visitors should be aware, however, that significant numbers of homeless "street people" frequent the Civic Center area at all times of the day and night.

WALKING TOUR *distance: .8mi*

Begin at the intersection of Market, Jones and McAllister Sts.

★**Hibernia Bank** – *1 Jones St. Interior not open to the public.* Ornamenting the downtrodden Tenderloin neighborhood that surrounds it, this delightful Beaux-Arts bank (1892, Albert Pissis) ranks among the city's most significant small buildings. Its design influenced many commercial architects to adopt the Classical idiom. Facing Market Street, the stately main entrance turns the corner of Jones and McAllister Streets with an ornate copper-domed vestibule supported atop Corinthian columns. Now a substation of the San Francisco Police Department, the interior was reconstructed following the 1906 fire; the elaborate banking hall remains unoccupied.

Walk southwest along Market St.

★**United Nations Plaza** – Linking Market Street with the Civic Center, this sleek, contemporary plaza (1980, Lawrence Halprin) commemorates the founding of the United Nations here in 1945. Brass inlays in the pavement mark the site's longitude and latitude, and a large fountain made of immense blocks of stone forms a striking centerpiece. In 1995, to celebrate the UN's 50th anniversary, the plaza was improved with additional stone markers. One of the blocks around the fountain is inscribed with extracts from President Franklin D. Roosevelt's speech to the US Congress proposing the UN, and a black, freestanding obelisk carries the full text of the Universal Declaration of Human Rights.

 Heart of the City Farmers Market
UN Plaza. ☎ *415-558-9455.* Wednesday and Sunday mornings, California's farm bounty finds its way to local kitchens via this cheerful, bustling market. The changing displays of fresh fruit and vegetables remind shoppers that beyond the hills of this cool, gray city lie places where seasons change.

Leading west from Market Street along the Fulton Street mall *(closed to vehicular traffic)*, the plaza is bordered by parallel rows of square columns carved with the names of United Nations member countries and the years in which they joined. Occurring in chronological order, the columns create, in effect, a passage through recent world history: the People's Republic of China in 1971, the two Germanies in 1973 and unified Germany in 1991, ending with Palau in 1994.

A large **sculpture** (**1**) of a rearing horse ridden by Simón Bolívar, the revolutionary who liberated South America from colonial rule, dominates the west end of Fulton Street mall.

Walk south on Hyde St. to Market St.

★**Orpheum Theater** – *1192 Market St. (at Hyde & 8th Sts.)* ⚹ ☎ *415-551-2000. www.bestofbroadway-sf.com.* Originally designed (1926, B. Marcus Priteca) to showcase vaudeville acts, this theater evokes a glorified, pre-Reformation Spain. The intricate facade is patterned after a 13C Léon cathedral, the high vaulted lobby ceiling is reminiscent of the Alhambra, and the auditorium ceiling is ringed with full-bodied lions. The 2,200-seat theater became a movie house in the 1930s but returned to its live-theater roots with the 1970 production of *Hair.* Meticulously restored in 1997-98, the opulent Orpheum continues to stage such Broadway hits as *Miss Saigon* and *Fosse!*

Walk back to UN Plaza and cross Hyde St.

James Lick Memorial (**2**) – Among the city's most engaging monuments (1894, Frank Happersberger) this sculptural amalgam stands on an axis with City Hall, between the old and new library buildings. A gift of the James Lick Trust, established by an eccentric mid-19C developer, the work depicts Eureka standing atop a 30ft central column. Around the base, allegorical female figures embody agriculture and commerce; tableaux depict scenes of a gold miner and a Spanish friar. Plaques carry the names and portraits of historically important individuals.

★**San Francisco Public Library** – *100 Larkin St. Open year-round Mon 10am–6pm, Tue–Thu 9am–8pm, Fri noon–6pm, Sat 10am–6pm & Sun noon–5pm. Closed major holidays.* ✕ ⚹ 🅿 ☎ *415-557-4400. http://sfpl.lib.ca.us.* Opened in 1996, San Francisco's new $137 million Main Library (James Ingo Freed & Cathy Simon) blends a contemporary take on Civic Center architecture with the latest in high technology. The gleaming exterior is sheathed in granite from the same quarry that provided stone for early Civic Center structures. The main facade, facing City Hall, reveals an updated version of Beaux-Arts classicism, while the Hyde Street elevation presents an angular, contemporary face. The seven-story interior, replete with catwalk bridges, shelves of books, artworks and an asymmetrical skylit atrium, boasts multimedia computers and access to electronic databases as well as to books and magazines. Changing displays of art and literature are presented in the lower-level Jewett Exhibition Gallery.

The Beaux-Arts-style former Main Library building, in the block north of the new library *(Larkin St. between Fulton & McAllister Sts.),* will have a new tenant in the fall of 2002. Having outgrown its longtime home in Golden Gate Park, the Asian Art Museum of San Francisco is relocating to the four-story venue (1917, George Kelham), incorporating the Chong-Moon Lee Center for Asian Art and Culture. The move will increase exhibit space by 30 percent at a cost of $151 million. Italian architect Gae Aulenti, best known for her redesign of a c.1900 train station into Paris' stunning Musée d'Orsay, drew up the plans for adaptive reuse of the erstwhile library—an E-shaped structure with three wings linked with a skylit indoor courtyard by steel footbridges. The collection is to be presented in timelines of recurring themes: Landscape, The Palace, Buddhism, The Local and the Foreign, and The Afterlife.

Cross Larkin & Grove Sts.

Bill Graham Civic Auditorium – *50 Grove St.* ☎ *415-974-4000. www.bill grahamcivic.com.* Originally completed for the 1915 Panama-Pacific International Exposition, Civic Auditorium (Arthur Brown, Jr.) has undergone many remodelings and name changes, most recently in memory of popular music promoter Bill Graham, who died in 1992. Banners and flags frequently bedeck the arcade of stone arches that form the Grove Street facade overlooking Civic Center Plaza. The 7,000-seat, four-story Beaux-Arts auditorium has long been one of the city's prime performance and special-event venues.

Cross Grove & Polk Sts. to City Hall.

★★**City Hall** – *1 Dr. Carlton B. Goodlett Pl. (bounded by Grove, McAllister & Polk Sts. and Van Ness Ave.). Open year-round Mon–Fri 8am–8pm, Sat–Sun noon–4pm. Closed major holidays. Guided tours Mon–Fri 10am, noon & 2pm; Sat–Sun 12:30pm & 2pm.* ✕ ⚹ 🅿 ☎ *415-554-5780. www.ci.sf.ca.us/cityhall.* Testament to San Francisco's civic pride, this monumental Beaux-Arts edifice, crowned by a magnificent dome, is considered by many to be San Francisco's most beautiful building. Designed by Arthur Brown, Jr., a graduate of the École des Beaux Arts in Paris, the building was completed in 1915 under the stewardship of populist mayor James Rolph, who had vowed to rid the city government of the corruption that contributed to the demise of the first City Hall.

The massive, four-story building occupies a rectangle covering two city blocks. Its splendid dome, trimmed with gold leaf, rises to a height of 307ft, about 13ft taller than the US Capitol Building in Washington DC. On the Van Ness Avenue facade, handsome Atlas-like telamones support the entrance. Doric pillars and colonnades along the porticoes, facades and dome reinforce the Classical idiom.

City Hall

Damaged in the Loma Prieta earthquake of 1989, the grand edifice closed in 1995 for $300 million worth of seismic retrofitting and historic restoration. It reopened in 1999 floating upon 600 "base isolators" (rubber and steel discs) planted beneath the building to dissipate earthquake motion.

Inside, a grand ceremonial marble staircase ascends to a spectacular, 181ft open rotunda, its east-facing section flanked by city government offices arranged according to bureaucratic hierarchy. The office of the mayor occupies the space directly beneath the central pediment on the Polk Street facade, with a balcony facing east onto Civic Center Plaza. Two grand public courts, skylit and with marble walls, extend from either side of the rotunda. The South Light Court displays historic exhibits from the **Museum of the City of San Francisco** (☏ 415-928-0289; www.sfmuseum.org), currently without a home of its own. (Other museum exhibits are in the nearby State Supreme Court Building.)

To the east of City Hall lies **Civic Center Plaza**, once the site of rallies, demonstrations and fiery speeches. The broad, beautifully proportioned space has been restored to its original 1912 design. Though frequented by throngs of street people, it retains its grand air.

Continue west on Grove St. Cross Van Ness Ave. and walk north.

★★**San Francisco War Memorial and Performing Arts Center** – *401 Van Ness Ave. Visit by guided tour (30min) only, year-round Mon 10am–2pm. Closed major holidays. $5 (includes tour of Davies Symphony Hall).* ⚔ & ☏ *415-552-8338 (ticket information p 51).* Flanking a formal courtyard designed by Thomas Church, these twin structures erected in memory of San Francisco's war dead served for decades as the city's center for the performing arts.

War Memorial Opera House – The first city-owned opera house in the US (1932, Arthur Brown, Jr.) hosted the plenary sessions that led to the establishment of the United Nations in 1945. The highly acclaimed San Francisco Opera and San Francisco Ballet perform here in an elegantly appointed 3,176-seat auditorium highlighted by a brilliant 27ft star chandelier. The proscenium, graced by Edgar Walter's gilded relief sculptures of two Amazons astride horses, is backed by a gold brocatelle curtain that weighs more than a ton. An 18mo, $84.5 million expansion and seismic retrofit was completed in 1997.

Veterans Building – Located north of the Opera House, this structure is home to city government offices and the intimate 928-seat **Herbst Theatre**, a venue for recitals, plays, lectures and public readings. The first-floor **San Francisco Art Commission Gallery** *(open year-round Wed–Sat noon–5:30pm; 3rd floor corridor open Mon–Fri 8:30am–5:30pm; ☎ 415-554-6080; http://sfac.sfsu.edu)* showcases work by emerging Bay Area artists.

Beneath fourth-story skylights is the **San Francisco Performing Arts Library and Museum** (**M**) *(open year-round Tue & Thu–Sat 11am–5pm, Wed 11am–7pm; library closed Tue; ☎ 415-255-4800; www.sfpalm.org)*. This nonprofit gallery and library presents exhibits on the city's arts heritage, from Barbary Coast bawdy houses to the present. A permanent research collection preserves news clippings, photographs, libretti, playbills and other items documenting the diverse history of Bay Area theater, music and dance, with special focus on influential local artists such as Lew Christensen and Isadora Duncan. Changing displays are mounted three to four times a year in a small entry gallery and adjacent corridor space.

Return to Grove St.

Louise M. Davies Symphony Hall – *Van Ness Ave. & Grove St. Visit by guided tour (30min) only, year-round Mon 10am–2pm from San Francisco War Memorial and Performing Arts Center.* ♿ 🅿 ☎ *415-864-6000. www.sfsymphony.org.* In contrast to the Beaux-Arts public buildings of Civic Center, this modern structure (1980, Edward Bassett) features a curving glass facade that reveals the lobby areas of the 2,743-seat hall. It is home to the San Francisco Symphony Orchestra. The elegant bronze sculpture *Large Four Piece Reclining Figure* (**3**) (1973) at the plaza entrance is by Henry Moore. Fletcher Benton's *Balanced Unbalanced T* (**4**) (1981) faces Franklin Street from Goldman Terrace.

② A Clean Well-Lighted Place for Books
601 Van Ness Ave.
☎ *415-441-6670.*
www.bookstore.com. Well-lighted it is, and it never closes before 11pm. Wander in for a public reading or a private browse at the city's largest independent bookstore, located in Opera Plaza. The music, cooking, fiction, children's and travel sections are particularly strong; check out the "staff recommends" cards with handwritten reviews tucked beneath selections.

3 • FINANCIAL DISTRICT★★

🚋 California Street. 🚍 bus 1-California, 2-Clement, 3-Jackson, 4-Sutter, 12-Folsom, 15-Third, 41-Union, 42-Downtown Loop; all streetcars Embarcadero or Montgomery St. stations. 🚇 Embarcadero or Montgomery St. stations.

Map p 77

This cacophonous forest of skyscraping steel, glass and stone, concentrated in a roughly triangular area north of Market Street along San Francisco's eastern bayshore, represents the heart of the city's financial community. Every large bank in California maintains a presence. Though modern in appearance, the district stands atop the city's historic core and includes some of San Francisco's oldest and most architecturally significant buildings.

Historical Notes

While San Francisco was born in 1776 at Mission Dolores and The Presidio, the roots of the modern downtown lie beneath the Financial District, where the village of Yerba Buena grew up in the early 1840s along what was then a sheltered bayfront. In 1846 US forces occupied the town at the outbreak of the Mexican-American War, and the following year Yerba Buena's name was changed to San Francisco. Irish surveyor Jasper O'Farrell laid out a street grid, designating the muddy path along the waterfront as **Montgomery Street** in honor of Captain John Montgomery, commander of the US forces who took the village. O'Farrell traced Market Street at a diagonal to the already established downtown grid, then laid another grid at a competing angle south of Market Street.

Until 1848, the sleepy community of some 300 souls served as a trading and supply center for oceangoing vessels that periodically sailed into the bay. By late 1894, with the discovery of gold in the Sierra Nevada foothills, the waterfront buzzed with activity and San Francisco boomed as the principal communication and supply conduit between the mining camps and the rest of the world. Dozens of vessels that sailed into the bay were abandoned by crews who jumped ship to head for the gold fields. Many empty boats served as impromptu warehouses and hotels until more substantial structures could be built. Wharves extended east of Montgomery Street to deep-water anchorage; the intervening mud flats were filled in with sand, dredgings and ship carcasses until the waterfront reached the line of the modern Embarcadero. Today, with a few exceptions such as the area of Jackson Square, very little remains of the Gold Rush city.

Wall Street of the West - Although San Francisco was molded by the Gold Rush, its role as financial center of the West Coast was cemented by silver. The immense fortunes engendered by Nevada's Comstock Lode during the 1860s brought stock exchanges, banks, the new transcontinental railroad and other commercial enterprises to the port city. Grand edifices arose in the Financial District, which quickly emerged as the commercial nexus of the West. By the 1890s, developments in construction technology made taller buildings possible, and Chicago-school skyscrapers such as the Mills Building and the Chronicle Building, both designed by Daniel Burnham, began to appear.

The great earthquake and fire of 1906 razed the Financial District, but within three years the area had been largely rebuilt. Many new buildings, such as the Bank of California, epitomized "City Beautiful" ideals, employing Classical motifs to create a visual sense of order and substance. Another burst of construction occurred in the late 1920s, when three office towers—the Hunter-Dulin, Russ and Shell Buildings—were completed. While each of these structures expresses different historical motifs, they share features common to the early Art Deco period, such as ornamental tops and setbacks on the upper stories. The Great Depression and World War II put a temporary halt to growth, but beginning in 1959 with the Crown Zellerbach building, dozens of skyscrapers rose. The construction wave culminated in the early 1970s with the city's two signature towers, the Bank of America Center and the Transamerica Pyramid.

The swift pace of wholesale change led preservationists to lobby for protection of many older buildings, and for strict limitations on the height and bulk of new ones. This movement resulted in the **Downtown Plan** of 1985, whose mandatory guidelines put a cap on the square footage of new construction allowed annually in the Financial District. As a result, most development now has shifted south of Market Street. Nonetheless, the hallowed crossing of Montgomery and California Streets remains the heart of financial San Francisco.

Visiting the Financial District – The Financial District is very much a place of business, and its character changes completely at different times of day. Workers clog the streets during morning and evening rush hours *(7-10am and 3-7pm)*. Garlicky aromas drift through the district by mid-morning as restaurants prepare for lunch; eateries fill to capacity at noon. Garage parking, though plentiful, is expensive; it's best to use the many buses, streetcars or cable cars that serve the area. Be alert to parking signs, as street parking is prohibited along certain thoroughfares during rush hours. The Financial District calms on weekends, particularly Sundays; many office buildings are closed outside of business hours.

When visiting the district, be sure to investigate office-building lobbies, many of which feature changing exhibitions of high-quality fine or decorative arts. Displays run the gamut from historic photographs to costume design and are well worth searching out. Some buildings boast rooftop or courtyard gardens, open to the public and ideal for taking a break or enjoying a picnic lunch.

WALKING TOUR *2.1mi*

Begin at the intersection of Post, Montgomery & Market Sts.

One Montgomery Street (**A**) – Standing at the symbolic entry to the "Wall Street of the West," this grand banking hall rose in the aftermath of the 1906 quake as the headquarters of First National Bank (later merged with Crocker Bank). The original section along Post Street, once a 14-story office tower, was designed by Willis Polk; above that entrance an ornate cast-iron canopy is graced with figures that flank a shield, inscribed with the words "Systematic Saving is the Key to Success." The ornate interior **banking hall★**, now a Wells Fargo branch bank replete with coffered ceiling and stately columns, was completed by Charles Gottschalk in 1921. The building was shortened in the 1980s and incorporated into the adjacent Crocker Galleria.

From the corner, walk west on Post Street and enter the **Crocker Galleria★** (1983, Skidmore, Owings & Merrill), an elegant shopping center that cuts through the middle of the block, its three tiers of commercial spaces topped by a barrel-vaulted

Crocker Galleria

© Robert Holmes

glass roof *(open year-round Mon-Fri 10am-6pm, Sat 10am-5pm;* ✗ ⅙ ▣ ☎ *415-393-1505; www. shopatgalleria.com)*. Pleasant cafes and deluxe boutiques such as Gianni Versace, Nicole Miller and Polo Ralph Lauren welcome tourists and workers from adjacent office towers. From the upper level of the Galleria, a stairway leads to a tranquil **rooftop terrace** *(follow sign to stairway or take elevator from bank entrance vestibule; open year-round Mon-Fri 7am-7pm)* atop One Montgomery.

Exit Crocker Galleria on Sutter St.

★★**Hallidie Building** – *130-150 Sutter St.* One of San Francisco's most noteworthy works of architecture, the seven-story office block was designed by Willis Polk (1917) and named for Andrew Hallidie, inventor of the cable car. Because the facade is formed by a modular grid of glass panes hanging from a sturdy reinforced concrete frame, the building is considered the world's first glass-curtain-walled structure, a precursor of contemporary commercial architecture. In the local offices of the American Institute of Architects, a small **gallery** *(6th floor; open year-round Mon-Fri 9am-5pm;* ⅙ ☎ *415-362-7397; www.aiasf.org)* offers changing displays of architectural drawings and photographs. A post office and a clothing store occupy the ground floor.

Walk east on Sutter St.

★**Hunter-Dulin Building** – *111 Sutter St.* This richly detailed building—completed in 1927 by the New York firm of Schultze and Weaver, designers of the Waldorf-Astoria Hotel—combines historical styles in a freewheeling manner. The main shaft, clad in granite-like terra-cotta panels, incorporates Romanesque arches and cast-iron spandrels embellished with medallions of mythical figures. Near the top, a central tower rises four floors to a mansard roof with gabled dormers. The elevator lobby boasts a painted, beamed ceiling and inlaid marble floor. Writer Dashiell Hammett set the office of his fictional hero, detective Sam Spade, in this building. The structure stands on the site of the Lick House, one of the West's premier hotels from the 1870s until destroyed in the 1906 earthquake and fire.

Walk to corner of Sutter & Montgomery Sts. and turn left.

Mills Building – *220 Montgomery St.* One of the few downtown structures to survive the earthquake and fire, this stately office building (1891) reflects the Chicago-school tenets of its designer, Daniel Burnham. The first in the city to be clad in decorative terra-cotta, the building was reconstructed after the quake by Willis Polk. A richly ornamented Romanesque archway forms the main entrance. The 22-story tower along the Bush Street facade was added in 1931 by Lewis Hobart. The environmental conservation group Sierra Club was established here in 1892.

★**Russ Building** – *235 Montgomery St.* Built in 1927, this 31-story Gothic Revival landmark (George Kelham) was the tallest tower on the West Coast until the 1960s. Filling an entire block of Montgomery Street, it is still a prime business address. A two-story give archway entrance leads to a striking **lobby**★ that features stone vaulting over cloister-like corridors, inlaid mosaic floors and elaborate elevator panels. Glass cases in the lobby display historic model ships from building owner Walter Shorenstein's collection.

Turn right at Pine St.

★**Pacific Exchange** – *301 Pine St. at Sansome St. Interior not open to the public.* Built in 1915 to house a US Treasury office, this proud structure was remodeled and enlarged with a tower in 1930. Ralph Stackpole, later a Coit Tower muralist, was commissioned to sculpt the remarkable pair of Social Realist-style monumental statues flanking the entrance. One granite figure depicts a trio of muscular men with a variety of tools, and a small boy with his right hand raised in a clenched fist; the other shows women harvesting grain and caring for children.

Backtrack to Montgomery St. and turn right.

★★ Bank of America Center – *555 California St. (enter via Montgomery St. plaza).* ✗ ⑤ The city's largest building, this 52-story, dark-red behemoth (1971, Skidmore, Owings & Merrill) competes with the Transamerica Pyramid for dominance of the skyline. It is West Coast headquarters for the Bank of America, founded in 1904 by A.P. Giannini as the Bank of Italy to serve the needs of Italian and other immigrants. (World headquarters moved to North Carolina in 1998 when the bank merged with NationsBank.)

The building contains 2 million square feet of office space. Its distinctive color comes from thick slabs of carnelian granite that wrap the faceted central shaft rising 780ft from street level. A grand, panoramic **view★★★** extends from the top-floor **Carnelian Room** lounge and restaurant *(take express elevator from Concourse Level; open to the public after 3pm)*; changing exhibits grace the Concourse Gallery and the main lobby, one floor above. The broad, open plaza along California Street is anchored by *Transcendence* (**1**) (1969, Masayuki Nagare), a dark, polished sculpture popularly dubbed "The Banker's Heart."

From the plaza, glance north at the contentious post-Modern design of **580 California Street** (1987, Johnson & Burgee), incorporating 12 faceless, hooded human figures eerily encircling the 20th floor.

Cross Montgomery St. and walk east on California St.

★ Merchant's Exchange Building (**B**) – *465 California St.* This 14-story office building (1903, Willis Polk) was the focal point of commerce in c.1900 San Francisco. Signals from its rooftop belvedere announced the arrival of ships through the Golden Gate. Badly damaged in the 1906 fire, it was quickly restored. Prolific architect Julia Morgan maintained an office on the 11th floor for most of her 46-year career.

From the Ionic columns at the entrance, walk though the barrel-vaulted elevator lobby to the commodious **Grain Exchange Hall★★**. Here, beneath marble columns and gilt capitals, merchants and traders convened to transact business. On the walls are 13 paintings by marine artist William Coulter, depicting the intricately rigged sailing vessels that once commanded San Francisco Bay. *(Though presently closed to the public, the hall may be included on some historical tours.)*

Return to Montgomery St. and turn right.

■ Belden Place

A delightful surprise is this one-block-long alley, extending from Pine to Bush Streets just east of Kearny Street. A piece of Old World Europe transplanted to San Francisco, it is lined with exquisite cafes—French, German, Italian, Greek and American—whose servers attend umbrella-covered tables, packed back-to-back, from one end of the lane to the other, during the lunch hours.

Dining at Belden Place

© Robert Holmes

★**Wells Fargo History Museum** (**M¹**) – 🔳 *420 Montgomery St. Open year-round Mon-Fri 9am-5pm. Closed major holidays.* ♿ ☎ *415-396-2619. www.wellsfargo history.com.* Concord coaches of Wells Fargo & Co. began carrying freight and passengers in 1852, and the company's gold-shipping and storage services complemented its growth as a bank. In this modern two-level gallery, Wells Fargo's inherent links to California history are told via photographs, documents, gold nuggets, bank notes and coins. Displays explore such topics as gold assaying, stagecoach robbery and telegraphing. Visitors can view a restored original coach and climb aboard a reconstructed one on the mezzanine to hear the recorded description of a harrowing cross-country stagecoach journey in the 1850s.

Continue north on Montgomery St. and turn left onto Commercial St.

Commercial Street – *Between Montgomery & Kearny Sts.* This narrow alley offers intriguing glimpses of early commercial San Francisco. Before landfill extended the waterfront to the Embarcadero, this block formed the foot of Long Wharf, which ran across the mud flats along the line of present-day Commercial Street to deepwater anchorage. Look east to see the towers of Embarcadero Center framing a fine view of the top of the historic Ferry Building, which stands at what once was the end of the wharf.

Tiny **Empire Park** offers a quiet refuge. Formerly known as Grabhorn Park, it was renamed in 1999 to honor "Emperor" Joshua Norton, an eccentric but beloved bankrupted businessman who held court on Commercial Street for 20 years in the 1860s and 70s. After Norton's funeral in 1880 drew a cortege of 30,000 grieving San Franciscans, visitor author Robert Louis Stevenson asked: "In what other city would a harmless madman, who supposed himself Emperor of the Two Americas, have been fostered and encouraged?"

On the opposite side of Commercial Street (*no. 605*), a plaque marks the location of the first building constructed on Yerba Buena Cove, a trading post built by the Hudson's Bay Company.

■ The Barbary Coast Trail

Through downtown San Francisco, large bronze medallions embedded in sidewalks at street corners indicate the course of the Barbary Coast Trail. Extending 3.8mi from the Old Mint at Fifth and Mission Streets to Aquatic Park at the foot of Van Ness Avenue, this urban stroll cuts through Chinatown, Commercial Street, Jackson Square, North Beach and Fisherman's Wharf, en route linking dozens of historic sites and a handful of museums. It is a fine introduction to the Gold Rush heritage of San Francisco. The brainchild of writer-historian Daniel Bacon, the privately sponsored trail officially opened in 1997 with implantation of the markers. (The city offered its assistance to the tourism-friendly venture by charging a $10,000 permit fee.) Walking-tour brochures, and Bacon's book, may be purchased at the **San Francisco Historical Society** (☎ *415-775-1111; www.sfhistory.org*) and other locations throughout the city.

Pacific Heritage Museum (**M²**) – *608 Commercial St. Open year-round Tue-Sat 10am-4pm. Closed major holidays and between major exhibitions.* ♿ ☎ *415-399-1124. www.citysearch.com/sfo/pacificheritage.* This elegant small museum displays changing exhibits of contemporary Asian art in an annex of the Bank of Canton. The bank building (1984, Skidmore, Owings & Merrill) incorporates the exterior walls and basement vaults of its predecessor, a US Subtreasury building (1877, William Appleton Potter), itself erected on the site of San Francisco's first mint. Interior windows on reveal the original basement coin vaults from different perspectives.

Backtrack to Montgomery St. and turn left. Cross Montgomery at Clay St.

Bank of San Francisco – *550 Montgomery St. Open year-round Mon-Thu 9am-4pm, Fri 9am-5pm.* ♿ ☎ *415-781-7810. www.banksf.com.* Within this small building is a gem of a **banking hall**★ clad in veined white marble. Egg-shaped, semiprecious stones are embedded between window arches. Originally the main San Francisco office of the Bank of Italy, the building was declared a National Historic Landmark in 1982 as the birthplace of branch banking. The hefty lock mechanism of the original vault may be seen in the banking hall.

Cross Clay St.

★★**Transamerica Pyramid** – *600 Montgomery St. www.tapyramid.com.* In the years since its 1972 completion, this bold pyramid has come to symbolize San Francisco, a role similar to New York City's Empire State Building or Chicago's Sears Tower. Designed by William Pereira to house the headquarters of the Transamerica Corporation, a leasing and financial institution, the elegant 48-story spire is

San Francisco's tallest building, rising 853ft from street level to the tip of its 212ft hollow lantern. The pyramid's slanted sides reduce the extent of its shadow on surrounding structures. The lobby gallery hosts changing exhibits of contemporary art and design. Although the public is denied access to upper floors, a lobby-level **Virtual Observation Deck** 🔲 ⚹ wired to rooftop monitors offers bird's-eye perspectives on the city in every direction.

The site was previously occupied by the Montgomery Block (1853), the premier office block on the West Coast, frequented by such diverse figures as Mark Twain and Sun Yat-sen before it was razed in 1959. Construction on the pyramid began a decade later. To the east, a peaceful grove planted with some 40 redwood trees forms a tranquil forest oasis.

Walk east on Clay St. and turn right onto Sansome St.

Transamerica Pyramid and Sentinel Building

© David R. Frazier

★**Old Federal Reserve Bank** – *400 Sansome St.* The facade of this classical Beaux-Arts gem (1924, George Kelham) makes a dramatic first impression with its eight 25ft Ionic columns and the row of federal eagles perched above its portico. The building exemplifies San Francisco's banking-temple tradition and the US government penchant for monumental architecture. Lobby walls and floors are finished in French and Italian marble, and doors are of solid bronze. Artist Jules Guerin, chief muralist for the Panama-Pacific International Exposition of 1915, painted the impressive "Traders of the Adriatic" mural. In 1984 the Fed moved its district headquarters to new offices on Market Street. The upper floors today house a law firm.

Cross Sacramento St. and continue south on Sansome St.

★★**Bank of California** – *400 California St.* Now the Union Bank of California, this exquisite, classically proportioned bank (1907, Bliss & Faville) displays the energy and resources put into rebuilding San Francisco after the 1906 fire. A regal, coffered ceiling tops the magnificent banking hall, embellished with Corinthian pilasters. Stairs lead down to the tiny **Bank of California Museum** (**M³**) 🔲 *(open year-round Mon-Fri 9am-5pm; closed major holidays; ⚹ ☎ 415-291-4653)*, displaying gold and silver currency circulated during the Gold Rush and Comstock mining bonanzas of the 19C.

Walk east on California St.

★★**First Interstate Center** – *345 California St.* Two angular towers linked by a glass-enclosed "sky bridge" cap this futuristic skyscraper (1987, Skidmore, Owings & Merrill). The building incorporated the facades of earlier historic structures, including the J. Harold Dollar Building (1920) and the Robert Dollar Building (1919), former steamship-line headquarters. Office spaces fill the lower 35 floors, while the top 11 stories house the luxurious **Mandarin Oriental Hotel** *(main entrance at 222 Sansome St.).*

Continue east on California St.

❶ Tadich Grill
240 California St.
☎ *415-391-1849.*
www.tadichgrill.com. Fresh fish is the fare, bulls and bears the topic of choice at this San Francisco institution, which began during the Gold Rush as a coffee stand. Go for the charcoal-grilled sole, the cold seafood salads, and for the no-nonsense service by white-jacketed waiters in long aprons, striding along the long, wooden bar.

★101 California Street – *101 California St.* This stepped-back glass silo (1982, Johnson & Burgee) has a three-story glass atrium that slices into the base of the building, acting as the main entrance. A triangular plaza runs south to Market Street.

Turn left on Davis St. Cross Sacramento St.

★Embarcadero Center – *Bounded by The Embarcadero and Clay, Sacramento & Battery Sts. Enter from Davis St. between buildings Two and Three and take the spiral stairs to the Promenade (3rd) Level.* ✕ ♿ ▯ The city's largest office and commercial complex, this series of four slab-like office towers (1982, John Portman and Assoc.) and the adjoining Hyatt Regency Hotel cover nearly 10 acres between The Embarcadero and the heart of the Financial District. Developed jointly by New York financier David Rockefeller and the San Francisco Redevelopment Agency, the center was constructed on the site of a produce market. A three-level shopping center occupies its lower floors, running along historic Commercial Street; pedestrian bridges traverse cross streets to link the four structures. More than a dozen sculptures dot public spaces, among them works by Jean Dubuffet and Louise Nevelson.

Linked to the east tower (Four Embarcadero Center) by a pedestrian bridge on the Promenade Level, the Hyatt Regency (1973) boasts an asymmetrical 17-story **atrium★**, one of the more awe-inspiring of the city's interior spaces.

Opening onto The Embarcadero from the east end of the complex is brick-paved **Justin Herman Plaza** 🧒, named for the president of the redevelopment agency in the 1960s. The angular forms of Vaillancourt Fountain (1971) invite exploration while enlivening the plaza's northeastern corner.

Cross The Embarcadero to the Ferry Building.

★★Ferry Building – *Description p 107.*

Cross The Embarcadero to the south side of Market St.

★One Market – *1 Market St.* Filling an entire block, this office complex was erected in stages, wedding the facade of the original Southern Pacific Railroad headquarters (1916, Bliss and Faville) to a futuristically redesigned interior (1995, Cesar Pelli and Assoc.). The belvedere of the red brick fortress is a focal point for California Street, which climbs Nob Hill to the west; the view southwest along Market Street extends to the summits of Twin Peaks.

Walk southwest on Market St. and cross Spear St.

Federal Reserve Bank of San Francisco – 🧒 *101 Market St. Lobby open year-round Mon-Fri 8:30am-4:30pm. Closed major holidays.* ♿ ☎ *415-974-3252. www.frbsf.com.* A vaulted loggia covers the bank's Market Street frontage, from which the bulk of the building (1982, Skidmore, Owings & Merrill) steps back in a series of terraces. In the lobby, the interactive **World of Economics★** exhibit offers entertaining but serious lessons in basic economics. Computer simulators enable visitors (pretending to be legislators, the US President or Chairman of the Federal Reserve) to adjust the rate of money growth, set interest rates or raise and lower taxes, and gauge the effect on the economy. The **American Currency Exhibit**, showcasing paper money from colonial to modern times, is presented off the lobby's west side.

Continue southwest on Market St. to Battery St.

One of the city's most energetic pieces of public sculpture, the **Mechanics Monument (2)** *(median at Market & Battery Sts.)* vividly memorializes the craftsmen who built San Francisco. Created by Douglas Tilden in 1894, the sculpture was dedicated to the memory of Peter Donahue, owner of the city's first iron foundry. Set atop a granite pedestal, the work depicts a team of muscular workers straining to punch a hole through a steel plate.

Cross Bush St., then Battery St. to its south side.

★Shell Building – *100 Bush St., intersection of Bush & Battery Sts.* Clad in light brown terra-cotta, this graceful Art Deco tower (1929, George Kelham) has a plain, 20-story central shaft that steps back to form a slender, richly ornamented top. Decorative motifs, including a large gilt shell over the entrance and abstract shell forms covering the parapets, represent the Shell Oil Corporation, which developed the property as its Western headquarters.

Next door, at **130 Bush Street** (1910, McDonald & Applegarth), stands one of the city's narrowest office buildings. Gothic-style ornamentation covers the 10-story, bow-fronted tower that measures just 20ft wide.

Continue west on Bush St. one block and cross.

★One Bush Street – Originally the Crown Zellerbach Building, now often called the Hambrecht & Quist Building (for its principal tenant), this distinctive tower is San Francisco's best example of International Style architecture. Designed by Hertzka & Knowles/Skidmore, Owings & Merrill in 1959, modeled after the latter firm's influential Lever House in New York City, the pale green glass box stands on concrete stilts above a broad plaza.

At its base is a sunken plaza anchored by a small, freestanding circular structure that houses an outlet of the Sharper Image chain. The One Bush Street lobby presents temporary art exhibits, ranging from photography to folk crafts, that rotate quarterly.

Cross Sutter St., turn right on Market St. and walk southwest to Montgomery St.

An angelic female perched atop a stone shaft, above a miner waving an American flag, is the most prominent element of the **Native Sons of the Golden West Monument (3)**, which honors the establishment of California statehood in 1850. Sculpted by Douglas Tilden in 1897, the statue was originally erected farther down Market Street, then moved to Golden Gate Park before being placed at its present location, at a prominent intersection, in 1977.

Cross Market St.

★★**Palace Hotel** – *2 New Montgomery St.* ✗ ㅤ ㅤ ㅤ *415-392-8600. www.sf palace.com.* This elegant hostelry at the edge of the Financial District figures prominently in San Francisco history. Constructed in 1875 by financier William Ralston as part of his plan to lure development south of Market Street, the Palace Hotel gained a reputation as the most opulent hotel in the West until gutted in the 1906 fire. It was immediately rebuilt and reopened in 1909 with great fanfare. Rivaling the Fairmont Hotel in sophistication and luxury, the new Palace quickly became the focal point of high society.

The former Grand Court, where passengers had once alighted from horse-drawn carriages, was transformed into an interior Garden Court where dignitaries sipped tea and champagne beneath flourishing palm trees. The hotel has hosted many luminaries, including seven US Presidents (Warren G. Harding died here in 1923). The long-standing landmark underwent a complete restoration in 1989-91, and is now a member of the Sheraton group.

© Robert Holmes

Garden Court, Palace Hotel

Enter at 639 Market Street and stroll down the main corridor to the glorious **Garden Court★★**, capped by a stunning canopy of intricately leaded art glass. The corridor boasts several display cases containing fascinating mementoes from hotel history, including photographs and scrapbooks, postcards, menus, china and wardrobe items. Also worth seeing is **Maxfield's**, a bar and restaurant *(off corridor near Market St. entrance;* ㅤ *415-512-1111)* with an allegorical mural of the Pied Piper of Hamelin by Maxfield Parrish.

Cross Market St., turn left and continue to Kearny St.

A cast-iron column rising from a small fountain, beloved **Lotta's Fountain** *(northeast corner of Market & Kearny Sts.)* was given to the people of San Francisco by entertainer Lotta Crabtree in 1875. Every April 18, around 5am, San Franciscans congregate here to commemorate the anniversary of the great earthquake and fire of 1906.

The intersection surrounding Lotta's Fountain once represented the heart of San Francisco's newspaper industry. The former **Chronicle Building** *(690 Market St.)*, erected in 1889 by Burnham & Root, remains the city's oldest office tower, though a 1962 remodeling obscured its original facade. Across Market Street lies the terra-cotta-clad **Hearst Building** *(691 3rd St.)*, an exuberant, Spanish Revival-style structure that was the longtime home of the *San Francisco Examiner*.

ADDITIONAL SIGHT

★★Jackson Square – *Bounded by Washington, Montgomery & Sansome Sts. and Pacific Ave.* Contrary to its name, San Francisco's oldest surviving commercial neighborhood is not a "square," but five square blocks of well-preserved mid-19C structures between North Beach and the Financial District. This former waterfront neighborhood was once the heart of the notorious **Barbary Coast**, the bawdy, Gold Rush-era district of saloons, theaters and burlesque houses that lined Pacific Avenue between Sansome Street and Columbus Avenue. The brick structures outlasted the great earthquake and fire of 1906; since the 1960s, many have been converted to upscale art galleries, design firms, law offices and antique stores— and more recently by dot-coms.

William Stout Architectural Books
804 Montgomery St.
☎ *415-391-6757.*
www.stoutbooks.com.
When books and magazines overflowed his apartment, architect Stout went into business as a bookseller. His space problem isn't solved: a huge selection of architectural titles, as well as art, photography, landscaping and other design-related themes, now overflow this charming shop, where architects gather to browse and network.

Today the two- and three-story buildings, with brick, cast-iron or stucco facades, create a cozily uniform departure from the neighboring towers of the Financial District. The oldest buildings lie along Montgomery Street a block north of the Transamerica Pyramid. The **Belli Building** (**C**) *(no. 722)* was constructed in 1851 on a foundation of redwood that literally floats upon former tidelands. First a tobacco warehouse, later a raucous nightclub where Lotta Crabtree got her start, it served as the law offices of famed attorney Melvin Belli ("King of Torts") from the 1960s until it was damaged in the 1989 earthquake. It is now undergoing reconstruction. The attached **Belli Annex** *(no. 726)*, a three-story brick Italianate built in 1852, marks the site of the first meeting (in 1849) of the California Freemasons. Next door, the two-story **Golden Era Building** (**D**) *(no. 730)* was built in 1852 as the home of the West's premier literary magazine, the *Golden Era*, whose contributors included Mark Twain, Bret Harte and Joaquin Miller.

Around the corner, the Italianate-style **Hotaling Warehouse** *(451-455 Jackson St.)* was constructed for whiskey distilling and storage in 1866. The building was rescued from the flames of the 1906 conflagration thanks to the valiant efforts of sailors, who strung a 1 in-diameter water hose over Telegraph Hill from their ships, and local firefighters. If the liquor had exploded, all of Jackson Square would have gone up with it. Wrote one dry-witted observer: "If, as they say, God spanked the town for being over frisky—why did he burn the churches down and spare Hotaling's whiskey?"

Pacific Avenue, the northern boundary of Jackson Square, was for years (before and after the earthquake) the rowdiest street in San Francisco. Many of its buildings were at one time saloons, dance halls, gambling parlors, brothels or boarding houses catering to transient sailors. Painted white pilasters and naked, dancing nymphs, sculpted in bas-relief on the exterior walls of the 1907 **Hippodrome** *(no. 555)*, are a vivid reminder of its post-earthquake heyday as the infamous Bella Union. Early-20C dances such as the turkey trot and chicken glide were popularized here, to the sounds of ragtime and Dixieland jazz bands, before spreading across the country.

4 • NOB HILL★★

🚃 all lines.
Map p 86

Nob Hill, which witnessed one of San Francisco's first infusions of wealth, today remains a vivid example of the city's diverse urban community. Cable cars trundle up and down the steep slopes, passing lovingly restored Edwardian homes and 1920s high-rise apartment buildings. Cozy bistros, flower shops and boutiques nestle together along the serene, tree-lined side streets. Sloping down to the southwest, Lower Nob Hill, bordered by Geary and Polk Streets, has a grittier feel, melding bustling theaters and restaurants with blockier residential buildings and quiet local taprooms.

Historical Notes

Nob Hill acquired its reputation as home to San Francisco's elite during the city's earliest years. In 1856 Dr. Arthur Hayne, a well-to-do dentist, became the first to settle on the craggy hill, ambitiously cutting a path through the scrub to the 376ft summit and erecting a modest home where the Fairmont Hotel stands today. Hayne was joined soon after by William Walton, a merchant who built a grander residence at the present-day corner of Washington and Taylor Streets. By the late 1860s, a handful of millionaires had purchased property and built homes near the summit, establishing it as the city's choicest residential locale.

The exclusive cachet was ensured after cable-car lines were installed on its steep flanks in 1873. Capable of transporting people and materials easily and regularly, cable cars opened the door to development of formerly inaccessible summits, and construction on the crest of Nob Hill boomed. As the rest of the city battled an economic depression prompted by the new transcontinental railroad (which brought low-cost East Coast goods to compete with higher-priced West Coast products), Nob Hill became what author Robert Louis Stevenson called "the hill of palaces," thanks in good part to a group of newly minted millionaires.

The Big Four – In 1859 four middle-class Sacramento merchants—**Leland Stanford, Charles Crocker, Mark Hopkins** and **Collis Huntington**—together purchased a modest number of shares in what seemed at the time an impossible venture: a railway across the western US. A decade later the transcontinental railroad was completed and their investments yielded millions of dollars in dividends. The four promptly moved to San Francisco, purchased lots on the summit of Nob Hill and built sprawling mansions where, according to Stevenson, they "gathered together, vying with each other in display, (and) looked down upon the business wards of the city." The hill was indirectly named for them: "Nob" is a contraction of "nabob," a term for European adventurers who made huge fortunes in India and the Far East.

In the 1880s the Big Four were joined on the hill by two "Bonanza Kings," Irish stock-market speculators who had extracted huge fortunes from Nevada's Comstock silver lode in 1873. **James Fair**, a former miner, bought Dr. Hayne's property, and **James Flood** erected his Italianate brownstone mansion, today the Pacific-Union Club, across Mason Street. Through the late 19C, large Victorian houses appeared on the flanks of the hill, near cable-car routes established along California and Powell Streets in 1878 and 1888 respectively. After its destruction by the great quake and fire of 1906, the area was rebuilt with tall, narrow Edwardian homes and high-rise apartments. Today Nob Hill maintains much turn-of-the-20C charm, although many wealthier San Franciscans now live in neighborhoods to the northwest, where larger plots accommodate palatial mansions in the spirit of the Big Four's legendary homes. Asian families populate the northeast slopes near Chinatown, and a large singles population occupies studios and small apartments to the southwest.

Visiting Nob Hill – Any time of day is a good time to visit, although early-morning sun sometimes obscures eastward views. As neighborhood denizens rush to work, t'ai chi practitioners congregate in Huntington Park. Traffic intensifies at the end of the work day, making street parking hard to find, but cable-car lines offer easy access from Union Square, the Financial District and Fisherman's Wharf. The Crown Room and Top of the Mark, Nob Hill's skyscraping watering holes, open in early evening, a good time to stop for tea or a cocktail and drink in glorious city views.

WALKING TOUR .6mi

Begin at the southwest corner of Powell & California Sts.

The first of the Big Four to build his mansion atop Nob Hill, Leland Stanford constructed an immense Italianate villa on this corner lot in 1876. Today it is the site of the **Stanford Court Hotel**, remodeled in 1972 from an elegant apartment building. The gray stone retaining wall encircling the block was built in the 1870s and was the only part of Stanford's mansion to survive the 1906 fire.

Walk west up California St.

Mark Hopkins Inter-Continental Hotel – *999 California St. at Mason St.* ✗ ♿ ▣ ☎ *415-392-3434. www.markhopkins.net.* In 1877 Mark Hopkins began construction of a sprawling Victorian mansion to rival Stanford's in elegance and ostentation. Hopkins died in 1878 before it was completed; in 1893 his widow donated the residence to the California School of Design, now the San Francisco Art Institute. The 1906 fire razed the structure, and in 1926 the Mark Hopkins Hotel rose in its place. It underwent a $51 million renovation in 2000. The hotel is crowned by the **Top of the Mark** *(open year-round Mon–Thu 3pm–1am, Fri–Sat 3pm–1:30am, Sun 4:30pm–1am; evening cover charge $6 Sun–Thu, $10 Fri–Sat)*, once a copper baron's penthouse; redesigned in 1939 as a swank Art Deco-style bar by Timothy Pflueger, it boasts panoramic **views**★★★ of the city and San Francisco Bay.

Cross California St.

★★ **Fairmont Hotel** – *Bounded by California, Mason, Powell & Sacramento Sts.* ✗ ♿ ▣ ☎ *415-772-5000. www.fairmont.com/Hotels/Index_SF.html.* With its opulent lobby, dignified facade and illustrious history, the Fairmont offers a glimpse of early-20C Nob Hill. Designed by James and Merritt Reid, its construction began in 1902 under the stewardship of Tessie Fair Oelrichs, James Fair's daughter. Work was nearly complete when the 1906 quake struck and fire swept the hill, leaving only the granite outer walls intact.

FISHERMAN'S WHARF

RUSSIAN HILL
NOB HILL

0   1/10 mi
0   100 m

MARINA DISTRICT

PACIFIC HEIGHTS

UNION SQUARE AREA

Architect Julia Morgan, early in her career, oversaw restoration and completion of the building in its original Italian Renaissance style. On April 18, 1907, exactly a year after the earthquake, the Fairmont reopened. It soon gained a reputation as the city's premier hotel. In 1945, the United Nations Charter was drafted in the elegant Garden Room; today, flags of UN-member countries above the hotel's main entrance commemorate the event. A modern tower was added in 1961.

In the ornate main lobby, massive marble pillars and wrought-iron balconies remain from Morgan's 1906 design. At the north rear of the hotel, a glass-walled exterior elevator rises slowly to the **Crown Room** restaurant *(open year-round Mon–Sat 4–9pm, Sun 10am–2pm & 6–9pm)*, renowned for its glorious views★★★.

Walk west on California St.

★Pacific-Union Club – *1000 California St. Not open to the public.* The only structure on Nob Hill to survive the 1906 blaze, silver baron James Flood's mansion was built in 1885 by English architect Augustus Laver at a cost of $1.5 million. Unlike other Nob Hill palaces, which were made of California redwood,

❶ The Tonga Room
Fairmont Hotel. ☎ 415-772-5278. Order anything with an umbrella at the Fairmont's Polynesian-style restaurant and "hurricane bar." Thatched umbrellas hover over rustic tables, and every half-hour a sprinkler system simulates a tropical rainstorm above the indoor lagoon. Don't miss the happy-hour buffet, or the floating live band.

Flood's 42-room Italianate home was built of Connecticut brownstone and withstood the 1906 earthquake, although the intense heat of the ensuing fire gutted the lavish interior. In 1908 architect Willis Polk shortened the central tower and added wings on two sides, softening the staunch vertical facade. The bronze fence surrounding it was patterned after a piece of lace favored by Flood's wife. Today the building is home to the private Pacific-Union Club, which traces its origins to 1852 and is considered the most exclusive men's club in the West.

Continue west on California St. and cross Taylor St.

★**Grace Cathedral** – *1051 Taylor St. at California St. Open year-round Mon–Fri & Sun 7am–6pm, Sat 8am–6pm, holidays 9am–4pm. Guided tours (1hr) Mon–Fri 1pm–3pm, Sat 11:30am–1:30pm, Sun 12:30pm–2pm, or by appointment.* ⚐ 🅿 ☎ 415-749-6300. www.gracecathedral.org. The third-largest Episcopal cathedral in the US anchors the crest of Nob Hill, its French Gothic spires soaring majestically over the city. Consecrated in 1964, the edifice occupies the lot formerly owned by Charles Crocker, whose huge, Second Empire-style mansion stood side-by-side with a Victorian villa he commissioned for his son as a wedding present. After both homes were destroyed in the 1906 fire, the family donated the land to the Episcopal diocese. Grace's cornerstone was laid in 1910 but construction did not begin until 1928 for financial and technical reasons. Work was halted by the Great Depression and again by World War II. The Notre Dame-inspired design by Lewis P. Hobart was executed in steel-reinforced concrete to withstand seismic tremors.

Set between the main entrance doors in the Gothic eastern portal, the bronze **Gates of Paradise** are the cathedral's most prized architectural feature. Duplicates of a set cast by Florentine sculptor Lorenzo Ghiberti (the originals adorn the Santa Maria del Fiore Cathedral Baptistry in Florence), the 16ft doors are divided into 10 richly ornamented panels illustrating scenes from the Old Testament. Inside the cathedral, dozens of stained-glass windows and murals depict a diversity of figures from saints to 20C luminaries, including Robert Frost, Franklin D. Roosevelt and Albert Einstein. The alterpiece, painter Keith Haring's *A Life of Christ*, was dedicated in 1995 by the AIDS Memorial Chapel Project. A magnificent Aeolian-Skinner organ, built in 1934 in American Classic style, resounds with 7,286 pipes. Two labyrinths invite exploration: a marble path to the right of the east entrance replicates France's Chartres Cathedral, and a second Chartres-inspired maze is woven into a large carpet near a Beniamino Bufano sculpture of St. Francis of Assisi.

Exit cathedral on Taylor St. and cross to the park.

Huntington Park – Banked slightly above street level, Huntington Park gracefully crowns Nob Hill. John McLaren, who designed Golden Gate Park and other Bay Area public gardens, oversaw the design and cultivation of this 1.75-acre plot, donated to the city after Collis Huntington's opulent mansion on the adjacent lot was destroyed in the 1906 fire. Blackwood acacias and sycamores thrive here, framing the 20C replica of Rome's Tartarughe ("Tortoise") Fountain that forms the park's centerpiece. Purchased in Italy by William Crocker's wife to beautify the family estate, this replica was moved here in 1955.

Walk east on Sacramento St. and turn left on Mason St.

Gates of Paradise, detail

© Robert Holmes

Getting A Grip: San Francisco's Cable Cars

More than 8 million visitors and San Franciscans annually ride the city's signature cable cars, a public transportation system invented and developed by Scotsman Andrew Smith Hallidie in 1873. Inspired by the work of his father, who had been awarded the world's first patent on iron-wire rope in 1835, 16-year-old Hallidie came to California in 1852, at the height of the Gold Rush, to build wire-rope transport systems for the mines. In his early 20s he moved to San Francisco, where he established a wire-rope manufacturing company and developed suspension bridges and cable tramways for the silver mines of Nevada's Comstock Lode. But it wasn't until 1869 that Hallidie first conceived of a similar system as a means of public transportation. Four years and $85,000 later, the idea that had been dubbed "Hallidie's Folly" took form as a primitive cable car line that ascended Clay Street between Kearny and Leavenworth Streets at 6mph.

California Historical Society, San Francisco. FN-25322

Andrew Smith Hallidie

A testament to the quality of Hallidie's design, today's cable cars work in much the same way as those of 1873. The concept is simple: Just as a constantly moving tow-rope pulls a skier up a snowy slope, huge loops of steel cable run at a continuous 9.5mph beneath Powell, Hyde, Mason and California Streets, powered by electric motors at the Cable Car Barn. To start the car moving, the "gripman"—in the middle of the car—operates a lever that extends down through a slot in the street. At the underground end of the lever, a "grip" closes and opens like a jaw on the moving cable. The tighter the grip closes, the faster the car goes. To reduce speed, the gripman opens the grip to release the cable; brakes are applied to stop. A conductor at the rear of the car helps with braking when necessary.

Because the soft metal dies, inside the jaws of the grip, are the only contact between the cables and the cars (which can weigh up to 10 tons), they must be replaced every four days. Likewise the cables, constructed of six strands of 19 wires twisted around a core of sisal rope, must be replaced every month or two through a labor-intensive process of cutting and splicing each individual strand. The track is inspected daily for imperfections, as are each car's three sets of brakes: wheel brakes, track brakes and emergency brakes. This is essential, considering the harrowing 18-21 percent grades the cars must negotiate.

Today the system, which was designated a National Historic Landmark in 1964, numbers 40 cable cars operating on three lines (Powell-Mason, Powell-Hyde and California Street). The entire system, including the powerhouse, was completely rehabilitated between 1982 and 1984, preserving this unique, colorful, characteristic part of San Francisco's past and present.

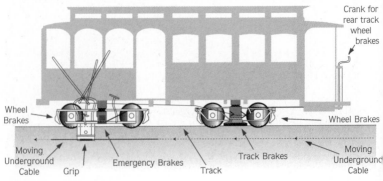

Crank for rear track wheel brakes

Wheel Brakes

Wheel Brakes

Moving Underground Cable

Grip

Emergency Brakes

Track

Track Brakes

Moving Underground Cable

★★ Cable Car Museum – ▥ *1201 Mason St. at Washington St. Open Apr–Sept daily 10am–6pm. Rest of the year daily 10am–5pm. Closed Jan 1, Thanksgiving Day, Dec 25.* ☎ *415-474-1887. www.cablecarmuseum.com.* This weathered brick building on the steep north slope of Nob Hill offers an up-close look at the nerve center of San Francisco's renowned cable-car system, the only one of its kind in the world. Besides serving as a powerhouse and car-storage barn, the structure houses a unique history museum.

On the upper level, a balcony overlooks the cable-car mechanism. Motors hum and giant wheels called "sheaves" rotate, powering continuous loops of cable for the system's three lines. Instructive panels affixed to the balcony railings and a video presentation *(16min)* explain how the system works. Historical displays tell the story of the cable cars from their invention, through their late-19C heyday, to the present. Other exhibits include historic photos, rudimentary hand tools and public transportation memorabilia. Among the treasured pieces is **Car No. 8**, only survivor of the Clay Street Hill Railroad, San Francisco's first cable-car line, which began operation in 1873. The car had been shipped to Chicago for the 1893 World's Columbian Exhibition and not returned; it thus fortuitously escaped the 1906 fire. On the lower level, a small viewing area offers a glimpse of the sheave room where the thick steel cables enter the building before being routed up to the main sheaves.

ADDITIONAL SIGHT

The Ritz-Carlton, San Francisco – *600 Stockton St. (between California & Pine Sts.)* ✕ ♿ ▯ ☎ *415-296-7465. www. ritzcarlton.com.* Built on the Chinatown flank of Nob Hill (1909, Napoleon Le Brun & Sons) as the West Coast headquarters of the Metropolitan Life Insurance Co., the original 80ft cube was expanded in 1914 and 1920 with two symmetrical wings. A facade of 18 Ionic columns supports an entablature that features hourglasses and lions' heads; while an allegorical figure ("Insurance") spreads its wings over two symbolic families from the portico above the entrance. A pair of annexes and a central garden court were added later. Met Life sold the building in 1973; for 11 years, until The Ritz purchased the building, it housed Cogswell College. After a four-year renovation, the luxurious hotel opened in 1991.

2 Swan Oyster Depot
1517 Polk St. ☎ *415-673-1101.* In the window, the day's catch stops sidewalk traffic; inside, jokes fly with the shucked shells.
Six brothers, their youngest sister and a friend or two preside over the 20-stool lunch counter, bantering with regulars, cracking crab legs and serving up buttery clam chowder, fresh seafood cocktails and oysters on the half shell while making strangers feel at home.

5 • NORTH BEACH★★

🚋 Powell-Mason. 🚍 bus 15–Third, 30–Stockton, 45–Union-Stockton or 39–Coit.
Map p 90

The erstwhile heart of San Francisco's Italian community and one of the city's oldest neighborhoods, this sunny district—nestling between bustling Fisherman's Wharf and the steep slopes of Telegraph Hill and Russian Hill—has become a prime residential haven for young professionals of diverse ethnic groups. Although shops and businesses from burgeoning Chinatown, to the south, slowly encroach across Broadway, the flavors and fragrances of North Beach's Italian roots still predominate, as evidenced by dozens of well-patronized trattorias, cafes and delicatessens. A onetime refuge for San Francisco's Beat counterculture, this neighborhood retains, to a certain degree, the close-knit character of a village.

Historical Notes

Only the name remains of the narrow stretch of sand that once formed the area's bayside border. As early as the 1850s, land-hungry speculators began dumping tons of fill material into the shallows that once lapped present-day Bay Street, eventually erecting a flourishing industrial zone atop the buried beach. Rough-and-tumble tent cities appeared on the sheltered southwest slope of Telegraph Hill in the early Gold Rush years. **Little Chile**, populated by treasure-seeking Chileans and Peruvians, sprang up near Kearny Street. Directly to the east between Broadway and Union Street stood **Sydney Town**, home of a notorious group of former Australian convicts, many of whom regularly terrorized their South American neighbors. Ships' crews carved chunks from the side of Telegraph Hill to provide ballast for their homeward voyages, the vessels having been vacated by the argonauts. The hillside scars remain visible today.

After the heady days of the Gold Rush, a polyglot mixture of newly arrived immigrants from Spain, France, Portugal, Germany and Italy moved into the valley, which subsequently became known as the **Latin Quarter**. Goats roamed the rocky crest of Telegraph Hill, where the working-class Irish had established an enclave on the eastern slope. Italian immigration, slow in the mid-19C, increased dramatically in the 1880s as successful émigrés brought their families from Europe. Newcomers from northern Italy disembarked at the foot of Sansome Street and stayed, attracted by North Beach's relatively warm microclimate, low rents and proximity to the wharves and canneries where many made their living. The Italian community gradually displaced other ethnic groups, and by 1900 the old Latin Quarter had given way to **Little Italy**.

The Best Minds of a Generation – As the children of Italian immigrants grew up, they also moved out, seeking agricultural opportunities in the rich Napa and Sonoma county farmlands. In the mid-50s, vacancies in North Beach had driven rents low enough to attract an anarchic assortment of poor and disillusioned—"beaten"— writers and artists bent on rejecting established societal and artistic norms. Calling themselves the **Beat Generation**, dubbed "beatniks" (by columnist Herb Caen), they adopted nonconformist bohemian lifestyles, smoked marijuana, drank red wine and espresso, listened to jazz and be-bop, and read poetry at favorite haunts like the Co-Existence Bagel Shop and The Place (both long since vanished). Of their principal gathering places, few remain: City Lights Bookstore, Vesuvio Café, Tosca Cafe and Caffé Trieste are rare survivors.

The movement inspired an outpouring of creative activity by its leading lights: poets Lawrence Ferlinghetti, Kenneth Rexroth, Gregory Corso and Allen Ginsberg; novelist Jack Kerouac; and visual artists Jay DeFeo and Robert LaVigne. The 1955 reading of Ginsberg's raw, apocalyptic poem "Howl" gave birth to the San Francisco Poetry Renaissance and an enduring cultural legend. "I saw the best minds of my generation destroyed by madness," Ginsberg intoned, "starving, hysterical, naked, draggin themselves through negro streets at dawn lookin for an angry fix. ..."

Within a decade, the movement was over, ruined in part by busloads of "square" tourists who overran North Beach in their search for "cool." By the mid-60s, the best minds of the Beat Generation had either passed away or moved on.

North Beach Today – Few in the counterculture could now afford the high rents of North Beach's surprisingly uniform, three- to four-story flats and apartment houses, built in a nine-year flurry of reconstruction after the 1906 earthquake and fire. The northward flow of families and businesses from Chinatown, begun in the 1960s as immigration restrictions on Asians eased, continues the district's long tradition of multiethnic coexistence. Many nonresident Italian Americans still consider North Beach home, returning often to shop, dine or gather at one of the venerable institutions still operated by descendants of the original owners.

Visiting North Beach – North Beach shows different faces at different times of the day. In the morning, a village atmosphere prevails as cafes fill with early-rising poets, eager job-seekers and neighborhood professionals stopping for a caffè latte before heading to work. The fragrances of baking bread and roasting coffee drift through the streets, and crowds gather to practice traditional t'ai chi exercises in Washington Square. In the evening, a younger international crowd takes over the bars, saloons and jazz clubs. Restaurants remain crowded until late night. Floodlights illuminate Coit Tower, Saints Peter and Paul Church, and other monuments. The annual **Italian Heritage Day Parade** (on Columbus Day in October) draws thousands to the streets of North Beach, as does the **North Beach Festival**, one of the oldest urban street fairs in the country, in mid-June. Public transport, serving all corners of North Beach, is strongly recommended, as parking is scarce and regulations are strictly enforced. It's best to climb Telegraph Hill on foot or take the 39–Coit bus from the Union Street/Columbus Avenue stop on the south side of Washington Square. Cars often wait in line over an hour to park at the summit. The hill's flanks are steep; wear sturdy shoes and pause frequently to rest and admire the wonderful vistas that extend over city and bay.

WALKING TOUR   *1.6mi*
Begin at the corner of Columbus Ave. & Broadway.

★**City Lights Bookstore** – *261 Columbus Ave. Open year-round daily 10am–midnight. Closed Thanksgiving Day & Dec 25.* ☎ *415-362-8193. www.citylights.com.* Founded in 1953 by poet Lawrence Ferlinghetti, this former beatnik hangout was the first all-paperback bookstore in America. It remains one of the best-known independent shops in the US, as much for its history as for its meandering layout, ambience and unique titles—many released by City Lights Publishers. In the upstairs poetry and Beat literature room, comfortable chairs encourage browsers to linger with their selections. Enlarged over the years, the store maintains its alternative reputation despite the presence on its shelves of clothbound books and other inevitable marks of changing times.

Across Jack Kerouac Alley from City Lights Bookstore lies **Vesuvio Café** *(255 Columbus Ave.;* ✗ ♿ ☎ *415-362-3370; www.vesuvio.com)*, another popular landmark of North Beach's Beat heyday. It was here that a black-clad crowd of beatniks gathered on October 13, 1955, before attending Ginsberg's now-legendary reading of "Howl" at the Six Gallery (long gone from its former Marina District location). Vivid paintings and leaded glass enliven the cafe's wood-trimmed walls, which are crammed with photos and memorabilia from the Beat era—even as employees now encourage patrons to desist from "rude" behavior by removing their berets.

Vesuvio Café

91

Just steps southeast on Columbus Avenue is the **San Francisco Brewing Company** *(155 Columbus Ave.;* ✗ ♿ ☎ *415-434-3344; www.sfbrewing.com)*, one of the first brew pubs in the US when it began producing its own beer in 1985. Established at the edge of the Barbary Coast in 1907 as the Andromeda Saloon, it attracted such diverse personalities as Jack Dempsey, a 1913 bouncer who became world heavyweight boxing champion, and Baby Face Nelson, public enemy no. 1, captured at the Andromeda by the FBI in 1939. Modern décor is characterized by historic photos and antiques, including the 1916 "Pukka Walla" fan of brass and palm fronds that rotates above the bar.

Walk north to Broadway, turn right and cross Columbus Ave.

As you cross, glance to your right for an impressive view of the Transamerica Pyramid. The **Sentinel Building** *(916 Kearny St.)*, a green, copper-trimmed, flat-iron-shaped office building (1905, Salfield and Kohlberg), rises in the foreground. Filmmaker Francis Ford Coppola purchased and restored the tower in the 1970s; on the ground floor, Café Niebaum-Coppola *(☎ 415-291-1700)* maintains a tasting lounge with vintages from the Napa Valley's Niebaum-Coppola Estate.

Broadway – *Broadway between Columbus Ave. & Montgomery St.* Though its reputation for danger, vice and sin has gentled in recent decades, the strip of sex shops and topless clubs along Broadway and Kearny Street harks back to San Francisco's less-than-savory past. Broadway's notoriety originated in the waterfront dives of Sydney Town in the 1850s, when a zone of dance halls, brothels, gambling dens and outlaw nests known as the **Barbary Coast** arose along lower Pacific Avenue, extending to present-day Jackson Square and parts of Chinatown. Sailors on shore leave enjoyed the strip's diversions at great peril: "Shanghaiing" was an all-too-common practice (the word, meaning "recruiting someone forcefully for maritime service," is said to have originated here). Civic pressure led to the cleanup of the Barbary Coast after the 1906 earthquake and fire, and bars offering exotic entertainment were restricted to Broadway, where they have persisted, mostly undisturbed, for years.

Several risqué venues opened in the 1960s and early 1970s, among them the Condor Club (now a sports bar) at the intersection of Broadway, Columbus and Grant Avenues. For several decades a neon figure of **Carol Doda**, the "queen of topless dancing," hung provocatively above the street, drawing scores of visitors. The cartoonish landmark was removed (and auctioned off piecemeal) in 1991, but several all-nude venues remain, catering mostly to curious college students and the occasional serviceman on shore leave.

Continue up Columbus Ave.

❶ Molinari Delicatessen

373 Columbus Ave. ☎ *415-421-2337.* Heady whiffs of parmesan, basil, salami and olives waft from this century-old North Beach institution. Neighborhood denizens pop in early to pick up handmade ravioli, tortellini, cheeses, olive oils and vinegars from Italy. Later in the morning, meats and cheese appear on the chopping block for the sandwich-at-the-desk and picnic-in-Washington Square crowds.

Molinari Delicatessen

© Robert Holmes

Coffee in North Beach

Black as night, strong as sin...

Long before every shopping mall and fast-food joint in America installed a coffee bar, before the Beats of the 50s were bolting shots of espresso in smoky cafés, the Italian-American residents of North Beach were drinking fine coffee. Today, with more than a dozen cafés and two traditional roasteries, North Beach is still a prime spot to enjoy some form of the bitter black liquid.

Espresso: Strong and black, made from finely ground, dark-roasted beans. Served in a demitasse, it is the base for all other coffee drinks. Called caffè romano when accompanied by a twist of lemon peel.

Caffè latté: Espresso with steamed milk, sometimes topped with foam. Often served in a tall glass.

Cappuccino: Espresso with a cap of milk foam. Served in a broad mug.

Mocha: Espresso with steamed milk and chocolate, topped with whipped cream. Also called "dessert."

Machiatto: Espresso "stained" with a drop of steamed milk. Served in a demitasse.

Caffè americano: Basic American-style coffee. In North Beach, even this is good.

Café au lait: American coffee with steamed milk.

© PhotoDisc, Inc

Columbus Avenue – Designed in 1872 as a direct path from the Financial District to the industrial zone growing along the northern waterfront, this broad, busy avenue traces the valley between Russian and Telegraph Hills, indiscriminately cutting across the city's square grid and creating several confusing six-way intersections. Called Montgomery Avenue at its construction, it was later renamed for Christopher Columbus to honor North Beach's Italian community. Today anchored by the Transamerica Pyramid, the thoroughfare extends through North Beach to The Cannery on Fisherman's Wharf. The blocks between Broadway and Filbert Street, lined with fragrant bakeries, garlicky trattorias, pungent delicatessens and aromatic cafes, preserve the soul of Italian North Beach.

Continue to Stockton St. and turn left.

The melding of cultures that distinguishes present-day North Beach is clearly visible in the block of Stockton Street between Vallejo and Green Streets. Asian markets and Chinese street signs rub shoulders with old-fashioned Italian shops advertising fresh *tagliarini* and imported olive oil.

North Beach Museum – *1435 Stockton St. (Bay View Bank), mezzanine level. Open year-round Mon–Thu 9am–4:30pm, Fri 9am–5pm. Closed major holidays.* ☎ *415-626-7070.* This small, bank-sponsored museum highlights North Beach's multiethnic heritage through changing displays and photo exhibits of the Chinese and Italian communities in the late 19C and early 20C. The museum features an 11-panel photographic panorama of San Francisco in 1877 by Eadweard Muybridge, as well as an especially fine collection of photos of North Beach, Fisherman's Wharf and Telegraph Hill during and after the 1906 temblor. Especially worth noting is Lawrence Ferlinghetti's handwritten poem "The Old Italians Dying."

Return to Columbus Ave. and continue northwest.

2 Caffeine and Conversation
For decades, North Beach denizens have stopped at the neighborhood's famed Italian coffeehouses to get their morning jolt. At **Caffè Trieste** *(601 Vallejo St.;* ☎ *415-392-6739),* or **Mario's Bohemian Cigar Store** *(566 Columbus Ave.;* ☎ *415-362-0536),* the price of a cup buys you a table for the day to work on your novel; the latter serves up the best focaccia sandwich going. Big windows at **Caffè Puccini** *(411 Columbus Ave.;* ☎ *415-989-7033)* and **Caffè Greco** *(423 Columbus Ave.;* ☎ *415-397-6261)* offer glimpses of daily life in North Beach. The coffee at **Caffè Roma** *(526 Columbus Ave.;* ☎ *415-665-3909)* comes fresh from a brass-trimmed roaster sitting in the window.

3 Beach Blanket Babylon

Club Fugazi, 678 Beach Blanket Babylon Blvd. (formerly Green St.). ☎ *415-421-4222. www. beachblanketbabylon.com.* Where else could you find Elvis and Madonna, Bill Clinton and Monica Lewinsky, Louis XIV and Whoopi Goldberg, Mr. Peanut and Snow White, and some of the most ludicrous hats ever created, together on the same stage? This outrageous spoof of current events and pop culture has played before packed houses eight times weekly at the same location since 1974, and is acclaimed as the longest-running musical revue in theater history.

★**Washington Square Park** – With a broad, sunny lawn and clusters of willow, cypress and sycamore trees, this pentagonal park occupies the heart of North Beach. The popular neighborhood gathering spot was donated to the city by its first mayor, John W. Geary, and set aside as a public park in 1847 by Jasper O'-Farrell, surveyor of San Francisco's downtown street grid. After Columbus Avenue sliced off its southwest corner (now called Marini Plaza) in 1873, the park was landscaped to Victorian taste with shade trees and a broad, curving path for promenading. Hundreds of refugees camped here during the year following the 1906 earthquake and fire. Today, elderly Asians gather each morning to practice *t'ai chi*, a graceful form of martial arts *(below)*, and Italian retirees spend hours on the benches facing Union Street. Visitors and locals alike often picnic on the grassy lawn.

Situated on the western side of the park, the bronze monument honoring San Francisco's heroic **Volunteer Firemen** (**1**) (1933, Haig Patigian) was erected through a bequest of Lillie Hitchcock Coit, San Francisco's firefighter-loving eccentric. A handsome bronze figure of **Benjamin Franklin** (**2**) stands at the center of the park; an inscription on its base refers to a time capsule buried in Washington Square Park in 1879 and opened a century later.

■ T'ai Chi

Early-rising visitors enjoying a morning trek through North Beach, Russian Hill, Nob Hill or other residential areas are likely to spy individuals or groups of people dressed in everyday clothes performing what appears to be a slow-motion outdoor ballet. *T'ai chi ch'uan*, an ancient, noncompetitive martial art, is practiced by many citizens as a form of exercise. The slow, meditative transitions between specified stances and positions is said to condition the body and relax the mind by harmonizing of the passive and active principles of *yin* and *yang*. Almost any serene plot can be a good place to perform this ritual, but groups tend to gather at Ina Coolbrith Park, Huntington Park, St. Mary's Square and especially Washington Square Park.

★**Saints Peter and Paul Church** – *666 Filbert St., north side of Washington Sq. Open year-round Mon–Fri 6:30am–4pm, weekends 6:30am–7pm.* ♿ ☎ *415-421-0809.* Built in Gothic Revival style with Italianate details, this handsome, twin-spired church (1924) is fondly known as the Italian Cathedral. Lawrence Ferlinghetti dubbed it "the marzipan church on the plaza," a description particularly true at night when floodlights bathe its cream-colored exterior. The imposing facade bears the opening line of Dante's *Paradiso*: "The glory of Him who moves all things penetrates and glows throughout the universe." The interior is warm and inviting, enclosed by an unusual flat ceiling of dark wood and illuminated by banks of votive candles and richly colored stained-glass windows. A spectacular, 40ft-high altar, made of Mediterranean marble and onyx, features a sculpted reproduction of da Vinci's *Last Supper*.

Screen legend Marilyn Monroe and baseball great Joe DiMaggio took wedding photos on the front steps of SS. Peter and Paul, contributing to the myth that they were married inside. (Both were in fact married in the church, though not to each other.) DiMaggio grew up in North Beach, and as a youth in the 1930s was a member of the church's boys' club—along with New York Yankees teammates Tony Lazzeri and Frankie Crossetti.

The church reflects North Beach's multiethnic character, offering Mass in English, Italian and Cantonese.

From the church, walk east up Filbert St. and climb the hill, following the "Stairs to Coit Tower" signs. To avoid the steep climb, take the 39–Coit bus from Washington Square.

★**Telegraph Hill** – The abrupt rise that punctuates the eastern edge of North Beach was named for a long-vanished semaphore erected atop its summit in 1849. A precursor to modern telegraph systems, the semaphore signaled the arrival of ships through the Golden Gate by varicolored flags hoisted along its two arms, positioned according to the type and nationality of the vessel. Gold Rush-era shacks and tent cities that dotted the steep, rocky flanks developed into working-class neighborhoods that persisted until the early 20C, when the automobile opened the way for wealthier citizens. Most of the structures on the hill (and in surrounding North Beach) burned to the ground during the 1906 fire, but houses on the east slope were saved by determined Italian Americans, who beat back the flames with blankets soaked in red wine.

© David R. Frazier

Coit Tower and Telegraph Hill

The tree-filled expanse at the hill's 274ft summit, today known as **Pioneer Park**, was donated to the city in 1876 by a group of businessmen intent on preserving the open space for future generations. The bronze statue of **Christopher Columbus** (**3**) at the center of the Coit Tower parking area was erected by the local Italian-American community. Panoramic **views**★★ from the summit encompass major landmarks including Twin Peaks, Lombard Street, the Golden Gate Bridge, Alcatraz and the Bay Bridge. On clear days, the East Bay hills come into view. As you gaze, listen for the sounds of barking sea lions drifting up from Pier 39.

★★**Coit Tower** – 〔Kids〕 *Summit of Telegraph Hill. Open May–Sept daily 10am–7:30pm. Rest of the year daily 10am–6pm.* 🅿 ☎ *415-362-0808.* Towering 180ft above a 32ft rectangular base, this fluted, concrete column (1934, Arthur Brown, Jr.) was an enduring gift to San Francisco's citizens from an unusual woman who wished to add "to the beauty of the city which I have always loved." Initially infamous for the heated social controversy incited by its lobby murals, Coit Tower ranks today among the city's best-known landmarks.

"Firebelle" Lillie – When **Lillie Hitchcock Coit** (1843-1929) was a child in San Francisco, daring teams of volunteers battled the many fires that regularly ravaged the city. It is said that one afternoon in the 1860s young Lillie, who had been saved from a fire during her childhood, came upon Knickerbocker Engine Company No. 5 struggling up Telegraph Hill en route to a blaze. Throwing down her schoolbooks, she rallied onlookers to help the firemen. In return, the company made her an honorary member. For the rest of her life, even as a wealthy widow in Paris, Coit wore a gold, diamond-studded fireman's badge everywhere she went; it was pinned to her clothing when her remains were cremated in 1929. In her will, she bequeathed $125,000 to the city, part of which paid for the statue of her beloved volunteer firemen in Washington Square Park. The bulk of the gift provided funds for Coit Tower, which, despite persistent local lore, was not designed to resemble a firehose nozzle.

California Historical Society, San Francisco. FN-13122

The Murals – The first major commission of the Depression-era Public Works of Art Project (PWAP), a New Deal initiative that engaged artists to decorate public buildings, the 19 fresco **murals**★★ in the lobby of Coit Tower were created in 1934. Working for an average of $31.22 a week, 26 local painters and numerous assistants labored for five months to produce a series of frescoes depicting contemporary life in California.

Lillie Hitchcock Coit (1843-1929)

④ Dining around the Square
Around Washington Square are some of North Beach's best (and best-loved) restaurants. It's not unusual to start at one, dine at another and cap the night at a third. At **Little City Antipasti Bar** *(Union at Powell St.; ☎ 415-434-2900)*, starters circle the globe, from quesadillas to ahi tuna to gravlax. At **Moose's** *(1652 Stockton St.; ☎ 415-989-7800)*, deal-makers dine, writers circulate, "How about those Giants?" is an opening gambit, and the food is first-rate. **Fior d'Italia** *(601 Union St.; ☎ 415-986-1886)*, which opened in 1886 (as the catering arm of a bordello), is the oldest continually operating Italian restaurant in the US; the service, decor and menu are old-fashioned and courtly. **Mario's Bohemian Cigar Store** *(566 Columbus Ave.; ☎ 415-362-0536)* is the place to stop for cappuccino and dessert.

While celebrating the state's abundance and diversity, the works contained powerful images that bluntly criticized the economic inequities of life during the Great Depression.

The murals' left-wing content raised the hackles of San Francisco's conservative elite. Fueling the controversy, a tense labor conflict smoldered along the waterfront at the base of Telegraph Hill, erupting into the longshoremen's Pacific Maritime Strike just as work on the murals drew to a close. The sometimes-violent strike crippled the entire West Coast and caused some to view any form of social criticism as radical agitation. Responding to civic pressure, the San Francisco Art Commission delayed the opening of Coit Tower and considered destroying the murals. After vigorous debate on both sides of the issue, only the most blatant (hammer-and-sickle) symbols of left-wing sympathy in Clifford Wight's mural (no. 4) were effaced, and the building was finally opened to the public in October 1934.

Visit – The murals display remarkable uniformity in both theme and style despite the fact that so many different artists created them. **California Industrial Scenes** (John Langley Howard) depicts the despair of the era through an image of a migrant family posing beside their disabled Model-T, while a group of well-to-do day-trippers gazes on them as if they were a tourist attraction. **The Library** (Bernard Zakheim) inspired controversy for its suggestion that the works of Karl Marx might offer a viable form of government. In **City Life** (Victor Arnautoff), perhaps the best-known mural, a bustling street scene none-too-subtly criticizes the indifference of urban dwellers to one another.

A brief elevator ascent *($3; purchase tickets in gift shop)* and a short flight of stairs take visitors to the observation deck. From here, panoramic **views★★★** sweep Angel Island and Marin County to the north, the Bay Bridge and Treasure Island to the east, downtown San Francisco to the south, and Russian Hill and the Golden Gate Bridge to the west.

From Coit Tower, descend the curving sidewalk along Telegraph Hill Ave. to the first corner and turn left at Filbert St.

★★ Filbert Steps – *Coit Tower to Sansome St.* Concrete and wooden stairs, descending this steep section of Filbert Street, comprise one of the city's most charming and surprising pathways. At **1360 Montgomery Street** (1937), the stairs pass a gleaming, Streamline Moderne apartment house that appeared in the 1947 film *Dark Passage* as the place where Lauren Bacall's character hid an escaped convict (Humphrey Bogart). Below Montgomery Street, the wooden staircase follows lushly landscaped garden terraces named for Grace Marchant, their original designer and a longtime neighborhood resident. Those who live along the steps today cultivate her verdant legacy, and the gardens flourish year-round. Inhabitants of the treehouse-like precincts along the pedestrian streets of **Darrell Place** and **Napier Lane** occupy handsome, mid-19C wooden cottages in styles typical of the vernacular architecture of the post-Gold Rush period. Note the simple facade at **no. 228** (1869), a delicately restored example of the Carpenter Gothic style, and the cottage at **no. 224** (1859).

At the bottom of the steps, cross Sansome St.

■ Jungle City

The relative warmth of Telegraph Hill and Washington Square attracts colonies of colorful parrots, descendants of household pets who escaped domestication. The parrots now form a curious and vocal part of North Beach's landscape, their loud screeches and brilliant colors enlivening Telegraph Hill's verdant flanks and the leafy canopies of Washington Square. Many of the birds also nest in the tall date palms that line Dolores Street in the Mission District.

Levi's Plaza – *Filbert St., between Sansome & Battery Sts.* Completed in 1982, this award-winning group of buildings (Hellmuth, Obata & Kassabaum) was designed to harmonize with the varying architectural styles of the surrounding neighborhood. Look west from the intersection of Battery and Filbert Streets to appreciate how its stacked-box profile mimics the houses marching steeply down Telegraph Hill. Administrative headquarters of Levi Strauss & Co., the complex boasts beautifully landscaped open spaces that serve as a placid haven amid the bustle of the nearby Embarcadero.

Walk north on Sansome St. to Greenwich St. and turn up the steps.

The **Greenwich Steps**, while not as lushly picturesque as the Filbert Street staircase, scale nasturtium-covered rocks and patches of fragrant anise along the ascent to the top of Telegraph Hill.

6 • RUSSIAN HILL★

🚋 Powell-Hyde or Powell-Mason.
Map p 86

Bounded by Francisco, Taylor, Pacific and Polk Streets, Russian Hill rises abruptly from the landfill flats of Fisherman's Wharf and North Beach Its precipitous flanks harbor a number of pre-1906 architectural gems and a rich history of literary activity. Topping 360ft at Vallejo Street between Taylor and Jones, and 294ft at Lombard and Hyde, the hill's two summits offer splendid views of Coit Tower, the Financial District, Alcatraz and the bay. Several secluded pedestrian stairways and paths negotiate the dips between the two peaks, making for beautiful, if vigorous, walks. Pleasant sidewalk cafes, restaurants, bars and shops on nearby Hyde and Polk Streets provide welcome places to eat, relax or browse.

Historical Notes

According to San Francisco lore, Russian Hill was named in the mid-19C when the graves of Russian seal hunters were discovered atop the crest of present-day Vallejo Street. After thousands of people turned out to see the city's first public hanging here in 1852, Joseph Atkinson built the first house on the south side of Russian Hill. Others followed, mainly working-class families who built simple wooden residences and climbed the steep slopes on foot. By the 1880s, cable-car lines had crept up Russian Hill's flanks and San Francisco's burgeoning population began eyeing the newly accessible heights. Small Victorian flats were built side-by-side with simple shingled cottages. A community of writers and artists moved in, securing Russian Hill's reputation as a bohemian enclave before upscale development took root.
From 1856 through the 1890s, Catherine Atkinson kept her home (at 1032 Broadway) open to such literary lights as Mark Twain, Ambrose Bierce, Robert Louis Stevenson and a group known as Les Jeunes, which included architect Willis Polk and poet Gelett Burgess. From the late 1860s until 1906, local literary maven Ina Coolbrith also hosted literary salons, inviting Twain, Bierce, Bret Harte, Charles Stoddard, George Sterling and others to her house at 1604 Taylor Street. For more than two decades after the 1906 quake and fire, the California Literary Society met in Coolbrith's upstairs flat at 1067 Broadway. In the 1940s Russian Hill provided the setting for several locally written mystery novels, and in 1952 Beat writer Jack Kerouac spent six months on the hill, staying with friends Neal and Carolyn Cassady at 29 Russell Street and working on several novels, including *On the Road*.
Unlike elite Nob Hill, Russian Hill continued to develop as a middle-class neighborhood, with small homes set relatively far apart and separated by gardens and wells. Although a few residential enclaves survived the 1906 fire, many homes were destroyed, and the ensuing architectural ferment of 1906-20 continues to define Russian Hill's aesthetic. Two- to four-story Edwardian buildings flourished, as did a number of pueblo-style stuccoes and Spanish and Art Deco apartment towers. Several less attractive high-rises were erected in the 1960s and 70s, blocking views; a 40ft height limit was imposed in 1974. Russian Hill today is a living testament to the city's architectural diversity. Its lofty heights, well-tended homes, and tranquil parks and gardens make it one of San Francisco's most picturesque neighborhoods.

Visiting Russian Hill – It's best to begin and end a visit to Russian Hill with a cable-car ride. Take the Powell-Mason line to Mason and Vallejo Streets to begin the walking tour, then pick up the Powell-Hyde line from the top of Lombard Street to finish. While not long, the route entails several steep climbs: Wear sturdy shoes.

WALKING TOUR *1mi*
Begin at Mason & Vallejo Sts. and walk west, climbing the left staircase.

Ina Coolbrith Park – A narrow plot of steep hillside bursting with Monterey pines, agave plants and hydrangea bushes along the Vallejo Street stairs, Ina Coolbrith Park was dedicated in 1931 as a memorial to the acclaimed poet and avatar of San Francisco's turn-of-the-20C literary community.

The niece of Mormon prophet Joseph Smith, **Ina Donna Coolbrith** (1841-1928) moved west with her family as a child. After spending her teenage years in Los Angeles, she moved to San Francisco in 1861. During the 1860s Coolbrith wrote poetry for and helped edit *The Californian* and the *Overland Monthly*, both highly esteemed literary journals, while spearheading the vibrant local salon scene. Later, during her long tenure as a librarian, Coolbrith encouraged writer Jack London and dancer Isadora Duncan in their artistic pursuits. The state legislature named her California's poet laureate in 1919.

From the Taylor Street stairhead, Coit Tower, the Bay Bridge and Yerba Buena Island are visible to the east through the trees. Begonias, zinnias and other blooming flowers garnish the paths that zigzag across the tiny park, and benches provide a peaceful place to rest.

Cross Taylor St. and continue up the Vallejo St. stairs to the summit.

Charming historic residences and outstanding eastward bay **views**★★ mark the summit of Vallejo Street. Tucked behind tall shrubbery and a redwood fence, the **Williams-Polk House**★ *(1013–1019 Vallejo St.)* was designed in 1892 by Willis Polk for Mrs. Virgil Williams, wife of a founder of the California School of Design (now the San Francisco Art Institute). The house is seven stories high on the side facing Broadway *(not visible)*. Inspired by the Arts and Crafts aesthetic, Polk embellished his creation with indigenous materials. So pleased was he with his design and with the view from the house that the architect waived his fee in exchange for quarters in the eastern third of the building.

The large, shingled structure at 1020 Vallejo Street contains the **Hermitage Condominiums** (1982, Esherick, Homsey, Dodge & Davis). The building occupies the former site of a one-story cottage that was home to the Rev. Joseph Worcester, an early proponent of the Arts and Crafts movement in the West. (Worcester himself had a hand in designing both his cottage and the Swedenborgian Church.) Many small cottages were demolished in the mid-20C to make way for large-scale building projects. Two of Worcester's original designs, the three-story, gable-roofed **Marshall Houses** *(1034 and 1036 Vallejo St.)*, both built in 1889, have survived the century largely unaltered.

Continue walking west to Florence Ln. on the left.

Screened by a charming, rose-covered fence, the shingled mansion at **40 Florence Lane** (1857) was remodeled by Willis Polk in 1891, and expanded nearly a century later by architect Robert A.M. Stern.

③ Swensen's Ice Cream

Union St. at Hyde St.
☎ *415-775-6818*. San Franciscans don't cope well with hot weather. When his troop ship sailed into the South Pacific, native son Earle Swensen, looking for the coldest place aboard, volunteered to make ice cream. Upon the war's conclusion, he opened shop here. The flagship in Swensen's fleet of 400 ice cream parlors holds only about a dozen customers, so most eat their cones out front while waiting for the cable car.

Cross the street to Russian Hill Pl.

Polk in 1916 built the houses at **1, 3, 5 & 7 Russian Hill Place**, which appear from the front as tiny Mediterranean-style cottages. The houses drop several stories at the back, however, presenting an imposing facade along Jones Street.

Turn right on Jones St. and walk north to Green St.

From the corner of Jones and Green Streets, fine **views**★★ extend to the north over Alcatraz. The 1000 block of Green features several beautifully restored Victorian-era earthquake survivors. The 1857 **Feusier Octagon House** at no. 1067 was sold in 1870 to Louis Feusier, a friend of Leland Stanford and Mark Twain; the handsome mansard roof was added several years later.

Return to Jones St. Turn left, continuing to Macondray Ln. Turn right and stroll to the wooden staircase.

★**Macondray Lane** – This enchanting little walking street, overhung by lush greenery, was one of Ina Coolbrith's favorite places to roam; it also appeared as "Barbary Lane" in author Armistead Maupin's serialized 1970s epic, *Tales of the City*. Turn-of-the-20C clapboard houses and modern glass condominiums share the cozily private lane.

Return to Jones St. and continue north, turning left on Union St. Turn right on Leavenworth St. and continue to Lombard St.

★★★**Lombard Street** – 🎦 Among San Francisco's most photographed tourist attractions, the 1000 block of Lombard Street boasts eight switchbacks in its one-block descent from Hyde to Leavenworth. The block's natural 27 percent grade was gentled to 16 percent in 1922, when cobblestones were used to pave the street. Today, roughly three-quarters of a million cars negotiate the hairpin turns each year, descending through banks of hydrangeas.

© Ron Watts/First Light

Lombard Street

Climb the stairs flanking the curves to Hyde Street, where **views**★★ extend north and east. From here, cable cars coast down to Ghirardelli Square and the Hyde Street Pier against a backdrop of Alcatraz and Angel Island.

ADDITIONAL SIGHT

★**San Francisco Art Institute** – *800 Chestnut St. Open year-round Mon–Fri 9am–5pm.* ✕ ♿ ☎ *415-771-7020. www.sfai-art.edu.* Founded in 1871, this prestigious fine-arts college occupies a Spanish Colonial Revival-style building (1926, Arthur Brown, Jr.), expanded in the béton brut style by English-born architect Paffard Keatinge Clay in 1969. A cultural center as well as a college, the institute welcomes the public to exhibits, galleries and avant-garde film screenings. Displays of student work change regularly in its open-air courtyard; temporary exhibits are mounted in the **Walter/McBean Gallery** *(open year-round Mon–Sat 11am–6pm).* The chapel-like **Diego Rivera Gallery** *(open year-round daily 9am–9pm; closed major holidays)* features *The Making of a Fresco Showing the Building of a City* (1931), a two-story mural by the famed Mexican artist. Rivera himself appears in the work, along with his wife, Frida Kahlo. From the rooftop deck, grand **views**★★ extend over Telegraph Hill and the northern waterfront.

4 San Francisco Art Institute Cafe
San Francisco Art Institute. ☎ *415-749-4567.* Wind your way through the art- and handbill-lined hallways to the Institute's broad back deck. Grab a sandwich, potato or daily entree— guaranteed to fill starving artists at rock-bottom prices—sit back and relax. The foreground of congregating students against a stunning backdrop of city, bay and sky may inspire you to bring out your brushes.

■ **Steepest Streets of San Francisco**

Filbert between Hyde and Leavenworth – **31.5 %** grade
Jones between Union and Filbert – **29 %** grade
Duboce between Buena Vista and Alpine – **27.9 %** grade
Jones between Green and Union – **26 %** grade
Webster between Vallejo and Broadway – **26 %** grade
Duboce between Alpine and Castro – **25 %** grade
Jones between Pine and California – **24.8 %** grade
Fillmore between Vallejo and Broadway – **24 %** grade

Powell-Hyde or Powell-Mason. █████ bus 2–Clement, 3–Jackson, 4–Sutter, 30–Stockton,
38–Geary or 45–Union-Stockton;
all streetcars Powell St. station. ███ Powell St. station.
Map opposite

Roughly bounded by Sutter, Taylor, Kearny and O'Farrell Streets, the Union Square area bustles as San Francisco's most vibrant and prestigious urban shopping district. Dominating the square itself, major department stores stand shoulder-to-shoulder with upscale boutiques and a turn-of-the-20C hotel. To the east, designer shops crowd in beside art galleries and specialty stores, and chichi cafes set up umbrella-shaded tables along secluded pedestrian lanes. To the west extends the city's theater district, where large and small venues mix with art galleries, hotels, all-night diners and exclusive social clubs.

Historical Notes

In 1850, San Francisco mayor John White Geary presented the city with Union Square Park, a precious gift during the height of the Gold Rush when land was at a premium. For the next two decades the neighborhood remained largely residential, staid Victorian homes and churches flanking the open square. Through the 1880s and 90s, the area grew increasingly commercial as merchants, attracted to the upscale, picturesque central square, rented the homes of wealthy residents who had relocated west to the more spacious environs of Pacific Heights. Sutter Street became the area's first fashionable shopping artery, followed by the streets flanking the square itself. Large retail establishments began appearing in 1896 when the **City of Paris** department store took up residence at the corner of Geary and Stockton Streets. Across the park at Geary and Powell, white-gloved porters opened the doors of the St. Francis Hotel for the first time in 1904. With its grand lobby, luxurious guest rooms and fine restaurants, the St. Francis, along with City of Paris and **Gump's** *(135 Post St.)*, an esteemed interior-design gallery, ensured Union Square's elite cachet.

The 1906 earthquake and fire nearly razed the district, but determined entrepreneurs lost no time in rebuilding. In 1908 the City of Paris rose anew; architects Bakewell & Brown preserved much of its original design and added a stained-glass rotunda reminiscent of one in Paris' Galeries Lafayette. The St. Francis was reconstructed and expanded that same year in its original Renaissance Revival style. In the blocks east of the square, Gump's was rebuilt, and new boutiques appeared along Maiden Lane. To the west, numerous theaters took root, many sporting Neoclassical facades. In the following decades, prestigious social clubs were founded in the area, among them the Romanesque Revival-style **Olympic Club** *(524 Post St.)*, the Moderne-influenced **Bohemian Club** *(624 Taylor St.)* and the **Metropolitan Club** *(640 Sutter St.)* for women only.

Today this preponderance of theaters and stores, along with numerous hotels, makes Union Square one of the city's liveliest districts. During the day, shoppers mob the stores around the square, especially **Saks Fifth Avenue**, **Neiman Marcus**, **Macy's** and the **DFS Galleria**, while flower vendors, shoeshine boys, buskers and panhandlers cram the sidewalks and traffic chokes the streets. At night, crowds shift west toward the Powell Street cable car lines and the theater district.

Visiting Union Square – Weekday mornings are the best time to shop; crowds throng the stores and sidewalks during afternoons and weekends. Most stores open at 10am. Small boutiques and galleries close around 5pm or 6pm, although large department stores remain open until 9pm or 10pm during sales and before the winter holidays. Visit at night during the Christmas season to see creative window displays and the square's enormous and brightly lit tree.

Public transport is plentiful; cable cars offer the best access to other downtown areas and Fisherman's Wharf. In morning and evening rush hours, street parking is hard to find and meter time is limited. Several parking garages dot the district; a large one lies beneath Union Square Park *(access from Geary St.)*.

The city sponsors many public events at Union Square throughout the year, including free concerts and a Cable Car Bell-Ringing Competition in late July. For a schedule, call the San Francisco Convention & Visitors Bureau. On Union Square at Stockton Street, a **TIX Bay Area** booth sells advance tickets and same-day, half-price tickets to live shows around the city *(open year-round Tue–Thu 11am–6pm, Fri–Sat 11am–7pm; www.theatrebayarea.org; ☎ 415-430-1140)*. Public restrooms are on either side of the ticket booth.

WALKING TOUR *distance: .5mi.*

Begin at the center of Union Square Park.

★**Union Square Park** – *Bounded by Post, Stockton, Geary & Powell Sts.* One of the few designated parks in Jasper O'Farrell's rigid street plan this 2.6-acre parcel was landscaped in the early 1850s and was named on the eve of the Civil War, when it hosted numerous rallies in support of the Union. In 1901 the **Dewey Monument (1)**, commemorating Admiral George Dewey's 1898 defeat of Spanish naval forces in the Bay of Manila, was erected at the center of the square. Newton Tharp designed the slender, 97ft granite Corinthian column and Robert Aitken cast the bronze figure of Victory—armed with wreath and trident—surmounting it. A five-story parking garage was built beneath the square in 1942, raising the park slightly above street level.

Union Square Park has hosted many heated demonstrations over the decades, but today its palm trees, Irish yews and boxwood hedges create a peaceful respite for workers, shoppers and passersby. Homeless people and street musicians avail themselves of the park's benches and retaining walls, while adventurous skateboarders take over in the evenings. A $6 million redesign of the park is tentatively planned for early in the 21C.

Union Square and Westin St. Francis Hotel

© Brigitta L. House/MICHELIN

Cross the square to the corner of Geary & Stockton Sts.

Neiman Marcus – *150 Stockton St. (at Geary St.). Open year-round Mon–Sat 10am–7pm (Thu 8pm), Sun noon–6pm. Closed Thanksgiving Day, Dec 25.* ✕ ♿ ☎ *415-362-3900. www.neimanmarcus.com.* With its rose-colored, harlequin-patterned granite exterior and rounded glass-and-aluminum entrance corner, this post-Modern department store (1982, Johnson & Burgee) marks a sharp architectural departure from the Renaissance-style, Baroque-ornamented City of Paris store that once stood here. The beloved City of Paris landmark was demolished in 1981, but its exuberant stained-glass **rotunda★** was preserved and today soars above the entrance foyer, framed by enameled, wrought-iron balconies. As befits its original surroundings, the rotunda depicts Paris' emblem, a sailing ship, and its motto, *Fluctuat nec Mergitur* ("He Floats but Does Not Sink").

Walk north up Stockton St. to Maiden Lane.

Maiden Lane – Once flanked with low-rent brothels, Maiden Lane was reincarnated after the 1906 fire as a quaint pedestrian street lined with maple trees, cafes, boutiques, salons and galleries. At no. 140 stands the **Frank Lloyd Wright Building★** (1949), the only structure in San Francisco designed by Wright and a forerunner to the famed architect's Guggenheim Museum in New York City. Now home to the fine collection of Folk Art International, the skylit gallery boasts a curvaceous inte-

Art Galleries and Rare Book Shops
49 Geary St. Collectors of art and rare books know they have to penetrate the bland facade here to find the treasure trove within. The second floor contains five antiquarian and rare book shops, and on the floors above, cavernous spaces designed to house Western Union machinery have been converted into galleries. Several art dealers specialize in photography.

rior with many circular and spiral motifs, including small round porticoes used as display cases, cutout porthole-like windows, a huge hanging planter and a ramp spiraling up to the second floor.

Return to Stockton St. and continue north.

Ruth Asawa Fountain (**2**) – 🧒 *Stockton St. deck (corner of Post St.), Grand Hyatt hotel.* This playful fountain (1972) by San Francisco sculptor Ruth Asawa represents a triumph of collective creativity. Asawa asked 250 city residents, ages 3 to 90, to sculpt city landmarks out of baker's dough. She cast the flour-and-water bas-reliefs in metal and arranged them around the fountain's cylindrical base in a map-like fashion. Look for whimsical depictions of the Transamerica Pyramid and Sutro Baths, juxtaposed with fantastic elements such as Superman in flight above Montgomery Street.

Continue north to Sutter St. and turn left.

★Four Fifty Sutter – *450 Sutter St. Open year-round Mon–Fri 8am–6pm, weekends & holidays 9am–2pm.* ✕ ♿ 🅿 ☎ *415-421-7221.* This 26-story tower (1929, Timothy Pflueger), housing medical and dental offices, is one of San Francisco's finest Art Deco skyscrapers. Elaborate Mayan motifs cover the spectacular gold-painted elevator lobby, adorn the plaster ceiling and decorate the undulating terra-cotta exterior all the way up to the top floor.

Continue west to Powell St. and turn left.

 Hang
556 Sutter St. Open year-round Mon–Sat 10am-6pm, Sun noon–5pm. ☎ *415-434-4264.* *www.hangart.com.* This spacious, relaxed showcase for emerging Bay Area painters and sculptors aims at luring new collectors by pricing most work under $2,000. Inspired by an engaging and knowledgeable young staff, rave reviews have showered Hang since its opening in mid-1998.

★★Westin St. Francis Hotel – *335 Powell St. Self-guided walking tour maps available at concierge desk.* ✕ ♿ 🅿 ☎ *415-397-7000. www.westin.com.* Internationally renowned, this elegant Renaissance and Baroque Revival structure fronts the entire west side of Union Square. Commissioned by millionaire Charles Crocker, it opened in 1904 as the Hotel St. Francis. After the 1906 fire, Bliss & Faville rebuilt and enlarged the hotel, which had previously occupied only half the block; it resumed business in 1907. In the decades since, celebrities and dignitaries have favored the St. Francis for its sumptuous interior, its central location and its emphasis on service, which extends to washing the coins given as change in the intimate Compass Rose bar and tearoom.

Today the hotel's early-20C grandeur is most evident in the beautiful entrance hall, where coffered ceilings, marble-sheathed Corinthian columns and ornate balconies create a luxurious ambience. The "Magneta" grandfather clock is a favorite rendezvous point for San Francisco socialites. A 32-story tower (William L. Pereira Assoc.) was added to the rear of the hotel in 1972. Visitors who brave the vertiginous ride up in its glass exterior **elevators** 🧒 are rewarded with expansive **views★★** of Union Square, the Financial District and the Bay Bridge.

Continue south on Powell St. to Geary St. Turn right.

Theater District – *Bounded by Sutter, Powell, Geary & Taylor Sts.* San Francisco's theater district contains about 10 venues ranging from spare, intimate houses to enormous, ornate, multi-balconied palaces. Grandest among the latter are the **Geary Theater★** *(415 Geary St.),* designed by Bliss & Faville in 1909, and the adjacent **Curran Theatre★** *(445 Geary St.),* by Alfred Henry Jacobs in 1922. Registered National Historic Landmarks,

❸ The Compass Rose
Westin St. Francis Hotel. ☎ *415-774-0167.* Step up from the St. Francis' main lobby to this elegant salon, faithfully recreated from its 1904 design. High tea is the afternoon specialty here, served with scones, berries in Grand Marnier cream, petits fours and tea sandwiches. Pay high, just for the pleasure of receiving your change in freshly washed coins.

the Geary and the Curran were con-structed of reinforced concrete in the Neoclassical style. The Geary's fancifully embellished terra-cotta columns and stolid exterior set off the Curran's Romanesque arches and mansard roof. Home to the celebrated American Conservatory Theater since 1967, the Geary was closed in 1989-96 for renovation and seismic retrofitting after suffering structural damage in the Loma Prieta earthquake. The Curran Theatre stages long-running Broadway shows since it opened. Nearby are the **Cable Car Theater** (**A**) *(430 Mason St.)* and the **Stage Door Theatre** (**B**) *(420 Mason St.)*, housed in the Native Sons Building; look for the medallion portraits of prominent California-born persons embedded in the building's facade. The Stage Door is now the home of the Ruby Skye nightclub *(☎ 415-693-0777)*; visit before 8:30pm (when cover charge is in effect) to view the sumptuous interior. *Consult Address Book for more San Francisco and Bay Area theater listings and ticket information.*

 The Redwood Room
Geary St. at Taylor St. in the Clift Hotel. ☎ *415-775-4700.* A single redwood tree (felled by lightning) provided the 22ft columns and all the wood paneling for this hotel bar completed in 1934. Sip a cocktail beneath the gilded reproductions of Gustav Klimt artworks that adorn the walls, and let the streamlined Art Deco fixtures soothe your senses.

8 • ALCATRAZ★★★

Blue & Gold Fleet ferry from Fisherman's Wharf.

A mere 1.5mi from the comforts of San Francisco, this infamous 12-acre island, now inhabited by scores of seabirds who nest among its crumbling ruins, once held scores of prisoners incarcerated atop its sheer cliffs. Aptly nicknamed "the Rock" and isolated from shore by the cold, treacherous currents that swirl through the bay, Alcatraz served variously as a fortress, military prison and US Federal Penitentiary until its conversion to a national park and museum in 1972. A visit to Alcatraz provides a haunting journey into one of the harshest chapters of American judicial history.

Historical Notes

The first Europeans to sight the barren island were Spanish explorers José de Cañizares and Juan Manuel de Ayala in 1775. Noticing the large number of cormorants nesting on the cliffs, they named the rocky spot *Isla de los alcatraces*, or "island of gannets," because the roosting birds reminded them of similar fowl that inhabited the waterways of Spain. With no fresh water and little natural vegetation, the island remained uninhabited until President Millard Fillmore designated it a military reservation in 1850 following the US takeover of California. Its location at the mouth of the bay made it a natural choice for a fortress, and construction on a garrison began in 1853. Though cannons were mounted on the island, advancing military technology soon rendered them obsolete; not one was ever fired in defense. In 1861 Confederate sympathizers and renegade US soldiers were incarcerated at the garrison, and in the 1870s its walls held Native American prisoners from various Indian wars in California and the West. In 1901 the last cannons were dismantled, and six years later regular troops abandoned the island, to be replaced by members of the US Military Guard.

A "Super Prison" – Mounting costs and increasing protest over conditions in the prison led to the 1933 transfer of the property to the US Department of Justice, which established a federal penitentiary on the island. Banishment to the maximum security facility on Alcatraz was reserved for the most "desperate and irredeemable criminals" in the federal system, including those designated "public enemies" and deemed a danger to society, even behind bars. The ratio of one guard to every three prisoners, a strict "no talking" rule, brutal isolation cells and a near-impenetrable security system quickly established Alcatraz's reputation as America's bleakest prison. Notorious inhabitants of "the Rock" included Al "Scarface" Capone, George "Machine Gun" Kelly, Alvin "Creepy" Karpis, and Robert "Birdman" Stroud (who, contrary to popular lore, never kept birds here).

Over the years, 36 men tried to escape from Alcatraz in 14 separate attempts, all of them apparently unsuccessful. Some of the escapees were captured, some were shot, and some disappeared forever in the cold, swift currents of the bay. The most notorious attempt, in which three inmates disappeared in 1962 and were presumed drowned or eaten by sharks (they were never seen again), raised serious questions about the prison's deteriorated condition. That, combined with the high cost of maintenance and the complaints of San Franciscans worried about the less-than-secure prison in their bay, led to the decision to close Alcatraz. After the last inmates were transferred in 1963, the island fell vacant until 1969, when a group of Native Americans occupied it. Citing an 1868 treaty granting them the right to claim uninhabited federal land, the group began efforts to establish a Native American cultural enclave. The occupation ended 19 months later, its goals unrealized. On October 12, 1972, Alcatraz was designated part of the Golden Gate National Recreation Area.

VISIT

Blue & Gold Fleet ferry departs from Pier 41 May–Sept daily 9:30am–4:15pm every 30–45min. Rest of the year daily 9:30am–2:15pm every 30–45min. Closed Jan 1 & Dec 25. $12.25 including audiocassette (highly recommended). Guided tours and ranger talks are frequently offered, hours vary and are posted daily on the island. Alcatraz After Hours tours are offered Apr–Oct Thu–Sun 6:15 & 7pm. Oct–Nov 4:15 & 5pm. Rest of the year 4:15pm. $22 including audiocassette. Reservations should be made at least one week in advance by calling ☎ 415-705-5555.

Note: Cold sea spray and strong winds often buffet the island, and pathways are rough. Wear protective clothing and strong, comfortable shoes. An Easy Access Program is available for the physically impaired. See ranger at entrance to island.

The ferry trip *(15min)* to the dock at Alcatraz offers stunning **views★★** of the San Francisco skyline, the Golden Gate Bridge and the imposing cliffs of the island. Graffiti from the Indian occupation can be spotted on the bluffs and dock buildings. At the ferry wharf, rangers provide an informative orientation near the landing, after which visitors are free to inspect the exhibit area on the lower floor of the Barracks Building (1867), view an **orientation video** *(12min)* in the theater, or climb the steep, switchback road past the ruins of the Post Exchange and Officers' Quarters to the cellhouse. Ranger-led talks and guided strolls in otherwise inaccessible parts of the island are occasionally offered; a list of the day's topics is available at the landing dock. Alcatraz After Hours offers a darker view of prison life: A haunting view of the city skyline, sometimes as it becomes obscured by fog, contributes to the sense of isolation inmates must have felt.

★★Cellhouse – *Self-guided audiocassette tour available at cellhouse entrance.* While most of the island's buildings have been reduced to ruins and turned over to raucous flocks of seabirds, the forbidding cellhouse is intact enough to provide a chilling glimpse into the bleak life of the federal prisoners who were sentenced here. Built by convicts in 1911, it was, for a time, the largest reinforced concrete structure in the world.

Visitors enter the building near the bunker-like control center, formerly an arsenal of arms and tear gas. Beyond the control center lies the Visitation Area, where prisoners were separated from visitors by thick plate glass, and spoke over a monitored telephone. Once inside the cavernous main room, visitors can stroll down "Broadway," the wide central passage between B and C Blocks leading to "Times Square," and step into a cramped, cold cell furnished with a regulation army cot, a folding table and chair and a squat, open toilet. Prisoners who violated the strict rules of Alcatraz were subjected to solitary confinement in the dank isolation rooms, or "dark holes," of D Block. The tear-gas canisters in the ceiling of the mess hall at the rear of the building were never used. Access to the recreation yard and library, now open for exploration, was a privilege awarded for good behavior.

Several concrete paths lead around the perimeter of the island where wild blackberry brambles, California poppies and coyote brush grow. Most of the land is not accessible to the public. The main road to the cellhouse and the western road from the cellhouse to the base of the recreation yard exit remain open year round.

Main Cell Block, Alcatraz Federal Prison (1956)

A waterfront promenade stretching some three miles from Fisherman's Wharf to China Basin. The Embarcadero ("boarding place" in Spanish) combines expansive views of the bay with public artworks, educational installations and recently built or renovated office and residential complexes. It forms one of the city's newest and most engaging public spaces.

Historical Notes

The vibrant hub of San Francisco's shipping and transportation industries from the Gold Rush until the 1950s, the Embarcadero took shape in the 1850s when landfill extended the shore from its natural line along present-day Montgomery Street. As San Francisco boomed through the late 19C, sailors, longshoremen and warehouse workers frequented the increasingly rowdy area, patronizing a growing number of gambling dens and union halls. Steamships, schooners and whalers embarked from the docks on commercial runs for shipping enterprises such as the Pacific Mail Steamship Company and the Alaska Packers.

Ferries from points across the bay began docking here before the turn of the 20C, and the waterfront swarmed with daily commuters until 1936, when rail service and auto lanes over the San Francisco-Oakland Bay Bridge siphoned away ferry traffic. Through the mid-20C, the Embarcadero's piers, rail yards and warehouses fell into disuse as shippers gradually transferred their activities across the bay to the better-equipped Port of Oakland.

In the early 1950s work began on the controversial **Embarcadero Freeway**, planned as a link between the Bay Bridge and the Golden Gate Bridge. Dominating the shoreline and blocking views of the Ferry Building and the bay, the elevated viaduct greatly diminished the waterfront's appeal, arousing San Franciscans' ire. Construction had reached Broadway before massive protest halted progress in 1959. By the late 1970s the Embarcadero south of Broadway had deteriorated in the shadow of the massive concrete roadbed. When the freeway was razed after being damaged in the 1989 Loma Prieta earthquake, revitalization efforts began in earnest.

A New Beginning – Ongoing redevelopment projects have revitalized this historic area with new public spaces, residential and commercial complexes and public art. Extending 3.2mi from Fisherman's Wharf to China Basin is **Herb Caen Way ...★**, a promenade named for the popular late *San Francisco Chronicle* columnist whose trademark ellipses punctuated many a morning read from 1938 to 1996. This long ribbon of sidewalk draws visitors, residents and swarms of joggers to enjoy glorious views of the bay, the Bay Bridge and the towers of the Financial District. At intervals along the walkway, attractive striped pylons—bearing interpretive text and photographs—draw visitors into colorful stories about local history. Fishermen gather at the end of **Pier 7** *(near Broadway)* with its old-fashioned wrought-iron railings and park benches, creaky wooden planking and expansive views of bay and city. The **Promenade Ribbon**, a linear sculpture made of concrete and glass block, is illuminated at night with a fiber-optic cable. Canary Island date-palm trees tower above the Embarcadero meridian, lined with elegant, double-torch street lamps.

South of the Ferry Building, brick warehouses and factories of the onetime waterfront industrial belt are reborn as residential and office spaces, some with trendy eateries. **Hills Plaza**, with its distinctive brick tower, is a noteworthy example; erected in 1924.

■ The Historic Streetcars of the F-Market Line

San Francisco's cable cars are not the city's only rolling history. Since September 1995, a colorful fleet of historic streetcars have glided up and down Market Street, a historical grace note amid the throngs of pedestrians, cars, buses and streetcars that swarm along the bustling thoroughfare. With the completion of new tracks in 2000, these beloved antiques now traverse the shoreline along The Embarcadero from China Basin to Fisherman's Wharf, south and north of Market Street, connecting with the BART light-rail system at a transit center near the Ferry Building.

Elegantly streamlined and colorfully painted, PCC cars were manufactured in the US from 1936 to 1952 and put into service throughout North America and Europe. They served on San Francisco's streetcar lines from 1948 to 1982. The rehabilitated cars today reflect not only the Muni green-and-cream colors, but also the color schemes of other cities where these streetcars were used, including Boston (orange, cream and silver), Baltimore (yellow and gray), Los Angeles (red, orange and gray) and Kansas City (cream, black and silver).

t originally housed the headquarters for Hills Brothers Coffee Company. New commercial and residential complexes enliven the west side of the Embarcadero from the Bay Bridge to new Pacific Bell Park at China Basin. En route, the thoroughfare passes attractive **South Beach Park**, anchored by Mark diSuvero's towering abstract sculpture *Sea Change* (**1**).

SIGHTS

★★**Ferry Building** – *Embarcadero at Market St.* Though its status as San Francisco's signature landmark has been supplanted by the Golden Gate Bridge and other monuments, the handsome Ferry Building remains one of the city's beloved historical markers. Designed by A. Page Brown of Colusa sandstone and anchored on 111 steel-framed concrete piers, the building was hailed at its dedication in 1898 as the most solidly constructed edifice in California, a claim that was roundly proved when it survived the great earthquake of 1906 with only its exterior stones loosened. The Ferry Building's 235ft clock tower, designed by Willis Polk, was inspired by the Giralda Tower on the Cathedral of Seville and boasts four huge (and accurate) clock faces.

© Robert Holmes

Ferry Building and Bay Bridge

Until completion of the Golden Gate and Bay Bridges in the late 1930s, the Ferry Building served as San Francisco's main transportation hub. An estimated 50 million people passed through it annually, commuters from Marin County and the East Bay, long-distance travelers from the transcontinental railroad terminus in Oakland. In 1956, after ferry traffic declined, the northern half of the structure was converted into office space, and in 1962 the southern half was remodeled to house government agencies. Today the World Trade Center occupies the north half of the Ferry Building.

Stroll behind the building to the wooden sundeck, where commuter ferries still depart for Sausalito and Larkspur in Marin County. Just north, another ferry offers service to Alameda, Oakland, Tiburon and Vallejo. The tranquil monument to Mohandas K. Gandhi (**2**) was donated to the city in 1988. The pier behind Gabbiano's restaurant offers sweeping **views**★ of the Bay Bridge and Yerba Buena and Treasure Islands.

The Jewish Museum San Francisco – *121 Steuart St. Generally open during exhibitions Thu, Fri & Sun 11am–5pm; call ahead as schedule may vary. Closed Jewish holidays.* ♿ ☎ *415-591-8800. www.jewishmuseumsf.org.* This award-winning museum mounts about three

❶ Farmers' Markets
Green St. at The Embarcadero. ☎ *415-353-5650.* Every Saturday morning, rain or shine, Bay Area organic farmers, bakers, cheese makers, pasta makers, fishmongers and florists gather to sell their wares. Chef tours, live music and cooking demonstrations are regular fixtures on the scene, as are seasonal fruit festivals and holiday celebrations.
A Tuesday Farmers Market (*11am–3pm*) is held opposite the Ferry Building in Justin Herman Plaza.

Rain Column, Rincon Center

© Robert Holmes

exhibitions per year, of two to three months each, to promote understanding of Jewish culture through art. Established in 1984, it maintains strong community ties via ongoing educational programs. Past exhibitions have included a controversial exploration of Jewish art during the 1950s and a glittering display of more than 100 menorahs. *Relocation of the museum to the refurbished Pacific Gas & Electric substation (1909, Willis Polk) on Jessie Street, opposite Yerba Buena Gardens, is projected for 2003.*

★**Rincon Center** – *101 Spear St. Open daily year-round.* ✗ ⅋ 𝗣 ☎ *415-777-4100.* This multistory shopping and residential complex (1989), a block south and west of the Ferry Building, boasts a panoply of stores and cafes. The former Rincon Annex Post Office (1940, Gilbert S. Underwood), which now functions as the center's **lobby**, remains its most gripping feature. Especially worthy of note are Russian-born artist Anton Refregier's **murals**★ depicting Northern California's rough-and-tumble history, beginning with the arrival of Sir Francis Drake in 1579 and ending with World War II. Completed in 1948 and rendered in broad, muscular strokes and bold colors that underscore Refregier's thematic emphasis on labor, struggle and war, these 27 panels provide an unsparing view of the wild West. Adjacent display cases present artifacts and photographs that further address Refregier's themes. In the lofty atrium off the lobby, an 85ft **Rain Column** (1988, Doug Hollis) forms the eye-catching centerpiece of a spacious food court.

★★**Pacific Bell Park** – ⁞⁞⁞⁞ �毱 *3rd & King Sts. Tours ($10) year-round daily 10am–2pm except when game conflicts. Coca-Cola Fan Lot (free) open year-round Tue-Sun 11am–5pm on non-game days, 2hrs before scheduled first pitch on days of home games. Game tickets $8–$42.* ✗ ⅋ 𝗣 ☎ *415-972-2000. www.sf giants.com.* Many baseball insiders consider San Francisco's new $319 million major-league stadium to be the finest in the world. Opened in April 2000, it couples the mood of an early-20C urban ballpark, such as Boston's Fenway Park or Chicago's Wrigley Field, with modern amenities. HOK Sport designed the 40,800-seat stadium to shield players and spectators from wind and fog; the field level slopes gently upward from the playing surface. From upper-level tiers, spectacular views extend to the city skyline, the Bay Bridge and Oakland beyond.

② **Java House**
Pier 40, The Embarcadero at Townsend St. ☎ *415-495-7260.* This tiny shack on the pier beside the South Beach yacht harbor recalls a time when longshoremen stopped in for burgers, beers and strong coffee. Pick up a tasty, dirt-cheap cheeseburger or tuna sandwich, settle down on a stool and get a taste of colorful, workaday San Francisco.

The park's main entrance is at **24 Willie Mays Plaza**, where a red-brick façade rises behind William Behrends' 9ft bronze statue of the Hall of Fame outfielder, who wore the number 24 throughout his playing career (1951-73). The **Coca-Cola Fan Lot**, above the left-field bleachers, features pop-bottle slides, a wiffleball field, speed-pitching and baserunning areas, and "the world's largest baseball glove," a huge sculpture of an old-time three-finger mitt. Behind the right-field wall, rare home runs may splash into **McCovey Cove** (named for another Hall of Fame Willie) a finger of China Basin where they are fished out by ardent boaters or by a team of Portuguese water dogs sponsored by comedian Father Guido Sarducci.

ADDITIONAL SIGHTS

★★San Francisco-Oakland Bay Bridge – *Open daily year-round. $2 toll westbound only from Oakland. Nonvehicular crossing of the bridge prohibited.* ☎ *510-286-4444. www.dot.ca.gov.* Though often overshadowed by the celebrity of the Golden Gate Bridge, this double-deck engineering marvel is a distinctive and beloved landmark in its own right. Begun in 1933 to alleviate traffic on the transbay ferries, which shuttled some 6 million cars between San Francisco and the East Bay, the project was financed by a $77 million federal loan during the nadir of the Great Depression. Engineers Charles H. Purcell, Charles E. Andrew and Glenn B. Woodruff joined forces with architect Timothy Pflueger to design the bridge, which had to cross 8.4mi of water—including approaches, its span is nearly eight times that of the Golden Gate.

To traverse the distance, the bridge was conceived as two structures meeting at Yerba Buena Island, a rocky promontory midway across the bay. The western section, comprising two 2,310ft suspension bridges, joins San Francisco and the island. The roadway hangs suspended from steel cables draped between four distinctive X-braced towers; a concrete pier rises 48 stories from the floor of the bay to anchor the two suspension bridges in the center. The eastern section, joining Yerba Buena Island and Oakland, is a cantilever-truss design—the roadway rests on steel-and-concrete piers joined by a network of steel beams. (A new, more seimically stable design is under examination.) Between the two sections, a tunnel pierces Yerba Buena Island; 76ft wide and 58ft high, its diameter may be the largest of any vehicular tunnel in the world.

Completed in November 1936, the bridge carried trains on its lower level and cars on its upper level for two decades. Today each deck bears five lanes of automobile traffic. Travelers on the westbound upper deck enjoy glorious **views**★ of the Financial District and the Embarcadero as they approach the city.

★Treasure Island – *Take I-80 east across the Bay Bridge; exit at Treasure Island/Yerba Buena Island exit, proceed to main gate. Viewpoint open year-round Sat–Sun.* Lying in San Francisco Bay midway between San Francisco and Oakland, this flat, man-made terrain was constructed in 1938 to host a world fair. The 400-acre island offers stupendous panoramic views as well as charming insights into a sometimes-overlooked chapter of San Francisco history.

The Pageant of the Pacific – As work on the Bay Bridge and the Golden Gate Bridge drew to a close, San Francisco boosters began planning a world fair to celebrate and to advertise the city's emergence from the Great Depression. For the fair site, the Army Corps of Engineers set to work creating an artificial island north of Yerba Buena Island, constructing a rectangular seawall and filling the space with bay dredgings and rubble excavated from the Bay Bridge tunnel. The city intended to locate its new airport on the site after the fair closed.

Opened on February 18, 1939, the **Golden Gate International Exposition of 1939-1940** drew more than 17 million visitors during its two-year run. In all, 36 nations and 31 states participated in the fair, themed "The Pageant of the Pacific" to prompt

Bay Bridge and Financial District from Yerba Buena Island

awareness of trade potential with Pacific Basin nations. Pan American Airways moved its then-innovative **China Clipper** seaplanes—offering passenger flights to Asia—from nearby Alameda to Treasure Island between 1939 and 1944, and visitors reveled in an extravaganza of exotic, Asian-inspired, Art Deco buildings and sculptures designed by a team of architects including Timothy Pflueger, Arthur Brown, Jr. and Lewis P. Hobart.

World War II brought an abrupt end to the jubilant celebration of Pacific relations. Most of the fair structures were demolished and the island became a naval training center for the duration of the conflict. By 1945, aerospace technology had so advanced that new aircraft required runways longer than Treasure Island could provide, and the city leased the site to the US Navy in exchange for land on the peninsula (site of present-day San Francisco International Airport). Naval Station Treasure Island operated at this scenic location from World War II until it closed in September 1997.

Today, while the City of San Francisco and the US Navy haggle over the island's uncertain future, public access is limited. The causeway at the gated entry area still affords a sweeping **view★★★** over the city, encompassing, from south to north, the suspension portion of the Bay Bridge, the San Francisco skyline and backdrop hills, the Golden Gate, Alcatraz, Mount Tamalpais, Angel Island and the North Bay, with the Richmond-San Rafael Bridge. The handsome Art Deco-style **Treasure Island Museum** (1937, George Kelham), once projected as the main San Francisco airport terminal, now is neither a museum nor transit hub; it holds offices of the City and County of San Francisco.

Addresses, telephone numbers, opening hours and prices published in this guide are accurate at press time. We apologize for any inconvenience resulting from outdated information. Please send us your comments:

    Michelin Travel Publications
    Editorial Department
    P. O. Box 19001
    Greenville, SC 29602-9001
    Email: TheGreenGuide-us@us.michelin.com

🚃 Powell-Hyde or Powell-Mason. 🚌 bus 19–Polk, 30–Stockton, 32–Embarcadero, 39–Coit or 44–Downtown Loop (Red Arrow).
Map pp 114-115

San Francisco's vibrant and colorful maritime legacy survives in this bustling and extremely popular district extending along the shoreline between Telegraph Hill and Fort Mason. Amid the historic sailing ships and converted piers and factories are a working fleet of fishing boats, a pod of vociferous and amusing sea lions and scores of boutiques and souvenir shops. Street performers and sidewalk seafood stands add to the carnival atmosphere along Jefferson Street. Quiet piers and unobstructed views of Alcatraz Island, Marin County and the Golden Gate Bridge make the wharf's western end one of the loveliest spots on San Francisco's waterfront.

Historical Notes

In 1853, **Henry "Honest Harry" Meiggs**, councilman, entrepreneur and later the most noto-rious embezzler of public funds in the city's early history, constructed a wharf extending 1,600ft from present-day Francisco and Powell Streets across North Point Cove into the bay. From its inception, Meigg's Wharf was an important center of industry. The ferry terminal to Sausalito was located at its far end, and a sawmill, a pipe works and a junk shop crowded its length. Shipbuilding flourished on the sands of North Beach, and visitors came down to the wharf to enjoy stunning bay views and the cheap beer, cracked crab and hot chowder at institutions like Paddy Gleason's Saloon and Abe Warner's Cobweb Palace.

In the 1860s, North Point Cove from Bay Street to the current shoreline was filled with rock blasted from the eastern face of Telegraph Hill, creating a flat stretch of land that became a manufacturing and industrial zone. A multitude of factories opened along the shore, including the Selby Lead and Smelting Works and the Pioneer Woolen Mill (later site of the Ghirardelli Chocolate Factory). Several railroads and piers were also built to serve the growing industries.

Home of the Pescatori – During the city's early years, fishermen tied up at several wharves along Vallejo, Green, Union and Filbert Streets. The 1872 legislation that authorized the construction of Columbus Avenue also directed the State Board of Harbor Commissioners to designate the Union Street Wharf "for the sole and exclu-sive use of the fishermen of the city." Development of downtown shipping zones, however, forced the fishermen to move twice—first in 1885 to the Filbert Street Wharf, and again in 1900 to their present home at the foot of Taylor Street.

Even before the fleet found its permanent mooring, Italians had established a virtual monopoly in all aspects of the fishing industry. After anti-Chinese legislation in the 1870s restricted commercial opportunities for the Asians, who previously had domi-nated the fishing industry, Genoese immigrants took to the seas and became the largest ethnic group on the bay. Over time, the Genoese fishermen (*pescatori* in Italian) were outnumbered by their compatriots from Naples, Calabria and Sicily. Today descendants of Sicilians dominate Fisherman's Wharf, from the fishing boats that con-tinue to depart from here to the wildly popular restaurants and sidewalk seafood stands that bear the names of their prominent Italian-American founders.

Through the first half of the 20C, fishing remained a major industry. As maritime tech-nology became more efficient, however, the bay and surrounding waters were overfished, forcing the boats to move farther and farther beyond the Golden Gate or to relocate altogether. By the 1950s the fleet's numbers had been severely reduced, and large sections of the old industrial zone had become rundown or abandoned.

Tidal Wave of Tourism – The opening of the National Maritime Museum in 1951 marked the beginning of the northern waterfront's rebirth as the city's most popular tourist destination. The area boomed in the 1960s when visionary developers began purchasing historic properties such as the California Fruit Canners Association building and the old Ghirardelli Chocolate Factory, converting them into architectural and commercial showpieces.

In years since, burgeoning tourism has sparked an explosion of related businesses, few of them linked to the maritime legacy that makes the wharf such an interesting place to visit. Street performers often block the already-crowded sidewalks with their mime and magic shows, juggling acts and music. Shopping complexes like The Anchorage and Cost Plus Imports share the once-industrial bayfill blocks with wharf-side seafood establishments that, while not usually considered "fine dining," provide fun-filled and scenic settings for dinner. Brightly lit T-shirt shops and souvenir stands line the south side of Jefferson Street along with several novelty museums, including the newly renovated, $15 million **Wax Museum at Fisherman's Wharf** (🧒 *145 Jefferson St.; open year-round Mon–Fri 9am–11pm, weekends 9am–midnight; $12.95;* ☎ *800-202-0400; www.waxmuseum.com).* Nearby is the **Ripley's Believe It or Not! Museum** (🧒 *175 Jefferson St.; open mid-Jun–Labor Day Sun–Thu 9am–11pm, Fri–Sat 9am–midnight, rest of the year Sun–Thu 10am–10pm, Fri–Sat 10am–midnight; $8.95;* ☎ *415-771-6188; www.ripleys.com).*

Sidewalk Seafood

A stroll along the north side of Jefferson Street between Jones and Taylor Streets leads through a symphony of smells and tastes whose overriding note is fresh seafood. The tradition of eating outdoors on the wharf dates from the early 20C, when Italian fishermen returning from early-morning runs grabbed steaming bowls of chowder from sidewalk stands before hurrying off to sell the day's catch. In 1916, Tomaso Castagnola began offering walkaway crab cocktails to tourists who came down to see the colorful fishing fleet. His success led Italian fishing families to set up their own steaming pots along the wharf from which they sold freshly cooked Dungeness crab. Even the opening of large, full-service restaurants in the 1930s could not diminish the popularity of the sidewalk stands.

Today, a ladle of creamy clam chowder in a hollowed-out loaf of sourdough bread has become a mandatory part of the San Francisco experience. Fresh crab, flown in daily when it is out of season here, continues to be the major attraction, and many of the crab sellers make a rhythmic show of cracking the sweet crustacean's 10 legs. Although nontraditional items such as pizza have recently appeared, the best fare on the wharf still comes from the sea—including shrimp or crab salad sandwiches on crusty sourdough rolls, freshly steamed Pacific rock lobster, prawn and crab cocktails, oysters, crab cakes, and an assortment of fried squid, fish and clams.

Through the glitter and the glitz, much of the area retains its salty flavor of old. As the San Francisco Bay fishery has resurged in number and variety, the number of fishing boats has likewise grown. Visitors who step off the main path will discover a series of working, albeit less-active piers, fabulous views of the bay and several evocative monuments to the city's maritime past.

Visiting Fisherman's Wharf – In summer and on most weekends throughout the year, massive crowds make movement on the sidewalks difficult, especially on the south side of Jefferson Street. During peak tourist seasons, tours to Alcatraz are often booked as far in advance as a week: Reserve as early as possible. In winter, when crab fishing is in full swing, the wharf is at its most interesting and least congested. Public transportation (bus, tram or cable car) is the best way to get here. Street parking in the area is scarce and meters are limited to two hours; regulations are enforced every day, including Sundays and holidays. Several well-marked lots along Jefferson Street between Taylor and Powell Streets, and a large garage across from Pier 39 *(Beach St. between Stockton & Powell Sts.* are expensive and often full. Other garages lie within the Anchorage Shopping Center *(Jones St. between Jefferson & Beach Sts.)*, Ghirardelli Square *(entrances from Beach St. or Larkin St.)* and Cost Plus Imports (entrance on Taylor St.).

Ferries for Sausalito, Tiburon and Angel Island leave from Pier 43 1/2. Check the signs carefully, as ferry operators also offer scenic bay cruises that depart from this pier. A new $2 million public ferry terminal at Pier 43 serves commuters to Vallejo.

The Blessing of the Fleet takes place the first weekend of October each year with a solemn procession from the SS. Peter and Paul Church *(p. 94)*.

SIGHTS

★Pier 39 – [Kids] *Open year-round Sun-Thu 11am–8pm, Fri-Sat 10am–8:30pm; later hours may apply in summer.* ✗ ♿ ☐ *($5.50/hr).* ☎ *415-981-7437. http://pier39.com.* Built over a dilapidated c.1900 pier, this festive, bi-level marketplace of shops and amusements ranks among the top tourist destinations in the state. On either side of its central passage lie rugged buildings covered with planks salvaged from Piers 3 and 34 prior to their reconstruction. After the Port of San Francisco lost its shipping supremacy to Oakland in the 1970s, Pier 39 was nearly demolished, but an ambitious redevelopment (1978) attracted all manner of shops from video arcades and novelty stores to confectioneries, clothing boutiques and seafood restaurants. A brightly painted, two-tiered carousel anchors the far end of the complex, and performers regularly take the stage behind it to entertain thousands of daily visitors.

Pier 39

A two-story, IMAX-style cinema mounts screenings of two **films**: *The Great San Francisco Adventure* and *The Living Sea (year-round daily 10am–6:30pm; $7.50 for one show, $10 for two; shows every 45min;* ☎ *415-956-3456).* The former film *(30min)* presents a humorous overview of the city's rough-and-tumble history featuring characters from its past and present, while *The Living Sea (40min, daily 11am only)* explores man's relationship with the marine environment. Near the end of the pier, the TurboRide Simulation Theater *($8 for one show, $16 for all four; shows every 15min;* ☎ *415-392-8872)* invites audiences to immerse themselves in four separate adventures—with race cars, dinosaurs, Indiana Jones-type temple explorers, and superstitions (as introduced by campy horror queen Elvira).

Adding to Pier 39's carnival atmosphere, a group of wild California **sea lions★** occupies the docks off its west side. Informal interpretive talks on the creatures are offered by volunteers from the **Marine Mammal Center** *(year-round weekends 11am–5pm;* ☎ *415-705-5500).* The reason for the sea lions' arrival here in 1990 is a mystery, but it is thought that they are members of the same colony that inhabits Seal Rocks, near Cliff House. Their raucous barking can be heard from as far away as the top of Telegraph Hill. A walk along the outer edge of the pier gives visitors a privileged view of the clowning sea lions, Alcatraz and the Bay Bridge.

Anchored off the H Dock on the opposite side of the sea lions from Pier 39 is **Forbes Island** *(Wed-Sun 5pm–10pm;* ☎ *415-951-4900; www.forbesisland.com),* a floating restaurant perched atop a 50ft-long artificial island. A pontoon boat delivers evening diners to a 40ft-tall lighthouse surrounded by bamboo and palm trees—700 engine-propelled tons of sand, topsoil, structure and white picket fence. The island's creator, Thor Kidoo, was inspired by *Jules Verne's 20,000 Leagues Under the Sea.*

★UnderWater World – [Kids] *Open Memorial Day–Labor Day daily 9am–9pm. Rest of the year daily 10am–8:30pm. Closed Dec 25. $12.95 ($15.95 includes IMAX movie). Behind the scenes tour (1hr 45min) Fri–Mon noon, 2 & 5pm; $25.* ♿ ☎ *415-623-5300. www.underworldsf.com.* Visitors here may enter and view the undersea world up close. Following a short video presentation and stroll through a selection of Northern California marine habitats, visitors descend via an ersatz "diving bell" to traverse a three-story, 707,000gal aquarium by way of a 300ft transparent acrylic **tunnel.** Marine biologists and naturalists point out 11,000 marine denizens of 193 species, including fish, sharks, rays and crabs.

★**Bay Cruises** – 🚸 A scenic cruise on San Francisco Bay offers visitors a new perspective of the city, from a peek at the underside of the Golden Gate Bridge to wide, glorious **views**★ of steep hills and imposing skyline. From the vantage point of the bay, visitors can learn about the history of San Francisco and get a glimpse of the waterfront as a busy, working port. The Blue and Gold Fleet's **Bay Cruise** *(departs Pier 39 May–Sept daily 10am–6:45pm; rest of the year daily 10am–4pm; round-trip 1hr; commentary; $17; ✗ & 🅿 ☎ 415-773-1188; www.blueandgoldfleet.com)* travels west along the shoreline, circles beneath the Golden Gate Bridge and passes very close to Alcatraz on the return, accompanied by English-language narration. The Red and White Fleet's **Golden Gate Bridge Cruise** *(depart from Pier 43 1/2 May–Sept daily 9am–6:15pm; rest of the year daily 10am–5pm; round-trip 1hr; commentary; $19 (including 1hr tour of USS Pampanito, below); ✗ & 🅿 ☎ 415-673-2900; www.redand white.com)* follows a similar route; individual headsets broadcast a well-produced narrative (available in six languages) that uses a combination of historical and dramatic voices, plus authentic sound effects.

★★**USS Pampanito** – 🚸 *Pier 45. Open Memorial Day–early Oct daily 9am–8pm (Wed 6pm). Rest of the year daily 9am–6pm (Fri & Sat 8pm). $7. ☎ 415-775-1943. www.maritime.org.* A World War II, Balao-class submarine built in the Portsmouth naval shipyard in 1943, this deep-diving, 311ft vessel made a half-dozen patrols during her two years of service in the Pacific, sinking six Japanese ships and damaging four others. In September 1944, the *Pampanito* and two other submarines jointly attacked a convoy of Japanese ships in the South China Sea carrying oil, raw rubber and other war supplies. After sinking several ships, the three subs pursued the surviving vessels out of the area. When the *Pampanito* returned a few days later, the crew spotted men clinging to pieces of wreckage; the 73 rescued were British and Australian prisoners of war who had been aboard the sunken vessels. That number—73—is commemorated on the *Pampanito*'s flag, displayed on the pier. Other informative panels describe the workings of a submarine and tell the story of the *Pampanito*'s construction and wartime service.

Visit – *Some physical agility is required to slip through the submarine's narrow corridors and small hatches.* The haunting, self-guided audio tour begins on the upper deck and moves from the rear (aft) torpedo room through the maneuvering room, engine rooms, galley, control room and officers' quarters to the cramped forward torpedo room, where members of the crew slept beside the massive weapons. A former commander of the sub narrates the audio tour, his matter-of-fact voice and understated descriptions effectively conveying the claustrophobia, fear and boredom that faced those who signed on for submarine duty. Pampanito veterans have added their personal accounts, complemented by sound effects and other historic recordings.

★**SS Jeremiah O'Brien** – 🚸 *Pier 45. Open year-round daily 9am–4pm. Closed Jan 1, Thanksgiving Thu & Fri, Dec 24, 25 & 31. $5. 🅿 ☎ 415-441-3101. Especially in fall and winter, the O'Brien may berth at Pier 32, south of the Bay Bridge off The Embarcadero; call to confirm hours & location.* This noble gray vessel formed part of the 5,000-ship armada that stormed Normandy Beach on D-Day in 1944. Launched on June 19, 1943, she was one of a fleet of 2,751 Liberty Ships that served as the backbone of the supply line to US armed forces in Europe and the Pacific during World War II. Lovingly restored and maintained by a crew of volunteers, the ship remains unaltered and fully operational. Self-guided tours cover all areas of the vessel, including the wheelhouse, engine room, crew's quarters, deckside guns and ship's store. On "steaming weekends" *(3rd weekend Jan–Apr, Jun–Sept & Nov)*, the crew fires up her triple-expansion steam engines, used in the blockbuster movie *Titanic* to replicate the engines of that ill-fated luxury liner. The O'Brien also welcomes visitors on all-day cruises of San Francisco Bay several times a year.

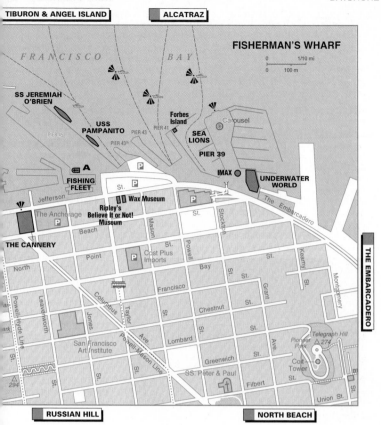

FISHERMAN'S WHARF

TIBURON & ANGEL ISLAND
ALCATRAZ
RUSSIAN HILL
NORTH BEACH

★**Fishing Fleet** – *North side of Jefferson St. between Jones & Taylor Sts.* The small, colorful fishing boats tied up at the docks just off Jefferson Street are remnants of an active and successful fleet that once numbered more than 450 vessels. Names like *Pico, Nina, San Giuseppe* and *Angelina,* painted on the sides of the boats, bear witness to the Italian roots of the city's fishing industry. In the late 19C, visitors came down to the wharf (then located at the foot of Filbert Street) to watch fishermen mend their nets or set sail in their sky-blue feluccas, lightweight boats with triangular sails and delicately pointed bows and sterns. Today the boats leave their berths very early in the morning to fish for rex and petrale sole, sea bass, mackerel, sand dab, rock cod, ling cod and herring in the waters outside the Golden Gate. Early-morning visitors will be rewarded with the sight of the fishermen returning to unload their catches along this and other piers behind the Jefferson Street Lagoon. For more than a century, this activity was the wharf's primary attraction, and it remains one of San Francisco's more evocative, if lesser known, sights. Although most of the fish sold in the city is now flown and trucked in, 20 million pounds of seafood still come into this port annually.

Visitors may take a self-guided tour of this active wharf area by following 30 interpretive signs, posted in 2000 by the Port of San Francisco and describing the history and current operation of the fishing industry.

A small, simple building of dark brown wood with a stained-glass ship's wheel over its door rests at the western foot of Pier 45. Erected in 1980 by the Fisherman's Wharf community, this **Fishermen's and Seamen's Memorial Chapel** (**A**) *(☎ 415-626-7070)* remains truly ecumenical, hosting christenings, bar mitzvahs, Latin masses, Buddhist memorials and weddings of all sorts.

★★**The Cannery** – *2801 Leavenworth St. at Jefferson St. Shops open year-round Mon–Wed 10am–6pm, Thu–Sat 10am–8:30pm, Sun & holidays 11am–6pm. Restaurant hours vary.* ✗ ⅙ ☎ *415-771-3112. www.thecannery.com.* Anchoring the west end of Jefferson Street, this airy, light-filled shopping complex belies its industrial origins. Built in 1907 as a packing plant for the California Fruit Canners Association, the building housed the most productive peach-canning operation in the world from 1916 to 1937. Rough economic times during the Great Depression forced the owner, Del Monte, to close the plant, and until a local developer purchased it in 1963, the building was used mainly as a warehouse.

Four external brick walls are all that remain of the original structure. The interior, completed in 1967, reveals a seamless modern design of open stairwells, bridges, spacious courtyards and meandering passageways lined with more than three dozen boutiques, restaurants and gourmet shops. On sunny days, the courtyard on the west side is a pleasant spot to relax with a cold drink and listen to street musicians. The Jacobean carved fireplace, intricate plaster ceiling and oak paneling in **Jack's Cannery Bar** on the ground floor date from 1609, and once belonged to the estate of newspaper tycoon William Randolph Hearst.

★★ **Hyde Street Pier** – 🔳 *Open May 15–Sept 15 daily 9:30am–5:30pm. Rest of the year daily 9:30am–5pm. Guided walks daily 11:30am, 12:30pm, 2:30pm & 4pm. Closed Jan 1, Thanksgiving Day, Dec 25. $5. ☎ 415-556-3002 or 415-561-6662. www.maritime.org/safrhome.shtml.* The historic ships and maritime artifacts on display at this long wooden pier evoke the era when San Francisco was an active and bustling port, with the sea its most important avenue of trade and transportation. Built as a ferry terminal in the years before construction of the Golden Gate and Bay Bridges, the Hyde Street Pier eventually became the mooring for six historic ships purchased and restored by the San Francisco Maritime Museum. The pier is now part of the **San Francisco Maritime National Historical Park**, which maintains what may be the largest historic fleet afloat. In addition to its six ships—all but one of which may be boarded and explored—the pier houses a turn-of-the-20C

© Robert Holmes

Historic Ships, Hyde Street Pier

"ark" (a flat-bottomed houseboat that served as a summer retreat on the bay), the 1850s-era office of Tubbs Cordage, several old tug boats and a **small boat shop** (**B**) that offers lessons in boat building and restoration. Demonstrations of seafaring skills are occasionally presented. The **Maritime Store** (**C**) at the entrance provides information about the park, and offers a vast array of books on maritime subjects.

★**Eureka** – *Right side of pier. Tour program year-round daily, noon.* This enormous side-wheel ferry, built in 1890 and still the world's largest wooden floating structure, could carry up to 2,300 commuters at a time. Originally named the *Ukiah*, the ship served as a railroad-car ferry until 1922, when she was rebuilt as the Eureka and launched as a passenger and auto ferry between Sausalito and San Francisco. After 1941 the *Eureka* plied the waters on the Oakland-San Francisco run until her giant walking-beam engine snapped in 1957. Today, visitors can sit on the restored commuter benches, wander the massive decks or operate a model walking-beam that stands beside the actual four-story, steam-powered engine. The ferry underwent a $2.7 million restoration in 1994 and has since been used as a stage set for the TV show *Nash Bridges*.

★**C.A. Thayer** – *Across from the Eureka. Tour program year-round daily, 11am.* Built in 1895 to haul logs of heavy Douglas fir between Washington and California, this venerable, three-masted wooden sailing schooner is one of only two such ships in the country (the other, the *Wawona*, is berthed in Seattle). Her single deck, open hold, shallow draft and relatively wide beam enabled her small crew to hold the 156ft craft steady in shallow, turbulent coves called "dogholes" as timber was loaded from the bluffs above. The *C.A. Thayer* served as a codfisher in 1925-31 and again in 1946-50. In the intervening years, she was used by the army as a barge to store empty shells from target practice at sea. Visitors who now descend into the ship's hold find themselves in a dark cave, its walls worn smooth by many loads of rubbing logs. Just above are the handsome captain's quarters and adjacent formal dining room. In the forecastle, a video *(11min)* recounts the story of the ship's last voyage. Deckhands in period costume often introduce the boat to groups of schoolchildren; sea chanteys are sung on board the first Saturday night of each month.

★★**Balclutha** – *End of pier on the left. Tour program year-round daily, 2pm.* Looming over the pier, virtually sparkling after a $1.5 million overhaul completed in June 1998, this three-masted, steel-hulled square-rigger was launched in Glasgow in 1886, rounding Cape Horn 17 times on voyages between Europe and California. A deep-sea cargo vessel measuring 301ft, the *Balclutha* carried wine, spirits, hardware and coal from European ports to San Francisco, returning to the continent loaded with California wheat. In 1904 her owners based her in San Francisco and she began a long career in the salmon industry, running cannery supplies and workers between Alaska and California. A promoter bought the ship in 1933, renamed her the *Pacific Queen*, and displayed her in various ports as a "pirate" ship. Following this ignominious stage of her career, she came to rest on the Marin mudflats, a near wreck. In 1954 the National Maritime Museum purchased and refurbished her, restoring her original name.

Today visitors admire the vast decks, inspect the bird's-eye maple cabinets and elegant Victorian furnishings of the captain's quarters, and try to imagine life in the cramped forecastle, where the crew slept. In the *Balclutha's* cavernous hold are displays of various anchors, mast riggings and rudders, ballast tubs and a model salmon cannery. Panels on deck give information about her history and workings.

In addition to these three ships, the steel-hulled steam tug *Hercules* (1907) and scow-schooner *Alma* (1891) are open for public viewing on a limited afternoon schedule, subject to weather. The New Jersey-built *Hercules* towed her sister ship through the Straits of Magellan on her maiden voyage, ranged north to Alaska until 1924, then towed railroad barges throughout San Francisco Bay before retiring in 1962. The *Alma* was typical of the broad, shallow, turn-of-the-century boats that carried bulk goods like hay, bricks and chicken feed along inland waterways from San Jose to Sacramento. Not open for visits, but moored for dockside viewing, is the paddle-wheel steam tug *Eppleton Hall* (1914), which operated on the River Wear near Newcastle upon Tyne, England, towing coal ships and barges.

Aquatic Park Beach – This small beach fronting a grassy lawn is one of the last stretches of open shoreline along the northern waterfront. The park and the beach were created in the 1930s as part of a WPA recreational complex. While most people consider the waters of San Francisco Bay too cold for swimming, intrepid members of the century-plus-old Dolphin Club and the South End Rowing Club still take daily dips here. Look for them among the swells in their brightly colored swim caps. Line fishermen frequent the 1,850ft **Municipal Pier** (1934), along with others seeking a quiet place to stroll.

❶ Buena Vista Cafe
2765 Hyde St. ☎ *415-474-5044.* Best known as the first bar in the US to serve Irish coffee (a heady concoction of Irish whiskey, coffee and whipped cream), this amiable bar sold its first steaming mug of the brew in 1952. Breakfast is served all day by aproned waiters who willingly direct visitors to local attractions.

★**National Maritime Museum** – *Beach St. at Polk St. Open year-round daily 10am–5pm. Closed Jan 1, Thanksgiving Day, Dec 25.* ☎ *415-556-3002. www.maritime.org/safrhome.shtml.* Resembling an ocean liner at berth on the edge of Aquatic Park, this unusual Streamline Moderne building (1939) houses a fine collection of maritime artifacts and historical displays. Its upper floors are recessed from a flat roof to create the impression of a ship's decks, a nautical effect enhanced by railings, porthole windows and cowl ventilators that look like smokestacks. It was built as the Aquatic Park Casino, centerpiece of the WPA's never-fully-realized recreational complex. Unusual slate intaglio reliefs by Sargent Johnson adorn its recessed doorway, while the interior boasts undulating undersea murals by Hilaire Hiler and a terrazzo floor designed by Richard Ayer, based on a shoal chart of the bay.

Occupying the building (which it shares with a senior center) since 1951, the museum forms part of the San Francisco Maritime National Historical Park. In the entrance hall, a large anchor, the hull of a scow schooner and three fine models (including one of the *Preussen*, a unique, five-masted square-rigger) whet visitors' appetites for other galleries. One collection is devoted to steam-powered ocean travel from post-Civil War to the 1980s; temporary exhibits are mounted elsewhere on the first floor. A larger exhibition hall *(2nd floor)* focuses on the 1850s-60s—the city's early years as a sea and inland port. Fisheries, whaling and shipbuilding are portrayed through unusual artifacts, including blubber-processing spoons and intricate figureheads from ships that once sailed San Francisco Bay; among them were trawlers and riverboats, ferries and yachts. Displays on the traditional arts of the sailor include knotting, modeling, whittling and scrimshaw carving. Large windows to the north, as well as an open observation deck *(3rd floor)*, offer grand views of the historic sailing ships at Hyde Street Pier.

★★**Ghirardelli Square** – *900 North Point St. between Polk, Larkin & Beach Sts. Open May–Dec Mon–Sat 10am–9pm, Sun 10am–6pm. Rest of the year Sun–Thu 10am–6pm, Fri–Sat 10am–9pm. Restaurant hours vary.* ✗ ♿ 🅿 ☎ *415-775-5500. www.ghirardellisq.com.* This famed shopping and dining complex, located within a series of renovated brick factories, is an extremely popular destination for visitors and one of the finest examples of San Francisco's dedication to preserving its historic buildings.

Born and trained in Rapallo, Italy, Domingo Ghirardelli came to San Francisco in 1849, eventually opening a small chocolate factory at 415 Jackson St. In 1865 he discovered that a bag of chocolate hung in a warm room would release its cocoa butter and that the remaining residue could be ground into a fine powder. This "broma" chocolate, as it was known, became the company's featured product. After Ghirardelli's retirement in 1892, his sons relocated the business, purchasing an entire city block including the Pioneer Woolen Mill (1859). Over the next 30 years, working with architect William Mooser, they transformed the complex into the Ghirardelli Chocolate Factory, adding a comfortable central courtyard where workers enjoyed picnic lunches. The now-famous **Clock Tower** (1916) and the enormous electric sign, lowered into place in 1915, beamed a comforting welcome to ships passing through the Golden Gate until they were darkened for defense purposes during World War II.

② Ghirardelli Chocolate Manufactory & Soda Fountain
In Ghirardelli Square.
☎ *415-474-1414.*
Find out all about chocolate from the first cocoa bean to the last sweet slurp at this bustling ice cream parlor. Break into the chocolate shell of the Alcatraz Rock, Strike it Rich with butterscotch and almonds, or experience your first Earthquake: a gargantuan sundae made of eight scoops, eight toppings, bananas, nuts and cherries.

The manufacturing operation relocated to a new factory across the bay in San Leandro in 1962. That left the old chocolate works imperiled until visionary shipping heir William Matson Roth stepped in. Purchasing the block, he set about an ambitious plan to redevelop it as a fine shopping and dining complex. The landmark redesign (1968, Wurster, Bernardi & Emmons) is renowned as one of the city's premier examples of adaptive reuse. Several new structures were added to the open courtyard, linking the upscale galleries, boutiques and restaurants housed in the old factory buildings. Exposed brick walls and highly polished hardwood floors have been preserved throughout the interiors, and pieces of obsolete chocolate machinery harken back to Ghirardelli Square's industrial origins.

11 • GOLDEN GATE BRIDGE★★★

𝖬𝖴𝖭𝖨 bus 28–19th Ave. or 29–Sunset
Map p 132

Stretching across the narrow strait of the Golden Gate above the swirling union of the Pacific Ocean and San Francisco Bay, this elegant Art Deco suspension bridge remains one of San Francisco's most beloved symbols.

Historical Notes

Imagined by a madman in 1869, proposed intermittently over the next four decades by saner visionaries, the bridge across the treacherous strait between the San Francisco Peninsula and Marin County elicited passionate emotions and aggressive resistance at every stage of its conception. Few took the idea seriously until 1916, when auto transportation was fast becoming a way of life. The city's Board of Supervisors commissioned the first feasibility study two years later.

Initial cost estimates for the structure ran as high as $100 million, but Joseph Strauss, a tireless and innovative engineer who already had built more than 400 bridges around the world, claimed that he could span the "unspannable" passage for a mere $27 million. Excited by Strauss' plan, citizens of counties from San Francisco to the Oregon border offered their financial and political support. Two major foes, however, stood in the way—the powerful Southern Pacific Railroad (sole owner of all transbay ferry operations), which stood only to lose from Strauss' railless design, and the US War Department, which feared that the bridge would hinder navigation and provide a target for enemy bombs in the event of war. Some naysayers claimed that the deep and turbulent waters of the bay were too treacherous for such an undertaking, and still others decried Strauss' estimate as being nearly $75 million too low.

For years parties on both sides wrangled. When the War Department withdrew its opposition in 1924, the Southern Pacific filed a battery of lawsuits designed to keep the project in litigation for decades. Soon thereafter, several counties that originally had backed the plan withdrew their support, citing danger and expense as reasons to abandon the construction attempt. Since no federal or state funding was to be allocated, the remaining counties faced an even greater financial burden if they wanted to be linked to the city across the bay. By the time the last obstacles were removed—the railroad finally dropped its lawsuits under public pressure—the Great Depression had crushed the economy and citizens couldn't afford the bonds issued for public support.

Golden Gate Bridge from Baker Beach

Larry Ulrich/Tony Stone Images

Then A.P. Giannini, visionary founder of the Bank of Italy, stepped forward and announced that his bank would finance the bridge. In January 1933, nearly 12 years after Joseph Strauss first submitted his proposal, groundbreaking ceremonies finally took place.

Spanning the Gate – Unemployed laborers turned out in droves to compete for plum jobs on the bridge once construction began. Not only did the project offer steady employment for thousands of men during the height of the Depression; it also provided the safest conditions yet found on a building site. Construction lore at the time held that one life would be lost for every million dollars spent. But Strauss and his principal assistant engineer, Clifford Paine, broke that grim law by enforcing unprecedented safety procedures that have since become standard, including safety belts, nets and filter glasses to block the blinding sun. Their stringency paid off: The first fatal accident, the toppling of a derrick onto a young steel worker, did not occur until the fourth year of construction. Only three months before the bridge opened, euphoria about the project's impending completion shattered when a scaffold suspended below the roadway tore loose and plummeted into the safety net, carrying a dozen men with it. The net held for an instant, then ripped open, dropping the victims into the deepest part of the channel. Two survived the plunge, but 10 men were lost in the vicious currents.

Despite this tragedy, the Golden Gate Bridge was hailed as a model of safety, economy and grace at its inauguration on May 27, 1937. A crowd of more than 200,000 surged across the span on foot on opening day. Automobiles followed next, continuing a week-long round of festivities celebrating the conquest of the "unbridgeable" Golden Gate. The final cost was around $35 million. Today, nearly 130,000 vehicles traverse the bridge daily, while pedestrians take to its sidewalks to admire its soaring towers, graceful cables and wondrous views.

The bridge itself can be viewed from afar at many points in San Francisco and Marin County, especially from Land's End, The Presidio, Marin Headlands, the Marina District and Fisherman's Wharf.

The Golden Gate Bridge

Measuring 1.7mi from end to end (with a suspension span of 1.22mi), the Golden Gate Bridge stood for many years as the world's longest suspension bridge until it was superseded by the Verrazano Narrows Bridge in 1964. Unlike more rigid types of bridges, a suspension bridge relies on gravity for its stability: the massive weight of the roadway, suspended from cables anchored on land, keeps the structure from falling. The cables provide enough flexibility for the midspan of the bridge to deflect transversely up to 27ft in high winds without jeopardizing the structure's integrity. There are five main components to a suspension bridge: piers, anchorages, towers, cables and a roadway, constructed in that order. The Golden Gate Bridge's two **piers** form the bases of the towers. The Marin pier stands close to shore, but the San Francisco pier had to be poured a quarter-mile offshore in 100ft of water because the nearer bedrock was deemed unstable. An oval concrete fender, 27.5ft thick at its top and as long as a football field, surrounds this southern pier, protecting it from battering waves and collisions. The two **anchorages**, each a collection

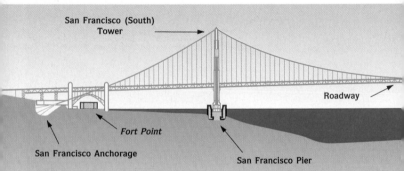

San Francisco (South) Tower

Roadway

Fort Point

San Francisco Anchorage

San Francisco Pier

- Length of suspended bridge: 6,450ft • Length of span between towers: 4,200ft
- Height of towers: 746ft • Combined weight of towers: 88 million lbs
- Dia. of cables: 36 3/8" • Total length of wire used in cables: 80,000 miles

VISIT

Viewing Area – ▦ *Access from US-101 or from Lincoln Blvd. $3 toll, southbound only. Pedestrian access to the bridge daily 5am–9pm east sidewalk only. ☏ 415-921-5858. www.goldengatebridge .org.* A cross section of a cable, a dignified statue of Joseph Strauss and panel displays lead from the parking area, through nearly five acres of manicured gardens of annuals and perennials. Just beyond, from a series of viewing platforms,

Bridging the Golden Gate (1937)

visitors can drink in the sight of the bridge's massive towers and cables. For closeup inspections, a stroll across the bridge on the east sidewalk is a must, but wear a jacket to ward off stiff winds. Walk to the center of the span for privileged **views★★** of Alcatraz, the Marin Headlands and the Pacific Ocean. From here, visitors can get a sense of Strauss' magnificent accomplishment by gazing up the sleek, looping cables that rise in a smooth arc to the top of the towers.

Cross to the **Vista Point** on the Marin County side for lovely **views★★** of the bridge from the north, backdropped by the forested hills of the Presidio.

At the city end of the bridge, the **Roundhouse**, built as a restaurant in 1938, is now a popular gift shop.

of massive concrete blocks able to withstand 63 million pounds of pull from the cables, were sunk into pits deep enough to hold a 12-story building. The twin steel **towers** rise 746ft (65 stories) above the piers, each supporting a total load of 123 million pounds from the two main cables. The massive **cables**, spun out of 80,000mi of wire, rest in saddles at the tops of the towers and are embedded into the anchorages on land. Under normal conditions (70°F and no load on the span), the cables bend the towers toward the shore by 6in. The steel-reinforced **roadway** hangs from ropes attached to the cables at 50ft intervals.

Since the Golden Gate Bridge's inauguration, weather conditions have forced it to close only three times. The bridge is continually maintained by a team of inspectors, electricians, ironworkers and painters. Since 1937, the bridge has been repainted repeatedly to prevent rust and corrosion from salt air, fog, high winds and auto exhaust. Its trademark shade of orange vermilion, dubbed "International Orange," was selected for aesthetic reasons.

- Clearance above highest tide: 220 ft • Weight of each cable anchorage: 240 million lbs
- Weight of cables, suspenders, accessories: 490 million lbs (24,500 tons)
- Total amount of steel used: 1.66 billion lbs. (83,000 tons)

12 • MARINA DISTRICT★

Ensconced on the northern waterfront between Van Ness Avenue, The Presidio and
Lombard Street, the Marina District is one of the city's most architecturally uniform
residential neighborhoods. Many blocks of pale, stucco facades are enlivened by an
abundance of Mediterranean Revival-style architectural details, including columns, tile
roofs, and arched windows and doors. The most desirable homes border the broad
swath of Marina Green and overlook San Francisco Bay.

Historical Notes

Early Spanish settlers were not attracted by the muddy, marshy inlet where the Marina
District now lies, although the high ground hemming it on either side greatly interested
military commanders charged with guarding the Golden Gate. Soldiers established The
Presidio on the rise to the west in 1776, and in 1797 emplaced a battery of five bronze
cannon atop the knoll now known as Black Point, to the east. The guns were never used
but in 1850 the site caught the eye of American military strategists who established an
army reservation there. To stave off Confederate attack during the Civil War, the Union
Army terraced Black Point and installed a new battery of 12 cannons. Like its predecessor, this battery never saw battle; it was eventually incorporated into Fort Mason.
Development came slowly to the mud flats, sand dunes and marshes between Black
Point and the Presidio. At the beginning of the 19C, dairy farms covered the hills and
valleys to the south (present-day Cow Hollow) and a roadhouse stood on the site of
the Palace of Fine Arts, an area then called Harbor View. In 1911, city boosters seeking
a favorable location for a world's fair—to promote the rebirth of the city after the
1906 earthquake and fire, and to celebrate the opening of the Panama Canal—decided
upon this largely empty tract. The Army Corps of Engineers erected a seawall along
the muddy waterfront and by 1913 had filled the 600 acres inside it with tons of

---

The Panama-Pacific International Exposition of 1915

As stewards of the West Coast's busiest port in the early 20C, San Francisco residents took keen interest in the construction of the Panama Canal. The resurrection
of the city from the 1906 earthquake and fire, and increasing competition from
the port at Los Angeles, heightened San Franciscans' resolve to celebrate the
canal's completion in a way that would unequivocally announce to the world that
the city was rebuilt, rejuvenated and ready to resume its place as the economic
and cultural center of the American Pacific coast.

On a 635-acre tract of reclaimed land, an esteemed group of architects, including
Louis C. Mullgardt, Bernard Maybeck, Willis Polk and William B. Faville, set about
designing a fabulous complex of pavilions representing 25 countries and 29 states.
From its opening day in February 1915, the fair dazzled the public with its attractions and architecture. Indirect lighting, an innovation of the era, accented a fantasy
city of Renaissance palazzos, Spanish missions, Classical temples and Byzantine domes.

PANAMA PACIFIC INTERNATIONAL EXPOSITION
SAN FRANCISCO CALIF. 1915.

sand and earthquake debris, creating a flat, attractive site upon which to erect the buildings of the Panama-Pacific International Exposition of 1915.

At the close of the fair, all of its structures were razed except the Palace of Fine Arts. Developers took over, laying out residential streets and building choice homes for sale. The Marina District, as it then became known, gained a reputation as a desirable middle-class address.

Ironically, the same uncompacted landfill laid down for a fair that advertised San Francisco's recovery from the 1906 earthquake proved disastrous during the Loma Prieta quake of 1989. The unstable ground beneath the Marina District liquefied during the tremor, causing several homes to collapse and heavily damaging dozens of buildings erected on the landfill. Today, however, the marks of Loma Prieta are largely erased and the Marina District remains an affluent residential neighborhood distinguished by its architectural harmony, its glorious views of the Golden Gate, and its tourist attractions at Fort Mason, the Palace of Fine Arts and the Exploratorium.

Visiting the Marina District – Marina Green, Chestnut Street, Union Street and intervening residential streets are pleasant for strolling by day or evening. Fort Mason Center's galleries, museums and other attractions are open by day, but most theater performances are held at night; call ☎ 415-979-3010 for recorded information about weekly events and cultural offerings. Maps and information about Fort Mason and the Golden Gate National Recreation Area are available at GGNRA headquarters at Upper Fort Mason. Street parking is usually available in the Marina District's residential areas, though time limits (usually 2hrs) are strictly enforced. Free public lots are located at Fort Mason Center *(entrance at Marina Blvd. & Buchanan St.)* and the Exploratorium *(westbound vehicles take Richardson Ave. to Lyon St. entrance; eastbound vehicles enter from Marina Blvd.)* but both fill up quickly afternoons and weekends. Limited free parking is available at Upper Fort Mason, in the Marina Yacht Harbor and along Marina Green. Walkers may enjoy strolling all or part of the Golden Gate Promenade, a popular and scenic byway that skirts Fort Mason and Marina Green on its 3.5mi route from Aquatic Park Beach to the Golden Gate Bridge.

The Great Palace of Machinery was vast enough for an airplane to fly through it. The Oregon state pavilion resembled the Parthenon, only using redwood trunks instead of marble pillars. Visitors were awed by a working scale model of the Panama Canal. At the center of the fairgrounds rose the Tower of Jewels, covered with more than 100,000 cut-glass jewels backed by tiny mirrors and suspended on wires, so that the tower appeared to shimmer in the breeze. Most beloved by San Franciscans was the Palace of Fine Arts. The fair was acclaimed far and wide as the most ambitious event ever hosted by the city, attracting nearly 20 million visitors in its 10 months of operation and earning a substantial profit—but ultimately failing to lure back the shipping business lost to Los Angeles' growing port. Constructed primarily of wood and plaster, most fair buildings were demolished at the exposition's close in December 1915. Of the original construction, only the Marina Yacht Harbor and the reconstructed Palace of Fine Arts remain today.

California Historical Society, San Francisco. James A. Heynemann Collection. FN-22832.

★FORT MASON

★Upper Fort Mason – The gentle slope and broad crown of a low hill overlooking the bay was a logical place for a military reservation. The Army failed to occupy the attractive site for more than a decade after 1850, however, and several well-to-do civilian families, in the interim, erected homes on Black Point before Union forces repossessed the property in 1863 during the Civil War. Named in 1881 for Col. Richard Mason, California's first military governor (1847-49), the outpost formed the western command center for the US Army during the Indian Wars of the late 19C. Gen. Frederick Funston's interim government established headquarters here in the anxious hours immediately following the 1906 quake, and tents were set up on the fort's broad meadow to house refugees from the devastated areas of the city.

Though operated as part of the Golden Gate National Recreation Area since 1972, Upper Fort Mason maintains the clean, orderly feel of a 19C Army command post. Military personnel still to occupy some of its many white, wood-frame buildings.

GGNRA Headquarters – *Bldg. 201, MacArthur St. Open year-round Mon–Fri 10am–5pm.* ♿ 🅿 ☏ *415-556-0561. www.nps.gov/goga.* Built in 1901, this three-story structure served briefly as an army hospital before its conversion to administrative offices after 1906. Inside, visitors may obtain abundant maps and information on GGNRA activities, and limited material on other national parks of the West.

Behind the headquarters building lies the charming **Fort Mason Community Garden**, a public plot where local residents may register for space to grow vegetables, flowers and root crops (more than 50 such gardens exist in the city). From the garden, a stroll along Pope Street leads past several examples of early military construction, including a wooden base chapel (1942). Originally a barracks, the American Youth Hostel at the head of the street dates from the Civil War period.

Black Point Battery – *North end of Franklin St.* In 1797, Spanish soldiers installed five-gun Batéria San José atop this serene bluff overlooking San Francisco Bay. The homes erected—without permission—by civilians in 1855 were confiscated by the army in 1863; several remain today along the east side of Franklin Street and are used as officers' quarters. Most prominent of the civilian "squatters" was explorer-politician John C. Frémont, whose house was demolished when Black Point was terraced for gun emplacements. Although the guns have been removed, Black Point Battery still offers lovely **views** east to tall-masted ships and small boats anchored off Aquatic Park, with the towers of downtown San Francisco and the hills of the East Bay beyond.

The Great Meadow – *Near Bay & Laguna Sts.* Site of a tent city erected to shelter thousands of refugees from the 1906 quake, this broad, undulating lawn today draws picnickers and sunbathers, and is the site of the annual September **San Francisco Blues Festival**. In the meadow stand a statue of the Madonna (**1**) by Italian-American sculptor Beniamino Bufano and a bronze figure of Bay Area Congressman Phillip Burton (**2**), whose efforts spearheaded creation of the GGNRA.

■ Golden Gate National Recreation Area

Embracing San Francisco's northern and western boundaries as well as Angel Island, Alcatraz and a large portion of coastal Marin County, the Golden Gate National Recreation Area was established by act of Congress in 1972. The 26,000-acre system of national parks, encompassing historic landmarks, military sites, redwood forests, beaches and undeveloped coastal lands, came about largely through the efforts of US Congressman Phillip Burton, who championed the movement to preserve the area's unused military lands as parks for nature conservation and recreation. Today the GGNRA attracts more than 25 million visitors annually.

GGNRA sites described in this guide include:

Alcatraz	San Francisco Maritime NHP
Fort Mason	Marina Green
Crissy Field	Fort Point NHS
The Presidio	Baker Beach
China Beach	Land's End
Cliff House	Ocean Beach
Fort Funston	Marin Headlands
Tennessee Valley	Muir Woods NM
Muir Beach	Stinson Beach

★**Fort Mason Center** – *Information* ☎ *415-441-3400. www.fortmason.org.* Built on landfill during the early 20C, this bayside complex of barracks, warehouses and docks served as the official embarkation point for Americans serving in Pacific theaters of war from 1910 through the Korean War. More than 1.5 million GIs and 23 million tons of cargo shipped out from its three sturdy docks during World War II, making Fort Mason the second largest Army port in the US at that time. This lower, bayside section of Fort Mason was decommissioned for civilian use in 1962 and was completely transformed as a cultural and community complex by 1977. Today its renovated military structures (dubbed "Landmark Buildings A-E") house theaters and performance spaces, museums, galleries, cafes, philanthropic organizations and other cultural venues. By day the center bustles with the comings and goings of museum visitors, performers and professionals.

Evenings draw theatergoers to any of several stages, including the **Cowell Theater**, built over the water on the middle pier, which also houses the Herbst Pavilion. The **Magic Theatre** *(Bldg. D, 3rd floor; ☎ 415-441-8822; www.magictheatre.org)* produces innovative plays from established and emerging writers; the **Young Performers Theatre** *(Bldg. C, 3rd floor; ☎ 415-346-5550; www.ypt.org)* specializes in dramatics for children; and the **Bayfront Theater** *(Bldg. B, 3rd floor; ☎ 415-474-8935; www.improv.org)* is home to improvisational "theatersports."

Worth a peek are the **San Francisco Children's Art Center** 〚Kids〛 *(Bldg. C, 1st floor; year-round Mon–Sat 9am–5:30pm; closed school holiday weeks; ᚴ ₽ ☎ 415-771-0292; www.childrensartcenter.org)*; and the **San Francisco Museum of Modern Art Rental Gallery** *(Bldg. A; open Memorial Day–Labor Day Thu 10am–9pm, Fri–Tue 10am–6.30pm; rest of the year Thu 11am–9pm, Fri–Tue 11am–6pm; closed major holidays; $9; ₽ ☎ 415-441-4777; www.sfmoma.org/museumstore/shop.html)*, where rotating exhibits of contemporary art are displayed on the ground floor and mezzanine. *General theater listings and ticket information pp 52-53; recorded Fort Mason Center event information* ☎ *415-979-3010.*

1 **Greens**
Fort Mason Center, Bldg. A. ☎ *415-771-6222.* Opened in 1979 by disciples of the San Francisco Zen Center, this gourmet vegetarian restaurant (its wine list is a national award winner) gets much of its produce from the center's Green Gulch Farm in Marin County. Reserve ahead for lunch or dinner, or stop in and rest your weary feet with coffee and a home-made scone while drinking in the lovely view of the bay and the Golden Gate Bridge.

Mexican Museum – *Bldg. D, 1st floor.* ᚴ ₽ ☎ *415-202-9700. www.mexican museum.org.* Closed during construction of a new home opposite Yerba Buena Gardens *(scheduled completion late 2002)*, the museum boasts a large collection of historic and contemporary Latin American arts and artifacts, as well as Chicano arts of the US. An ongoing schedule of public events and lectures includes monthly Diego Rivera mural tours *(1st Wed of each month, 3pm; 155 Sansome St.).*

J. Porter Shaw Library – *Bldg. E, 3rd floor. Open year-round Tue 5pm–8pm, Wed–Fri 1pm–5pm, Sat 10am–5pm. Closed major holidays.* ᚴ ₽ ☎ *415-556-9870. www.nps. gov/safr.* Operated by the San Francisco Maritime National Historical Park, whose headquarters are one floor below, this library of maritime history maintains a collection of about 32,000 books plus oral history archives, sea chanteys, recorded interviews, vessel registers, photographs and other nautical items centering on West Coast shipping and whaling. The Oceanic Society also maintains its offices here and launches whale-watching cruises *(p 134)* from the adjacent Marina Yacht Harbor weekends year-round.

San Francisco African American Historical & Cultural Society – *Bldg. C, 1st floor. Open year-round Wed–Sun noon–5pm. $2. Guided tours available.* ᚴ ₽ ☎ *415-441-0640.* Changing exhibits highlight achievements, people and events related to the African-American experience, particularly in California. The museum also mounts exhibits of work by African-American artists.

Museo ItaloAmericano – *Bldg. C, 1st floor. Open year-round Wed–Sun noon–5pm. Closed major holidays. $3.* ᚴ ₽ ☎ *415-673-2200. www.museoitaloamericano. org.* In addition to a permanent exhibition of modern Italian and Italian-American art and temporary displays of work by contemporary artists, this museum and cultural center sponsors community education programs, including Italian language classes.

San Francisco Craft & Folk Art Museum – *Bldg. A. Open year-round Tue–Fri & Sun 11am–5pm, Sat 10am–5pm. Closed major holidays. $3. Guided tours (45min) available 1st Wed & 2nd Fri 1:30pm, 1mo advance reservations required.* ₽ ☎ *415-775-0990. www.mocfa.org.* Offering rotating exhibits of historical folk art and contemporary crafts from around the world, this small museum also operates a wonderful gift shop selling an international assortment of handmade toys, art and mementos.

COW HOLLOW

Despite its homely name and prevailing residential character, Cow Hollow is best known for its charming, trendy shops and restaurants housed in attractive Victorians along bustling Union Street. Wedged below the flats of the Marina District at the foot of steeply rising Pacific Heights, the rolling "hollow" was known as Golden Gate Valley in the mid-19C, when herds of cattle from more than 30 dairy farms grazed upon its dales and hills. The availability of bovine carcasses also attracted tanneries, slaughterhouses and related industries. By the 1870s, the valley was dubbed "Cow Hollow" for its less endearing pastoral qualities. Wealthy residents of Pacific Heights complained about the stench rising from the valley until, in 1891, the city ordered the businesses closed and the "hollow" filled in.

Developers readily transformed Cow Hollow's pastures into a respectable neighborhood of two- and three-story wood-frame houses. Buildings along Union Street, the main thoroughfare, survived the earthquake and fire of 1906, and the area enjoyed a boom as it greeted merchants and residents fleeing the burned-out areas of San Francisco. Local businesses catered primarily to

neighborhood shoppers until the 1950s, when antique shops, furniture showrooms and interior decorators began renting Union Street's Victorian storefronts, attracting clients from other parts of the city. Other fashionable shops and restaurants followed suit, converting Victorian houses and courtyards for retail use and increasing Union Street's popularity as a shopping district. Although later refurbishments have in some cases teetered toward preciousness, much of Cow Hollow's genteel, early-20C architecture survives intact, along with several evocative reminders of its rural past.

★**Union Street** – Lined with refurbished Victorians, Union Street's eight-block retail district between Van Ness Avenue and Steiner Street invites leisurely exploration. Pedestrians are free to wander through pleasant courtyards and

Shopping on Union Street

© Robert Holmes

patios, between and behind old houses now converted to boutiques, galleries, arts-and-crafts shops and small, urbane restaurants. Particularly attractive are the bed-and-breakfast inns of **Charlton Court** *(south side of Union St. between Laguna & Buchanan Sts.)*, a quiet lane thought to have once served as a depot for milk wagons. The house and barn (c.1870) of James W. Cudworth, Cow Hollow's first dairyman, still stand behind a palm tree at no. 2040; they now house designer boutiques. A roofed passage at no. 2164/2166 leads to an old barn and leafy carriage yard, where plants and garden ornaments are displayed for sale. Cow Hollow's most unusual building, visible to the north from the corner of Union and Webster, is the former main temple of the **Vedanta Society of Northern California** *(2963 Webster St.)*. Built by Joseph Leonard in 1905 after a design by Swami Trigunatita, the three-story wooden building sports an ecumenical medley of ornamentation intended to represent religions and cultures of the world.

2 **La Nouvelle Patisserie** *2184 Union St. ☎ 415-931-7655.* Tender brioches and flaky croissants provide the chorus line for a show-stopping lineup of glorious French pastries, including chocolate ganache sponge cake, napoleons with caramelized topping and towering croquembouche, all created by master patissier Jean-Yves Duperret.

St. Mary the Virgin Episcopal Church – *2325 Union St. at Steiner St. Open year-round Mon–Fri 9am–5pm, Sun during services. Closed major holidays and Christmas week.* ♿ ☎ *415-921-3665. www.smvsf.org.* Partially hidden behind its fence and lych-gate, this charming church (1891) evokes the feel of an English country parsonage, though its wooden frame and redwood-shingle cladding herald the Arts and Crafts style characteristic of northern California architecture. Peace and tranquillity pervade the quiet, A-frame sanctuary and grounds. The gushing spring in the entry courtyard was used to water dairy herds, and is one of Cow Hollow's most beguiling reminders of its bucolic past.

★Octagon House – *2645 Gough St. at Union St. Open Feb–Dec 2nd & 4th Thu. & 2nd Sun, noon–3pm. Closed major holidays. Contribution requested. Guided tours (30min) available.* ☎ *415-441-7512.* Built in 1861 by William C. McElroy, this small house was moved from a nearby lot to its present site in 1953 by the National Society of Colonial Dames of America in California, which uses it as a museum for its collection of decorative arts from the Colonial and Federal periods. The two-story structure took its curious shape from Orson Squire Fowler's popular 1848 book, *A Home for All*, which theorized that octagonal houses provided more light, space and ventilation than conventional square-cornered houses, and were consequently healthier. The interior floor plan was substantially altered when the central stairwell was moved to the west by its present owners. Most of the rooms on the second floor, which is naturally lit by a central octagonal cupola that protrudes above the main roof, retain their original dimensions.

The museum displays many fine pieces of early American furniture, portraits, samplers, looking glasses, pewter and silverware, as well as examples of ceramics and other decorative items from the lively import trade during the Colonial era and early Republic. One room houses a collection of signatures and handwritten documents by all but two of the signatories to the Declaration of Independence, including Thomas Jefferson, John Hancock, Benjamin Franklin and John Adams.

ADDITIONAL SIGHTS

Chestnut Street – The four blocks of Chestnut Street between Divisadero and Fillmore Streets, about halfway between Union Street and Marina Green, comprise the Marina District's main commercial avenue. A pleasant thoroughfare for shopping, dining and strolling, Chestnut Street projects a comfortable, friendly, middle-class atmosphere reminiscent of a small-town main street.

③ California Wine Merchant
3237 Pierce St. ☎ *415-567-0646.* For more than two decades, owners Greg and Deborah O'Flynn have tracked the astonishing growth and variety of California wines. You won't see the big names here: Their no-gimmicks shop, once the refrigerated portion of a defunct creamery, specializes in vintages from top-of-the-line, small-production wineries in California and the Pacific Northwest.

Marina Green – Encompassing an expansive stretch of Marina District waterfront between Webster and Scott Streets, this broad, 10-acre greensward is popular with locals for its stiff breezes—ideal for kite-flying—and for its stupendous **views★★** of San Francisco Bay, the Golden Gate Bridge and yachts anchored offshore. A favored spot of sunbathers, in-line skaters, volleyball players and joggers, the lawn is bordered by handsome dwellings in a diverse array of architectural styles. Most were built in the 1920s and incorporate Spanish and Italian Baroque details inspired by the 1915 Panama-Pacific International Exposition.

Enclosed by a 1,500ft jetty extending parallel to Marina Green, the **Marina Yacht Harbor** encloses a flotilla of boats, many of them belonging to members of the private St. Francis Yacht Club, which occupies an attractive, tile-roofed structure (1928, Willis Polk). Visitors who brave the walk to the end of the jetty can see the "wave organ," a sculpted jumble of concrete and stone embedded with pipes, each with one end sunk beneath the surface of the harbor. One hears the gurgling "music" of the sea, theoretically, by putting an ear to an exposed pipe end.

★★Palace of Fine Arts – *Baker & Beach Sts.* Ranking among San Francisco's best-known landmarks, this grand rotunda and peristyle were replicated from structures designed by renowned architect Bernard Maybeck to house art exhibits for the 1915 Panama-Pacific International Exposition. The original building, designed to be impermanent, was framed in lath and chicken wire and covered with a plaster and burlap-fiber mixture called "staff," its surface sprayed to resemble travertine. When the buildings of the fair were torn down to make way for residential development, aesthetically minded citizens lobbied to spare the Palace of Fine Arts. No efforts were made to strengthen the building, however, and it slowly disintegrated until a plan for restoration was made in 1962. Workers made casts of the columns, statuary and artistic details, and the building was entirely reconstructed in concrete and steel between 1964 and 1967.

Maybeck's design was purely romantic in concept, inspired largely by the work of 18C engraver Giovanni Piranesi and *The Isle of the Dead*, a 19C painting depicting a royal tomb. Maybeck himself described the building as "an old Roman ruin" and stated his intent to project sadness. Reinforcing the sense of mystery and melancholy, the female figures sculpted by Ulric Ellerhusen along the top of the peristyle face inward, their faces buried in their arms.

© Edward Thomas

Palace of Fine Arts

The rotunda, 110ft high and 135ft across, is decorated with eight large panels carved in low relief. Angels look down from the interior of the dome; two of the original 14ft angels are preserved inside the Exploratorium. On clear, calm days, the large duck pond spreading from the foot of the rotunda reflects mirror images.

★★**Exploratorium** – Kids *3601 Lyon St. Open Memorial Day–Labor Day daily 10am–6pm (Wed 9pm). Rest of the year Tue–Sun 10am–5pm (Wed 9pm). Closed Thanksgiving Day & Dec 25. $9, children 6-17 $5; free 1st Wed.* ✗ ᕫ ▢ ☏ *415-561-0360. www.exploratorium.edu. (Tactile Dome $3 additional admission; entry at 10:15am, noon, 1:45pm, 3:30pm, 5pm & 6:45pm; reservations suggested;* ☏ *415-561-0362.)* Located in the cavernous, semicircular structure behind the Palace of Fine Arts rotunda, this innovative museum of science, art and human perception has served as a model for similar science museums around the world since its opening in 1969. The Exploratorium's creator, physicist Frank Oppenheimer, maintained a novel philosophy that a museum can best teach science through "hands-on" participation.

The museum boasts more than 650 exhibits in physics, electricity, life sciences, thermodynamics, weather, light, psychology, linguistics, sense perception and a host of other subjects. By pushing buttons, rotating wheels, peering through prisms, activating motors, engineering arches, arranging chimes, shouting into tubes and performing a wide variety of other actions, visitors set experiments in motion, observe the results and speculate on the causes. Instructions and explanations accompany each exhibit, and staff members are available to answer questions. Among the most popular exhibits are the miniature **tornado demonstration**; the photosensitive **Shadow Box**, where people's shadows are temporarily recorded on a wall; and the **distorted room**, where visitors can enter an optical illusion. New exhibits are continually being developed in the extensive workshops adjacent to the main floor, in full view of visitors.

Not to be missed is the soundproof, pitch-black **Tactile Dome**, a multilevel crawl chamber through which visitors must find their way only by sense of touch. It is not recommended for claustrophobes.

Addresses, telephone numbers, opening hours and prices published in this guide are accurate at press time. We apologize for any inconvenience resulting from outdated information, and we welcome corrections and suggestions that may assist us in preparing the next edition. Please send us your comments:

Michelin Travel Publications
Editorial Department
P. O. Box 19001
Greenville, SC 29602-9001
Email: TheGreenGuide-us@us.michelin.com

13 • THE PRESIDIO★★

MUNI 8 bus 28–19th Avenue, 29–Sunset, 41–Union, 43–Masonic or 45–Union-Stockton. Map pp 132-133-

For more than two centuries, The Presidio's privileged setting on 1,480 acres overlooking the Golden Gate earned it a reputation as the most beautiful military installation in North America. Residents and visitors are drawn to the lushly forested expanse to enjoy its handsome and eclectic mix of architectural styles, its traces of San Francisco's military history, and the spectacular views extending from its miles of wooded trails. Closed as an army base in 1994, The Presidio is now administered by a federal trust agency in partnership with the National Park Service.

Historical Notes

Selected as the site of the northernmost military installation of the far-reaching Spanish colonial empire, The Presidio (the word means "military garrison") was dedicated on September 17, 1776, by Lt. José Joaquin Moraga. Originally an adobe quadrangle about 300yds on each side located approximately where the Main Post now stands, The Presidio was San Francisco's first European settlement, predating Mission Dolores by a month. The Spanish never considered the outpost to be of primary importance despite its strategic location at the mouth of the bay. Official disinterest, combined with decades of rain, earthquakes, wind and salt air, kept the lonely fortress in a perpetual state of disrepair, even after Mexico acquired it (along with independence from Spain) in 1821.

The Presidio's outlook changed in 1846 when John C. Frémont and a group of civilians staged the capture of the crumbling, largely defenseless fort from the Mexican government. The American flag was raised over the decaying garrison following cession of California to the US in 1848. San Francisco's growth as a commercial hub during the Gold Rush caused President Millard Fillmore to issue an executive order in 1850 reserving the property for military use. Over the next decade the fort was restored and enlarged, while other installations were erected around the bay, including Fort Point and Alcatraz.

Bulwark of National Defense – The timing of this military construction was fortuitous. Following the outbreak of the Civil War, defense of San Francisco Bay moved to top priority from the Union's point of view. Gold and silver from California and Nevada mines were at stake. The Presidio undertook a major military buildup to guard against invasion by Confederate forces.

Following the Civil War, The Presidio housed US troops engaged in conflicts with the Modoc, Apache and other Native American tribes across the West. Between 1886 and 1976, the magnificent eucalyptus, cypress and pine forests—in all, 100,000 trees of 200 species—were planted in military rows on the rolling lands of the base, both to beautify it and to protect its barren, sandy, windswept terrain from erosion. The coastal defense batteries along the bayfront also were constructed. After 1898, as frontier outposts across the West were closed, The Presidio served as the launching pad for American expansion into the Pacific. During the Spanish-American War, thousands of soldiers camped on the grounds before sailing for the Philippines.

The presence of a large, standing army proved vital at the time of the 1906 earthquake and fire. Presidio troops helped maintain order as martial law was proclaimed, and more than 16,000 refugees camped on the fort's open lands. When the US entered World War I, troops trained here for combat in France. During World War II, The Presidio became headquarters for the Western Defense Command, as nearly 2 million troops shipped out from San Francisco. In the 1950s the base was named the command center for Nike missile defense of the bay and served as headquarters for the Sixth US Army until 1994.

Swords to Plowshares – In 1962 the site was named a National Historic Landmark District. When the Golden Gate National Recreation Area (GGNRA) was created a decade later, Congress tagged The Presidio, whose military importance had waned, for future inclusion in the park. In 1989 The Presidio was designated for closure as part of a general defense reduction and consolidation, and on October 1, 1994, the Sixth Army marched off the grounds for the last time as The Presidio came under the supervision of the National Park Service. The remnants of the earliest 18C structures were discovered beneath the Main Post parking lot in 1996, shedding new light on what was believed to be the size of the original Presidio.

Today an official unit of the GGNRA, the property is managed by **The Presidio Trust**, a presidentially appointed, nonprofit board charged with maintaining The Presidio's aesthetic, ecological and historic integrity while weaning it from federal dollars by 2013. About 80 percent of Presidio lands are under the direct aegis of the trust, while coastal areas are managed by the National Park Service. Ensuring public access to the fine Greek, Colonial, Mission and Mediterranean Revival and Victorian buildings on the grounds, as well as to trails and unique natural habitats, is central to every decision. So, too, is protecting the rights and privacy of a community of 800 households and over 150 organizations.

In order that The Presidio may become self-supporting, administrators are examining large-scale leasing options. The most high-profile would allow renowned filmmaker George Lucas to develop the former Letterman Army Medical Center complex (1899), on the east side of The Presidio, as a 23-acre campus for the digital arts, incorporating a seven-acre "Great Meadow." Already occupying 12 buildings of the complex is the **Thoreau Center for Sustainability** *(1014 Torney Ave. at Gen. Kennedy Ave.; ☎ 415-561-6327; www.thoreau.org)*, whose 60 member organizations are dedicated to environmental and social-justice issues. Their often-eclectic causes range from waste management and women's empowerment to the preservation of indigenous ancestral lands and the use of tree-free fiber in paper and textiles. The Smithsonian Institution, meanwhile, is pondering the establishment of a West Coast affiliate at The Presidio.

Visiting The Presidio – Visitors may enter The Presidio by one of its three historic gates, or by **Lincoln Boulevard** from the southwest; the latter skirts the Coastal Defense Batteries, offering stunning views in the south-to-north direction. The Lombard Gate (Lombard St. at Lyon St.), the most widely used entrance, is convenient to the Marina District and the Palace of Fine Arts; those entering here may stop at the **Presidio Trust Information Center** *(448 Letterman Dr.; ☎ 415-561-5300; www.presidiotrust.gov)* for maps and brochures. The Presidio Boulevard Gate *(Presidio Blvd. at Pacific St.)* and the Arguello Boulevard Gate *(Arguello Blvd. at Pacific St.)* provide entry from the southern border of The Presidio. From all three gates, signs point the way to the Main Post. Parking lots abound on the property. Check the weather before setting out—coastal fog often lingers longer here than in other areas of the city, and a jacket or sweater may come in handy.

Located in the heart of the Main Post, the **William Penn Mott Jr. Visitor Center** *(102 Montgomery St.; open year-round daily 9am–5pm; closed Jan 1, Thanksgiving Day, Dec 25; & ▣ ☎ 415-561-4323; www.nps.gov/prsf)* is a good place to begin a visit. It offers maps, books, museum displays (including historic dioramas), a 15min slide show and walking-tour brochures. *(Visitor Center access is limited during seismic retrofitting in 2001-02.)* Inquire about temporary shows mounted nearby at the **Herbst International Exhibition Hall** *(385 Moraga Ave. at Montgomery St.; ☎ 415-441-3400)*, a former commissary renovated to house traveling exhibitions with a historical perspective.

Formerly a private club reserved for Presidio officers, the Arnold Palmer-designed **Presidio Golf Course** *(300 Finley Rd. at Arguello Gate; ☎ 415-561-4653)* today welcomes all golfers to tackle its 18 scenic holes. Popular jazz brunches *(reservations essential)* are hosted in the clubhouse every weekend. A 2.5mi stretch of the **Bay Area Ridge Trail** extends through The Presidio; designed for hikers and bikers, it marks the start of the c.1,000mi Juan Bautista de Anza National Historic Trail between The Presidio and southern Arizona's Tubac Presidio.

SIGHTS

★★ **Main Post** – Although no longer the efficient headquarters of a bustling military base, the Main Post remains the focal point of activity at The Presidio. The stately brick **barracks★** (c.1890) stretching along Montgomery Street, on the west side of the large central Parade Ground, once housed soldiers of the Spanish-American War. The dignified row today contains The Presidio's main visitor center and offices of the GGNRA. At the southern end of the Parade Ground stands **Pershing Square**, site of the home of Gen. John "Black Jack" Pershing, later commander of the American Expeditionary Forces in Europe during World War I. Pershing's wife and daughters

Barracks, Main Post

© Brenda Tharp

131

perished in a 1915 blaze that destroyed the house (a son survived); a flagpole signifies its location. A nearby monument marks the corner of the original adobe and thatched-roof Presidio compound built by the Spanish in 1776. On either side stand two bronze cannon, cast in the late 17C and brought here to protect the little Spanish fort.

Nearby is the tiny **California Indian Museum & Cultural Center** (**M¹**) *(97 Arguello Blvd. at Moraga Ave.; open Mon–Fri 8am–5pm;* ☎ *415-561-3992; www.cimcc.indian .com)*, which offers a photo portrait gallery and stages lectures on native history, arts and traditions. Just west, on a low rise, the **Main Post Chapel** *(130 Fisher Loop; Tue–Wed 10am–2pm;* ☎ *415-561-3930)* features a 1930s WPA mural by artist Victor Arnautoff. Diverse spiritual traditions often hold ceremonies and events here. At the chapel's east end is a small Vietnam memorial.

The **San Francisco Film Centre** *(39 Mesa St.;* ☎ *415-561-3456)* has revamped one Mission-style barracks building on the east side of the Parade Ground as a home for numerous small moviemakers and publishers, with production facilities and a screening room. Together with Robert Redford's Sundance Cinemas, the Film Centre

THE PRESIDIO-GOLDEN GATE BRIDGE

RICHMOND DISTRICT & PRESIDIO HEIGHTS

has proposed to renovate and expand the historic **Presidio Theatre** *(99 Montgomery St. at Moraga Ave.)* as a home for independent and international films.

Tree-lined Funston Avenue, one street further east of the Parade Ground, was once reserved for officers. The Neoclassical and Italianate cottages (1862-63) at the southern corner, known as **Officers' Row★**, originally faced west but were turned towards the east in 1878 to present a more pleasant aspect to visitors. An ongoing dig by University of California archeology students has turned up 150,000 artifacts from this era. Further along Funston Avenue, more elaborate residences representing several Victorian substyles were reserved for higher-ranking officers.

★**San Francisco National Military Cemetery** – *Entrance off Sheridan St. at Lincoln Blvd.* In 1884 The Presidio's 28-acre burial ground was designated a National Military Cemetery, allowing any US veteran the privilege of being buried here. Graves date from as far back as the Civil War. Well-known persons laid to rest here include Gen. Frederick Funston, acting Presidio commander during the 1906 earthquake and fire, and US Rep. Phillip Burton, sponsor and champion of the GGNRA. Eucalyptus and pine woods surround the cemetery.

A short distance away, beneath the Crissy Field Avenue overpass leading to the Golden Gate Bridge, lies a small **Pet Cemetery** [Kids], worth a quick peek to see the whimsical, and often poignant, headstones marking the graves of generations of Presidio household pets.

Crissy Field – *Crissy Field Ave. off Lincoln Blvd.* Strollers, picnickers, dog walkers and kite fliers share this broad, flat field with board sailors, who on fine days raise colorful sails for a few brisk turns on wind-whipped waves. Once a soggy marsh, the field was drained and filled for the 1915 Panama-Pacific International Exposition, then covered with 70 acres of asphalt as an Army aircraft test site from 1919 to 1936. (Many original buildings still stand, including hangars that once housed cloth biplanes.) The National Park Service has undertaken a three-year, $32-million project to restore the original tidal marsh, beach and dunes, anchoring them with native grasses and other plants. It is scheduled to culminate in spring 2001 with the opening, in a former commissary, of **Crissy Field Center** *(*[Kids] *Mason St. west of Halleck St.;* ☎ *415-427-4779; www.crissyfield.org)*, whose exhibits and programs are to focus on the convergence of urban and natural environments. At the western end of the field is the former commander's residence, now headquarters for the State of the World Forum established by ex-Soviet Union President Mikhail Gorbachev. Adjacent, in the former Fort Point Coast Guard Station (1890), are offices of the National Oceanic and Atmospheric Administration (NOAA) and Farallones Marine Sanctuary Association.

Gulf of the Farallones National Marine Sanctuary Visitors Center (**M²**) – [Kids] *993 Marine Dr. Open year-round Wed–Sun 10am–4pm. Closed Jan 1, Thanksgiving Day, Dec 25.* 🅿 ☎ *415-561-6625. www.farallones.org.* Exhibits describe research and conservation efforts in the 948sq mi sanctuary, whose boundaries embrace Marin County coastlines to the mean high-tide mark and the rocky Farallon Islands (26mi west of the Golden Gate), home to the largest concentration of breeding seabirds in the continental US. The sanctuary also harbors more than two dozen species of marine mammals. In the visitor center are a live tidepool tank; interactive computer displays outlining such sanctuary activities as whalewatching, birdwatching, fishing and kayaking; and murals depicting life in the Gulf of the Farallones and adjacent Cordell Bank sanctuaries.

■ A Whale of a Time

Few experiences may be more thrilling, and perhaps more unsettling, than tossing in salty swells on a small boat beyond the sight of land, surrounded by a good dozen of the largest creatures ever to inhabit the earth.

Such may be the predicament of those who venture into the Gulf of the Farallones National Marine Sanctuary. This stretch of sea is extraordinarily rich in krill, tiny shrimp-like crustaceans that are the favorite food of baleen whales. Blue whales, who may consume four tons in a single day, grow to 100ft long and 200 tons in weight; in summer and fall, these gargantuan creatures converge near the Farallon Islands, spouting and raising their fins and tails as they roll in the waves. Agile humpback whales may approach boats at closer proximity. In winter, gray whales, migrating between Alaska and Baja California, pass through these seas; they may be accompanied by newborn calves as they travel north in spring.

Unless you own your own boat, the only practical way to visit the sanctuary is aboard a marine research vessel. The Oceanic Society's naturalist-led *New Superfish*, a 63ft motor vessel, accommodates 50 passengers and crew ($50-$65; ☎ *415-474-3385; www.oceanic-society.org)*; it departs Fort Mason Center weekend days (except late May and December) year-round. Though bound for the Farallon Islands, it may turn back short of the avian-rich rocks, depending upon what marine life or inclement weather it encounters en route.

Fort Winfield Scott – *Entrance on Kobbe Ave. near Park Blvd.* A horseshoe-shaped group of white, Mission Revival-style barracks, Fort Winfield Scott was built in 1910 to house the Coast Artillery Corps. The only complex in The Presidio of uniform architectural style, Fort Scott provides a quiet, attractive setting from which to view the piers of the Golden Gate Bridge.

★**Coastal Defense Batteries** – Scattered along the cliffs that border Lincoln Avenue between Fort Point and Baker Beach, these crumbling concrete bunkers offer spectacular **views★★★** of the sea, the Marin Headlands and the Golden Gate Bridge. Linked by the Coastal Trail, the batteries were constructed between 1853 (at Fort Point) and 1910 to protect San Francisco Bay from invasion by sea. As with most of the fortifications around the bay, however, their guns were never fired in defense.

The best way to enjoy the view is to stroll along the Coastal Trail south from the Golden Gate Bridge toll plaza through Battery Cranston (1897), Battery Marcus Miller (1891), Battery Boutelle (1900) and Battery Godfrey (1895) to the Fort Scott Overlook. At **Battery Chamberlin** (1902), overlooking Baker Beach further down the Coastal Trail, the public may assist in cleaning, loading and firing a 50-ton "disappearing" gun the first full weekend of each month *(Sat–Sun 10am–2pm)*.

★**Baker Beach** – *Bowley St. off Lincoln Ave., southwest corner of The Presidio.* Perhaps the most popular beach in San Francisco, as much for its smooth sand as for the high dunes that protect it from all but the coldest winds, Baker Beach attracts two types of beachgoer. The southern end, near the parking lot, draws families and adolescents. The northern end, with its more dramatic view of the Golden Gate Bridge and the sage-covered cliffs, is popular with devotees of nude sunbathing—an activity tolerated (though not officially permitted) on federal land.

ADDITIONAL SIGHT

★**Fort Point National Historic Site** – Kids *Scheduled to close for 3–4yrs during retrofitting work on Golden Gate Bridge, to begin sometime in 2001. Until then, open year-round Wed–Sun 10am–5pm. Closed Jan 1, Thanksgiving Day, Dec 25. Guided tours (30min) and self-guided audio headset tours ($2.50; 45min) available.* 🄿 ☏ *415-556-1693. www.nps.gov/fopo.* Tucked beneath a steel arch at the southern anchorage of the Golden Gate Bridge, this impressive, multistoried brick-and-granite fort stands as a fine example of Civil War-era masonry and military architecture. Designed as the first of three enormous fortifications to guard the entrance to San Francisco Bay (the other two were to be built on Alcatraz Island and at Lime Point, now the northern anchorage of the bridge), Fort Point was erected in 1861 atop the site of Castillo de San Joaquín (1794), an abandoned Spanish gun battery.

The original design, calling for a rectangular structure of granite blocks, was modified (after construction began) to a brick fortress with defensive towers on the east and west. Master brickmasons were hired to build the structure; their fine craftsmanship remains evident throughout. As the Civil War approached, the US military, anticipating Confederate attacks on San Francisco Bay, ordered the uncompleted and unarmed fort occupied. For months a garrison stood guard over empty gun casements.

Like other military installations around the bay, Fort Point's ordnance was never fired in defense. By 1885 its guns were considered obsolete and were removed for scrap. Long periods of minimal occupation or complete abandonment followed, with the thick walls occasionally serving as a damp, lonely barracks for unlucky companies of soldiers.

Initial plans for the Golden Gate Bridge placed Fort Point on the exact spot where Joseph Strauss, the bridge's designer, intended to sink the southern anchorage. After visiting the fort, Strauss was so impressed by the quality of its masonry that he designed a massive steel arch over the fort to preserve it.

Visit – Restored and rebuilt by the National Park Service in the 1970s, Fort Point provides visitors with an excellent glimpse into military life on the California coast in the late 19C. Information panels throughout the building detail the history of the fort and the lives of the soldiers stationed there. Just inside the "sally port," the only entrance to the structure, lies a Spanish bronze cannon (1684), saved from Castillo de San Joaquín, and a huge 1844 Rodman cannon, typical of those that once guarded the Golden Gate. *(Cannon drill demonstrations are presented daily at noon & 2:30pm)*. To the right of the sally port, the former sutler's store (post exchange) houses a visitor center, bookstore and small theater presenting slide shows and short films about the fort and the Golden Gate Bridge.

Handcut granite spiral staircases lead to the upper tiers, with their intricate masonry and arching ceilings. Officers' quarters and privates' barracks are hung with historical photographs, and there are exhibits documenting the experiences of 20C African-American soldiers and the wartime contributions of American women. From the top-level barbettes, visitors can marvel at a unique and stunning **view**★★ of the southern pier and underbelly of the Golden Gate Bridge.

14 • GOLDEN GATE PARK★★★

ⓂⓊⓃⒾ bus 5–Fulton, 21–Hayes or 44–O'Shaughnessy.
Map p 139

Encompassing more than 1,017 acres of meadows, gardens and public buildings, verdant Golden Gate Park is the largest cultivated urban park in the US. Stretching 3mi inland from Ocean Beach to Stanyan Street, the roughly .5mi wide park accommodates 27mi of footpaths and 7.5mi of equestrian trails, all linking an enchantingly natural, yet entirely man-made, landscape of lakes, waterfalls, swales and woods.

Historical Notes

As San Francisco prospered in the 1860s, William Ralston and others began laying plans for a city park to rival designs for Central Park, at that time under construction in New York. They selected a roughly rectangular tract of the sandy scrublands known as the Outer Lands as an affordable, if not quite ideal, location. When Mayor H.P. Coon consulted Frederick Law Olmsted, designer of Central Park, the famous landscape architect eyed the dunes and advised that large trees would never grow on the site. Undaunted, city planners in 1871 contracted engineer and surveyor William Hammond Hall to build a park on the maligned tract.

Raising a bulwark behind Ocean Beach to deflect ocean winds, Hall graded the inland dunes into gentle hills and valleys, securing them by sowing barley, lupine and ammophila grass. When this natural matting had taken root, he began to plant trees. Starting on the eastern end of the park, Hall laid out roads in a meandering fashion, partly to discourage speeding but also to imitate the leisurely ambience of a rural road. His urbane carriage entry, a narrow strip of greenery called the **Panhandle**, today harbors the park's largest and oldest trees.

By the late 1870s, the new park was a resounding public success. Corrupt city officials, however, embezzled budgeted funds, neglected maintenance and allowed private concessionaires to stake claims to park land. Falsely accused of corruption in 1876, Hall resigned his commission as park superintendent. Golden Gate Park plunged into a decline that went unchecked until 1886, when a new civic administration asked Hall to return as an adviser.

"Uncle John" – In 1890 Hall appointed **John McLaren** (1846-1943) as the new park superintendent. Born in Stirling, Scotland, McLaren cut his horticultural teeth working as a gardener on great Scottish estates, and in Edinburgh's Royal Botanical Gardens, before coming to California in 1872. Prior to his park appointment, McLaren landscaped large estates for wealthy Bay Area patrons and tended his commercial plant nursery in nearby San Mateo.

Fondly known as "Uncle John" by his staff and an admiring public, the cantankerous McLaren ran Golden Gate Park with a forceful, patriarchal hand. Believing that a park should provide a sylvan refuge from city life, McLaren fought hard against new buildings, concessions, statues and other urban encroachments. Continuously battling would-be developers, personally planting millions of flowers, bulbs and trees, and tirelessly driving himself and his gardeners toward perfection, McLaren devoted himself to the park for 53 years. In addition, he found time for other projects, including Buena Vista Park, Huntington Park and the 1915 Panama-Pacific International Exposition. By the time of his death at 97, McLaren had succeeded in cultivating one of the world's most varied gardens.

The Midwinter Fair of 1894 – Four years after McLaren's appointment, journalist Michael H. de Young, inspired by the World's Columbian Exposition of 1893 in Chicago, successfully convinced city officials that San Francisco should mount its own fair at Golden Gate Park to promote the city's splendid winter climate. Five fancifully domed and spired buildings and a 266ft Electric Tower were erected around a quadrangle called the Great Court, and the California Midwinter International Exposition of 1894 (also called the Midwinter Fair) opened on January 27. All of California's counties, four other states and more than 19 foreign countries participated, drawing some 2.5 million visitors during its six months of operation. Today visitors flock to the site, now the **Music Concourse**, to hear Sunday concerts in Spreckels Bandshell (1899), and to tour the park's outstanding art museums and the natural-history exhibits and planetarium of the California Academy of Sciences.

Besides its exalted role as a leafy retreat, Golden Gate Park has served many uses during the 20C. Refugees set up temporary homes here after the 1906 earthquake. Thousands flocked here during the "Summer of Love" in 1967, when hippies hung out and crowds gathered for mass celebrations and concerts at Speedway Meadow. For most San Franciscans, Golden Gate Park serves as a big backyard—a place for family picnics, neighborhood baseball games, outdoor sports and contemplative strolls.

SIGHTS

★Conservatory of Flowers – *Conservatory Dr. W. & John F. Kennedy Dr. Closed through 2002 for repair.* ☎ 415-346-4234. This ornate Victorian glass palace shelters more than 20,000 rare and exotic plants under an octagonal central dome and two flanking wings. Golden Gate Park's oldest structure, the lacy white wood-frame building was prefabricated in Dublin, Ireland, modeled after the famous glasshouses of London's Kew Gardens; it was shipped to the San Jose estate of James Lick for installation. Arriving after Lick's death in 1876, the disassembled structure was purchased by a consortium of San Francisco businessmen led by Leland Stanford, and donated to Golden Gate Park. Seasonal blooms in formal geometric designs grace the parterres in front.

John McLaren Rhododendron Dell – *John F. Kennedy Dr. at 6th Ave.* At the heart of this 20-acre, spring-blooming garden stands a statue of John McLaren (**1**) contemplating a pinecone. The life-size proportions and quiet, natural pose contrast pointedly with the host of heroic bronze figures that surround the nearby Music Concourse, an ironic contradiction to McLaren's lifelong campaign to keep statues from cluttering the park's natural scenery. Stroll to the nearby bower of enormous tree ferns to experience the sensation of having entered a world of giants.

Practical Information ....Area Code: 415

Getting There – 🚌 from Market St. take **5-Fulton, 21-Hayes** and walk into park from 8th Ave. & Fulton St., or take **71-Haight–Noriega** or **N-Judah** and connect with **44-O'Shaughnessy** or walk from 9th Ave. From Fisherman's Wharf (Van Ness Ave. & North Point St.), take southbound **42-Downtown Loop**, **47-Van Ness** or **49-Van Ness/Mission** down Van Ness, transfer at McAllister St. to **5-Fulton**, walk into park at 8th Ave. From Union Square, take **38-Geary**, transfer to **44-O'Shaughnessy** at 6th Ave. From the east, Fell St. leads directly into the park, which is bounded by Fulton & Stanyan Sts., Lincoln Way and the Great Highway; Park Presidio Blvd. enters from the north, 19th Ave. from the south. Call ☎ 673-6864 for more information.

Getting Around – Golden Gate Park is laced with curving drives that emerge to connect with the city's street grid at 20 points along the park perimeter. Two main thoroughfares traverse from east to west: John F. Kennedy Dr. (north) and Martin Luther King, Jr., Dr. (south). On Sundays and most holidays, Kennedy Dr. between Kezar Dr. & 19th Ave. is closed to vehicular traffic. On Saturdays, Middle Dr. W. closes between 19th Ave. & King Dr. (south of the Polo Field). **Parking** (street and lots) is available throughout the park, although spaces fill quickly on sunny Sundays. Disabled-parking spaces are located in the Music Concourse *(fee charged weekends & holidays)*. The primary botanical and cultural attractions are situated in the park's eastern half; recreation areas occupy the western section.

Visitor Information – Park maps and event information are available at the **Beach Chalet** visitor center *(p 148)* or at **McLaren Lodge** *(501 Stanyan St. at east entrance to park; open year-round Mon–Fri 8am–5pm; ☎ 831-2700; www.parks.sfgov.org)*. The *Golden Gate Park Explorer Pass ($14)* allows the visitor one-time access to the park's main cultural attractions (California Academy of Sciences *p 146*, Asian Art Museum *p 141* and Japanese Tea Garden *p 138*); passes are available at the Academy of Sciences and the Visitors Information Center at Hallidie Plaza *(p 56)*. **Food** concessions are located in the Concourse area, Children's Playground and Stow Lake boathouse; the California Academy of Sciences and the Beach Chalet.

Recreation – Public sports facilities include baseball/softball diamonds at Big Rec Ball Field *(☎ 753-7024)* and tennis courts *(☎ 753-7027)* north of the Children's Playground. Guided horseback trail rides depart from Golden Gate Park stables located north of Golden Gate Park Stadium *(reservations required; ☎ 668-7360)*. Pedal, electric and row boats may be rented at Stow Lake *(open year-round daily 10am–4pm; ☎ 752-0347)*. The nine-hole Golden Gate Park Golf Course is located near 47th Ave. & John F. Kennedy Dr. *(☎ 751-8987)*. Paved biking and skating trails ramble the park; Middle Dr. W. is a car-free skaters' haven on Saturdays, while a portion of John F. Kennedy Dr. is dedicated to skaters and bicyclists on Sundays & holidays *(rentals at several shops along Stanyan St., and behind Stow Lake Boathouse; ☎ 668-6699)*. Extensive hiking paths wind through the park, and a variety of free walking tours are conducted May–Oct (♿ ☎ 263-0991; www.frp.org).

Children's Playground – ▨ *Kezar Dr.* ✗ A pioneering concept when it opened i 1888, this municipal playground was centered on the sandstone Sharon Building which provided refreshments, stored play equipment and stabled goats for th kids' "barnyard." Today it is a venue for art classes for children and adults Redesigned in 1978, the playground has swings and slides, a sandbox, a pla structure and a new, goat-free version of the barnyard. The magnificent Herschel Spillman **Carrousel★**, its princely stable of carved wooden animals under a dom supported by 16 fluted columns, was built in 1912 and restored in 1984 *(ope Memorial Day–Labor Day daily 10am–6pm; rest of the year Fri–Sun 10am–4:30pm closed Jan 1, Thanksgiving Day, Dec 25; $1/adult, 25¢/child; ☎ 415-753-5210)*

★★Japanese Tea Garden – ▨ *Hagiwara Tea Garden Dr. Open Apr–Oct dail 9am–5:30pm. Rest of the year daily 8:30am–5pm. $3.50. ✗ 🅿 ☎ 415-831-2700* Harboring a delightful maze of winding paths, stone lanterns, ornamental ponds bonsai, a wooden pagoda, a Zen garden and a teahouse, this tranquil, five-acre gar den has been a premier attraction since it was built for the Midwinter Fair of 1894

© Michael S. Yamashita

Japanese Tea Garden

After the fair closed, the garde continued operating under th direction of master gardene Makoto Hagiwara, who als tended the tea concession and i credited with inventing the for tune cookie here in 1909. A plaque by the front entranc honors the memory of Hagi wara and his family.

The garden is most colorfu around April, when its cherr trees burst into bloom. The ex quisitely crafted ceremonia gateway at the front entrance i a traditional feature of Japanes shrines. Inside, the steeply arch ing wooden **Moon Bridge (2** takes its name from the orb formed by the bridge and its re flection in the pond below. Nea the center of the garden sits a 10.5ft statue of *Amazarashi no-hotoke-Buddha* ("the Bud dha who sits through sun an rain without shelter"); cast in Japan in 1790, it is the larges bronze Buddha outside Asia Visitors enjoy sipping green te and nibbling delicate cookies in the open-air **teahouse (3)**.

★★Strybing Arboretum – *Martin Luther King, Jr., Dr. at 9th Ave. Open year-round Mon–Fri 8am–4:30pm, weekends & holidays 10am–5pm. Guided tours (1hr) avail able Mon–Fri 1:30pm, weekends 10:30am & 1:30pm. Contribution requested. ✗ 🄳 ☎ 415-661-1316. www.strybing.org.* Covering 70 acres of rolling terrain, this out standing botanical collection comprises 6,000 species of plants from all over th world. Arranged around a large, central lawn, its varied gardens shelter seclude benches and gentle pathways that invite leisurely contemplation. The arboretum emphasizes regions of Mediterranean climate, with significant collections from California, the Cape Province of South Africa, southwestern Australia and Chile Other attractions include a hillside garden of succulents; the New World Clou Forest, where special mist emitters supplement the San Francisco fog; the verdan Redwood Nature Trail; the Primitive Plant Garden of moss, lichen, cycads, horse tails, tree ferns and conifers; and the Moon-Viewing Garden, where East Asia plants grow around a reflecting pond in a landscape inspired by classical Chinese and Japanese principles. The adjacent Garden of Fragrances and Biblical Garde share a handsome retaining wall built of stones removed from a medieval Spanish monastery purchased by William Randolph Hearst, who had it dismantled an shipped to Golden Gate Park for reassembly. A fire destroyed the crates and iden tifying markings, leaving a great pile of indistinguishable stones from which th Park Department has drawn over the decades for a variety of masonry projects Housed in the County Fair Building to the west of the Arboretum's main entrance the **Helen Crocker Russell Library of Horticulture** *(open daily year-round 10am-4pm closed major holidays)* maintains more than 12,000 volumes and presents exhibits *(changing quarterly)* of botanical prints and other art.

GOLDEN GATE PARK
EASTERN SECTION

N ←

0 _____ 100 m
0 _____ 1/10 mi

Shrader St.
Grove St.
Hayes St.
Fell St.
Panhandle
Oak St.
Page St.
Haight St.
Waller St.
Beulah St.

Stanyan St.

McAllister St.
Fulton St.

McLaren Lodge

Kezar Drive

Children's Playground

CARROUSEL

Kezar Stadium

Frederick

Carl

Arguello Blvd.
2nd Ave.
3rd Ave.
4th Ave.
5th Ave.
6th Ave.
8th Ave.
10th Ave.
12th Ave.
14th Ave.
16th Ave.

Cabrillo

Fulton

Way
St.

CONSERVATORY OF FLOWERS

John F. Kennedy Drive

MacLaren Tennis
Lily Pond

Rhododendron Dell

1

Stow Lake

CALIFORNIA ACADEMY OF SCIENCES

Music Concourse

M.H. de Young Memorial Museum

Middle Drive East

Shakespeare Garden

Spreckels Bandstand

ASIAN ART MUSEUM

JAPANESE TEA GARDEN

3
2

Post Garden

Big Rec Ball Field

County Fair Bldg.

Library of Horticulture

STRYBING ARBORETUM

Lincoln
Hugo
Way

5th Ave.
7th Ave.
9th Ave.
11th Ave.
13th Ave.
15th Ave.
17th Ave.
19th Ave.
21st Ave.
23rd Ave.

Mann Luther King Jr. Drive

Park Presidio Blvd

John F. Kennedy Drive

Rail Presidio Bypass Drive

Fulton

Pioneer Log Cabin

428
Strawberry Hill

Stow Lake

4

Pavilion

Cross Over Drive

Prayer Book Cross
5

Blue Heron

Transverse Drive

Lloyd Lake

Portals of the Past

Speedway Meadow

Middle Drive West

Elk Glen Lake

Shakespeare Garden – *Martin Luther King, Jr., Dr. & Middle Dr. E.* Established in 1928, this small English garden nurtures plants mentioned in the works of William Shakespeare. The locked box in the back wall contains a bust of the Bard, a copy cast from the sculpted image at the poet's tomb. That image was carved by Gerard Johnson after Shakespeare's death in 1616. *Visitors who wish to see the bust must make prior arrangements at the McLaren Lodge (p 137).*

Stow Lake – 🚆 *Stow Lake Dr.; access from John F. Kennedy Dr. or Martin Luther King, Jr., Dr.* Serving as the park's main irrigation reservoir, this moat surrounding Strawberry Hill is the largest of the 15 man-made lakes and ponds that dot Golden Gate Park. Swarms of waterfowl share the water with a flotilla of small boats which may be rented from the boathouse on the northwest shore. The 428ft summit of Strawberry Hill, reached by footpath, is the highest point in the park and was famed for its panoramas of the city before trees grew to block the view. Constructed in 1894, a **waterfall** (**4**) named for industrialist Collis P. Huntington cascades 125ft from the summit to the surface of the lake. A decorative Chinese moon-viewing pavilion stands on the island's eastern shore. Immediately north of Stow Lake, **Prayer Book Cross**, a 57ft Celtic cross carved of sandstone, dominates the hill above **Rainbow Falls** (**5**).

M. H. de Young Memorial Museum – *Closed during construction of new building in 2001-05.* ☎ *415-863-3330. www.thinker.org.* Badly damaged in the 1989 Loma Prieta earthquake, the original de Young Museum has been earmarked for demolition. In its place will rise a new building by Herzog & de Meuron, a Swiss architectural firm whose designs include London's new Tate Gallery of Modern Art (2000).

A partner with the California Palace of the Legion of Honor in a single administration called the **Fine Arts Museums of San Francisco**, the de Young specializes in American fine and decorative arts from the pre-Columbian era to the present. It also has significant holdings in textiles, African and Oceanic art.

Historical Notes – The de Young Museum was established by **Michael H. de Young**, co-founder of the *San Francisco Chronicle.* Inspired by the World's Columbian Exposition in Chicago in 1893, de Young pulled together a similar spectacle, the California Midwinter International Exposition, the following year. When the fair closed, he persuaded the city's Park Commission to preserve the Egyptian Revival-style Fine Arts Building as a museum dedicated to the memory of the great fair. It opened in 1895.

Collecting with more enthusiasm than connoisseurship, de Young began to amass a great miscellany of artwork, historic artifacts and natural-history exhibits. One of the early purchases, *Caius Marius Amid the Ruins of Carthage* (1807) by US painter John Vanderlyn—a bold if unsuccessful attempt to establish an American school of monumental history painting—was significant enough to attract the interest of benefactors. Among them was the Rockefeller family. In 1978 Blanchette and John D. Rockefeller III bequeathed their extraordinary personal collection of American painting and works on paper—a gift of some 137 works that propelled the de Young to first-class status among American art museums.

Louis C. Mullgardt, architectural coordinator of the Panama-Pacific International Exposition of 1915, added east and central sections in 1919 and 1921 to the original Fine Arts Building, itself demolished as unsafe in 1929. The west wing, present home of the Asian Art Museum, was completed in 1965. When the Asian moves in 2002 to new quarters at Civic Center, however, its wing, like the rest of the de Young, will be leveled.

The Collections – The de Young's **American art★★** collection reveals great depth in portrait, landscape and genre painting, with special emphasis in *trompe l'œil* still life. Decorative work highlights furniture, silver, glass and porcelain. **Arts of the Americas★** feature ceremonial and funerary objects, some in gold and jade, from Mesoamerica and South America before 16C European intrusion. Indigenous art from the west coast of North America includes fine basketry, storage containers for intertribal "potlatch" gatherings, and rare 19C totem poles in which depictions of ancestral animal spirits rise one from another.

The museum's holdings of world **textiles** include the finest collection of high-quality Anatolian *kilims* (flat-woven pileless tapestries) outside Turkey. The **African art** exhibit contains pieces from a cross-section of agricultural sub-Saharan cultures, mostly West African. The small but beautiful collection of the **art of Oceania** concentrates on the pre-World War II arts of Polynesia, Melanesia and Micronesia.

Since 1970, the two Fine Arts Museums of San Francisco have shared conservation and education resources, while the division of functions—the Palace of the Legion of Honor is devoted solely to European art, from antiquity to modern—promotes acquisition without competition or duplication. Current plans aim at strengthening the de Young's profile in early-20C American and late-20C Bay Area art, with a view to presenting contemporary art in the context of earlier traditions. Already, the de Young has accepted 14 Gottardo Piazzoni murals for transfer from the old Main Library into which the Asian Art Museum is moving.

The New de Young – The new three-story museum building is slated for completion in 2005. To be constructed of recycled redwood, eucalyptus and copper, it will occupy two fewer acres of parkland than the existing building, but will boast nearly double the gallery space. According to the architect's plans, patrons will enter through a glass-flanked esplanade to a grand public area for civic events. Skylights and windows will flood the galleries with natural light. First-floor rooms will hold 20C American art and the ancient and native arts of the Americas. The second floor will feature the African and Oceanic collections, and will contain a light-controlled area with a study center for the textile collection. Temporary shows will be presented in the basement level. A 10-story Education Tower with an observation deck will rise at the museum's northeast corner; a courtyard café and outdoor sculpture parks will surround the new building.

★★THE ASIAN ART MUSEUM

Open Wed–Sun 9:30am–5pm (1st Wed 8:45pm). Closed major holidays; closes permanently Oct. 7, 2001, in preparation for move to Civic Center. $7 (free 1st Wed). Tours (1hr) by request. ✗ ♿ ▣ ☏ *415-379-8880. www.asianart.org.*

Possessing what is today considered the finest collection of Asian art in the nation, this museum was born of the efforts of collector and Olympic advocate Avery Brundage. With particular strengths in Chinese art, including jades, ceramics, ritual bronzes and paintings from the Ming and Qing dynasties, the collection of some 12,000 works also boasts the nation's most comprehensive assemblage of Japanese art. There also are significant holdings of Indian and Southeast Asian religious statuary, and Korean, Himalayan and Near Eastern artwork.

Historical Notes – The museum's founder, **Avery Brundage** (1887-1975), represented the US in the decathlon during the 1912 Olympics in Stockholm, Sweden, and enjoyed an extremely prosperous career as an engineering executive before being appointed to the International Olympic Committee in the 1920s. During his extensive travels around the world in this capacity, he became fascinated by East Asian cultures, adopted a Taoist philosophy, and launched a collection of Japanese woodblock prints and netsuke—carved bone toggles used to fasten men's kimono sashes. His passion for collecting broadened in the 1930s to embrace 3,000-year-old Chinese bronzes, Chinese ceramics and objects from Korea, Southeast Asia, India and its neighbors, and the Middle East.
By the 1950s, Brundage began to search for a permanent museum that could conserve and display his then-uncataloged collection of 5,000 pieces. Anticipating closer relations with Pacific Rim nations, and believing his museum would be a "bridge of international knowledge and respect," he selected San Francisco—with its growing reputation as a gateway to the Pacific Rim—as an ideal location. After protracted negotiations, Brundage presented a portion of his collection to the city in 1959. The city-owned Asian Art Museum opened in 1966. Following Brundage's death in 1975, the museum continued to acquire and catalog Asian artwork. Other benefactors stepped forward to donate works, including important collections of Indian miniature paintings, Thai ceramics, and other Chinese and Japanese works. Able to display only 12 to 15 percent of the collection at any given time, the museum has long outgrown its present home. In the early 1990s, the city decided to relocate the Asian and its Chong-Moon Lee Center for Asian Art and Culture to the Beaux-Arts-style, former Main Library building at Civic Center. The four-story venue will increase exhibit space by 30 percent at a cost of $151 million. The museum will close at Golden Gate Park in October 2001 and is scheduled to reopen at the Civic Center in November 2002.

Visiting the Asian Art Museum – Three galleries to the left of Gruhn Court, the central hall, host high-quality temporary exhibitions. Against the court's west side, the brilliant Treasure Wall, designed after Qing dynasty Empress Dowager Cixi's treasure case in Beijing's Forbidden City, contains colorful ceramics, sculptures and carvings from throughout Asia and serves as an overview of the museum's collections. Chinese and Korean galleries are on the first floor; the second floor houses the Japanese, Himalayan, Southeast Asian and Indian galleries; Near Eastern artifacts are displayed along the second-floor loggia. To accommodate its limited display space, the museum regularly rotates exhibits so that even objects of primary importance are not always on view.

★★Chinese Art *1st floor*

Comprising over half the museum's holdings, the Chinese collection numbers some 6,000 bronzes, sculptures, paintings and decorative arts. The works exemplify the beauty and diversity of Chinese art from Neolithic times to the present, while the comprehensive collection of pottery, vases, tableware and figurines thoroughly illustrates the momentous history of ceramics in China.

The Neolithic Age in China yielded a wealth of earthenware pottery, stone craft and jade. The museum's oldest pot, a small earthenware **bottle** from the Yangshou culture, dates from 4800–3600 BC. **Oracle bones**, created by priests to divine the future, represent the first evidence of written language in China. Neolithic artisan were already producing **jades** in the characteristic doughnut shape, called *bi*, which has remained a popular finished shape for jade throughout Chinese history. Harder than steel, jade was revered for its durability, and was believed to possess a life preserving property.

Shang dynasty ritual bronzes, made to contain tomb offerings, include three-legged pots called *ding*, decorated on the outer surfaces with intricate spirals and monster heads. A highlight is a **ritual vessel** (12C BC) shaped like a rhinoceros. Composite animals and decorative surface carvings characterize later Zhou dynasty bronzes. Depleting resources of bronze caused the Han dynasty government to ban the placement of ritual bronzes in tombs except among aristocrats, resulting in alternative use of pottery tomb offerings. Stoneware and lacquerware also developed during this era; the museum owns China's oldest-known **lacquer vessel** (1 AD) with a maker's mark.

Indian influences permeate early works of Chinese Buddhist art. Among them i the earliest known Chinese **Buddha image** (AD 338), a gilt bronze representation o the Indian prince who became the Buddha—recognizable by its extended earlobe and a cranial protuberance signifying wisdom. The worldly confidence of the Tang dynasty encouraged an appreciation of simplicity, exemplified by the draperies on Buddhist images. Their cultural dynamism also shows in secular works, particularly in the **sancai tomb figures**—three-color ceramic statues depicting horses, Bactrian camels and foreign traders. The Tang dynasty also developed cobalt-blue glazes and true porcelain, a hard, white ceramic of kaolin clay that rings when struck.

■ Highlights of the Chinese Dynasties

Neolithic Period (c.5000–16C BC): Regional cultures emerge, with distinct craft traditions in clay, stone, bone, basketry and textiles.

Shang Dynasty (1122–1028 BC): Transition to Bronze Age is marked by the rise of cities and rival clans. Remarkable piece-mold technique is invented for casting shapely bronze vessels.

Zhou Dynasty (1122–256 BC): Prosperity during unsettled era of state-making creates a market for objects of extreme technical refinement and splendor.

Qin Dynasty (221–206 BC): Short-lived dynasty marks beginnings of imperial China; the Great Wall is unified and a common script is established.

Han Dynasty (206 BC–AD 220): Major dynasty forges a single Chinese nation and imposes a long period of peace marked by expansion and the coming of Buddhism. Prosperity encourages trade along the Silk Road, bringing in foreign influences. The decorative dragon becomes prominent, along with layered and inlaid bronzework.

Six Dynasties (AD 317–589): Empire splits into rival states.

Sui Dynasty (AD 581–618): Empire is reunited; Grand Canal is built. Potters improve glazing techniques.

Tang Dynasty (AD 618–907): Expansive dynasty blossoms into powerful nation, open to foreign trade and spreading Chinese influence, especially to Japan. Aristocratic burial rites are increasingly elaborate; tomb furnishings proliferate in quality and quantity. Buddhism flourishes. **AD 907-1125:** Empire breaks down into individual states, including the northern **Liao dynasty** (937-1125).

Song Dynasty (AD 960–1279): Humanistic age of extreme aesthetic richness is renowned for fine and varied ceramics and painting. Nomads establish **Jin dynasty** (1115-1234) in the north, but the court moves south to Hangzhou and continues to govern as a sub-dynasty known as the **Southern Song** (1217-1279).

Yuan Dynasty (AD 1279–1368): Mongol dynasty favors blue-and-white porcelains to trade with Islamic nations.

Ming Dynasty (AD 1368–1644): Return to native rule is a classic age of blue-and-white wares.

Qing Dynasty (AD 1644–1911): Period of foreign rule under Manchus features ceramics of brilliant color and eggshell translucency. Contact with West increases.

Horse with Bridle, Tang Dynasty

Asian Art Museum of San Francisco, Avery Brundage Collection

Ceramics reached a peak during the Song dynasty with the development of green celadon glazes, light-blue Jun ware and the opaque, glassy, blue-green glaze of Longquan ware. A rougher form of pottery was introduced to Japan during this dynasty, ironically carried home from southern Chinese monasteries by Japanese monks. Particularly interesting are the bronze wire burial suit and bronze mask from the short-lived Liao dynasty.

During the Yuan dynasty, potters added kaolin clay, making glazes thicker and more opaque. The Ming dynasty is noted for the proliferation of glazing and decorating techniques, five-color ware. Western tastes were profoundly influenced by the blue-and-white ware exported from the late Ming dynasty onward.

Unlike post-Renaissance art from the West, which relies on a fixed perspective, Chinese (and Japanese) **landscape painting** traditionally employs a "floating" perspective that invites the eye to enter the painting and to move from feature to feature, promoting a meditation on nature. The museum's broad collection focuses on Ming and Qing masters and includes monumental landscapes and still-life scrolls from the 13C to the present. The museum also holds many examples of **calligraphy**, emphasizing the different script styles of the Ming dynasty.

★Korean Art *1st floor*

The 500-odd objects of the Korean collection include hanging scrolls, stoneware ceramics from the Three Kingdoms and United Silla periods (57 BC–AD 935), gold jewelry, ash-glazed funerary pottery (cinerary ware) and celadon-glazed vessels from the Koryo period (AD 918–1392). Though less prolific than the Chinese, Korean potters produced many unique ceramic forms, including gourd-shaped bottles with red-pigment celadon glaze. Two slate **daggers** (c.500–600 BC) are the museum's oldest Korean artifacts. Important Buddhist objects include sculptures, bronze vessels and implements, paintings, lacquerware and furniture. A gilt bronze sculpture of *Amitabha Buddha* (8C), the largest specimen of such quality in a Western collection. Exceptional portraits include *Buddha Amitabha and Eight Great Bodhisattvas* (14C) and *A King of Hell* (16C).

★★Japanese Art *2nd floor*

With more than 4,200 objects, the Japanese holdings are the most comprehensive in the US. Highlights are screens and scroll paintings, ceramics, bronzes, religious sculptures, swords and decorative arts. The museum also has splendid collections of *netsuke* miniatures in horn and ivory, and Japanese calligraphy representing different styles and formats from the 12C–20C.

Among prehistoric treasures are earthenware pottery, bronze *dotaku* (bells), mirrors and weapons, and a wealth of *haniwa* (retaining posts for burial mounds) fashioned in the shapes of animals, houses, boats and people. Sculptures of the Nara to Meiji periods were made of wood, bronze and dry-lacquer, a technique that involves applying lacquer-soaked cloths to a clay core that is later removed. Many Buddhist temples of various sects were built with powerful statues of ferocious guardians standing on misshapen demons: "dwarves of ignorance." Buddhist sculpture and painting reached their zenith during the Kamakura period, as the

■ History of Japan

Prehistoric Age (c.12,000 BC–AD 552): Contact with China and Korea after c.300 BC brings new technologies to pottery; metal tools and bronze bells (*dotaku*) develop. In **Kofun Period** (AD 250–552), imperial Japan takes form.

Asuka to Nara Periods (552–710): Buddhism enters Japan from China via Korea. Along with religious influences, Japan imports Chinese writing, tea and styles of architecture, sculpture and painting.

Heian Period (794–1185): Capital moves from Nara to Heian-kyo (now Kyoto).

Kamakura Period (1185–1333): Rise of the warrior class of samurai. Zen (a Buddhist sect encouraging intellectual spiritualism based on meditation) arrives from southern China. The arts and the tea ceremony become secularized.

Muromachi Period (1333–1573): Under strong shogunate rule, a flourishing of Zen—and reaction against it—infuses the arts, particularly painting and the tea ceremony.

Momoyama Period (1573–1615): Warlords battle for control of Japan while Western traders and missionaries make their first landings on the Japanese coast.

Edo Period (1615–1868): The shogun Tokugawa Ieyasu moves the capital to Tokyo and seals the country from foreign arrivals; a strict class structure (samurai, farmers, craftsmen and merchants) is established. Ensuing prosperity allows the diffusion of art through a broad swath of society.

Meiji Period (1868–1912): Following the 1853-54 visit of US Commodore Matthew Perry, Japan is compelled to abandon isolationist policies and open trade with the US and Europe. Modernization becomes paramount after a new imperial government overthrows the weakening Tokugawa shogunate.

arrival of Zen inspired artistic expression characterized in painting by monotone landscapes that fade to blankness. The demand for **samurai swords** pushed the manufacture of Japanese steel to a high art, involving ritual instructions that required repeated pounding, folding and immersions in water.

Nearly 200 screens (only a handful on display at any time) represent major schools and styles of painting. Among them are the colorful Yamato-e style, monochrome Kanga landscapes, and the abstract, minimalist Haboku (splashed ink) style, a technique expressive of Zen spontaneity. By the middle of the Muromachi period non-religious painters of the Kano school—which rejected the narrative traditions of painting to emphasize poetic simplicity of image and line—plied their arts on large screens that were used for blocking drafts and brightening dark castles.

A traditional **Japanese tea ceremony exhibit** displays a whisk for frothing the tea and roughly formed Temmoku teaware—a reflection of the secular Japanese appreciation for *wabi* (poverty) and *sabi* (rusticity).

The arrival of Western missionaries during the turbulent Momoyama period served as a favorite subject of secular painters. Many painting schools flourished during the Edo period, as did the arts of lacquerware, ceramics and stage drama. Highly decorated items from this era include *inro* (small cases for personal effects), a fine koto (13-stringed zither), an exquisitely lacquered palanquin, and woodblock prints. The Meiji period enriched contact between Japanese artists and the outside world, reaffirming traditional arts and introducing new themes, styles and techniques.

★Tibetan and Himalayan Art *2nd floor*

This fascinating gallery contains about 300 items from Nepal, Tibet and Bhutan, overwhelmingly religious art including scriptures, gilt bronze sculptures of Hindu and Buddhist gods, and Nepalese and Tibetan scroll paintings known as *thangkas*. Both Hindu and Buddhist subjects are popular and coexist peacefully in vivid Nepalese paintings. Exhibits embrace spectacular shrines produced by Newar artisans from the 8C–19C, mostly metalwork inlaid with semiprecious stones.

Tibetan arts are influenced by Nepal, India and China. Buddhism in Tibet dates from the 7C, introduced by the Chinese and Nepalese queens of King Srongtsen Gampo. The dominant school, Tantrism, is based on the belief that enlightenment can be achieved through esoteric practices. Tibetan artworks, with fantastic, terrifying and beautiful imagery, are unique expressions of Buddhist practice and wisdom. Ritual implements are made of precious metal and gems, and even human bone. Most common in Tibet are the bell (*drilbu*) and thunderbolt (*dorje*), respectively representing the feminine attribute of wisdom and the male property of skillful means, both necessary for enlightenment.

Bhutan is renowned for textiles woven on backstrap and floor looms in cotton, wool and silk. Patterns, usually with stripes—vertical for men and horizontal for women—differ between households.

The museum's *thangka* collection is one of the largest in a public American institution. These scrolls—120 examples from the 12C–20C—are made of sized cotton and brilliantly painted. Only a few are exhibited at any given time.

★★Indian Art *2nd floor*

A wealth of religious statuary in stone, bronze, terra-cotta and wood represents sculptural styles from every regional school and spans all major periods of Indian art from the 3C BC to AD 19C. The collection also boasts carved ivories, jades and fine miniature paintings, as well as artists' prints of British India (c.1780–1910). The distinctive Gandhara style developed in what is now southern Afghanistan and northern Pakistan. As Gandhara was situated at a crossroads on the Silk Road between East and West, its sculpture reflects a Hellenistic and Roman style of carving, illustrated by a splendid rendition of a 2C–3C Bodhisattva adorned with earrings, mustache, flowing robes, elaborate hairstyle and copious jewelry. Outstanding are eight fragments of **friezes** depicting the life of Shakyamuni, the Indian prince who became the Buddha, from birth (emerging from the right side of his mother, Maya) to his death on a couch while teaching his grieving disciples. More typical in flavor is the Hindu and Jain sculpture of Mathura, capital of the Kushan empire. Most South Indian sculpture employed hard granitic rock, though bronze statues were also created. The Mysore region produced delicate schist carvings: an example is a seated Ganesha (13C)–one of 14 museum statues of the elephant-headed god—which regularly receives "offerings" from museum patrons. Sandstone dominated sculpture in central and western India. Many works decorated the outsides of temples; a prominent example is a 5C **lingam**, a phallic symbol and cult image of the Hindu god Shiva. Pala sculptures from east India were carved in a fine-grained schist that permitted intricate details, smooth surfaces and technical sophistication. The style directly influenced Southeast Asian and Himalayan art.

■ Selected Hindu Deities

Brahma: The Creator, one of the Hindu triad of supreme gods.

Devi: A Hindu goddess whose many forms include Uma, consort of Shiva; Parvati, mother of Ganesha; and ferocious Durga, slayer of the Buffalo Demon.

Ganesha: The elephant-headed son of Shiva and Parvati, beloved as the god of wisdom and wealth.

Krishna: An incarnation of Vishnu, among the most beloved of Hindu gods. Krishna is often depicted as a handsome young man with blue skin.

Shiva: The Destroyer, most widely worshipped of the chief gods, wears his hair matted, carries a cobra and trident, and appears as teacher, itinerant wanderer or force of destruction. By clearing chaff for new growth, he is also a creator.

Vishnu: The Preserver, one of the Hindu triad of supreme gods. Vishnu wears a crown and carries a conch, lotus, discus and club, and can take many forms.

★Southeast Asian Art *2nd floor*

The collection comprises more than 500 pieces from mainland and insular Southeast Asia (Thailand, Burma, Laos, Cambodia, Vietnam, Malaysia, Indonesia and the Philippines). Sculptures constitute much of the collection, which has grown to include textiles (especially Thai and Lao silks), weaponry (highlighted by examples of the sinuous gilt *kris*, a Malay-Indonesian dagger), jewelry and manuscripts. Hindu and Buddhist sculptural motifs influenced by Indian art have been vigorously reinterpreted: A spectacular example is a 12C Cambodian carved-stone lintel depicting an army of monkeys attacking a demon from the Indian epic *The Ramayana*. The holdings also include an important collection of Thai ceramics.

Islamic and Ancient Persian Art *2nd floor loggia*

The museum owns about 450 Near Eastern objects spanning 6,000 years from prehistoric through Islamic medieval periods, including painted earthenware, glazed ceramics and metal objects. Particularly fine are the Luristani bronzes (c.1000–650 BC) and ceramics from the 15C Timurid dynasty of Tamerlane, who ruled from Samarkand.

★★CALIFORNIA ACADEMY OF SCIENCES

🅺🅸🅳🆂 *Open Memorial Day–Labor Day daily 9am–6pm (1st Wed of month to 8:45pm). Rest of the year daily 10am–5pm. $8.50. Guided tours (2hrs 30min) available.* ✕ ♿ 🅿 ☏ *415-750-7145. www.calacademy.org.*

The oldest scientific institution in the West, the California Academy of Sciences has maintained its sense of mission—to explore and interpret the natural world—while celebrating nature's biodiversity and the endlessly varied survival strategies among its species. Three separate divisions compose this multifaceted institution: the Natural History Museum, one of the 10 largest in the world, harboring more than 14 million specimens; the Steinhart Aquarium, oldest in the US, presenting more than 185 exhibits; and the Morrison Planetarium, taking the theme of development over time beyond the limits of Earth and into the far reaches of space.

Historical Notes – Founded in 1853 in a surge of post-Gold Rush enthusiasm for knowledge about California's physical environment, the Academy of Sciences began as a clubby group of naturalists who collected specimens and presented scholarly papers in an office on Clay Street. As public interest in its educational and information-gathering efforts increased, the Academy began to function as a natural-history museum. In 1891 the organization took up residence at 833 Market St., in a building bequeathed by local philanthropist James Lick. Charles Crocker and Leland Stanford were among those who donated funds for an exhibit to display birds, mammals, plants and other specimens from the collections.

The Market Street building and most of its contents were destroyed by the earthquake and fire of 1906, but the institution had become so popular that San Francisco's citizenry voted to re-establish it in Golden Gate Park. The first unit of the present facility, the North American Hall of Birds and Mammals, opened in 1916. Subsequent developments expanded the natural-history museum and added the Steinhart Aquarium in 1923 and the Morrison Planetarium in 1952.

Today, interactive computerized stations and study collections enable the Academy's legion of scientists to share their current research discoveries with visitors. Eight departments—Anthropology, Aquatic Biology, Botany, Entomology, Herpetology, Ichthyology, Invertebrate Zoology and Geology, and Ornithology and Mammalogy—maintain impressive holdings and pursue active research. The **Biodiversity Resource Center** (**A**) provides access (through videotapes, optical laser disks and CD-ROM databases) to information on efforts to preserve biodiversity worldwide. The **Academy Library** holds 170,000 books and 2,100 current journals.

Visiting the Academy of Sciences – From the ticket booth, visitors enter **Cowell Hall**, where the skeleton of a tyrannosaur extends a greeting from an era that ended 65 million years ago. The hall hosts temporary exhibits and the Academy Store, selling books, gift items and contemporary art. Steps lead down to a cafeteria that opens onto a cheerful patio. Natural-history exhibit halls extend to the sides, while the Steinhart Aquarium lies directly opposite, across the Fountain Courtyard.

CALIFORNIA ACADEMY OF SCIENCES

★★Natural History Museum

In this section of the tripartite Academy, interpretive exhibits invite visitor participation. In addition to the permanent displays, two major special exhibitions are mounted each year in **Wattis Hall**.

★Wild California – This long, cavernous hall originally housed the North American Hall of Birds and Mammals. Current dioramas present habitat groups in California's widely varied multitude of ecosystems, including bobcats prowling the glades of an oak woodland, pronghorn antelopes grazing the plains of the Great Basin, and grizzly bears clawing for roots on a mountain slope. Intensely magnified exhibits depict underwater and kelp-forest bio-communities. Wall-mounted speaker phones give detailed information related to video sequences shown on monitors at each habitat. At the far end of the hall, behind a replicated battleground for life-size elephant seals, a saltwater **surge tank** (**B**) recreates the surf zone on the rugged Farallon Islands off San Francisco's Pacific Coast.

In the **Gem and Mineral Hall** *(adjacent to Wild California)*, displays drawn from the Academy's permanent collection distinguish gems from minerals and minerals from rock. Specimens are organized from simplest to most complex chemical composition and are grouped according to type and structure, with special attention to their physical and optical qualities. Among thousands of minerals, only 70 are classified as gems—for their purity, rareness, beauty and durability.

★African Safari – Denizens of Africa's tropical heart inhabit the masterfully painted dioramas of this enormous, barrel-vaulted hall. Created in 1934, the room exhibits giraffes, antelopes, gazelles and other large herbivores sustained by savanna grasses over most of the African continent. Their carnivorous predators, including lions, cheetahs, jackals and leopards, illustrate the interdependence of the region's life forms. The most dramatic exhibit is the **Watering Hole** (**C**), showcasing a populous and interdependent community of animals gathered to drink while lighting effects and sounds—recorded on location in Africa—mimic a shortened version of the diurnal cycle. Adjoining this hall is the **African Experience**, an interactive play area for younger children.

The **Elkus Collection** focuses on the evolution of art and culture among indigenous peoples of western North America. Traditional and contemporary pottery, basketry, metalwork, weaving, woodcarving and painting are featured—from the Pueblo, Hopi and Navajo of the Southwest to the Haida and Inupiat of Canada and Alaska. In the **Far Side of Science** (**D**) gallery, original cartoons by Gary Larson embody the artist's zany take on the scientific method. The **Human Cultures Gallery** showcases changing anthropological and photographic displays.

★Earth and Space Hall – Visitors can discover earthquakes, volcanoes and space exploration through exhibits designed to promote understanding of the Earth's position in the solar system and the dynamic forces within it. Sundials, pendulums, chronometers and navigational devices illustrate the ways time and distance have been measured throughout history. Other displays examine space voyaging and the Hubble space telescope. Step on a scale to find out how much you'd weigh on various planets, view a moon rock collected by astronauts on the Apollo 17 mission, or watch an immense Foucault pendulum knock down a peg every 22 minutes to confirm the Earth's rotation beneath its swing.

Perhaps most memorable are the images screened in the **EarthQuake Theater**, a 15min show *(standing room only)* that simulates tremors as strong as 8.3 on the Richter Scale—equal in magnitude to the great San Francisco quake of 1906.

★★Life Through Time – *Self-guided audio tours ($1) available for rental at main ticket booth.* This challenging, yet enormously informative, permanent exhibit—subtitled "The Evidence for Evolution"—traces adaptations of body structures over 3.5 billion years. An interactive computer program called "LIFEmap" allows users to select a life form and explore its sequence of development, learning through the use of branching diagrams how all living things are interconnected and why certain forms are more closely related than others. An entire wall composed of striated layers of fossil-bearing rock shows relative geological age, and the highlight exhibit, **Age of Dinosaurs**, traces changes in morphology as the immense creatures adapted to life on land—and then failed to adapt to abrupt geological change.

★Morrison Planetarium

🔲 *Enter at Earth and Space Hall. Shows Jul–Aug Mon–Fri 11:30am, 12:30pm, 2pm & 3:30pm, weekends noon–4pm hourly. Rest of the year Mon–Fri 2pm, weekends 11am–4pm hourly. Laser shows weekends 5pm. Closed Thanksgiving Day & Dec 25. $2.50 (laserium $7).* ♿ ☎ *415-750-7141. www.calacademy.org/planetarium.*

The Academy's planetarium was the first to be constructed entirely in the US. Its star projector, the instrument that casts images upon the central dome, was successfully improvised in 1948 by Academy technicians who had gained expertise making and repairing optical instruments for the US Navy during World War II. The planetarium staff produces six shows a year on such topics as recent discoveries, celestial navigation and upcoming events: comets, meteor showers and eclipses.

★ Steinhart Aquarium

Kids *Open same hours as California Academy of Sciences. Guided tours (1hr) available. ☎ 415-750-7145. www.calacademy.org/aquarium.*

Founded in 1923, the oldest operating aquarium in the US boasts an unusually diverse collection of fish from around the globe. Strolling past the various aquariums, visitors learn why fish school, see how environmental degradation affects undersea life, explore the effects of wave action, witness camouflage techniques enabling ocean and freshwater fish to blend into their various habitats, and observe symbiotic partnerships (such as that between grouper and wrasse).

Visit – In the steamy **Swamp** near the aquarium's entry, dim-eyed crocodilians laze about in foliage-filtered light. Proceed clockwise around the **Reptiles and Amphibians (E)** to the darkened hall where freshwater and saltwater fish glide and glimmer in lighted tanks. Don't miss the display of fish that use electricity for communication and defense (the electric eel may be hard to spot when inactive). Next to the **Penguin Environment**, with its breeding colony of South African black-footed penguins (sometimes called "jackass penguins" for their characteristic braying noise), lies the **Coral Reef**, an entire symbiotic community of coral plants and invertebrate animals. The reef is among the first ever to be maintained in an aquarium. The intriguing **Fish Roundabout★** places visitors in the center of a doughnut-shaped, 100,000-gallon tank to observe the schooling behavior of fast-swimming ocean fish. At its base, the **Touch Tidepool** draws children, especially, to extend fingers toward a sea anemone's tentacles or study the underside of a starfish. *(Visitors can watch fish being fed at 1:30pm daily, penguins at 11:30am & 4pm daily.)*

ADDITIONAL SIGHTS IN THE PARK

The western section of Golden Gate Park, from Stow Lake to the ocean, abounds with great stretches of meadows, woods, sports facilities and minor attractions. Reflected in Lloyd Lake, the portico known as **Portals of the Past** is all that remains of a Nob Hill mansion destroyed in the earthquake and fire of 1906; it was moved here in 1909 to commemorate the disaster. Halfway to the ocean from Stow Lake lies the immense **Polo Field**; although it no longer hosts polo matches, simultaneous football, rugby, soccer and lacrosse games are often held here, and runners, bicyclists and equestrians avail themselves of its concentric tracks.

At **Spreckels Lake**, model-boat enthusiasts launch their own radio-controlled vessels. A bit farther west along John F. Kennedy Drive, at the **Bison Paddock** **Kids**, a small herd of the shaggy beasts grazes under eucalyptus trees.

In the park's northwest corner, the small but beautifully cultivated **Queen Wilhelmina Tulip Gardens** *(bloom early spring)* provide a setting for the **Dutch Windmill★** **Kids** (1902), one of the world's largest, which pumped water for park irrigation until 1929. The windmill was restored for decorative purposes in 1981. Its companion, the **Murphy Windmill** (1905) in the park's southwest corner, still awaits restoration.

★ Beach Chalet – *Open year-round daily 9am–6pm. Closed Dec 25. Guided tours (30min) available.* ✗ ♿ 🄿 ☎ *415-751-2766.* The last structure ever designed by architect Willis Polk, this Spanish Colonial-style pavilion (1921)—bordering the Great Highway on the park's western edge—operated for years as a workingman's bar. The structure is graced with some of the city's finest WPA-funded **murals★**, frescoes executed in 1937 by Lucien Labaudt. Contrary to the toil honored in the Coit Tower murals, the Beach Chalet scenes depict recreation and diversion. The frescoes have been carefully restored and the building's main floor modified to serve as a park **visitor center**. An elegantly sinuous bannister, designed by Labaudt in the form of a serpent and carved of honey-hued magnolia wood, leads to a second-floor brew pub and restaurant.

15 • HAIGHT-ASHBURY

🚌 bus 6–Parnassus, 7–Haight, 33–Stanyan, 37–Corbett, 43–Masonic, 66–Quintara or 71–Haight-Noriega; streetcar N–Judah.
Map opposite

Although more than three decades have passed since the Human Be-In and Summer of Love, a countercultural ethos still clings to Haight-Ashbury, usually called "the Haight." Named for two streets intersecting at its heart, this neighborhood draws hordes of young people to its parks and sidewalks, thrift stores and coffeehouses. With 90 percent of its housing stock predating 1922, the Haight boasts some of the city's loveliest Victorian homes, attracting a steady influx of ambitious remodelers since the mid-1970s. Today this area, nestled between Golden Gate Park and its Panhandle, Buena Vista Park and Frederick Street, manages to nurture both its turn-of-the-20C roots and its anarchic ones to create a colorful, eclectic community.

Historical Notes

Culture... – Before the early 1870s, the neighborhood was a sandy scrubland sparsely populated by farmers. As San Francisco's population skyrocketed, a committee of city officials—Supervisors Ashbury, Clayton, Cole, Shrader and Stanyan among them—determined the city's westward expansion. In addition to establishing a street grid (imposing their own names on several streets), the supervisors reserved large spaces for public use, including Golden Gate Park and its Panhandle.

As these parks developed, a resort area took shape in the neighborhood surrounding Stanyan Street. The Haight Street Cable Railroad began regular runs from Market Street in 1883; hotels, restaurants, saloons and shops appeared; and a California League baseball field was built in 1887 north of Waller Street. Beginning in 1895 **The Chutes**, an amusement park on the south side of Haight Street between Cole and Clayton streets, drew large crowds with its vaudeville theater, zoo, carnival rides and 300ft water slide. Property values quintupled and new homes proliferated so rapidly that the architectural style of the day, Queen Anne, continues to characterize the Haight more than a century later.

By the early 1900s the area was predominantly residential. As the baseball field and amusement park were dismantled, new shops and restaurants opened along Haight Street between Stanyan Street and Masonic Avenue. For two decades, the neighborhood remained solidly middle-class. In the 1920s the advent of the automobile opened relatively far-flung Twin Peaks and the Sunset District to development, diminishing the Haight's appeal as a "streetcar suburb." During the Great Depression, many Haight-Ashbury homes were sold or divided into apartments; rents plunged and buildings deteriorated as absentee ownership rose.

... And Counterculture – By the 1950s the neighborhood hosted an eclectic mix of students, gays, blacks and beatniks fleeing tourist-ridden North Beach. A decade later, the Haight blossomed into a countercultural haven, celebrating rock music, mind-altering drugs and free love. An estimated 20,000 people crammed into Golden Gate Park in January 1967 for Timothy Leary and Allen Ginsberg's **Human Be-In**, an anti-establishment celebration featuring poetry readings and rock concerts. Jerry Garcia's Grateful Dead held court at 710 Ashbury St.; neighbors included Janis Joplin and members of Jefferson Airplane. Together these musicians invented the wandering, melodic San Francisco Sound that catapulted them to international fame. Haight-Ashbury reached its peak later that year during what became known as the **Summer of Love**, when some 75,000 young people flocked to the neighborhood, sleeping in Golden Gate Park and attending free rock concerts and parties.

In 1968, many hippies left the Haight for rural communes, and heroin replaced LSD and marijuana as the drug of choice. By 1971, more than a third of the shops on Haight Street were boarded up, and violent crime soared. Yet the neighborhood survived to experience a gentrification movement later that decade. Crime dropped as incomes and property values rose. By 1980 the Haight had re-emerged as the middle-class enclave it had been a century before.

Hanging in the Haight

Today the Haight is more mainstream than it was during its late 60s heyday. Despite citizen protest, several chain stores have appeared in the neighborhood, and a new wave of upscale designer-clothing shops and restaurants have opened to serve young professionals. But disaffected youths still congregate on street corners and in Golden Gate Park, along with middle-aged denizens whose appearance seems only to have grayed since 1967. Quirky collectors flock to the area's comic shops and vintage magazine stores, and hipsters hang out in Haight Street cafes. Even as the Queen Annes are restored to their late-19C beauty, vestiges of the 60s live on.

Residential Architecture – Hundreds of unique, eye-catching Victorian period houses, most in the Queen Anne style, adorn Haight-Ashbury. Characterized by asymmetrical massing, a panoply of external surfaces and designs, bay windows and sometimes turrets, the homes date primarily from the building boom of the 1880s and 90s. Because houses in the Haight were so much in demand, Queen Annes were frequently built in rows of four or five similar structures, but a variety of color and detailing options provided ample opportunity for homeowners to distinguish their abodes from their neighbors'. A stroll along Central Avenue or Page, Masonic or Waller streets reveals fanciful examples of Queen Annes, many restored during the gentrification trend that swept the neighborhood in the 1980s and 90s. The rows at **1214-1256 Masonic Avenue** and **1315-1335 Waller Street★** embody the spirit of the style.

SIGHTS

★Haight Street – Lined with coffee shops, clothing stores, nightclubs and restaurants, Haight Street from Stanyan Street to Central Avenue bustles day and night. The narrow sidewalks teem with skaters, shoppers, tourists and occasional street performers; incense wafts from New Age shops; and rock music pulses from frenetic thrift stores where patrons wait in line to trade old duds for new duds. While the buildings here are not the district's most distinguished, some, like the colorful, curvaceous structure at **no. 1679-81** (1904, James F. Dunn), display a certain charm. At the corner of Haight and Clayton stand the Haight-Ashbury Free Clinics, providing free, quality health care since 1967.

 Bound Together: An Anarchist Book Collective *1369 Haight St.* ☏ *415-431-8355.* For over two decades, this outlet has served up required reading for the counterculture: books, magazines and pamphlets on alternative thinking, vegetarianism, and the remaking of a new society on the ruins of the old. The store keepers are volunteers, often writers, easy to talk to and ready to answer questions.

Buena Vista Park – Rising abruptly south of Haight Street, this sylvan hill boasts a children's playground, two secluded tennis courts and tantalizing glimpses of the city from between the trees that crowd its steep slopes. The 36.5-acre park was reserved for public use in 1867, and John McLaren supervised the planting of cypress, live oak, pine and eucalyptus trees during the early 1900s. In recent years, non-native plants have been removed and underbrush cleared from the hillside. Visitors who make the bracing climb along footpaths to the summit are rewarded with sweeping **views** of San Francisco residential areas stretching away toward bay and ocean.

★St. Ignatius Church – *650 Parker Ave. at Fulton St. Open year-round Sun–Fri 8am–5pm, Sat 8am–6pm.* ☎ *415-422-2188. www.stignatiussf.org.* This imposing domed Renaissance Revival church (1914, Charles J. Devlin), on the campus of Jesuit-affiliated University of San Francisco, features two 213ft towers on either side of a facade dominated by Corinthian columns, atop Ionic columns, separated by a portico. A campanile at the northeast corner houses a three-ton bell cast in England in 1859.

The interior design is based on early Christian basilicas. A deeply coffered ceiling, free-standing columns and arches offer a dramatic framework for the sanctuary, whose paintings, iconography and ornate stained-glass windows were added between 1938 and 1962. A polychrome white-oak baldachin stands over an altar of Italian marble with Moroccan onyx inlays, containing relics of St. Ignatius.

ADDITIONAL SIGHTS

Josephine D. Randall Jr. Museum – Kids *199 Museum Way, Corona Heights. From Haight St., take Masonic Ave. south to Roosevelt Way; turn left, then right after three blocks on Museum Way. Open year-round Tue–Sat 10am–5pm. Closed major holidays.* ☎ *415-554-9600. www.randallmuseum.org.* This family-oriented science museum sits at the end of a dead-end street with a view over the Mission District. Interactive exhibits include a lapidary studio, a greenhouse, a seismology laboratory and a live-animal nursery. School science fairs are staged throughout the year. Public classes include such subjects as mushrooms, spiders, telescope making, carnivorous plants and "Zen and sawdust."

★★Twin Peaks – Kids *From Haight St. drive south on Clayton St. to Carmel St.; cross and continue up Twin Peaks Blvd. to Christmas Tree Point on the left.* These two high points dominate the horizon west of downtown and are visible from more areas of the city than Mt. Davidson, highest point in San Francisco at 929ft. The two distinct but adjacent peaks reach 904ft (north peak) and 922ft (south peak).

Postcard Row: Alamo Square Victorians

© PhotoDisc, Inc.

The row of Victorians located at 710-720 Steiner St., between Hayes and Grove Streets, strikes a familiar chord with most San Francisco visitors. One of the most photographed vantages in the city, "Postcard Row" stands before a remarkable, snapshot-ready backdrop featuring many city landmarks, including the Bank of America Center and the Transamerica Pyramid. Lush, grassy Alamo Square Park, across the street, conveniently allows photographers ample time to focus.

Distinguished externally by window and door treatments and by color, the three-story, wooden, gable-roofed houses were completed in 1895 and sold for $3,500 apiece by Irish-born carpenter and real-estate developer Matthew Kavanagh, who lived at no. 722 from 1892-1900. All seven homes are private, one- or two-family dwellings, although no. 716 was divided into seven apartments from the 1920s until the 1950s. The J. Frank Moroney house at no. 710, distinguished by its jewel-encrusted stained-glass windows and ornate gable, originally belonged to a socialite couple from New York, then changed hands a half dozen times throughout the century. The house was extensively renovated in 1967, and was sold for $87,500 in 1974.

Most visitors content themselves with the grand **panorama**★★★ of the north and east sides of the city from the parking lot at Christmas Tree Point, although it is possible to climb up the grassy slopes of either peak for a view to the west as well. On clear days, Mt. Diablo to the east in Contra Costa County, and Mt. Tamalpais, to the north in Marin County, come into view.

Architect Bernard Maybeck, who designed the Palace of Fine Arts for the 1915 Panama-Pacific International Exhibition, had grandiose plans for Twin Peaks, including a great monument at the summit with waterfalls cascading to the valley below. The plans never materialized. Today visitors and locals throng the viewpoint, particularly on weekend afternoons.

■ **San Francisco Viewpoints**

San Francisco offers vistas at nearly every turn, from urban cityscapes to natural landscapes. Viewpoints on this list are guaranteed to delight (weather permitting); each view rates★★★. See individual sight descriptions for more information.

Alamo Square – The quintessential postcard view of the downtown skyline looming behind a row of picture-perfect Victorians.

Angel Island – An oasis of tranquillity in the middle of the bay. Mt. Livermore's summit offers an unobstructed 360° view of the entire Bay Area.

Coit Tower – A sweeping yet intimate overview encompasses the northern waterfront, Marin County and East Bay as well as the quieter corners of North Beach and Russian Hill.

Land's End – An enchanting and dramatic overview of sea, rocky coastline, sweeping tide and Golden Gate Bridge.

Marin Headlands – Turnouts along Conzelman Road provide ample opportunity to soak in an ever-broadening panorama of bay, bridge and city.

Mount Diablo – One of the region's most extensive panoramas encompasses not just the Bay Area but a good bit of the rest of California.

Mount Tamalpais – A virtual map of the Bay Area spreads from this peak. Low-lying fog makes the view especially interesting, as the summit remains clear while building tops and bridge piers poke up through the puffy white layer.

Treasure Island – An outstanding scape of the famed towers of the Financial District, with the Ferry Building and Bay Bridge in the foreground.

Twin Peaks – One of the city's best-known and most-frequented tourist stops, a good place to get an overall impression of the city's layout.

---

16 • JAPANTOWN

ᙏᙏᙏ bus 38–Geary, 2–Clement, 3–Jackson or 4–Sutter.
Map p 155

Known as Nihonmachi by local residents, Japantown is a locus of Japanese-American cultural life in the Bay Area. Its tidy, six-block core, bounded by Fillmore, Sutter and Laguna Streets and Geary Boulevard, displays some of the city's finer groupings of well-maintained Victorian houses alongside neat but simple modern buildings, many with stucco and half-timbered exteriors that evoke the traditional countryside architecture of Japan. By comparison with teeming Chinatown, Japantown is a much more subdued, orderly and open neighborhood, both architecturally and socially. Its well-organized identity is perhaps best epitomized by the Japan Center shopping, dining and entertainment complex at the heart of the community.

Historical Notes

A few Japanese came to San Francisco after the Meiji revolution of 1868 but arrivals did not peak until the first decade of the 20C. Anti-Asian sentiment slowed Japanese immigration considerably by the 1920s. Most new arrivals settled in the South of Market area, but when that neighborhood was devastated by the earthquake and fire of 1906, residents took refuge in the Western Addition. The new community, popularly known as Little Osaka, harbored about 7,000 Japanese-American residents within a 20-block rectangle formed by Fillmore, Pine, Octavia and O'Farrell streets.

Little Osaka was abandoned during World War II when anti-Japanese hysteria following the Pearl Harbor attack culminated in Executive Order 9066, forcing the evacuation of 112,000 Japanese-Americans to internment camps. Empty residences soon were inhabited by an influx of civilian workers, many of them black, who came to fill wartime shipyard jobs. After the war's end, many Japanese Americans returned to San Francisco, though few resettled in the old neighborhood. Diminished from its prewar size, Japantown took on its present appearance in the late 1960s and 70s when massive urban-renewal projects cleared blocks of Victorian housing and widened Geary Boulevard. Since then, new construction has generally echoed Japanese architectural themes.

Visiting Japantown – Japantown comes alive in the evening when diners and movie-goers flock to its many restaurants and its celebrated AMC Kabuki 8 Theatre complex. The greatest crowds gather on festival days. During the spectacular **Cherry Blossom Festival** in mid- to late April, thousands congregate to enjoy Japanese arts and crafts, foods and music, taiko drumming, dancing and a colorful parade.

SIGHTS

Japan Center – *1737 Post St., between Geary Blvd., Fillmore & Laguna Sts. Open daily year-round. Most shops open daily 10am–6pm, restaurants & lounges later. Closed Jan 1, Thanksgiving Day, Dec 25.* ✗ ♿ 🅿 ✉ *415-922-6776.* Reminiscent of contemporary Japanese architecture—and therefore more blandly international than traditional in style—this five-building complex (1968, Minoru Yamasaki) of galleries, shops, restaurants, cinemas and the deluxe Radisson Miyako Hotel serves as a focal point for community celebrations. Its most striking Japanese touch is the **Peace Pagoda** (**1**), inspired by the miniature round pagodas dedicated to eternal peace by Empress Koken more than 1,200 years ago in Nara, Japan. Rising 110ft above the plaza in five copper-roofed concrete tiers, the pagoda is capped by a golden ball atop a copper spire, symbolizing virtue.

 Kabuki Springs & Spa
1750 Geary Blvd. in Japan Center. ✉ *415-922-6000. www.kabukisprings.com.* A sojourn in this day spa will revive even the most bone-weary traveler. The Joie de Vivre hotel group has kept its traditional Japanese baths while adding a full range of modern spa treatments, including ayurvedic rebalancing and seaweed wraps. Sign up for one of several other plans including steams, hot soaks and *shiatsu* massage, and emerge relaxed, refreshed and squeaky clean.

From the Peace Plaza, stroll west through the Kintetsu and Kinokuniya buildings, linked by an arching bridge over Webster Street. They are home to a colorful row of Japanese restaurants, galleries, music and video stores, electronics stores, antiques shops, a Japanese bookstore and the Ikenobo Ikebana (flower-arranging) Society. The complex's westernmost building houses the AMC Kabuki 8 Theatres, a popular venue for first-run films and for the annual **San Francisco International Film Festival** in April and May.

Buchanan (Nihonmachi) Mall – *Buchanan St., between Sutter & Post Sts.* This quiet, attractive outdoor pedestrian street (1976) evokes the atmosphere of a Japanese village, with cobbled paving and "half-timbered" buildings. A small police *koban* (kiosk) stands at the Post Street end of the mall near a hardware store, while traditional restaurants and shops selling Japanese furniture, stationery, chinaware, gifts, kimonos and publications line its sides.

Konko Church of San Francisco – *1909 Bush St. Open year-round Mon–Sat 6:30am–6pm, Sun 8am–3pm. Guided tours (1hr) available; reservations recommended.* ✉ *415-931-0453.* With a handsome "half-timbered" exterior surface and timbers jutting from the roof, this steel-frame building (1973, Van Bourg, Nakamura & Associates) blends traditional Japanese aesthetics with modern engineering. The interior incorporates a traditionally austere, natural-wood Shinto altar—frequently graced with offerings of food and flowers—with Christian influences such as pews. English-language services are held Sundays. Inspired by a Japanese farmer's revelation in 1859, the Konko (Eternal Golden Light) sect of Shintoism advocates earthly happiness and respect for all life by encouraging reverence for the Principal Parent of the Universe *(Tenchi Kane no Kami)* and by practicing personal meditation.

2 Soko Hardware
1698 Post St. ✉ *415-931-5510.* Nestling up to hammers and screwdrivers, a glorious array of housewares such as tatami mats, mulberry wrapping paper, rice cookers and flower-arranging supplies brings Japan to San Francisco. Downstairs you'll find Japanese tools and plastic-shrimp sushi displayed next to sink faucets and extension cords.

Sokoji-Soto Zen Buddhist Temple – *1691 Laguna St.* ☎ *415-346-7540.* Dedicated in 1984, this overseas-mission temple building is handsomely clad with half-timbered stucco facing. Images of Koso-Dogen Zenji and Taiso-Keizan Zenji, celebrated as the founders of the Soto sect of Zen, flank the golden image of Shakyamuni Buddha at the center of the elaborate altar. The temple is attended by monks in traditional robes.

⋆**Buddhist Church of San Francisco** – *1881 Pine St. Open year-round Mon–Fri 10am–5pm, Sat 9am–noon. English language service Sun 9:30am. Closed major holidays. Guided tours (1hr) available; reservations suggested. Contribution requested.* ☎ *415-776-3158. http://userwww.sfsu.edu/~regman/bcsf.htm.* This most exquisite of Japantown temple interiors occupies the second floor of an otherwise unprepossessing building (1938, Gentoko Shimamato). It is capped by a stupa, a bell-shaped pagoda, containing relics of the Buddha presented by the Thai royal court in 1935. The Jodo Shinshu (True Pure Land) sect of Buddhism has long adopted such American cultural influences as pews, pulpit, homily books and an organ, but the golden altar embodies Japanese tradition. A small standing image of Amida Buddha occupies the central position, raising his right hand in a sign of wisdom and lowering his left in compassion. He is flanked on the right by an image of Shinran Shonin (1173-1262), founder of the Jodo Shinshu sect. Worshipers leave offerings of flowers, fruit and sweets in gratitude.

Jodo Shinshu's **Buddhist Churches of America** headquarters, founded here in 1898, share this building with a separate entrance *(1710 Octavia St., ☎ 415-776-5600).*

ADDITIONAL SIGHT

⋆⋆**The Cathedral of St. Mary of the Assumption** – *1111 Gough St. at Geary Blvd. Open year-round daily 6:45am–4:30pm. Guided tours available Apr–Oct Mon–Sat 9am–noon. Organ recitals Sun 3:30pm.* ♿ 🅿 ☎ *415-567-2020. www.stmary cathedralsf.org.* Sheathed in white travertine marble and visible from miles around the city, San Francisco's third Catholic cathedral—best known simply as "St. Mary's"—crowns a shallow rise known as Cathedral Hill. Commissioned after a fire burned down its Van Ness Avenue predecessor in 1962, the striking, contemporary cathedral (Pier Luigi Nervi & Pietro Belluschi, with McSweeney, Ryan & Lee) was dedicated in 1971.

Enter through the main doors facing Geary Boulevard to see the bronze overpanel, an image of Christ rising above human figures to represent the ecumenical search for God throughout civilization. Backed by stained glass, the overpanel is also impressive when viewed from the interior.

The building's most daring design attribute is its reinforced concrete **cupola**, formed of hyperbolic paraboloids that join to enclose a soaring atrium. At the level of the congregation, clear glass panels afford fine views of the city. Unobstructed views of the massive marble altar can be had from all 2,400 seats. Narrow stained-glass windows rise steeply from the four compass points to meet at the cupola's apex, forming a brilliant cross 190ft above the sanctuary floor. Suspended on wires 75ft above the altar is a contemporary **baldachin**, a shimmering canopy of anodized aluminum rods designed by Richard Lippold to sparkle in the slightest breeze. A magnificent, 4,842-pipe Ruffatti organ perches on a concrete pedestal. Cast-bronze shrines by Enrico Manfrini and Mario Rudelli depicts events in the lives of Mary and Jesus.

17 • PACIFIC HEIGHTS⋆⋆

🚌 bus 3–Jackson, 22–Fillmore, 24–Divisadero, 41–Union,
45–Union-Stockton or 83–Pacific.
Map opposite

Stretching along a high east-west ridge between Van Ness Avenue and The Presidio, this elegant residential neighborhood holds some of the city's finest houses and loveliest views. The name Pacific Heights connotes San Francisco wealth, and its reputation is fully deserved: no other neighborhood gives a grander vision of the life of affluent San Franciscans.

Historical Notes

The area today known as Pacific Heights occupies a favored location equidistant from San Francisco's three main historic centers: Mission Dolores, The Presidio and the commercial area around Yerba Buena Cove (today the Financial District). Trails linking these three centers converged near the highest point of the ridge, called the *divisadero*, but the neighborhood's precipitous streets were not developed until late in the 19C, after other areas of the city had already been established. In the mid-1850s the street grid was extended west from Van Ness Avenue, but as late as 1880 only a few houses had been built here.

Improvements in public transportation, notably the invention of the cable car, brought the area within easy reach of downtown, and at the end of the 1870s Pacific Heights experienced its first of many real-estate booms, focused upon the easternmost edges of the district. The city's most successful merchants constructed huge mansions along Van Ness Avenue. Almost all were destroyed in the great earthquake and fire of 1906, many of them having been dynamited by the US Army to create a firebreak.

Ornament by Formula – Throughout the late 19C, on smaller parcels all over Pacific Heights, speculative developers built more modest but still impressive homes. Often erecting between five and ten houses at a time, side-by-side on the narrow lots, contractors followed formulaic plans but decorated the exteriors in a variety of ornamental motifs, from Gothic to Italianate to many combinations thereof. The prefabricated decorative elements earned these houses the nickname "Gingerbread," and the many surviving examples are among San Francisco's most cherished architectural treasures. In the decade following the 1906 catastrophe, many wealthy San Franciscans who had lost homes on Nob Hill and elsewhere resettled in Pacific Heights, attracted by the neighborhood's bay views and peaceful, noncommercial ambience. Most of the district's largest homes date from this period, a time of great energy in every aspect of San Francisco's civic life. Along Broadway, for example, Comstock mining magnate James Leary Flood built a pair of mansions, each of which would cost $25 to $50 million today, while many bankers, industrialists and other civic leaders built stately homes. Only the very rich could afford to maintain such massive and money-consuming establishments, and beginning in the 1920s, apartment towers were built to lodge the city's elite on a more modest scale. Some of these buildings today rank among San Francisco's most desirable residences, their full-floor units rising 10 or more stories and offering splendid views. Smaller, more conventional apartments aimed at young professionals working in downtown offices arose in the eastern half of Pacific Heights during this period. Today many Pacific Heights mansions house schools or consulates, such as those of Italy *(2151 Broadway)* and Germany *(1960 Jackson St.)*, but the vast majority remain private homes. One of the few earthquake survivors, the Haas-Lilienthal House, today is the city's finest house museum. Although choice residential areas have appeared in other parts of the city, the neighborhood retains its reputation as a preferred address of moneyed San Francisco.

An Architectural Smorgasbord – Pacific Heights' wealthy denizens spent fortunes ensuring that their residences reflected their financial and social status. As a result, the neighborhood constitutes a showcase of design. A slow meander along its quiet streets reveals examples of almost every architectural style and period that exist in San Francisco. Elite taste leaned toward refined, Classical motifs. Many architects looked to the Italian Renaissance palazzo for inspiration, and most followed the rules and precepts established by the École des Beaux Arts in Paris, which many of them had attended. Stone or brick was a popular building material, and designs tended to follow one consistent historical style rather than mix aspects from different periods. Apart from the palaces and mansions of San Francisco's elite, the great majority of homes here were built in the 1880s and 90s for well-to-do families by speculative developers, usually without the services of an architect. Almost all of these "Gingerbread Victorians" were built of wood, with molding, trim and other decorative elements ordered from pattern books and catalogs then widely available to the mass market. Fish-scale shingles, ogive-arched window frames and finely carved verge boards could be bought directly from lumber mills and added to the design at the whim of the builder or homeowner.

Visiting Pacific Heights – Bear the terrain in mind when planning a visit to the "heights." Streets ascend and descend abruptly, sometimes as much as 100ft in one block, to accommodate the willy-nilly fluctuations of the landscape. Public transportation is handy, and street parking is generally easier to find on the west side of the neighborhood than elsewhere in the city.
To get a sense of life in Pacific Heights, visit during early evening when the people who live here jog the streets or walk their dogs. The area also enjoys breathtaking sunset vistas from its many viewpoints.

SIGHTS

★★**Haas-Lilienthal House** – *2007 Franklin St. Visit by guided tour (1hr) only, year-round Wed noon–3pm & Sun 11am–4pm. Closed major holidays. $5. ☎ 415-441-3004. www.sfheritage.org.* One of San Francisco's few Victorian-era residences open to the public, this imposing gray edifice (1886, Peter R. Schmidt) is among the last survivors of the many ornate single-family houses that once filled this eastern Pacific Heights neighborhood. This elegant residence typifies the architectural aspirations of the city's upper-middle class at the end of the 19C—whereas the grandiose mansions atop Nob Hill were for the affluent elite. Constructed for William Haas, a prominent wholesaler, it passed to his daughter and son-in-law, Alice and Samuel Lilienthal, in 1916. After Alice's death in 1972, her family donated the house to the Foundation for San Francisco's Architectural Heritage, which currently maintains it as a house museum and headquarters.

The exterior embellishments are typical of the Queen Anne style and include a variety of patterned siding, ornately bracketed gables and a deceptive corner tower with windows 10ft above the floor. The basement, which at times was used as a ballroom, now holds a display of photographs showing the house in its pre-1906 neighborhood context. Upper-floor rooms, including two parlors, a dining room and one of the original six bedrooms, are furnished in a range of decorative styles dating from the 1880s to the 1920s.

> **Cars Dawydiak**
> *Bush St. at Franklin St.*
> ☎ *415-928-2277.* The Bay Area—not too hot, not too cold, steep hills, two-lane highways—is sports-car territory. This longstanding dealer (pronounced "da-WID-ee-yak") specializes in European sports models from 1955 to the 1990s, with an emphasis on Porsches. Daydream among the 25-30 cars in the 8,000sq ft showroom; the knowledgeable sales staff is happy to answer questions.

★★**Spreckels Mansion** – *2080 Washington St.* Of all the many grand mansions in Pacific Heights, none is more ostentatious than the elaborate French Baroque-style palace built in 1913 for sugar magnate Adolph Spreckels and his wife, Alma de Bretteville Spreckels. The main facade consists of a series of five arched windows separated by pairs of ornate Ionic columns. The house—now owned by romance novelist Danielle Steel—faces onto lushly landscaped **Lafayette Park**. The rear gardens, which drop steeply down to Jackson Street, boast a covered swimming pool.

★**Broadway Mansions** – *Broadway between Fillmore & Buchanan Sts.* These two elegant blocks of Broadway bear witness to the emergence of Pacific Heights as home to San Francisco's elite after the 1906 earthquake. One of the finest buildings in the city is the former **Flood Mansion**★ *(no. 2222)*, designed by local architects Bliss and Faville in 1912 for James Leary Flood. The house is a refined

Spreckels Mansion

© Robert Holmes

and beautifully crafted version of an Italian Renaissance palazzo, its Tennessee marble hung on an earthquake-resistant steel frame. A pair of brick mansions, both dating from the same period, stand alongside the Flood Mansion; all three now house private schools.

Just south of Broadway, the **Bourn Mansion** *(2550 Webster St.)* was designed by Willis Polk in 1896 for William Bourn, the mining magnate for whom Polk also created the magnificent Filoli estate south of San Francisco. Designed as a pied-à-terre, the stately home contains only two bedrooms; rough clinker brick softens the Classical formality of the facade. Most unusually, the design plays down the importance of the entrance, which is set back in a deep vestibule beneath the upper-floor balcony.

In the block east of Webster lie two other remarkable mansions, the stately **Italian Consulate** *(no. 2151)*, and the blue-and-gray, Baroque Revival-style **Hamlin School** *(no. 2120)*. James Flood had the latter (1901) constructed on land owned by his sister, then moved to the Flood Mansion after its completion. It too is now a private school.

★**Fillmore Street** – Lively, inviting and unpretentious, Pacific Heights' only commercial district lies along Fillmore Street between Jackson and Bush streets. Its art cinema, boutiques, bookstores, restaurants and cafes are good places to take a break while walking around the neighborhood.

South of California Street, Fillmore runs past the Japan Center and across Geary Boulevard through the heart of the Western Addition. To the north, it reaches the edge of Pacific Heights at Broadway, where it offers one of the city's finest bay **views**★ before dropping swiftly down into Cow Hollow and the Marina District.

Alta Plaza Park – 🧒 *Bounded by Jackson, Scott, Clay & Steiner Sts.* Set aside as a public park when the city annexed the Western Addition in the mid-1850s, the lush green oasis of Alta Plaza lies at the heart of Pacific Heights. Basketball and tennis courts and a children's playground occupy the center of the park, and the green lawns are a favorite picnic spot. Terraces drop down on Alta Plaza's south side, forming a distinctive ziggurat of concrete and shrubbery.

The houses facing the terraces are among the oldest in Pacific Heights: a series of elaborate Italianate Victorian houses at **2637-2673 Clay St.**, all designed and built by the same contractor in 1875.

On the north side of the park, Jackson Street features a pair of houses created by two influential turn-of-the-20C architects whose use of Classical Beaux-Arts models contrasts with the lighthearted playfulness of other Victorian-era designs. The former Music and Arts Institute at **2622 Jackson St.** was the first of architect Willis Polk's many commissions in the city. Built of stone in 1894 and styled like a Renaissance-era Tuscan villa, the house was acclaimed by *The San Francisco Examiner* as "the first Classical residence in San Francisco." Nearby, the angular brick facade of **2600 Jackson St.** was designed by Ernest Coxhead and built in 1895 by industrialist Irving Scott as a wedding present for his daughter.

18 • RICHMOND DISTRICT
and PRESIDIO HEIGHTS

Richmond District: MUNI bus 38–Geary, 1–California, 2–Clement or 4–Sutter.
Presidio Heights: MUNI bus 3–Jackson or 43–Masonic.
Map opposite

One of San Francisco's most ethnically diverse neighborhoods and a haven of the middle class, the Richmond District is a relatively flat expanse of undistinguished row houses sandwiched between Masonic Avenue to the east, California Street to the north, Golden Gate Park to the south and the Pacific Ocean to the west. Just to the north, between California Street and The Presidio, lies Presidio Heights, a wealthier residential enclave comprised largely of spacious, single-family homes.

Historical Notes

Although they are today socially and economically distinct, the Richmond District and Presidio Heights both were once part of the Outer Lands, a vast expanse of scrub plants and dunes extending from the developed areas of the city to the Pacific Ocean. Recluses and outlaws took refuge in the "Great Sand Waste," as it was called, and cemeteries occupied its eastern edge. In the final two decades of the 19C, Adolph Sutro purchased vast amounts of the sandy acreage cheaply, opening the land for development. He built a steam railway along the present course of California Street to his Cliff House and monumental bathhouse at Land's End.

Construction in the Richmond District proceeded quickly after the 1906 earthquake and accelerated after a municipal railway line began operating along Geary Boulevard in 1912. Two years later, Mayor Jim Rolph ordered all San Francisco's cemeteries closed and removed south of the city limits to the town of Colma, spurring construction of yet more single-family row houses until the Great Depression struck in 1929. These new tracts drew residents of broad ethnic diversity, including White Russians fleeing the 1917 Russian Revolution, Jews from Eastern Europe and, after World War II, Japanese-Americans returning from internment camps. Chinese-Americans have formed the largest ethnic group since the 1970s, but the 1990s witnessed a resurgence of Russian immigration.

Presidio Heights developed more slowly, lot by lot, as wealthy families hired architects to build unique, often palatial homes. A casual stroll through the neighborhood, especially along Pacific Avenue, Jackson Street and Washington Street, reveals a broad variety of architectural styles including Norman, Tudor, Italianate, Queen Anne and Romanesque. Specially designed door knockers, mailboxes, gates, gardens and a host of other intriguing ornamental details add to the visual appeal. Particularly worth noting is **Roos House** *(3500 Jackson St.)*, a massive, half-timbered residence designed in 1909 by renowned Arts and Crafts practitioner Bernard Maybeck.

SIGHTS

San Francisco Columbarium – *1 Loraine Ct., north of Anza St., east of Arguello Blvd. Open year-round Mon–Fri 10am–5pm, weekends 10am–2pm. Guided tours (1hr 30min) available, 1-week advance reservations required.* ♿ 🅿 ☎ *415-221-1838.* Owned and operated by the Neptune Society of Northern California, a cremation organization, this copper-roofed, Neoclassical rotunda recalls the days when cemeteries covered the Richmond's shallow dunes. Erected in 1898 as part of the Oddfellows Cemetery, the columbarium was spared when the graves were removed to Colma in 1914. Today it contains more than 4,400 niches for cremated remains, including those of several prominent San Francisco families. The flamboyant interior is adorned with a mosaic-tile floor, stained-glass windows and skylights, and brightly painted plaster filigree. Individually decorated niches, arranged around four circular levels, flush out the passions and personalities of the deceased.

Clement Street – The more charming of the Richmond's main shopping thoroughfares (the other being Geary Boulevard), Clement Street is popular for its markets, bookshops and household-goods stores. Locals and visitors alike flock here for its excellent yet understated restaurants. The 12-block stretch between Arguello and Park Presidio boulevards is sometimes known as "New Chinatown" because so many of its residents have relocated from downtown's Chinatown. Although Asian restaurants predominate, a culturally diverse community thrives on Clement Street with its Continental bistros, Russian and Italian restaurants, Irish pub, dessert parlor, Western saloon and other diversions.

★Temple Emanu-El – *2 Lake St. Visit by guided tour only, year-round Mon–Fri 1–3pm. Closed Jewish holidays. $15.* ♿ ☎ *415-751-2535. www.emanuelsf.org.* Rising 150ft from the ground and visible for miles, this synagogue's spectacular, orange-tiled, Byzantine-style dome crowns a massive, architecturally unified complex of offices and meeting halls. Designed by Sylvain Schnaittacher, John Bakewell and Arthur Brown, Jr., the building was dedicated in 1926 as the third synagogue for the venerable Reform Jewish congregation, founded in San

Francisco in 1850. Outside the sanctuary doors, a cloistered courtyard is dotted with plants named in the Old Testament as well as a lion-headed fountain. Visitors enter through the vestibule, its ceiling decorated with a brilliant blue and yellow fresco of a star-studded sky.

The temple, which seats 1,700, is lit by two stained-glass windows representing fire (west) and water (east). Four massive bronze chandeliers symbolize the tears of the Jews. At the altar, the Ark of the Covenant stands beneath a marble canopy, housed in a gilded bronze tabernacle box inlaid with cloisonné; the box was built in London by Californians Frank Igerson and George Dennison.

1 V. Breier Contemporary and Traditional Craft
3091 Sacramento St.
☎ *415-929-7173.* This charming shop displays an eclectic mix of folk art, furniture and contemporary crafts, much of it produced by Bay Area artists. Ceramics and glass occupy the front room, while sculpture ornaments the garden out back.

The synagogue is home to the **Elizabeth S. and Alvin I. Fine Museum**, whose permanent and temporary exhibits in the temple foyer integrate Jewish art and history into the congregational mind set. The permanent collection includes many antique ritual household objects, tapestries and manuscripts.

Immediately north of the synagogue is **Presidio Terrace**, an exclusive residential enclave since 1905. Pass through the gate to admire elegant homes, many by noteworthy architects, including no. 15 (1905, Bakewell & Brown), no. 34 (c.1910, George Applegarth) and no. 36 (1911, Julia Morgan).

Sacramento Street – The discreet but charming stretch of Sacramento Street between Lyon and Spruce Streets forms the elite shopping district of Presidio Heights. More subdued than popular Union Street or Fillmore Street, Sacramento Street's upscale boutiques, intimate restaurants and small cinema cater to a mostly local clientele.

★★**Swedenborgian Church** – *2107 Lyon St. Open year-round Mon–Fri 9am–5pm, Sun service 11am.* ☎ *415-346-6466. www.sfswedenborgian.org.* This diminutive, lovingly crafted wood-and-brick chapel, officially named the Church of the New Jerusalem, is better known as the Swedenborgian Church after Swedish scientist, philosopher and religious writer Emanuel Swedenborg, whose doctrines inspire the

Swedenborgian Church, interior

© Robert Holmes

congregation. A fine example of Arts and Crafts design and construction, the church was conceived in 1895 by the congregation's founder, the Rev. Joseph Worcester, himself an architect who enlisted the help of many talented friends. Bruce Porter sketched the design from an Italian original, while A. Page Brown served as chief architect and Bernard Maybeck as draftsman. Willis Polk designed the adjacent Parish House.

The church interior replicates the natural beauty of a California woodland. A massive fireplace along the west wall warms the entrance on chilly mornings. The ceiling is supported by bark-covered branches of native California madrone. Landscape painter William Keith contributed the pastoral scenes of the California countryside along the north wall, while Porter designed the windows along the south wall to admit a view of garden trees. The solid chairs were built by hand, without nails, of maple wood and woven tule rushes from the Sacramento River delta. A giant clam shell near the altar is the baptismal font in which poet Robert Frost, among many others, was submerged and sanctified as an infant. Outside, herringbone-patterned brick walkways frame lush gardens planted with trees and shrubs from around the world, symbolizing universality.

Lyon Street Steps – *Between Broadway & Green St.* Too steep for vehicular traffic, this part of Lyon Street was landscaped around 1915 and today forms one of the city's most attractive public spaces. Dropping toward the bay from the west end of Broadway along the eastern wall of the Presidio, the steps offer a memorable **view★★** out over the great reddish dome of the Palace of Fine Arts across the bay to Angel Island and Mt. Tamalpais. Flower beds and other plantings soften the carefully choreographed, Beaux-Arts stairs, landings and balustrades, and benches offer a place to rest while taking in the view. The corner of Broadway and Lyon offers pedestrian access to the forests of the Presidio; three blocks south stands the Swedenborgian Church.

San Francisco Fire Department Pioneer Memorial Museum – Kids *655 Presidio Ave., between Bush & Pine Sts. Open year-round Thu–Sun 1–4pm.* & ☎ *415-558-3456. www.sffiremuseum.org.* This converted firehouse garage houses a wonderful collection of historic fire engines, including the city's first hand-drawn pump cart (1849). Historical displays, photos and memorabilia, including eclectic collections of fire extinguishers, helmets, hydrants and uniforms, tell of the city's several devastating fires—including the conflagration of 1906—and of heroic figures from San Francisco's firefighting past.

Particularly worth noting is the helmet that belonged to Lillie Hitchcock Coit, the eccentric booster of the San Francisco Fire Department; an ornate certificate proclaims her an honorary member of Knickerbocker Engine Co. No. 5. Visitors may also inspect the modern-day fire engines and equipment in adjacent Firehouse no. 10.

② HomeChef
3527 California St.
☎ *415-668-3191.*
www.homechef.com. Stop into this elegantly stocked store for gourmet cooks to browse among specialty ingredients, equipment and other supplies. Just down the street, at 3501 California St. (upstairs), sign up for the HomeChef cooking school, which offers onetime and series classes covering everything from Mediterranean meals to Thai treats.

19 • CASTRO DISTRICT and NOE VALLEY

bus 24–Divisadero; streetcars F–Market, K–Ingleside, L–Taraval
or M–Oceanview to Castro St. station;
Map pp 164-165

Bounded roughly by 16th, 22nd, Douglass and Dolores streets, the lively, 44sq-block Castro District forms the heart of San Francisco's vibrant gay community, as well as the geographical center of the city. Bars, restaurants, trendy clothing stores and boutiques crowd together along Castro, Market and 18th Streets, while residential side streets lined with beautifully refurbished Victorians invite leisurely exploration.

Historical Notes

Part of a 4,000-acre land grant given to San Francisco's last Mexican mayor, José de Jésus Noe, the present-day Castro District and neighboring Noe Valley were used primarily for cattle-ranching and sheep-grazing until shortly after the Gold Rush. In 1854, during a citywide wave of land speculation, a wealthy produce merchant named John Meirs Horner bought much of Noe's ranch, platted a street grid, and began peddling land tracts to working-class Irish and German immigrants. By 1887 the Market Street Cable Railway extended down Castro Street, linking Eureka and Noe valleys and opening the 21st Street summit to development.

As the district sustained only minor damage in the 1906 earthquake and fire, campgrounds for refugees were quickly erected. Many of the temporary residents opted to stay, and a tight-knit working-class community thrived well into the 1920s, when a commercial building boom graced Castro Street with the majestic Castro Theatre and several other fine structures. The district's social fabric changed after the Twin Peaks Tunnel opened in 1917, leading some residents to relocate to newly developing areas to the west. The Great Depression forced many landowners to divide and rent out single-family homes; federal housing subsidies in the 1950s further encouraged the working-class families' slow march out of the city.

A New Alternative – The area experienced a marked change in the early 1970s when gay San Franciscans began purchasing the homes vacated by the working class. Gay bars appeared along Castro Street in 1972 and the Castro District became a gay enclave, overt about its new identity thanks to the social liberalization of the period and significant gains in gay civil rights. In 1977 residents of the Castro were instrumental in electing **Harvey Milk**, one of their own, to the city's Board of Supervisors, making him the first openly gay elected official in US history. Milk's life and career were cut short the following year when he and then-Mayor George Moscone were gunned down at City Hall by City Supervisor Dan White. In 1978, largely due to the presence of gay men in city and state political arenas, San Francisco passed the Gay Bill of Civil Rights, forbidding discrimination in housing and employment on the basis of sexual orientation.

Crisis struck the neighborhood in the 1980s with the onset of the AIDS epidemic. In response, public-education organizations, support groups and health-news clearinghouses have taken root all over the Castro. Today an upbeat, neighborly attitude pervades the district. On thronged commercial thoroughfares, dance music pulses in many shops, whose creative, sometimes outrageous window displays are among the most eye-catching in the city. Along the quiet residential streets, rainbow flags, symbolizing gay liberation, brighten the windows of many Victorian homes.

Visiting the Castro District – During the day, the Castro hums with the comings and goings of residents and visitors. Shoppers flood Castro Street and its cross streets, where neighbors stop and chat on crowded sidewalks. At night, neon signs of bars and the spectacular Castro Theatre light up, dance music is ratcheted up a few notches, denizens and visitors alike put on their finery and the air buzzes with palpable energy.

Street parking in the area can be exceedingly difficult to find. Many public transportation lines serve the area, most stopping at Harvey Milk Plaza (Castro Street station) at the intersection of Market, 17th and Castro streets.

In October, the **Castro Street Fair** draws large crowds to hear local rock bands perform and to see the work of local artists and entrepreneurs.

CASTRO DISTRICT

Castro Street – Flanked with bookstores and bars, salons and cafes, the bustling shopping strip between Market and 19th streets has served the neighborhood since the 1850s. Named for Vincent Castro, an early Mexican rancher, the busy thoroughfare overflows day and night with foot and car traffic.

In recent years, **Market Street** between Castro and Church streets has also become a vibrant shopping strip. Full-grown Canary Island palm trees were planted along the median in 1994, adding a welcome touch of green. In 1995, the refurbished streetcars of the historic F-Market line began clanging through, balancing the trend-setting designer clothing boutiques, funky gift shops and tony new restaurants with a charming touch of the past.

At the southwest corner of Market and Castro streets is **Harvey Milk Plaza**, dedicated in late 1997 on the 20th anniversary of Milk's election to office. Above a simple memorial flies a huge eight-color rainbow flag, the universal symbol of sexual diversity that was created in the Castro.

Milk lived in a blue Victorian at **575 Castro St.** His apartment was above his camera store, his campaign headquarters in the rear of the building. Today, a mural of Milk, clad in a T-shirt adorned with a rainbow flag, gazes from an upstairs window. At once an idealist and a realist, Milk wrote in an eerily prescient letter one year before his death: "In the event that I am killed by an assassin's bullet, may that same bullet shatter every closet door."

The AIDS Memorial Quilt

Invoking both an American tradition of quilting and a historic practice of honoring the dead with national monuments, the AIDS Memorial Quilt, sponsored by the NAMES Project Foundation, represents a unique, moving response to the epidemic of Acquired Immune Deficiency Syndrome that has asserted itself throughout the world since the early 1980s. Composed of coffin-sized 3ft-by-6ft panels, each handmade in memory of someone who died of the virus, the quilt tours the world in sections, to increase AIDS awareness and to raise funds for North American AIDS-service organizations.

The idea for the quilt originated with Cleve Jones, a San Francisco gay-rights activist. In 1985, after learning that more than 1,000 city residents had died of AIDS-related illnesses, Jones asked participants in the 1985 memorial march for Harvey Milk to carry signs bearing the names of friends and acquaintances who had succumbed to the virus. At the end of the march, the posters were affixed to the facade of the San Francisco Federal Building, and the resulting patchwork resembled a quilt.

In 1986, Jones founded the NAMES Project, and in spring 1987 he made the first cloth panel in memory of his best friend. Soon, handmade panels adorned with such diverse materials as spray paint, leather, sequins and photographs began arriving at the NAMES Project headquarters in San Francisco. In 2001 headquarters were moved to Atlanta, Georgia.

In October 1987, when the quilt was displayed for the first time in Washington DC, it comprised 1,920 panels and covered a space larger than a football field. A 1996 display in the capital was made up of an estimated 41,000 panels, covering roughly 29 football fields. But while the rapid expansion of the quilt constitutes a serious and moving reminder of the growing proportions of the epidemic, its panels remain very personal. Colorful, quizzical, kitschy, campy, each individual square celebrates the uniqueness, spirit and joie de vivre of one who has died.

★**Castro Theatre** – *429 Castro St. Open year-round daily, at showtimes. Theater interior also accessible on Cruisin' the Castro tour.* ♿ ☎ *415-621-6120.* Declared a San Francisco Historic Landmark in 1977, this splendid Spanish Renaissance Revival theater (1922, Timothy Pflueger) represents the city's finest example of early-20C movie-palace architecture. The front exterior facade features Spanish Colonial-style ornamentation above the low-hanging marquee and a huge, pink-neon sign, both added in 1937. The grand, 1,520-seat interior's gently curved green and gold-leaf ceiling, two-story proscenium framed by columns and an ornate lintel, and sumptuous murals combine to create a magical ambience. Attend one of the two nightly screenings to hear resident musicians playing the Mighty Wurlitzer organ, which slowly rises from the orchestra pit for the performance, then sinks back down as the lights dim.

Screening kitsch classics, foreign movies, silent-era gems and low-budget experimental films most of the year, the Castro Theatre also hosts several annual film festivals, including the San Francisco International Film Festival and the Gay and Lesbian Film Festival.

NOE VALLEY

Cradled in the lowlands south of the Castro District, Noe Valley features wide, Victorian cottage-lined streets intersecting a quaint, bustling shopping strip. Like the Castro, the neighborhood was part of José Noe's huge ranch until well into the 1850s, and harbored a thriving community of working-class immigrants through the mid-20C. In the 1970s the area gained popularity with hippies and artists, and the enclave was nicknamed "Nowhere Valley" and "Granola Valley" due to its relative isolation and liberal-thinking population.

Today residents can only wish for such anonymity: Noe Valley in recent years has become a desirable neighborhood for young professionals starting families. Its colorful commercial thoroughfare, **24th Street** *(between Dolores & Diamond Sts.)*, retains its modest appeal. During the day, the awning-covered sidewalks fill with

1 **Joseph Schmidt Confections**
3489 16th St. Open Mon–Sat 10am–6:30pm. ☎ *415-861-8682.* Think of this place as an art gallery where chocolate is the medium. *Objets d'art* range from truffles to chocolate fish, tulips, mushrooms, even graduation mortar boards. Flavors and shapes change with the seasons, but the city's perennially cool climate keeps the art from melting.

2 **Isak Lindenauer Antiques**
4143 19th St. Open Sat–Mon 11am–6pm. ☎ *415-552-6436.* This small antiques dealer began specializing in Arts and Crafts and Mission-style furniture and fixtures in 1973, long before the styles were widely collected. It's well worth a stop— Lindenauer might have just taken delivery of a new shipment of Gustav Stickley pieces, his specialty.

3 **Global Exchange**
3900 24th St. Open Mon–Sat 10am–7pm. ☎ *415-648-8068.* A fair return to the craftsperson is the idea behind this nonprofit shop. Handicrafts from 40 countries (many of them developing nations) show up in this small space. Children's overalls from Guatemala, soapstone carvings from Kenya and Indonesian slide whistles are typical of the variety of attractively priced items for sale. Another Global Exchange store is in Berkeley at 2840 College Ave.

denizens walking dogs and pushing strollers; cafes overflow with latte-sipping, newspaper-reading customers; and designer clothing shops, bookstores, flower stands and wine merchants beckon shoppers with creative window displays.

20 • MISSION DISTRICT★

🚌 bus 14–Mission, 22–Fillmore, 33–Stanyan or 48–Quintara/24th St.
🚇 16th St. or 24th St. station.
Map pp 164-165

Embracing numerous peoples and cultures while maintaining a festive Latino flavor, San Francisco's oldest neighborhood occupies a vast area roughly bounded by Potrero Avenue and Dolores, 14th and Cesar Chavez Streets. A series of hills ripples along the scenic western edge of the district, offering some protection against chill fogs and ocean winds; as a result, "the Mission" boasts one of the city's warmer microclimates. The vibrant, gritty, colorful heart of the Mission District thrives along 24th Street, a narrow, tree-lined thoroughfare jammed with small shops, groceries, *taquerías* and restaurants.

Historical Notes

In 1776, Spanish explorer Juan Bautista de Anza staked out the location for a Catholic mission in this warm valley near an Ohlone settlement. On June 29 of that year, Franciscan priests Pedro Cambón and Francisco Palou celebrated Mass to establish the new mission, dedicating it to St. Francis of Assisi. A primitive village grew up in the vicinity of the mission compound, but the surrounding lands remained largely uncultivated because the soil was poor. After secularization in 1834, wealthy Californio ranchers used the property for cattle grazing, although Yankee squatters' rights prevailed after the US won the Mexican-American War in 1848.

Like the rest of San Francisco, the Mission District boomed with the onset of the Gold Rush. In 1851, a 40ft-wide plank road was laid through the marshy South of Market area, providing a connection to the flourishing downtown waterfront and opening the neighborhood to development. A street grid was platted, with 16th Street serving as the main commercial thoroughfare. Although several wealthy San Francisco families built lavish weekend homes in the area, the Mission District mostly attracted working-class people. Many of them were immigrants from Germany and Scandinavia—and, later, Italy and Ireland—who had arrived on trade vessels and stayed to work in the shipyards and factories of the burgeoning city.

Latino Enclave – Much of the district survived the earthquake and fire of 1906, and many of those left homeless by the conflagration resettled here. Working-class families moved in, drawn to jobs available in burgeoning factories, breweries and warehouses. Throughout the 1920s, Mexicans fleeing the revolution in their homeland swelled the ranks of Latinos in the core of the Mission; in subsequent decades, new waves of first- and second-generation Latinos replaced many European-descended families. Social and political unrest in Central and South America since the 1970s has fueled a steady influx of new immigrants from these regions.

The area east of Valencia and south of 16th Street today remains predominantly Latino and largely working-class. In the industrial northeast corner of the district, artists and dot-com entrepreneurs have begun to transform empty warehouses into sleek living and working spaces, studios and theaters, giving rise to a small but trendy cafe and bar scene. On the western edge of the district, chic new restaurants and watering holes have begun to crop up beside secondhand bookstores and thrift shops, drawing a wealthier crowd into what had been an inexpensive enclave for avant-garde artists, students and political activists.

Visiting the Mission District – During the day, and especially on weekends, the Mission District's commercial thoroughfares hum with activity. Shops and sidewalks teem with people, lines lead out the doors of the most popular *taquerías*, and strains of salsa music fill the air. At night, restaurants and bars on Valencia Street, and on 16th and 22nd between Valencia and Guerrero streets, fill to capacity until last call. While many parts of the Mission are safe, the neighborhood's rough-and-tumble character can be intimidating. At night, keep to Valencia and 16th Streets and the areas south and west of them, except to access the BART stations on Mission Street. Street parking is relatively easy to find, though meters and time limits are strictly enforced day and night.

Exuberant celebrations occur regularly, including *Cinco de Mayo (1st Sun in May)*, *Carnaval San Francisco (Memorial Day Sun)*, the *Latino Summer Fiesta (second Sat in Sept)*, and *Halloween San Francisco (Oct 31)*. For information, contact the Mission Economic Cultural Association ☎ 415-826-1401.

SIGHTS

★**Mission Dolores (Mission San Francisco de Asís)** – *16th & Dolores Sts. Open daily 9am–4pm. Closed Jan 1, Easter Sunday, Thanksgiving Day, Dec 25. $2 contribution requested. ♿ ☎ 415-621-8203. www.bgmm.com/missions/dolores.htm.* Flanked by a historic cemetery and a lavishly ornamented 20C basilica, San Francisco's oldest extant structure serves as a distinct reminder of the city's Spanish heritage and a repository of early European history.

The sixth mission in the Alta California chain was first established in 1776 near the present-day corner of Camp and Albion Streets, two blocks east of its present site. A nearby lake named for Our Lady of Sorrows (Nuestra Senora de los Dolores) gave the mission its centuries-old nickname, Mission Dolores. The present chapel was completed in 1791, though poor soil and illness among the neophytes impeded the mission's growth. By the time it was secularized in 1834, the neophytes had largely abandoned it, and the property was occupied by squatters during the raucous days of the Gold Rush. The Catholic Church reacquired the property in 1860, erecting a series of larger churches alongside the old chapel to accommodate a growing congregation. The present **church★** (1918), with its gloriously ornate Churrigueresque facade, was designated a basilica in 1952.

Visit – A remarkably sturdy structure, the **chapel★★** has survived major earthquakes in 1868, 1906 and 1989 as well as abandonment and neglect. Today it appears much as it did in 1791, thanks to a conscientious restoration program completed in 1995. Cement stucco covers 4ft-thick adobe walls, while amber-colored windows bathe the interior in warm light. The ornate, hand-carved reredos and side altars were imported from Mexico in 1780, and bronze bells occupying niches high in the chapel's front exterior facade were brought as gifts in 1792, 1795 and 1797. The remarkable, multicolored motifs painted on the high, beamed ceiling are patterned after Ohlone basket designs.

A small passage north of the chapel contains a splendid **diorama** of the mission as it appeared in 1799; the model was created for the Golden Gate International Exposition of 1939-40. The mission's small **museum (M)** houses shards and shreds of artifacts discovered during restorations, as well as baptismal records and vestments dating from the colonial period. A section of the wall plaster is cut away and covered with glass to show the thick adobe bricks within. On the south side extends a tranquil **cemetery★**; here, amid verdant, varied plantings, are buried many of San Francisco's early leaders, including Luis Antonio Arguello (1784-1830), first governor of California under Mexican rule; Francisco De Haro (1803-1848), first mayor of San Francisco; and many others whose names grace nearby streets.

Dolores Street – *Between 16th & 21st Sts.* Rolling hills, lofty palm trees and an eye-catching assemblage of architectural styles characterize this attractive stretch of Dolores Street. At 18th Street, Mission Dolores' architecture is echoed in the huge, red-tile-roofed Mission High School (1926, John Reid, Jr.); exemplifying the city's diversity, its student body hails from more than 30 countries. Lush, hilly **Mission Dolores Park**, stretching from 18th to 20th Streets on the west side of Dolores Street, was laid out in 1905 and served as a cemetery for two Jewish temples.

Five Hundred Years of Resistance, detail (1993) © by Isaías Mata

■ Speaking Walls: The Murals of San Francisco

San Francisco tallies more than 500 wall paintings within its 49sq mi. Some record traditional history. Others serve as vibrant pictorial voices for communities without expression in mainstream art institutions—groups united by race, ethnicity, class, gender or politics. The great Mexican muralist **Diego Rivera** visited the city during the early 1930s, executing important works at the San Francisco Art Institute and the Pacific Exchange. Fresco murals at Coit Tower and the Beach Chalet reflect Rivera's influence during this period. During the late 1960s, **David Alfaro Siqueiros** improved techniques for outdoor painting, and the Mission District witnessed an explosion of outdoor art the following decade. The fences, walls and garage doors of Balmy Alley, off 24th Street, were originally decorated by schoolchildren. Many Mission District artists painted their first murals in the alley, including Patricia Rodríguez, Graciela Carillo and Irene Pérez, who later founded Mujeres Muralistas, a group of women artists who pictured the beauty of their cultures. Many of those early murals were subsequently replaced in the 1980s by the **PLACA** group—this time with themes of the struggle for peace in Central America.

Following is a brief list of some exceptionally interesting murals. For more information, call the **Precita Eyes Mural Arts Center** *(2981 24th St. near Harrison St., ☎ 415-285-2287; www.precitaeyes.org)* which offers lectures and walking tours of Mission District murals *(Sat 11am, $5; Sat–Sun 1:30pm, $10)*.

Las Lechugueras (1983) by Juana Alicia; Taquería San Francisco, 24th & York Sts.

New World Tree (1987) by Juana Alicia, Susan Cervantes, Raúl Martínez; Mission Pool, 19th St. near Valencia St.

Silent Language of the Soul (1990) by Juana Alicia and Susan Cervantes; Cesar Chavez Elementary School, Shotwell & 22nd Sts.

The Dream Theater Murals (1991) by Neil Levine; Little Hollywood Launderette (interior), Market St. at Laguna St.

Five Hundred Years of Resistance (1993) by Isaías Mata; St. Peter's Church, 24th St. at Florida St.

Maestrapeace (1995) by various women artists; Women's Building, 3543 18th St.

Prime Time/No Time and *Just Us* (1980), *Venceremos* (1981) by Ray Patlan; New College of California Law School (interior), 50 Fell St.

Life of Washington by Victor Arnautoff; George Washington High School (interior), 32nd & Anza Sts.

Chinese American History (1988) by Victor Fan; YMCA playground, 855 Sacramento St.

Other mural locations described elsewhere in this guide include:

South of the park is **Liberty Street** *(between 20th & 21st Sts.)*, lined with Victorians dating from the 1860s. All major styles are represented, including Italianate *(no. 109)*, Stick *(nos. 111-121)*, and Queen Anne *(no. 123)*.

★**24th Street** – *Between Mission & Potrero Sts.* This lively, tree-lined shopping strip exudes the gritty, exuberant aura of the Mission District. Community residents flock here daily to pick up produce, meats, cheeses and baked goods from the many tiny shops and markets. Bright awnings shadow fruit stands overflowing with exotic picks; salsa music pours from music stores and slow-moving cars; Spanish rolls off the tongues of shopkeepers and shoppers alike; and a host of modest eateries serve up a plethora of Latin American cuisines.

Stroll down **Balmy Alley**★ *(between Treat & Harrison Sts.)* to admire the colorful murals adorning nearly every garage door and wall surface. Occupying an unassuming corner storefront, **Galería de la Raza** *(corner of 24th & Bryant Sts.)* has sustained and nurtured the Chicano art movement since 1970 through exhibitions, events, and performances. The gallery showcases new artists along with established ones; exhibits, which change every four to six weeks, reflect Chicano and Latino social and cultural issues.

4 **Studio 24**
2857 24th St. Open Tue–Sat noon–6pm. ☎ *415-826-8009.* Adjacent to Galería de la Raza, this colorful retail shop stocks handcrafts and contemporary and traditional folk art from Mexico and Central and South America.

5 **St. Francis Fountain**
2801 24th St. Open Mon–Fri 11am-9pm, Sat-Sun 11:30am-8pm. ☎ *415-826-4200.* The city's only surviving soda fountain, built in 1916, was last remodeled (pink on pink) the year Harry S Truman was elected president: 1948. Take a booth or a stool at the counter and sip a soda or belly-up to the house gut-buster challenge: five scoops of different flavors of ice cream, two toppings, whipped cream and a banana.

Valencia Street – *Between 16th & 23rd Sts.* A profusion of coffeehouses, restaurants, thrift stores and bars has sprung up in recent years along this section of Valencia Street and the cross streets linking it to Guerrero Street, transforming the former working-class neighborhood into a trendy "new Bohemia." While still a bit down at the heel, the area has become a magnet for the young and the hip, and for Arabic immigrants as well as Latin American. Regulars drift through its coffeehouses, used bookstores and thrift shops by day; at night, strolling mariachi bands enliven its teeming restaurants, bars and clubs.

Levi Strauss & Company – 🅺🅸🅳🆂 *250 Valencia St. Visit by guided tour (1hr 30min) only, year-round Tue–Wed 9 am, 11am and 1:30pm. Reservations required. Closed 1st 2 weeks in Jul & late Dec–early Jan.* & ☎ *415-565-9159. www.levi strauss.com.* Located in an attractive, canary-yellow building (1906), this factory represents a tiny link in the enormous, international Levi's chain. In 1873, German-born Levi Strauss and his partners patented the design he had developed while in San Francisco making "waist-high" overalls for miners during the Gold Rush. The design included the now-famous back-pocket design and reinforced copper rivets. The guided tour includes a video *(10min)*, a tour of the Levi's museum and a stroll through the loud factory floor where jeans are designed and sewn.

21 • SOUTH OF MARKET

🚌 bus 9–San Bruno, 12–Folsom, 14–Mission, 19–Polk, 27–Bryant or 42-Downtown Loop.
🚇 Powell St., Civic Center or Van Ness Ave. stations.
Maps p 171

San Francisco's hardscrabble history meets its high-tech future in the area known as South of Market, a heterogeneous industrial zone bounded by Market, Townsend and 13th Streets and The Embarcadero. Like New York City's SoHo (which inspired South of Market's sobriquet, "SoMa"), the area is largely dominated by warehouse and factory structures. Yet this quarter pulses with some of the city's most vibrant cultural activity. On and around 3rd and 4th Streets, the redevelopment project now known as **Yerba Buena Gardens** has attracted several renowned museums and galleries, along with an enormous convention center and the soul of the burgeoning multimedia ("dot-com") industry. Constraints on development in the neighboring Financial District have brought new office towers to SoMa's northeastern fringe. Elsewhere, erstwhile industrial buildings are reborn as sleek, spacious restaurants, ultrahip clubs, theaters, lofts and cafes.

Historical Notes

In 1847, Irish engineer and surveyor Jasper O'Farrell platted the area with streets parallel and perpendicular to Market Street, a 120ft-wide thoroughfare laid diagonally through the city from The Embarcadero to Twin Peaks. Anticipating industrial development on this flat terrain fronting the bay, O'Farrell planned SoMa's blocks four times larger than those north of Market, and made the streets twice as wide. Gasworks, shipyards, refineries, foundries and breweries took root along the waterfront, and workers settled in boardinghouses near The Embarcadero and in a large tent community euphemistically called "Happy Valley." Wealthy business owners built elegant Victorian mansions atop nearby **Rincon Hill**, a high sand ridge separating Yerba Buena Cove and Mission Bay. At the foot of the hill lay South Park, an attractive enclave of Georgian townhouses encircling a private oval common.

Wharves, factories and shanties quickly occupied the land-filled waterfronts of Yerba Buena Cove and Mission Bay, and in 1869 Rincon Hill was bisected to facilitate industrial traffic. As unattractive development on the flats continued to encroach on their elite enclave, well-to-do San Franciscans deserted South of Market, particularly after the 1873 invention of the cable car made it possible to build on Nob Hill and other slopes west of downtown. The neighborhood gained the nickname "South of the Slot" once the Market Street cable-car line was established in 1876.

Neighborhood in Transition – After the earthquake and fire of 1906 razed the sector, SoMa population remained largely male and working-class. That didn't change until the 1950s, when real-estate developers recognized South of Market's potential as an adjunct to the Financial District. Today architects, graphic designers, performing artists, filmmakers and cyberartists make SoMa their home. New apartments and condominiums, particularly along The Embarcadero and around South Beach, have encouraged an influx of downtown workers to take up residence. A proliferation of clothing manufacturers' outlets draws bargain-hunters by the busload.

The lively after-dark scene—mainly between 8th and 10th streets, and along 11th Street between Folsom and Harrison streets—offers dance clubs and discos, microbreweries and bistros, theaters, galleries and experimental performance spaces in converted industrial buildings. The recent completion of Pacific Bell Park at China Basin, and the ongoing construction of new cultural complexes near Yerba Buena Gardens, presages the continuation of SoMa's seemingly perpetual state of transition.

SIGHTS

Old Mint – *88 5th St. Not open to the public.* With its six great Doric columns and pyramidal granite staircase, the Old Mint (1874, Alfred B. Mullet) remains one of San Francisco's finest Neoclassical buildings. Made of brick with stone facing, the structure served as a US Mint from 1874 to 1937, narrowly surviving the fire of 1906 when employees, with the help of soldiers and a tiny firehose, fought the flames to save $200 million in silver and gold. The building's grand entrance, elevated 12ft above the sidewalk, suggests power and indomitability. The structure was designated a National Historic Landmark in 1966. Damaged in the 1989 earthquake, the Old Mint closed its doors in 1995.

South Park – *Bounded by 2nd, 3rd, Brannan & Bryant Sts.* Modest apartment houses, unique shops and charming cafes flank this sedate, tree-filled, oval-shaped park, bringing a touch of gentility to a warehouse-dominated neighborhood. Designed in the early 1850s to resemble London's Berkeley Square, South Park, like nearby Rincon Hill, was home to high society until the early 1870s. Writer Jack London was born nearby in 1876 (a plaque marks his birth site at 601 3rd St.). Today the eclectic surface treatments of South Park's homes and storefronts bear witness to the growing presence of design firms in the neighborhood.

NAMES Project Foundation – *310 Townsend St. at 4th St. In 2001 the NAMES Project Foundation moved the quilts national headquarters to Atlanta, Georgia. www.aidsquilt.org.* The foundation's national headquarters are located near China Basin, opposite the CalTrain terminal. The Project sponsors the AIDS Memorial Quilt (p. 162), at 42,000mi long the largest community art project in the world, which it stores here. Visitors are welcome to step inside to view the panel storage areas or to inquire about sewing workshops.

Folsom Street – A hive of activity for alternative society, this street—and those adjoining it between 6th and 11th Streets—may hold the greatest concentration of nightclubs in San Francisco. Once a center for the stud-and-leather-clad fringe of gay culture, Folsom Street's draw today is more diverse, though not a lot tamer. Ground zero for the tattooed and body-pierced set is 11th and Folsom, where queues form outside places like the **DNA Lounge** *(375 11th St.; ☎ 415-626-1409)*, the **Paradise Lounge** *(308 11th St.; ☎ 415-861-6906)* and the **Cat Club** *(1190 Folsom St.; ☎ 415-431-3332)*. Nearby, cavernous dance clubs like **Endup** *(401 6th St.; ☎ 415-357-0827)* and **Ten 15 Folsom** *(1015 Folsom St.; ☎ 415-431-1200)* pack in the crowds.

By day, explore Folsom Street by walking west from 7th Street, passing numerous clubs that open only after dark. Don't miss **Brainwash** *(1122 Folsom St.; ☎ 415-861-3663)*, which combines a bar and grill with a laundromat. Improvisational comedy is a regular feature in its upstairs theater, Above Brainwash. A block west, **New Langton Arts** *(1246 Folsom St.; ☎ 415-626-5416)* is a mainstay of contemporary SoMa culture. The nonprofit gallery and experimental performance space offers cutting-edge exhibitions in mixed media, including visual arts, video, theater, music and literature.

Two venerable nearby churches were built by early-20C working-class ethnic communities. The 1906 **Ukrainian Orthodox Church of St. Michael** *(345 7th St. at Harrison St.; ☎ 415-861-4066)* was a spiritual rock for a sizable colony of Ukrainian immigrants. A double stairway flanked by palm trees approaches its twin-towered façade. **St. Joseph's Church** *(1415 Howard St. at 10th St.)*, now closed due to earthquake damage, anchored an Italian community; built in 1912, its twin towers form a Neo-Baroque façade.

 Slim's
333 11th St. ☎ 415-255-0333. Reggae, jazz, country and alternative acoustic all have a home at this longstanding nightclub, but mosh-diving and head-slamming do not, as a sign on the wall warns. Bonnie Raitt, Melissa Etheridge and Pearl Jam all have appeared at the popular venue, owned by veteran rocker Boz Skaggs. Clubbers can dine on the balcony or dance on the huge floor.

Potrero Hill

This eclectic residential neighborhood in the heights south of SoMa features windswept streets, lovely views, comfortable commercial strips and historic factories that recall the area's industrial origins. Many design studios have recently relocated along De Haro Street between 16th and Mariposa streets; trendy cafes and restaurants do an active business here. **Eighteenth Street** between Arkansas and Mississippi streets harbors a cozy commercial strip of shops and restaurants, boasting scenic **views**★ of downtown from its north-south cross streets.

★**Basic Brown Bear Factory** – 🅺🅸🅳🆂 *444 De Haro St. Open year-round Mon–Sat 10am–5pm, Sun noon–5pm. Closed major holidays. Guided tours (30min) daily 1pm, Sat also 11am ($12 including small bear). ⅋ ☎ 415-626-0781. www.basicbrownbear.com.* Within this diminutive gray warehouse resides a veritable Santa's workshop. A small crew of workers cuts, sews and stuffs virtually every size and shape of teddy bear imaginable—from the long-legged Natalie Bear, reminiscent of early toy bears, to the mammoth California Bear, hunched over on all fours. The two front rooms of the factory are stacked floor-to-ceiling with stuffed and unstuffed bears; visitors may select and stuff their own.

An entertaining guided tour leads from the showroom to the cutting room, where bears are cut en masse from patterns; to the sewing room, where the pieces are stitched together and eyes attached; then to the stuffing room, where polyester fill is blown into the bears by a machine invented to stuff life jackets during World War II. Guides relate the nuts and bolts of bearmaking and recount the history of teddy bears, from the story of how they were named (in 1903, for US President Theodore Roosevelt) to how they were made to be safe and durable for kids. The Bear Factory has a smaller outlet at The Cannery on Fisherman's Wharf.

 Butterfield & Butterfield Auctioneers and Appraisers
220 San Bruno Ave. ☎ 415-861-7500. Previews occur two or three weekends a month at the largest US auction house outside New York City. Specialties include California paintings, fine and rare wines, American and European arms and armor, Asian art, memorabilia and prints. Around the corner at Butterfield West, less pricey items go on the block two weekends a month, luring those who like the idea of finding a treasure and landing it for a pittance.

Anchor Brewing Company – *1705 Mariposa St. Gift shop open year-round Mon–Fri 9am–5pm. Brewery visit by guided tour (90min) only, year-round Mon–Fri 2pm. Reservations required (1–2 wks in advance for Mon–Wed tours, 4–8 wks for Thu–Fri tours). Closed major holidays. ⅋ ☎ 415-863-8350. www.anchorbrewing.com.* Housed in an attractive, Art Deco factory (1937), Anchor Brewing Company has earned a national reputation for brewing **Anchor Steam Beer**, a tart, amber lager. The company sparked a 1990s trend in the US toward beers produced by small manufacturers, or microbreweries.

Founded in 1896, Anchor began as one of many local breweries that aimed at quenching San Franciscans' thirsts. By 1965, the brewery, then located at 8th and Bryant Streets, was ready to close its doors until Fritz Maytag, heir to the Maytag appliance fortune, bought the company. Maytag struggled for more than a decade to perfect his brew. He moved the operation to its present location in 1979.

Inside, the second-floor tasting room is arranged like an old-fashioned pub, with a long oak bar and brewery memorabilia decorating the walls; on tap is every Anchor brew made. Guided tours include a visit to the factory's main room, where barley, hops and malt begin the long transformation into beer, and to the high-speed bottling room.

EXCURSION

Golden Gate Railway Museum – *Hunters Point Naval Shipyard. From US-101 south of downtown, take Cesar Chavez St. east to 3rd St.; turn south to Evans Ave., then east to Hunters Point. Follow signs past security station to museum. Open year-round weekends 10am–4pm, weekdays by appointment.* ☎ *415-822-8728. www.ggrm.org.* Train buffs love this out-of-the-way curiosity, where Bay Area railroad history is brought back to life in antique equipment (c.1899-1962) and described by enthusiastic volunteers. On display are nearly 50 steam and diesel locomotives, passenger cars (including Pullman sleepers, articulated coaches and baggage cars) and freight cars (including flatcars, refrigerator cars and cabooses). The Rent-a-Loco program *($125-$300/hr)* enables visitor to train in the operation of an antique engine and run it a short distance on the track.

22 • YERBA BUENA GARDENS★★

🚌 bus 14–Mission, 15–Third, 30–Stockton or 45–Union-Stockton.
🚇 Montgomery St. or Powell St. stations.
Map opposite

The contemporary heart of the South of Market district, this once-rundown industrial zone has evolved into the cultural hub of San Francisco. With six museums (and two more soon to open), the city's principal convention center, a performing-arts center, a children's center and a high-tech shopping-and-entertainment complex, it pulses with activity from morning until late at night.

At the core of one of the biggest urban-renewal projects in the US is Yerba Buena Gardens, a 5.5-acre park that opened in 1993 between 3rd and 4th, Mission and Howard Streets. Adjacent neighborhoods, once home to retired sailors and longshoremen and the urban poor, now bustle with architecture and graphic-design firms, film and software-production studios, trendy restaurants and nightclubs. Along the fringe of Market Street just one block north of the Gardens, new high-rise hotel and office towers are sprouting, outside the jurisdiction of stricter building codes in the adjacent Financial District.

Historical Notes

For more than three decades, beginning in the 1960s, San Francisco's urban rede-velopment agency cast its eyes south across Market Street. Politics and litigation played a strong hand, as residents fought planners and real-estate developers to prevent their declining community from becoming a high-rise ghetto.

The first big step took place in 1981 with the completion of **Moscone Convention Center** (Hellmuth, Obata and Kassabaum) on the south side of Howard Street. Later addi-tions came in 1988 and 1991, bringing total exhibition space to 442,000sq ft. (The Moscone West annex, now under construction across Howard and 4th Streets, is to open in 2003.) A sports arena originally was scheduled for construction in the block north of the convention center. But citizen voices won out, and a multicultural focus was agreed upon. Its centerpiece became the Yerba Buena Gardens.

With the opening in 1995 of architect Mario Botta's brilliant San Francisco Museum of Modern Art, the Yerba Buena area's future was virtually secure. In 1999, Sony Entertainment launched its four-story, all-ages Metreon complex; a 10-acre children's recreation and education center, the Rooftop at Yerba Buena Gardens, rose above Moscone Center. Beside venerable St. Patrick's Church, facing the park block on its north, construction will soon begin on a plaza to be shared with the Jewish Museum and the Mexican Museum, both relocating to new buildings here. Museums of history, photography and cartoon art are a mere block east or west. Indeed, the Yerba Buena Gardens area seems to be in a perpetual state of transition.

Visiting Yerba Buena Gardens – Most museums and galleries, including the San Francisco Museum of Modern Art, open at 11am; most are closed certain days of the week, but may (as in the case of SFMOMA) stay open late one evening. At midday, office workers gather on the Esplanade for lunch and enjoy free concerts held regu-larly in the outdoor bandshell *(for performance schedule* ☎ *415-978-2787).*

Surface lots dot the areas around Yerba Buena Gardens, and street parking is usually easy to find after rush hour ends around 7pm. The large garage at 5th and Mission Streets offers abundant parking in a convenient location.

SIGHTS

★**Yerba Buena Center for the Arts** (**A**) – *3rd & Mission Sts. Open year-round Tue–Wed & Sat–Sun 11am–6pm, Thu–Fri 11am–8pm. Closed major holidays. $6. Tours available Thu 6:30pm & Sat 1pm.* & ☎ *415-978-2787. www.yerba buenaarts.org.* Exploring such issues as race, class, gender, history, technology and art itself, the changing exhibitions in this low-slung, modernistic building (1993, Fumihiko Maki) reflect the cultural diversity and experimental élan of the Bay Area. Designed to resemble an ocean liner—its tall flagpole suggesting a mast and the angled Mission Street facade recalling a stern—the $44 million structure contains a 6,700sq-ft performance space, two cavernous first-floor galleries and a sculpture plaza. Upstairs, a high-tech gallery accommodates film, video and multimedia installations, while an open terrace overlooks the large downstairs gallery and spacious lobby. Temporary exhibitions of work by emerging artists rotate with shows by internationally renowned artisans.

Immediately south of the galleries stands the 750-seat **Yerba Buena Center for the Arts Theater** (**B**) (1993, James Stewart Polshek and Partners). Exposed steel cross beams emphasize its boxy, geometrical design, accented by red and yellow flourishes around the lobby and entranceway. The theater hosts local and touring performance groups that share the center's goal of promoting multiculturalism.

Esplanade (**C**) – Incorporating gently rolling hills, trees, gardens, eclectic sculptures and an outdoor performance area, the manicured Esplanade is a quiet haven. Paths meander about the ground level, which lies atop an underground extension of Moscone Center. The south side is dominated by *Revelations*, a site-specific memorial to Dr. Martin Luther King, Jr. Behind an exhilarating waterfall, 50ft wide and 20ft high, are 12 glass panels engraved with quotations from the civil-rights leader's speeches and writings. It was the joint work of sculptor Howard Conwill, poet Estella Majoza and architect Joseph De Pace.

On a second-story terrace, the Sister City Garden features plants and shrubs from the 14 international cities that nurture cultural and political relations with San Francisco. Fine sculptures stud the Esplanade, including wild-eyed *Shaking Man* by Terry Allen *(terrace level)* and *Deep Gradient/Suspect Terrain*, a 20ft steel-and-glass sinking "ship" by John Roloff in the east garden.

★**Metreon–A Sony Entertainment Center** (**E**) – 🆔 *101 4th St. at Howard St. Open year-round daily 10am–10pm.* ✗ & ☎ *415-369-6000. www.metreon.com.* This four-story, 350,000sq ft retail and entertainment complex offers a businesslike façade to city traffic but an open and inviting front to the Esplanade. Within the

$85-million center are a 15-screen cineplex and IMAX theater, seven restaurants and numerous stores. Most encourage potential buyers to interact with their wares, including software programs (in **microsoftSF**), electronics devices (in **Sony Style**), compact discs (in **Hear Music**) and computer games (in **PlayStation**).

Three interactive attractions cater, respectively, to young children, older children and the child in everyone. **Where the Wild Things Are** is a whimsical playhouse based upon Maurice Sendak's popular kids' book. **The Way Things Work** uses film and machinery to explore basic physics in everyday technology, per the works of architect-illustrator David Macaulay. **Airtight Garage** is a cutting-edge electronic games arcade designed by graphic novelist Jean "Moebius" Giraud.

Rooftop at Yerba Buena Gardens (D) – ▦ *750 Folsom St. Open year-round daily 10:30am–11pm.* ✕ ⬧ ☎ *415-777-3727. www.yerbabuena.org/ybgsafetynet, maps/rooftop.html.* This $56 million children's complex atop the west wing of Moscone Center's South Hall is highlighted by an illuminated, glass-enclosed Charles Looff carousel (constructed c.1906 and subsequently a fixture at the Playland-at-the-Beach amusement park). It includes a year-round ice-skating rink, a 12-lane bowling center, an interactive playground and learning garden, a labyrinth of hedges, and an outdoor amphitheater. Rooftop's cornerstone is **Zeum★** *(▦ 221 4th St.; open year-round weekends & holidays 11am–5pm, mid-Jun–Aug Wed–Fri noon–6pm; $7;* ⬧ ☎ *415-777-2800; www.zeum.org),* a 34,000sq ft high-tech studio and theater for the visual and performing arts, designed by architect Adele Naude Santos.

★★San Francisco Museum of Modern Art

151 3rd St. Open Memorial Day–Labor Day Thu–Tue 10am–6pm (Thu 9pm). Rest of the year Thu–Tue 11am–6pm (Thu 9pm). Closed major holidays. $9 (free 1st Tue, 1/2 price Thu 6pm–9pm). Guided tours (1hr) available. ✕ ⬧ ☎ *415-357-4000. www.sfmoma.org.*

San Francisco's premier showcase for modern art occupies an innovative contemporary building that makes a striking new addition to the city's skyline. After an extended and awkward tenancy in its longtime quarters at Civic Center, the museum (popularly known as "SFMOMA") is coming of age in its new home facing Yerba Buena Gardens.

Growing Pains – The present-day museum began in 1871 as the San Francisco Art Association, a group of artists and art lovers determined to promote artistic expression and appreciation in the Bay Area. Housed at the Palace of Fine Arts after the Panama-Pacific International Exposition of 1915, the organization, renamed the San Francisco Museum of Art, moved in 1935 to new quarters in the War Memorial Veterans Building at Civic Center. Founding director Grace McCann Morley conceived an ambitious program of more than 70 shows a year highlighting pivotal movements and seminal works of contemporary art, and the museum quickly gained a reputation for bringing new and challenging works before the public eye. It organized the first solo exhibitions of works by then-unknown artists Arshile Gorky, Clyfford Still, Jackson Pollock, Robert Motherwell and Mark Rothko. As early as 1970, despite several expansions and renovations, problems inherent in the Veterans Building space—lack of climate control, no ground-floor presence, insufficient gallery space and inadequate storage—inhibited the flow of donations and caused certain important traveling shows to bypass the Museum of Art. In 1988, the board of trustees initiated massive fundraising efforts to begin construction of a new home for the museum on land situated across from Yerba Buena Gardens. Swiss architect Mario Botta, reputed for humanistic modernism and skillful use of natural light, was selected to design the new space, with Hellmuth, Obata & Kassabaum, Inc. as the architect of record. The commission represented Botta's first building in the US and his first major museum.

Modern Home for Modern Art – Botta's design is a striking composition of symmetrically arranged, stepped-back, brick-clad masses. Though at first glance the building appears simple and blocky, fine brickwork creates a rhythmic play of light and shadow across its exterior, and such details as exposed expansion joints are worth a careful look. Piercing the center of the building is a massive shaft, set off from the red-brown brick by stripes of alternating black and white stone. Botta created a huge skylight by slanting the top of the cylinder toward 3rd Street and facing the slanted surface with glass. This great central oculus serves as both beacon and receptor: It announces the museum's presence in the cityscape while suffusing the building's upper galleries and atrium with natural light.

Botta, who studied and worked extensively in Italy and was much influenced by that country's public architecture, envisioned the museum's interior street level as a piazza-like urban space. Paved in alternating bands of polished and unpolished black marble, the stunning central **atrium★★** leads to a stylish cafe, a bookstore, a 299-seat theater, classrooms and special-events spaces. Its open design reveals the building's spatial arrangement at a glance, giving a clear sense of five levels arrayed around the great, catwalk-crossed tower shaft and accessed by a majestic stairway.

In the galleries, the colors of structural and finish materials provide a neutral backdrop for artworks. The blacks and grays of stone and the slickness of glass and steel play against the somber warmth of wood tones. Nordic birch sheathes the wainscoting, and the maple floors are sprung to reduce foot fatigue.

The Collections – Now numbering more than 20,000 works of art, the permanent collection was initiated in 1935, just six years after the Museum of Modern Art was founded in New York City. The initial gift of 36 works—including Diego Rivera's *The Flower Carrier*—was presented by local insurance magnate Albert M. Bender, one of the institution's founding trustees. Through the 20C the holdings grew steadily in size and scope while staying true to the museum's contemporary bent. Acquisition of painting and sculpture remained a focus, with major donations bestowed by influential San Franciscans such as architect Timothy Pflueger (whose landmark Pacific Telephone Building backdrops the museum building to the east), Elise Stern Haas and Harriet Lane Levy. American abstract artist Clyfford Still's gift of 28 paintings is one of the treasures of the museum's holdings. Today the painting and sculpture collections represent all major movements of modern art, with significant strengths in early Modernism and works by California and Bay Area artists.

As early as 1936, the museum began to present photography as a fine-art medium, and gifts of works by Alfred Stieglitz, Ansel Adams, Imogen Cunningham and other members of the Group f.64 augmented the photography collection. An initial architectural show in 1940 gave rise to the museum's Department of Architecture and Design; further exhibitions of the work of such noted architects as Le Corbusier and American designers Charles and Ray Eames have helped to secure the museum's reputation in this field. The Department of Media Arts, established in 1988 and one of only five such curatorial chairs in the US, celebrates the Bay Area's position as a hub of activity in video, film, digital and on-line works.

Visit – First-time visitors are advised to take the interactive CD-ROM-based audio tour *($3; rental table on 1st floor)* recorded by museum curators and directors; the tour provides excellent insights into the collection and its highlights. Stop by the computer-equipped study alcove *(2nd floor)* where users can sample various programs, among them a survey of key ideas and issues in 20C art with reference to the permanent collection, and a multimedia archive of California artists. The museum's library and graphic-arts research center *(lower level)* are open to the public by appointment only.

5 **Caffe Museo**
In SFMOMA. ☎ *415-357-4500.* Glowing woods and fixtures match the museum's decor at this elegant cafe, the perfect place to refresh with an espresso, a vegetarian pasta, a focaccia sandwich or other light, Italian fare. Eat in, or take a table on the sidewalk to view the comings and goings at Yerba Buena Gardens across the street.

Don Myer Photography/San Francisco Museum of Modern Art

Cityscape I (1963) by Richard Diebenkorn

In addition to hosting important traveling shows, the museum maintains an active program of changing thematic exhibitions from the permanent collection. Much gallery space is reserved for this purpose. Only part of the permanent collection is on view at any given time.

Second floor – Paintings, sculpture and works of architecture and design drawn from the permanent collection occupy galleries here. Though artworks are frequently rotated, visitors are likely to see mainstays of the painting collection. Henri Matisse's landmark *Femme au Chapeau* (1905) created outrage when it was exhibited at the Paris Salon d'Automne of 1905; critical response to the painting, and to similar works exhibited with it, gave rise to the term "Fauvism" to describe the use of vivid, non-naturalistic colors. Georges Braque's *Violin and Candlestick* (1910), created during the height of Cubism, represents objects simultaneously from multiple points of view. A small gallery rotates works by Paul Klee, who participated briefly in the *Blaue Reiter* movement; the 100 Klee works promised the museum by benefactor Dr. Carl Djerassi span the length of the Swiss artist's career. Visitors should not miss Mexican muralist Diego Rivera's sympathetically idealized paean to peons, *The Flower Carrier* (1935), nor self-taught artist Frida Kahlo's insightfully detailed portrait of herself and her husband, *Frieda and Diego Rivera* (1931), which she painted especially for museum trustee Albert Bender, her friend and patron. Jackson Pollock's immensely influential *Guardians of the Secret* (1943), one of the museum's most important pieces, opened the gateway to American Abstract Expressionism as well as to Pollock's own "drip" period. One gallery is dedicated to selections from the museum's 30 huge, abstract canvases by Clyfford Still.

Berkeley painter Joan Brown's *Noel in the Kitchen* (c.1964) embodies the Bay Area Figurative movement's return to recognizable subject matter in the aftermath of Abstract Expressionism. Other California artists whose work may be on view include Richard Diebenkorn, Elmer Bischoff, David Park, Robert Arneson, Edward Keinholz, Wayne Thiebaud and Bruce Connor. Works by Jasper Johns, Robert Rauschenberg and Pop artists James Rosenquist and Andy Warhol reflect the styles that evolved in the postwar period in reaction to Abstract Expressionism. Other noteworthy works include paintings by Pablo Picasso, Joan Míro, Salvador Dalí, Georgia O'Keeffe, Roy Lichtenstein and Mark Rothko.

The Department of Architecture and Design taps its permanent collection to present frequently changing shows on furniture, graphic arts, building design and even urban design.

Third Floor – Lower ceilings here keep scale appropriate to exhibitions of photography and works on paper. The museum's 9,000-piece photography collection is international in scope and rich in both historic and contemporary holdings. Strengths include works by mid-20C American masters Edward Weston, Imogen Cunningham, Ansel Adams, Edward Steichen, Diane Arbus, Margaret Bourke-White, Robert Mapplethorpe and Alfred Steiglitz (including one portrait of his wife, painter Georgia O'Keeffe).

Fourth and Fifth Floors – These two levels are devoted to the exhibition of large-scale, contemporary pieces and installations, sometimes including works from the permanent collection. The entire floor is engineered to handle the technical requirements of experimental work, and movable nonbearing walls allow the spaces to be reconfigured as necessary. Natural light washes the white surfaces of these high-ceilinged upper galleries, though subtle screens and filters can adjust its quality. Be sure to venture across the fifth floor's dramatic steel bowstring-truss **catwalk★** soaring 125ft over the lobby floor for a superb (if decidedly vertiginous) overview of the central shaft.

Additional Sights

★Pacific Telephone Building – *140 New Montgomery St.* This 30-story building (1925, Timothy Pflueger) was the only skyscraper south of Market Street for decades. Today the restored building still boasts an elegant terra-cotta facade and brass doorways topped by ogee arches. The elegant **lobby★** features black marble walls and columns, an intricate plaster ceiling with Asian motifs, and display cases with memorabilia illustrating the building's history. The modest **Pacific Bell Museum & Archives** *(enter from lobby; open Tue–Thu 10am–2pm;* ☎ *415-542-0182)* has a variety of offbeat exhibits on telephone history.

★Friends of Photography at the Ansel Adams Center (G) – *655 Mission St. Open year-round daily 11am–5pm (1st Thu to 8pm). Closed Jan 1, Thanksgiving Day, Dec 25. $5.* ♿ ☎ *415-495-7000. www.friendsofphotography.org.* Newly ensconced in a larger gallery space, this award-winning museum exhibits fine historic and contemporary photographs and works in other visual media. Established in 1989, the center was named for San Francisco-born artist **Ansel Adams** (1902-1984), whose dramatic photographs of the American Southwest brought photography newfound respect as an art form in the 1930s. In these early works, as well as in his later Sierra Club books and photographs of Japanese-Americans interned during World War II, Adams sought to fuse his passions for social justice and environmental preservation with his desire to bring photography recognition in the larger artistic community. The Friends of Photography, founded in 1967 by Adams and other renowned artists and historians, continue to promote the photographer's goals. One gallery of the museum is primarily dedicated to Adams' life and work.

California Historical Society – *678 Mission St. Open year-round Tue–Sun 11am–5pm. $3 (free 1st Tue).* ♿ ☎ *415-357-1848. www.calhist.org.* The state's official historical research organization, founded in the late 19C, carries out an active program of collection and exhibition on California's colorful, rambunctious past. In its attractive building (1922), the society maintains holdings *(available for study by appointment)* of books, manuscripts, original documents, journals, maps, photographs and fine and decorative arts covering the great sweep of California's history, with some publications dating from the 17C. A spacious public gallery on the first level houses changing thematic exhibits curated by society staff, as well as traveling exhibits organized by other historical institutions. There also is an excellent specialty bookshop off the lobby.

St. Patrick's Catholic Church (**F**) – *756 Mission St. Open year-round daily 6:30am–6:30pm. Concerts Wed 12:30pm.* ♿ ☎ *415-421-3730.* Founded by Irish immigrants during the golden days of 1851, St. Patrick's first red brick church was erected on this site in 1872, and served working-class families through the late 19C. Destroyed by the quake and fire of 1906, it was rebuilt in 1909 in Gothic Revival style using many of the original bricks. Fire scars still mark some walls. Green-veined Irish marble lines the vestibule; stained-glass windows depict scenes from the life of St. Patrick; even the vestments are embroidered with Celtic patterns. Ironically, the congregation is now largely Filipino in ancestry, and mass is celebrated in the Tagalog language as well as in English.

Wednesday noontime concerts of classical music, featuring local and touring professional artists, are offered year-round (☎ *415-777-3211).*

A broad pedestrian plaza, under construction on the site of a former parking lot east of St. Patrick's, will be shared with the **Mexican Museum** (☎ *415-202-9700)* and **The Jewish Museum San Francisco** (☎ *415-788-9990).* Both are scheduled to move into new facilities opposite Yerba Buena Gardens by 2003.

Marriott San Francisco Hotel – *55 4th St.* ✗ ♿ 🅿 ☎ *415-896-1600* Although adjacent buildings tend to obscure its futuristic 39-story profile, this Postmodern building (1989, Anthony Lumsden) is a modern landmark. The Marriott's neo-Deco silhouette and fan-shaped windows once led to its being labeled "the Jukebox" by a local columnist. It is best viewed looking south down Grant Avenue from Chinatown.

Cartoon Art Museum (**M²**) – Kids *814 Mission St., 2nd floor. Open year-round Tue–Fri 11am–5pm, Sat 10am–5pm, Sun 1–5pm. Closed major holidays. $5.* ♿ ☎ *415-227-8666. www.cartoonart.org.* Housed in the former *Call-Bulletin* newspaper building, this museum displays comics that wed drawing and text to sometimes humorous, sometimes shocking effect. Founded in 1984 to foster appreciation of cartoon art, the museum has since amassed an 11,000-piece permanent collection, including work dating from the late 18C. Samples of these works are displayed alongside temporary exhibits of international and local cartoonists, many of whom use the medium to critique the status quo.

Peanuts Cartoonist's Self-portrait

© Charles Schulz/Cartoon Art Museum

Society of California Pioneers – *300 4th St. at Folsom St. Open year-round Tue–Fri & 1st Sat 10am–4pm. Closed major holidays. $3 (may vary by show).* ♿ ☎ *415-957-1849. www.california pioneers.org.* This showcase for 19C and early 20C treasures, collected by descendants of pre-1850 Californians, opened in September 2000 catty-corner from Moscone Center. On the first floor, the Seymour Pioneer Museum presents changing theme exhibits on California history drawn from the permanent collection of 6,000 artifacts and 50,000 photographs. On the second floor, the Moore Gallery offers early portraits and landscapes by the likes of Thomas Hill and William Keith, as well as prints and lithographs. The third floor holds the Sullivan Library, a research center open by appointment.

Oceanfront

23 • SUNSET DISTRICT and LAKE MERCED

MUNI bus 18–46th Ave., 23–Monterey, 28–19th Ave., 29–Sunset,
or 48–Quintara–24th St.; streetcar L–Taraval, M–19th Ave. or N–Judah.

Bounded on the east by Stanyan Street, on the west by the Pacific Ocean and on the north by Golden Gate Park, the Sunset District encompasses a broad, flat grid of regularly spaced residential streets with row after orderly row of tract houses. Most attractions lie along the coast or scattered around natural Lake Merced in San Francisco's southwesternmost corner.

Historical Notes

Part of the wind- and fog-scoured expanse of sand dunes known as the Outer Lands during the city's early decades, the Sunset is today a wind and fog-scoured expanse of stucco row houses. They were erected after construction of a streetcar tunnel under Twin Peaks opened the area to residential development in the 1930s. During the ensuing building frenzy, contractors literally raced each other up and down the newly platted streets, throwing up affordable, mass-produced row houses. Although derided by architectural critics for their "cookie-cutter" sameness, the bungalows nonetheless offered the possibility of home ownership to people of less-than-substantial means. The Sunset's two most interesting neighborhoods, **Forest Hill** (east end of Taraval St.) and **St. Francis Wood** (east end of Sloat Blvd.), predate the Twin Peaks tunnel.

The Sunset District harbors the main campus of San Francisco State University and the medical center of the University of California at San Francisco. Extending across the district's southern border is Lake Merced, a pleasant body of water that is a popular recreation destination for the golf course and biking and running trails that line its shores. The area's most visible landmark is the distinctive **Sutro Tower**, a pronged, red-and-white-striped television transmitter perched atop Mt. Sutro, which rises above the district on the northeast. The tower is the city's tallest structure.

SIGHTS

★**Ocean Beach** – KID MUNI bus 18–46th Ave. or 48–Quintara-24th St.; streetcars L–Taraval or N–Judah. This expansive beach creates a broad, sandy seam between San Francisco and the Pacific Ocean. Pounding surf and a dangerous undertow make swimming here unwise, although schools of surfers in gleaming wetsuits often paddle out from the beach at the foot of Taraval Street to await the perfect wave. A paved **promenade**, landscaped with dune-stabilizing grasses and shrubs, extends north 3mi from Sloat Boulevard to just south of Cliff House, making the beach extremely popular with bikers, walkers and runners.

1 PJ's Oyster Bed
737 Irving St. at 9th St.
☎ *415-566-7775.* This informal, popular "Bayou by the Bay" serves hearty, delicious seafood and oysters. Come in good voice or be muted by the roar of music, patrons and steam-inhaling fans. Portions are hearty—for each meal you eat, you'll have a second to take home.

2 Casa Aguila
1240 Noriega St. at 20th St.
☎ *415-661-5593.* The owners circulate sangria, chips and salsa to sustain the inevitable crowd of patrons-in-waiting outside this small, imaginatively decorated Mexican restaurant. Helpings are huge, especially the signature dish, *la parillada*, a mound of seafood, pork, chicken or some of each, served on a flame-heated stand.

Sigmund Stern Grove – *Parking entrance on Vale St., off Crestlake Dr., 1 block north of Sloat Blvd. between 19th Ave. & Sunset Blvd.* MUNI *bus 23–Monterey or 28–19th Ave. Open year-round daily 10am–6pm. Concerts: mid-Jun–mid-Aug Sun 2pm.* ✕ 🅿 ☎ *415-252-6252. www.sterngrove.org.* Presented to the city as a park in 1931 by Rosalie Stern in memory of her husband, Sigmund, this 33-acre sylvan "grove" lies at the bottom of an east-west-running ravine. Redwoods and fragrant eucalyptus trees hem the sides of the narrow valley surrounding Stage Meadow, which forms a natural amphitheater. Free musical performances are staged as part of a popular, long-running concert series endowed by Mrs. Stern in 1938. Music lovers of every stripe bring blankets and picnic fare to enjoy concerts in a range of musical styles from jazz to opera. Pre-performance lectures and demonstrations are held just east of Stage Meadow in the dignified, Victorian **Trocadero** (1892), built by earlier landowner George M. Greene and popular as a saloon before Prohibition.

★**San Francisco Zoo** – [Kids] *Sloat Blvd. at 45th Ave.* [MUNI] *bus 18–46th Ave. or 23–Monterey; streetcar L–Taraval. Open year-round daily 10am–5pm. $9. Guided tours (1hr) available Sat 11am.* ✗ ▣ ☎ *415-753-7080. www.sfzoo.org.* Set on 125 undulating acres on the southern fringe of the Sunset District, San Francisco's zoo has overcome its fog-draped site and dispiriting institutional history to welcome some 900,000 visitors a year.

The zoo's original plan took shape in the 1930s, a legacy of the WPA-assisted public construction common among zoos of that era. By the 1980s, its diminutive concrete enclosures had been eclipsed by the cageless, "natural habitat" displays adopted by other zoos in the country. In 1993, with the zoo facing loss of its accreditation, a partnership was formed between the city and the nonprofit San Francisco Zoological Society to manage it and raise funds for physical renovation, species conservation and breeding programs.

In 1997, San Franciscans approved a $48 million bond to rebuild two-thirds of the zoo by 2004, focusing on more naturalistic habitats for its 1,000 denizens—including an African savanna and new quarters for lions, elephants, rhinos, chimpanzees, orangutans and the fauna of Madagascar. Improved visitor amenities, including shops and food outlets, will cluster near a new main entrance. The Lurie Education Center and Koret Animal Resource Center were scheduled to open in 2001 as a first step.

Visit – For now, begin your visit with a ride on the **Safari Tram** *(30min; $2.50)*, then return to linger at spots of particular interest. Just past the entrance, the **Children's Zoo** *(open mid-Jun–Labor Day daily 10:30am–4:30pm; rest of the year daily 11am–4pm)* features meerkats and prairie dogs, an insect zoo, terrariums at kids' eye level, and a petting barnyard where human youngsters can make friends with domestic animals. Admire the graceful inhabitants of **Flamingo Lake**, then continue to the superb **Primate Discovery Center★**, where 15 species of rare and endangered monkeys and prosimians cavort and swing in open atriums. The adjacent **Aye-Aye Forest** houses endangered aye-ayes, the first breeding pair of these rare nocturnal primates to be exhibited in public. A spur trail leads to **Gorilla World**, a lushly landscaped, one-acre domain where a six-member society of lowland gorillas acts out the rules of its own hierarchy.

For a glimpse of animal life below the Equator, stroll left from the main entrance to the **Australian Walkabout**, an outdoor habitat for kangaroos (one of them albino), wallabies and emus. Nearby are the **Billabong**, home to waterfowl from Down Under; **Koala Crossing**, patterned after an Outback station; and **Rainbow Landing**, an aviary aflutter with colorful lorikeets. **Puente al Sur** ("Bridge to the South") features such Latin American creatures as capybaras, tapirs and Andean condors. The **Feline Conservation Center**, near the zoo's South Gate, harbors small and medium-sized cats—including snow leopards, jaguars and panthers—for breeding and study. Visitors to **Penguin Island** can view the world's most successful breeding colony of Magellanic penguins. Detour to the **black rhinoceros** enclosure where, chances are, 30yr-old Ellie will be nursing another child: In 2000, she gave birth to her 13th. Other animals on view may include tigers (Siberian and Sumatran) and bears (spectacled, polar and Kodiak). Before departing, take a spin around the track on **Little Puffer** *($2)*, a miniature turn-of-the-20C steam train gleamingly restored and brought back from premature retirement.

Fort Funston – *Enter from Rte. 35 (Skyline Blvd.) just south of John Muir Dr.* [MUNI] *bus 18–46th Ave.* ☎ *415-239-2366.* This expansive former military post overlooking the Pacific Ocean was established in 1898 during the Spanish-American War. As with all of San Francisco's coastal fortifications, it was never tested in combat. Originally called the Laguna Merced Military Reservation, the fort was renamed in 1917 in honor of General Frederick Funston, the Presidio co-commandant who organized military forces to maintain order in San Francisco in the aftermath of the 1906 earthquake and fire. With the approach of World War II, heavy cannonry was installed; Battery Richmond Davis, built in 1938, held two 16in guns. In a strategy worthy of Lewis Carroll, destination-less "roads" were created within Funston's grounds at this time to confound any invaders arriving by sea.

Today the former military lands (decommissioned in 1963) are managed by the Golden Gate National Recreation Area as a 250-acre park. Ice plants cloak the dunes atop bluffs that rise 200ft above a clean sand beach; these dunes are considered among the finest hang-gliding spots in the US. Visitors gather on a wooden viewing deck for expansive shoreline vistas and to watch the aerialists in flight with their colorful craft. The grounds are also a popular place for urbanites to run their dogs. The north end of the park is a stopover for migratory Central and South American bank swallows, which burrow into the bluffs and nest there from April through July. At that time, the habitat is closed to public visitation.

Visit – Stop at the small **visitor center** *(open year-round weekends noon–4pm;* ♿ ▣ ☎ *415-239-2366)* at the edge of the parking lot (once a Nike missile site) to take in displays on Fort Funston's history, and to acquire park maps and other information. Knock on the adjacent park rangers' door for information when the visitor center is closed. The nearby Environmental Science Center maintains a native plant nursery behind the structures. Scenic **Sunset Trail** *(.75mi)* meanders atop the windswept dunes and past Battery Davis before looping back to the parking lot. Long-distance hikers may link this trail to other sections of the Coastal Trail for a 4.7mi walk to Cliff House or a 9.1mi ramble to Fort Point.

San Francisco State University – *1600 Holloway Ave. at 19th Ave.* bus *18–46th Ave. or 29–Sunset; streetcar M–19th Ave.* 415-338-1111. *www.sfsu.edu.* Founded in 1899 as a teacher-training college, this was the first normal school in the US to require a high-school diploma for admission. The college had a high national profile during the late 1960s, as student protests against racial discrimination, the Vietnam War, the military draft and "irrelevant" college classes culminated in November 1968 in the longest campus strike in history. Acting university president S.I. Hayakawa refused to give in to the students, and strife finally ended in March 1969 with both sides claiming victory. A lasting legacy was the establishment of the nation's first School of Ethnic Studies and an expanded Black Studies Department. Today the 93-acre campus claims nearly 27,000 students. An emphasis on multiculturalism is evident at the **Art Department Gallery** *(upper level of Fine Arts Bldg., between Tapia Dr. & Cesar Chavez Student Center; open Sept–May Mon–Sat noon–4pm; closed major holidays;* 415-338-6535*)*, whose changing exhibits focus on notable artists of African, Asian and Hispanic ancestry. Two Ruth Asawa sculptures stand on either side of the lobby. Inquire in the gallery for a self-guided map to campus sculptures.

The Poetry Center and American Poetry Archives *(Humanities Bldg., Tapia Dr. opposite Fine Arts Bldg.;* 415-338-2227*)*, founded in 1954 with a gift from W.H. Auden, harbors the world's largest videotaped collection of poets and authors reading their own works—more than 2,000 in all. The **Sutro Library** *(480 Winston Dr., north campus; open Mon–Sat 10am–5pm; closed major holidays;* 415-731-4477*)*, a part of the California State Library system, has one of the West's earliest and largest genealogical collections, inherited from the estate of Adolph Sutro.

Cayuga Playground – *Cayuga & Naglee Aves., one block west of Alemany Blvd.* bus 29–Sunset. This urban oasis, the work of gardener Demetrio Braceros, uplifts an otherwise-downtrodden neighborhood. From the stumps of fallen trees, Braceros has carved the likenesses of the Virgin Mary and Jesus, Michael Jordan, Princess Di and others, including a menagerie of animals. He has woven twigs and branches into fences, railings and benches; designed two walking paths, the Garden of Eden Trail and the New Trail of Hope; planted flowers, vegetables and fruit trees, and wrote inspirational messages on rocks with beautiful calligraphy.

24 • SUTRO HEIGHTS and LAND'S END★★

bus 18–46th Ave. or 38–Geary
Map pp 180-181

The rugged northwest corner of San Francisco, between Ocean Beach and Lincoln Park, has drawn visitors to its rocky cliffs and sheltered coves since Ohlone Indians camped here. Comprising ghostly ruins, a historical roadhouse, brush-lined trails and breathtaking views, this stretch of the Golden Gate National Recreation Area (GGNRA) provides an impressive natural refuge at the edge of bustling San Francisco.
Its highlight is the California Palace of the Legion of Honor, San Francisco's preeminent repository for European art. Extending its pristine colonnaded wings toward the rugged shores of the Golden Gate, the museum enjoys a spectacular setting amid the Monterey pines and cypresses of Lincoln Park.

Historical Notes

Settlement came slowly to San Francisco's coastline. In the early days of the gold rush, a few intrepid Europeans tried to homestead here, but it wasn't until the mid-1850s that Seal Rock House, an early precursor to today's Cliff House, was constructed near the shore, drawing city dwellers on Sunday beach outings. In the mid-1860s, prominent San Francisco families—including the Crockers, Stanfords and Hearsts—adopted the area as their summer playground. In the last two decades of the 19C, however, the area lost its upper-class cachet, largely thanks to a populist-minded entrepreneur named Adolph Sutro.

The Comstock King – In 1851, at the age of 21, Prussian-born **Adolph Sutro** (1830-98) arrived in San Francisco in search of Gold Rush riches. After establishing himself as a tobacconist, the self-educated engineer relocated in 1860 to Virginia City, Nevada, where fortunes were being made from the Comstock Lode. Silver, not gold, lay in the lode's blue clay, but mining proved treacherous due to poor ventilation and water in the shafts. Sutro designed a 4mi-long passage beneath the silver vein, wrangling for nearly 15yrs with banks, mine owners and investors over funds to build it. When the Sutro Tunnel finally opened, its brilliant engineer was dubbed the Comstock King.

Adolph Sutro in his Library (c.1885)

Marilyn Blaisdell Collection

A shrewd businessman, Sutro sold his shares in the tunnel just prior to the crash of the mine stock in 1880. Returning to San Francisco, he quickly invested his fortune in land, eventually coming to own 1/12 of all the property in the city, including hundreds of acres of wind-swept sand dunes between downtown and the ocean. His enormously popular Sutro Baths, his lush estate atop Sutro Heights, his 5-cent railway and his rebuilt Cliff House ballooned the oceanfront's fame as a favorite leisure destination for pleasure-seeking San Franciscans of every economic stripe.

A Popular Playland – By 1921 a beachside entertainment zone of dance halls, rides and other amusements had sprung up between Sutro Heights and Golden Gate Park. Renamed **Playland-at-the-Beach** in 1928, the strip resounded with shrieks of pleasure from the Big Dipper roller coaster and sprightly music from a Looff carousel (since restored and moved to the new Rooftop at Yerba Buena Gardens). Streetcars brought revelers from downtown to practice their marksmanship in the shooting galleries, whoosh down the Fun House slide and munch on waffles, hot dogs and chocolate-covered ice-cream cookie sandwiches.

By the mid-20C Playland had fallen into seediness; it succumbed to the wrecking ball in 1972. In the mid-1970s much of San Francisco's west coast, including Ocean Beach, Sutro Heights and Land's End, were acquired by the National Park Service as part of the GGNRA. Today this region's dramatic natural beauty, its most enduring resource, has again become its central attraction.

Visiting Sutro Heights and Land's End – This area is very popular with visitors, especially in summer. Parking spaces just in front of Cliff House tend to fill quickly, but lots may be found above Sutro Baths on Merrie Way; across Point Lobos Avenue from Merrie Way; and at Fort Miley beside the *USS San Francisco* memorial.

Note that the cliffs are unstable: When hiking, keep to designated paths. When exploring near the water, never turn your back on the ocean as waves can be extremely unpredictable. High tides tend to arrive suddenly, and sneaker waves—large waves that rise without warning—pose a threat to the careless.

SUTRO HEIGHTS

★Cliff House – *1090 Point Lobos Ave. Open year-round Mon–Thu 9am–10:30pm. Fri–Sat 8:30am–11pm.* 🍴 ♿ 🅿 ☎ *415-386-3330. www.cliffhouse.com.* Best known for its spectacular setting, Cliff House perches atop a high bluff overlooking the Pacific Ocean. Although today's modern structure lacks the awe-inspiring grandeur of Adolph Sutro's version, it recalls the area's heyday as San Francisco's preeminent leisure destination.

The present building is the third incarnation of a white clapboard roadhouse erected in 1863 by real-estate tycoon Charles Butler, who hoped to spark Coney Island-style development of the adjacent coastal area. By the 1880s it had acquired a somewhat unsavory reputation as a gambling hall to which "gentlemen" repaired for afternoon trysts. Adolph Sutro, who bought the property in 1881, cleaned up its tawdry image and remade it as a family resort, building the Sutro Railroad to transport the general public to and from the city.

This first Cliff House burned to the ground on Christmas Day 1894, but Sutro lost no time in hiring architects Emile Lemme and C.J. Colley to design its replacement: a flamboyant, eight-story, many-spired confection resembling a French chateau.

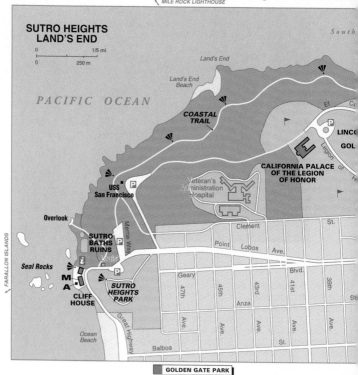

Critics decried Sutro's extravagance, but the public loved the ornate castle and its restaurants, art galleries, luxurious parlors with panoramic ocean views, private lunch rooms and observation tower 200ft above the sea. Its glory was short-lived, however—the building survived the 1906 earthquake only to succumb to fire the following year.

In 1909 the Reid Brothers, architects of the Fairmont Hotel, designed the third and present Cliff House. The resort remained popular through Prohibition, but was abandoned for extended periods in the mid-20C. Many times renovated and modernized, Cliff House was acquired by the National Park Service in 1977.

Today visitors enjoy stiff breezes, stunning **views★★** of Ocean Beach, and glimpses of brown pelicans, cormorants and—in certain seasons—sea lions roosting on **Seal Rocks**, just offshore. A GGNRA **visitor center★** *(open year-round daily 10am–5pm; closed Jan 1, Thanksgiving Day, Dec 25; 1hr guided tours available, reservations required; ⚙ 🅿 ☎ 415-556-8642; www.nps.gov/goga)* on the lower deck offers maps and information, as well as photos of Cliff House, Ocean Beach and Sutro Baths as they appeared at the turn of the 20C.

Cliff House (1896-1907)

Musée Mécanique (M) – 📷 *Open Jun–Aug daily 10am–8pm. Rest of the year Mon–Fri 11am–7pm. weekends & holidays 10am–8pm.* ♿ 🅿 ☎ *415-386-1170.* Situated opposite the visitor center on the lower terrace, this gallery contains a curious collection of antique mechanical amusements, including coin-operated player pianos and orchestrions, mobile dioramas made entirely of toothpicks, and penny-arcade picture machines. Many of the mechanisms were collected from Playland, most notably "Laughing Sal," whose rambunctious guffaws—audible from a considerable distance—recall the days when small change could still buy a laugh. Historic photographs of Playland line several walls, and a room at the rear houses modern arcade games.

Camera Obscura (A) – 📷 *Open year-round daily 11am–sunset. Closed rainy & foggy days. $1.* ♿ 🅿 ☎ *415-750-0415.* Housed in a small building near the Musée Mécanique, this curious instrument employs a mirror and two opposing lenses to magnify and project views of the surrounding area onto a 6ft parabolic screen. The motorized contraption completes a 360° rotation every 6min, giving visitors close-up views of Ocean Beach, Seal Rocks and the rugged coastline stretching away to the north.

★**Sutro Baths Ruins** – *Access by footpath from Louis' Restaurant or steps from the end of the Merrie Way parking lot.* The haunting vestiges of the once-grand Sutro Baths lie in a cove just north of Cliff House. Lupine and ice plants cover the hills surrounding the concrete foundations that hardly evoke the magnificence of the disappeared structure they once supported. Sea birds bathe in the brackish pools. A tunnel, originally used to dump dirt dredged from the baths, pierces the bluff to the north, leading to a stretch of craggy coastline. The tunnel crosses a sea cave where the sound of rushing waves reverberates on rocky walls. Above the tunnel, an upper path leads to an **overlook** from which the remains of long-grounded ships can be spotted at low tide.

★★**Coastal Trail** – *3.4mi loop. From the Merrie Way parking lot, follow the sandy path to the wide main trail. www.nps.gov/goga.* This well-maintained loop provides an invigorating walk along San Francisco's northwesternmost headland, a wild, heavily wooded shoreline boasting spectacular **views**★★★ of the ocean, the Golden Gate Bridge and the Marin Headlands. For part of its length, the lower trail follows an old railroad bed atop sheer bluffs that plunge abruptly to swirling waters. Eucalyptus trees scent the hills rising to the south, while Monterey pines and firs hold the crumbling cliffs in place with gnarled, winding roots. Stairs scale the steeper inclines, and several smaller trails lead off the main path, one of them to the secluded Land's End Beach often frequented by members of the city's gay community. The main trail, narrow and winding in places, leads to a viewing platform overlooking the posh Sea Cliff neighborhood. Walk down the steps to the end of the overlook for a lovely view of rocky Eagle's Point.

The return route leads up from the overlook to follow a wide, paved berm along El Camino del Mar through the **Lincoln Park Golf Course**★. These city-owned public links, landscaped by John McLaren in 1909, boast spectacular views from the fairways. Pass to the right of the California Palace of the Legion of Honor through a parking lot above the golf course to rejoin the footpath, which leads to the trail's end at the Fort Miley parking lot. Across from here, part of the bullet-torn bridge of the **USS San Francisco** commemorates the commander and crew of this vessel, which was heavily damaged in the naval Battle of Guadalcanal (1942).

★**Sutro Heights Park** – *Point Lobos Ave. at 48th Ave.* The grounds of Adolph Sutro's former estate occupy a striking promontory overlooking Cliff House and Ocean Beach. Although the residence was demolished in 1939, the property remains a paradise of well-tended lawns and stately groves of distinctive trees. Sutro chanced upon the commanding site in 1881 during a leisurely buggy ride and purchased it forthwith. The original small cottage was enlarged to a comfortable, though not opulent, country home. Sutro lavished his attention on the grounds, importing drought-resistant flowers and trees from all over the world,

Sutro Baths

Adolph Sutro's most beloved contribution to San Francisco was the fabulous Sutro Baths, an elaborate and luxurious public swimming facility the millionaire erected among the rocks below his Sutro Heights estate. In 1891, construction began on the three-story, glass-domed structure, designed by Sutro to utilize tidal ebb and flow to fill and empty its pools. After its completion in 1894, city dwellers paid 5 cents to travel out to the baths on Sutro's own railroad. From the Greek-inspired entrance portal, they descended a grand stairway bounded by palm trees to a cavernous main hall with seven saltwater swimming pools, ranging in temperature from bathwater-warm to ocean-cold. Patrons could change into rented woolen swimming suits in one of 500 private dressing rooms, lounge on bleachers seating 5,300 people, dine in any of three restaurants, or simply wonder at an astounding display of artifacts and curiosities collected by the Comstock King. There were seven slides, one for each pool, and 30 swinging rings strung above the 1.8 million gallons of water.

Despite their enormous popularity, the baths operated at a financial loss, and in 1934 Sutro's heirs covered part of the swimming pools with a skating rink and basketball courts. After World War II, the deteriorated pools were closed. The skating rink continued to operate until 1966, when plans were made to demolish the structure and build apartments on the site. A fire of unexplained origin hastened the building's demise but the apartments were never built and the National Park Service acquired the property in 1980.

including Norfolk Island pines, Canary Island date palms and Monterey cypresses. He designed a wind-powered watering system, built a large glass conservatory for delicate plants, and installed more than 200 statues of mythical and historical figures, many of questionable artistic merit. Ever the populist, Sutro placed a sign at the entrance inviting the public "to walk, ride, and drive therein." After his death in 1898, Sutro's daughter Emma continued this open-door policy, bequeathing the estate to the city as a public park in 1938. In 1976, the National Park Service acquired Sutro Heights.

Visit – Two stone lions, copies of originals now housed in Park Service archives, flank the park's entrance. To the left of the broad driveway, figures of a stag and the goddess Diana rise among the foliage. Sutro's glass conservatory (now demolished) stood to the east of the circular drive that served as a carriage turnaround. A white Victorian gazebo—originally the property's wellhouse—lies to the west on a grassy lawn where intricate carpets of brightly colored flowers once flourished. Follow the wide dirt path past the gazebo, veering left off the main driveway to Sutro's now-overgrown viewing parapet to enjoy some of the area's finest ocean **views★★**; on the clearest days, the Farallon Islands, a protected wildlife refuge 26mi offshore, can be spied on the horizon. Descend the stone stairs to see the lovely terraced gardens on its sheltered south side, replanted by the WPA after Sutro Heights became a public park.

★★CALIFORNIA PALACE OF THE LEGION OF HONOR

100 34th Ave. at El Camino del Mar, Lincoln Park. Open year-round Tue–Sun 9:30am–5pm. Closed major holidays. $8 (free 2nd Wed). Guided tours available. ✗ ⚐ ▣ ☏ *415-863-3330. www.thinker.org.*

A gift to San Francisco from **Alma de Bretteville Spreckels,** this museum houses her personal collection of great sculptures by Auguste Rodin, plus a treasury of European, particularly French, art.

Historical Notes – Born in San Francisco to impoverished European immigrants, Alma de Bretteville (1881-1968) inherited the energy of her hard-working mother and the imagination of her father, whose pride in the faded nobility of the French de Bretteville lineage instilled in his daughter a sense not only of personal destiny but of noblesse oblige. Alma grew into a statuesque, willful, mostly self-educated woman who defied convention in many ways. After several years of a socially unacknowledged liaison, she married sugar magnate **Adolph Spreckels** in 1908. In 1914 she met and fell under the influence of American-born dancer Löie Fuller, the toast of Belle Epoque Paris, who convinced her that her destiny was to become a great patron of the arts with Löie as her agent and chief advisor.

Today the Legion of Honor still expresses the determined grandeur of Alma, who would have liked to have grown up in an art-filled palace and perhaps sought vindication of her social status in the construction of this one. At her request, the building (1924, George Applegarth) was modeled after the 1915 Panama-Pacific International Exposition's French Pavilion. The pavilion was itself a version of the Hôtel de Salm, a 18C Parisian residence designated by Napoleon in 1804 as the Palais de la Légion d'Honneur. (That building's semicircular rotunda so impressed Thomas Jefferson that he incorporated it into his design for Monticello.) On Armistice Day 1924, the new museum was dedicated to the 3,600 Californians who had perished in World War I, declaring the wish of the founders to "honor the dead while serving the living."

Visiting the Legion of Honor – Arrayed with neoclassical symmetry around the central rotunda, the 19 main-floor galleries present a selective, chronologically organized survey of medieval to modern European art. (The Medieval and Renaissance period collections normally displayed in galleries 1 through 5 have been replaced by other exhibitions during construction of the new de Young Museum.) Throughout the main floor, paintings are exhibited with sculptures, textiles and decorative arts of the same period. Large galleries on the lower level host temporary exhibitions, along with rotating displays of works from the Achenbach Foundation for Graphic Arts. The Achenbach Study Center permits computer access to digitized images by subject as well as by artist and title. Greek, Etruscan, Roman and Egyptian antiquities and porcelain collections are shown here, and the museum's bookstore, café and theater are also located on the lower level.

The Thinker by Auguste Rodin

The Collection

Dance-related art and European decorative arts initially formed the core of the museum's holdings, along with one of the finest collections of works by French sculptor Auguste Rodin (1840-1917) outside the Musée Rodin in Paris. Alma, introduced to Rodin in 1914, acquired many of the pieces during the artist's lifetime, when his sculptures were cast by his favorite *fondeur*, Alexis Rudier. The museum now owns 106 sculptures by Rodin, of which the most famous, *The Thinker* (1880), greets visitors in the museum's Court of Honor.

In 1950, the Legion received the city-owned **Achenbach Foundation for Graphic Arts**. This immensely important body of works on paper today numbers 80,000 prints, drawings, photographs, and illustrated books, including the 3,000-work archive of Crown Point Press and special collections of theater and dance designs, Asian miniatures and prints, and early photography.

Along with the M. H. de Young Memorial Museum, the Legion of Honor forms the Fine Arts Museums of San Francisco, whose European collections it houses. The museum reopened in 1995 after a three-year overhaul to seismically strengthen the building while expanding and improving the interior. Although the structure had to be gutted in the process, its shell remained intact. A square-based glass pyramid was added to the outdoor Court of Honor, offering homage to I.M. Pei's famed glass structure at the Louvre; like Pei's pyramid, this one serves as a skylight for spaces on the lower level.

Mannerism and Baroque Art – *Galleries 6 & 7*. The progressively idealized human form and increasingly secular subject matter of High Renaissance art yielded around 1520 to the figural elongation and harsh coloring associated with Mannerism. El Greco was a master of this style: In his *St. John the Baptist* (c.1600), a strange play of light, like that of an electrical storm, charges the picture and the elongated central figure.

The Baroque style, which emerged in Rome around 1600 as a conscious reaction to the artificiality of the Mannerist style, reflects the scientific discoveries of the period, including the inventions of the telescope and microscope. Revolutionary ideas were interpreted with great variety by each national school. Representation of movement in space and time, and a fascination with light effects and the emotional state, contribute to the style's unmistakable vigor and theatricality. Especially worth note are the Georges de la Tour companion portraits, *Old Man* and *Old Woman* (c.1618); and *Samson and the Honeycomb* by Il Guercino (c.1657), which exemplifies the Baroque style with rounded forms, individualized faces, blowing trees, flying hair and a sumptuous play of light.

The Rococo style flourished in mid-18C France. Jean-Antoine Watteau, François Boucher, Jean-Honoré Fragonard and Venetian painter Giovanni Battista Tiepolo all employed a rich profusion of ornament, asymmetrical motifs, pastel colors and exquisite craftsmanship to create an ambience of pleasure. A **marquetry table** (1680-90), a marvel of inlaid oak, fruitwood, metal, horn and tortoise shell, merits careful inspection; the work is attributed to André-Charles Boulle, a renowned French cabinetmaker who was retained by Louis XIV to create pieces to ornament Versailles.

Rodin Sculpture – *Galleries 8, 10 & 12*. Skylights and high, arched windows bring a changing play of natural light over the surfaces of great works by Auguste Rodin, widely acknowledged as the "father of modern sculpture." Gallery 10 displays large casts, including the justly famous

Burghers of Calais (cast c.1889), *The Kiss* (cast c.1887) and *The Three Shades* (cast c.1880). (*Burghers* and *The Kiss* are sometimes displayed in smaller versions to make room for other, less-well-known Rodin sculptures.) Rodin's raw, unfinished bases proclaim his struggle to wrest form and meaning from mass—a stylistic trait shared by the sculptor's inspiration, Michelangelo. Sculptures by Rodin contemporaries share gallery 12.

Galleries 9 and 11 are period spaces containing examples of the museum's fine collection of 18C furniture and ormolu-mounted ceramics.

18C-19C British Art – *Gallery 13.* Founded in 1768, the Royal Academy of the Arts moved to elevate British painting to a significant current within the mainstream of European art. Guided by its president, Sir Joshua Reynolds, the academy championed history painting but also encouraged portraiture and landscape. Reynolds' *Anne, Viscountess Townshend* (1779) places the subject against a carved relief suggesting ancient Greece. By the early 19C, landscape painting, thanks in particular to Thomas Gainsborough (*Landscape with Country Carts*, c.1784) and John Constable, emerged as the primary genre. Later artists such as John Martin interpreted the elements in a more dramatic manner. Examples of *chinoiserie* decoration include a scarlet-lacquered bureau-cabinet and a commode by Pierre Langlois.

Dutch and Flemish Art – *Galleries 14 & 15.* Protestant Holland and Catholic Flanders split politically in the early 17C, forging divergent artistic styles. In the Netherlands, Rembrandt and his school documented the citizenry and their surroundings in portraits, still lifes, landscapes and genre paintings. One fine example, by the master himself, portrays sea captain *Joris de Culerii* (1632). Artists centered around Flanders continued under the patronage of monarchy and Church, employing richer colors and concentrating on religious subjects. Anthony van Dyck's *Portrait of a Lady* (c.1620) communicates the aristocratic status of its subject, while *The Tribute Money* (c.1612) by Flemish master Peter Paul Rubens employs sumptuous color and drama, expressing a Counter-Reformation mission to attract the faithful. Smaller Dutch pictures, such as Willem van Aelst's remarkable still life, *Flowers in a Silver Vase* (1663), detail everyday life in a great center of commerce, while Flemish works express their connection to aristocracy. Frans Pourbus the Younger's *Portrait of a Lady* (1591), though formal and restrained, depicts clothing materials of great richness—all in black, the color most fashionable at the turn of the 16C.

European Neoclassicism – *Gallery 16.* The excavations of Pompeii and Herculaneum in the mid-18C inspired new enthusiasm for antiquity, expressed in art through the sober elevation of civic virtue and public morality in reaction to the exuberance of the rococo. First among the revolutionary painters was Jacques-Louis David, who became a foremost exponent of the new classicism following the exhibition of his *Oath of the Horatii* at the Paris Salon of 1785; two of his paintings are in this gallery. One of David's most successful pupils was the portraitist Baron François Gerard, court painter to Napoleon. Pierre-Henri de Valenciennes' *A Capriccio of Rome with the Finish of a Marathon* (1788) reflects the classical landscape tradition of the 17C master Poussin. Fine French silver by Martin-Guillaume Biennais and Henri Auguste is on view in this gallery.

The Fine Arts Museums of San Francisco

View of Rome: The Bridge and Castel Sant'Angelo with the Cupola of St. Peter's (1827) by Jean-Baptiste-Camille Corot

19C European Art – *Galleries 17 & 18.* Europe in the 19C, with Paris as its nominal capital, witnessed one of the richest and most complex periods in Western art. Reflecting the radical changes in social, political and intellectual spheres, a wide variety of artistic styles rapidly evolved. Jean-Baptiste-Camille Corot (*View of Rome: The Bridge and Castel Sant'Angelo with the Cupola of St. Peter's*, c.1827) pioneered landscapes based on sensations of light and color, influencing the Barbizon School and later the Impressionists. *Equestrian Portrait of Charles V* (c.1814) by Théodore Géricault displays the restless searching and dash of Romanticism, and Jean-Léon Gérôme's *The Bath* (c.1880-85) reveals a new exoticism, with the white-fleshed bather passive amid the vivid Islamic tiles of the oriental setting. Another remarkable work is Konstantin Makovsky's *The Russian Bride's Attire* (1889), which depicts costumes from various periods of Russian history in attendants' dresses.

In the late 19C, painters began to develop a new visual vocabulary to record their close scrutiny of nature and contemporary life. Depicting the transient moment with spontaneous brushwork, blurred outlines and colors in vibrant interrelation, the Impressionists were rejected by the Paris Salon of 1873; in response, they mounted their own, immensely influential exhibition. Realism and themes of modern urban life absorbed artists such as Edgar Degas (*Musicians in the Orchestra*, 1870) and Edouard Manet (*At the Milliner's*, 1881). Works by Pierre-August Renoir, such as *Landscape at Beaulieu* (1893), show the dissolution of outline into warm color. *Eiffel Tower* (1889) reveals Georges Seurat's experimentation with pointillism, a technique in which adjacent dots of color are "read" by the viewer's eye to produce a coherent image. Paul Cézanne's *Forest Interior* (c.1898) anticipates Cubism in its rendering of a constructed scene from more than one viewpoint.

20C European Art – *Gallery 19.* A great wave of artistic experimentation broke over Europe soon after the beginning of the 20C, inaugurating movements such as Cubism, Futurism, German Expressionism and Surrealism. Anchored by a late Claude Monet *Water Lilies* (c.1914-17), the gallery showcases two of Pablo Picasso's stylistic transformations; two paintings demonstrating Henri Matisse's mastery of abstract design and color; and works by other innovative 20C artists such as Georges Braque and Salvador Dalí. A black lacquer and straw table and chairs by creative designer Armand-Albert Rateau are also on view here.

ADDITIONAL SIGHTS

★**Sea Cliff** – *Entrance from El Camino del Mar at 27th Ave.* This secluded residential enclave forms a strikingly civilized corner amid San Francisco's wild coastal landscape. Curving, gently sloping streets accommodate the neighborhood's rolling terrain, winding among luxurious Mediterranean-style homes sheathed in brick or pale stucco. Most buildings here date from the 1920s. An early local example of planned residential development, the quiet, elegant neighborhood is considered one of the city's most desirable addresses. Actor Robin Williams is among the celebrities who own homes here.

China Beach – 🚸 *End of Seacliff Ave. off El Camino del Mar at 27th Ave. Parking available at beach entrance or on El Camino del Mar.* Fringing a gentle cove, this pleasant strip of sand is one of the few places in the city where swimming is safe, though its cold ocean waters tempt few. Sheltered from the Golden Gate's incessant winds by a jutting headland, the beach was nicknamed for Chinese fishermen who camped here in the 19C. Large shower rooms, a broad deck and a small grassy area with tables and barbecue grills make China Beach a favored place for sunning and recreation.

Further reading

Adventuring in the San Francisco Bay Area by Peggy Wayburn (1995, Sierra Club Books)

Berkeley Landmarks: An Illustrated Guide to Berkeley, California's Architectural Heritage by Susan Dinkelspiel Cerny (1994, Berkeley Architectural Heritage Assoc.)

The Best of Herb Caen: 1960–1975 (1991, Chronicle Books)

Big Alma: San Francisco's Alma Spreckels by Bernice Scarlach (1990, Scottwall Assoc.)

The Dashiell Hammett Tour by Don Herron (1991, City Lights Books)

The Earth Shook, the Sky Burned: A Moving Record of America's Great Earthquake and Fire: San Francisco April 18, 1906 by William Bronson (1996, Chronicle Books)

Golden Gate National Recreation Area (Golden Gate National Park Assoc.)

> Guide to the Parks
>
> Alcatraz: Island of Change
>
> Cliff House & Lands End: San Francisco's Seaside Retreat
>
> Fort Point: Sentry at the Golden Gate
>
> Marin Headlands: Portals of Time
>
> Muir Woods: Redwood Refuge

Post and Park: A Brief Illustrated History of the Presidio of San Francisco

Roughing It by Mark Twain (1871; reprint 1972, University of California Press)

San Francisco Almanac by Gladys Hansen (1995, Chronicle Books)

San Francisco Architecture by Sally B. Woodbridge and John M. Woodbridge (1992, Chronicle Books)

San Francisco Invites the World: The Panama-Pacific International Exposition of 1915 by Donna Ewals and Peter Clute (1991, Chronicle Books)

San Francisco Memoirs: Eyewitness Accounts of the Birth of the City compiled and introduced by Malcolm E. Barker (1994, Londonborn Publications)

San Francisco Stories: Great Writers on the City edited by John Miller (1990, Chronicle Books)

Tales of the City by Armistead Maupin (1994, HarperPerennial)

Tamalpais Trails by Barry Spitz (1995, Potrero Meadow Publishing Company)

This is San Francisco: A Classic Portrait of the City by Robert O'Brien (1994, Chronicle Books)

Two Years Before the Mast by Richard Henry Dana (1840) (1986, Penguin Books)

West from Home: Letters of Laura Ingalls Wilder, San Francisco, 1915 edited by Roger Lea MacBride (1995, HarperCollins Publishers)

Vineyards Along the Silverado Trail, Napa Valley

© Robert Holmes

Excursions

25 • BERKELEY★★

Population: 103,343.
🚇 Berkeley station.
Maps pp 196 and 198

Intellectual and cultural vitality characterize this university city, remarkable for its academic invention, political turmoil, social experimentation and vibrant artistic, architectural and culinary expression. Although the University of California campus has always been the powerhouse behind Berkeley's sometimes-celebrated, sometimes-reviled dynamism, the majority of the city's inhabitants live and work at some remove from academia, in urban communities that stretch from the largely industrial "flatlands" of Ocean View, through the downtown business precinct along Shattuck Avenue, to the beautiful, tree-filled neighborhoods of Claremont, Elmwood and the North Berkeley hills.

Historical Notes

Like Oakland, the lands of present-day Berkeley pastured cattle before becoming part of Luis María Peralta's Rancho San Antonio in 1820. The land was eventually overtaken by squatters. In 1852, Francis Kittredge Shattuck subdivided lands along the middle course of Strawberry Creek into farms; the nearest town, Ocean View, sprang up more than a mile away along the bay shore. Not until the 1860s, when a site on the upper forks of Strawberry Creek was selected for an institution of higher learning, did shops and hotels begin to sprout along Shattuck's farm road, today's **Shattuck Avenue**. In 1866 the fledgling community at the edge of the undeveloped campus was named after the Irish bishop and philosopher George Berkeley (1685-1753), author of the oft-quoted line, "Westward the course of empire takes its way." For the next four decades, after it merged with Ocean View, the town grew up steadily around "Cal," as the university is called. In the aftermath of San Francisco's great earthquake and fire of 1906, a tidal wave of new settlers flooded Berkeley and housing tracts filled the farm and grazing lands. By 1916, wooden buildings along Shattuck Avenue had been replaced with substantial masonry structures, many of which still stand today.

Cultural Ferment – Berkeley has long enjoyed a reputation for attracting intellectuals, idealists and eccentrics whose diverse and often highly cultivated tastes have left their mark on the city's history, architecture and ambience. While Beaux Arts aesthetics and pockets of greenery became the hallmark of campus architecture in the early 20C, builders beyond the university property integrated leafy yards and landscaped footpaths with neighborhoods of highly original and imaginative architecture. A gastronomic version of this passion for art and nature swept Berkeley in 1971 when Alice Waters opened her famed Chez Panisse restaurant, giving rise to California Cuisine and lending the moniker **Gourmet Ghetto** to upper Shattuck Avenue (between Rose & Virginia Sts.).

Today Berkeley revels in its numerous fine restaurants—including a rich array of ethnic eateries—located on Shattuck and in the neighborhoods along **Solano Avenue★** in north Berkeley, **Telegraph Avenue** just south of the UC campus, and behind the early-20C storefronts of the **Elmwood** shopping district (along College Ave. at the intersection of Ashby Ave.). Bookstores, cinemas, coffee houses and craft shops also thrive in these areas. In particular, the erstwhile industrial sector along **4th Street** (north of University Ave.) has become a popular shopping area with a quirky, if somewhat upscale, bent. Just off this strip, Takara Sake U.S.A. (708 Addison St.; ☎ 510-540-8250) offers sips of Sho Chiku Bai in the tasting room of the largest sake brewery in the US.

Berkeley's penchant for idealism fueled the student protest movements of the 1960s, spreading its reputation as a hotbed of radicalism. Though now considerably mellowed from the late 70s and early 80s—when the city government cultivated its own foreign policy, promoted itself as a model for socialism, and was widely referred to as "the People's Republic of Berkeley"—the city retains many reminders of its radical heyday.

Visiting Berkeley – Stop at the Berkeley Convention & Visitors Bureau **Visitor Information Center** (2015 Center St. 1st floor; open year-round Mon–Fri 9am–5pm; closed major holidays; ♿ ☎ 510-549-7040, hotline: 510-549-8710; www.visitberkeley.com) for maps and information. Guided tours of the UC Berkeley campus depart from the **Campus Visitor Center** (101 University Hall, 2200 University Ave.; open year-round Mon–Fri 8:30am–4:30pm; closed Dec 25–Jan 1; 90min tours Mon–Sat 10am & Sun 1pm; ♿ ☎ 510-642-5215; www.berkeley.edu).

Although the student population diminishes during spring, summer and Christmas vacations, Berkeley bustles day and night throughout the year. Restaurants and coffeehouses near campus hum from morning to late evening, and theaters, bookstores and cinemas offer a wide variety of entertainment.

ADDRESS BOOK

Dining in the East Bay

Please see explanation on p 42.

Chez Panisse – *1517 Shattuck Ave., Berkeley.* & ☎ *510-548-5525. www.chezpanisse.com. Closed Sun.* **$$$$ California.** California cuisine was born in this Craftsman-style restaurant in 1971, under the watchful eye of culinary doyenne Alice Waters. Just-picked organic greens and baby vegetables pair up with free-range meat and fish fresh from the sea to create stellar prix-fixe menus that change nightly. Upstairs, the more casual **Café at Chez Panisse** serves simpler—and less expensive—fare for both lunch and dinner.

Bay Wolf – *3853 Piedmont Ave., Oakland.* & 🅿 ☎ *510-655-6004.* **$$$ Mediterranean.** Established in 1975, Bay Wolf reigns as a longtime favorite of East Bay residents. The full gamut of Mediterranean-area cuisines contributes to a changing menu, served in a romantic setting in a refurbished Victorian home.

Brazio – *3421 Blackhawk Plaza Circle, Danville.* & 🅿 ☎ *925-736-3000.* **$$$ Italian-Tuscan.** A wood-oven grill for pizzas and steaks is a focal point of this sophisticated restaurant, just a stone's throw from the Blackhawk Museum. In warm weather, diners enjoy patio seating beside a pond fed by small waterfalls.

Oliveto – *5655 College Ave., Oakland.* & ☎ *510-547-5356.* **$$$ Italian-Florentine.** With an upstairs view on the bustling Rockridge neighborhood, Oliveto offers seasonal cuisine in a country trattoria setting. Chef Paul Bertolli, formerly of Chez Panisse, pairs pastas and polenta with fresh fish and game.

Caffe Centro – *2132 Center St., Berkeley.* & ☎ *510-981-8373. Closed Sun.* **$$ Mediterranean.** Baked Fanny Bay oysters, goat-cheese ravioli, rosemary-skewered shrimp, and braised rabbit in mustard sauce are but a few of the items on Jean-Pierre Moulle's casually chic downtown Berkeley eatery.

Santa Fe Bar & Grill – *1310 University Ave., Berkeley.* & 🅿 ☎ *510-841-4740.* **$$ California.** Lodged in a 1904 rail depot, this landmark grows its own produce in an adjoining garden. The menu offers the likes of rack of lamb with a parsnip purée, and grilled salmon with a leek confit. A jazz pianist performs nightly.

Bette's Ocean View Diner – *1807 Fourth St., Berkeley.* & ☎ *510-644-3230. Breakfast and lunch only.* **$ American.** There's no ocean view, but this classic diner—with its chrome jukebox and model train circling overhead—is a good stop for classic and unsusual (soufflé pancakes with chocolate) breakfasts.

Picante – *1328 Sixth St., Berkeley.* & ☎ *510-525-3121.* **$ Mexican.** This upscale taqueria gets raves from locals for its fresh ingredients, homemade chorizo tacos and tamales of braised pork, butternut squash and poblano chiles.

Staying in the East Bay

Please see explanation on p 42.

The Claremont – *41 Tunnel Rd., Berkeley.* ✗ & 🅿 ⚓ ☎ *510-843-3000. www.claremontresort.com. 279 rooms.* **$$$$** A mere 20-minute drive from downtown San Francisco, the castle-like Claremont Resort and Spa was considered a country getaway when it opened in 1915. Today, between the fitness center, full-service spa, tennis club, pools and day camp for kids, there's no excuse to be bored here. Ask for a room in the new wing with its spacious marble baths and custom-made furniture.

Lafayette Park Hotel – *3287 Mount Diablo Blvd., Lafayette.* ✗ & 🅿 ⚓ ☎ *925-283-3700. www.woodsidehotels.com. 140 rooms.* **$$$$** A French provincial-style oasis west of Walnut Creek, this gracious hotel extends its elegance to antique-furnished guestrooms, which surround a trio of courtyards.

Waterfront Plaza Hotel – *10 Washington St., Oakland.* ✗ & 🅿 ⚓ ☎ *510-836-3800. www.waterfrontplaza.com. 144 rooms.* **$$$$** In the heart of Jack London Square, right on the Oakland waterfront, this fine hotel is centrally located for ferry, BART or auto access to attractions throughout the Bay Area.

Hotel Durant – *2600 Durant Ave., Berkeley.* ✗ & 🅿 ☎ *510-845-8981. www.hoteldurant.com. 140 rooms.* **$$$** You can almost hear ghosts of students past charge through this renovated six-story 1928 hotel, next to the University of California campus. Historic late-19C and early-20C photos line corridor walls.

The French Hotel – *1538 Shattuck Ave., Berkeley.* & 🅿 ☎ *510-548-9930. 18 rooms.* **$$** Clean, cozy rooms here attract a variety of international travelers. Many prefer eating at the in-house café over wandering Berkeley's "Gourmet Ghetto."

■ The Free Speech Movement

As early as the 1930s, UC students had railed against social injustice. But political events of the 50s and 60s stirred a stronger reaction and fueled Berkeley's reputation for radical behavior.

The first rumblings of the Free Speech Movement began with opposition to the House Un-American Activities Committee hearings of Sen. Joseph McCarthy and the would-be invasion of Cuba's Bay of Pigs during the Kennedy Administration. Soon civil-rights marches and Vietnam War protests catapulted the city to the forefront of national attention. On Sept. 30, 1964, the university's Board of Regents called in police to break up a peaceful sit-in demonstration by students at Sproul Plaza. Subsequent years were marked by a campaign of harsh reprisals against students who dared to declare their right to self expression. Then-Gov.ernor Ronald Reagan sent riot police and the National Guard to squelch demonstrations with tear-gas assaults, mass arrests and even a 17-day campus occupation.

Conflict reached its apex in spring 1969, when Berkeley residents attempted to turn an abandoned piece of university land, three blocks south of the campus, into "Power to the People Park." Trees and flowers were planted in April, but a month later, the Regents re-staked their claim by having fences built around the park. Rioting predictably ensued, with hundreds injured and one man killed by a stray bullet. The fence was not removed until 1972. People's Park today is an unstated and unspectacular memorial to that epoch.

Street parking near the campus is difficult to find, and posted restrictions throughout Berkeley are strictly enforced. Try the city pay lots on Allston Way or Center St., located three blocks from the Campus Visitor Center. University parking garages usually fill by afternoon during term; small pay lots are found farther away at the Botanical Garden, and the Lawrence Hall of Science, both connected to the main campus by shuttle *(50¢)*. Neighborhoods away from the campus offer easier street parking. From San Francisco, it's best to take BART to the Berkeley station and either walk one block east (uphill) to the campus or ride a campus perimeter shuttle bus from Shattuck Avenue to Mining Circle *(operates year-round Mon–Fri 7am–6pm; 25¢; ☎ 510-642-5149)*.

★★UNIVERSITY OF CALIFORNIA, BERKELEY *Map p 196*

The first and most prestigious campus of the acclaimed University of California system, UC Berkeley is noteworthy for its varied architecture and profuse landscaping, its outstanding museums and research collections, its notoriety in the 1960s and 70s as a hotbed of student activism, and its myriad contributions to human knowledge, especially in the field of nuclear physics.

The university owes its creation to clergymen scholars from the eastern US, led by the Rev. Samuel Hopkins Willey and the Rev. Henry Durant, who chartered the College of California in Oakland in 1854. Seeking to expand two years later, the trustees acquired lands on the twin forks of Strawberry Creek, officially dedicating their enterprise in 1861 at **Founders' Rock (1)**, still visible on campus today *(corner of Hearst Ave. & Gayley Rd.)*.

In 1864, landscape architect Frederick Law Olmsted was commissioned to plan the college grounds and an adjacent residential neighborhood. Olmsted aligned the campus on an east-west axis, but a shortage of funds curtailed construction of this initial plan. In 1867, the college merged with the state-sponsored Agricultural, Mining and Mechanical Arts College, and the new institution was dedicated the following year as the University of California.

Athens of the West – At the turn of the century, noted philanthropist and university regent **Phoebe Apperson Hearst** financed a competition to expand construction of the main campus "with landscape gardening and architecture forming one composition." Supported by Hearst moneys and state funds, architect John Galen Howard set out to make Berkeley the "Athens of the West," establishing Beaux-Arts as the hallmark architectural style with a phalanx of white granite buildings sporting red-tile roofs and Neoclassical ornamentation. In the course of expansions during the first half of the 20C, campus architecture diversified with the addition of buildings by such noteworthy architects as Bernard Maybeck, Julia Morgan, George Kelham and Arthur Brown, Jr.

In addition to its 178-acre main campus, the university embraces 1,054 acres in the steep Berkeley Hills, including lands occupied by the Lawrence Berkeley Lab *(not open to the public)*. Founded by Ernest O. Lawrence (1901-1958) as the Radiation Laboratory in 1936, the laboratory housed several progressively more powerful cyclotrons that fueled profound breakthroughs in 20C physics, including Glenn Seaborg's 1941 discovery of plutonium, an event that heralded the Atomic Age.

Today, with 14 separate colleges and schools, 1,460 faculty members and an ethnically diverse student body that numbers some 30,000, UC Berkeley ranks among the nation's leading universities. Many of its graduate programs are annually rated at or near the top of national standings, and Berkeley graduates earn more PhDs than those of any other American university. Eight Nobel laureates are among the current faculty: three physicists, two chemists, two economists and a poet. An active center of culture and sports, the campus hosts frequent concerts, film screenings, club meetings, lectures and sporting contests. The year's biggest sporting event is the November football game against cross-bay archrival Stanford University—called, simply, The Big Game.

Walking Tour

Begin at West Gate (Oxford St. between University Ave. & Center St.).

Planted in 1877, the **Eucalyptus Grove** on the south side of University Drive contains the tallest hardwood trees in North America. Some measure nearly 200ft high.

★**Valley Life Sciences Building** – The largest academic building in the nation when it was completed (1930, George Kelham), this massive pseudo-Egyptian "temple" to science supports dense rows of immense pilasters; it is intriguingly decorated with bas-relief tableaux, American bison skulls, saber-tooth tiger heads, griffins and other designs. The interior, renovated in 1994, houses laboratories and world-class natural-history specimen collections, including the **Museum of Paleontology**★ (**M**[1]) 🧒 *(open year-round daily 8am–5pm; ♿ ☎ 510-642-1821; www.ucmp.berkeley.edu)*. One of the oldest (1921), largest and most important collections in the country, it contains more than five million invertebrates and 135,000 catalogued vertebrate specimens, including the largest triceratops skull ever found, giant clams, a frozen mammoth *(not on display)*, an ichthyosaur skeleton and the assembled skeleton of a *Tyrannosaurus rex.* Only a small portion of the collection is displayed at any given time, in cases spread over three floors surrounding the central spiral staircase.

Walk east of the building on the pedestrian walkway, past the flagpole. Beyond California Hall, turn uphill toward the Campanile.

Campanile Way passes among a quartet of monumental Neoclassical structures, all designed by John Galen Howard, including **California Hall** (**A**) (1905), **Durant Hall** (**B**) (1912) and **Wheeler Hall** (**C**) (1918), headquarters of the English department. The grandest of the four structures, **Doe Library**★ (1911; additions in 1917 and 1995) recalls a Roman temple with a Corinthian colonnade on its northern facade. As the university's central book repository, the library manages holdings of more than eight million bound volumes and 90,000 periodicals, housed throughout the campus and in its extensive underground "stacks." On the ground floor, the wood-paneled **Morrison Library** provides a cozy haven for casual readers. Upstairs, note the barrel-vaulted Reference Room and the old circulation hall with its magnificent coffered bronze ceiling and suspended lamps.

Bancroft Library (**D**) – *Open year-round Mon–Fri 9am–5pm, Sat 1–5pm. Hours may vary during university holidays.* ♿ ☎ *510-642-3781. www.lib.berkeley.edu.* This annex (1948, Arthur Brown, Jr.) on the east side of the Doe Library stores rare books, manuscripts, archival materials and special collections, including the

Sather Gate, UC Berkeley

© Robert Holmes

country's largest assemblage of manuscripts, notebooks and papers belonging to author Mark Twain. The Bancroft is famed for its holdings of Western Americana amassed by 19C San Francisco bookseller Hubert Howe Bancroft (1832-1918). Treasures periodically rotated through the library anteroom include paintings of the old West, first editions and printed posters. The **Plate of Brass** displayed was long believed to have been left by Sir Francis Drake when he landed on the California coast in 1579. Metallurgists have since demonstrated that the plate, discovered in Marin County in 1936, is a clever hoax.

South of the Bancroft Library stands the oldest building on campus, the red-brick **South Hall** (**E**) (1873, David Farquharson), built in the French Second Empire style. Once the university president's office, the building now houses the School of Information Management and Systems.

Ascend the stairs to the Campanile.

★★**The Campanile (Sather Tower)** – ▦ *Open year-round Mon–Fri 10am–4pm, Sun 10am–2pm & 3–5pm. Closed Dec 25–Jan 1. $1. ☏ 510-642-5215. www.berkeley .edu:80/visitors/campanile.html.* Modeled on the bell tower in Venice's St. Marks Square, this 307ft, steel-framed, granite-clad shaft (1914, John Galen Howard) is crowned by a quartet of obelisks surmounted with bronze urns, and a soaring central spire capped by a bronze lantern. A memorial to university benefactor Jane K. Sather, the Campanile houses a carillon of 61 bells. From its open-air observation platform, arched windows frame panoramic **views**★★ of the Berkeley hills, downtown Oakland, San Francisco Bay and intriguing geometry of the campus, with Campanile Way delineating the east-west axis drafted in Olmsted's campus plan of 1864. When school is in session, carillonneurs at a keyboard play the bells from an enclosure at the platform's center in a fascinating, if deafening, performance *(Mon–Sat 7:50am, noon & 6pm; Sun 2pm).*

Walk north from the Campanile, turning right at the first corner.

Hearst Memorial Mining Building – This granite-clad Beaux-Arts building (1907, John Galen Howard and Julia Morgan) was named for Sen. George Hearst, who made his fortune in mining. The facade bears three archways and a row of corbels carved to resemble men and women straining to support the massive wooden cornices. Normally housing offices, laboratories and classrooms, the building was emptied for seismic upgrading in 1998, a $67-million project expected to continue through 2001.

Walk south across Mining Circle and cross University Dr.

The route passes **Le Conte Hall** (**F**), the physics building where J. Robert Oppenheimer (1904-1967), Edward Teller and other physicists drafted a blueprint of the first atomic bomb in the summer of 1942.

Turn right, then left, crossing Strawberry Creek under an arch with a Latin inscription, and over a concrete footbridge.

At the lush green known as Faculty Glade, a path beside Strawberry Creek leads east behind the partially wood-shingled **Faculty Club** (**G**) (1902, Bernard Maybeck), which blends beautifully with the surrounding oaks, laurels and redwoods. After crossing and recrossing the creek on adjacent bridges, pass behind the redwood log **Senior Hall** (**H**) (1906, John Galen Howard) and turn left onto a flagstone path that leads past the cabin to the brown-shingled **Women's Faculty Club** (**J**) (1923, John Galen Howard), ensconced in a pretty English garden.

Pass along the front of the club, climb steps and cross to ascend a broad stairway on the north side of Cheit Hall.

The assemblage of buildings constituting the **Haas School of Business**★ (1995, Moore/Ruble/Yudell/VBN) projects the atmosphere of a prosperous quarter in a north German city, complete with street lamps, gabled roofline, multi-paned windows and an enclosed parapet walk above its arching western gateway. Pass under the eastern portal arch to Piedmont Avenue, and look left to the concrete, Tudor Revival "castle" of **Bowles Hall** (**K**) (1929, George Kelham), rising magnificently on a hillside and surmounted by chimneys, gables and steep, red-tiled roofs. Hidden by trees a little farther to the north, the 8,500-seat outdoor **Hearst Greek Theater** (1903, John Galen Howard and Julia Morgan) was modeled after the ancient amphitheater at Epidarus. Directly across the street stands **California Memorial Stadium** (1923, John Galen Howard), home field for the Cal Bears football team. The public is welcome to recall the glory of past heroes in its Hall of Fame *(open 1st Thu of month, 10am–3pm; ☏ 510-642-4056).*

Turn right and walk to Bancroft Ave.

International House (**L**) – *2299 Piedmont Ave. ✗ ♿ ☏ 510-642-9490. http:// ihouse.berkeley.edu:7002.* Iberian flourishes highlight this residential and cultural center (1930, George Kelham), the Berkeley branch of a movement to encourage cultural exchange between Americans and foreigners. A Moorish domed tower and balconies dominate the exterior. Many of the large public rooms and hallways inside, including the Great Hall and the International Cafe, reveal traditional Spanish decorative elements such as red-tile floors, carved-wood doors and iron chandeliers.

Walk down the south side of Bancroft Ave.

★UC Berkeley Art Museum – *2626 Bancroft Way. Open year-round Wed–Sun 11am–5pm (Thu 9pm). Closed university holidays. $6.* ✗ & ☎ *510-642-0808. www.bampfa.berkeley.edu.* Housing one of the largest university art collections in the US, the museum was born in 1963 when Abstract Expressionist painter Hans Hofmann (1880-1966), having left Nazi Germany with the aid of two UC professors, donated 45 paintings and $250,000 to the university. The distinctive building (1970, Mario Ciampi, Richard Jorasch and Ronald Wagner) unfolds like a paper fan. Its stark, spacious interior features 10 cantilevered exhibition terraces linked by ramps and stairs. In addition to Hofmann's work (displayed in gallery A on a rotating basis), the 9,000-piece permanent collection is strong in 20C art, pre-20C European painting, Asian ceramics and painting, and contemporary art. Sculpture is displayed in an outdoor garden that wraps around the north and west sides of the building. The museum also mounts changing exhibitions from university and traveling collections.

Associated with the museum, but now in its own nearby campus home, the renowned **Pacific Film Archive★** *(2575 Bancroft Way;* ✗ & 🅿 ☎ *510-642-1412)* preserves 8,000 films, videos and rare prints of classic films emphasizing Japanese, Soviet and American art cinema *(shows year-round nightly, hours vary; closed university holidays; $6).*

Backtrack up Bancroft Ave. to College Ave. and cross the street to Kroeber Hall.

Phoebe Hearst Museum of Anthropology (**M²**) – *103 Kroeber Hall. Open year-round Wed–Sun 10am–4:30pm (Sept–May Thu 9pm). Closed major & university holidays. $2.* & 🅿 ☎ *510-643-7648. www.qal.berkeley.edu/~hearst.* Among the country's most significant anthropological research museums, the Hearst was established around a core collection obtained in a series of expeditions funded by Phoebe Apperson Hearst, starting in 1899. Today the **collections★** have grown to contain some 4 million artifacts from around the world, with emphasis on California archaeology, ancient Peru, Classical Greece and Italy, ancient Egypt, Central American textiles and ethnological artifacts from West Africa, Oceania and the Arctic and sub-Arctic regions. Varied temporary exhibitions are drawn from this vast collection.

Painted Cloth (1000-1450 AD), Chimú Capac Culture, Peru

A single permanent exhibit displays the handicrafts of Ishi, who in 1911 appeared in Oroville, California, on the verge of starvation. Believing him to be the last surviving member of the Yahi tribe, Berkeley anthropologist Alfred Louis Kroeber invited Ishi to live at the museum (then located in San Francisco), where he was encouraged to demonstrate the techniques of his native culture by making tools and crafts until his death in 1916.

Rising across the courtyard northeast of Kroeber Hall, the 10-story concrete **Wurster Hall** (**N**) (1964, DeMars, Escherick, Olsen) is a striking example of the Brutalist style.

Passing between Morrison and Hertz Halls, turn left at Faculty Glade and follow the creek downstream.

Pause at the wall of the old brick powerhouse to admire Byzantine-inspired mosaics created in 1936 by WPA-sponsored artists Helen Bruton and Florence Swift. The scenes depict a group of artists, musicians and dancers.

Continue west to Sproul Plaza.

Sather Gate – Spanning the broad pedestrian entrance to the main campus, this monumental, filigreed bronze gateway (1910, John Galen Howard) arches between four granite pillars capped by banded glass globes. Telegraph Avenue once met the campus at Sather Gate, but the commercial zone was cleared to Bancroft Avenue in the 1950s and replaced in 1960 by **Sproul Plaza★**. Best known as the site of student protests in the 1960s and 70s, the plaza draws students, musicians and other entertainers, protesters, political campaigners, street preachers and eccentrics of every stripe. Commemorating its revolutionary birthright, a 6in circle at the center of the plaza is ceremonially declared an extraterritorial zone "not subject to any entity's jurisdiction."

On the plaza's east side stands Sproul Hall, which houses university administrative offices. The King Student Union complex on the west side contains food services, bookstores, sundry shops and Zellerbach Auditorium, the university's largest enclosed performance venue.

Additional Sights on Campus

★UC Botanical Garden – *200 Centennial Dr. Open Memorial Day–Labor Day daily 9am–7pm. Rest of the year daily 9am–4:45pm. Closed Dec 25. $3 (free Thu). Guided tours (1hr) available Thu, weekends 1:30pm.* ⚐ ▯ ☏ *510-643-2755. www.mip.berkeley.edu/garden.* Some 13,000 species of plants grace the slopes of Strawberry Canyon in a sylvan setting above the main campus, overlooking the bay. University scientists have nurtured exotic plants collected from the wild since 1890, though this 34-acre site was established in the 1920s. Most of the garden is organized geographically, representing flora of Asia, Africa, the Mediterranean and Europe, New Zealand, Australia, Meso-America, North America and California. Thematic gardens nurture palms and cycads, old roses and Chinese medicinal herbs. A sequoia forest and redwood grove are located across Centennial Drive.

Lawrence Hall of Science – ▭ *1 Centennial Dr. Open year-round daily 10am–5pm. Closed Labor Day, Thanksgiving Day, Dec 24–25. $7, children 5–18 $5.* ▯ ▯ ☏ *510-642-5132. www.lhs.berkeley.edu.* Dramatically situated high in the Berkeley hills, this futuristic museum (1968, Anshen and Allen) is dedicated to teaching children about physics, biology, chemistry, navigation, mathematics, computers and lasers through interactive exhibits, laboratories and a comprehensive program of classes. The planetarium complements an active Saturday-night astronomy program. Frequently changing temporary exhibits feature mechanical creatures, the mysteries of chemistry, and a variety of science topics ranging from prehistoric life to space travel. The **view★★** from the front patio overlooks much of the northern Bay Area. On the hillside above the Hall of Science looms the Silver Space Sciences Laboratory *(not open to public)*.

SIGHTS IN BERKELEY

★Telegraph Avenue – *Between Bancroft & Dwight Ways.* From morning through late evening this compelling thoroughfare flows with students, bibliophiles, crafts sellers, street people and tourists, all of whom frequent its many coffeehouses, bookstores, eateries and shops.

East of the avenue, sandwiched between Dwight Way and Haste Street, **People's Park** remains a potent symbol of Berkeley radicalism. Seized from the university by students and political activists in 1969, the park sparked a series of riots and running battles between police and protesters before a sort of truce was reached, in which the city of Berkeley manages the property in partnership with the university. Some space today has been turned into community gardens, even as students relax in the grass and read beside homeless transients.

★★ **First Church of Christ, Scientist** – *2619 Dwight Way at Dana St. Visit by guided tour (45min) only, year-round 1st Sun of each month 12:15pm, or by reservation. Public services Sun 11am & Wed 8pm.* ▣ ☎ *510-845-7199.* Bernard Maybeck's masterwork (1910) harmonized a wealth of styles, yet copied none, in a unique, Arts and Crafts structure of surpassing beauty and serenity. The church fuses multiple rooflines—typical of a Japanese temple—with Spanish tiles and rectangular, fluted columns supporting trellises hung with wisteria. In the shape of a Greek cross, the sunken auditorium is naturally lit by side windows and diagonally spanned with arching beams, imparting a feeling of great spaciousness. The milled woodwork in the ceiling beams and the interior furnishings, all of which Maybeck himself designed, show exquisite craftsmanship.

★ **Judah L. Magnes Museum** – *2911 Russell St. Open year-round Mon–Thu & Sun 10am–4pm. Closed major & Jewish holidays. Guided tours (1hr) available Wed & Sun or by appointment.* ☎ *510-549-6950. www.magnesmuseum.org.* Set amid shaded grounds landscaped by John McLaren, an imposing mansion (1908) houses the nation's third-largest museum of Jewish history and art. Named for a prominent San Francisco rabbi, the museum sponsors changing exhibits *(main level)* highlighting Jewish history and the works of 19C and 20C Jewish artists and photographers. Galleries on the upper level are reserved for rotating exhibits of ceremonial and cultural items from the museum collections, including Hanukkah lamps, amulets, Bibles, Torah pointers, wedding robes, Torah cases and arks, and Sephardic artifacts from around the world.

★ **Claremont Resort** – *41 Tunnel Rd., end of Ashby Ave. Open daily year-round.* ✗ ⚐ ▣ ☎ *510-843-3000. www.claremontresort.com.* Looming like a white castle in the hills between Berkeley and Oakland, this stately old hotel (1915, Charles Dickey) forms the centerpiece of an upscale resort. The proposal to build it originally was floated in the first decade of the 20C by three East Bay businessmen, one of whom subsequently won the entire property from his partners in a game of checkers. A reputation for dullness dogged the hotel for many years, largely because laws forbade the sale of liquor within a mile of the UC Berkeley campus. An enterprising student actually measured the distance in 1936, however, and discovered that the southern end of the hotel lay beyond the mile radius; the following year, the Terrace Lounge opened on the "wet" side of the invisible line, where it remains to this day. (The Claremont rewarded the student with free drinks for the rest of her life.) International tournaments have been played on the hotel's 10 tennis courts, and its full-service spa draws a devoted following.

Tilden Regional Park – 🔟 *From Berkeley take Spruce St. north to Grizzly Peak Blvd., cross and make a sharp left on Cañon Dr. Follow signs to the Nature Area. Open daily year-round dawn–dusk.* △ ✗ ⚐ ▣ ☎ *510-635-0135. www.ebparks.org.* Sprawling over 2,078 acres on the eastern side of the ridge above Berkeley, this predominantly undeveloped preserve offers varied attractions to people of all ages, including swimming and fishing in **Lake Anza**, golf, pony rides, picnicking, group camping, hiking trails, a petting zoo and miniature train rides. Also here are the walking paths of the **Tilden Nature Study Area** *(open year-round Tue–Sun 10am–5pm; closed Jan 1, Thanksgiving Day, Dec 25; guided tours available weekends;* ⚐ ▣ ☎ *510-525-2233).* Within the park, the 10-acre **Botanic Garden** *(open year-round daily 8:30am–5pm)* cultivates the world's largest collection of California native plants. Landscaped on picturesque terraces along the banks of Wildcat Creek, the garden's more-than-1,500 species are divided into 10 separate sections that correspond with geographical regions of the state.

❶ Bookstores on Telegraph
The stretch of Telegraph Avenue between Haste Street and Dwight Way has satisfied many a Berkeleyite's literary longings. **Cody's** *(no. 2454; ☎ 510-845-7852)*, one of the largest independent bookstores in the Bay Area, stocks general interest books, with specialties in computers, psychiatry, fiction and children's books. **Moe's** *(no. 2476; ☎ 510-849-2087)* sells good used books on four floors; an antiquarian section occupies the top floor. Metaphysics and religion are the specialties at **Shambhala**, *(no. 2482; ☎ 510-848-8443)* along with witchcraft, meditation and acupuncture. At the end of the block, **Shakespeare & Co.** *(no. 2499; ☎ 510-841-8916)* stocks its tall shelves and narrow aisles with used books, including a number of discounted review copies.

❷ Peet's Coffee & Tea

*2124 Vine St. at Walnut St.
☏ 510-841-0564.* Berkeley-born Peet's places nearly as much value upon educating customers about coffee as it does to making a sale. The three-decade-old anchor store of the popular Peet's chain doesn't have a sign out front—regulars know where to go. Bean up while perusing the wide variety of coffee fixings and paraphernalia for sale.

Northgate – This neighborhood was named for its location immediately outside the north entrance to the University of California campus. Above the first block of Euclid Avenue, lined with pleasant shops and restaurants, the rise where Ridge Road intersects with Le Conte Avenue has been dubbed "Holy Hill" for its uncanny concentration of theological schools.

Paramount among the venerable institutions is the Graduate Theological Union *(2465 Le Conte Ave.)*, a Georgian Revival mansion built of red clinker-brick in the 1920s. The GTU administers a union of nine schools and 1,400 students as well as the **Flora Lamson Hewlett Library (P)** *(2400 Ridge Rd.; ☏ 510-649-2500)*, one of the country's largest theological collections.

Walter J. Ratcliff's Holbrook Building *(1798 Scenic Ave.)*, an impressive Tudor Revival structure, is part of the Pacific School of Religion, oldest seminary in the western US. Its **Badè Institute of Biblical Archaeology (M³)** displays a fine collection of Old Testament (1000–800 BC) antiquities, including the unique Seal of Jaazaniah. They were excavated in the early 20C by Dr. William Badè at Tell en-Nasbeh (thought to have been the biblical Mizpah of Benjamin) in Israel *(open year-round Tue & Thu 10am–3pm, closed major holidays & last week in Dec; guided tours by reservation only; ☏ 510-849-8272; www.psr.edu/bade)*. The Institute also features a collection of 300 historic Bibles from the 15–18C, a gallery of contemporary theological art and a table that once belonged to naturalist John Muir.

Thornberg Village★, better known locally as Normandy Village *(1817-1839 & 1781-1783 Spruce St.)*, lies two blocks west of Holy Hill. Erected in 1927-28 in "Hansel and Gretel" style by William R. Yelland, the residential complex is a storybook

OAKLAND

fantasy of Gothic arches and towers, playful brickwork, eccentrically peaked rooflines, faux-leaded windows, carved-wood gargoyles, handcrafted lanterns, cobbled drives and meandering stairways.

North Berkeley Hills – Long a magnet for well-educated residents with cultivated tastes, the steep hills north of the UC Berkeley campus earned their reputation for high aestheticism after the turn of the 20C, when streets were laid out along hill contours instead of the more typical grid pattern. Encouraged by the Hillside Club, a social organization with strong interests in preserving the natural beauty of the hills, developers introduced landscaped footpaths and stairways to complement the Arts and Crafts and brown-shingled houses that dominated the neighborhood, and that are still recognized as the hallmark of residential architecture in Berkeley. When a wildfire destroyed between 500 and 600 neighborhood homes in 1923, many residents rebuilt in an eclectic array of period revival styles inspired by Norman castles, Swiss chalets, Spanish missions, Tudor mansions, Italian villas, and Japanese and classic Greek temples.

Today the area offers pleasant if strenuous strolls along its streets and paths, including **Rose Walk** (linking Euclid & LeRoy Aves.) and **La Loma Steps** (between LeRoy Ave. & Buena Vista Way). At the heart of the neighborhood, the four-acre **Berkeley Municipal Rose Garden★** (Euclid Ave. north of Bayview Pl.) flourishes on terraces that descend down the canyon of Codornices Creek. Funded by WPA grants, the garden was completed in 1937, and today contains more than 3,000 rose bushes of 250 species. One spectacularly eccentric house, the **Hume Cloister** (**Q**) (2900 Buena Vista Way), replicates a 13C French monastery. An even more unusual structure, the **Temple of the Wings** (**R**) (2800 Buena Vista Way) with a pair of Corinthian colonnades joined to a central dance stage, was designed by Bernard Maybeck and completed in 1914.

26 • OAKLAND★

Population: 367,230
🚉 12th Street/City Center or Lake Merritt station.
Alameda/Oakland ferry to Jack London Square.
Map p 201

Directly across the bay from San Francisco, linked to it by the San Francisco-Oakland Bay Bridge, bustling Oakland boasts a large and busy port, gleaming waterfront and civic-center districts, an exceptional museum and a profusion of ambitiously restored mid-19C to 20C residential and commercial buildings.

Historical Notes

After the founding of Mission Dolores in San Francisco, the native Ohlone lands of the East Bay provided pasture for mission cattle. In 1820, when Luis María Peralta retired from military duties in nearby San Jose, the king of Spain granted him 44,800 acres of East Bay rangeland. Embracing the future sites of Oakland, Piedmont, Emeryville and Berkeley, Rancho San Antonio prospered by shipping tanned cowhides to eastern US markets from the family's bayside boat landing, the Embarcadero de Temescal. The Gold Rush of 1849 signaled the end of the pastoral life on Rancho San Antonio as large numbers of prospectors traveling from San Francisco passed through the contra costa, the "opposite coast," en route to the Sierra Nevada goldfields. Interlopers soon began to log and mill East Bay redwood forests, and squatters carved out farms on the fringes of the ranch. The Peraltas eventually lost most of their lands as a town began to take shape near the former site of the Embarcadero de Temescal.

Boom and Decline – Incorporated on May 4, 1852, and named for its expansive groves of oak trees, the young settlement of Oakland soon acquired a wholesome reputation as a quiet community of houses, shops, churches, farms and schools, with regular ferry service to the woollier city across the bay. The arrival of the transcontinental railroad in 1869 established Oakland as a regional transportation hub, and shops, hotels and restaurants sprang up along 8th, 9th and Washington Streets—the area today known as Old Oakland. When the 1906 earthquake and fire devastated San Francisco, Oakland sheltered more than 150,000 refugees, many of whom elected to remain.

Skyscrapers grew up along Broadway through the early 20C, and the city was joined to San Francisco by the Bay Bridge, the largest civil engineering project of the time. Oakland's population grew by a third during the years of World War II when the Kaiser Shipyards attracted thousands of workers. With the end of the war, however, came economic decline and social unrest. In the 1960s Oakland suffered through race riots and rising rates of urban poverty and violent crime. Natural disasters also took their toll—the Loma Prieta earthquake of 1989 collapsed the "Cypress Structure" section of the double-deck I-880 freeway through West Oakland, while a devastating hill fire in 1991 razed substantial residential areas.

A Gradual Rebuilding – Although vacant storefronts continue to haunt Broadway, major civil-engineering programs have brought a measure of recovery to downtown. The expanded, modernized **Port of Oakland** now ranks among the top 20 in the world. In addition, the opening of eight BART stations in Oakland in 1974, the re-establishment of passenger ferry service to San Francisco in 1989, and the completion of a new Amtrak passenger station in 1995 renewed Oakland's traditional role as a Bay Area transportation center. The City Center and Jack London Square areas underwent massive redevelopment in the 1980s, and work along the waterfront is continuing. Meanwhile, the city has aggressively preserved its rich architectural heritage, buying and refurbishing scores of Victorian and 20C houses and commercial buildings in Old Oakland and Preservation Park. Gentrified neighborhood shopping precincts, including **Piedmont Avenue** *(between MacArthur Blvd. and Pleasant Valley Ave.)* and **College Avenue** in the Rockridge district, attract shoppers and diners by day and evening.

Guiding the renaissance in downtown Oakland is Mayor Jerry Brown, an austere counterculturalist known as "Governor Moonbeam" for the ecologically and spiritually based policies he promoted during two terms as California governor (1974-82). Elected Oakland's urban chief by a landslide in 1998, he has been a strong voice in strengthening public safety, education and the arts.

Visiting Oakland – Downtown Oakland bustles only during weekday business hours, by far the best time to visit the area. Parking is available in downtown garages, but it's best to take BART to the 12th Street/City Center station. That station is also convenient to Chinatown and Old Oakland.

The Lake Merritt BART station accesses the Oakland Museum of California and the south side of Lake Merritt. Parking is available in the museum's basement garage and on the north and west sides of the lake.

Jack London Square offers abundant garage parking, with discounts offered to patrons of the square's shops and restaurants. The immediate waterfront area is a pleasure to explore on foot throughout the day and evening, though the Oakland Produce Market is best seen in the early morning. The **Alameda-Oakland Ferry** from San Francisco docks near Jack London Square after crossing the bay.

For maps and visitor information, contact the **Oakland Convention & Visitors Bureau** *(475 14th St., Suite 120; ☎ 510-839-9000; www.oaklandcvb.com).*

SIGHTS

Downtown 🚇 *12th St./City Center station.*

City Hall – *1 Frank Ogawa Plaza. Open year-round Mon–Fri 9am–5pm. Closed major holidays.* ⅏ ☎ *510-444-2489.* The present-day center of downtown Oakland was ordained by city planners to be the dynamic intersection where Broadway, San Pablo Avenue and 14th Street converged. Since the opening of City Center in the 1980s, the focus of business has shifted one block south, but City Hall still dominates that prominent intersection (now eclipsed by parks and pedestrian walkways). A vaulting symbol of the city's progressive spirit, when it was completed in 1914 (Palmer, Hornbostel & Jones), the 18-story shaft rises from a three-story Beaux Arts podium, capped by a Baroque-style clock tower. Inside, an elegant staircase leads from the lobby to a third-floor Council Chamber.

★**Oakland City Center** – *Between Broadway and 12th, 14th & Clay Sts. Open year-round Mon–Fri 6am–6:30pm, Sat 10am–4pm.* 🍴 ⅏ 🅿 ☎ *510-628-8490. www.oaklandcitycenter.com.* The pleasantly landscaped John B. Williams Plaza conducts pedestrians via escalators upward from the sunken BART station to this open-air mall. At its center stands a brightly painted metal **sculpture (1)** by Roslyn Magzilli entitled *There* (1988). The title is a jocular allusion to Gertrude Stein's famous (and usually misinterpreted as spiteful) observation—"There is no there there"—following a visit to her childhood hometown after an absence of many years. To the west, three-story rows of modern commercial buildings, designed by Horace Gilford, frame a striking view of the Federal Building's twin towers. East from the plaza, sight lines converge on the 21-story **Oakland Tribune Building** *(13th & Franklin Sts.).* The jaunty landmark (1923, Edward Foulkes), designed to recall an Italian campanile but capped with a copper-clad, French chateau-style roof, housed the offices of *The Oakland Tribune* until the newspaper moved to Jack London Square in 1992.

★**Ronald V. Dellums Federal Building** – *Between 12th, 14th, Clay & Jefferson Sts.* Some 5,000 employees occupy the offices of this monumental, twin-towered structure, the largest building in Alameda County. Completed in 1993, the limestone-clad towers contain federal courts, offices and a public auditorium, and are linked by a 75ft glass rotunda that serves as a lobby. A marble-and-granite map of the Bay Area spreads across the rotunda floor.

Preservation Park – *13th St. & Martin Luther King, Jr. Way.* ☎ *510-874-7580. www.oaklandnet.com/community/preservation/index.html.* These 16 splendidly landscaped Victorian homes were relocated from their original sites and restored as a charming office park. Labels recount the history of each of the houses, which span the decades from about 1870 to 1910. Worth a special visit is the Italianate **Pardee Home Museum**★ *(672 11th St.; visit by 90min guided tour only, year-round Fri–Sat noon; closed major holidays; $5;* ☎ *510-444-2187; www.pardeehome.org)*, family mansion of two Oakland mayors: Enoch Pardee and, later, his son George. The latter also held the office of California governor from 1903-07. Built in 1868, the mansion is maintained as it was in 1981 at the death of George Pardee's daughter. Tours reveal a hodgepodge of furnishings and thousands of objets d'art collected and displayed by George's wife.

★**Old Oakland** – *Bounded by Broadway and 7th, 10th & Washington Sts. Walking tours May–Oct;* ☎ *510-238-3234.* This restored historic district formed the heart of downtown Oakland during the 1870s. Today it remains an extraordinary grouping of 19C commercial buildings. The shops, hotels and restaurants were built between 1868 and 1880 for the throngs of travelers passing through the Central Pacific passenger depot at 7th and Broadway (terminus of the first transcontinental railroad); the sturdy, two- and three-story structures were restored in the 1980s. Splendid showcases of Victorian craftsmanship, they display a medley of brick and granite masonry, elegant cornices and elaborate ornamentation.

❶ G.B. Ratto & Co.
821 Washington St. at 9th St. ☎ *510-832-6503.* An Oakland institution, this venerable specialty-food emporium has catered to the particularities of East Bay tastes for 100 years. Linger over the lengthy cheese counter beneath hanging salamis, then wend your way to the café in back.

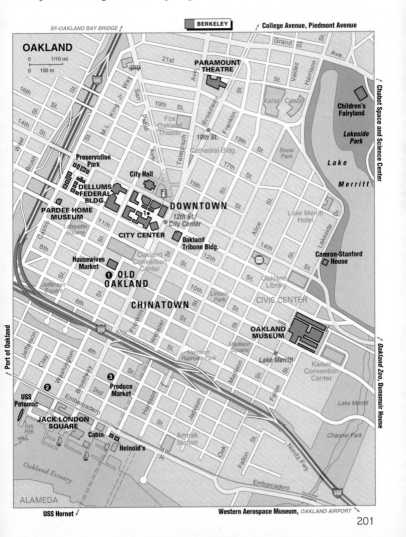

Exotic culinary items abound at the commodious **Housewives Market** *(9th & Washington Sts.; open year-round Mon-Sat 9am-6pm)*, which shelters an ethnically diverse emporium of food counters, produce and fish markets, butcher shops and other stalls.

Oakland Chinatown – *Bounded by Broadway and 7th, 10th & Harrison Sts. ☎ 510-208-6080 (Oakland Asian Cultural Center).* Although the first Chinese immigrants arrived in Oakland in the early 1850s, they gathered in the present nine-square-block quarter during the 1870s. Unlike its San Francisco counterpart, Oakland's Chinatown does not court tourists, although many visitors enjoy exploring the bustling array of shops and markets, and tasting Asian foods.

★★**Paramount Theatre** – *2025 Broadway.* 🚇 *19th St. Visit by guided tour (2hrs only, year-round 1st & 3rd Sat 10am, $1. Closed major holidays. ☎ 510-465-6400. www.paramounttheatre.com.* This monumental movie palace (1931, Timothy Pflueger) is one of the nation's finest examples of Moderne design. The building's resplendent Art Deco detailing describes flowers, foliage, birds and people in addition to the more abstract designs typical of the style. Authentically restored in 1973, it is now owned by the city as a performing-arts facility.

The exterior boasts two majestic tile mosaics of puppeteers, divided by the towering Paramount sign. The amber-colored *Fountain of Light* dominates the lobby; the glass sculpture appears to be rising in spectacular billows toward a green-lit grillwork ceiling. With seating for nearly 3,000 people, the lavish auditorium features a gold-lit filigreed ceiling, and paneled side walls sculpted in bas-relief scenes of maidens and warriors. Ralph Stackpole sculpted the horsemen on the orchestral panel above the stage. A Wurlitzer organ mounted on a hydraulic lift rises to stage level for performances. Also worth a gaze are the splendidly decorated men's and women's restrooms, the curving foyers, and the women's Black Lacquer Smoking Lounge.

Nearly as fantastic, though now closed, is the nearby **Fox Oakland Theater** *(1815 Telegraph Ave.).* Built in 1928 (Diggs, Weeks & Day), this exotic, Moorish-style movie palace conjures visions of Arabian Nights. In its day, it was grander than anything on Hollywood Boulevard.

Waterfront *Southwest of downtown.*

★**Jack London Square** – 🚌 *Along the Embarcadero from Clay to Alice St. Farmers' market year-round Sun 10am–2pm. ✗ ♿ ☎ 925-426-5420. www.jacklondonsquare.com.* Stretching along the busy Inner Harbor of the Oakland Estuary southeast of Broadway, this once-gritty dock area has been developed as an attractive pedestrian-friendly complex. In addition to shops, restaurants, hotels, cinemas, a farmers' market and a yacht harbor, it has become the East Bay's hippest nightlife district. Oakland's Amtrak passenger lines, Oakland Estuary water-taxi service, and ferries from San Francisco converge near the marina.

 Yoshi's
510 Embarcadero West.
☎ *510-238-9200.*
www.yoshis.com. The top venue for jazz in the San Francisco Bay Area is, perhaps surprisingly, not in San Francisco at all but in a Japanese restaurant just off Jack London Square. The cabaret-style theater, open nightly, presents many of the biggest names in contemporary jazz music— including, in late 2000, Branford Marsalis, Shirley Horn and Earl Klugh.

The square was named for writer Jack London, who lived in Oakland as a boy and young man. His adventurous spirit is recalled in the historic **Jack London Cabin**, a reconstruction from original timbers of the rustic, single-room log cabin that London occupied during the winter of 1897-98 while prospecting for gold in the Yukon Territory.

Near the cabin stands one of London's favorite watering holes, **Heinold's First and Last Chance Saloon** *(56 Jack London Sq. ☎ 510-839-6761),* built in 1883 from the timbers of a whaling ship. Heinold's was also patronized by authors Ambrose Bierce, Joaquin Miller and, for a short time, Robert Louis Stevenson. Still operating as a bar, it was declared a National Literary Monument in 1997. A floor contorted by the 1906 earthquake (and never repaired) holds three small tables and a half-dozen barstools; wonderful historical photos cover the walls.

USS Potomac – *FDR Pier, end of Clay St. (Visitor center opposite at 540 Water St. Dockside tours year-round Wed & Fri 10am–1:15pm, Sun noon–3:15pm; $5. History cruises (2hrs) mid-Mar–mid-Nov alternating Thu & Sat by reservation (☎ 510-627-1215); $30. 📷 ☎ 510-839-8256. www.usspotomac.org.* Franklin Delano Roosevelt's presidential yacht is berthed at Jack London Square. The 165ft former Coast Guard cutter was built in 1934 and officially recommissioned as a US Navy vessel for the use of the Commander in Chief two years later.

Today the *Potomac* has been renovated to match its appearance when it served as a presidential retreat on the Potomac River and along the Atlantic seaboard. Points of interest include the Presidential Cabin, the engine room and a radio room from which Roosevelt made a national broadcast on March 29, 1941.

Corrugated metal awnings roof the sidewalks of the **Oakland Produce Market** *(2 blocks east of Jack London Square)*. From early morning to early afternoon, workers on forklifts shuttle crates of fresh fruits and vegetables between waiting trucks and warehouse buildings, some of which have been brokering wholesale produce since 1917. Some warehouse bays have been converted to restaurants.

 Oakland Grill
301 Franklin St. at 3rd St.
☎ *510-835-1176.* Get to this produce district eatery around 8am to down a hearty breakfast against a backdrop of fruits and vegetables being unloaded and readied for sale. All four buildings on this nostalgic corner sport corrugated metal awnings. Just to say you did it, try the scrambled egg whites, listed on the menu as "Ono Yoko."

Lake Merritt Area   *East of downtown.* 🚇 *Lake Merritt station.*

Lake Merritt – *Bounded by Lakeside Dr. and Grand & Lakeshore Aves.* The shores of this 155-acre saltwater tidal lake offer a haven of green serenity near the bustling heart of the city. The shimmering expanse of water was a marshy tidal slough until 1869, when Dr. Samuel Merritt, an ex-mayor who owned land on its shores, dammed the outlet at 12th Street to create the lake. In 1870, he successfully lobbied the California legislature to declare it an official wildlife refuge. Although many private landowners built mansions at its edge, the city eventually secured the properties and turned them into public parkland. A pleasant esplanade winds around the lake's 3.5mi shoreline, broadening on the northern side into **Lakeside Park** *(Bellevue & Grand Aves.)* This lush oasis of 122 oak-shaded acres includes a bandstand, show gardens, and **Children's Fairyland** 🎠 *(1520 Lakeside Dr.; open Apr–mid-Jun & mid-Sept–Nov Wed–Sun 10am–4pm; mid-Jun–early Sept daily 10am–4:30pm, weekends 5pm; Dec–Mar Fri–Sun 10am–4:30pm; $3.25; ✗ ♿ 🅿 ☎ 510-238-6876)*, an amusement park for the very young.

Camron-Stanford House – *1418 Lakeside Dr. Visit by guided tour (1hr) only, year-round Wed 11am–4pm & Sun 1pm–5pm, rest of the week by appointment. Closed Jan 1 & Dec 25. $4.* 🅿 ☎ *510-444-1876.* This sedate Italianate residence (1876) on the southwest shore of Lake Merritt was home to a succession of prominent figures, including Josiah Stanford, brother of railroad magnate Leland Stanford. The mansion served as the first Oakland Public Museum from 1910 until 1967, when most of the exhibits were removed for storage pending completion of the new Oakland Museum building. The interior was painstakingly restored to its 19C appearance and reopened for public tours in 1978. The lower floor still exhibits some of the original museum's Oakland history collections, while the main floor showcases Victorian-era interior decoration and furnishings.

© Robert Holmes

Lake Merritt

★★Oakland Museum of California – 🎟 *1000 Oak St. Open year-round Wed–Sa*
10am–5pm (1st Fri 9pm), Sun noon–5pm. Closed Jan 1, Jul 4, Thanksgiving Day
Dec 25. $6 (free 2nd Sun). Guided tours weekends 1:30pm or by appointment
✕ ⚫ 🅿 ☏ 510-238-2200. www.museumca.org. A city showpiece, this 7.7-acre
cultural complex celebrates California's natural and human history and its art
A setting for public art and celebration, the museum's innovative garden
—a geometric weave of landscaped passages, courtyards, terraces and stairways—
encourage visitors to explore the building from its sunken central lawn court to it
scenic rooftops.

In the early 1960s, city officials and private individuals launched a massive publi
campaign to build a grand new museum complex that would help revive inner-cit
Oakland. The facility consolidated three existing collections—the Snow Museum
which focused on natural history; the Oakland Public Museum, devoted to Nativ
Californian ethnology and the state's pioneer history; and the Oakland Art Museum
Internationally acclaimed architect Eero Saarinen was the leading candidate to desig
the museum when he died unexpectedly in 1961. His colleague, Kevin Roche, wa
then chosen to undertake the project. With assistance from architectural technolo
gist John Dinkeloo, Roche created a series of tiered horizontal galleries around
central courtyard, overhung with terraced roof gardens. Composed solely of rein
forced concrete, plate glass and wood, the building's strongly angular lines ar
graced by statuary and softened with flowers, shrubs and trees—including orchar
varieties like olive and pear that recall the state's important agricultural roots. Th
museum opened in 1969 to rave reviews, with *New York Times* critic Ada Louis
Huxtable calling it "one of the most thoughtful revolutionary structures in the world.
The three main departments—natural sciences, history and art—occupy the prin
cipal halls on three separate levels of the building. The **Great Hall** features majo
traveling exhibitions, art shows and temporary presentations drawn from th
museum's own collections.

★Natural Sciences Gallery – *1st level.* Inspired by Elna Bakker's book *An Island Calle*
California, this hall (also known as the Hall of California Ecology) is arranged t
guide visitors on a walk eastward through central California to experience th
astounding breadth and richness of the state's geography and biodiversity. Detaile
dioramas of native flora and fauna re-create eight distinct biotic zones that stretc
across the middle of the state: the Coastline, the foggy Coastal Mountains, the dr
Inner Coast Ranges, the Central Valley, the Sierra Slope, the High Sierra, the sage
brush deserts of the Great Basin, and the rocky Mojave Desert. Located off th
main hall is the Aquatic California Gallery, where realistic displays in resin illustrat
life in the state's coastal and delta waters, salt marshes and freshwater stream

★Cowell Hall of California History – *2nd level.* The hall's permanent exhibition–
California: A Place, A People, A Dream—traces the state's human history throug
historical tableaux and displays of 6,000 artifacts. Beginning with **First People**, th
exhibition reveals the diversity of California's native cultures through their rituals
basketry, fetishes, stone tools and clothing. In **Explorers, Priests and Colonists**, the hard
ships and successes of the Spanish-Mexican period are explored through churc
artifacts, navigational equipment, a sample of an adobe wall and the tools of th
early colonists. **Immigrants and Settlers** are recalled in a model pioneer's cabin wit
its rustic kitchen. **Adventurers and Goldseekers** re-creates the raucous boom times c
the mid-19C, complete with an archetypal assay office and 5oz of gold nuggets
Founders, Organizers and Developers chronicles the lives of Victorian-era citizens throug
displays of day-to-day paraphernalia from home, city and farm, including a rura
"mud wagon," a millionaire's black carriage and a gleaming fire truck. Finally
Seekers, Innovators and Achievers celebrates the 20C "California Dream" of a better lif
for all who come here, whether surfers, Hollywood stars, backpackers, beatniks
hippies, immigrants or Silicon Valley inventors. (This exhibit, unfortunately, has no
been made current since 1984.)

At the rear of the hall sits Ivan and Elliot Schwartz's striking sculpture, *Dreamers*
created by fusing masks, cast from the faces of real Californians, to clothed figure
and spraying all with white plaster. A special gallery features changing exhibits o
historical subjects, and three computer stations provide in-depth information.

★★Gallery of California Art – *3rd level.* Devoted to works by artists who have lived, worke
or studied in California, the collection contains paintings, sculptures, drawings
prints, photographs and mixed-media works from the early 19C to the presen
Visitors may take a counter-clockwise course through the gallery for a chronolog
ical progression. Of special note are the 19C California landscapes, includin
paintings of the Sierra Nevada by Thomas Moran, Albert Bierstadt, Thomas Hi
and William Keith. The museum holds the largest collection of work from Californi
Arts and Crafts practitioners Arthur and Lucia Kleinhans Mathews, includin
murals, frames and furniture. California Impressionist works are represented b
Guy Rose, Joseph Raphael and E. Charlton Fortune, and by the Oakland-base
"Society of Six" landscapists: William Clapp, August Gay, Selden Gile, Mauric
Logan, Louis Siegriest and Bernard von Eichman.

The collection includes works by Richard Diebenkorn, Elmer Bischoff, David Park and other adherents to the Bay Area Figurative movement, as well as by Abstract Expressionists Clyfford Still, Mark Rothko, Sam Francis, Frank Lobdell and Hassel Smith. Later 20C works by Wayne Thiebaud, Robert Bechtle, David Hockney and Bruce Conner share space with contemporary sculptures by Deborah Butterfield, Manuel Neri and ceramist Robert Arneson. The museum owns the world's largest collection of Dorothea Lange's photographs and negatives, and photography by Eadweard Muybridge (an early San Francisco panorama) and such group f.64 members as Edward Weston, Ansel Adams and Imogen Cunningham.

ADDITIONAL SIGHTS

★Chabot Space & Science Center – Kids *10000 Skyline Blvd. Exit I-580 at Park Blvd.; continue east across Rte. 13, then right on Mountain Blvd., which becomes Ascot Blvd. Climb to ridgetop, then right on Skyline Blvd. Open year-round Tue–Sat 10am–5pm, Sun noon–5pm. Planetarium & MegaDome Theater also open Fri–Sat 7–9pm, observatory Fri–Sat 7–10pm. Closed Jan 1 & Dec 25. Museum $8 (children 4-12 $5.50), planetarium or theater $8.75 (kids $6.50), two venues $14.75 (kids $11), full access $19.75 (kids $15.50).* ╳ ♿ 🅿 ☎ 510-336-7300. *www.chabotspace.org.* Thirteen years in the making, this impressive 86,000sq ft hilltop center opened in August 2000 on 13 acres of parkland, at a cost of $76.5 million. Within are an acclaimed planetarium and theater, hands-on exhibits and science labs, and powerful telescopes that invite public access. The surrounding site has an amphitheater and a natural garden.
To the right of the main entrance, in the East Building, the 243-seat **Ask Jeeves Planetarium** can project up to 9,000 stars with fiber-optic technology and its Zeiss projector. To the left, the 210-seat **Tien MegaDome Theater** presents such 70mm films at "To Be an Astronaut" and "SolarMax." Between the two, the **Your Place in the Universe** exhibit features 3-D displays about Earth, the solar system and the Milky Way galaxy. The second-level **Hall of California Astronomy** harbors an exhibit on observatories and the manufacture of telescopes and other instruments.
A sky bridge leads to the West Building, with its **virtual space-flight center** (the Challenger Learning Center) and a full-size replica of the International Space Station's laboratory and living modules. Solar and meridian-transit **telescopes** are attached to this building; beyond is a historic 8in refractor telescopes, moved from the original 1883 Oakland Observatory. Weekend viewing *(free)* is offered at a 20in refractor nicknamed "Rachel." A 36in telescope is planned.

Oakland Zoo – Kids *9777 Golf Links Rd., just east of I-580. Open late May–Labor Day daily 10am–5pm, rest of the year daily 10am–4pm. Closed Thanksgiving & Dec 25. $6.50.* ╳ ♿ 🅿 ☎ 510-632-9525. *www.oaklandzoo.org.* This small but friendly zoo, an integral part of Knowland Park since 1936, boasts more than 400 native and exotic animals of 108 species in 58 different exhibits. Among the most popular are chimpanzees, elephants and lions, as well as sun bears in Rain Forest Canyon. A 2/3-size replica of a **Civil War-era train** *(open year-round daily 11am–4pm; $1.50)* pulled by a steam locomotive, winds through the southern part of the zoo. The 15min **Sky Ride** *(open daily in summer, rest of the year weekends 11am–4pm; $2)* soars over grazing American bison and tule elk.

★Dunsmuir House and Gardens – *2960 Peralta Oaks Ct., off 106th Ave. just south of Knowland Park. Grounds open Feb–Dec Tue–Fri 10am–4pm; $2. May–Sept also Sun noon–3pm; free. Mansion tours Apr–Sept Wed 11am & noon; May–Sept also 1st Sun, 1 & 2pm; $5.* ♿ 🅿 ☎ 510-615-5555. *www.dunsmuir.org.* Built by Alexander Dunsmuir, son of a wealthy British Columbia coal baron, this historic 50-acre estate is one of Oakland's unsung highlights. Dunsmuir had the house built in 1899 as a wedding gift for his wife, Josephine; but on the couple's honeymoon in New York, Alexander took ill and died. Josephine lived in the house for fewer than two years before her own death. The estate was purchased by banker I.W. Hellman Jr. in 1906; his family held the property until the early 1960s, when it was purchased by the City of Oakland.

Visit – House tours begin at the quaint **Dinkelspiel House**, built for the Hellmans' daughter Florence in the early 1930s. The long driveway to the mansion leads through a meadow landscaped in part by John McLaren, best known for his work in Golden Gate Park. Camperdown elms, hornbeams and bunya-bunya are among the trees here. A new pavilion above the meadow is a venue for concerts, lectures and other special events.
The centerpiece of the estate is **Dunsmuir House**. The 37-room mansion was built in Neoclassical Revival style by San Francisco architect J. Eugene Freeman, who adapted Georgian and Federal styles with symmetrical facades, hipped or gabled roofs and Palladian windows. Embracing more than 16,000sq ft in three stories, the house presents a Tiffany-style dome, 10 fireplaces and inlaid parquet floors. Roads lead south beyond the mansion to a historic farm area. Of note is the **Carriage House**, with mahogany-paneled walls and wrought-iron horse feeders.

Western Aerospace Museum – *8260 Boeing St. (Building 621), off Earhart Rd. North Field, Oakland Airport. Open May–Sept Tue–Sun 10am–5pm, rest of the year Wed–Sun 10am–4pm. $6.*   *510-638-7100. www.aerospace.org/wam home/htm.* A vintage (1940) hangar built as a training facility for World War I aircraft mechanics is home to this surprising museum. On display are such historic aircraft as Naval fighters and a sister craft to the L-10 piloted by Amelia Earhart. The impressive Ahrens Collection offers 1/72 scale-model US military aircraft; other exhibits feature women and African American aviators, aerial photography, air racing, and Col. Jimmy Doolittle's 8th Air Force.

Outdoors is the Short Solent four-engine Flying Boat *(tours $2)*, built in 1946. Almost 90ft long, with the tip of its tail 37ft above the ground, the plane was designed to take off and land exclusively in water. Converted to luxury passenger service in 1949, it became the property of reclusive billionaire Howard Hughes in 1959. Following his death, it was rescued and restored.

★★USS Hornet – *Pier 3, Alameda. Take Atlantic Ave. north off Webster St. (Rte. 61) and follow signs. Open year-round Wed–Mon 10am-5pm. Closed Thanksgiving Day & Dec 25. $10.*   *510-521-8448.* Commissioned in November 1943, this Essex-class aircraft carrier was the eighth in a line of US naval vessels to be named *Hornet*; it replaced the seventh USS *Hornet*, a carrier sunk in October 1942 at the Battle of Santa Cruz in the Solomon Islands. With a length of 894ft, the 41,200-ton ship was designed to carry up to 3,400 servicemen and an attack force of F6F Hellcat fighters, TBM Avenger torpedo bombers and SB2C Helldiver dive bombers. Steaming from Pearl Harbor in March 1944, the USS *Hornet* moved quickly to the forefront of the Pacific war. In action at Iwo Jima in June 1944, air crews shot down 67 Japanese aircraft, commencing an extraordinary string of victories that earned the ship seven battle stars, and her pilots Navy records for the number of planes shot down in one month (255) and in a single day (72). At the invasion of Okinawa in April 1945, the *Hornet* scored the first crippling hits on the largest battleship of its day, the 72,000-ton *Yamato*, which was sunk in the battle. When 60ft seas buckled its flight deck during a severe typhoon in June 1945, the carrier was forced to retire to the US for repairs. The *Hornet* ended the war with a combat record of 1,420 aircraft, 42 cargo ships, 10 destroyers, a carrier, a cruiser and a battleship destroyed. Despite having endured 59 attacks, the *Hornet* never sustained a single hit by bomb, torpedo or Kamikaze pilot.

The *Hornet* also served in the Vietnam War. It achieved a place in history in May 1969 when it retrieved astronauts Neil Armstrong, Buzz Aldrin and Michael Collins—the crew of Apollo 11—upon their return from the first manned moon mission. The splashdown in the Pacific was witnessed live by President Richard Nixon from the *Hornet*'s bridge, and by the largest television audience in history. Later that year, the *Hornet* also retrieved the returned astronauts of Apollo 12. The ship was decommissioned in June 1970 and declared a National Historic Landmark in 1991.

Visit – Boarding the ship on its vast **Hangar Deck,** where aircraft were stored between sorties, visitors may view a short orientation program and peruse a gallery of historic photographs before commencing self-guided tours.

At mid-ship, a set of painted footprints marks the first steps of Apollo 11's lunar astronauts back on "earth," when they walked from the retrieval helicopter to quarantine in a customized trailer; an adjacent exhibit highlights that event. A 5min **flight simulator** *($3)*, equipped with computer-generated film and hydraulic lifts, permits visitors to experience the sensation of launching and landing an aircraft on a carrier deck.

Steep, narrow ship ladders climb to the sprawling **Flight Deck,** above which rises the massive "Island" or control tower. Visitors may climb to the Navigation Bridge, where the captain and officers piloted the ship, and the Flag Bridge, where the fleet admiral commanded a task force of support ships. From the Primary Flight Control Bridge overlooking the runways in the aft of the control tower, the "Air Boss" monitored the takeoffs and landings of aircraft.

Descending to the **Second Deck,** below the Hangar Deck, visitors may tour the refurbished officers' quarters, lounge and dining hall, the Marine Detachment quarters, the enlisted men's mess and the engine room.

27 • AROUND THE EAST BAY

East of the ridge line backdropping Berkeley and Oakland, pleasant suburban towns dot a series of hills and valleys overshadowed by Mt. Diablo. Visible from many of San Francisco's loftier viewpoints, this regal peak looms over the San Ramon and Diablo Valleys, which drain north to the narrow Carquinez Straits in the northeast part of San Francisco Bay. Martinez, Concord, Walnut Creek, Alamo, Danville and other residential communities spread over the valley floors, while exclusive developments extend higher into the grassy hills. The historic Solano County towns of Vallejo and Benicia guard either end of Carquinez Straits.

SIGHTS

★**Mount Diablo State Park** – Kids *North Gate Rd., 35mi from San Francisco. From Oakland, take Rte. 24 east through the Caldecott Tunnel to Walnut Creek. Continue east on Ygnacio Valley Rd. for 2.5mi; take a right on Walnut Ave., which turns into North Gate Rd. after 1.5mi and leads another 12mi to the summit. Park open year-round daily 8am–dusk. Closed during very high fire-risk days. $5/car.* △ 🅿 *Summit Museum open Memorial Day–Labor Day Wed–Sun 11am–5pm. Rest of the year Wed–Sun 10am–4pm.* 🅫 🅿 ☎ *925-837-2525. www.mdia.org.* The sweeping, panoramic **view**★★★ from the 3,849ft summit of Mt. Diablo is said to encompass more than 40,000sq mi. That would make it the second most extensive view over land from any point on earth, after Africa's Mt. Kilimanjaro. On clear days, the naked eye can easily pick out such far-flung landmarks as San Francisco (27mi west), the Farallon Islands (62mi west), Mt. Lassen (165mi northeast), the Sacramento River Delta to the north, and the long wall of the Sierra Nevada range to the east. A good pair of binoculars can bring Yosemite National Park's El Capitan (130mi east) into focus. From this remarkable vantage point, Colonel Leander Ransom in 1851 established the Mt. Diablo Base and Meridian, used to make the first surveyed maps of Northern California and Nevada. A year later, R.D. Cutts mapped the state's northern waterways for the Coast Survey from here.

Both survey marks still can be seen upon the rock now enclosed by the small **Summit Museum**, built of locally quarried sandstone by the Civilian Conservation Corps in 1940. Exhibits within the museum focus on Mt. Diablo's geology and its natural and human history; telescopes mounted on an observation deck assist viewing of distant sites. *Note: summer fogs often obscure views.*

On the mountain's flanks are extensive outcrops of fossilized seashells and prehistoric mammal bones. The park also is home to some 400 plant species, as well as deer, cougar, coyote, bobcat and about 200 species of birds, including bald eagles. Mt. Diablo offers camping, picnicking, hiking on more than 150mi of trails, and climbing in the weird sandstone formations known as **Rock City**. A new visitor center is under construction in the Mitchell Canyon section of the park.

Lindsay Wildlife Museum – Kids *1931 First Ave., Walnut Creek, 45mi from San Francisco. From Oakland, take Rte. 24 east, turning north on I-680. Turn left at the Treat/Geary Exit onto Geary Rd.; left again on Buena Vista Ave.; then right on First Ave. Open mid-Jun–Labor Day Tue–Sun 10am–5pm. Rest of the year Tue–Fri noon–5pm, weekends 10am–5pm. Closed week following Labor Day. $5.* 🅫 🅿 ☎ *925-935-1978. www.wildlife-museum.org.* This small community-oriented natural-history museum is both an educational center and the largest wildlife-rehabilitation hospital in the US. Injured animals that cannot be returned to the wild live out their days here, under conditions carefully designed to satisfy both their physical and psychological needs. Eagles, hawks and other raptors roost on perches, while squirrels, coyotes and other mammals cavort below eye level. Live reptiles and amphibians, as well as mounted insect collections, introduce yet more local fauna.

★★**Eugene O'Neill National Historic Site** – *Kuss Rd., Danville, 28mi from San Francisco. Visit by guided tour (2hrs 30min) only, year-round Wed–Sun 10am & 12:30pm (shuttle pickup times). Reservations required. From I-680 east of Oakland (between Rte. 24 & I-580), exit at Sycamore Valley Rd.; National Park Service van picks up visitors in adjacent park-and-ride lot for drive to Tao House. Closed Jan 1, Jul 4, Thanksgiving Day, Dec 25.* ☎ *925-838-0249. www.nps.gov/euon.* Situated on a scenic knoll in the shadow of the Las Trampas wilderness, this modest yet comfortable dwelling was home for more than six years to playwright **Eugene O'Neill** (1888-1953). Author of nearly 60 plays, winner of four Pulitzer Prizes for drama, and the only American playwright to win the Nobel Prize for Literature (in 1936), O'Neill is one of the nation's best known and most influential dramatists.

Tragedy and Triumph – The son of a successful traveling actor, Eugene O'Neill was born in a New York City hotel and raised largely "on the road" by a loving but troubled family. O'Neill's personal life was filled with difficulties. His mother was addicted to morphine and his brother to alcohol. Both of his sons—Eugene Jr. (1910-50) and Shane (1919-77)—committed suicide and he was bitterly estranged from his daughter, Oona (1925-91), following her 1943 marriage to much-older comic actor Charlie Chaplin. Suffering from tuberculosis, alcoholism and severe depression himself, O'Neill overcame his afflictions to find fulfillment first as a seaman and ultimately as a playwright. His heavily autobiographical tragedies helped transform American theater from an arena of pure entertainment into a high art form. O'Neill's six years at Tao House, a then-remote home he built with his third wife—Carlotta (née Hazel Tharzing, 1888-1965), an actress and a former Miss California—were among the happiest and most productive of his life. In 1936, the intensely private O'Neills bought 158 acres of almond and walnut orchards on the flank of Las Trampas Ridge, attracted by the site's remoteness and its handsome views of Mt. Diablo and the San Ramon Valley. Designed by architect Frederick Confer, their white, two-story Monterey-style house was built of concrete

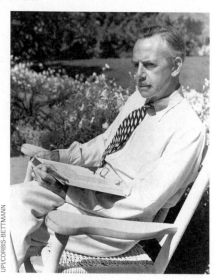

blocks (baselite) intended to re
semble adobe brick, with
black-tile roof and verandas or
the second floor. The coupl
christened their home **Tao Hous**
after Carlotta's taste for chi
noiserie and Eugene's interes
in the Taoist philosophy. Her
O'Neill wrote six plays, includ
ing four of his greatest: *The Ice
man Cometh*, *Hughie*, *A Moo
for the Misbegotten* (whose in
tended setting is thought to be
the old barn on this property
and his masterpiece, *A Long
Day's Journey into Night*.

O'Neill's degenerative illness
and an inability to hire local as
sistance during World War
forced the couple to sell th
house in February 1944 and re
turn to the East Coast, wher
the playwright died in 1953
After the property became
National Historic Site in 1980
the National Park Service begar

Eugene O'Neill (1937)

efforts to restore the home and furnishings to their original appearance.

Visit – On the downstairs floor, guided tours lead through the kitchen, living room
guest room (which hosted Bennett Cerf, Somerset Maugham and John Ford), and
"Rosie's Room," named for O'Neill's cherished player piano. Upstairs are O'Neill'
writing den, which he furnished in a style fitting for a shipboard cabin, and the couple'
bedrooms—the writer's still containing his original bed, an antique Chinese opium
couch from Gump's. The 13-acre site also preserves the pool built for the playwright
an avid swimmer, and the grave of the O'Neills' beloved Dalmatian dog, Blemie.

⋆⋆**Blackhawk Museum** – Kids *3700 Blackhawk Plaza Cir., Danville. 33mi from Sa
Francisco. Exit I-680 at Sycamore Valley Blvd. (which becomes Camino Tassajara
and continue 5mi to Blackhawk Plaza. Open year-round Wed–Sun 10am–5pm
Closed Jan 1, Thanksgiving Day, Dec 25. $8. Guided tours (1hr) available week
ends 2pm.* ⅙ 🅿 ☎ *925-736-2277. www.blackhawkauto.org.* At the eastern en
of Blackhawk Plaza—a beautiful, Mediterranean-style luxury shopping comple
landscaped with a cascading artificial creek—rises the rose-granite and glass façade
of this museum. It houses a stunning collection of some 120 beautifully restored
vintage automobiles spanning the decades from the 1890s to the 1960s
Informatively labeled and attractively arranged through two levels, the rare and
historic vehicles are presented as works of art. From the ground floor, an interio
hall leads to the Moving Inspirations Art Galleries, comprising nearly 4,000 piece
of automotive art and memorabilia.

⋆**John Muir National Historic Site** – *4202 Alhambra Ave., Martinez. 30mi from
San Francisco. Take I-80 northeast from Oakland to Rte. 4 East; exit at Alhambr
Ave. and turn left. Open year-round Wed–Sun 10am–4:30pm. Closed major holi
days. $2.* ✗ ⅙ 🅿 ☎ *925-228-8860. www.nps.gov/jomu.* This comfortable hom
surrounded by orchards formed part of the 2,600-acre fruit ranch owned by **Joh
Muir** (1838-1914). The legendary conservationist resided here during the fina
decades of his life, tending orchards and writing many works that have since
become landmarks of the environmental movement.

Born near Dunbar, Scotland, Muir arrived in Wisconsin with his family at the age
of 11. Detesting the drudgery of farm work, he eventually departed to pursue the
life of a wandering botanist, walking first to the Gulf of Mexico in 1867, wher
he took ship passage for San Francisco. His many visits to the Sierra Nevad
invoked a lifelong love for rugged wilderness. A fine scientist and gifted writer
Muir published observations of nature that attracted a following among East Coas
readers and opened minds to the then-novel idea of conserving wilderness lands
Muir helped found and served as the first president of the Sierra Club, and even
tually prevailed upon the US Congress to bolster the young National Park
movement with new or expanded parklands in the Sierra Nevada and elsewhere

Visit – Built in 1882 by Muir's father-in-law, Dr. John Strentzel, this two-story
Italianate frame residence was John Muir's home from 1890 until his death. Th
house today reflects the Victorian proclivities of the Strentzel family more thar
Muir's own simple tastes. The conservationist wrote many of his influential book
in the second-floor "scribble den," which retains his original desk and objects col
lected on his trips throughout the US.

Muir himself planted the large *Sequoia giganteum* (giant sequoia) that grows sturdily near the northwest corner of the house. The park also preserves a number of grape vines and pear, peach, cherry, fig, orange, pomegranate, apricot and plum trees, and beyond, 326 acres of land on Mt. Wanda. Beyond the orchard stands the **Martinez Adobe** (1849), the home of Vicente Martínez, who received it as part of an early 19C land grant of 17,750 acres.

A film on Muir's life is shown in the visitor center. Muir and his family are interred in a nearby graveyard that is not open to the public.

Benicia – *34mi from San Francisco. Take I-80 northeast from Oakland across the Carquinez Bridge, then east on I-780 to 2nd St. exit in Benicia.* ☎ *707-745-2120.* Established on part of General Mariano Vallejo's vast land holdings, this small, friendly community on the north shore of the Carquinez Straits was named for Vallejo's wife. The town—second to be incorporated in the state—grew up along 10 blocks of First Street north of the waterfront, today a pleasant boulevard of cafes and shops. From February 11, 1853, to February 25, 1854, Benicia served as the California state capital. **Benicia Capitol State Historic Park** *(115 West G St.; open year-round daily 10am–5pm; closed Jan 1, Thanksgiving Day, Dec 25; $2;* P ☎ *707-745-3385)* preserves the old brick statehouse, furnished as it may have been during its 12-months-plus tenure.

Benicia Arsenal – *From 1st St. drive east on Military East, pass through the old army gate and follow signs to the Camel Barn and the Clocktower.* The US Army founded a military reservation in Benicia in 1849, establishing the Benicia Arsenal the following year. One of four US arsenals at the time, it served until it was deactivated in 1964, after which it was converted to the Benicia Industrial Park. Many of the old military buildings today house offices and artists' studios, some of which are open to the public. Among historic reminders of the army's presence are the oldest military cemetery in the Pacific states (1849), the turreted arsenal storehouse known as the Clocktower (1859), the commandant's house, and the **Camel Barn Museum** *(2060 Camel Rd.; open year-round Wed–Sun 1–4pm; $2;* & P ☎ *707-745-5435)*, where the army auctioned camels in 1864 after experimenting with them as pack animals in the North American deserts.

Port Chicago Naval Magazine National Memorial – *Concord Naval Weapons Station, 38mi from San Francisco. Take I-80 northeast from Oakland to Rte. 4 East; exit at Port Chicago Hwy. and proceed to main gate. Open by appointment only (24hr advance reservation required).* & P ☎ *925-838-0249. www.nps.gov/poch.* This somber memorial was dedicated on July 17, 1994, on the 50th anniversary of a World War II munitions explosion that killed 320 mostly African-American military and civilian workers. Wayside exhibits line a brick walkway that leads to the Suisun Bay tidal basin, where the memorial stands. Names of all victims are etched into its polished black granite. Inland, a chapel and visitor center contains further exhibits.

Vallejo Naval & Historical Museum – *734 Marin St., Vallejo. Open year-round Tue–Sat 10am–4:30pm. $1.50.* & P ☎ *707-643-0077.* Located in the former Vallejo City Hall (1927), this fine small museum has five galleries that recount regional history. It highlights the naval presence with a submarine periscope that is installed through the roof for a 360-degree view of the city.

Walking tours of the **Mare Island Naval Shipyard**, in adjacent San Pablo Bay, are arranged through the museum. The US Navy purchased Mare Island in 1852 and assigned David Farragut ("Damn the torpedoes, full speed ahead") as its first commandant. The base grew to become the largest ship construction and repair site in the world. Tours take in 19C-20C housing of many styles, a hospital complex, dry docks and other facilities.

★**Six Flags Marine World** – ▥▥▥ 🎟 *2001 Marine World Pkwy., Vallejo. 30mi from San Francisco. Take I-80 northeast from Oakland and exit at Rte. 37. Blue & Gold Fleet ferry departs from Pier 39 (San Francisco) to Vallejo daily 8:45am–7:40pm. One-way 1hr; $7.50. Shuttles depart Vallejo dock for the park. Package including park admission $40; call for information (Blue & Gold Fleet* ☎ *415-705-5555). Park open mid-Mar–Memorial Day Fri 10am–6pm, Sat 10am–8pm, Sun 10am–7pm; Memorial–Labor Day Mon–Thu 9am–8pm, Fri & Sun 9am–9pm, Sat 9am–10pm; Labor Day–end Sept Fri 10am–6pm, Sat 10am–9pm, Sun 10am–8pm; Oct Fri–Sat 10am–11pm, Sun 10am–9pm. Closed Nov–mid-Mar. $39.99, children under 4ft tall $19.99.* ✗ & P($7). ☎ *707-643-6722. www.sixflags.com/marine world.* This 160-acre, landscaped park combines three distinct elements—it's a zoo, an oceanarium and an amusement park rolled into one—while entertaining and educating visitors about conservation issues with various shows and exhibits. Beginning as a modest theme park in 1968 in Redwood City, 25mi south of San Francisco, it was renamed Marine World Africa USA in 1972 after a merger with a Southern California wildlife park, and relocated in 1986 to its present site in Vallejo. The Six Flags chain of theme parks acquired Marine World in 1999.

Visit – A visit to the park is best structured around seven live animal performances presented up to four times daily in various outdoor amphitheaters *(shows last 20-30min; map and daily schedule available at entrance)*. Prominent are the bottle-nosed acrobats of **Dolphin Harbor**; the **Killer Whale Show**, in which an orca dives, cavorts and splashes the audience; and the **Wildlife Theater**, where the presentation of exotic animals from around the world furthers appreciation for endangered species. There also are seal, sea-lion and tropical-bird displays. Visitors pass through a transparent viewing tunnel as sharks swim overhead in **Shark Experience★**; hand-feed giraffes at the **Giraffe Dock**; team up in a game of tug-of-war with pachyderms at **Elephant Encounter**; watch frisky walruses through a glass-walled tank at the **Walrus Experience★**; and explore the steamy jungle setting of the **Butterfly Habitat★** in search of brilliant tropical specimens. The **Tiger Island Splash Attack★** provides an underwater viewing window on 400-pound Bengals.

Also worth visiting are a saltwater aquarium, the **Marine Research Center** and an animal nursery. **Looney Tunes Seaport** is a children's ride and amusement area. In the **Batman Water Thrill Spectacular**, a team of stunt skiers take part in myriad waterborne antics. Among the most popular rides are the **DinoSphere TurboRide**, a three-dimensional motion simulator that carries visitors past a life-sized, mechanical Tyrannosaurus and through an erupting volcano, and **Monsoon Falls**, in which rafters plunge over a 55ft rapid. The half-dozen roller-coasters are even better known; they include **Medusa**, called the world's first "flying" roller coaster, which travels at 65mph through seven inversions; and **Roar**, a classic wooden coaster that drops more than 10 stories at speeds above 50mph.

Killer Whale Show, Marine World

28 • MARIN HEADLANDS★★

🚍 bus 76–Headlands (Sundays and holidays only)
Map p 214

Rising north of the Golden Gate, these 15sq mi of pristine coastal lands encompass windswept ridges, sheltered valleys, sandy coves and scattered vestiges of the area's military history. Protected since 1972 as part of the Golden Gate National Recreation Area (and by the US Army before that), the Marin Headlands offer unequaled views of the city-fringed bay, the Golden Gate Bridge elegantly overlapping San Francisco's skyline, and the vast Pacific Ocean stretching away to the western horizon.

Historical Notes

The headlands' strategic importance became evident to US forces soon after their takeover of California in 1846. A fort was planned at Lime Point (today the north pier of the Golden Gate Bridge) to complement Fort Point and Alcatraz in guarding the mouth of the strait. The fort was never built, but other defenses—batteries, bunkers and gun emplacements—appeared along the bluffs. Many installations rapidly grew obsolete, to be replaced by newer armaments at Forts Baker, Barry and Cronkhite. No gun was ever fired in defense, and today the grounds of the forts harbor a multitude of abandoned coastal defense installations ranging from post-Civil War earthen bunkers to Cold War-era Nike missile sites.

Thickly covered with coastal grasses, sagebrush, coyote brush and oak woodlands, the headlands provide habitat for lizards and snakes, elusive bobcats and foxes, and blacktailed deer. In spring, lupine, Indian paintbrush and other colorful wildflowers decorate the hillsides. Lagoons and coves attract stately egrets and herons, while fleets of brown pelicans patrol the coastal waters, and offshore rocks provide haven for seals, sea lions and nesting shorebirds.

Visiting the Marin Headlands – By car, follow US-101 north across the Golden Gate Bridge and exit at Alexander Ave. (2mi); follow Marin Headlands signs. For visitors without cars, 🚍 bus 76-Headlands offers hourly transit between San Francisco and Fort Cronkhite on Sundays and holidays.

In summer, ocean-born fogs pour over these hills, freshening the air but obscuring the stunning views of the bridge, bay and city. In fall and spring—the best seasons to visit—the hills bask in sunshine. If possible, avoid crowds by going on weekdays; Sundays are especially popular. There are four campgrounds (primitive and modern) in the headlands, and hiking, biking and fishing opportunities abound. For information and reservations, contact the Marin Headlands Visitor Center *(p 212)*.

SIGHTS

Fort Baker – *From San Francisco, follow US-101 north across the Golden Gate Bridge to the Alexander Ave. exit, just past Vista Pt. At Bunker Rd., turn left and follow signs to the Bay Area Discovery Museum.* Named in honor of Col. Edward Dickinson Baker, a Civil War hero and friend of Abraham Lincoln, this attractive group of buildings and batteries was the first military post on the north side of the Golden Gate. Eight small batteries were constructed between 1873 and 1943, including the still-visible Battery Yates (1905) near Cavallo Point—the easternmost tip of Horseshoe Cove.

Today, the section east of the bridge, called **East Fort Baker**, is home to the Army's 91st Division Reserve, a US Coast Guard station, the Presidio Yacht Club and a children's museum. Stroll the bluffs overlooking Horseshoe Cove for dramatic **views★★** of the Golden Gate Bridge. The **Bay Trail** *(.25mi)* along the shore east of Cavallo Point offers views of the East Bay, Angel Island and Alcatraz while skirting the habitat of the endangered Mission Blue butterfly.

★**Bay Area Discovery Museum** (**M**) – 🧒 *Open mid-June–mid-Sept Tue–Sun 10am–5pm. Rest of the year Tue–Thu 9am–4pm, Fri–Sun 10am–5pm. Closed major holidays. $7.* 🍴 ♿ 🅿 ☎ *415-487-4398. www.badm.org.* One of the Bay Area's excellent children's museums, this complex of six learning-oriented halls delights children ages 1 to 10. In the **Entrance Pavilion**, young computer whizzes head for the multimedia computer center to check out the latest educational CD-ROM programs before heading off to the science room or maze of illusions. The **San Francisco Bay★** building highlights some of the activities and animals of the bay. Kids pretend to go crabbing off a pier, explore an undersea tunnel, or fish for salmon on the Discovery Boat. The **Architecture and Design** building helps young visitors learn how to build bridges and other structures, design interiors, or be pretend-engineers on a high-rise construction project. The **ToT SpoT**'s whimsical, multicolored rooms safely occupy kiddies 3 and under, and the **Art Room** offers a variety of drop-in art activities. There's also a science lab, a ceramics studio, a media center and the **Maze of Illusions**, with 45 different visual effects.

Cove Beach, Marin Headlands

Conzelman Road** – *From Fort Baker, return to Alexander Ave., turn right toward US-101, pass under the freeway and continue to Conzelman Rd., following signs for Marin Headlands.* This gloriously scenic route snakes along the Headlands' rugged bluffs past abandoned military batteries. Turnouts provide ample opportunity to drink in outstanding **views** of San Francisco Bay, the Golden Gate Bridge and the Pacific. Stop at **Battery Spencer** *(.25mi)*, a massive concrete casement built in 1896 to house three cannons, for a formidable city view framed by the looming north pier of the bridge. The curious can crawl into a command station overlooking a gun mount. **Battery Construction 129** *(1.75mi)*, highest gun battery in the US, was begun in 1942 to house a 16in gun capable of firing shells over 20mi; construction halted in 1944 and the battery was left unarmed. From mid-August to mid-December, **Hawk Hill***, just above Battery 129, draws legions of birders to witness the southward migration of raptors—eagles, hawks and falcons—plying the only such flyway on the West Coast.

Beyond Battery 129 the road crests and becomes a winding one-way passage that curves down along the precipitous edge of a high sea cliff. Entering decommissioned Fort Barry, it heads past Battery Rathbone-McIndoe (1905) to Batteries Alexander (1905), Wallace (1918) and Mendell (c.1905). From the latter, views extend west and north over the coastal headlands, guano-covered Bird Rock, Rodeo Valley and the stark barracks and buildings of Fort Cronkhite. Point Bonita can be seen due south of Battery Mendell.

*****Point Bonita Lighthouse** – 🔟 *From the end of Conzelman Rd., follow lighthouse signs to trailhead for hike (.5mi) to Point Bonita (sturdy shoes advised). Open year-round Sat–Mon 12:30–3:30pm. Guided tours (45min) weekends 12:30pm.* 🄿 ☎ *415-331-1540. www.nps.gov/goga.* Perched on the rocky tip of Point Bonita, this small lighthouse has helped guide mariners through the Golden Gate since 1855. Though automated in 1981, the sentinel still employs its original Fresnel lens, through which beacons of light were beamed to 19C passenger ships, lumber schooners and naval fleets of both world wars. Extensive restorations to the lighthouse were completed in 1996.

*****Marin Headlands Visitor Center** – 🔟 *From Conzelman Rd. take Field Rd. to the corner of Bunker Rd. Open year-round daily 9:30am–4:30pm. Closed Thanksgiving, Dec 25. Call ahead for schedule of guided tours (1-2hrs).* ♿ 🄿 ☎ *415-331-1540. www.nps.gov/goga.* Located in Fort Barry's former post chapel (1941), this ranger station/visitor center mounts excellent, hands-on natural history displays and exhibits on the human inhabitants of the headlands—Coast Miwok, 19C *vaqueros* (Mexican and Native American cattle ranchers), Portuguese dairy ranchers, lighthouse keepers, and soldiers. Browse the well-stocked bookstore for books, field guides and maps.

Near the visitor center lies Missile Site SF 88L, a former **Nike missile site,** one of several around the bay. Its original but unarmed Nike missiles are open to the public for viewing *(open year-round Wed–Fri & first Sun of each month 12:30–3:30pm; call in advance for guided tours;* ♿ 🄿 ☎ *415-331-1540).*

ADDRESS BOOK

Dining in Marin County

Please see explanation on p 42.

Lark Creek Inn – *234 Magnolia Ave., Larkspur.* ♿ ⓟ ☎ *415-924-7766.* $$$
American. Just over the Golden Gate Bridge, this charming inn occupies a spacious Victorian house surrounded by towering redwoods. Creative approaches to traditional dishes—such as Caesar salad and Yankee pot roast—demonstrate an elegant simplicity. Sunday brunch is served outdoors on the patio during good weather.

Ondine – *558 Bridgeway, Sausalito.* ♿ ☎ *415-331-1133. Dinner & Sun brunch only.* $$$ **Asian fusion.** Chef Seiji Wakabayashi melds the influences of his native Japan and other Pacific Rim cuisines with California ingredients to create dishes like abalone chowder, seaweed-crusted halibut, and rack of lamb with a wasabi port demi glace. The restaurant's windows look out on San Francisco Bay.

Buckeye Roadhouse – *15 Shoreline Hwy., Mill Valley.* ♿ ⓟ ☎ *415-331-2600.* $$$ **American.** A gourmet touch is given hearty home cooking in a wilderness-lodge atmosphere here. You can't go wrong with the "smoky barbecue" or roast chicken.

Dragonfly – *1546 Redwood Hwy., Corte Madera.* ♿ ⓟ ☎ *415-927-8889.* $$ **Chinese.** This elegant restaurant offers gourmet Mandarin and Szechuan specialties in sophisticated surroundings that belie its shopping-mall location. A contemporary jazz duo performs in the bar.

Guaymas – *5 Main St., Tiburon.* ♿ ☎ *415-435-6300.* $$ **Mexican.** Diners sip margaritas and dine on Jaliscan-style tacos, tamales and more gourmet dishes, while enjoying a panoramic view of Angel Island and the San Francisco skyline.

Savanna Grill – *55 Tamal Vista Blvd., Corte Madera.* ♿ ⓟ ☎ *415-924-6774.* $$ **Southern.** Chef Steve Simmons calls his cuisine "gourmet Southern comfort food." Typical fare: grilled shrimp with red-curry peanut sauce, and sage-crusted game hen with shiitake-mushroom macaroni and cheese. Live jazz plays nightly.

Grey Whale Inn – *12781 Sir Francis Drake Blvd., Inverness.* ⓟ ☎ *415-669-1244.* $ **American.** Not far from Point Reyes, the Grey Whale offers patio seating where diners can enjoy pizzas and sandwiches while watching dusk fall.

Staying in Marin County

Please see explanation on p 48.

The Harbor House Inn *5600 S. Hwy. 1, Elk.* ✗ ♿ ⓟ ☎ *707-877-3203, www.theharborhouseinn.com. 10 rooms and cottages.* $$$$ Though north of Marin County along the southern Mendocino coast, this luxurious rural inn—built by lumber-company executives in 1916 atop challenging ocean cliffs—is a worthy place to rest one's head and dine during a northbound excursion from Point Reyes.

Waters Edge – *25 Main St., Tiburon.* ♿ ⓟ ☎ *415-789-5999. www.marin hotels.com. 23 rooms.* $$$$ Located on the downtown Tiburon waterfront, this stylish new luxury boutique hotel offers stunning views and modern comfort. Most rooms have private bay balconies; all have fireplaces.

Mill Valley Inn – *165 Throckmorton Ave., Mill Valley.* ♿ ⓟ ☎ *415-389-6608. www.millvalleyinn.com. 25 rooms.* $$$ French doors open onto private decks or balconies overlooking a redwood grove or the streets of charming Mill Valley. Breakfast, included in the room rate, is served at an in-house espresso bar.

Mountain Home Inn – *801 Panoramic Hwy., Mill Valley.* ♿ ⓟ ☎ *415-381-9000. www.bnbinns.com/mountainhome.inn. 10 rooms.* $$$ High on the slopes of Mt. Tamalpais, this B&B sits at a popular trailhead for hikers and mountain bikers.

Alta Mira Hotel – *125 Bulkley Ave. off Princess St., Sausalito.* ✗ ♿ ⓟ ☎ *415-332-1350. 31 rooms.* $$ Alta Mira means "high view" in Spanish, and that's just what this quaint 1927 inn offers over San Francisco Bay. Mediterranean in styling, it has an eclectic variety of rooms but remains a local favorite.

Hostelling International–Point Reyes – *On Point Reyes National Seashore, 8mi from Bear Valley Visitor Center in Point Reyes Station.* ♿ ⓟ ☎ *415-663-8811. www.norcalhostels.org. 44 beds.* $ Situated off Limantour Road, 2mi from the Pacific and 25mi from the Lighthouse, this simple hostel offers a common kitchen and other shared facilities.

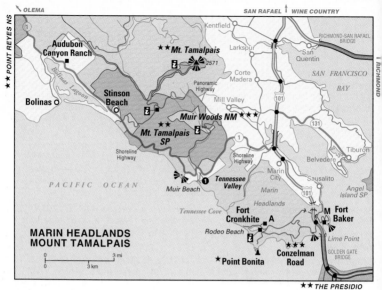

Fort Cronkhite – *Follow Bunker Rd. to Mitchell Rd. and continue along Rodeo Lagoon to beach parking lot.* Named for World War II commander Maj. Adelbert Cronkhite, the fort housed gun batteries and a Nike missile battery. A set of well-preserved former barracks still stands sentinel on the fort's grounds.

The waters off Fort Cronkhite's **Rodeo Beach** draw surfers, although dangerous currents and cold temperatures make it unsafe to swim. From the beach parking area, the Coastal Trail leads to Battery Townsley *(.5 mi)*.

The Marine Mammal Center (**A**) – Kids *1065 Fort Cronkhite. Follow signs from Bunker Rd. Open year-round daily 10am–4pm. Closed Jan 1, Thanksgiving Day, Dec 25. Guided tours (30min) by reservation.* ♿ 🅿 ☏ *415-289-7325. www.tmmc.org.* Since opening in 1975, this animal hospital for wild creatures has rescued, rehabilitated and released hundreds of injured and sick marine mammals found on the California coast. Visitors can see adult and juvenile sea lions and seals in various stages of recuperation. The center also conducts marine-mammal research and runs educational marine environmental programs.

ADDITIONAL SIGHT

Tennessee Valley – *From the Golden Gate Bridge, take US-101 north to the Mill Valley/Stinson Beach (Hwy. 1) exit. Continue .5mi to Tennessee Valley Rd. Turn left and continue 1.5mi to trailhead parking lot.* This peaceful valley was named for the *SS Tennessee*, a 210ft steamer that ran aground on the beach here in dense fog on March 5, 1853. The ship was carrying 600 passengers from Panama to San Francisco. All survived, but the ship was destroyed.

The valley, once part of the Rancho Saucelito, was later home to several Portuguese dairy ranches. Today the ranches are gone and the valley forms part of the GGNRA. A pleasant, easygoing hiking road *(2mi)* wanders down the inland valley to Tennessee Cove and the ocean. Herds of black-tailed deer have replaced the dairy cattle, hawks soar overhead and great horned owls hoot from eucalyptus trees along the way.

The geographic focal point of southern Marin County, kingly Mt. Tamalpais *(tam-ul-PIE-us)* towers majestically over San Francisco from the north. Its rocky, 2,571ft summit affords some of the Bay Area's finest views, while its flanks harbor an extraordinary abundance of trails, meadows, forests and other enticements to delight lovers of natural beauty and outdoor sports. Largely undeveloped, its terrain protected as state and national parklands or county watershed, it has been a treasured recreation resource for Bay Area urbanites for more than a century.

Historical Notes

Coast Miwok tribes made their home on the bay and ocean fringes of Mt. Tamalpais for at least 3,000 years prior to European exploration and settlement of the area. The mountain itself was considered sacred. In 1772, Spanish explorers Don Pedro Fages and Padre Juan Crespí named the mountain La Sierra de Nuestro Padre de San Francisco ("The Mountain of Our Father of San Francisco"). Its present name is thought to have been derived from the Coast Miwok words *tamal*, meaning "bay," and *pa* (later corrupted by the Spanish to *pais*), meaning "mountain."

Trail, Rail and Carriage – In the decades following the Gold Rush, residents and visitors looked to the mountain for leisure and recreation, traveling to its scenic slopes by ferryboat, stagecoach and train. Hiking trails were established and in 1884, a wagon road to the west peak was built. By 1896 tourists could ascend from the foothill town of Mill Valley to the summit aboard the steam-powered Mill Valley and Mt. Tamalpais Scenic Railway (later known as the Mt. Tamalpais and Muir Woods Railway). Dubbed the "Crookedest Railroad in the World," the train chugged along a steep 8.2mi route, negotiating 281 curves along the way. In 1907, a "gravity car" line to Muir Woods was installed, wherein passengers glided silently down from the summit to the Muir Woods Inn before hiking or riding horse-drawn carriages to the redwood forest. The railway ceased operation in 1930.

The work of preserving Mt. Tamalpais' unspoiled beauty was set in motion by **William Kent**, an ardent and wealthy Marin County conservationist and state representative. Between 1905 and 1928, Kent made numerous gifts of land to the state and federal governments; his donations and political lobbying helped create Muir Woods National Monument and Mount Tamalpais State Park, and resulted in the mountain's present status of public ownership.

A nature lover's paradise, Mt. Tamalpais is blessed with abundant wildlife and a tremendous variety of vegetation. Some 300 species of birds have been seen soaring above the peaks or flitting in the treetops, including red-tailed hawks, turkey vultures, black ravens, Stellar's jays, quail, wrens and pileated woodpeckers. Black-tailed deer, Western gray squirrels, Sonoma chipmunks and brush rabbits all make their homes here. Nocturnal bobcats are present but rarely seen, and sightings of mountain lions and coyotes have been reported in recent years, though most large mammals were hunted out in the early 1800s.

Visiting Mt. Tamalpais – Roads through the park offer spectacular vistas of ocean, bay and rugged hills. **Shoreline Highway** (Rte. 1) takes a cliff-hugging route along the coast: From San Francisco, take US-101 north over the Golden Gate Bridge to the Mill Valley/Stinson Beach exit and turn left onto Rte. 1. The most direct route winds up the mountain's southern ridges on the **Panoramic Highway, Pantoll Road** and **Ridgecrest Road** to a vista point near the summit: from Shoreline Highway, turn right on Panoramic Highway and follow the signs to Mt. Tamalpais. The **Muir Woods Road** branches off the Panoramic Highway.

The mountain is a favored recreation destination at all times of the year. Trails and unpaved fire roads offer more than 210mi of hiking, biking and equestrian paths. For maps and information on weather and trail conditions, contact the GGNRA headquarters at Fort Mason or the Mount Tamalpais State Park **Pantoll ranger station** *(intersection of Panoramic & Stinson Beach Hwys.; open year-round daily 8am–dusk;* ☐ ☎ *415-388-2070).*

Spring is a fine time to visit, as myriad small creeks run full, grassy ridges wear a lush green coat, and wildflowers festoon the slopes. In summer, thick fogs can blanket the mountain's lower slopes; yet the summit is often sunny and can afford extraordinary views of fog-wrapped San Francisco Bay.

While it is possible to visit all sights described on Mt. Tamalpais in one day, visitors may wish to plan more leisurely visits to individual sights.

SIGHTS

★★**Mount Tamalpais State Park** – *18mi from San Francisco. Take US-101 north to Rte. 1 (Shoreline Hwy.); continue to Panoramic Hwy. and turn right, following signs to the park. Open year-round daily 7am–dusk. Closed during high fire-risk days. $2/car.* ⚠ *(reservations ☎ 800-444-7275)* ☐ ☎ *415-388-2070. http:// cal-parks.ca.gov/north/marin/mtsp239.htm.* The park began as a 200-acre gift from William Kent and was later enlarged through the efforts of local hiking clubs, which helped acquire an additional 520 acres. Today it completely surrounds Muir Woods National Monument. Nature lovers flock to Mt. Tam's spectacular trails year-round, and summer brings theatergoers to the Mountain Theatre, a woodsy natural amphitheater with terraced stone seats, that mounts popular musicals and theatrical performances on weekends in May and June *(E. Ridgecrest Blvd., just east of intersection with Pantoll Rd. ☎ 415-383-1100)*.

East Peak – *From the Pantoll ranger station, take Pantoll Rd. to Ridgecrest Blvd. and continue toward the summit.* Numerous turnouts, picnic spots, trailheads and scenic overlooks mark the long ascent to a parking area a quarter-mile below the top of Mt. Tamalpais. From here, cities, towns and majestic bay appear as if on a giant raised relief map, backdropped to the east by Mt. Diablo, 35mi away. The 360-degree panorama is one of the finest **views**★★★ in the Bay Area. On exceptionally clear winter days, the snow-capped Sierra Nevada mountains are visible 140mi to the east, as are Mt. St. Helena to the north and the Farallon Islands to the west. Vegetation at this elevation consists mostly of the brushy mix of scrub oak and red-barked manzanita known as chaparral. From the East Peak parking lot, a short but rocky and strenuous path *(.3mi)* leads to the summit fire lookout, rebuilt in 1937 by the Civilian Conservation Corps *(closed to the public)*. The **Verna Dunshee Trail** *(.7mi)* makes a level, paved loop around the summit.

> ### ■ A Cradle for Mountain Biking
>
> In the early 1970s, a group of local bicycle enthusiasts began modifying and equipping their traditional balloon-tired "cruiser" bikes to withstand travel across Mt. Tamalpais' rugged trails and fire roads. Riding and racing such bikes became a local passion, and ensuing years brought increasing technological innovations that resulted in today's sophisticated "mountain bikes." Mt. Tamalpais continues to attract a steady stream of bicycling enthusiasts, many of whom make the strenuous ascent to the summit on the unpaved Old Railroad and Eldridge grades.

Many trails guide hikers and bicyclists to East Peak and other points around the park. One of the more popular mountain-bike routes starts from a trailhead at **Mountain Home Inn**, a bed-and-breakfast lodge built on the site of a historic railroad inn *(810 Panoramic Hwy.; park in public lot across from the inn)*. The path ascends on unpaved fire roads that follow, in part, the old railway grade. Hikers may prefer to start higher on the mountain, at Pantoll, where several possible routes lead to the summit. Another popular destination is the **West Point Inn** (1904), a rustic wooden structure situated on a ridge just below the summit. Hikers, equestrians and bicyclists congregate here to refill water bottles, relax on the shady veranda and take in panoramic **views**. From the inn, the Old Railroad Grade continues to East Peak.

★★★ **Muir Woods National Monument** – ▦ 🄺🄸🄳🄸 *17mi from San Francisco. Take US-101 north to Rte. 1 (Shoreline Hwy.); continue to Panoramic Hwy. and turn right, then left on Muir Woods Rd. Open year-round daily 8am–sunset. Guided tours (1hr) Fri–Sun 1pm. $2.* ✗ ⅃ 🄟 ☎ *415-388-2596. www.nps.gov/muwo.* Situated on the slope of Mt. Tamalpais along Redwood Creek, Muir Woods harbors one of the largest stands of ancient coast redwoods in the Bay Area. The tranquil grove of majestic red-barked trees, some 1,100 years in age, attracts more than 1.5 million visitors annually.

A Tree-Lover's Monument – The world's tallest trees, coast redwoods *(Sequoia sempervirens)* can attain heights equal to that of a 36-story building. They are among the few conifers that can sprout from knotty outgrowths, called burls, as well as reproduce by seeds. The absence of resin in the trees' 6in- to 12in-thick bark, coupled with the high tannin content of the wood, renders them resistant to fire, insect damage and disease, enabling them to live for hundreds of years. Muir Woods is a relatively young grove; its oldest trees are more than a millennium old. California's tallest, oldest redwoods thrive well to the north of here in the Redwood Empire *(consult The Green Guide to California)*.

Prior to the arrival of Europeans on the west coast, millions of acres of primeval redwood forest blanketed the coastal reaches of California and southern Oregon; aggressive logging has since wiped out all but 150,000 acres. Much of Mt. Tamalpais' virgin redwood forest was logged in the years following the Gold Rush, but the trees in present-day Muir Woods escaped the lumbermen's saws and axes, owing to their relative inaccessibility. The forest became a national monument in 1908 after William Kent donated 295 acres of land in Redwood Canyon to the federal government in 1907, insisting that the park be named for conservationist John Muir. In a letter of thanks to Kent, Muir wrote "This is the best tree-lover's monument that could possibly be found in all the forests of the world."

Visit – Begin at the visitor center and adjacent bookstore, which stock trail maps and information about local natural history. From the visitor center, six miles of trails (some paved) wind about the forest floor, following the paths of Redwood Creek and Fern Creek. The **Main Trail** *(1mi)* crosses over a series of wooden bridges, looping under a dense canopy of mature redwoods that rise like spires toward the heavens. Amid groves of living trees, trunks of fallen giants lie in various states of decay in a lush undergrowth of sword ferns, azaleas and horsetail, a primitive plant whose ancestry dates back 300 million years. Muir Woods' most impressive trees stand in **Cathedral Grove** and **Bohemian Grove**, site of the park's tallest tree, measuring 253ft *(tree is unmarked)*.

© Brenda Tharp
Muir Woods National Monument

The Main Trail connects to the Hillside Trail *(1.9mi loop)* or to the Ocean View, Lost and Fern Creek trails *(3.1mi loop)*. Trails in the monument also connect with unpaved hiking trails in Mount Tamalpais State Park.

ADDITIONAL SIGHTS

Muir Beach Overlook – *17mi from San Francisco. Take US-101 to Rte. 1 (Shoreline Hwy.); from Muir Woods, take Frank Valley Rd. 2.5mi and turn right on Rte. 1.* Steps lead down to a railed promontory that affords sweeping **views**★★ of the coast to the north and south. The hooded concrete burrows on the bluff behind the promontory were installed during World War II; signs illustrate how the stations were designed to target enemy vessels.

South of the overlook, Shoreline Highway passes **Muir Beach**, a small, scenic stretch of sand situated at the mouth of Redwood Creek. Tables and grills make this an excellent spot to relax, though dangerous tides and currents make swimming inadvisable.

 The Pelican Inn
Junction of Rte. 1 and Pacific Way (Muir Beach Rd.). ☎ *415-383-6000.* This thoroughly British country inn and pub was created by a fourth-generation pub owner from Surrey, England. Pub fare and pints of British and Irish brews are served up in a low-beamed dining room and at a candlelit Tudor-style bar.

Stinson Beach – *Rte. 1, 5mi north of Muir Beach Overlook.* Called Willow Camp in the late 19C, this charming beach town is a popular stop for coastal travelers. Its small but inviting assortment of restaurants and art galleries, bookstore, surf shop and outdoor Shakespeare theater draws visitors and residents from throughout San Francisco and Marin County. The excellent **beach**★★, one of the few in the area safe for swimming (when it's not being patrolled by sharks), is the town's principal attraction. In addition to swimmers, the 3.5mi sandy crescent draws surfers, sunbathers and kayakers. Stinson Beach is the finishing point for the annual Dipsea Race in which runners traverse Mt. Tamalpais from Mill Valley.

Audubon Canyon Ranch – 🖼 *4900 Shoreline Hwy. (Rte. 1), 3.5mi north of Stinson Beach. Open mid-Mar–mid-Jul weekends & holidays 10am–4pm, Tue–Fri 1–4pm by appointment. $10 donation suggested.* 🅿 ☎ *415-868-9244. www.egret.org.* This 1,000-acre bird sanctuary is located in a woodsy canyon adjacent to Bolinas Lagoon. In spring, the center's grounds and trails are open for observing great blue herons and white egrets nesting in the trees. A small museum mounts interesting exhibits on local geology and natural history.

Bolinas – *5mi north of Stinson Beach. Take first left turn off Rte. 1 north of Bolinas Lagoon.* In a captivating setting on an off-the-beaten-path peninsula between the Pacific Ocean and Bolinas Lagoon, this picturesque community has in recent decades developed a reputation as an insular outpost of counterculture. Settled in 1835 on the Baulenes Rancho land grant, the town boomed during the Gold Rush when schooners came here to load timber destined for building sites in San Francisco. Today, the quaint downtown features a charming bar, a health-food store, several cafes and a small local history **museum and art gallery** *(48-50 Wharf Rd.; open Fri–Sun 1–5pm; closed Dec 25.* ⅙ ▯ ☎ *415-868-2006).* The pleasant beach near downtown attracts swimmers, surfers and sunbathers.

30 • POINT REYES NATIONAL SEASHORE★★

Map p 220

Windy, wave-swept and often cloaked in fog, the Point Reyes Peninsula is an enchantingly varied expanse of wilderness 40mi north of San Francisco. Jutting from the west Marin County pasturelands into the Pacific Ocean, this 30mi coastal wedge harbors long sandy beaches, lush forests, rugged sea cliffs and vast wetlands, all populated by diverse animal, bird and marine life. Laced by 140mi of trails, the 102sq mi peninsula was designated a national seashore in 1962.

Historical Notes

Formed by the San Andreas Fault, the Point Reyes peninsula rides on the eastern edge of the Pacific tectonic plate, creeping northwesterly at about 2in per year while the adjacent North American plate travels westward at a slower rate. The two plates meet in a rift zone that runs south through the Olema Valley and northwest beneath narrow Tomales Bay, which separates the peninsula from the rest of Marin County. The jut of land was thrust more than 16ft northwest of the mainland by the great earthquake of 1906. A legacy of the peninsula's ancient journey along the San Andreas Fault is its granite backbone, **Inverness Ridge**, which has geologic origins in the Tehachapi Mountains 300mi to the south. Five million years ago, the peninsula occupied the site of present-day Monterey Bay; someday it will be an island sliding toward the Gulf of Alaska.

'White Bancks and Cliffes' – For thousands of years, Point Reyes was home to Coast Miwok Indians. The peaceable Miwoks harvested acorns and berries, fished for shellfish and salmon, and hunted deer and elk. In summer 1579, Francis Drake, an English explorer sponsored by Queen Elizabeth I, turned south from his search for a Northwest Passage and anchored his ship, the *Golden Hind*, for repairs in the vicinity of Point Reyes. The "faire and good baye" he described is thought to be the protected bay now known as Drakes Bay. Drake claimed his landfall for England, calling it "Nova Albion" after "the white bancks and cliffes" (resembling the blanched palisades of England's Dover coast) that rise over Drakes Beach.

In the next decades the area was visited by Spanish explorers, including Sebastián Vizcaíno, who in 1603 named it La Punta de Los Reyes or "Point of the Kings." In 1792, British Captain George Vancouver gave Drakes Bay its name. But Francis Drake's claim to Nova Albion was never upheld by Vancouver nor other English visitors. The area became a distant colony of Spain. After Mexican independence in 1821, Point Reyes became a center for cattle ranching, remaining so after the US takeover of California. In the 1950s, development threatened to change the peninsula forever, but fierce preservation efforts led to the creation of the Point Reyes National Seashore in 1962. Numerous historic cattle ranches, dating from the 1850s to 1870s, continue to operate within the park's boundaries, and drivers must be ready to pause for herds crossing the roads.

SIGHTS

Bear Valley Area

★ **Bear Valley Visitor Center** – 🄺🄳🄸 *Open year-round Mon–Fri 9am–5pm, weekends & holidays 8am–5pm. Closed Dec 25.* ⅙ ▯ ☎ *415-663-1092. www.nps.gov.* Rangers on duty at this attractive, barn-like park headquarters provide information, answer questions, take campsite reservations, and post times and meeting places for guided hikes and other interpretive programs. The bookstore stocks a wide variety of posters, postcards and natural-history publications, including books about Point Reyes. Spend time in the center's fine **exhibit hall,** where displays on coastal wetlands, birdwatching hot spots, marine mammals and cultural history provide an introduction to the peninsula.

From the Visitor Center parking lot, the pleasant, easy **Earthquake Trail★** 🄺🄳🄸 *(.6mi)* invites strollers to see the dramatic effects of ground-shifting that took place during the 1906 quake, whose epicenter was in this rift zone. One spot on the trail shows how a wooden fence split and separated as it rode with the moving ground. Also leading from the parking lot, the **Woodpecker Nature Trail** 🄺🄳🄸 *(.7mi)* offers a quick introduction to the natural wonders of Point Reyes.

Practical Information..Area Code: 415

Getting There – From San Francisco take US-101 north to Mill Valley/Stinson Beach exit (Rte. 1); continue on Shoreline Hwy. (Rte. 1) to Bear Valley Rd. (27mi). For a quicker if less dramatic route, continue north on US-101 to the Greenbrae exit (10mi) to Sir Francis Drake Blvd. west, turn right on Rte. 1 and take the first left onto Bear Valley Rd.

When to Go – Weather conditions can change dramatically from one area to the next on the peninsula; visitors should always be prepared for cool winds and damp conditions. The autumn months are usually mildest. Winter, the rainiest season, is the best time to see migrating gray whales.

Visitor Information – Stop by the Bear Valley Visitor Center for maps and information on recreation, lodging and seasonal events. Other information centers are located at Drakes Beach and Point Reyes Lighthouse. Point Reyes National Seashore information may be accessed on the Internet at www.nps.gov/pore.

Accommodations – **Bed-and-breakfast** inns and **cabins** are available in Inverness, Olema and Point Reyes Station. A hostel is located at Point Reyes (☎ 663-8811). The six camping areas on the peninsula range from primitive to modern; for reservations call Bear Valley Visitor Center (four campgrounds, all for hikers and bikers; ☎ 663-8054); Tomales Bay State Park (one campground for hikers and bikers; *no reservations necessary*); or the private Olema Ranch (one campground, cars welcomed; ☎ 663-8001).

Recreation – **Hiking**: easy and strenuous trails; stop at Bear Valley Visitor Center for maps and information. **Biking**: on roads and designated trails; rentals in Olema and Point Reyes Station. Guided **horseback** trail rides: Five Brooks Stables (☎ 663-1570). **Birdwatching**: Point Reyes Bird Observatory (west of Bolinas); Estero de Limantour (east of Drakes Estero). **Whale Watching**: Point Reyes Lighthouse.

Morgan Horse Ranch – Kids *Open year-round daily 10am–4:30pm.* P ☎ 415-663-1763. Situated just behind the Visitor Center, this 100-acre ranch maintains a herd of more than a dozen compact, muscular Morgans used by park rangers for backcountry patrol. A self-guided tour of the ranch (which includes a blacksmith's shop, pole barn and stables) trots visitors through two centuries of history about the Morgan, the first American breed of horse.

Kule Loklo – Kids A short walk *(.5mi)* from the Visitor Center, this re-created Coast Miwok village offers a glimpse into the lifestyle and culture of the peninsula's native inhabitants. The village's structures, built according to authentic Miwok techniques, include redwood-bark shelters, an underground sweat lodge and a ceremonial dance house. At the time of Francis Drake's visit, some 100 Miwok villages similar to this one were scattered across present-day Marin and south Sonoma counties.

★ **Bear Valley Trail** – *8.2mi round-trip. Trailhead near Visitor Center.* Hikers, bikers, joggers and equestrians range this wide, easygoing path along Coast Creek. Traversing redwood forests and picnic-perfect Divide Meadow, the trail ends at the Arch Rock **viewpoint** overlooking the ocean. Several more-strenuous trails branch off the Bear Valley Trail, including the Sky, Glen and Old Pine trails; the Coast Trail intersects it near Arch Rock.

Limantour Beach – *From the visitor center, drive 1.5mi north on Bear Valley Rd. Turn left on Limantour Rd. and continue 6mi.* This splendid curve of land along Drakes Bay is famous for its fine **views** of the white cliffs of Point Reyes. At the northern end, the shoreline narrows to form Limantour Spit, which separates the wildlife-rich waters of Limantour Estero (*estero* is Spanish for "estuary") from the deeper waters of Drakes Bay. From September through May, Limantour Estero and nearby Drakes Estero are major wintering and migratory grounds for shorebirds and seabirds. Come at low tide to explore numerous tidepools.

Point Reyes Peninsula Area

The tip of Point Reyes, protruding some 15mi into the Pacific Ocean, has for centuries constituted a severe hazard for mariners making their ways along the California coast. Numerous ships have met their demise here, lost in the dense fogs and stormy weather that frequently drape the exposed jut of land. High winds and heavy surf rake the northwest-facing bluffs and pound the sands; beaches and estuaries on the southeast side enjoy sheltered, peaceful conditions.

Sonoma County Coast ↑

Mount Vision – *From Bear Valley Rd., veer left onto Sir Francis Drake Blvd. and turn left on Mt. Vision Rd.* From the overlook enroute to Mt. Vision's 1,282-ft summit, sweeping **views★★** extend over Point Reyes, Drakes Estero and the rolling Pacific Ocean. The narrow, winding road continues to the peak, where hikers can connect to several different trails scaling the flanks of Inverness Ridge.

West of Mt. Vision Road, take Drakes Estero exit off Sir Francis Drake Boulevard to **Johnson's Oyster Farm** *(open year-round Tue–Sun 8am–4:30pm;* ♿ 🅿 ☎ *415-669-1149)*, a family-owned purveyor of freshly harvested shellfish.

Drakes Beach – *Follow signs from Sir Francis Drake Blvd.* Here, visitors enjoy one of the peninsula's most serene stretches of sand, sheltered from pounding surf and stiff ocean winds. Gentle waves lap the shore, and the adjacent estuary attracts birds (and birdwatchers) year-round. The small **Kenneth C. Patrick Visitor Center** here provides information and exhibits on the marine ecosystem of Drakes Bay *(open Memorial Day–Labor Day Fri–Tue 10am–5pm; rest of the year weekends & holidays only 10am–5pm; closed Dec 25;* 🍴 ♿ 🅿 ☎ *415-669-1250).*

Point Reyes Beach – *Follow Sir Francis Drake Blvd. southwest 4.7mi from Mt. Vision Rd.; turn right at sign to North Beach.* The wide, splendid, 12mi strip comprising **North Beach** and **South Beach** faces northwest—directly into the strongest winds and roughest surf of the open ocean. The beaches offer glorious walks, but strong currents make them unsafe for swimming, surfing or wading.

★★Point Reyes Lighthouse – 🔲 *End of Sir Francis Drake Blvd.; parking area is 22mi from Bear Valley Visitor Center. .5mi walk to visitor center & lighthouse, open year-round Thu–Mon10am–4:30pm, weather permitting.* ☎ *415-669-1534. www.nps.gov/pore.* Perched halfway down the sheer south face of precipitous Point Reyes headland—considered perhaps the foggiest and windiest point in the continental US—this beacon guided countless mariners for more than a century, from 1870 to 1975. A steep staircase of 308 steps *(closed when winds exceed 40mph)* descends to the station, where visitors can admire the three-ton Fresnel lens cast in 1867. The brass-mounted light, still fully operational, is visible for more than 24 nautical miles.

On clear days, the headlands offer excellent **views★★★** of the coast, the Farallon Islands to the southwest and distant San Francisco. The spot is popular with birders (more than 370 species have been recorded in the area) and with whale-watchers, who congregate here to spy gray whales as they pass close to shore during their annual migration season *(Dec–Apr)*. Sea lions and seals perch on rocky abodes just east of the point. Chimney Rock is one of the best places to spot elephant seals in the Bay Area.

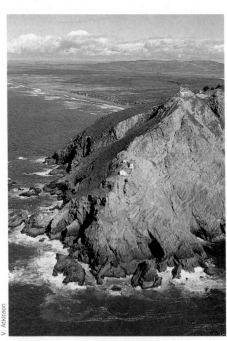

V. Atkinson

Point Reyes Lighthouse

Tomales Point Area

Dairy and cattle ranches blanket the peninsula's northern point, set between the Pacific Ocean to the west and Tomales Bay to the east.

Pierce Point Ranch – Kids *From Bear Valley Visitor Center, take Sir Francis Drake Blvd. north 7.5mi. Turn right on Pierce Point Rd. and continue to its end. Open year-round dawn–dusk.* ⟁ ▣. Established in 1858 by Vermont dairy farmer Solomon Pierce, this pastoral spread of farm buildings remains the only one of the park's 26 historic dairy and cattle ranches open to the public. A self-guided tour leads among the ranch buildings, while exhibits describe such farm activities as butter churning and hay collecting.

The wide, mile-long stretch of **McClures Beach** *(turn left at end of Pierce Point Rd.; follow steep .5mi dirt path to beach)* is bounded by granite outcrops. At the south end, a narrow passageway through the rocks *(accessible only at low tide)* opens onto a pocket beach where cormorants nest on Elephant Rock.

The lands surrounding the beach and the ranch today form a 2,600-acre reserve for a flourishing herd of **tule elk**, reintroduced in 1978; these animals once roamed the entire peninsula before being hunted out in the late 19C. More than 150 white-spotted **axis deer** graze on the moors between Marshall Beach Trail and Estero Trail, and a similar number of **fallow deer** range over the peninsula; one-fifth of them sport pure white coats.

Tomales Bay State Park – *5mi north of Inverness. Open year-round daily 8am–sunset. $2/car.* ⚔ ⚠ *(hiker/biker sites only)* ⟁ ▣ ☎ *415-669-1140. http:// parks.ca.gov/north/marin/tbsp237.htm.* Tiny **Heart's Desire Beach** and Shell Beach offer excellent opportunities for swimming and wading in sheltered Tomales Bay. Follow interpretive signs along the **Nature Trail** *(.5mi)* to Indian Beach, where a traditional native shelter can be visited.

ADDITIONAL SIGHT

Point Reyes Station – *2mi north of Olema by Rte. 1.* This small town grew up as a dairy center and stop along the North Pacific Coast Railroad. Although bakeries, restaurants, art galleries and antique shops now occupy some of its late-19C structures, dairy ranchers still swap stories at the local diner and load up supplies at the feed barn, preserving the community's bucolic atmosphere.

EXCURSION

Sonoma County Coast – North of Point Reyes Station, Highway 1 snakes along the precipitous Pacific coastline for 74mi before entering Mendocino County *(see The Green Guide to California)*. Spectacular views abound of steep, rocky cliffs pummeled by roiling surf. Sleepy seaside towns and state parks punctuate the wild shoreline, which nurtures a variety of birds and marine animals.

Bodega Bay – *34mi north of Point Reyes Station.* The second-largest salmon port on the Pacific coast bears the name of Spanish explorer Juan Francisco de la Bodega y Cuadra, who reached its sheltered anchorage in October 1775. Commercial fishing took off in the 1940s; today, the waterfront bustles with the comings and goings of some 300 boats. From the bluffs atop **Bodega Head** *(3mi off Hwy. 1 on Eastshore Rd., north of Bodega Bay)*, on the far side of the bay, stretch splendid **views★** of the coast from Point Reyes to Fort Ross. Between January and May, the bluffs are a popular spot for whale watching.

Six miles east in **Bodega** is the building *(17110 Bodega Lane)* that served as the schoolhouse in Alfred Hitchcock's classic film *The Birds* (1962). Originally the Potter School (1873), the Italianate structure has been converted into a bed-and-breakfast inn.

★Sonoma Coast State Beaches – *Extending 18mi, Bodega Head to Meyers Gulch, just north of Jenner. Open daily year-round. $2/car.* ⚠ *($16; reservations required).* ⟁ ▣ ☎ *707-875-3483. http://parks.ca.gov/north/russian/scsb209.htm.* This spectacular strip of coast affords striking seascapes and numerous opportunities for fishing, hiking, camping, sunbathing and beachcombing. Rocky outcrops separate the 15 small, sandy crescents that punctuate the shoreline. Some of the most dramatic **views★** are from **Duncan's Landing** *(5mi north of Bodega Dunes)*.

One of the most accessible of the Sonoma Coast beaches is **Goat Rock Beach★** *(8mi north of Bodega Dunes)*, at the mouth of the Russian River, where visitors enjoy a unique **view** of river and ocean barely separated by a narrow spit of sand. From November to March, throngs of resident harbor seals vie with fishermen to catch schools of salmon that return each year to spawn.

Turnouts abound on this stretch of highway. North of Jenner, the road becomes a series of switchbacks winding high above the ocean *(average speed 25mph)*. Several miles south of Fort Ross, the road flattens out and marine terraces appear on the left.

★★ Fort Ross State Historic Park – *22mi north of Bodega Bay. Open year-round daily 10am–4:30pm. Closed Thanksgiving Day, Dec 25. $2/car.* ⟁ ▣ ☎ *707-847-3286. http://parks.ca.gov/north/russian/frshp207.htm.* Built high on a desolate promontory above a sheltered azure cove and flanked by forested mountains to the east, Fort Ross reigned as Russia's easternmost outpost for nearly 40 years. This strategically located stronghold provided a base from which colonists hunted sea otters for their valuable pelts and supplied food to Russia's more remote outposts in Alaska.

Settlement Rossiia (Russia), as the colony was christened, was established in 1812 by members of the Russian-American Company. The first colonists, a group of 25 Russians and 80 Alaskan Aleuts (recruited for their skill in hunting sea otters), negotiated with the resident Kashaya Pomo Indians for land before constructing the garrison. Several hundred people subsequently led a peaceful existence cultivating the land and its resources, but by the mid-1830s, California's sea otter population and the colony was abandoned.

The present fort has been partially restored to its early appearance. A short, paved loop trail *(.5mi)* leads from a **visitor center**—offering displays on the history of the fort and earlier Pomo tribes—through a cypress grove to the fort. Constructed of redwood and modeled after traditional edifices in Siberia, the stockade contains six structures of clean, simple lines. Most buildings are replicas; only the **Rotchev House** *(north wall)* is partially original. The **officials' quarters** *(southwest wall)* display artifacts evoking the fort's early days.

The small **chapel**—first Russian Orthodox church in North America outside Alaska— boasts a distinctive, hexagonal tower and round cupola. This building is the third incarnation of the original structure that was erected in 1825 but collapsed during the 1906 earthquake.

Salt Point State Park – *9mi north of Fort Ross. Open year-round daily dawn–dusk. $2/car. Closed during inclement weather.* △ ▣ ☏ *707-847-3221. http://parks.ca .gov/north/russian/spsp248.htm.* Named for the substance that Native Americans once collected from submarine crevices for preserving seafood, this 6,000-acre park runs along 4mi of coastline. Divers favor the site for its underwater **Gerstle Cove Marine Reserve**. Off the shores of the cove, seals sun themselves on glistening rocks. The adjacent **Kruse Rhododendron State Reserve** *(entrance 3mi north of Salt Point)* protects 317 acres studded with thickets of coast rhododendron that succeeded vegetation razed years ago by a forest fire. This site is best visited from April to June, when the towering rhododendrons burst into bloom.

31 • SAUSALITO★
Population: 7,036
Map p 224

Nestled into the bay side of the Marin Headlands just a few miles north of the Golden Gate Bridge, this upscale residential community draws throngs of visitors on sunny days and weekends. Sausalito's winding streets, sophisticated boutiques and lush hillsides dotted with attractive homes and gardens create a relaxed yet cultured ambience, and its privileged setting affords some of the finest views of San Francisco and the bay islands.

Historical Notes

On the afternoon of August 5, 1775, the Spanish supply ship *San Carlos*, under the command of Lt. Juan Manuel de Ayala, dropped anchor just outside the Golden Gate. Ayala's first mate and six crew members, sent ashore to explore potential anchorage sites, became the first Europeans to enter the bay from the sea. Ayala named their chosen anchorage after the trees they found growing along freshwater streams (the Spanish word *sauces* means "willows").

Sausalito's first Anglo settler, **William Richardson**, arrived in San Francisco Bay in 1822 at age 27, while serving as first mate on a British whaler. Fluent in Spanish and conversant in several other languages, he became the first to build a habitation in San Francisco, then called Yerba Buena. In 1825, having acquired Mexican citizenship, Richardson married the daughter of the *comandante* of The Presidio. Through family connections, he later acquired title to the 19,572-acre Rancho del Saucelito, which stretched from the Marin Headlands to Stinson Beach on the west side of the peninsula. In 1849, after the US takeover of California, his property came under dispute and he was forced to sell the southern portion of the land.

Railroad and Shipping Hub – Early attempts to develop the area failed and in 1868 1,164 acres were acquired by a group of San Francisco businessmen intent on developing a resort and residential community. In 1875, the North Pacific Coast Railroad extended its tracks from San Rafael to Sausalito. Trains carrying lumber from the northern redwood forests halted here to unload their cargoes onto a fleet of ferryboats that carried travelers and commerce between rural Marin County and booming San Francisco.

In 1942, three months after the US entered World War II, the US Maritime Commission hired the W.A. Bechtel Company to construct a new West Coast shipyard capable of quickly building standard **Liberty Ships** and oil tankers. Bechtel selected 210 acres of undeveloped Sausalito waterfront as the site of the new facility, known as Marinship. In 1942-43, 75,000 men and women poured into the town to build vessels for the American war effort.

Beginning just previous to the war—in the years following the 1937 completion of the Golden Gate Bridge—Sausalito also experienced an influx of writers, artists, poets and other free-spirited souls. They found inexpensive refuge in the hulks of retired ferryboats and in houseboats made from the hulls of old military landing craft. The close-knit community of "floating home" dwellers persists today, continuing the 1890s tradition of houseboating on Richardson Bay.

Visiting Sausalito – *From San Francisco, take US-101 over the Golden Gate Bridge to the Alexander Ave. exit, just past Vista Point; continue 2mi to Bridgeway Blvd. Street parking and public lots in Sausalito fill to capacity on weekends, leaving drivers with no option but to park on residential streets high on the hillsides. A good alternative is to take a ferry; they depart regularly from Pier 41 at Fisherman's Wharf (year-round Mon–Fri 10:40am–8pm; weekends & holidays 10:40am–6:25pm; Memorial Day–Labor Day Sat only to 10:15pm; no service Jan 1, Thanksgiving Day, Dec 25; 30min; $6/one way; ✗ ♿ 🅿 Blue & Gold Fleet ☎ 415-705-5555; www.blueandgoldfleet.com) or the Ferry Building (year-round Mon–Fri 7:05am–8pm; weekends & holidays 10:50am–6:55pm, May–Sept 8:05pm; no service Jan 1, Thanksgiving Day, Dec 25; 30min; $5/one-way; ✗ ♿ 🅿 Golden Gate Ferry ☎ 415-923-2000; www.transitinfo.org/GGT/). A visitor information kiosk at the ferry landing provides free brochures and other information.*

SIGHTS

★**Bridgeway Boulevard** – This attractive thoroughfare skirting Sausalito's waterfront was originally called Water Street. The name was changed to Bridgeway in 1937, as highway engineers had planned to route Golden Gate Bridge automobile traffic directly through Sausalito. An alternate route above the village was ultimately selected and Bridgeway instead became the anchor of a charming commercial district of restaurants, cafes, galleries, retail shops and inns like the **Casa Madrona** *(801 Bridgeway; ☎ 415-332-0502)*, a restored Victorian villa (1885) nestled on the wooded hillside overlooking the yacht harbor.

Near the ferry landing, across from the Mission-style Sausalito Hotel and The Inn Above Tide, is tiny **Plaza Viña del Mar**. The plaza honors the city of Viña del Mar, Chile, one of Sausalito's two sister cities (the other is Sakaide, Japan). Created by resident Sausalito architect William Faville, designer of much of San Francisco's 1915 Panama-Pacific International Exposition, the park features an Italianate fountain and two whimsical, elephant-shaped light standards originally created for the fair. South of the ferry landing, Bridgeway's wide sidewalks offer delightful **views**★★ of San Francisco, the bay, Alcatraz and Angel Island.

Sausalito Visitor Center & Historical Exhibit – *780 Bridgeway. Open year-round Tue–Sun 11:30am–4pm. Closed major holidays. ♿ 🅿 ☎ 415-332-0505. www.sausalito.org.* Occupying a former ice house, this small museum's displays trace the history of Sausalito from the days of the Coast Miwok to the present. Particularly interesting are photographs of the Golden Gate Bridge under construction, and portraits of such famous residents as actor Sterling Hayden; Sally Stanford, a San Francisco madam-who became mayor of Sausalito; and infamous rum-runner and bank robber "Baby Face" Nelson.

Sausalito Yacht Harbor – Just north of the visitor center, a forest of masts rises above Sausalito's vast flotilla of sail and motor yachts. Visitors can walk along the boardwalk fronting the harbor and on individual piers for close-up views of luxury watercraft. Several houseboats can be seen from the public walkway at the north end of the harbor.

Bulkley Avenue – *From Bridgeway, follow Princess St. (first street south of Plaza Viña del Mar) to Bulkley Ave. and turn right.* A walk up shady Bulkley Avenue, through the hills that backdrop Sausalito's waterfront, brings visitors to elegant homes and contemporary compounds embellished by elaborate gardens and forests of pine, oak, acacia and eucalyptus trees. The **Alta Mira** *(125 Bulkley Ave.; ☎ 415-332-1350)*, a sprawling, Spanish-style hotel built in 1927, commands spectacular bay **views**★★ from its terrace. Opposite, the **First Presbyterian Church** (1909, Ernest Coxhead) is a striking example of the Shingle style; note its intricate wooden exterior. Just past the church, tiny **Excelsior Lane** descends the precipitous slope to Bridgeway.

 The Inn Above Tide
39 El Portal; ☎ 415-332-9535.
www.innabovetide.com. Guests at this charming luxury inn—the first Bay Area lodging to be built over the water—can be excused for thinking they're afloat. All 30 rooms, most with fireplaces, face onto the water. Seals and pelicans glide past private balconies as sailboats materialize from the bay's haunting fog. At night, the San Francisco skyline is startlingly bright.

Marinship – *From downtown, follow Bridgeway north 1mi to Marinship Way and turn right.* This complex of warehouses and docks is all that remains of the huge shipbuilding facility that transformed Sausalito during World War II. In 1942 and 1943, more than 90 vessels were constructed here, including 15 Liberty Ships, 62 T-2 oil tankers and 16 Navy oilers, all in record time. Working three shifts around the clock, seven days a week, workers built the ships with amazing speed; one 10,000-ton tanker, the SS *Huntington Hills*, was built and delivered to America's forces in the Pacific in just 33 days. When the American fleet gathered in Tokyo Bay on August 14, 1945, to accept Japanese surrender, eight Marinship-built tankers were present, including the yard's flagship, the USS *Tamalpais*.

★**Bay Model Visitor Center of the US Army Corps of Engineers** – Kids *2100 Bridgeway. Open Memorial Day–Labor Day Tue–Fri 9am–4pm, Sat 10am–6pm. Rest of the year Tue–Sat 9am–4pm.* ♿ 🅿 ☎ *415-332-3870. www.spn.usace.army.mil/bmvc.* Located in a former Marinship warehouse, this 1.5-acre scale model of the San Francisco Bay and Sacramento-San Joaquin Delta was originally conceived to test the effect on the shallow bay of proposed dams. The dams were never built. Today the model serves as an educational and interpretive tool to simulate the tides, currents, salinity and other water-flow aspects of the vast estuary system; it normally is in full operation on Fridays and Saturdays, with 15min demonstrating the passage of a 24hr period.

The self-guided tour of the model includes an introductory video ("Water: The Link to Civilization") and interactive displays on environmental issues and long-term bay management strategy. Visitors walk above and beside the sprawling miniature representation of 343sq mi of bay, delta and Pacific coastline. Near the lobby is a fascinating **display**★ on Marinship and Sausalito's World War II shipbuilding years. Outside the Bay Model, stroll to the waterfront to see the massive 1915 steam schooner *Wapama*, which once hauled lumber up and down the Pacific coast. The wooden ship, drydocked on a barge alongside the pier, is under extensive restoration by a team of volunteers *(call ☎ 415-556-3002 for information on Saturday barge tours).* It forms part of the collection of the San Francisco Maritime Park.

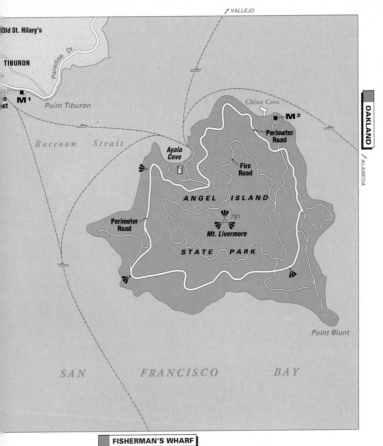

FISHERMAN'S WHARF

32 • TIBURON and ANGEL ISLAND★

Map above

A breezy maritime ambience, a historic Main Street, a bustling waterfront promenade and popular restaurants lure visitors to this charming bayside village at the southern tip of the Tiburon peninsula.

Historical Notes

Lt. Juan Manuel de Ayala, the first European to visit the area, named Punta de Tiburon (Shark Point) during his 1775 voyage to explore and chart San Francisco Bay. Tiburon formed part of an 1834 Mexican land grant, the Rancho Corte Madera del Presidio, deeded to Irish immigrant John Reed. In 1884, it became a busy railroad town when a branch line of the San Francisco and North Pacific Railroad (later the Northwestern Pacific Railroad) was built along the peninsula, making it possible to travel from San Rafael and the Redwood Empire to San Francisco via train and ferry. Today, roads and a bike path along Richardson Bay mark the route of the long-defunct railroad, but traces of late-19C Tiburon still shape the character of the downtown area.

Visiting Tiburon – Ferries from San Francisco's Fisherman's Wharf offer the easiest and most scenic transportation to Tiburon, especially on crowded summer weekends. *(Ferries depart Pier 41 year-round Mon–Fri 11am–5pm, May–Sept weekends & holidays 9:30am–6:30pm, Sat only 10:15pm; rest of the year 10:40am–5:50pm; commuter service via San Francisco Ferry Building year-round Mon–Fri 6am–7:15pm; additional Fri & Sat evening departures in summer; no service Jan 1, Thanksgiving Day, Dec 25; 30min; $5.50; ✗ ♿ ▯ Blue & Gold Fleet ☎ 415-705-5555; www.blueandgoldfleet.com).*

Driving from San Francisco, take US-101 north 6mi to the Tiburon Blvd. (Rte. 131) exit; continue 4mi to the town center. Parking lots are located on Tiburon Blvd. next to the Boardwalk Market, on Main St. next to the Tiburon Playhouse movie theater, and at Point Tiburon (enter from the traffic circle at the end of Tiburon Blvd.).

Visitor information is available from the **Tiburon/Belvedere Chamber of Commerce** *(☎ 415-435-5633; www.tiburon.citysearch.com).*

SIGHTS

Main Street – Weekends and pleasant afternoons bring throngs of visitors to Tiburon's charming Main Street, where colorful, false-fronted buildings evoke the atmosphere of the late 19C. Walkways skirt the shore and numerous waterside restaurants welcome visitors to relax on outdoor decks. Ferryboats docking from San Francisco and Angel Island add to the cheerful hubbub.

West of downtown, Main Street turns sharply north to become pleasant **Ark Row**, where trees shade a charming collection of grounded houseboats, or "arks," that once floated on the bay as summer residences. Now transformed as boutiques and small shops, these unusual structures retain much of their yesteryear appeal with such decorative adornments as arched roofs and tiny columns. Most date from the late 19C.

■ Arks Around the Bay

Through the late 19C and early 20C, numerous San Franciscans spent their summers aboard floating homes known as "arks," moored off the shores of Sausalito and other southern Marin County towns such as Tiburon. Popular summer retreats, these quaint structures enhanced the good life on San Francisco Bay and Richardson Bay. Some of them have been preserved on land as shops and homes on Bridgeway (north end of Sausalito Yacht Harbor) and "Ark Row" (downtown Tiburon). A refurbished ark is displayed at the Hyde Street Pier in San Francisco.

Tiburon Railroad-Ferry Depot Museum (M¹) – *1920 Paradise Dr., 3 blocks east of ferry landing. Open Apr–Oct Wed & Sun 1–4pm. Rest of the year by appointment only. Contribution requested.* ☎ *415-435-1853.* The only dual-use rail-and-ferry station west of New York's Hudson River, Donahue Depot (1884) was once the key link between San Francisco and the Redwood Empire. It was not retired from active use until 1968. Now on the National Register of Historic Places, it contains a c.1900 model of Point Tiburon and walls of historic photos.

★The China Cabin – *52 Beach Rd.; turn west from Tiburon Blvd. Open Apr–Oct Wed & Sun 1–4pm. Rest of the year by appointment only. Contribution requested.* ☎ *415-435-1853.* Resting atop pilings in Belvedere Cove, this beautiful, Victorian-era social salon was salvaged from the *SS China* (1866), a wood-hulled sidewheel steamer that once traversed the Pacific Ocean from San Francisco to Hong Kong and Yokohama for the Pacific Mail Steamship Company. The interior, restored to its full, gilded grandeur, offers a tantalizing glimpse of the elegance and luxury of 19C social salons.

Old St. Hilary's – *Upper end of Esperanza St. From Tiburon Blvd. turn east on Beach Rd. and follow signs across Mar West St. (.7mi). Open Apr–Oct Wed & Sun 1–4pm. Rest of the year by appointment only. Contribution requested.* ♿ 🅿
☎ *415-435-1853.* Perched on a hillside above town, this former Roman Catholic church (1888) represents an excellent example of the Carpenter Gothic style. The historic landmark is surrounded by **St. Hilary's Preserve**, which protects 217 species of wildflowers, two-thirds of them native to the Tiburon Peninsula. Scenic paths lead through the preserve, where the wildflowers bloom much of the year.

Richardson Bay Wildlife Sanctuary – *376 Greenwood Cove Rd., 3.2mi west of downtown off Tiburon Blvd. Open year-round dawn–dusk.* ☎ *415-388-2525.* Administered since 1961 by the National Audubon Society, this bayside refuge has its headquarters in the 1876 **Lyford House** *(tours Nov–Apr Sun 1–4pm)*, an 1876 Victorian built by a prominent 19C doctor, Benjamin Lyford. A 2.6mi walk from here follows Richardson Bay along the former railroad track bed.

★★ANGEL ISLAND STATE PARK

This hilly, forested island, separated from Tiburon by tide-swept Raccoon Strait, is a peaceful oasis amid busy San Francisco Bay. Over its long history of human habitation, the 750-acre island—largest in the bay—has served as a Coast Miwok haven, a Spanish land-grant cattle ranch, a US military base, a quarantine station and an immigration facility.

The island was christened Isla de Los Angeles (Angels Island) by Lt. Juan Manuel de Ayala in 1775. After years of military use and a period (1910-40) when it served as an immigration station, the island was declared surplus property by the federal government in 1948. In 1954, citizen groups led by Marin County conservationist Caroline Livermore persuaded the California State Park Commission to acquire 37 acres surrounding Ayala Cove. In 1963 the entire island (with the exception of a Coast Guard installation at Point Blunt) became part of California's state park system. Today it draws runners, hikers, bikers and campers to its myriad trails, lofty campsites and tranquil picnic spots.

Visiting Angel Island – Angel Island is pleasant throughout the year, though summer fogs can obscure its stunning views of San Francisco and the bay. On weekends, especially during the summer, recreation enthusiasts flock to its trails and campsites. *Open year-round daily 8am–sunset; Visitor Services open Apr Wed–Sun, May–Oct daily, Nov & Mar weekends only.* △ ⚑ & ☏ *415-435-1915. www.angelisland.com.*

The Cove Cafe offers light lunch fare and outdoor dining. Open-air motorized tours *(1 hr; audio commentary; $11.50)* and **mountain bike** rentals *($10/hr or $25/day)* are available through Angel Island Tram Tours *(☏ 415-897-0715).* Sea Trek offers **sea kayak** tours *(all-day guided tour $100, reservations required, ☏ 415-488-1000).* Limited overnight **camping** is available by advance reservation only *(☏ 800-444-7275, http://parks.ca.gov/travel/index.htm).*

Ferries depart from **Tiburon** *(Apr–Sept Mon–Fri 10 & 11am, 1 & 3pm, weekends 10am–5pm each hour; rest of the year Wed–Fri call for schedule, weekends 10 & 11am, 1 & 3pm; one-way 10min; $5.50 round-trip & park admission; Angel Island-Tiburon Ferry ☏ 415-435-2131).* From Pier 41 in **San Francisco** *(Apr Wed–Sun 10am–12:15pm, May–Oct Mon–Fri 10am–12:15pm, weekends & holidays 9:30am–11:45am & 2pm; rest of the year Mon–Fri 10am, weekends & holidays 10:40am; one-way 20min; $10.50 round-trip & park admission;* ⚑ & *Blue & Gold Fleet ☏ 415-705-5444).* From **Oakland** and **Alameda** *(May–Oct weekends 10:50am & 11am, respectively; round trip 1hr; $13;* ☐ *Alameda/Oakland Ferry ☏ 510-522-3300).* From **Vallejo** *(May–Oct weekends 9am; call for weekday schedule; 55min; $13; ☏ 707-643-3779).*

Visit

Ayala Cove – Ferries dock at this cozy little cove named for Lt Juan Manuel de Ayala, who anchored his ship here for a month in 1775. The cove's broad sweep of lawn is a popular picnic spot. Stop at the state park **visitor center** for maps and brochures, and to take in exhibits on the island's history.

Perimeter Road – *5mi loop. Trailhead to left of Ayala Cove.* This mostly paved road rings the island's forested flanks and offers an easy, scenic stroll past military installations and garrisons recalling the island's human history. From various points along the road, **views★★★** take in the jagged San Francisco skyline, shiplike Alcatraz and the Golden Gate Bridge spanning the mouth of San Francisco Bay. From the main path, spur roads and trails lead to several fine beaches and enclaves of historic buildings. At China Cove (North Garrison), a barracks that formerly housed Chinese, Russian, Japanese and South American immigrants today houses a small **museum★** (**M²**) *(visit by 45min guided tour only, May–Oct weekends & holidays 11am–3:30pm).* The **Fire Road** *(3mi loop)* circumscribes the island at a higher elevation, providing bikers and hikers a more challenging route.

Mt. Livermore – The 781ft summit of the island's central peak, accessible from Ayala Cove by the moderately strenuous Northridge *(2mi)* and Sunset *(2.5mi)* trails, offers an unobstructed **panorama★★★** sweeping over San Francisco, the bay and the communities surrounding it. The mountain was named for Caroline Livermore, leader of the movement to preserve Angel Island.

ADDITIONAL SIGHT

San Rafael Arcángel Mission – *10mi north of Tiburon at 5th Ave. & A St. in San Rafael. Take Rte. 131 to US-101 north and continue to Central San Rafael exit. Chapel open year-round daily 6am–4:30pm (gift shop 11am–4pm). Closed major holidays.* ☏ *415-456-3016.* The 20th and penultimate mission of the California chain was founded in 1817 as an *asistencia* to Mission Dolores in San Francisco. The branch mission was used as a sanitarium for San Francisco parishioners in failing health, and was named for the patron saint of bodily healing. The buildings were razed in 1870; the current replica on the site dates from 1949. Fragments from the original church are on display in the mission's gift shop.

Addresses, telephone numbers, opening hours and prices published in this guide are accurate at press time. We apologize for any inconvenience resulting from outdated information, and we welcome corrections and suggestions that may assist us in preparing the next edition. Please send us your comments:

Michelin Travel Publications
Editorial Department
P. O. Box 19001
Greenville, SC 29602-9001
Email: TheGreenGuide-us@us.michelin.com

Lying inland within a two-hour drive of San Francisco, the Napa Valley and Sonoma County thrive on the abundant sunshine and fertile soil that produce grapes for some of North America's finest wines. Though vineyards flourish along many of California's inland coastal areas from Eureka to San Diego County, and even as far east as the foothills of the Sierra Nevada, these areas just north of San Francisco have garnered a reputation as the state's preeminent winemaking regions. Visitors and locals flock here, drawn by the temperate climate, varied natural beauty and acclaimed wineries that make the Wine Country one of California's foremost tourist destinations.

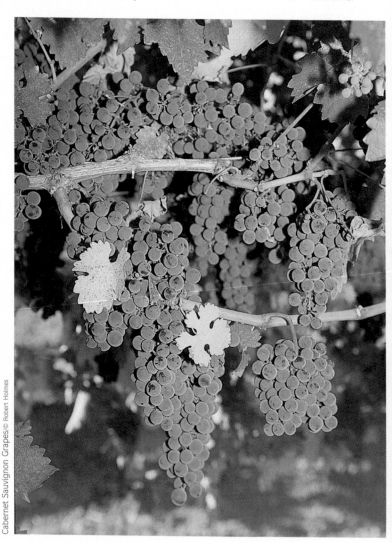

Cabernet Sauvignon Grapes/© Robert Holmes

Historical Notes

Cuttings of Criollas grapevines traveled north from the Baja Peninsula during the late 17C, transported by Franciscan padres as they established the mission chain in Alta California. Wines made from these "mission" grapes were used primarily for trade and for sacramental purposes; their quality would be considered poor by today's standards. In the early 1830s a French immigrant propitiously named Jean-Louis Vignes (*vigne* is French for "vine") established a large vineyard near Los Angeles using cuttings of European grapevines *(Vitis vinifera)*, and by the mid-19C winemaking had become one of southern California's principal industries.

In 1857 **Agoston Haraszthy** (1812-69), a Hungarian immigrant, purchased a 400-acre estate in Sonoma County, named it Buena Vista, and cultivated Tokay vine cuttings imported from his homeland. The grapes flourished, inspiring Haraszthy to envision northern California as a mecca for the production of premium wines. In 1861, bolstered by promises of state funding from Governor John Downey, Haraszthy traveled to Europe to gather assorted varieties of *vinifera* cuttings for experimentation in California soil. Upon his return, the state legislature refused to uphold Downey's commitment, claiming that it was unfair for the state to favor any single industry. Undeterred, Haraszthy persisted in distributing (at his own expense) some 100,000 cuttings, training the area's grape growers (many of them European immigrants) and testing varieties with different soil types. The quality of California wines steadily improved, and areas around San Francisco began to supersede southern California as the state's principal viticultural region.

Boom and Bust – Successful application of Haraszthy's discoveries created a veritable boom in the wine industry throughout the Napa and Sonoma Valleys in the last decades of the 19C. Among the wineries established during this period were **Gundlach-Bundschu (1)** (1858), founded by Bavarian immigrant Jacob Gundlach; **Charles Krug (2)** (1861), first winery in Napa Valley; and **Schramsberg Vineyards** (1862), first of the region's hillside wineries to hew storage caves out of rock. Other renowned names of the present-day wine industry, including **Beringer, Beaulieu** and **Inglenook**, also were established during this period.

As the 19C drew to a close, northern California grapevines fell prey to phylloxera, a root louse that attacks susceptible *vinifera* plants. Entire vineyards were decimated. Researchers at the University of California, in concert with French grape growers who had experienced similar devastation in the 1850s, discovered they could combat phylloxera by replanting vineyards with disease-resistant wild-grape rootstocks from the midwestern US, onto which *vinifera* cuttings had been grafted. The rebuilding process was slow, but the wine industry achieved a modicum of recovery by the early 20C only to find itself faced with growing opposition from the American temperance movement. On January 29, 1919, the US Congress ratified the 18th Amendment prohibiting the manufacture, sale, importation and transportation of intoxicating liquors in the US.

Prohibition – Prohibition brought California's winemaking industry to a near-standstill as grapegrowers converted their vineyards to the cultivation of other crops. Licenses were granted to only seven California wineries (including the Christian Brothers, Beringer, Sebastiani and Beaulieu Vineyards) to produce wines for sacramental and medicinal use. Home production of "non-intoxicating" grape juice for private consumption was also permitted, though limited to 200gal/yr per family.

In 1933, when Prohibition was repealed by the 21st Amendment, wine growers again were faced with the prospect of rebuilding their industry. The Great Depression slowed the reclamation of vineyards and the organization of related trades and distribution systems, and it was not until the early 1970s that the demand for fine table wines rose and California's wine industry was fully re-established.

Wine Country Today – In recent decades the Napa and Sonoma valleys have experienced tremendous development. Besides significant increases in vineyard acreage, the late 20C witnessed an explosion of small-scale operations, some housed in old wineries updated with state-of-the-art equipment. Researchers at the University of California at Davis' renowned Department of Viticulture and Enology develop new methods of grape cultivation and winemaking, while advisory boards oversee quality control, and trade associations work to promote California wines throughout the world.

Today the Wine Country, moving beyond its traditional role, has become a center for fine art and gastronomy. Napa's new American Center for Wine, Food and the Arts, scheduled to open in late 2001, is the latest indication. Trendy restaurants evince a growing dedication to the joys of pairing food and wine. In 1995 the renowned Culinary Institute of America installed a campus in the former Christian Brothers/Greystone Cellars winery, and critics nationwide have dubbed chef Thomas Keller's French Laundry in Yountville as the finest restaurant in the US. Recent years have seen the rise of a new generation of showplace operations—among them Opus One, Clos Pegase, Codorniu Napa and The Hess Collection Winery—that combine wine production with the display of fine art and innovative architecture.

Viticulture and the Art of Winemaking

The Wine Country is organized into **Approved Viticultural Areas**, each suitable for the cultivation of certain types of grapes. Growing conditions vary among these areas, depending upon soil type and climate. Volcanic activity in the region has produced porous soils in which wine grapes thrive, but soil depth and moisture vary from region to region, as do mineral levels.

Weather is considered the most important factor affecting the cultivation of wine grapes, which require a long growing season of hot days and cool nights. In the Wine Country, grapes ripen slowly from April to October, giving flavors and acids plenty of time to develop. The average annual rainfall of 33in occurs mostly between November and May. Differences in elevation, proximity to the sea and exposure to sun, fog and wind create numerous microclimates, each affected by factors as seemingly slight as a dip in a mountain ridge or the tilt of a slope.

Reading a Wine Label

Who made the wine and where was it bottled? Where and when were the grapes grown? How much alcohol is contained therein? The label on a bottle of wine says all of this and more. Labeling information is regulated by the US Treasury Department's Bureau of Alcohol, Tobacco and Firearms, and certain elements are required by law.

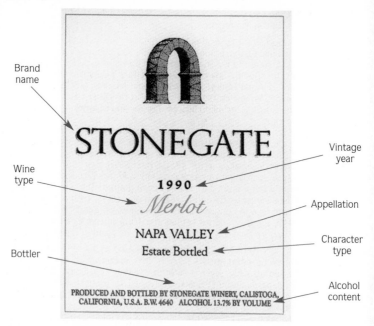

Brand name

Wine type

Bottler

Vintage year

Appellation

Character type

Alcohol content

STONEGATE

1990

Merlot

NAPA VALLEY

Estate Bottled

PRODUCED AND BOTTLED BY STONEGATE WINERY, CALISTOGA, CALIFORNIA, U.S.A. B.W. 4640   ALCOHOL 13.7% BY VOLUME

Required elements:

Brand name – May be the name of the producer, or a secondary or special brand name of the producer.

Wine type – If 75 percent of the grapes used in the wine are of one type, such as Chardonnay, Zinfandel or Pinot Noir, that name must appear on the label as the name of the wine. Otherwise the wine may be called "table wine" or take a generic name such as Burgundy or Chablis.

Appellation – This is the geographic origin of the grapes used in making the wine. In order for the name of an Approved Viticultural Area, such as Napa Valley, to appear on the label, 85 percent of the grapes used must come from that particular area. If the appellation is a county such as Napa or Sonoma, the grape content from that appellation must be 75 percent. If the appellation is the state of California, the wine must be produced entirely of California-grown grapes.

Bottler – The name of the bottling winery may be different from that of the brand name. "Produced and Bottled by" indicates that at least 75 percent of the wine was fermented by the bottler. "Made and Bottled by" indicates that at least 10 percent of the wine was fermented by the bottler.

Alcohol content – Table wines may contain 7 to 14 percent alcohol by volume; aperitif wines 15 to 24 percent; dessert wines 14 to 24 percent or greater. There is no requirement for sparkling wines.

Optional elements:

Vintage year – The year in which the grapes were grown may only appear on a label if 95 percent of the grapes used in the wine were harvested that year.

Character type – Additional information such as "Estate Bottled" indicates that the vineyard is managed by the winery, and that the vineyard and the winery are located within the stated appellation.

Vineyard – If the label indicates a specific vineyard, 95 percent of the grapes used must come from that vineyard.

Practical Information..Area Code: 707

Getting There

By Car – Consult individual entries for directions to the **Napa Valley** *(p 234)*, Sonoma Valley *(p 242)* and the **Upper Sonoma-Russian River Region** *(p 247)*.

By Bus – **Greyhound** service to Napa, Sonoma & Santa Rosa (☎ *800-231-2222*); **Golden Gate Transit** to most cities in Sonoma County (☎ *415-923-2000*).

General Information

When to Go – The best times to visit the Wine Country are in the spring, when yellow mustard plants blossom in the vineyards before the summer's heat sets in; and in the fall, when temperatures are comfortable, the sun shines without fail, and winemakers begin the harvest and crush (pressing of grapes). Advance reservations are recommended for lodging and attractions in summer and fall.

Visitor Information – Contact the following agencies to obtain maps and information on recreation, accommodations and seasonal events: **Napa Valley Tourist Bureau** *(PO Box 3240, Yountville CA 94599;* ☎ *944-1558)*; **Napa Valley Conference & Visitors Bureau** *(1310 Napa Town Center, Napa CA 94559;* ☎ *226-7459; www.napavalley.com)*; **Napa Valley Vintners Association** *(899 Adams St., St. Helena CA 94574;* ☎ *963-3388; www.napavintners.com)*; **Sonoma Valley Visitors Bureau** *(453 1st St. E., Sonoma CA 95476;* ☎ *996-1090; www.sonomavalley.com)*; **Sonoma County Tourism Information** *(401 College Ave., Ste. D, Santa Rosa CA 95401;* ☎ *800-576-6662)*; **Sonoma County Wineries Association** *(5000 Roberts Lake Rd., Rohnert Park CA 94928;* ☎ *586-3795)*; **Santa Rosa Convention & Visitors Bureau** *(9 Fourth St., Santa Rosa CA 95401;* ☎ *571-5949; www.visitsantarosa.com)*; **Russian River Wine Roads** *(PO Box 46, Healdsburg CA 95448;* ☎ *433-4335)*. For a copy of the **Napa Valley Guide** or the **Sonoma County Guide** *($7)*, which include complete information on accommodation, dining and shopping, call ☎ 538-8981.

Accommodations – Charming **bed-and-breakfast inns** can be found in towns along Rte. 29 (Napa Valley), Rte. 12 (Sonoma Valley) and US-101 (Russian River Valley). Larger **hotels** are located in Napa, Sonoma and Santa Rosa. Bed-and-breakfast and hotel reservation services include: **B&B Style** (☎ *942-2888 or 800-995-8884)*, **Napa Valley Reservations Unlimited** (☎ *252-1985)*, **Napa Valley Tourist Bureau Reservations** (☎ *258-1957)*, and **Bed and Breakfast Association of Sonoma Valley** (☎ *938-9513; www.sonomabb.com)*. It is wise to reserve well in advance as the best accommodations fill up during peak tourist season. Year-round **camping** is available at Bothe-Napa Valley State Park (☎ *942-4575)* and Sugarloaf Ridge State Park (☎ *833-5712)*, and at Lake Sonoma (☎ *433-9483)*.

Recreation

Ballooning – Balloon tours *(3-5hrs)* depart at sunrise and fly year-round. Prices range $115–$195/person and may include a champagne brunch after the flight. Advance reservations required. Prices can vary with the number of passengers carried; inquire when booking. Napa Valley companies include **Adventures Aloft** (☎ *944-4408)*, **Bonaventura Balloon Company** (☎ *944-2822)* and **Napa Valley Balloons Inc.** (☎ *944-0228)*. Sonoma County companies include **Above the Wine Country Balloons and Tours** (☎ *829-7695)* and **Air Flambuoyant** (☎ *838-8500)*.

Biking – A good way to enjoy the gentle, rolling terrain of the Wine Country is by bicycle. Rental shops offering trail information are in Napa, Sonoma and Calistoga. Weekend and day **bicycle tours** of the area *(equipment provided; day trip $95;* **Get-Away Adventures** ☎ *763-3040; www.getawayadventures.com)*. The same firm offers hiking, canoeing and kayaking trips of 1-6 days, $95-$1,589 all-inclusive.

Farmers' Markets – These bustling markets offer local produce, poultry and other farm products (arrive early for the best selection): **Napa Valley Farmers' Market** *(Old Railroad Depot, St. Helena; May–Nov Fri 7:30am–11:30am;* ☎ *252-2105)*, **Thursday Night Market** *(4th & East Sts., Santa Rosa; May–Sept Thu 5pm–8:30pm;* ☎ *545-1414)*, **Sonoma Farmers Markets** *(Plaza; early Apr–Oct Tue 5:30pm–dusk; Depot Park; year-round Fri 9am–noon;* ☎ *538-7023)*, **Healdsburg Farmers Market** *(North & Vine Sts.; late May–late Dec Sat 9am–noon; Plaza; Jun–Oct Tue 4pm–6pm;* ☎ *431-1956)*.

Sightseeing – **California Wine Country Tours** take passengers by motor coach through Marin County to the Sonoma Valley *(9hrs; depart San Francisco Transbay Terminal year-round daily 9am; $43; Red & White Fleet;* ☎ *415-447-0597)*. The **Napa Valley Wine Train** leaves from downtown Napa and offers dining and wine tasting on a 3hr excursion (☎ *253-2111; www.winetrain.com)*.

ADDRESS BOOK

Dining in the Wine Country

Please see explanation on p 42.

Please see explanation on p 42.

La Toque – *114 Rutherford Cross Rd., in the Rancho Caymus Inn, Rutherford.* & 🅿 ☎ *707-963-9770. www.latoque.com. Dinner only. Closed Mon & Tue.* **$$$$ California-French.** Cozy up to the stone fireplace here for straightforward French-inspired cuisine. Designed to be a "progression of flavors"—paired with wines, of course—the nightly changing five-course prix-fixe menu (cheese course is optional) frequently features Sonoma foie gras, diver scallops, and Niman Ranch beef and pork. Dessert is followed by coffee and *mignardises.*

John Ash & Co. – *4330 Barnes Rd., Santa Rosa.* & 🅿 ☎ *707-527-7687.* **$$$ California.** In a secluded restaurant surrounded by vineyards at the Vintners Inn, 4mi north of Santa Rosa, chef Jeffrey Madura blends fresh seasonal ingredients with his own enthusiasm in dishes like seared sea bass with orzo pasta, figs and prosciutto, and filet of beef accompanied by ravioli filled with porcini mushrooms and foie gras.

Tra Vigne –*1050 Charter Oak Ave., St. Helena.* & ☎ *707-963-4444.* **$$$ Italian.** Italian for "among the vines," Tra Vigne represents renowned chef Michael Chiarello's successful attempt to bring the cooking of southern Italy to northern California. Although the menu focuses on seasonal ingredients—asparagus in spring, mushrooms in autumn—dishes such as crispy herb gnocchi with braised lamb shanks, and fritto misto with tomato vinegar remain classics. Grab an espresso at Cantinetta to enjoy in the brick courtyard, surrounded by grapevines.

Mustards Grill – *7399 St. Helena Hwy., Yountville.* & 🅿 ☎ *707-944-2424. www.mustardsgrill.com.* **$$$ American.** A long-standing Wine Country favorite, this casual ranch-style restaurant on Highway 29 draws winemakers and industry VIPs for its fresh cuisine and top-notch international wine list. The menu ranges across American regional dishes with nods to continental and Asian touches. Don't leave without tasting the sublimely thin and crispy onion rings with house-made ketchup.

Dempsey's Restaurant & Brewery – *50 E. Washington St., Petaluma.* & ☎ *707-765-9694.* **$$ American.** Organic vegetables and fruits from the Red Rooster Ranch dominate the menu at this indoor-outdoor eatery beside the Petaluma River. Vegetarians can look past the wood-oven pizzas, chicken and chops to ZLT sandwiches (with zucchini) and Indian-style lentil cake.

The Wine Country's current production is based primarily on descendants of the *vinifera* cuttings introduced by Agoston Haraszthy in the 19C. Best adapted to Wine Country growing conditions is the **Cabernet Sauvignon**, a small, blue-black grape from the Médoc district of France's Bordeaux region that produces a rich, full red wine. The Burgundy region's **Pinot Noir** grape is used for both table wine and California sparkling wine. Other red wine grapes from Europe include **Cabernet Franc**, **Petite Sirah**, **Napa Gamay** (derived from France's Gamay Beaujolais) and **Zinfandel**, now grown chiefly in California.

Some of California's finest white wines are made from **Chardonnay**, the premier white grape of France's Chablis and Burgundy regions. Chardonnay produces a dry, richly flavored wine. The **Sauvignon Blanc**, used in the making of French Sauternes and Pouilly-Fumé, grows well in the Wine Country's cooler areas. The **Pinot Blanc**, of the same family as the Burgundy's Pinot Noir, is an important ingredient in many sparkling wines. Other white European varieties include **Riesling** and **Chenin Blanc**.

From Vine to Barrel to Bottle – Once grapes have achieved desired levels of sugar and acid, they are picked by hand or machine and placed into a stemmer-crusher device. Here paddles remove the stems and break the skins to produce a soupy mixture of seeds, skins and juice called **must**. In the making of white wines, the must is pressed immediately, usually in a device known as a **bladder press**. The pressed juice is clarified, inoculated with yeast, transferred to tanks, and left to ferment. During **fermentation**, which can last from three days to six weeks, the yeast organisms consume the sugar in the grapes, creating ethyl alcohol, carbon dioxide and heat. If left unchecked, this heat can speed the fermentation process, completing it before desired flavors have had time to develop. To control the temperature, modern stainless-steel fermentation tanks are equipped with dimpled cooling sheaths or "jackets" that control the duration of fermentation. In the making of red wines, fermentation occurs before pressing; thus, skins and seeds are left in contact with the juice, imparting rich, dark colors and tannins to the fluid.

Tuscany – *1005 First St., Napa.* ♿ ☎ *707-258-1000*. **$$ Italian-Tuscan**. Diners who can't get into Tra Vigne are delighted to find Tuscany in the bustling heart of the city of Napa. Dishes like fresh salmon-and-mussel stew with artichokes, and rotisseried rabbit in pancetta, may be followed by a memorable tiramisu.

Staying in the Wine Country

Please see explanation on p 48.

Meadowood – *900 Meadowood Lane, St. Helena.* ♿ ☎ *707-963-3646. www.meadowood.com. 85 rooms.* **$$$$** A private estate built in the early 1960s, Meadowood was expanded in the 70s to become an elite and secluded resort destination. Just off the Silverado Trail, the resort makes a perfect perch for Wine Country adventures. Rustic cottages dotting a cool wooded grove bring guests down to earth, while service remains heavenly. Golf, tennis, a full spa, and the excellent Restaurant at Meadowood round out the amenities.

La Residence – *4066 St. Helena Hwy. N., Napa.* ♿ ☎ *707-253-0337. www.laresidence.com. 20 rooms.* **$$$$** A gracious bed-and-breakfast complex in a rural setting near the town of Napa, La Residence sprawls across two acres of gardens framed by towering oak and pine trees. Handsome antique décor and personalized hospitality make this a good Wine Country choice.

Villagio Inn & Spa – *6481 Washington St., Yountville.* ♿ ☎ *707-944-8877. www.villagio.com. 112 rooms.* **$$$$** Reminiscent of a Tuscan village—with two-story villas surrounding lush gardens and vineyards, fountains and waterways, swimming pools and tennis courts—the Villagio combines its resort atmosphere with a health spa. Rates include a champagne continental breakfast.

Beazley House – *1910 First St., Napa.* ♿ ☎ *707-257-1649. 11 rooms.* **$$$** Napa's first bed-and-breakfast when it opened in 1981, this antique-filled 1902 Colonial Revival mansion still ranks among the valley's best. Five of the rooms are in a replicated carriage house; all are within walking distance of downtown.

Sonoma Hotel – *110 W. Spain St., Sonoma.* ♿ ☎ *707-996-2996. www.sonomahotel.com. 16 rooms.* **$$$** From the stone fireplace in the lobby to the claw-foot tubs in the guest rooms, the hotel exudes country charm. German immigrant Henry Weyl erected this building on Sonoma's town square in 1880 as a dry-goods store and community center. In its current incarnation, the beautifully restored hotel offers cozy rooms equipped with rustic iron headboards and twig nightstands.

Camellia Inn – *211 North St., Healdsburg.* ♿ ☎ *707-433-8182. 9 rooms.* **$$** A home-like hideaway in the charming Russian River Valley, this Italianate-style Victorian offers nightly wine tastings and eclectic antique décor.

After fermentation the wine may be again clarified of impurities by filtration, centrifuging or **racking** (a process in which wine is transferred from tank to tank, leaving the settled sediments behind).

In the last clarification, called **fining**, substances such as clay, gelatin or egg whites may be introduced; sediments and impurities adhere to these materials, which are then easily removed.

Many wines are **barrel-aged** in white-oak barrels; aging can last from a few months to several years. Certain varieties require a blending stage in which various wines are mixed to achieve desired flavors. Some wines are bottled before the final aging period.

Visiting the Wine Country – To fully experience the region's relaxed pace and easygoing character, it's best to select no more than four wineries per day for tasting, and to limit guided tours to one or two per day.

Many wineries offer self-guided tours. Auto traffic, especially during peak seasons, can be heavy. Travelers on tight schedules should bear in mind that although the Wine Country is blessed with lush vegetation, inspiring vistas and an enviable climate, tourist attractions other than wineries are few. Visitors for whom wines and winemaking hold limited appeal should plan less time to visit the region.

Picnicking is one of the joys of a visit to the Wine Country. Attractive picnic areas grace many wineries, and numerous delis and roadside markets offer abundant, often elegant takeout fare, wines and nonalcoholic beverages.

Wineries described in the following sections have been selected and rated on their historic, architectural and cultural merits. A comprehensive, updated listing of wineries is available in the *Wine Country Guide to California*, published annually by *Wine Spectator* magazine and available at bookstores, newsstands and visitor centers.

33 • NAPA VALLEY★★

www.napavalleyonline.com

Map p 240

Cradled between two elongated mountain ranges, this world-renowned valley extends roughly 35mi in a northerly direction from San Pablo Bay to Mt. St. Helena. The Napa Valley is home to some of California's most prestigious wineries, many of them clustered thickly along Route 29 as it passes through the towns of Napa, Yountville, Oakville, Rutherford, St. Helena and Calistoga. Others dot the more tranquil Silverado Trail to the east and the intervening crossroads.

Access – From San Francisco (55mi), drive north on US-101; exit at Rte. 37 and drive east to Rte. 121. Turn left (north) on Rte. 121 and continue to Rte. 29 north. For a quicker if less scenic route, drive north on I-80 to Rte. 37 west and continue to Rte. 29 north.

SIGHTS *described from south to north.*

Napa – Originally settled in 1832, this sprawling city on the banks of the Napa River experienced its first significant population boom during the post-Gold Rush period. Weary miners and vacationing San Franciscans made their way upriver from San Francisco Bay to the then-peaceful little resort town. Riverboat captains and bankers established businesses and elegant Victorian residences through the late 19C, transforming Napa into an active shipping and administrative center. Now Napa County's largest city with 66,548 residents, it still serves as a gateway for the abundance of wines and agricultural goods produced in the verdant Napa Valley. The name is derived from a Native American word meaning "plenty."

Downtown – *1st & 2nd Sts. between Main & Randolph Sts.* At the friendly heart of downtown Napa, the venerable **Goodman Building** (1901), with its gray stone façade *(1219 1st St.),* is now home to the research library and museum of the Napa County Historical Society. Just across the street and one block north, an enormous contemporary **Clock Tower** overlooks the site where the first Magnavox speaker was invented in 1915 (a bronze sculpture of a vintage speaker commemorates the achievement). Other noteworthy buildings include the Italianate **Napa Opera House** *(1018 Main St.),* constructed in 1879, closed in 1914, and currently underoing renovation for use as a performance space; and the stately, ornate **Winship-Smernes Building** *(948 Main St.).*

Victorian Neighborhoods – *South and west of downtown.* Residential neighborhoods hold a wealth of elegant houses from the late 19C and early 20C. A stroll or a slow drive in the vicinity of **Jefferson, First, Third** or **Randolph Streets** reveals numerous well-restored homes built in the Italianate, Queen Anne, Eastlake and Shingle styles characteristic of Victorian architecture around the turn of the 20C.

American Center for Wine, Food and the Arts – *1st St. between Soscol Ave. & Silverado Trail, Napa.* ✗ ⅙ 🅿 ☏ *707-257-3606. www.theamericancenter.org.* This $70-million cultural and educational center is scheduled to open in late 2001 on 12 river-bend acres just east of downtown Napa. Winemaker Robert Mondavi was the founding visionary and primary contributor, but trustees also include home-living entrepreneur Martha Stewart, chefs Julia Child and Alice Waters, *Wine Advocate* publisher Robert Parker and artist Wayne Thiebaud.

At the center, professional chefs, winemakers and artists will share their passions with visitors through cooking and wine-tasting classes, outdoor concerts, garden tours, films and lectures. A core exhibit—**Soil and Spirit, the Quest for Nourishment**—will interpret the distinctiveness of American culture and lifestyle as seen through food and drink, themselves shaped by factors of history and geography.

★★The di Rosa Preserve—Art & Nature – *5200 Carneros Hwy. (Rte. 121), Napa (2.5mi west of Rte. 12). Visit by guided tour (2hr 30min) & reservation only, Jun–Sep Mon, Wed & Thu 9:25am & 12:55pm, Tue 12:55 & 6:25pm, Sat 9:25 & 10:25am. Rest of the year, Tue–Fri 9:25am & 12:55pm, Sat 9:25 & 10:25am. $10.* 🅿 ☏ *707-226-5991. www.dirosapreserve.org.* René di Rosa, son of a US ambassador to Italy, came to San Francisco from Yale University in the 1950s as a young newspaper reporter. Enamored with the Beat culture prevalent in North Beach at that time, he began supporting undiscovered artists by purchasing their work. In 1960, he purchased 460 acres of abandoned vineyards in the Carneros area of lower Napa Valley, converting the 1886 stone winery into his home.

Di Rosa's first love remained art. As the years passed, he and his late artist wife, Veronica, amassed a personal collection of more than 1,500 works—produced in the greater San Francisco Area in the last half of the 20C—by 650-plus artists, many of whom have become famous. Robert Arneson, Joan Brown, Bruce Conner, Manuel Neri and William T. Wiley are among those whose works are represented here. Styles, media and subject matter vary widely, reflecting a history of the enigmatic city's creative energies. Much of the collection is avant-garde; other pieces, like an outdoor Meditation Chapel, are dramatic and thought-provoking.

234

In 1997, di Rosa opened the preserve to visitors, who now park beneath an earthen dam (on which graze mock sheep) and are shuttled past a 35-acre lake to the historic residence and galleries. Di Rosa himself will sometimes join tours, sharing anecdotes and expressing his whimsical taste in art.

★**Codorniu Napa** – *1345 Henry Rd. From downtown Napa take Rte. 29 south to Rte. 121. Turn right and drive west 4mi, turning right on Old Sonoma Rd. Turn left on Dealy Ln. then veer left on Henry Rd. Continue .3mi to driveway entrance. Open year-round daily 10am–5pm. Closed Jan 1, Thanksgiving Day, Dec 24–25. Guided tours (30min) available 11am & 2pm. $4-$6 (tasting fee).* ♿ 📷 ☎ *707-224-1668.* In 1872 the Codorniu family of Barcelona became Spain's first producers of sparkling wine made in the *méthode champenoise* tradition. Their Napa Valley operation occupies an innovative contemporary structure (1991, Domingo Triay) at the foot of Milliken Peak. Sloping, grass-covered earth berms bury the winery's walls, maintaining consistently cool temperatures in storage and production areas within. From the entrance plaza a view extends eastward over the lower Napa Valley. Galleries around a serene courtyard hold 16C-17C European winemaking equipment and changing displays of works by local artists.

★★**The Hess Collection Winery** – *4411 Redwood Rd. From Rte. 29 in Napa take the Redwood Rd./Trancas exit and drive west on Redwood Rd. 6mi to winery entrance. Open year-round daily 10am–4pm. Holidays 10am–2pm. Closed early Jan, Easter Sunday, Thanksgiving Day, Dec 25. $3-$4 tasting fee.* ♿ 📷 ☎ *707-255-1144. www.hesscollection.com.* Nestled in a remote southwestern corner of the Napa Valley on the slope of Mt. Veeder, this beautifully renovated structure contains one of the nation's largest and finest private art collections open to the public, as well as a state-of-the-art winemaking facility. The original stone structure (1903) was acquired by the Christian Brothers in the early 1930s to house the Mont LaSalle winery. In 1983, Swiss entrepreneur Donald Hess leased the property, transforming the upper floors into galleries to exhibit his outstanding collection of works by contemporary American and European artists. Francis Bacon, Robert Rauschenberg and Frank Stella are among those represented, along with such lesser-known artists as Rolf Iseli, Theodoros Stamos, Arnulf Rainer, Lynn Hershman and Magdalena Abakanowicz.

Through wide windows in the stairwells, visitors strolling through the sweeping galleries glimpse the steel tanks and ultra-modern bottling room of the winery. A graceful audiovisual presentation *(12min)* focuses on the seasonal beauty of the vineyards and highlights the unique process of making wine in a mountain region. The property adjacent to The Hess Collection Winery is graced by the **Christian Brothers Retreat and Conference Center** (3) *(4401 Redwood Rd.;* ☎ *707-252-3810; www.christianbrothersretreat.com),* a Mission Revival-style complex (1932) of residential, religious and school buildings interspersed with serene courtyards.

Yountville – This small community of 3,400, ranging along the east side of Route 29, was named for George C. Yount (1794-1865), a North Carolina frontiersman who established vineyards here in 1836 on a portion of the 11,814 acres granted him by the Mexican government. Today Yountville's charming inns, trendy bou-

---

① French Laundry
6640 Washington St., Yountville. ☎ *707-944-2380.*
www.frenchlaundry.com.
Some critics say the French Laundry—lodged in a century-old stone laundry building reminiscent of a European country inn—is the best restaurant in the US. Chef Thomas Keller, masterful in the preparation of sophisticated and creative French cuisine, offers five-course prix-fixe dinners ($70-$80) and a 10-course "chef's tasting menu" ($105) nightly. A sommelier matches wines on request. The price is worth it for a special occasion. Make reservations two months ahead.

© Robert Holmes

tiques and excellent eateries make it a popular base for visitors to the southern Napa Valley. Of particular note is the historic brick Groezinger winery (1870), now restored as **Vintage 1870**, a center for specialty shops and boutiques.

★**Napa Valley Museum** (**M**¹) – *55 Presidents Cir. From Rte. 29/Yountville exit, drive west .3mi toward Veterans Home. Museum is on right. Open year-round Wed–Mon 10am–5pm. Closed major holidays. $4.50.* & 🅿 ☎ *707-944-0500. www.napavalleymuseum.org.* The highlight of this innovative museum (1998, Fernau and Hartman) is an impressive multimedia display entitled **California Wine: The Science of an Art ★★.** An interactive audiovisual program allows visitors to experience a full year in Napa winemaking, exploring soils, climates and microclimates, grape growth, rootstocks, pests, cloning, varietal characteristics, harvest, crushing, fermentation, racking, storage, blending and bottling.

An upper gallery features **The Land and People of the Napa Valley,** with exhibits that describe the artistic, cultural and environmental heritage of the region. Additional temporary exhibits range from history to art.

★★**Domaine Chandon** – *1 California Dr. From Rte. 29/Yountville exit, drive west .2mi toward Veterans Home. Entrance is on right. Open Apr–Oct daily 10am–7pm. Rest of the year Wed–Sun 10am–7pm. Closed Jan 1, Thanksgiving Day, Dec 25. Guided tours (45min) available. Tasting fee.* ✗ & 🅿 ☎ *707-944-8844. www.chandonusa.com.* Visitors to this innovative winery complex (1973) are introduced to French winemaking tradition with a dash of California visual style and appeal. Commissioned by Moët-Hennessy, owners of France's famed Moët et Chandon, the modern structures of gray concrete harmonize with the sweeps and curves of the surrounding terrain; the arched ceilings are reminiscent of traditional wine caves in France's Champagne region.

In the entrance hall, an attractive gallery highlights skills and trades related to winemaking; an informative guided tour explains the principal stages of sparkling wine production according to the *méthode champenoise.* Informative guided tours cover the principal stages involved. An upscale restaurant is located within the visitor center; its outdoor terrace allows picturesque glimpses of the beautifully landscaped winery grounds, old oak trees and vineyards.

★**Opus One** – *7900 St. Helena Hwy (Rte. 29). Visit by guided tour (1hr) only, year-round daily 10:30am–3:30pm. Closed Jan 1, Easter Sunday, Thanksgiving Day, Dec 25. Reservations required. $25 (tasting fee).* & 🅿 ☎ *707-944-9442. www.opusonewinery.com.* Every detail of this innovative structure (1991, Johnson Fain & Partners)—from the French-style white limestone walls to the California redwood pergola crowning the building—testifies to the unique international collaboration that created Opus One, the first ultra-premium winery in the US. In 1970, Baron Philippe de Rothschild of Pauillac, France, approached Napa Valley vintner Robert Mondavi to discuss a joint winemaking venture based in California. Although the team produced its first vintage in 1979, a decade passed before ground was broken for the innovative structure that houses the winery today.

Visitors pass through an olive tree-studded courtyard before entering the dramatic reception hall. Works by well-known artists grace the walls and open spaces of the comfortable Salon, where Continental antiques blend seamlessly with luxurious contemporary furnishings. Descending a grand staircase shaped like the inside of a barrel, visitors enter an elegant tasting room and walk into the semicircular Grand Chai, or cellar, where row upon row of oak barrels stained with wine-colored bands curve into the distance on either side.

■ **Méthode Champenoise**

Most sparkling wines produced in the Wine Country are made by the *méthode champenoise* developed in 17C France by Dom Perignon, a Benedictine monk. In this process, a still wine traditionally blended from Pinot Noir and Chardonnay grapes is inoculated with yeast and sugar, bottled, capped and allowed to ferment a second time. The carbon dioxide gas retained in the bottle infuses the wine with bubbles, creating pressures of up to 110 pounds per sqare inch inside the bottle. The bottle is then stored on its side for as many as six years to let the wine age.

Following aging, the wine is clarified by "riddling," a painstaking process of turning and lifting the bottles daily, bit by bit, until they are nearly upside down, so that yeast and sediments gather in the neck. The wine must then be "disgorged": The neck of the bottle is immersed in a brine solution so that the sediments within it freeze; when the bottle is then uncapped, pressure from within forces out the plug of frozen sediment. A *dosage* of sugar and brandy or other wine is added to the bottle before final corking and labeling.

© N. Kerby

Opus One Winery

★Robert Mondavi Winery – *7801 St. Helena Hwy. (Rte. 29), Oakville. Open year-round daily 9am–5pm. Closed Jan 1, Easter Sunday, Thanksgiving Day, Dec 25. Guided tours (45-90min, $10); reservations recommended.* ⌖ 🅿 ☏ *707-259-9463. www.robertmondavi winery .com.* Constructed in 1966, this striking building anticipated a new generation of modern wineries designed to showcase art and architecture as well as wine. Sculptor Beniamino Bufano's figure of St. Francis with outstretched arms greets visitors beneath the monumental arched entry to the complex, and temporary exhibits of works by local artists are regular features at the winery. A popular Summer Music Festival and a winter concert series are held here annually.

★★St. Supéry – *8440 St. Helena Hwy. (Rte. 29), Rutherford. Open May–Oct daily 9:30am–6pm. Rest of the year daily 9:30am–5pm. Closed Jan 1, Thanksgiving Day, Dec 25. Guided tours (1hr) available. $3 (tasting fee).* ⌖ 🅿 ☏ *707-963-4507. www.stsupery.com.* The modern winery structure houses a comprehensive **Wine Discovery Center★**, featuring in-depth displays on seasonal viticulture, the wine-making process, soil types and appellations. Especially interesting is the SmellaVision exhibit, a "nose-on" display where visitors can sniff eight characteristic aromas associated with Cabernet Sauvignon or Sauvignon Blanc varietals, and examine the color variations for each type of wine. Adjacent to the winery is a model vineyard with detailed panels and exhibits explaining how vines are trained, trellised and pruned according to the variety of grape.

 Oakville Grocery
7856 St. Helena Hwy. (Rte. 29). ☏ *707-944-8802.* French white-truffle oil, raspberry-peach-champagne jam, fresh crusty breads, more than a dozen types of olives and the best-stocked cheese counter in the Napa Valley lure visitors and locals to this tiny but deliciously crammed grocery for picnic or pantry supplies. Assemble a feast of meats, cheeses, breads and pâtés, and the friendly and knowledgeable staff will help you pick the perfect complementary wine from an impressive array of local vintages.

Also on the property is the charming Victorian home built by Joseph Atkinson, the first vintner to own the property. The house *(visit by 3hr guided tour only)* has been restored with period pieces to reflect the life and times of an 1880s winemaker.

★★Niebaum-Coppola Estate Winery – *1991 St. Helena Hwy. (Rte. 29), Rutherford. Open year-round daily 10am–5pm. Closed Jan 1, Easter Sunday, Thanksgiving Day & Dec 25. $7.50 tasting fee. Guided tours (1hr 30min) available daily 11am & 2pm. $20 (includes tasting fee).* ⌖ 🅿 ☏ *707-968-1161. www.niebaum-coppola.com.* The imposing stone winery (1882) at the center of the Niebaum-Coppola estate was built by Gustave Niebaum, a Finnish sea captain and enterprising founder of Inglenook Wines (1879). Most of Niebaum's property, including his Victorian home and 1,600 acres of adjacent land, was purchased in 1975 by filmmaker Francis Ford Coppola (*The Godfather* trilogy) and his wife Eleanor. The massive building, known as the Inglenook Chateau, and a portion of the original vineyards remained in the hands of Heublein, Inc., until 1995, when the Coppola family acquired the entire estate, thus restoring the historic property to its original proportions.

A tree-lined courtyard surrounds a reflecting pool in front of the Inglenook Chateau, which is thought to have been the first gravity-flow winery in the valley. Upon entering the building, visitors can peek into the **Captain's Room** (1889) on the right, a replica of Niebaum's ship's quarters that includes 17C stained-glass windows, 16C Flemish wine cups and a 400-year-old lamp. The Centennial Museum, an intriguing monument to film and winemaking, reflects the careers of both of the winery's charismatic owners, Niebaum and Coppola.

★**St. Helena** – *Rte. 29, 12mi north of Napa.* A picturesque main street graces this charming town of 5,400 at the heart of the Napa Valley. Plentiful and widely varied accommodations, intriguing and innovative restaurants, and a central location close to a number of popular wineries make St. Helena an excellent base for exploring the entire valley.

★**Robert Louis Stevenson Silverado Museum** (**M²**) – *1490 Library Ln. From Main St. northbound, turn right on Adams St., cross the railroad tracks and turn left. Open year-round Tue–Sun noon–4pm. Closed major holidays. Contribution suggested.* ♿ ▣ ☎ *707-963-3757.* Housed in a pleasant gallery within the town library building, this small, memorabilia-packed museum is devoted to the life and works of Robert Louis Stevenson (1850-94), renowned and beloved author of such popular 19C stories as *Treasure Island, Kidnapped* and *A Child's Garden of Verses.* Stevenson honeymooned in a cabin on the slopes of Mt. St. Helena in summer 1880 and immortalized this Napa experience in his book *The Silverado Squatters.* The museum's holdings—comprising photographs, books, manuscripts and the author's personal artifacts—are considered second in importance only to the Stevenson collections at Yale University's Beinecke Library.

■ The Silverado Quaffer

When Robert Louis Stevenson honeymooned in the Napa Valley in 1880, he expressed his affection for the region's fledgling wine industry in word and taste.

"I was interested in California wine," he wrote in *The Silverado Squatters.* "Indeed, I am interested in all wines, and have been all my life, from the raisin wine that a schoolfellow kept secreted in his play-box up to my last discovery ...

"Wine in California is still in the experimental stage; and when you taste a vintage, grave economical questions are involved. ... Meanwhile, the wine is merely a good wine; the best that I have tasted better than a Beaujolais, and not unlike."

Stevenson was particularly fond of the **Schramsberg Vineyards** (*1400 Schramsberg Lane off Petersen Lane west of Rte. 29;* ☎ *707-942-4558*). "Mr. Schram's place ... is the picture of prosperity," the author scribed. "I was tasting wines in the cellar. To Mr. Schram this was a solemn office; his serious gusto warmed my heart; prosperity had not yet wholly banished a certain neophite and girlish trepidation, and he followed every sip and read my face with proud anxiety. I tasted all. I tasted every variety of Schramberger, red and white Schramberger, Burgundy Schramberger, Schramberger Hock, Schramberger Golden Chasselas, the latter with a notable bouquet, and I fear to think how many more."

★★**Beringer Vineyards** – *2000 Main St. (Rte. 29), north of downtown St. Helena. Open year-round daily 9:30am–5pm. Closed Jan 1, Thanksgiving Day, Dec 25. Guided tours (45min) available.* ♿ ▣ ☎ *707-963-7115. www.beringer.com.* The Napa Valley's oldest continuously operating winery was established in 1876 by Jacob and Frederick Beringer, German immigrants who arrived in the US in the 1860s. The brothers' winery escaped the worst of the legislative strictures of Prohibition because they acquired a license to produce wine for religious and medicinal purposes. Extending into the sloping hillside behind the complex are over 1,000ft of tunnels where the temperature remains a constant 58°F, an ideal environment for aging wine.

The centerpiece of the property is the stately **Rhine House** (1883), constructed by Frederick Beringer as his residence. Modeled after the Beringer ancestral home in Germany, the 17-room mansion features elegant woodwork, inlaid floors and exceptional **stained-glass windows★**. The regal oleander trees about the property were planted at the turn of the century by Jacob Beringer.

The Culinary Institute of America at Greystone – *2555 Main St. (Rte. 29), north of downtown St. Helena. Cooking demonstrations (☎ 707-956-2358) year-round daily 10:30am & 1:30pm, weekends also 3:30pm; reservations suggested; $7.50. Campus Store & Marketplace (☎ 707-967-2309) open year-round daily 10am–6pm. Restaurant (☎ 707-967-1010) open year-round daily 11:30am–*

10pm. Closed major holidays. ✗ ♿ 🅿 *www.ciachef.edu.* The massive stone **building★** looming over Rte. 29 was erected in 1889 by William Bourn as Greystone Cellars, a cooperative effort by Napa Valley winegrowers in need of aging and storage facilities. The largest freestanding stone building in California when it was built, the winery changed hands several times before being purchased in the 1950s by the Christian Brothers, a Catholic teaching order.

Today the building houses the West Coast campus of the renowned Culinary Institute of America, which offers continuing education for professionals in the food, wine, health and hospitality fields. Visitors are welcome to explore the delightful herb gardens or browse through the Campus Store & Marketplace, a lively culinary retail outlet

Wine Cellar

© Robert Holmes

with a pastry café. In the Wine Spectator Greystone Restaurant, professional chefs expertly prepare meals in an open kitchen.

The Institute also houses a whimsical **corkscrew collection** of more than 1,800 wine openers, some dating from the 18C. The collection was assembled over a period of 40 years by Brother Timothy, cellarmaster of the Christian Brothers.

Bale Grist Mill State Historic Park – Kids *3369 St. Helena Hwy. (Rte. 29), 3mi north of downtown St. Helena. Open year-round daily 10am–5pm. Closed Jan 1, Thanksgiving Day, Dec 25. $1. Guided tours (30min) available.* ♿ 🅿 ☎ *707-942-4575. http://cal-parks.ca.gov/north/silverado/bgm251.htm.* From the parking area, a pleasant, sylvan path leads to this charming historic **grist mill★**, powered by a 36ft waterwheel. Established in 1846 by Edward T. Bale, an Englishman who married a niece of Gen. Mariano Vallejo, the mill ground into flour the grain harvested by Napa Valley farmers. The wooden mill and waterwheel, which ceased operation about 1905, are partially restored.

Docent tours and an audiovisual presentation provide a good introduction to the milling process, and weekend demonstrations allow a look at the mill in action *(call for demonstration schedule)*. Interpretive displays focus attention on the milling process and on local pioneer history. Visitors can purchase flour and cornmeal milled on site.

★★Sterling Vineyards – *1111 Dunaweal Ln., 6.8mi north of St. Helena via Rte. 29 (entrance on right). Open year-round daily 10:30am–4:30pm. Closed Thanksgiving Day, Dec 25. $6 (includes tramway & wine tasting).* ♿ 🅿 ☎ *707-942-3344. www.sterlingvineyards.com.* Perched like a secluded Greek monastery on a 300ft knoll rising abruptly from the valley floor, this complex of pristine white buildings (1969, Martin J. Waterfield) is one of the Napa Valley's architectural grace notes. Visitors ascend to the winery from the parking area by a hushed ride on the vineyard's **aerial tramway** Kids, from which tranquil views extend over the surrounding area. At the summit, follow informative panels on a self-guided tour through the winery, past colorful examples of tile work, across terraces with **views★** of the northern Napa Valley, and under campaniles representing a contemporary take on traditional mission-style bell towers. The collection of eight bells dating from the early 18C was acquired for Sterling Vineyards in 1972 from London's church of St.-Dunstan-in-the-East.

★Clos Pegase – *1060 Dunaweal Ln., 6.8mi north of St. Helena via Rte. 29 (entrance on left). Open year-round daily 10:30am–5pm. Closed Jan 1, Easter Sunday, Thanksgiving Day, Dec 25. $2.50 (tasting fee). Guided tours (30min) daily 11am & 2pm.* ♿ 🅿 ☎ *707-942-4981. www.clospegase.com.* Housed in a harmonious sprawl of terra-cotta and earth-toned structures at the base of a small volcanic knoll, Clos Pegase (1987, Michael Graves) is a striking example of the Napa Valley's variety of architectural styles. The winery is named for Pegasus, the famed winged horse of Greek mythology, who is said to have first created wine when he struck his hooves to the ground of Mt. Helicon, unleashing the Spring of the Muses and irrigating a vineyard below.

Conceived as a temple to wine and art, the monumental winery complex reveals architect Graves' signature view of themes from classical antiquity, reflected in oversized columns, triangular pediments and an open central atrium. Selections from owner Jan Shrem's private art collection appear throughout the winery, from the tasting room walls to niches in the 20,000sq ft of storage caves hewn into the knoll of volcanic tufa *(caves open to the public by guided tour only)*. Shrem's residence, also designed by Graves, crowns the knoll *(not open to the public)*.

★**Calistoga** – *Rte. 29, 6mi north of St. Helena.* Founded in 1859 in the shadow of Mt. St. Helena, this residential and resort town of 4,700 unites the flavor of the late-19C frontier era with 20C modernity. Thermal activity in the area, manifested in numerous geysers and hot springs, fueled Calistoga's development as a resort where tourists flocked to "take the waters"; local Native Americans had long sworn by their medicinal properties. According to legend, Calistoga founder **Sam Brannan** (1819-88) stumbled upon the town's name by confusedly (some say drunkenly) declaring it "The Calistoga of Sarafornia" (Saratoga of California) after upstate New York's famed Saratoga Hot Springs. Today, hot-spring spas continue to fuel the town's popularity, though Calistoga is equally well-known for its bottled mineral water.

False-front facades along **Lincoln Avenue**, the town's main thoroughfare, provide a charming frontier flavor, as does the historic **Railroad Depot** *(1458 Lincoln Ave.).* Erected in 1868 to serve the long-defunct Napa Valley Railroad Company, the structure now houses shops, a restaurant and the visitor center.

★**Sharpsteen Museum (M³)** – 🎫 *1311 Washington St., 2 blocks north of Lincoln Ave. Open Apr–Oct daily 10am–4pm. Rest of the year daily noon–4pm. Closed Thanksgiving Day & Dec 25. Contribution requested.* ♿ 🅿 ☏ *707-942-5911. www.sharpsteen-museum.org.* The highlight of this small museum is an intriguing assemblage of miniature **dioramas** recreating scenes of Calistoga's colorful past. Founded in 1979 by Ben Sharpsteen—one of Walt Disney's original 11 animators and later an Oscar-winning producer—the museum also features a collection of early-19C photos, a restored stagecoach and assorted artifacts pertaining to the town's history. Adjoining the museum building is a **cottage** from Sam Brannan's resort, relocated from its original site and fully refurbished to appear as it would have during Calistoga's resort heyday.

3 Ca'Toga Galleria d'Arte
1206 Cedar St., Calistoga.
☏ *707-942-3900.*
www.catoga.com.
Venetian fresco artist Carlo Marchiori's gallery is a remarkable piece of classical Italy transported to the Wine Country. Animal and Commedia dell'Arte themes dominate the eclectic collection, highlighted by a painted terrazzo floor (a chart of the pre-Copernican universe) and barrel-vaulted ceiling (a mural of mythological constellations). Those enamored with Marchiori's style may also purchase tickets to tour his estate, Villa Ca'Toga, just north of Calistoga *(May–Oct Sat 11am).*

★**Old Faithful Geyser** – 🎫 *From Calistoga drive east on Lincoln Ave.; bear left on Grant St. and continue 1mi. Turn left on Tubbs Ln. Entrance on the right. Open Apr–Oct daily 9am–6pm. Rest of the year daily 9am–5pm. $6.* 🍴 ♿ 🅿 ☏ *707-942-6463. www.oldfaithfulgeyser.com.* Located at the foot of Mt. St. Helena, this privately owned geyser is one of the world's three known "faithful" geysers, so named for their regular eruptions (the others are located at Yellowstone National Park and in New Zealand). Approximately every 40 minutes, the geyser spews a column of superheated water some 60ft into the air in a splendid shower of droplets and steam.

★**Petrified Forest** – 🎫 *6mi west of Calistoga. Drive north on Rte. 128; turn left on Petrified Forest Rd. Open Jun–Sept daily 10am–6pm. Rest of the year daily 10am–5pm. Closed Thanksgiving Day & Dec 25. $4.* ♿ 🅿 ☏ *707-942-6667. www.petrifiedforest.org.* A circuit trail through this small, privately owned forest winds past the stone remnants of giant redwoods that were petrified more than three million years ago when Mt. St. Helena erupted, covering the surrounding area with ash and molten lava. Among the highlights is The Giant, an ancient redwood 60ft long and 6ft in diameter.

■ CALISTOGA MUD BATHS AND MINERAL SPRINGS

Volcanic activity in the northern Napa Valley has produced numerous geysers and hot springs, many of which have been harnessed to fuel Calistoga's famed and popular spas. A basic mud bath package, including mud bath, herbal wrap and mineral whirlpool bath, lasts about an hour, and costs $60-$70. Other options include massages, facials and mineral pool soaks.

Calistoga Spa Hot Springs – 1006 Washington St.	☏	707-942-6269
Wilkinson's – 1507 Lincoln Ave.	☏	707-942-4102
Golden Haven Hot Springs – 1713 Lake St.	☏	707-942-6793
Indian Springs – 1712 Lincoln Ave.	☏	707-942-4913
Mount View Spa – 1457 Lincoln Ave.	☏	707-942-5789
Eurospa – 1202 Pine St.	☏	707-942-6829
Calistoga Oasis – 1300 Washington St.	☏	707-942-2122
Nance's Hot Springs – 1614 Lincoln Ave.	☏	707-942-6211
Lincoln Avenue Spa – 1339 Lincoln Ave.	☏	707-942-5296

Auberge du Soleil

180 Rutherford Hill Rd.,
off the Silverado Trail.
☎ 707-963-1211.
www.aubergedusoleil.com.
The breezy terrace of this
elegant country inn offers
the wine-weary traveler an
unparalleled view across the
Napa Valley. Select a meal
from the inspired and highly
acclaimed California-French
menu in the dining room,
or sip a fizzy lemonade
al fresco while contemplating
the silvery acres of olive
trees that surround the inn.

Robert Louis Stevenson State Park –
*7mi north of Calistoga. Take Lincoln Ave.
east; turn left at the Silverado Trail and
right at Rte. 29. Open year-round daily
dawn–dusk.* 🅿 ☎ 707-942-4575.
*www.cal-parks.ca.gov/north/
silverado/rlssp215.htm.* This largely undeveloped park provides an excellent opportunity for hikers and bikers to explore
the rugged, picturesque slopes of Mt. St.
Helena (4,343ft). On its ascent to the
summit, a trail passes the site (near an
abandoned silver mine) where Robert
Louis Stevenson and his wife, Fanny Os-
borne Stevenson, spent their honeymoon
in 1880. After 1mi, the trail emerges
from the forest to join an unpaved fire
road to the summit; from the road,
sweeping **views**★★ extend over the north-
ern Napa Valley and beyond. Another trail winds 6mi east below cliffs of volcanic
origin.

★**Silverado Trail** – Running parallel to Route 29 along the eastern edge of the Napa
Valley between Napa and Calistoga, this scenic road offers a tranquil, relaxed alternative to the often traffic-choked main highway. Its many dips and curves
accommodate the rolling terrain at the base of the ridges bordering the valley, and
acres of serene vineyards are punctuated by numerous wineries. Horseback riders
and bikers are a common sight. Several crossroads link the pastoral Silverado Trail
with Route 29, allowing visitors ample opportunity to sample both aspects of the
Napa Valley.

34 • SONOMA VALLEY★★

www.sonoma.com

Map p 240

The Sonoma Valley is agriculturally and topographically more diverse than the Napa
Valley. Anchored by the historic town of Sonoma, the valley dominates the southern
portion of Sonoma County, where vineyards and wineries rub shoulders with orchards
and fields. The region enjoys a reputation for excellent produce and other farm products, as well as for wines. Approved Viticultural Areas here include Los Carneros,
Sonoma Valley and Sonoma Mountain. Most wineries lie in the vicinity of Sonoma and
along or near Rte. 12 as it leads through the town to Santa Rosa and to the Upper
Sonoma-Russian River Region.

Access – From San Francisco (49mi), take US-101 north; exit at Rte. 37, continue
to Rte. 121 and turn left (north). Continue to Rte. 12 and turn left to Sonoma.

SIGHTS

★★**Sonoma** – *Map opposite*. Site of the California mission chain's northernmost and
final outpost, this charming community of 8,800, set amid the sun-soaked orchards
and vineyards of the Sonoma Valley, is the Wine Country's most historically significant town.

Sonoma was born in 1823 with the founding of the San Francisco Solano Mission.
Nearby, the Mexican government established a military outpost to guard against
the threat of Russian encroachment from Fort Ross, 30mi north. After missions
were secularized in 1834, Gen. Mariano Vallejo was assigned to oversee distribution of the mission lands and to establish a pueblo at Sonoma.

The town's central plaza was the scene on June 14, 1846, of the **Bear Flag Revolt**,
an uprising of American settlers disgruntled with Mexican control of California.
Hoisting a white flag emblazoned with a brown bear and a star, the group proclaimed California an independent republic. A month later, US forces captured
Monterey, declared California a US possession, and effectively ended the short-lived
republic. Formally incorporated in 1850, Sonoma flourished as a supply and trade
center for the area's farms and nascent winemaking industry.

The town retains the charming flavor of that period, though today its historic adobe
buildings, occupied by shops, restaurants and inns, stand beside contemporary
structures. Several noteworthy examples of 19C residential architecture grace the
streets south and west of the plaza, where attractive dwellings display elements
of the Mission, Bungalow and Monterey Colonial styles.

Sonoma State Historic Park★★, headquartered near the Toscano Hotel, maintains and operates the town's key historic sites, including the San Francisco Solano Mission, the Sonoma Barracks, the Toscano Hotel, the Vallejo Home and Petaluma Adobe. *All sights open year-round daily 10am–5pm. Closed Jan 1, Thanksgiving Day, Dec 25. Guided tours available weekends noon–2pm. $1 ticket includes all sights.* 🅿 ☎ *707-938-1519. www.parks .sonoma.net/sonoma.html.*

★**Plaza** – *Bounded by Spain St., 1st St. W., Napa St., & 1st St. E.* Laid out by Mariano Vallejo in 1835, Sonoma's eight-acre plaza is the largest of its kind in California. Anchored at its center by the **City Hall**

① Sonoma Cheese Factory
2 Spain St. ☎ *707-996-1931.* Step off the plaza to taste any of 11 varieties of Jack cheese made at this diminutive "factory," one of the area's largest cheese producers. A gloriously stocked gourmet deli offers a broad selection of local delicacies in addition to fine Sonoma Jack products, perfect for stocking a picnic basket or for sampling on the side terrace.

(1908), an eye-catching Mission Revival structure of roughly hewn basalt, the plaza today is attractively landscaped, laced with walkways and dotted with duck ponds, benches and play areas. On the east side of the Plaza, the **Sonoma Valley Visitor Center** *(453 1st St. E.,* ☎ *707-996-1090)* is lodged in a restored Carnegie Library building (1913). A dramatic bronze **statue** (**1**) near the northeast corner depicts a soldier raising the Bear Flag, commemorating the 1846 revolt. Shady yews, sycamores and plane trees create a peaceful atmosphere amid the bustle of surrounding streets.

★**San Francisco Solano Mission** – *E. Spain St. & 1st St. E.* ♿ ☎ *707-938-9560.* Founded in 1823 by Father José Altamíra, California's final mission was part of a Mexican government effort to strengthen its holdings against potential Russian invasion. The original wooden church and other structures, destroyed during an uprising in 1826, were replaced by adobe buildings the following year. The mission operated until secularization in 1834, when Mariano Vallejo dismantled the property and erected a parish chapel on the site of the original church.

About half of the original mission complex remains standing. It includes the chapel and part of the priests' quarters, restored around 1912. Displays of period furnishings and artifacts retell mission history. They precede an impressive collection of watercolor **paintings** depicting the California missions, executed by Norwegian artist Chris Jorgensen (1859-1935). In the restored chapel, the Stations of the Cross and framed paintings are authentic to the mission period.

Across Spain Street *(no. 217)* stands the **Blue Wing Inn** (1840), an attractive, symmetrical adobe structure that formerly served as a saloon and hotel. The enormous wisteria vine winding along its second-story balcony blooms luxuriantly in March and April.

★**Sonoma Barracks** – *Spain St. & 1st St. E.* This spacious, two-story adobe structure (1841), its wide balcony overlooking the plaza, housed Mexican troops stationed here to guard Sonoma. Following US occupation of California, the barracks served various American regiments during the Mexican-American War. Now a museum of the historic park, the barracks contain displays illustrating aspects of Sonoma's history, including artifacts from the various periods of Mexican and American settlement. To the right of the entrance, the re-created sleeping quarters appear as they might have during military occupation, with cots and bunks in neat rows. A video presentation *(22min)* highlights the northern frontier and the life of Mariano Vallejo. An interpretive store sells reproduction 19C toys and gifts.

Adjacent to the barracks lies the historic **Toscano Hotel** *(viewing windows open year-round daily 10am–5pm; docent tours Sat–Mon 1–4pm; closed Jan 1, Thanksgiving Day, Dec 25; contribution requested;* 🅿 ☎ *707-938-1519),* built as a general store in the 1850s and converted to a boardinghouse in the 1880s for Italian immigrants working in nearby quarries. Today the wood-frame building's fancy Victorian furnishings belie its rough-and-tumble origins. Visitors can peek into cramped upstairs sleeping rooms, examine an intricate hair sculpture fashionable in the mid-19C, or explore the restored kitchen and dining room behind the main building.

Train Town | *PETALUMA ADOBE SHP*

★ Lachryma Montis (Vallejo Home) – *North end of 3rd St. W., .5mi from the plaza. Leave the plaza by W. Spain St. and turn right on 3rd St. W.* ☎ *707-938-9559.* The elegant Gothic Victorian home (1852), set amid attractively landscaped grounds, was named "tear of the mountain" in Latin for the mountain spring on the property. The lovely residence served as the final home of Mariano Vallejo, one of Mexican California's most powerful and colorful figures.

Born in Monterey, **Mariano Vallejo** (1807-90) rose quickly through Mexican military ranks during the first part of his life, becoming commandant of San Francisco's Presidio at age 24. In 1834, Gov. José Figueroa commissioned him to administer the secularization of the Sonoma mission and the founding of a pueblo and defense outpost. In return, Vallejo received 44,000 acres of land near Petaluma, which he developed as a private ranch. Two years later he was appointed commander of all Mexican troops in California. Although he did not contest the American takeover of California, Vallejo was jailed briefly during the Bear Flag Revolt. He was elected to California's first state senate in 1850 and served as mayor of Sonoma (1852-60) before retiring at Lachryma Montis.

The airy, spacious interior of the four-bedroom house is furnished to reflect the period when Vallejo lived there. It provides a delightful picture of his genteel lifestyle. Also on the property is a brick storehouse containing a small interpretive center and collection of artifacts from the 19C, among them a graceful French phaeton used by Vallejo and his family for excursions into town. A stroll through the well-tended grounds reveals a walkway around the spring, small outbuildings and guesthouses, and several orange trees that blossom in the spring and perfume the gardens with a delicious sweet scent.

★★ Buena Vista Winery – *18000 Old Winery Rd. From downtown Sonoma drive east on Napa St., turn left on 7th St. and right on Lovall Valley Rd., then left on eucalyptus-lined Old Winery Rd. for .5mi to the winery. Open year-round daily 10:30am–5pm. Closed Jan 1, Thanksgiving Day, Dec 25. Guided tours (30min) Jul–Sept 11am & 2pm, rest of the year 2pm.* ⊡ ☎ *707-938-1266. www.buenavistawinery.com.* Sonoma County's first premium winery occupies a pleasantly rolling site amid eucalyptus, oak and bay laurel trees. It was founded in 1857 by Agoston Haraszthy. Today, Buena Vista wines are made at another facility 5mi southeast of Sonoma.

Visitors may peer through an iron gate into Haraszthy's renowned **wine cellars**, dug into the limestone hill behind the winery by Chinese laborers in 1863. The stone **Press House** (1862), reputed to be California's oldest remaining winery building, today boasts a handsomely refurbished interior; the wooden beams are original. The second-floor gallery hosts an artist-in-residence program featuring works by local artists and craftspeople.

★ Sebastiani Vineyards – *From downtown Sonoma drive east on Spain St. and turn left on 4th St. E. Open year-round daily 10am–5pm. Winery visit by guided tour only (30min) 10:30am–4pm. Closed Jan 1, Dec 25.* ♿ ⊡ ☎ *707-938-5532. www.sebastiani.com.* This sprawling winery incorporates sections of a livery stable purchased by Italian immigrant Samuele Sebastiani in 1904. Sebastiani transformed the stone structure into a wine cellar; construction of additional buildings progressed throughout the first half of the 20C. The winery's reception room displays rudimentary casks, crushers and other equipment from the early part of the century. On the guided tour, visitors see Sebastiani's two 60,000gal oak fermentation tanks, reputed to be the largest in the world outside of Heidelberg, Germany. Scattered throughout the winery are more than 300 wooden cask heads and doors embellished with whimsical **carvings** executed from 1967 to 1984 by local artist Earle Brown.

Train Town – 🧒 *20264 Broadway, 1mi south of the Plaza on Rte. 12. Open Jun–Sep daily 10am–5pm. Rest of the year Fri–Sun & holidays 10am–5pm. Closed during heavy rain. $3.75.* ♿ ⊡ ☎ *707-938-3912. www.traintown.com.* An old-fashioned carousel and a working scale-model railroad make Train Town a fine destination for families with small children. Passengers big and little sit on benches in low, open-top train cars for a 20min ride through 10 acres of landscaped countryside with bridges, tunnels, waterfalls and miniature buildings. The train stops midway at a petting zoo, where anyone so inclined can touch a goat or a pony. Train souvenirs and fairground snacks add to Train Town's old-time carnival atmosphere.

★★ Jack London State Historic Park – *10mi from Sonoma. 2400 London Ranch Rd., in Glen Ellen. From Sonoma, drive 5mi north on Rte. 12, turn left on Madrone Rd. and right on Arnold Dr. Continue into Glen Ellen and turn left on London Ranch Rd. Open Apr–Oct daily 9:30am–7pm. Rest of the year daily 9:30am–5pm. Museum closed Jan 1, Thanksgiving Day, Dec 25. $3/car. Guided tours (1-2hrs) available.* ⊡ ☎ *707-938-5216. www.parks.sonoma.net/JLPark.html.* Sprawling among peaceful hills in the shadow of Sonoma Mountain is the 800-acre "Beauty Ranch," home of writer Jack London (1876-1916) during the last years of his life. Today a state park, the ranch commemorates this beloved American author of such adventure stories as *The Call of the Wild* (1903) and *The Sea Wolf* (1904).

Sailor on Horseback – Born illegitimately in San Francisco in 1876, Jack London was raised in Oakland, where as a boy he labored in the city's canneries and mills. His huge capacity for hard work and his love of adventure were united with a voracious appetite for books. The poverty-stricken boy was encouraged in his reading at the Oakland Free Library by poet Ina Coolbrith. By age 16, London used his small savings to buy a sloop, the *Razzle Dazzle*. Living a reckless life on the Oakland docks, raiding oyster beds by night on San Francisco Bay, London was introduced to his lifelong nemesis of alcoholism in the waterfront bars, where he also began to nurse his socialist sympathies. He joined a sealing expedition to Siberia and joined the Klondike Gold Rush in 1897. Forced by scurvy to return to Oakland the following year, London directed his energies to writing stories of his adventures in the far north. His first short story, published by the *Overland Monthly*, earned him only $5 but launched a hugely successful career as a novelist, foreign correspondent, short-story writer and lecturer.

In 1905 London, by then renowned as an author and advocate of socialism, purchased a run-down ranch in the hills near Glen Ellen and settled there with his second wife, Charmian. In 1911 the Londons began construction of Wolf House, a massive four-story mansion of hand-hewn lava boulders and redwood logs. Its 26 rooms and nine fireplaces occupied 15,000sq ft. On the night of August 22, 1913, a month before the couple was to move in, a fire roared through the house, leaving only stone walls. Crushed, the Londons never rebuilt Wolf House, but continued to live in a small cottage on the ranch. Jack London died there in 1916 at the age of 40 of uremic poisoning.

Visit – Erected by Charmian London in 1919 as her residence, with the intention of making it a museum to honor her husband, the rustic stone **House of Happy Walls★ (A)** today serves as the park visitor center. The massive building contains memorabilia of both Londons, including artifacts from the author's life and work, letters, photographs, clothing and objects amassed during the couple's world travels, notably Pacific meanderings aboard their boat, the *Snark*.

A trail *(1.2mi round-trip; trailhead at House of Happy Walls)* winds through rolling meadows and forests to the ghostly ruins of **Wolf House★**, in the heart of a glade overlooking a peaceful valley. A short detour from this trail leads to the Londons' gravesite atop a peaceful hill.

© N. Kerby

Wolf House Ruins, Jack London State Historic Park

The **Beauty Ranch Trail★** *(.5mi loop; accessible from the upper parking lot)* wanders about the property past stables, silos, a piggery and the Londons' modest cottage *(open weekends)*. More extensive hiking trails lead throughout the park and up the steep slope of Sonoma Mountain *(summit located on private property)*.

★★**Petaluma Adobe State Historic Park** – *3325 Adobe Rd., Petaluma, 10mi from Sonoma. Leave Sonoma by Rte. 12 south; turn right on Leveroni Rd., left on Arnold Dr. & right on Rte. 116; continue 3mi and bear right on Adobe Rd. Continue 3.25mi to fork in road; turn sharply right and proceed .25mi to park entrance on right. Open year-round daily 10am–5pm. Closed Jan 1, Thanksgiving Day, Dec 25. $2.* ⌂ ☎ *707-938-1519. www.parks.sonoma.net/adobe.html.* In 1834, Mariano Vallejo established a 100sq mi ranch headquarters on this hilltop site overlooking the rolling Sonoma County countryside. Rancho Petaluma thrived, producing cattle, horses, sheep and voluminous crops of grain until Vallejo leased out the property in September 1850.

The state of California took it over in 1951. Today the restored two-story dwelling, one-half its original size, re-creates the atmosphere of a prosperous 19C ranch with interpretive displays on history and especially the Californio lifestyle. Authentic period pieces decorate Vallejo's personal chambers and other rooms upstairs; ground-floor rooms are outfitted with looms, kitchen tools and candle-making equipment. In the courtyard stand hive-shaped ovens once used to prepare meals for the adobe's residents. Living history demonstrations are occasionally mounted in spring and summer *(call for dates and times)*.

★**Petaluma** – *12mi west of Sonoma via Rte. 116 west from Rte. 12. Tourist information* ☎ *707-769-0429. www.petaluma.org.* Set astride the Petaluma River in a fertile valley 40mi north of San Francisco, this agricultural town of 50,913 grew from a hunters' camp to a grain-shipping port in 1852. The **Great Petaluma Mill** *(Petaluma Blvd. N. & B St.; restored as a shopping complex)*, once the region's largest feed mill, survives as a testimony to the city's early industry. In 1879 Lyman Byce put Petaluma on the map when he invented a new incubator for the mass production of poultry. Dubbed the "World's Egg Basket," Petaluma shipped as many as 600 million eggs per year until high labor and feed costs caused the decline of the poultry industry after World War II. The city today remains a dairy center; its wholesome appearance has led it to become a film site for such movies as *American Graffiti* and *Peggy Sue Got Married.*

The **Old Petaluma** historic district *(north of B St. along Petaluma Blvd. N. & Kentucky St.)* reflects the town's Victorian heritage. River commerce and poultry generated the revenue used to build grand cast-iron buildings at the turn of the 20C. Widely used in the construction of commercial buildings in the mid- to late 19C, cast iron was molded and sold in prefabricated parts. It thus provided an inexpensive way to reproduce the ornately carved cornices and columns that distinguished the architectural styles of the day. In addition to its low cost and ease of use, cast iron was thought to protect buildings from fire, a notion that later proved false.

Petaluma's finest row of ironfront architecture *(Western Ave. between Kentucky St. & Petaluma Blvd.)* is bounded on the north corner by the Italianate **Mutual Relief Building** (1885) and on the south by the **Masonic Hall** (1882), topped by a landmark clock tower. Nearby, the **McNear Building** *(15-23 Petaluma Blvd. N.),* with its elegant row of second-story arches, actually incorporates two structures; the original (1886) and the addition (1911) were owned by one of Petaluma's first families. It embraces the Mystic Theater, where the World Wristwrestling Championship *(*☎ *707-778-1430)* is held each October. Garlands, wreaths and marbled columns constitute some of the rich detail that distinguishes the facade of the **Old Opera House★** *(149 Kentucky St.),* built in 1870 to host minstrel shows and theater productions.

Free walking tours of the historic downtown, led by costumed docents, depart twice weekly *(May–Oct Sat–Sun 10:30am)* from the **Petaluma Historical Library & Museum** *(20 4th St.; open year-round Mon, Thu–Sat 10am–4pm, Sun noon–3pm; closed major holidays;* ☎ *707-778-4398).* The sandstone Classical Revival building (1906, Brainerd Jones), a former Carnegie library, houses a collection of artifacts related to local history The building's free-standing, stained-glass dome is the largest in California.

The **Heritage Wall** (1998, Steve della Maggiora) muralizes Petaluma history on a full exterior wall of a building *(Petaluma Blvd. N. & Washington St.)* that once housed the world's only pharmacy for chickens. City maps and other information are available from the Petaluma Area Chamber of Commerce *(799 Baywood Dr.;* ☎ *707-769-0429; www.petaluma.org).*

Marin French Cheese Company – *7500 Red Hill Rd.; 9mi south of Petaluma via D St. Extension. Open year-round daily 8am–5pm. Closed Jan 1, Thanksgiving Day, Dec 25.* ✗ & ▯ ☎ *707-762-6001.* Nestled among tranquil hills next to a tree-shaded pond, the factory offers a behind-the-scenes glimpse of the cheese-making process, from separating the curd to aging the cheese and packaging the final product. A sales room carries a full line of the company's products.

Consult the address book section at the beginning of the guide and the practical information section at the end for a wealth of travel tips, useful addresses and phone numbers, details on shopping, recreation, entertainment and information about annual events.

This region of northern Sonoma County comprises three principal viticultural areas: the Russian River Valley, the Dry Creek Valley and the Alexander Valley. Other smaller areas include Knight's Valley, Green Valley, Northern Sonoma and Chalk Hill.

The lovely **Russian River Valley** follows the curving path of the Russian River as it meanders south through Healdsburg and veers west toward the coast, passing picturesque wineries, rolling vineyards and brooding stands of redwood trees. Swimming, canoeing and kayaking are popular sports on the river where it passes through the resort communities of Forestville, **Guerneville**, Monte Rio and Duncans Mills, and the surrounding forests offer ample opportunities for hiking and camping.

Hemmed by majestic mountain ridges, the **Alexander Valley** extends along the Russian River east and north of Healdsburg. Small, rustic wineries dot the curves and corners of Route 128 as it wanders across a pastoral landscape of vineyard-covered foothills. The 20mi-long valley was named for Cyrus Alexander, a Pennsylvania trapper who settled here in the 1840s.

The delightful **Dry Creek Valley★** extends from the Warm Springs Dam on Lake Sonoma to just south of Healdsburg. Approximately 12mi long, the narrow valley is laced with small, winding roads that meander among vineyards, beneath canopies of trees and across the valley floor. Zinfandel grapes have been grown here, and in the Alexander Valley, for more than a century.

Access – From San Francisco take US-101 north to Santa Rosa (49mi) or to Healdsburg (64mi).

SIGHTS

Santa Rosa – *Exit US-101 north at 3rd St.* The sprawling city of 126,891 is the commercial hub and seat of Sonoma County. Incorporated in 1858, Santa Rosa experienced a population and development boom after the opening of the Golden Gate Bridge and World War II. It was the home of botanist Luther Burbank (1849-1926) and cartoonist Charles Schulz (1922-2000), as well as collector Robert Ripley (1893-1949) of *Believe It or Not!* fame.

US-101 bisects the old and new sections of town. Santa Rosa's historic district, known as **Railroad Square** *(bounded by 3rd, Davis & 6th Sts. and the railroad tracks),* is west of the freeway; it comprises a charming cluster of restored brick and stone buildings constructed in 1870 to serve the Santa Rosa & North Pacific Railroad. Today the square has been transformed into an attractive group of offices, specialty shops, boutiques, restaurants and inns; a visitor center occupies the former train depot *(☎ 707-577-8674; www.visitsantarosa.com).*

East of US-101 and the Santa Rosa Plaza shopping mall is the downtown area, centered on **Courthouse Square** *(Mendocino & Santa Rosa Aves. at 3rd & 4th Sts.).* Framed by fountains, the grassy swath is a popular site for outdoor concerts.

Northeast of downtown are lovely residential streets lined with well-preserved late-19C Victorian homes. One of the finest, located at 1015 McDonald Avenue, was featured in Walt Disney Studios' 1960 movie *Pollyanna.*

 Hotel La Rose
308 Wilson St.; Santa Rosa. ☎ 707-579-3200. *www.hotellarose.com.* A charming historic hotel in Railroad Square, the La Rose was built in 1907 of locally quarried sandstone. Fully renovated, it offers modern rooms with Victorian touches, both in the main building and in a contemporary bank of suites across 5th Street. Josef's restaurant serves fine French cuisine, and a continental breakfast is included in the moderate room rates.

★Luther Burbank Home & Gardens – *Sonoma & Santa Rosa Aves. Home visit by guided tour (30min) only, Apr–Oct Tue–Sun 10am–3:30pm; $3; gardens and Carriage House Museum open year-round daily.* ᕲ ☎ 707-524-5445. *www.luther burbank.org.* Visitors can tour the modest home of the renowned botanist, who moved to Santa Rosa from Massachusetts in 1875, or stroll among lush gardens. Burbank's extensive experiments in plant hybridization—resulting in such now-commonplace strains as the Russet Burbank potato, the Shasta daisy and the Santa Rosa plum—produced more than 800 new varieties of fruits, nuts and vegetables and earned him a reputation as magician of the botanical world.

In the renovated carriage house, displays tell the story of Burbank's life and work. The simple furnishings of his charming Greek Revival home bear witness to the horticulturalist's simple lifestyle, although he clearly had many high-powered friends: photos show him with the likes of Henry Ford and Thomas Edison, Jack London and John Muir, Helen Keller and Paramahansa Yogananda.

Before he acquired a large property outside Santa Rosa, the grounds surrounding Burbank's home served as his laboratory. The gardens were beautifully redesigned in 1960 and renovated in 1992, and today feature many of Burbank's experimental hybrids, including some 100 varieties of roses.

Church of One Tree – *Juilliard Park, across Santa Rosa Ave. from Burbank Home. Closed to the public.* ☎ 707-543-3282. Constructed of boards from a single 275ft redwood tree, this now-dilapidated Gothic Revival church formerly housed a small museum dedicated to the life and discoveries of native-son Ripley, creator of the *Believe It or Not!* cartoons.

★**Sonoma County Museum** (**M¹**) – *425 7th St. Open year-round Wed–Sun 11am–4pm. Closed major holidays. $2.* ⁂ **P** ☎ *707-579-1500. www.pressdemo.com/scmuseum.* Santa Rosa's former post office (1909), designed in the Classical Revival style, now showcases the art, history and culture of Sonoma County. Historical exhibits cover the period from the early 18C, when Miwok, Pomo and Wapo peoples occupied the area, through the growth of the wine industry and recent population growth; they include scale models of historical buildings and an interactive fiber-optic map tracing settlement patterns. Landscapes by William Keith and Thomas Hill are among works presented in the California Gallery of 19C painting. Six to 10 temporary exhibits are presented each year, often interpreting the cultural heritage of segments of the county's population.
A $22-million museum expansion is scheduled to begin in 2001, with completion by 2004. Corridors will link the old post office to a main exhibit building, a courtyard café and a 200-seat auditorium, increasing existing space by four times.

Charles M. Schulz Museum and Research Center (**M²**) – *1 Snoopy Pl., off W. Steele Ln. & Hardies Ln. Exit US-101 north at Steele Ln. and turn left.* ⁂ **P** ☎ *707-579-4452. www.charlesmschulzmuseum.org.* For nearly 50 years, until his death in early 2000, Santa Rosa resident Charles Schulz wrote and illustrated the world's most popular comic strip, *Peanuts.* The often funny, often poignant, always memorable saga of underachiever Charlie Brown and his overachieving dog, Snoopy, appeared in 3,000 newspapers in 75 countries and 40 languages, and was read by hundreds of millions of people.
C. David Robinson's design for this private museum, scheduled to open in fall 2001, reflects Schulz's modest, low-key personality and the sense of community evident in the comic strip. The museum hopes to build an understanding of cartoonists and cartoon art while telling the story of Schulz's life and career, integrating artists who influenced Schulz and whom he in turn influenced. As well, the museum will celebrate the *Peanuts* characters through rotating exhibits of 7,000 original comic strips and examples of 50 years of product items. A 100-seat auditorium will present films; outside will be gardens and other exhibits.

Snoopy's Gallery and Gift Shop – 🧒 *1665 W. Steele Ln. Open year-round daily 10am–6pm. Closed major holidays.* ⁂ **P** ☎ *707-546-3385 or 800-959-3385. www.snoopygift.com.* Lovers of *Peanuts* enjoy a visit to this gallery, where memorabilia, cartoons and original drawings are displayed on the mezzanine level.

Redwood Empire Ice Arena – *1667 W. Steele Ln. Open year-round daily; closed major holidays. Call for hours.* ✗ ⁂ **P** ☎ *707-546-7147.* Schulz himself directed the construction of this Swiss chalet-style arena in 1969. Concerts as well as ice shows are held inside. The facility includes the **Warm Puppy Café**, where Schulz had a Snoopy-like breakfast of jelly donuts every morning.

★**Healdsburg** – Founded in 1857 by Harmon Heald, a migrant farmer-turned-merchant, tranquil Healdsburg *(HEELDS-burg)* sits at the confluence of the Alexander, Dry Creek and Russian River valleys. Several excellent restaurants and inns make it an ideal starting point for forays into these areas. At the heart of this town of 9,600 is picturesque, one-acre **Plaza Park** *(Healdsburg Ave. and Plaza, Center & Matheson Sts.)*, scene of numerous civic festivals and events. Dozens of different species of trees grown in and around the plaza; request a walking-tour brochure, "Tree Walk of Healdsburg," from the Healdsburg Area Chamber of Commerce *(217 Healdsburg Ave.;* ☎ *707-433-6935).*
The town today is promoting itself as a "Carmel of the Wine Country," with restaurants, galleries and spas to counter its Monterey Peninsula prototype. The Spa Off The Plaza *(706 Healdsburg Ave.;* ☎ *707-431-7938)*, lodged in a 1909 Craftsman-style building, is one such establishment offering day-spa services.

Healdsburg Museum (**M³**) – *221 Matheson St., 2 blocks east of the plaza. Open year-round Tue–Sun 11am–4pm. Closed major holidays.* ⁂ **P** ☎ *707-431-3325.* Housed in a beautifully preserved former Carnegie Library building, this small museum contains a collection of artifacts from indigenous peoples and from California's Mexican period. Highlights include photographs, Pomo Indian baskets, grinding rocks and weapons, bringing to life upper Sonoma's colorful history.

© Robert Holmes

Harvest at Jordan Vineyards, Alexander Valley

★**Simi Winery** – *16275 Healdsburg Ave., Healdsburg. Open year-round daily 10am–4:30pm. Closed Jan 1, Easter Sunday, Thanksgiving Day, Dec 25. Winery visit by guided tour (1hr) only, daily 11am, 1 & 3pm.* ♿ 🅿 ☎ *707-433-6981. www.simi-winery.com.* Founded in 1883 by Italian immigrants Giuseppe and Pietro Simi, this winery today boasts some of the oldest vines and stone cellars in California along-side an ultra-modern winemaking facility. The massive stone cellars were built in two phases, visible in the building's two types of stonework. In the mid-1880s, Chinese workers constructed the original south side, as well as railroad tracks that still run through the middle of the property. (They were once used to ship bottles directly from the cellars.) The north side was constructed in 1904 by Italian masons under the direction of Isabel Simi, Giuseppe's daughter, who (according to local lore) took over management of the winery at age 14 when her father and uncle died of influenza. Legend has it that after Prohibition, with the winery all but bank-rupt, Isabel rolled a barrel onto the old highway and offered free sips of wine, thereby establishing California's first tasting room.

A guided tour takes visitors through the historic stone cellars and into a high-tech fermentation center that is considered one of the finest in the state.

★**Ferrari-Carrano Winery** – *9mi north of Healdsburg at 8761 Dry Creek Rd.* ☎ *707-433-6700. www.ferrari-carrano.com.* Five acres of stunning parterre gardens surround a spectacular Italianate villa that is the focus of this fine estate. Visitors enter through wrought-iron gates, meandering along garden paths, past a rippling stream flanked by exotic shrubs and colorful beds of annuals and perennials. An Italian court-yard provides the formal entrance to the Renaissance-style **Villa Fiore** (1997), its stone columns and arches rising above the Dry Creek Valley. From an elegant tasting room and wine shop, a curving stone staircase descends to a vaulted, cobblestone-floored viewing area, revealing more than 1,100 French oak barrels aging fine red wines.

★**Lake Sonoma** – *11mi north of Healdsburg by Dry Creek Rd. www.parks.sonoma .net/laktrls.html.* Nestled in the coastal foothills of northern Sonoma County, this elongated lake was created in 1983 when the Warm Springs Dam was constructed at the confluence of Warm Springs and Dry creeks. Now a popular recreation area, Lake Sonoma offers a plethora of activities including boating, swimming, fishing, picnicking, hiking and camping in and around its sapphire waters.

★★**Visitor Center and Fish Hatchery** – 🎦 *3333 Skaggs Springs Rd. Open year-round daily 9:30am–4:30pm (hours may vary by season).* ⚠ *($10-$32)* 🅿 ☎ *707-433-9483. www.spn.usace.army.mil.* Displays of craftwork and artifacts in the Visitor Center exemplify the traditions and beliefs of the indigenous Pomo people, and the effects of the arrival of Hispanic and Caucasian settlers. Informative panels illustrate geo-logical formations and thermal activity in the area.

The adjacent state-of-the-art hatchery building, created by the US Army Corps of Engineers to mitigate environmental disruption of Dry Creek caused by the Warm Springs Dam, offers a rare opportunity to observe the spawning and hatching of steelhead trout and coho (silver) and chinook salmon. Fish climb an inclined channel or "ladder" into the hatchery where they are held, sorted and spawned— activities visible from a mezzanine-level interpretive center. *Viewing times: Jan–Mar for steelhead trout; early Oct–Dec for salmon. Call ahead to verify.*

Lake Sonoma Overlook – *2.5mi from Visitor Center via Stewarts Point Rd.; follow signs.* Designed in harmony with its natural surroundings, the wood-timbered overlook offers soaring **views**★★ of the lake, dam and surrounding mountains, including Mt. St. Helena in neighboring Napa Valley.

★Hop Kiln Winery – *6050 Westside Rd., 6mi southwest of Healdsburg. Open year-round daily 10am–5pm. Closed Jan 1, Easter Sunday, Thanksgiving Day, Dec 25.* ▣ ☎ *707-433-6491. www.hopkilnwinery.com.* This historic **hop barn★** (1905), one of the finest examples of its type, functioned as part of northern California's hop-growing industry. Hops were dried in three huge wooden kilns, resembling giant inverted funnels, before being pressed and baled for shipment to area breweries. The kiln was renovated as a winery in 1975.

★Korbel Champagne Cellars – *13250 River Rd., 2.5mi northeast of Guerneville. Visit by guided tour (50min) only, May–Sept daily 10am–3:45pm each hour. Rest of the year daily 10am–3pm. Closed Easter Sunday, Thanksgiving Day & Dec 25.* ✗ ㊡ ▣ ☎ *707-824-7000.* In the early 1870s, Czech immigrants Anton, Francis and Joseph Korbel acquired a lumber mill at this site on the sloping banks of the Russian River. By the end of that decade, having largely denuded the surrounding hillsides of their redwoods, the Korbels planted grapevines among the stumps. Construction of a large, handmade-brick winery building was completed in 1886 for the production of brandy and sparkling wine.

The highlight of a visit to Korbel is an informative guided tour covering both historic and contemporary processes of *méthode champenoise* sparkling-wine production. Enjoy a wander through the 250-variety antique **rose garden** *(guided tours May–Sept Tue–Sun 11am, 1 & 3pm)* on the slope below the Korbel family summer home. Stroll through the old train depot, formerly the terminus of the Fulton-Guerneville branch of the Northwest Pacific Railroad. After dining in the restaurant or picking up picnic food in the deli, you can take an impromptu tour of the Russian River Brewing Company—Korbel's response to visitors with champagne tastes but beer budgets.

★Armstrong Redwoods State Reserve – 🄺🄸🄳🄴 *2mi north of Guerneville on Armstrong Woods Rd. Open year-round daily 8am–one hour past sunset. $2/car. Guided tours (30min) available by reservation.* △ *(in adjacent Austin Creek State Recreation Area)* ▣ ☎ *707-869-2015. www.parks.sonoma.net/Armstrng.html.* Lush, dense forests of varied species of trees surround a 500-acre grove of ancient redwoods that survived 19C logging operations thanks to the conservationist efforts of Col. James Armstrong. Today the grove forms the heart of an 800-acre state park that boasts some of Sonoma County's finest surviving redwood trees. A self-guided nature trail *(.5mi)* passes through cool, fern-laced glades.

36 • PALO ALTO★

Tourist information ☎ 650-324-3121 or www.batnet.com/pacc

Map of principal sights p 12

An affluent college town of about 59,000 situated between the marshlands of San Francisco Bay and the Santa Cruz Mountains, Palo Alto derives its name from the twin-trunked coast redwood under which Gaspar de Portolá camped on his 1769 expedition. Now single-trunked and timeworn, **El Palo Alto**, "the tall tree," still stands in a small park by the railroad tracks off Alma Avenue. It remains the official symbol of Stanford University.

★★STANFORD UNIVERSITY

Circled by Campus Dr. E. & W., west of El Camino Real (Rte. 82) via Palm Dr. Visitor information at entrance to Quadrangle and in lobby of Memorial Auditorium (open year-round Mon–Fri 8am–5pm, weekends 9am–5pm; closed Dec 18–Jan 4). Student-led campus tours (1hr) depart Memorial Auditorium year-round daily 11am & 3:15pm. ✗ ᵫ 🅿. ☎ 650-723-2560. www.stanford.edu.

Established by railroad magnate Leland Stanford, this renowned institution sprawls across 8,180 acres. Its gracious, Spanish-flavored Richardsonian Romanesque buildings are shaded by eucalyptus, bay and palm trees.

Born on a farm in New York, the university's founder, **Leland Stanford** (1824-93), was a lawyer by training and an opportunist by nature. He moved to California during the Gold Rush, became state governor, then president of the Central Pacific Railroad, a high-risk venture that earned him a fortune.

In 1884 Stanford and his wife, Jane, lost their only child, 15yr-old Leland, Jr., to typhoid fever. The bereft couple, declaring that "the children of California shall be our children," set out to establish a university on the grounds of their Palo Alto ranch. Stanford directed it to be built on flat land in the form of a parallelogram. Architect Charles Allerton Coolidge and landscape architect Frederick Law Olmsted jointly conceived the campus plan and the low, arcaded buildings of the university, which opened in 1891. Two years later, Stanford died at age 69 and his wife was left to shoulder the 1890s financial depression that threatened the existence of the university. By the early 20C, with the economic crisis resolved, Stanford University was on its way to becoming a solid, and eventually celebrated, academic institution. Though the campus suffered severe earthquake damage in 1906 and 1989, it has remained an architecturally impressive institution, it has remained a leading academic and research center, with a current enrollment of some 14,000 students. Among its 1,455 faculty members are 12 Nobel laureates, four Pulitzer Prize winners, and 20 recipients of the National Medal of Science.

The northwest corner of campus still holds the original **Red Barn** *(Fremont & Electioneer Rds.)*, original Victorian stables built by Leland Stanford more than a century ago. Extending beside it is the **Stanford Golf Course** *(Junipero Serra Blvd. & Campus Dr. W.)*, where the world's best golfer, Eldrick "Tiger" Woods, first achieved teen-age fame as two-time national amateur champion.

★**Main Quadrangle** – The main entrance road from downtown Palo Alto leads up Palm Drive to the historic heart of campus. The expansive, tiled courtyard is bordered by the university's 12 original colonnaded buildings and anchored by the magnificent **Memorial Church**★★ *(open year-round Mon–Fri 8:30am–5pm; guided tours Fri 2pm; ☎ 415-723-1762)*. Built in 1903 by Jane Stanford to commemorate her husband, the church features elaborate Byzantine-style mosaics, stained glass and a renowned 7,777-pipe organ equipped to play Renaissance and Baroque music.

★**Hoover Tower** – *Observation deck open year-round daily 10am–4:30pm. Closed between academic quarters. $2. ᵫ ☎ 650-723-2053.* The landmark 285ft campanile houses part of the Hoover Institution on War, Revolution and Peace, a public-policy research center inspired by university alumnus Herbert Hoover. Two museum galleries *(both sides of entrance hall)* are devoted to the considerable accomplishments of Hoover and his wife, Lou Henry Hoover. The top of the tower features a 35-bell carillon and an observation deck offering panoramic views of the campus and of San Francisco and the Bay Area to the north.

★**Iris & B. Gerald Cantor Center for Visual Arts** – *Lomita Dr. & Museum Way. Open year-round Wed & Fri–Sun 11am–5pm, Thu 11am–8pm. Closed major holidays. ✗ ᵫ 🅿 ☎ 650-723-4177. www.stanford.edu/dept/SUMA.* This university museum houses a dazzling, eclectic collection of 20,000 pieces of ancient to contemporary sculpture, paintings, crafts and ceremonial artworks from Africa, Oceania, Asia, Europe and the Americas. Noted for its cultivated eclecticism, it is renowned for its ambitious collection of more than 200 Rodin sculptures.

■ Herbert Hoover

One of Stanford University's most illustrious alumni was Herbert Hoover (1874-1964), a member of the institution's first class in 1891 and a graduate in geology. Hoover traveled the globe as a mining engineer for nearly two decades—managing mines in Russia, China, Burma and Australia—before entering public life in 1914, when he established a humanitarian relief organization in Europe. His role as an adviser to President Woodrow Wilson led to his appointment as secretary of commerce in the Harding and Coolidge administrations of the 1920s. Hoover subsequently was elected US President in 1928 and served one term.

In 1945, Hoover was called back to public service by President Harry Truman to coordinate dispersal of food to 28 nations during a post-Second World War famine. He served as an adviser to President Dwight Eisenhower in the 1950s.

Before he died at age 90, Hoover wrote more than 30 books and expanded a world-renowned library that he had established at Stanford in 1919. He maintained an office on the 11th floor of the Hoover Tower, built in 1941.

Formerly the Leland Stanford Jr. Museum, the Canton's precursor was founded by Leland and Jane Stanford as a memorial to their son, an amateur collector of eclectic tastes. Junior's well-rounded collections formed the nucleus of the museum (1894, Percy and Hamilton), designed after the National Archaeological Museum of Athens and built of reinforced concrete. When it opened, it was both the first neoclassical and largest private museum in the US.

Although Jane Stanford bolstered the collection by donating 15,000 additional objects before her death in 1905, the early museum closed after suffering heavy damage in the earthquake of 1906. For half a century, the building was assigned for use by other university departments. The museum was revived in the 1950s, but severe structural damage during the Loma Prieta earthquake of 1989 again forced its closure. The university responded with an ambitious campaign to retrofit the original 72,000sq ft building, while architect James Polshek & Partners designed a rectangular, 42,000sq ft addition of steel, glass and stucco. It reopened in 1999.

The result, renamed after major contributors and bolstered by additional collections, is now a premier university teaching museum that illustrates comparative objets d'art from a broad spectrum of cultures and eras.

Visit – Designed by Venetian artist Antonio Paoletti, the 13 mosaics across the front facade of the original building illustrate the progress of civilization through learning and arts. Three pairs of massive entry doors, each weighing 600 pounds, are encased in bronze panels depicting examples of ancient architecture. The two-story entry hall, clad in marble and with floors of terrazzo, is presided over by a statue of Athena. Flanking the entrance, the two original wings exhibit the Classical, historical and international collections, while the new addition—behind the entry hall—houses contemporary art and rotating exhibits. Two courtyards are devoted to sculpture.

A central gallery behind the entry lobbies acknowledges the museum's origin in the **Stanford Family Memorabilia**. It includes family portraits, curios from young Leland's collections, the boy's death mask, and the **Golden Spike** from the ceremonial completion of the first transcontinental railroad.

★**Rodin Sculpture Garden** – ☎ 415-723-3469. Located on the southwest side of the Cantor Center, this one-acre garden displays 20 large-scale bronze casts by French sculptor Auguste Rodin, including his famed *The Gates of Hell* (1880-1900). A half-dozen casts from Rodin's series *The Burghers of Calais* are also displayed in a courtyard on the Serra Street side of the Main Quad. Elsewhere on campus are sculptures by such prominent artists as Joan Miró, Alexander Calder and Henry Moore. A free *Guide to Outdoor Sculpture* is available at the adjacent art museum and the campus visitor information booth.

Stanford Linear Accelerator Center – *2575 Sand Hill Rd., just east of I-280, Menlo Park. Visitors center open year-round daily Mon–Fri 8am–5pm; guided tours (2hrs) by reservation.* ✗ ᔕ ▣ ☎ *650-926-2204. www.slac.stanford.edu.* Operated by the university for the US Department of Energy, SLAC opened in 1961 as a research facility in particle physics. Within this 480-acre facility, which includes a 2mi-long linear accelerator, scientists probe the structure of matter on atomic and subatomic levels with x-rays and particle beams. In the small visitor center, exhibits describe such discoveries as quarks and explore successes in biomedical and environmental research. Also displayed is a skeletal cast of an ancient walrus-like mammal, *Paleoparadoxia*, found at during excavation at SLAC.

ADDRESS BOOK

Dining in the South Bay and Peninsula

Please see explanation on p 42.

A.P. Stump's – *163 W. Santa Clara St., San Jose.* & ☎ *408-292-9928. www.apstumps.com.* **$$$ New American.** Lodged in the 1883 Masson-LeFranc Building in downtown San Jose, this cavernous restaurant features weekend jazz on an outdoor patio. The creative menu offers such entrées as grilled quail with black-truffle gnocchi and filet mignon with potato and hazelnut fritters.

Evvia Estiatorio – *420 Emerson St., Palo Alto.* & ☎ *650-326-0983. http:// evviaestiatorio.com.* **$$$ Greek.** No stodgy Balkan eatery, Evvia's open kitchen focuses on Californian approaches to Aegean classics. You'll get spanakopita (spinach pie) and moussaka (lamb-eggplant casserole), to be sure, but also octopus with roasted bell peppers and salmon with a tomato-ouzo sauce.

Rue de Paris – *19 N. Market St., San Jose.* & ☎ *408-298-0704. www.ruede paris.com. Dinner only. Closed Sun.* **$$$ French.** Best of its kind in the Silicon Valley, this romantic restaurant is adorned with hand-painted murals of Paris street scenes. Diners may start with escargots, continue with a beef or seafood entrée, and treat themselves to a Grand Marnier soufflé for dessert.

E&O Trading Company – *96 S. First St., San Jose.* & ☎ *408-938-4100. www.eotrading.com. Closed Sun.* **$$ Asian fusion.** Capturing the essence of a legendary 19C friendship between an Indonesian spice merchant and a British ale trader, this intriguing restaurant focuses on grills and small plates of Indian and Southeast Asian cuisines. Colorful, casual décor enhances the experience.

Moss Beach Distillery – *Beach Way & Ocean Blvd., off Hwy. 1, Moss Beach.* & ☎ *650-728-5595. www.mossbeachdistillery.com.* **$$ American.** Built in the 1920s as a Hollywood retreat, this historic building became a Prohibition-era hideout for bootleggers. It's now a steak-and-seafood eatery where diners can take in beautiful sunsets while whale-watching from an outdoor patio.

Peninsula Fountain & Grill – *566 Emerson St., Palo Alto.* & ☎ *650-323-3131.* **$ American.** This classic 1923 soda fountain endeavors to keep its menu and prices as authentic as its atmosphere. Cheeseburgers and milkshakes highlight the menu, which also includes such items as meatloaf and fried chicken.

Staying in the South Bay and Peninsula

Please see explanation on p 48.

The Fairmont San Jose – *170 S. Market St., San Jose.* ✗ & 🅿 🌫 ☎ *408-998-1900. www.fairmont.com. 541 rooms.* **$$$$$** Catering primarily to business travelers, this 20-story grand hotel in the heart of downtown will increase its size by nearly 50 percent with the completion of a new tower by the end of 2001. Guestrooms are elegant and sophisticated.

Stanford Park Hotel – *100 El Camino Real, Menlo Park.* ✗ & 🅿 🌫 ☎ *650-322-1234. www.woodsidehotels.com. 163 rooms.* **$$$$$** Near Stanford University, this handsome inn boasts room with vaulted ceilings, granite fireplaces, English yew-wood armoires and writing desks, and courtyard views. Its warm décor and guest library contribute to a high-brow academic flavor.

Hotel De Anza – *233 W. Santa Clara St., San Jose.* ✗ & 🅿 ☎ *408-286-1000. www.HotelDeAnza.com. 101 rooms.* **$$$$** Built in 1931, fully renovated six decades later, the historic De Anza retains an Art Deco-era appeal. Rooms are spacious and contemporary; not only do guests get a morning paper with their coffee, they're invited to "raid the pantry" for late-night deli snacks.

Costanoa Coastal Lodge & Camp – *An hour's drive south of San Francisco on Hwy. 1, Pescadero.* & 🅿 ☎ *650-879-1100. www.costanoa.com. 52 units.* **$$** A "base camp for coastal adventures" near the Año Nuevo State Reserve, Costanoa offers three types of accommodation—a stylish 40-room lodge, a set of cabins favored by families and couples willing to share a bath, and a handful of tent bungalows. A general store and spa complete the complex.

EXCURSIONS

NASA Ames Research Center – *Moffett Field, Mountain View. From US-101, take Moffett Field exit; turn right to main gate, then left .4mi on R.T. Jones Rd. to Gate 17C. Visitor center open year-round Mon–Fri 8am–4:30pm.* ☎ *650-604-6274. www.arc.nasa.gov.* Founded in 1939 at a former naval air field as an aircraft research laboratory, this 430-acre facility has been a part of the National Aeronautics and Space Administration since 1958. Now the hub of NASA information technologies, Ames also is the lead NASA agency in the study of gravity, astrobiology and Mars exploration, to name but a few. The center harbors the world's largest wind tunnel and several advanced flight simulators.

Open to the public is a visitor center, in a facility once used to evaluate early space capsule designs, that showcases the center's research and discoveries—including planetary exploration concepts, space-suit technology and oblique wing research.

★★**Filoli** – *13mi north of Palo Alto at Woodside and 30mi south of San Francisco; take I-280 to Edgewood Rd.; exit west, turn right on Cañada Rd. and continue 1.3mi to gate. Visit by guided tour (2hrs) mid-Feb–Oct Tue–Thu, reservations required. Visit by self-guided tour Thu–Sat 10am–3pm. $10. ⅹ(Tea Room) �& ▯ ☎ 650-364-8300. www.filoli.org.* Nestled into the inland side of the Coast Range's heavily wooded foothills, this 654-acre estate is precariously situated astride the San Andreas Fault. Yet its elegance exemplifies the gracious lifestyle made possible at the turn of the 20C by fortunes derived from several of California's great economic forces: mining, real-estate speculation, water development and agriculture.

The formal Italian Renaissance gardens and U-shaped, "Modified" Georgian Revival mansion (1915-17, Willis Polk) were commissioned by William Bourn II (1857-1936), owner of the Empire Mine in Grass Valley; at the time, Empire was California's most productive hard-rock gold mine. Bourn was also president of the Spring Valley Water Company, consisting of Crystal Springs Lake and its adjacent lands, and it was here that he sited his 43-room country estate. Filoli (named for a favorite Bourn credo, *Fight for a just cause; Love your fellow man; Live a good life*), with its large, mature trees spreading shadows over acres of well-kept lawns, still expresses the confidence of settled rural wealth.

After the deaths of Bourn and his wife in 1936, Filoli was acquired by its only other owner, William P. Roth. Roth died in 1963. His widow, Lurline Roth, who expanded but did not redesign the gardens, donated Filoli to the National Trust for Historic Preservation in 1975.

★★**Mansion** – The ground floor features furniture and art from both the Bourn and Roth families; an extensive collection of 17C-18C Irish and English furnishings and decorative arts bequeathed by Melville Martin in 1998; and a smaller number of gifts and pieces on loan from the Fine Arts Museums of San Francisco.

House tours commence in the Reception Room, where a 17ft-by-33ft Persian carpet (19C), woven over three generations, covers the floor. The kitchen features an impressive ship's stove acquired in 1942 from the Matson Navigation Company, owned by Lurline Roth's father. The grand ballroom, with its 22ft ceilings, is adorned with Ernest Peixotto murals (1925) depicting Ireland's Lakes of Killarney and Muckross House, an 11,000-acre estate given by the Bourns to their daughter on her marriage in 1910. Ruins of a Franciscan abbey destroyed by Oliver Cromwell in 1644 are preserved in distant imagery in the murals.

★★★**Gardens** – Designed by Bruce Porter with continuing assistance from Isabella Worn, this 16-acre botanical wonder (1917-20) successfully combines the formal with the natural. Planned as a sequence of outdoor "rooms," each with its own horticultural and seasonal delights, the gardens are aligned along the same north-south axis as the house, extending the lines of the mansion's transverse hallway. Some of the most interesting plants were gifts or purchases from foreign governments, disposing of display specimens after the 1915 Panama-Pacific International Exposition. Many of the column-shaped Irish yews, used as pillars in Filoli's garden "architecture," started as cuttings from the yews at Muckross. All floral arrangements on display in the mansion are supplied by the gardens.

Hiller Aviation Museum – ⓚ 601 Skyway Rd., San Carlos, just off US-101 north at Redwood Shores Pkwy. Open year-round daily 10am–5pm. Closed major holidays. $7. ☎ 650-654-0200. www.hiller.org. Exhibits proceed chronologically through the history of manned flight, with special emphasis on the greater Bay Area. One of the earliest aircraft displayed is the 1883 Gull, a fully controllable glider invented by John J. Montgomery, a Santa Clara University engineering professor. Montgomery later was killed testing his third glider prototype in 1911—the same year the Curtiss Pusher landed and took off from the first "aircraft carrier," the USS *Pennsylvania*, in San Francisco Bay. Further exhibits progress from early fixed-wing aircraft to blended and oblique wing designs, and include such innovations as the Flying Platform and the high-altitude Boeing Condor. Many of the aircraft on display have been refashioned piece-by-piece by resident craftsmen, whose current projects may be viewed through the windows of the Restoration Workshop.

Coyote Point Museum for Environmental Education – ⓚ 1651 Coyote Point Dr., San Mateo, east of US-101 via Poplar Ave. or Dore Ave. exits. Open year-round Tue–Sat 10am–5pm, Sun noon–5pm. Closed Jan 1, Thanksgiving Day, Dec 24-25. $3 (free 1st Wed). ☎ 650-342-7755. www.coyoteptmuseum.org. Geared toward teaching children the natural environment of the Bay Area, this museum offers an interactive walk "from the mountains to the bay" with small animals and an aquarium. A wildlife habitat features more than 40 species of indigenous live animals. From eucalyptus- and pine-shrouded Coyote Point, there are magnificent views of the San Francisco and Oakland skylines. Adjacent Coyote Point Recreation Area ($4) has nature trails, a beach and a saltwater marsh as well as picnic grounds, a marina and a fishing jetty.

Tourist information ☎ 408-283-8833 or www.sanjose.org
Map of principal sights p 12

Now California's third largest city with some 870,000 residents, the self-proclaimed "capital of Silicon Valley" bustles with high-tech prosperity. In San Jose's revitalized downtown, stately old buildings mix with modern high-rises amidst palm-lined plazas and avenues. Spread through the city are a number of unusual museums, from innovative new ones to "mysterious" older ones.

Historical Notes

Spanish administrators chose this site in the fertile Santa Clara Valley in 1777 for the founding of El Pueblo San José de Guadalupe, the first civilian settlement in Alta California. The new farming community on the banks of the Guadalupe River supplied food to soldiers quartered in the presidios in San Francisco and Monterey. Twenty years later, the San José Mission was founded 13mi to the north. In 1849, three years after the American takeover of California, members of the state's Constitutional Convention chose San Jose as the state capital, an honor it held for several months before the seat of government was moved to Vallejo.

From the mid-19C to mid-20C, agriculture remained San Jose's chief industry. Abundant flowering orchards attracted weekend tourists who came from throughout the Bay Area to enjoy "the Garden City in the Valley of Heart's Delight." In the postwar period, the character of Santa Clara County changed dramatically as structures housing electronics industries began to sprout in place of the orchards, and by the late 1960s "Silicon Valley" had encompassed San Jose. Such computer giants as IBM, Hewlett-Packard, Apple, Novell and Adobe Systems developed facilities in the city and in neighboring communities. San Jose today ranks as the 11th largest city in the US.

Visiting San Jose – The downtown heart of San Jose, focused around **Plaza de Cesar Chavez** *(Market St. & Park Ave.)*, site of frequent civic festivals, bustles seven days a week. Most museums and other visitor attractions are open daily except Mondays. Parking is not much of a problem on weekends, when most offices are closed. Validated parking is available at many downtown garages. The **Valley Transportation Authority (VTA)** light-rail system *(☎ 408-321-2300; www.vta.org)* runs 24 hours daily, linking most hotels and attractions at a nominal cost.

For maps and visitor information, contact the **San Jose Convention & Visitors Bureau** *(333 W. San Carlos St., Suite 1000; ☎ 408-283-8833 or 888-726-5673; www.sanjose.org)*. Or stop by the **Visitor Information & Business Center** in the San Jose McEnery Convention Center *(W. San Carlos & Market Sts.; open year-round Mon–Fri 8am–5pm, weekends 11am–5pm; ☎ 408-977-0900)*.

The best way to experience the high-technology ambience of Silicon Valley might be on a guided tour, as most firms are not normally open to the public. **Tech Tours** *(☎ 408-358-0768; www.tech-tours.com)* incorporate a history of the late-20C development of the valley.

Plaza de Cesar Chavez

SIGHTS

★★The Tech Museum of Innovation – 🧒 *20 S. Market St. at Park Ave. Open July 5–Labor Day Fri–Wed 10am–6pm, Thu 10am–8pm. Rest of the year Fri–Wed 10am–5pm. Closed Dec 25. $8 each for museum and theater; $13.50 combined ticket. ✗ ᕕ ☎ 408-294-8324. www.thetech.org.* This state-of-the-art, interactive exhibit hall (popularly known as "The Tech") is designed to encourage the spirit of innovative curiosity, characteristic of the original techno-tinkerers of Silicon Valley. Housed in a domed, mango-colored building with azure highlighting, The Tech is entertaining for all ages, but specifically courts the youthful "information generation" with playful, participatory exhibits in such fields as communications, microelectronics, space exploration, robotics and biotechnology.

Established in 1990, the museum increased its size six-fold (to 132,000sq ft) when it moved to its present site in 1998. A fascinating mobile sculpture, George Rhoads' *Science on a Roll*, enlivens the side-entrance sidewalk on Park Avenue, where crowds gather outside to watch a continuous sequence of clanging and clattering billiard balls travel by ramps and elevator through a precisely synchronized mechanical maze.

Visit – The main entrance is on the middle floor of a three-story atrium. Escalators lead up and down to exhibit floors. On the Upper Level, exhibits in **"Life Tech: The Human Machine"** *(gallery 1)* invite adults and children to test their reactions on a virtual Olympic bobsled ride; design a human-powered bicycle, boat or airplane; and tour a virtual operating room that depends on non-invasive technologies for diagnosis and treatment of the human body. **"Innovation: Silicon Valley and Beyond"** *(gallery 2)* provides a glimpse of robotics and computer-generated design, encouraging visitors to try their hands at inventing a roller coaster or high-tech bicycle, or in creating a three-dimensional self-portrait with a laser scanner. One display relates how companies design and manufacture silicon microchips in a "cleanroom," an industrial innovation that sparked Silicon Valley's heady propulsion to the forefront of the technology revolution.

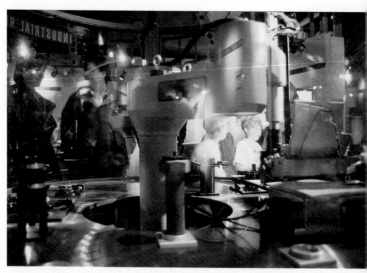

Robotic Artist at Work

Descending to the Lower Level, changing exhibits in **"Center of the Edge"** portray state-of-the-art technology now under development. Visitors to **"Communication: Global Communications"** *(gallery 3)*, may create and manipulate their own film clips, cartoons or multimedia images in the electronic Digital Studio, or create a personalized internet "newspaper" on the computer. In **"Exploration: New Frontiers"** *(gallery 4)*, budding explorers may pilot a robotic submarine, test-drive a remote-control planetary rover, design an earthquake-proof building, or test hand-eye coordination with a laser affixed to a space-age chair.

Adjacent to the ground-floor street entrance, the 295-seat **Hackworth IMAX Dome Theater** screens documentary films on a hemispherical screen that covers 80 percent of the dome, engulfing the audience with images and sound.

San Jose Museum of Art – *110 S. Market St. Open year-round Tue–Sun 10am–5pm (Thu 8pm). Closed Jan 1, Thanksgiving Day, Dec 25. $7 ($3.50 Thu 5–8pm). ✗ ᕕ ☎ 408-294-2787. www.sjmusart.org.* Established in 1933 in an old sandstone Richardsonian Romanesque post office (1892) and expanded in 1991 with a modern wing of glass, aluminum and concrete, the museum faces upon

Fairmont Plaza. At any one time, four major exhibits are presented; rotated quarterly on a staggered schedule, they may feature cutting-edge paintings, sculpture, photographs and installation art by California artists, as well as nationally significant traveling shows. Three Dale Chihuly glass chandeliers above the main entrance are the only permanent pieces in the collection. Wall text is in Vietnamese and Tagalog as well as Spanish and English, an indication of the great ethnic variety in the South Bay area.

The Cathedral Basilica of Saint Joseph – *80 S. Market St. Open year-round daily.* ☎ *408-283-8100. www.stjosephcathedral.org.* Founded in 1803 as a small adobe church, hub of the first Catholic parish in California, this beautiful building was constructed in 1877 by Brian Clinch—a devout architect who read the New Testament in Greek. The cathedral was dedicated as a minor basilica in 1997. The impressive interior is worth a visit.

San Jose Museum of Quilts & Textiles – *110 Paseo de San Antonio at 3rd St. Open year-round Tue–Sun 10am–5pm (Thu 8pm). Closed major holidays & between shows. $4 (free 1st Thu).* ♿ ☎ *408-971-0323. www.sjquiltmuseum.org.* Regularly changing exhibits focus on works by traditional and contemporary quilt and woven tapestry artists. Costumes and dolls from various ethnic communities suggest the diversity of design and craft traditions.

★**Children's Discovery Museum of San Jose** – 🧒 *180 Woz Way, off W. San Carlos St. at Rte. 87. Open mid-Jun–Labor Day Mon–Sat 10am–5pm, Sun noon–5pm; rest of the year, closed Mon. Closed Jan 1, 2nd week of Sept, Dec 25. $6.* 🍴 ♿ ☎ *408-298-5437. www.cdm.org.* Housed in a whimsical purple structure (1991, Ricardo Legorreta) that resembles building blocks, this bilingual (English-Spanish) museum dominates Guadalupe River Park. Hands-on exhibits and programs are geared to families and school-age children. Highlights include **Streets**, an intersecting corridor demonstrating the workings of urban infrastructure; **Current Connections**, an introduction to electricity; interactive arts and nature exhibits; and activity areas designed to teach cultural diversity. A variety of performers are featured in the museum's theater.

★**Peralta Adobe and Fallon House** – *175 W. St. John St. at San Pedro St. Visit by guided tour (90min) only, year-round Tue–Sun 11am–4pm. Closed major holidays. $6.* ♿ ☎ *408-993-8182. www.historysanjose.org.* Ensconced amid the modern structures of downtown, an early-19C adobe and a luxurious Italianate mansion recall San Jose's Spanish Colonial beginnings and its early-19C growth.
Erected for Thomas Fallon, a flamboyant former guide with the Frémont party who had married a Californio land-grant heiress, Fallon House was the grandest residence in San Jose when it was completed in 1855. Among other luxurious accoutrements, the mansion boasted marble fireplaces, elaborately decorated ceilings and woodwork carefully painted to look like oak. After serving as a hotel and a restaurant through the early 20C, it was acquired by the city and painstakingly restored. The lower level contains an excellent small museum detailing San Jose's development from Spanish Colonial pueblo through the American period.
Across the street, the modest Peralta Adobe was the residence of Luís María Peralta, a high-ranking pueblo official and wealthy landowner. The bedroom of the structure appears as it would have around 1800 (note the intriguing, suspended cradle), while the living room, or *sala*, is more elaborately furnished as it would have been around 1840.

Kelley Park — 🧒 *1300 Senter Rd. at Story Rd., 3mi southeast of downtown via S. 1st St. & Keyes St. Open year-round daily dawn–dusk. $4.* 🍴 ♿ 🅿 ☎ *408-277-4191.* The former orchard estate of Judge Lawrence Archer, a San Jose mayor, and his daughter and son-in-law, Louise and Frank Kelley, this 156-acre park on Coyote Creek contains a variety of attractions. **Happy Hollow Park and Zoo** (🧒 *open year-round 10am–5pm, closed major holidays;* ☎ *408-295-8383)* harbors more than 150 animals, including a jaguar and a pygmy hippo; children's rides, and a puppet theater. Broad shaded lawns attract throngs for weekend picnics. There's also a Greek-style amphitheater and a miniature train linking the zoo and the historical museum.

★**Historical Museum in Kelley Park** – *1650 Senter Rd. at Phelan Ave. Open year-round Tue–Sun noon–5pm. Closed Jan 1, Thanksgiving Day, Dec 25. $6 (including tour).* 🍴 🅿 ☎ *408-287-2290. www.historysanjose.org.* This 25-acre complex evokes life in San Jose around the turn of the 20C. The museum comprises some two dozen historic homes and shops, a third of which are re-creations; the remainder were relocated from their original sites.
Centered around a grassy shaded plaza, the complex is notable for its 115ft reproduction of the **San Jose Electric Tower**, a fanciful metal-beamed pyramid of street lights; and the **H.H. Warburton Doctor's Office**, with its medical and dental paraphernalia. Other highlights include the **Print Shop**, where traditional typesetting and printing techniques are demonstrated, and a brick reproduction of the city's **Chinese Temple**, featuring an elaborately carved Cantonese wooden altar from the original 1880s temple.

★ **Japanese Friendship Garden** – *Open year-round daily 10am–dusk.* ♿ 🅿($4) ☎ *408-277-5254.* The meticulously landscaped 6.5 acres, built in the early 1960s, are modeled after Korakuen Garden in Okayama, Japan, San Jose's sister city. Paths wind past stone lanterns, a small pagoda and a variety of flora, including flowering cherry trees and carefully placed conifers. On the upper level, a large pool—populated by brightly colored *koi*, turtles, ducks and blue herons—is spanned by a lovely Moon Bridge. A waterfall pours over ornamental rocks into a lower pool, site of a tea-house. The shapes of the two ponds resemble the Japanese characters for *kokoro*, a word designating heart and soul.

Overfelt Gardens – *Educational Park Dr., .25mi north of McKee Rd., 5mi east of downtown via Julian St. Open year-round daily dawn–dusk.* ♿ 🅿 ☎ *408-251-3323.* This 33-acre park was the lifelong home of Mildred Overfelt (1873-1967), whose father established a prosperous grain and dairy farm here in the 1850s. The original ranch house still stands. Highlight of the park is the **Chinese Cultural Garden**; its monuments include a 30ft statue of ancient philosopher Confucius overlooking a reflecting pond, and pavilions dedicated to nationalist statesmen Sun Yat-sen and Chiang Kai-shek. Three lakes attract abundant waterfowl and aquatic life.

Winchester Mystery House – 🚻 *525 S. Winchester Blvd. Visit by guided tour only, year-round daily; call for schedules. Three tours are offered: Winchester Estate (1hr) $13.95; Behind the Scenes (90min) $10.95; combination tour $21.95.* ✗ ♿ 🅿 ☎ *408-247-2101. www.winchestermysteryhouse.com.* This strange, rambling 160-room Victorian hodgepodge is the creation of Sarah Winchester, widow of rifle magnate William Wirt Winchester. After purchasing an eight-room San Jose farmhouse in 1884, she added to it compulsively until her death in 1922. Local legend avers that Mrs. Winchester was guided in her architectural excesses by the ghosts of those who had lost their lives to Winchester firearms. Now largely unfurnished, the house is notable for its collection of Tiffany and European **art glass**. The **Historic Firearms Museum** on the grounds displays an international collection of pistols and rifles.

★ **Rosicrucian Egyptian Museum** – *1342 Naglee Ave. at Park Ave. Open year-round*

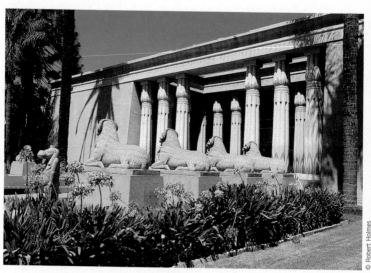

© Robert Holmes

Rosicrucian Egyptian Museum

daily 10am–5pm. Closed Jan 1, Thanksgiving Day, Dec 24-25. $7. ♿ 🅿 ☎ *408-947-3636. www.rosicrucian.org.* Modeled after the Temple of Amon at Karnak, the exterior is dominated by a columned entryway and gold-paneled doors incised with hieroglyphs. The interior features one of the most extensive displays of Egyptian and Mesopotamian artifacts on the West Coast, numbering some 5,000 pieces. Note in particular the display on mummification *(gallery A)*, with painted coffins; **sarcophagi**; human and animal remains, including an unsheathed, mummified body; and a full-scale reproduction of a Middle Kingdom **Rock Tomb** *(visited by guided tour only)*.

Displays of Egyptian pottery, jewelry, glass, funerary objects, writing implements and statues of deities *(galleries B, C & D)* range from the pre-Dynastic period (4800 BC) to the Coptic period (late 2C–mid-7C AD) and include Babylonian, Sumerian and Assyrian cylinder seals and cuneiform tablets.

The museum is located on the edge of **Rosicrucian Park**, a five-acre city block filled with statues, gardens and Egyptian- and Moorish-style buildings that serve as head-quarters for the English Grand Lodge of the nonsectarian Rosicrucian Order, AMORC (Ancient and Mystical Order Rosae Crucis). Rosicrucian Park was established in 1927, when the order's imperator, H. Spencer Lewis, established its headquarters in San Jose. The grounds now house research and administrative buildings, an auditorium, a **planetarium** and the museum.

EXCURSIONS

Santa Clara de Asís Mission – *2.5mi northwest of downtown San Jose, on Santa Clara University campus. From San Jose, follow The Alameda (which becomes El Camino Real) to campus entrance. Open year-round daily 8am–6pm. Closed Dec 26–Jan 1.* & ▯ ☎ *408-554-4023.* Established on the banks of the Guadalupe River in 1777, the eighth California mission was founded as an additional outpost in the vicinity of San Francisco Bay, but was moved in 1781 to its present site on higher ground. Padre Junípero Serra officiated at the laying of the cornerstone for an impressive adobe church that was completed in 1784. Surrounded by fertile lands, the mission prospered until an earthquake destroyed the complex in 1812. A new church, completed in 1814, served first as a mission, then as a parish chapel, until it was destroyed by fire in 1926. The current building resembles the original 1784 adobe.

Visit – Offset by a campanile, the **church** exterior features statues of saints and a roof covered in clay tiles gleaned from the ruins of earlier mission structures. Today encased in redwood, the wooden cross standing in front of the church dates to the 1777 founding of the mission. The painted ceiling of the Victorian-style interior replicates the original design of Mexican artist Augustín Davila.

The simple **St. Francis Chapel** *(behind the main sanctuary)* contains an original wall, ceiling and floor. To the left of the church lies a landscaped **quadrangle** where a number of plants (olive trees, roses and wisteria) survive from the mission days. Across from the entrance to the mission lies the **De Saisset Museum** *(open year-round Tue–Sun 11am–4pm; closed major holidays; reduced hours between exhibitions;* ☎ *408-554-4528; www.scu.edu/deSaisset)*, a university museum devoted to world art and California history. The main level features temporary exhibits of selections from the museum's permanent collection of 16–20C European and American art; Asian art and African art.

★**Triton Museum of Art** – *1505 Warburton Ave. at Lincoln St., Santa Clara, 2 blocks north of El Camino Real. Open year-round Tue 10am–9pm, Wed–Sat 10am–5pm.* & ▯ ☎ *408-247-3754. www.tritonmuseum.org.* Ensconced in a tranquil seven-acre park, this modern museum displays an eclectic collection of Native American and Western art in three skylit galleries. The **Austen D. Warburton Collection of American Indian Art and Artifacts★** spans several centuries of basketry, pottery and other artifacts from California, Southwest and Pacific Northwest tribal traditions. Selections from the permanent collection, displayed in a gallery to the right of the central rotunda, include a 19C Albert Bierstadt landscape, an 18C William Hogarth engraving and a 17C Rembrandt etching. Temporary exhibits emphasize the diversity of contemporary art in the San Francisco Bay Area. A sculpture garden nestles outside the museum walls.

★★**Intel Museum** – *2200 Mission College Blvd., Santa Clara. Open year-round Mon–Fri 9am–6pm, Sat 10am–5pm. Closed major holidays.* & ▯ ☎ *408-765-0503. www.intel.com/go/museum.* As the world's largest semiconductor company, the Intel Corporation invented the technology—in 1968—that put computer memory on tiny silicon chips rather than in magnetic fields. Interactive exhibits here in the company headquarters walk visitors through the principles of transistor technology, from identification of conductors to chip design and production. The use of these chips in personal computers, through the current Pentium IV processor, and future practical applications is also examined.

To make a silicon chip, sand is chemically purified, converted into crystal ingots, melted with added trace chemicals and cooled, then ground to a uniform diameter and sliced into grooved wafers. A photolithographic etching process forms the multi-layered transistors on a chip; aluminum is patterned on the wafer to make electrical connections that complete the transistor. Remarkably, a microprocessor today contains 50-100 million transistors, and circuitry lines are 1/500th the width of a human hair.

Paramount's Great America – ⫘ 🎟 *2401 Agnew Rd., Santa Clara, off US-101 at Great America Pkwy., 6mi north of San Jose. Open weekends 10am mid-Mar–Jun & Sep–Oct; daily 10am Easter week & Jun–Aug. Closing times vary. $39.99.* ✗ & ▯ ☎ *408-988-1776. www.pgathrills.com.* This 100-acre amusement park, originally opened in 1976, is a favorite of roller-coaster fanatics. Its nine coasters include the new **Stealth**, which races up to 50mph as "the world's first and only true flying coaster," according to Paramount. Among other thrill rides are the inverted **Top**

Gun jet-coaster, the 210ft **Drop Zone** tower, the **James Bond 007** motion simulator, and three water rides, including the 50ft drop of **Whitewater Falls**. Scooby-Doo and the characters from Nickelodeon's *Rugrats* series greet children in more family-oriented areas. There's a full entertainment schedule including IMAX shows, numerous shops and restaurants.

San José de Guadalupe Mission – *19mi northeast of San Jose in Fremont, .5mi south of I-680 at second Mission Blvd. exit (Rte. 238). Open year-round daily 10am–5pm. Closed Jan 1, Easter Sunday, Thanksgiving Day, Dec 25. Contribution requested.* & ☎ *510-657-1797.* The 14th mission in the California chain was founded by Padre Fermín Lasuén in 1797 and named for St. Joseph. The mission's first permanent adobe church was completed in 1809. Before secularization in 1834, San José was one of the most prosperous missions in California. During the Gold Rush, the mission served as a rooming house and general store for gold seekers on their way to the southern mother-lode mines. In 1858 the mission complex was returned to the Catholic Church, but a massive earthquake 10 years later destroyed the old adobe church, and a wooden Gothic-style structure was erected in its place. In the early 1980s work began on the careful reconstruction of the original adobe church that occupies the site today.

Within the simple, unadorned exterior walls, the church interior reflects the 1833-40 period, featuring an ornate gold-leaf replica of the reredos and historic **statuary**. Note the statue of St. Joseph (c.1600) from Spain and that of the Virgin (18C) from Mexico; rear side altars display statues of Christ (early 19C) and St. Bonaventure (1808). The hammered copper baptismal font (1830s) was painted by Augustín Davila, painter of the interior of the original church.

A small garden separates the church from the original adobe **padres' quarters**, which now house a museum of mission history featuring Native American and church artifacts.

★**Don Edwards San Francisco Bay National Wildlife Refuge** – *Marshlands Rd., Fremont; from I-880 or Rte. 84 at east end of Dumbarton Bridge, take Thornton Ave. to refuge road. Visitor center open year-round Tue–Sun 10am–5pm. Closed major holidays.* & 🅿 ☎ *510-792-0222. www.r1.fws.gov/sfbnwr.* The largest urban wildlife refuge in the US sprawls across 20,000 acres of salt marsh, tidal sloughs, mudflats and rolling hills at the southern end of San Francisco Bay. More than 200 species of waterfowl, shorebirds and migratory birds live, breed and/or feed in the refuge, which was dedicated in 1972 and renamed for a former congressman in 1995.

From the bluff-top **Visitor Center**, an extensive system of trails follows boardwalks and bridges across tidal flats. Within the center are excellent interpretive exhibits on life in the refuge, as well as an auditorium and observation deck. More trails extend through managed wetland habitat from an **Environmental Education Center** (*Los Esteros Rd., Alviso; from Rte. 237, turn right at Zanker Rd. for 2mi; open year-round Mon–Fri 8am–4:30pm;* ☎ *408-262-5513).*

Ardenwood Historic Farm – 🖼 *34600 Ardenwood Blvd., Fremont, just north of Rte. 84. Farm and house open Apr–mid-Nov Tue–Sun 10am–4pm. $5 ($1 Tue–Wed & Sat). Rest of the year, grounds open same hours. Closed Thanksgiving Day, Dec 25.* ⚒ & 🅿 ☎ *510-796-0663. www.ebparks.org/parks/arden.htm.* Ardenwood offers 21C visitors an opportunity to view and participate in activities common at a late-19C farm. George Washington Patterson built a ranch house here in 1857; as his property grew into a prosperous estate, his home was expanded in Queen Anne style in 1889 and surrounded by elaborate Victorian gardens. Many original buildings, including the **house** *(visit by guided tour only)*, remain standing. Weekend programs include the planting, tending and harvesting of organic crops, and demonstrations of cooking, farm chores and blacksmithing. The **Farmyard Café** serves lunches *(open seasonally Thu–Fri 11am–2pm, weekends 10am–4pm).*

38 • SAN MATEO COUNTY COAST

Map of principal sights p 12

Untouched by the sprawl of the city to its north or the urbanized peninsula area to its east, coastal San Mateo County is geographically isolated by the San Gregorio and Santa Cruz mountain ranges and protected against development by the lack of a practical commuter route.

Route 1 narrows to two lanes as it wends its way south from Pacifica through the pastoral farming and fishing villages of Moss Beach, Princeton, San Gregorio and Pescadero. South of Half Moon Bay, the east side of the highway skirts a gently undulating landscape patterned with fields of flowers, wholesalers' greenhouses, and rows of artichoke and brussels sprout plants; pumpkin patches vividly dot the landscape in autumn. To the west extend ocean beaches, superb spots for strolling, picnicking, tidepooling and wildlife observation, though rip currents and frigid water temperatures make swimming inadvisable. From January to April, at many points along the drive, **gray whales** may be seen only a few hundred yards offshore, making their annual migration between summer feeding grounds in the Arctic and their winter home off the coast of Mexico's Baja Peninsula.

The notorious stretch of highway known as **Devil's Slide** forms a gateway to the coast from San Francisco. Just south of Point San Pedro, the highway narrows and swerves around steep cliffs dramatically striated with rock layers upthrust from ancient marine sediments. Rock slides have closed the road on several occasions in recent years, but conservationists fear that replacing it with a tunnel or inland route would encourage development of the delightfully rural coastal towns to the south.

Visiting San Mateo County Coast – From San Francisco drive south on Hwy. 1 (19th Ave.) or Rte. 35 (Skyline Blvd.), which intersects Hwy. 1 south of Daly City. To return to San Francisco, either retrace the route or take Rte. 92 east from Half Moon Bay, then continue north on I-280. Mileage to each sight is calculated from the preceding sight. The car fee at park entrances allows any same-day state park visit.

In summer, the coast is often cool and foggy; the weather clears in spring and fall. Reservations are necessary to visit the wildlife protection areas at Año Nuevo State Reserve during the breeding season from December through March; the spectacle is well worth the effort of advance planning. Swimming is inadvisable along the San Mateo County Coast due to cold water and hazardous surf; beware of sneaker waves when venturing close to shore. For information on camping and other park-system amenities, contact the **California State Parks Bay Area District Office**, *(250 Executive Park Blvd., Suite 4900, San Francisco CA 94134-3306; ☎ 415-330-6300)*.

DRIVING TOUR *50mi*

Sanchez Adobe Historic Site – *100 Linda Mar Blvd., Pacifica, 9mi south of San Francisco via Hwy. 1. Open year-round Tue–Thu 10am–4pm, weekends 1–5pm. ☎ 415-359-1462.* Reflecting many periods of California history, this adobe was built in 1848 as the home of Don Francisco Sanchez. Artifacts recall the site's prior use as an Ohlone village, a Spanish mission farm and a cattle ranch; it later became a general's residence, a hotel, a Depression-era speakeasy and an artichoke storage facility. Restored in 1953, it has been refurbished and is open for self-guided tours.

Point Montara Lighthouse – *5mi. 16th St. off Hwy. 1, Montara. ☎ 415-728-7177. http://parks.ca.gov/central/bayarea/pmls282.htm.* Built in 1875 as the Point Montara Fog Signal and Light Station, this picturesque beacon house—a naval training base during World War II—has been a youth hostel since 1980.

★**James V. Fitzgerald Marine Reserve** – 🧒 *2mi. California Ave. at N. Lake St., Moss Beach, west of Hwy. 1. Open year-round daily dawn–dusk. 🅿 ☎ 650-728-3584.* Extensive shale reefs bridge the expanse between land and sea, creating tidepools richly populated with myriad marine life, including limpets, barnacles, mussels, sea urchins, starfish, anemones, chitons, hermit crabs, sponges and abalone. Rangers help visitors search the wonders of the pools and lead explorations during low tide. A small visitor center identifies specimens.

Pillar Point Harbor – *2.4mi.* A granitic headland extends from the coast here, creating a sheltered harbor that serves as an anchorage for local fishermen. Fresh fish is sold daily from boats and fish markets, and simple seafood restaurants serve up steaming chowder, seafood cocktails and fresh fish and chips. Whale-watching cruises depart from the wharf during the season *(depart Jan–Apr weekends & holidays 10am & 1:30pm; round-trip 3hrs; commentary; reservations required; $25; 🅿 Huck Finn Sportfishing Center ☎ 650-726-7133 or 800-572-2934; http://usafishing.com/Halfmoon.html).*

Francis Beach – 🧒 *4.1mi. Foot of Kelly Ave. in Half Moon Bay, .6mi west of Hwy. 1. Open year-round daily 8am–sunset. $2/car. ⚠ ($16) ♿ 🅿 ☎ 650-726-8819. http://parks.ca.gov/hmbsb277.htm.* The Half Moon Bay State Beach system extends 4mi to the north of this flat, sandy expanse, and includes Venice and Dunes beaches. Francis Beach provides a welcome departure from the coast's typically rocky beaches. Dune grasses fringing the shoreline provide habitat for snowy plovers. Picnic tables overlook the ocean from the day-use area, and a Coastside Trail *(3mi)* lures hikers and bikers. The skull of a blue whale entangled in a fisherman's net in 1988 is visible near the entry booth. A new visitor center, with exhibits on regional history and natural resources, opened in fall 2000.

San Gregorio State Beach – *11mi. Open year-round daily 8am–sunset. $2/car 🅿 ☎ 650-879-2170. http://parks.ca.gov/central/bayarea/sgsb273.htm.* This broad, sandy beach lies at the mouth of San Gregorio Creek. Walk north at low tide to see dramatic, cavelike erosion at the base of the sandstone bluffs, or stroll atop to spot whales in season.

Pescadero State Beach – *4.4mi. Open year-round daily 8am–sunset. $2/car at north entrance only, free at south & central entrances.* 🅿 ☏ *650-879-2170. http://parks.ca.gov/central/bayarea/psb227.htm.* From the bluffs that loom over this popular beach, views extend west over the Pacific and the San Mateo County coastline. East of Route 1, extensive walking trails penetrate the **Pescadero Marsh Natural Preserve**, a 510-acre freshwater/brackish coastal marsh. Migratory birds plying the Pacific Flyway stop here to rest, drawing flocks of birdwatchers, especially in late fall and early spring. Binoculars are helpful. *Guided walks of marsh year-round (weather permitting) Sat 10:30am & Sun 1pm. Meet in Central Pescadero parking lot, watch for signs off Rte. 1 just south of Pescadero Creek.*

Pebble Beach – 🚸 *2.1mi. Open year-round daily 8am–sunset. $2/car.* 🅿 ☏ *650-879-2170. http://parks.ca.gov/central/bayarea/bhsb266.htm.* Breaking waves here deposit glistening, many-colored pebbles onto the beach from an offshore quartz reef *(note: it is illegal to remove pebbles).* This part of the coast bears spectacular displays of **tafoni**—lacy, filigree-like formations wrought by erosion on the face of weathered stone. Pebble Beach is the northernmost unit of **Bean Hollow State Beach**, accessible from here by car or via a 12-station clifftop nature trail *(1mi).* Harbor seals occasionally may be seen sunning themselves on the wet rocks below the trail, or vying with swooping cormorants for fish.

★**Pigeon Point Light Station** – 🚸 *3mi. Visit by guided tour (50min) only, Sept–Jun weekends 11am–4pm. Jul–Aug Fri–Sun 11am–4pm (weather permitting). $2.* 🅿 ☏ *650-879-2120. http://parks.ca.gov/central/bayarea/ppls281.htm.* Built in 1871, this starkly graceful lighthouse tower was automated in 1926. The lantern room contains the original Fresnel lens, a device consisting of 1,008 glass prisms that shape light from a central lamp into a horizontal beam intense enough to be visible many miles out at sea. The point itself offers lovely views of the coast and surrounding landforms. A self-guided tour of the grounds explains the light station's past in vivid detail. The lighthouse outbuildings today house a unit of the American Youth Hostel Association.

★**Año Nuevo State Reserve** – 🚸 *6.6mi. Open year-round daily 8am–sunset. Elephant seal rookery open Apr–Sept daily 8am–6pm, Oct–Nov daily 8am–4pm. Rest of the year by appointment only. Closed 1st 2 weeks in Dec.* 🅿*($2)* ☏ *650-879-0227. Seal Walks guided tours (2hr 30min) Dec 15–Mar 31 daily 8:45am–2:15pm every 15min. Closed Dec 25. Reservations recommended 8 weeks in advance. $4.* ☏ *650-879-0227 or 800-444-4445. http://parks.ca.gov/central/ bayarea/ansr228.htm.* This 4,000-acre coastal reserve encompasses a rocky offshore island *(not open to the public)* and a wildly beautiful promontory of bluffs and beaches. The promontory is the largest mainland rookery between Baja and northern California for **northern elephant seals**. From December through March, the seals gradually congregate here, the females coming ashore to give birth to single pups and joining "harems" dominated by massive, 2.5-ton alpha bulls. Violent clashes between males over harem control are common. In spring and summer, seals again come ashore to molt.

Continue another 22mi to Santa Cruz (see The Green Guide to California). Rte. 17 returns northeasterly to San Jose, about 30mi.

Elephant Seal Pup, Año Nuevo State Reserve

■ Santa Cruz

The archetypal California beach community, Santa Cruz *(tourist office: ☎ 831-425-1234)* curves around the northern end of Monterey Bay 22mi south of Año Nuevo State Reserve. Founded in 1791 with the Mission Exaltación de la Santa Cruz, it became a hub for a wide range of industries, including lumbering, fishing, limestone quarrying, tanning and agriculture. In the late 19C, the Southern Pacific Railroad came to town and soon thereafter, Santa Cruz became a thriving seaside resort. With the establishment of a University of California campus in the hills above the city in the mid-1960s, the resort milieu was overlaid with a college atmosphere that attracted artists and craftspeople to the area. The population now exceeds 50,000.

The **Santa Cruz Beach Boardwalk**★★ (Kids *open May–Aug daily 11am, Sept–Apr weekends & holidays noon; closing hours vary;* ✕ 🕭 🅿 ☎ *831-426-7433, www.beachboardwalk.com)*, built in 1904, remains the oldest amusement park in California. Its renovated boardwalk features turreted and brightly painted buildings and rides fronting a wide bay beach *(swimming inadvisable because of dangerous currents)*. Both the **Giant Dipper** (1924)—a .5mi-long wooden roller coaster—and the **Looff carousel** (1911)—the work of the respected Danish woodcarver Charles I.D. Looff—enjoy the status of national historic landmarks. Nearby, the **Cocoanut Grove Banquet and Conference Center** (1907) is famous for its now-renovated Grand Ballroom, where such musicians as Artie Shaw, Benny Goodman and Xavier Cugat once performed with their big bands. A few blocks west, the broad **municipal wharf** stretches into the bay and is lined with tackle shops and eateries. A magnificent **view** of the Boardwalk extends from its decks. North of the waterfront stands the **Santa Cruz Surfing Museum**, honoring local surfing personalities and their equipment. The one-room museum is housed in the Mark Abbott Memorial Lighthouse *(West Cliff Dr.)* and includes an informative exhibit on West Coast shark attacks between 1926 and 1996, as well as various models of surfboards *(open year-round Mon, Wed–Sun noon–4pm; closed Jan 1 & Dec 25, & Wed in winter; contribution requested;* 🕭 ☎ *831-420-6289)*.

The **Santa Cruz City Museum of Natural History** *(1305 E. Cliff Dr.)*, on a cliff above the bay, covers the natural history of the area and includes an exhibit of artifacts and fossils detailing the Ohlone Indians' way of life *(open year-round Tue–Sun 10am–5pm; closed major holidays; $2 contribution requested;* 🕭 🅿 *www.cruzio.com/~scmuseum ☎ 831-420-6115)*.

Santa Cruz Mission and State Historic Park *(Mission Plaza off School St.; open year-round Thu–Sun 10am–4pm; $2;* 🕭 ☎ *831-425-5849)* preserves the site of the original mission (1791). This 12th mission, named in honor of the Holy Cross, suffered at the hands of ruffianesque settlers in the nearby pueblo of Branciforte. After achieving a peak population of 531 neophytes (smallest of all the missions), Santa Cruz declined slowly; following secularization, its structures were destroyed by earthquakes, fires and floods. In 1931 a small replica of the adobe church was erected 200ft from the original site.

A seven-room **barracks** is the only structure remaining from the original mission complex. Built in 1824 to house converts, it was later occupied by Californio and Irish citizens; the Californios remodeled the structure by encapsulating it within a Victorian-style house, thus protecting its adobe walls from dissolving. Today restored to its 1840s appearance, it is maintained by the state park system.

The **University of California, Santa Cruz**★ *(follow Bay St. northwest to main entrance on Coolidge Dr.)* is renowned for its distinctive architecture and spectacular **setting**★★ in the lush hills above Santa Cruz amid groves of redwood trees. Eight distinct college campuses surround an academic and administrative core that serves 10,000 students. In 1965 the state university system purchased 2,000 acres of land and carefully integrated 14 original structures from the 1860s Cowell Ranch into the new campus. The **Mary Porter-Sesnon Art Gallery** *(☎ 831-459-2314)* at Porter College and the **Eloise Pickard Smith Gallery** *(☎ 831-459-5667)* at Cowell College mount changing exhibits of contemporary art; the **arboretum** is devoted to exotic flora, particularly from South Africa, Australia and New Zealand (Empire Grade, .3mi west of main entrance; open year-round daily 9am–5pm; closed Thanksgiving Day & Dec 25; 🅿 ☎ *831-427-2998)*.

Six miles north of Santa Cruz is **Henry Cowell Redwoods State Park**★ *(Rte. 9; open year-round daily 6am–dusk; $3/vehicle;* △ 🕭 🅿 ☎ *831-335-4598)*. Trails weave through the woodlands of this biotically diverse 1,760-acre tract, bisected by the San Lorenzo River and notable for its fine stands of coast redwoods. The **Redwood Grove Trail** *(.8mi; begin south of parking lot)* loops past the park's largest trees, some towering 300ft.

Roaring through the Cowell Redwoods, the **Roaring Camp & Big Trees Narrow-Gauge Railroad** (Kids *Graham Hill Rd., Felton; Apr–Nov daily, Dec–Mar weekends only; call for schedule;* ✕ 🕭 🅿 ☎ *831-335-4484; www.roaringcamprr.com)* departs from a former logging camp site. The commercial steam-train tour (6mi, 75min) penetrates deep into the ancient redwood forest, snaking around hairpin turns and negotiating steep switchbacks before arriving near the summit of Bear Mountain.

Mission District Mural

Practical
Information

Calendar of Events

Listed below is a selection of San Francisco's many popular annual events; some dates may vary annually. For more information about events in the Bay Area, consult the periodicals listed on p 276 or contact the San Francisco Convention and Visitors Bureau (☎ 415-391-2000; www.sfvisitor.org).

Spring & Summer

1st Sun in Apr	**Street Performers Festival** *Pier 39*	415-705-5500
Easter Sunday	**Easter Parade & Hat Promenade** *Union St.*	415-885-1335
late Apr	**Cherry Blossom Festival** *Japan Center*	415-563-2313
late Apr–early May	**San Francisco International Film Festival** *various locations*	415-931-3456
May–Oct	**Shakespeare at the Beach** *Stinson Beach*	415-868-9500
1st Sun in May	**Cinco de Mayo Festival** *Mission District*	415-826-1401
1st weekend in May	**A Fair to Remember** *Golden Gate Park*	415-750-8340
3rd Sun in May	**Bay to Breakers Race** *The Embarcadero to the Great Highway*	415-808-5000, ext. 222
Memorial Day Sun	**Carnaval San Francisco** *Mission District*	415-826-1401
Jun–Oct	**California Shakespeare Festival** *Orinda*	510-548-3422

VISITOR CENTERS
1 Beach Chalet
2 Cliff House
3 Fort Mason - GGNRA HQ
4 McLaren Lodge
5 Presidio Main Post
6 San Francisco Convention & Visitors Bureau Information Center

RECREATIONAL AREAS
1 3Com Park
2 Candlestick Point
3 Coastal Trail
4 Crissy Field
5 Fort Funston
6 Fort Mason Piers
7 Golden Gate Golf Course
8 Golden Gate Promenade
9 Land's End
10 Lincoln Park Golf Course
11 Pacific Bell Park
12 Pier 7
13 Presidio Golf Course

TRANSPORTATION
1 Ferry Building
2 Golden Gate Ferries
3 Oakland International Airport
4 San Francisco International Airport
5 Transbay Bus Terminal

TOUR DEPARTURE POIN
1 All About Chinatown
2 Blue & Gold Fleet Cruises
3 City Guides Mural Tour
4 Cruisin' the Castro
5 Dashiell Hammett Tour
6 Mangia North Beach
7 Pacific Heights Walking Tour
8 Precita Eyes Mural Tour
9 Red & White Fleet Cruise
10 Wok Wiz Chinatown Adventure Tours and Chinese Heritage Wa

1st weekend in Jun	**Union Street Spring Festival** *Union St. between Gough & Steiner Sts.*	415-441-7055
3rd weekend in Jun	**Juneteenth Celebration** *Kimball Park, Geary & Steiner Sts.*	415-229-1220
3rd weekend in Jun	**North Beach Festival** *Grant Ave. & Green St.*	415-989-6426
mid-Jun	**Dipsea Race** *Mill Valley to Stinson Beach*	415-331-3550
mid-Jun–mid-Aug	**Stern Grove Midsummer Music Festival**	415-252-6253
last weekend in Jun	**Lesbian/Gay/Bisexual/Transgender Pride Celebration** *Castro District*	415-864-3733
Jul-Aug	**Summer Music Festival** *Robert Mondavi Winery, Napa Valley*	707-226-1395
July 4	**Fourth of July Waterfront Festival** *Fisherman's Wharf*	415-705-5500
3rd Thu in Jul	**Cable Car Bell-Ringing Championship** *Union Square*	415-923-6202
late Aug–mid-Dec	**Renaissance Pleasure Faire** *Vacaville*	800-523-2473
Sept	**Shakespeare in the Park** *Golden Gate Park*	415-422-2222
Labor Day weekend	**Sausalito Art Festival** *Marinship Park*	415-332-3555
2nd Sat in Sept	**Ghirardelli Chocolate Festival** *Ghirardelli Square*	415-775-5500
2nd Sat in Sept	**Latino Summer Fiesta** *Mission District*	415-826-1401
mid-Sept	**San Francisco Fringe Festival** *Theater District*	415-931-1094

SHOPPING

The Anchorage
Baker Hamilton Square
The Cannery
Crocker Galleria
Embarcadero Center
Ghirardelli Square
Macy's
Neiman Marcus
Pier 39
Saks Fifth Avenue
San Francisco Shopping Centre

PUBLIC SERVICES

1 American Express Company
   Travel Service
2 City Box Office
3 Tix Bay Area
4 Walgreens 24hr Pharmacy

ENTERTAINMENT VENUES

1 Cable Car Theater
2 Center for the Arts
3 Club Fugazi
   (Beach Blanket Babylon)
4 Cowell Theater
5 Davies Symphony Hall
6 Fillmore Auditorium
7 Geary Theater
8 Herbst Theatre
9 Slim's
10 Theatre on the Square
11 War Memorial Opera House
12 The Warfield

next to last weekend in Sept	San Francisco International Art Exposition *Fort Mason Center*	312-587-3300
next to last weekend in Sept	San Francisco Blues Festival *Great Meadow at Fort Mason*	415-979-5588
next to last weekend in Sept	Autumn Moon Festival *Chinatown*	415-982-6306
last weekend in Sept	Festival of the Culinary Arts *Polk & Turk Sts.*	415-249-4640
last Sun in Sept	Folsom Street Fair *South of Market*	415-861-3247
Oct	Artspan Open Studios *various locations*	415-861-9838
1st weekend in Oct	Fleet Week *Embarcadero & Fisherman's Wharf*	415-705-5500
1st Sun in Oct	Castro Street Fair *Castro & Market Sts.*	415-467-3354
2nd Sun in Oct	Italian Heritage Parade & Festival *Fisherman's Wharf & North Beach*	415-989-2220
mid-Oct–early Nov	San Francisco Jazz Festival *various locations*	415-788-7353
3rd weekend in Oct	International Vintage Poster Fair *Fort Mason Center*	415-546-9608
late Oct–early Nov	Grand National Rodeo, Horse & Stock Show *Cow Palace*	415-469-6057
Oct 31	Halloween San Francisco *Civic Center*	415-826-1401
2nd week in Nov	Film Arts Festival of Independent Cinema *Castro & Roxie Theaters*	415-552-8760
3rd Fri in Nov	Embarcadero Center Holiday Lights Celebration *Justin Herman Plaza*	415-772-0753
Dec	Festival of Lights *Fisherman's Wharf*	415-705-5500
Feb	Festival of Winter Classical Concerts *Robert Mondavi Winery, Napa Valley*	707-226-1395
Feb (date varies)	Chinese New Year Parade & Celebration *Chinatown*	415-391-9680
2nd week in Feb	Sex Tour 2001 *San Francisco Zoo*	415-753-7165
last weekend in Feb	Pacific Orchid Exposition *Fort Mason*	415-546-9608
2nd or 3rd Sun in Mar	St. Patrick's Day Parade *Embarcadero to Civic Center*	415-731-0924

Planning the Trip

Consult the pages shown for detailed practical information about the following areas: **Golden Gate Park** p 137, **Point Reyes National Seashore** p 218 and the **Wine Country** p 231.

Visitors may contact the following agencies to obtain maps and information on points of interest, accommodations and seasonal events.

San Francisco Convention & Visitors Bureau
PO Box 429097, San Francisco CA 94142

☏ 415-391-2000
www.sfvisitor.org

Berkeley Convention & Visitors Bureau
2015 Center St., Berkeley CA 94704

☏ 510-549-7040
www.berkeleycvb.com

Marin County Convention & Visitors Bureau
1013 Larkspur Landing Cir., Larkspur CA 94939

☏ 415-499-5000
www.visitmarin.org

Napa Valley Conference & Visitors Bureau
1310 Napa Town Center, Napa CA 94559

☏ 707-226-7459
www.napavalley.org

Oakland Convention & Visitors Bureau
475 14th St., Suite 120, Oakland CA 94612

☏ 510-839-9000
www.oaklandcvb.com

San Jose Convention & Visitors Bureau
333 W. San Carlos St., San Jose CA 95110

☏ 408-295-9600
www.sanjose.org

San Mateo County Convention & Visitors Bureau
111 Anza Blvd., Suite 410, Burlingame CA 94010

☏ 650-348-7600
www.sanmateocountycvb.com

Santa Rosa Convention & Visitors Bureau
9 Fourth St., Santa Rosa CA 9540

☏ 707-577-8674
www.visitsantarosa.com

San Francisco's Seasons

The San Francisco Bay Area enjoys a temperate climate year-round. Although temperature variation from season to season is slight, weather conditions can change quite suddenly in the course of a day, and from area to area. Inland temperatures are usually higher than those along the bayshore and especially the oceanfront. Nighttime lows tend to stay between 45°-55°F.

The key to comfort when visiting the region is dressing in layers. Shorts and other light clothing are rarely practical. In the **spring** and **summer**, daytime highs average in the 60s, although the infrequent fog-free day can bring sunny skies and temperatures in the 80s. The busiest tourist season is July and August; visitors should make advance reservations whenever possible and expect long lines for the more popular attractions. The region's glorious views are at their finest during the clear days of **autumn**, when daytime temperatures in the 70s make exploring the area quite comfortable. Rain is the norm during the **winter** months; 80 percent of the annual precipitation occurs between November and April, and temperatures fluctuate little throughout the day, hovering between 45° and 60°F.

Fog is an important weather determinant: its presence causes temperatures to drop, making a sweater or jacket necessary. Spring fogs occur in the early morning and generally lift by mid-day. Fog persists throughout the day in coastal areas during summer, though it may burn off over inland areas before returning in the evening. Autumn days are relatively fog-free. Winter fogs usually occur inland, leaving coastal areas in the clear.

© Donovan Reese/Tony Stone Images

San Francisco Temperature Chart
(recorded at San Francisco International Airport)

Month	avg. high	avg. low	Precipitation
Jan	56°F (13°C)	41°F (5°C)	4.6in (11.7cm)
Apr	63°F (17°C)	47°F (8°C)	1.5in (3.8cm)
Jul	71°F (21°C)	53°F (12°C)	0.04in (0.1cm)
Oct	70°F (21°C)	51°F (10°C)	1.0in (2.5cm)

Getting to San Francisco

BY AIR

San Francisco International Airport (SFO) – ☎ *650-876-7809. www.flysfo.com.*
13.5mi south of San Francisco. Most international and domestic flights arrive and
depart from SFO. **Airport Information Booths** *(open year-round daily 8am–midnight)* are
located on the upper and lower levels of all terminals. Computerized information kiosks
are located in baggage-claim areas, adjacent to the booths. **Restaurants** are located on
upper levels of terminals. Smoking is prohibited throughout the terminal buildings. A
medical clinic is located on the lower level of the International Terminal *(open 24hrs
daily)*. Most public transportation departs from the lower level of each terminal;
for information call the **Ground Transportation Hotline** ☎ 800-736-2008 *(weekdays
7:30am–5pm)* or access the airport's website.
SFO's new **International Terminal** opened in December 2000. The 2.5 million sq-ft facility
effectively doubled the airport's size. The world's largest structure to be built upon
seismically sensitive base isolators, it boasts "common-use" technology that enables
different airlines to share ticket counters and its 24 gates for top efficiency. The **Louis
A. Turpen Aviation Museum** is housed in a re-creation of the airport's original 1930s passenger lounge. Still proceeding, as part of SFO's $2.4 billion expansion, are
construction of a front-door BART station and an intra-airport light-rail-transit system
(both scheduled by 2002).

Taxis – Taxis depart near the yellow columns outside all terminals on the lower-level
center island. Taxi service to downtown San Francisco takes approximately 20–30min
and costs between $21–$34.

Shuttles – ☎ *510-893-7665 or 800-736-2008.* Numerous companies offer transport
between SFO and hotels in downtown San Francisco and surrounding areas. Shuttles
depart near the center island outside all terminals on the upper level *(curbside service
from airport 8am–midnight, $10-$14.50)*. Pre-arranged shuttle service departs from
the lower level, courtyards 2 and 3 *(24hrs daily by reservation only, $9–$21)*.

Public Transit – **SamTrans, CalTrain-SFO Shuttle** *(free)* and **BART-SFO Express** depart from the
upper-level roadway at the International and North Terminals. Follow "Public Transit"
signs to bus stops, where schedules and fares are posted. Information may also be
accessed at the **Airport Information Booths** or computerized kiosks located next to the
booths in baggage-claim areas.

Rental Cars – *p 274.* Rental-car agency service counters are located on the lower level
of each terminal. Conduct all business in the terminal before boarding shuttles for
transport to rental-car lots.

Oakland International Airport (OAK) – *www.flyoakland.com.* ☎ *510-577-4000.*
*7.5mi south of downtown Oakland; 17mi southeast of downtown San Francisco, allow
1hr transit time.* This smaller, easy-to-navigate airport handles both domestic and
international flights. Information booths are located near main entrances *(open daily
8am–8pm)*.

Taxis and Shuttles – Taxi stands are located outside Terminals 1 and 2. Service to downtown San Francisco 35–40min, $40–$45; to downtown Oakland 15–20min, $22.
Shuttles to hotels and to the surrounding area depart from the traffic island outside
each terminal. Fares and transit time vary according to destination. Companies offering
service to San Francisco include **A-1 Shuttle Services** *(☎ 888-698-2663)*, **Air-Transit Shuttle**
(☎ 510-568-3434), **City Express Shuttle** *(☎ 510-481-0444)*, **International Shuttle** *(☎ 510-
430-2700)* and **Superporter Express** *(☎ 877-337-8737)*. In all, 44 shuttle companies
offer service; many require advance reservations.

Public Transit – **BART** *(p 274)* offers service from OAK to San Francisco and East Bay
stations. Shuttle to Coliseum Station departs in front of Terminals 1 and 2. For
information ☎ 510-465-2278. Local bus service is provided by **AC Transit** *(☎ 510-
817-1717)* Line 58. Buses connect with BART and mainline bus routes.

Rental Cars – *p 274.* Service counters are located in each terminal near the baggage
claim area. Rental cars are located in front of the terminals.

BY TRAIN

The **Amtrak** rail network offers a relaxing alternative for the traveler with time to spare.
Advance reservations are recommended to ensure reduced fares and availability of
desired accommodations. Passengers can choose from first-class, coach, sleeping cars
and glass-domed cars allowing a panoramic view. Fares are comparable to air travel.
Major long-distance routes to the Bay Area are the *Zephyr* from Chicago via Denver
and Salt Lake City *(49hrs)* and the *Coast Starlight* from Los Angeles *(11hrs)*. Short-
distance routes include the *Capitols* via Sacramento or San Jose and the *San Joaquins*
via Bakersfield. The nearest **Amtrak station** to San Francisco is located across the bay
at 5885 Landregan St. in Emeryville; a shuttle bus transports passengers from the
station to four locations in San Francisco: the Ferry Building, Hyatt Embarcadero, Pier
39 and San Francisco Centre *(one-way 20min; free)*. Travelers from Canada should

inquire with their local travel agents about Amtrak/VIARail connections. **All-Aboard Pass** allows up to 45 days travel nationwide (limited to three stops). **USA RailPass** (not available to US or Canadian citizens or legal residents) offers unlimited travel within Amtrak-designated regions at discounted rates; 15- and 30-day passes are available. Schedule and route information: ☏ 800-872-7245 (toll-free in North America only; outside North America, contact your local travel agent).

CalTrain offers service between San Francisco and San Jose. Schedule and route information: ☏ 415-495-4546.

BY BUS

Greyhound provides access to San Francisco at a leisurely pace. Fares are generally lower than other forms of public transportation. **Ameripass** allows unlimited travel for 7, 15, 30 or 60 days. Some travelers may find long-distance bus travel uncomfortable due to the lack of sleeping accommodations. Advance reservations suggested. *(Schedule and route information: ☏ 415-495-6789 or 800-231-2222; www.greyhound.com).*

BY CAR

Map p 12. San Francisco is easily accessible by major interstate highways. US-101 and I-280 enter the city from the south. I-80 crosses the Bay Bridge from Berkeley and Oakland *($1 bridge toll for westbound traffic only)*. US-101 provides access to San Francisco from the north, across the Golden Gate Bridge into San Francisco *($3 bridge toll for southbound traffic only)*.

International Visitors

BEFORE YOU GO

In addition to the agencies listed on p 268, visitors from outside the US can contact the San Francisco Convention & Visitors Bureau's foreign language information lines *(Français ☏ 415-391-2003; Deutsch ☏ 415-391-2004; Español ☏ 415-391-2122; Japanese ☏ 415-391-2101)* or the US embassy in their country.

Foreign Consulates – In San Francisco, international visitors can contact consulates of their country of residence. Major consulates include:

Country	Address	☏
Australia	1 Bush St.	415-362-6160
Brazil	300 Montgomery St.	415-981-8170
Canada	555 Montgomery St.	415-834-3180
China	1450 Laguna St.	415-674-2900
France	540 Bush St.	415-397-4330
Germany	1960 Jackson St.	415-775-1061
Japan	50 Fremont St., 23rd Floor	415-777-3533
Mexico	870 Market St., Suite 528	415-392-5554
United Kingdom	1 Sansome St., Suite 850	415-981-3030

Entry Requirements – Citizens of countries participating in the Visa Waiver Pilot Program (VWPP) are not required to obtain a visa to enter the US for visits of fewer than 90 days. For more information contact the US consulate in your country of residence. Citizens of non-participating countries must have a visitor's visa. Upon entry, nonresident foreign visitors must present a valid passport and round-trip transportation ticket. Canadian citizens are not required to present a passport or visa to enter the US, although identification and proof of citizenship may be requested (a passport or Canadian birth certificate and photo identification are usually acceptable). Naturalized Canadian citizens should carry their citizenship papers. Inoculations are not generally required, but check with the US embassy or consulate before departing.

Health Insurance – The United States does not have a national health program. Before departing, visitors from abroad should check with their insurance company to determine if their medical insurance covers doctors' visits, medication and hospitalization in the US. Prescription drugs should be properly identified, and accompanied by a copy of the prescription.

US Customs – All articles brought into the US must be declared at the time of entry. **Prohibited items:** plant material; firearms and ammunition (if not intended for sporting purposes); meat or poultry products. For further information contact the US embassy or consulate before departing, or the US Customs Service, San Francisco Port Director, *(open Mon–Fri 8am–4:30pm; 555 Battery St.; ☏ 415-782-9210).*

1 penny= 1 cent

10 dollar bill

1 dollar bill= 100 cents

dime= 10 cents

5 dollar bill

nickel=5 cents

quarter=25 cents

20 dollar bill

MONEY

Currency Exchange – Many banks located in the downtown area offer foreign currency exchange. Visitors can also exchange currency at San Francisco International Airport on the upper and lower levels of the International Terminal and in Area F, North Terminal.

Credit Cards and Travelers Checks – *p 275.*

Taxes and Tipping – *p 275.* Prices displayed or quoted in the US do not generally include **sales tax** (8.5% in California). Sales tax is not reimbursable. It is customary to give a small gift of money (a **tip**) for services rendered, to waiters, porters, chamber maids and cab drivers. The word "tip" originally was an acronym for "to insure promptness."

GENERAL INFORMATION

Driving in the US – *p 274.* Visitors bearing valid driver's licenses issued by their country of residence are not required to obtain an International Driver's License to drive in the US. Drivers must carry vehicle registration and/or rental contract, and proof of automobile insurance at all times. Rental cars *(p 274)* in the US are usually equipped with automatic transmission, and rental rates tend to be lower than those overseas. Gasoline is sold by the gallon (1 gal=3.8 liters) and is cheaper than in other countries. Most self-service gas stations do not offer car repair, although many sell standard maintenance items. Road regulations in the US require that vehicles be driven on the right-hand side of the road. Distances are posted in miles (1mi=1.62km).

Electricity – Voltage in the US is 120 volts AC, 60 Hz. Foreign-made appliances may need AC adapters (available at specialty travel and electronics stores) and North American flat-blade plugs.

Mail – *p 276.*

Temperature and Measurement – In the US temperatures are measured in degrees Fahrenheit and measurements are expressed according to the US Customary System of weights and measures.

Equivalents

Degrees Fahrenheit	95°	86°	77°	68°	59°	50°	41°	32°	23°	14°
Degrees Celsius	35°	30°	25°	20°	15°	10°	5°	0°	-5°	-10°

1 inch = 2.54 centimeters	1 foot = 30.48 centimeters
1 mile = 1.609 kilometers	1 pound = 0.454 kilograms
1 quart = 0.946 liters	1 gallon = 3.785 liters

Telephone – Instructions for using public telephones are listed on or near the phone. The cost for a local call from a pay phone is 35¢ (any combination of quarters, nickels or dimes). Some public telephones accept credit cards, and all will accept long-distance calling cards. Most hotels add surcharges for telephone calls. Unless otherwise indicated, most telephone numbers listed in this guide that start with "800," "888" or "877" are toll-free in the US only.

Getting Around

PUBLIC TRANSPORTATION

The San Francisco Municipal Railway (Muni) *(see below)* operates an extensive network of transportation lines using diesel and electric buses, light-rail streetcars and cable cars. Bus service to other areas is provided by **Golden Gate Transit** *(☎ 415-923-2000)*, serving Marin, Contra Costa and Sonoma Counties; **SamTrans** *(Mon–Fri 6am–10pm, weekends 8am–8pm, holidays 8am–3pm; ☎ 650-508-6455)*, serving San Mateo County; and **AC Transit** *(☎ 510-817-1717)*, serving Alameda and Contra Costa Counties. All arrivals/departures in San Francisco occur at the Transbay Terminal. The Bay Area Rapid Transit (BART) *(p 274)* commuter rail line links San Francisco with cities in the East Bay including Oakland and Berkeley. **CalTrain** *(☎ 415-495-4546)* commuter rail service runs between San Francisco and San Jose. The **Bay Area Traveler Information System** provides information on traffic conditions, routes and fares for all transportation systems in the San Francisco Bay Area *(☎ 415-817-1717)*. Transit Information for all agencies serving the nine-county San Francisco Bay area may be accessed online at www.transitinfo.org.

San Francisco Municipal Railway (Muni)

949 Presidio Ave., Room 238, San Francisco CA 94115; ☎ 415-673-6864, www.sfmuni.com. System maps *($2)* are sold at newsstands, map shops, some bookstores and the Muni main office *(in the summer tourist season, route maps may be difficult to find and may be purchased by mail; $2.50)*. System timetables are available from the Muni main office. In this guide, recommended transit lines are indicated with the **Muni** symbol.

Buses – Muni buses generally operate daily 5:30am–12:30am, every 4-20min; some routes on major corridors run 24hrs/day (**owl service** *designates late-night schedule*). Route number, name and destination are indicated on the front of the bus. Buses with the route name in black-and-white make all stops; green-and-white make limited stops, and red-and-white provide express service to destination only. Pickup points are recognizable by covered shelters and Muni signs (route numbers and names are clearly marked). Route maps are posted in bus shelters. More than half of the routes are accessible to riders with disabilities, and Muni is diligently expanding this service *(Muni Accessible Services ☎ 415-923-6142)*.

Metro Streetcars – Muni's five-line light-rail system runs underground below Market Street from The Embarcadero; surfacing to offer street-level transportation along The Embarcadero, eastern bayshore and outlying neighborhoods. The J-Church, K-Ingleside and M-Oceanview lines operate daily 5:30am-12:30am. The L-Taraval and N-Judah lines operate 24hrs/day (buses provide owl service). All lines run every 5-15min weekdays and every 10-20min evenings and weekends.

© Robert Holmes

San Francisco's Roller-Coaster Roads

Cable cars – *p 88*. As San Francisco's whimsical symbols, cable cars provide access to many attractions, including Chinatown and Fisherman's Wharf. Three lines operate daily 6am-12:30am, every 5-15min. The **Powell-Hyde** (PH) and **Powell-Mason** (PM) lines zigzag from Powell and Market Streets in the Union Square Area over Nob Hill to Fisherman's Wharf. The **California** (C) line runs along California Street through Chinatown from Market Street to Van Ness Avenue. Brown-and-white signs along the route indicate stops. Cable cars run in the middle of the streets, between the car lanes. Wait until the cable car comes to a complete stop before boarding or disembarking (on either side of the car). Watch out for oncoming traffic.

Historic Streetcars – *p 106*.

Fares – Bus and streetcar fares are $1 (exact fare required), cable cars $2 (change given). Discounted fares available for children, senior citizens and disabled persons. Transfers *(free)*, valid for buses and streetcars only and good for two changes, are issued when fare is paid. The Muni Passport allows unlimited travel on all systems for one day *($6)*, three days *($10)* and seven days *($15)*. They also entitle holders to discounts at many attractions. Muni Passports are sold at the Visitor Information Center *(p 56)*, TIX Bay Area *(p 53)* and Muni main office.

Bay Area Rapid Transit (BART)

800 Madison St., Oakland CA 94607-2688. ☎ *510-464-6000. www.bart.org.* This fast commuter rail line links San Francisco and East Bay cities including Oakland and Berkeley. BART runs Mon–Fri 4am–1:30am, Sat 6am–1:30am and Sun 8am–1:30am. Free route maps and schedules are available at stations. Machines sell tickets in each station, with fare determined by destination; not all machines provide change. Fares are discounted for children, senior citizens and disabled persons. Direction of trains is indicated on video monitors above boarding platforms. In this guide, recommended stations are indicated with the bà symbol.

Ferries *p 57*

Taxis

All San Francisco taxicab companies share the same rate schedule: $1.70 for the first mile and $1.80 for each additional mile. Taxis may not be readily available; it's best to call for a pickup. There are no extra fees for baggage handling or for assisting passengers with physical disabilities. The major cab companies in San Francisco are **Yellow Cab** ☎ 415-626-2345, **Veterans** ☎ 415-552-1300 and **National** ☎ 415-648-4444. (Others may be found in the Yellow Pages telephone directory.)

DRIVING IN SAN FRANCISCO

San Francisco Road Conditions: ☎ *415-557-3755.* Given the efficiency of public transportation, and the ease by which many sights are reached on foot, a car is not necessary in San Francisco. However, a car is recommended for visiting areas such as Marin County or the Wine Country. Roads are often congested and public parking lots expensive. Street parking, difficult to find, requires strict attention to posted curb colors and correctly curbed tires *(see "Parking" information below)*. **Rush hours**, the peak transit times for business commuters, occur weekdays 7:30am–9am and 4pm–6pm. Visitors are encouraged to avoid driving during these times.

Road Regulations – The maximum **speed limit** on major expressways is 65mph in rural areas and 55mph in and around cities. Speed limits within the city range from 25mph in residential areas to 35mph on major streets. Use of **seat belts** is mandatory for driver and passengers. Child safety seats are required for children under 4 years old or weighing less than 40 pounds (seats available from most rental car agencies). Drivers must always yield the **right of way** to cable cars and pedestrians.

Parking – When parking on a hill, drivers must block front wheels against the curb (facing downhill turn wheels *toward* curb, facing uphill turn wheels *away* from curb); use of parking brake is mandatory. Restricted parking is indicated by the color of curb: **red** (no standing or parking), **yellow** or **black** (loading zone), **white** (limited to 5min), **green** (limited to 10-30min), **blue** (reserved for the disabled). Neighborhood parking by permit only in many areas; check street signs carefully. Parking prohibited during posted street-cleaning times.

Car Rental

Major rental-car agencies maintain locations downtown and at San Francisco and Oakland airports. Most agencies rent only to persons at least 25 years old, although some will rent to younger drivers for a daily surcharge. A major credit card and valid driver's license are required. Some agencies also require proof of insurance. The average daily rate for a car ranges from $30–$40. Sales tax on car rentals is 8.5%.

Rental Company	Reservations ☎
Alamo	800-327-9633
Avis	800-331-1212
Budget	800-527-0700
Dollar	800-421-6868
Enterprise	800-325-8007
Hertz	800-654-3131
National	800-227-7368
Thrifty	800-331-4200

(Toll-free numbers may not be accessible outside of North America.)

General Information

Business Hours – Most businesses operate Mon-Fri 8am–5:30pm. Banks are usually open Mon-Fri 9am–3pm; some may have extended or Saturday hours. Department stores and shopping centers operate Mon-Sat 9:30am–8pm, Sun 11am–6pm; many extend their hours between Thanksgiving and Christmas. Smaller shops and stores (except those in Chinatown) are closed on Sundays.

Time Zone – San Francisco is on Pacific Standard Time (PST), 3hrs behind Eastern Standard Time (EST) and 8hrs behind Greenwich Mean Time (GMT). Daylight Savings Time (clocks advanced 1hr) is in effect for most of the US, including California, from the first Sunday in April until the last Sunday in October.

Major Holidays – Most banks and government offices in the San Francisco area are closed on the following legal holidays *(many retail stores and restaurants remain open on days indicated with *)*:

New Year's Day	January 1
Martin Luther King, Jr.'s Birthday*	3rd Monday in January
Presidents' Day*	3rd Monday in February
Memorial Day*	Last Monday in May or May 30
Independence Day*	July 4
Labor Day*	1st Monday in September
Columbus Day*	2nd Monday in October
Veterans Day*	2nd Monday in November
Thanksgiving Day	4th Thursday in November
Christmas Day	December 25

Money – Most banks are members of the network of Automatic Teller Machines (ATMs), which allows visitors from around the world to withdraw cash using bank cards and major credit cards 24hrs a day. ATMs can usually be found in banks, airports, grocery stores and shopping malls. Networks (Cirrus, Honor, Plus) that are serviced by the ATM are indicated on the machine. To inquire about ATM service, locations and transaction fees, contact your local bank, Cirrus (☎ *800-424-7787*) or Plus (☎ *800-843-7587*). For cash transfers, **Western Union** (☎ *800-325-6000; www.westernunion.com*) has agents throughout the Bay Area. Banks, most stores, restaurants and hotels accept **travelers checks** with picture identification. In San Francisco, **American Express Company Travel Service** offices are located at 560 California St., 455 Market St., 124 Geary St. and 333 Jefferson St. ☎ 415-536-2600. To report a lost or stolen **credit card**: American Express ☎ 800-528-4800; Diners Club ☎ 800-234-6377; MasterCard ☎ 800-307-7309; Visa ☎ 800-336-8472.

Taxes and Tipping – In California, the sales tax is 8.5%; cold food items are exempt. Hotel occupancy tax is 14% (not included in quoted hotel rates). Tax percentages in other areas (including Berkeley, Oakland, Marin County and the Wine Country) may vary. In restaurants, it is customary to tip the server 15-20% of the bill. At hotels, porters should be tipped $1 per suitcase and hotel maids $1 per day of occupancy. Taxi drivers are usually tipped 15% of the fare.

Liquor Law – The legal minimum age for purchase and consumption of alcoholic beverages is 21. Proof of age is normally required. Most bars stay open until 2am. Almost all packaged-goods stores sell beer, wine and liquor; legal hours of sale are 6am–2am.

TELEPHONE

Area Codes ☎

San Francisco (including Marin County)	415
Peninsula cities (south of Daly City, including San Mateo County)	650
East Bay (including Berkeley and Oakland)	510
East Bay (including Contra Costa County)	925
Wine Country	707

Important Numbers

Police/Ambulance/Fire (emergency, *24hrs*)	911
Police (non-emergency, *24hrs*)	415-553-0123
Physician Referrals (*Mon–Fri 9am–5pm*)	415-353-6566
Dental Referrals (*24hrs*)	415-421-1435
House Calls USA (*24hrs*)	800-468-3537

24hr Pharmacies

Walgreens	3201 Divisadero St. (Marina District)	415-931-6417
	498 Castro St. (Castro District)	415-861-3136
	25 Point Lobos Ave. (Richmond District)	415-386-0736
Time		415-767-8900
Weather		415-936-1212

Major TV Networks

ABC	Channel 7	FOX	Channel 2
CBS	Channel 5	NBC	Channel 4
CNN	Channel 3	PBS	Channel 9

Major Radio Stations

88.5 FM	Public Radio	102.1 FM	Classical	680 AM	Sports/talk
93.3 FM	Country	103.7 FM	Jazz	810 AM	News/talk
97.3 FM	Rock	104.5 FM	Alternative	1550 AM	News/talk

Newspapers and Magazines – San Francisco's two main daily newspapers are the *San Francisco Chronicle* (morning) and the *San Francisco Examiner* (afternoon). The Sunday edition, the *Chronicle-Examiner* is published jointly and features an extensive arts-and-entertainment supplement. Two weekly alternative papers, *The San Francisco Bay Guardian* and the *SF Weekly*, both published on Wednesday, offer different perspectives of the city as well as diverse and comprehensive entertainment sections. These free publications are available in newspaper boxes and cafes. the *Bay Area Reporter* and the *San Francisco Bay Times* cater to the gay community. In addition, many neighborhood groups publish papers featuring upcoming events and social happenings in their areas.

Mail – Post offices located throughout the San Francisco Bay Area operate Monday–Friday 8am–5pm (some have extended weekday and Saturday hours). First-class rates within the US: letter 34¢ (1oz), postcard 20¢. Overseas: letter generally 80¢ (1oz), postcard or aerogramme 70¢. Letters and small packages can be mailed from most hotels. Stamps and packing material may be purchased at many convenience and drugstores, and at post offices. Businesses offering postal and express shipping services are located throughout the city *(see Yellow Pages of phone directory under Mailing Services)*. Postal Service Information Line *(Mon–Fri 8am–6pm;* ☎ *800-725-2161; www.usps.gov)*.

Fax Services – Many hotels, and businesses that offer copying or mailing services, will send or receive faxes for a per-page fee.

Safety Tips – San Francisco is considered a relatively safe city, but visitors should heed the following common-sense tips to ensure a safe and enjoyable visit:

- Avoid carrying large sums of money, and don't let strangers see how much money you are carrying.

- Keep a firm hold of purses and knapsacks, carry your wallet in your front pocket, and avoid wearing expensive jewelry.

- Stay awake when riding on public transportation, and keep packages close by. Muni and BART vehicles are equipped with devices that enable riders to notify personnel of emergencies.

- Always park your car in a well-lit area. Close windows, lock doors and place valuables in the trunk.

- Exercise caution when visiting or traveling through the **Tenderloin** (roughly bounded by Golden Gate Ave., Van Ness Ave., O'Farrell St. and Mason St.), the **Western Addition** (the blocks immediately west of Civic Center, and south of Japantown); and the **Mission District** (the blocks east of Valencia and north of 16th Streets).

Earthquake Precautions – Although severe earthquakes are infrequent, they are also unpredictable, and earthquake preparedness is a fact of life in the San Francisco Bay Area. If an earthquake strikes when you are **outside**, move to an open area away from trees, buildings or power lines. If you are in a **vehicle**, decrease speed, pull to the side of the road and stop. Do not park on or under bridges; sit on the floor of the vehicle if possible. If you are in a **building**, stand within a doorway or sit under a sturdy table. Stay away from windows and outside walls. Remain in a safe place until shaking stops, and be prepared for aftershocks. If possible, listen to the radio or TV for advisories.

TIPS FOR SPECIAL VISITORS

Children

Throughout this guide, sights of particular interest to children are indicated with a Kids symbol. Many of these attractions offer special children's programs. Most attractions in San Francisco offer discounted admission to visitors under 18 years of age. In addition, many hotels offer family discount packages, and some restaurants provide a children's menu.

Travelers with Disabilities

Throughout this guide, full wheelchair accessibility is indicated in admission information accompanying sight descriptions by a ♿ symbol. All **BART** trains and stations and most **Muni** lines are wheelchair-accessible. The *Muni Access Guide* gives helpful hints for disabled persons using the system *(free from Muni Accessible Services, 949 Presidio Ave., San Francisco CA 94115; ☎ 415-923-6142, TTY 415-923-6366; www.sfmuni.com).* Both transit services offer discounts to persons with disabilities; contact telephone numbers on pp 273-274 for more information. Disabled visitors can obtain a temporary parking permit from the Department of Motor Vehicles *(1377 Fell St., San Francisco CA 94117; ☎ 415-557-1179).*

A Wheelchair Rider's Guide to San Francisco Bay and Nearby Shorelines provides a wealth of information about many sights in the Bay Area *(free from the California State Coastal Conservancy; ☎ 510-286-1015).*

Disabled travelers using **Amtrak** and **Greyhound** *(pp 270-271)* should contact these companies prior to their trip to make special arrangements and receive useful brochures. For information about travel for individuals or groups, contact the Society for the Advancement of Travel for the Handicapped, *(347 5th Ave., Suite 610, New York NY 10016; ☎ 212-447-7284; www.sath.org).*

Senior Citizens

Most attractions, hotels and restaurants offer discounts to visitors age 62 and older (proof of age may be required). For information regarding events, policies and programs contact the Senior Citizen Information Line, ☎ 415-626-1033. Additional information may be obtained from the American Association of Retired Persons (AARP), *(601 E St., NW, Washington DC 20049; ☎ 202-434-2277; www.aarp.com).*

Accommodations

San Francisco offers a wide range of accommodations, from elegant hotels *($200-$500/night)* to moderately priced motels *($75/night and up).* The majority of hotels are clustered around the Union Square Area. Rates tend to be higher at Nob Hill, Financial District and Fisherman's Wharf establishments. Many motels can be found along Lombard Street in the Marina District. Amenities usually include television, restaurant and smoking/non-smoking rooms. More elegant hotels also offer workout facilities, room service and valet service. Downtown hotels normally charge a daily fee in excess of $20 for parking; all room rates are subject to a 14 percent city hotel tax. Breakfast is not usually included. A similar variety of lodgings is available in the East Bay. Hotels are listed in the *San Francisco Lodging Guide ($3 with the San Francisco Book)* from the San Francisco Convention and Visitors Bureau *(p 268).*

Hotels/Motels – San Francisco is well-known for its proliferation of small, often independently owned "boutique" hotels. These small luxury inns reflect the historic flavor of the city in ways that large, modern lodgings cannot. Three local hotel groups that enjoy pairing their properties with individuals are the **Kimpton Group** *(222 Kearny St., Suite 200, San Francisco CA 94108; ☎ 415-397-5572; www.kimptongroup.com).* **Joie de Vivre Hotels** *(567 Sutter St., San Francisco CA 94102; ☎ 415-835-0300; www.sftrips.com)* and **Personality Hotels** *(639 Sutter St., San Francisco CA 94102; ☎ 415-202-8700; www.personalityhotels.com).*

Major national hotel chains are widely represented in the Bay Area. Locations include:

Best Western	800-528-1234 www.bestwestern.com	Mandarin Oriental	800-622-0404, www.mandarin oriental.com
Choice Hotels	800-424-6423 www.choicehotels.com	Marriott	800-228-9290, www.marriott.com
Hilton	800-445-8667 www.hilton.com	Pan Pacific	800-327-8585, www.panpac.com
Holiday Inn	800-465-4329 www.holiday-inn.com	Radisson	800-333-3333, www.radisson.com
Hyatt	800-233-1234 www.hyatt.com	Ramada	800-228-2828, www.ramada.com
Inter-Continental	800-662-4455, www.interconti.com	Ritz-Carlton	800-241-3333, www.ritzcarlton .com
ITT Sheraton	800-325-3535, www.sheraton.com	Westin	800-228-3000, www.westin.com

Reservation Services

Accommodations Express
www.accommodationsexpress.com   800-906-4685

California Reservations
www.californiares.com   800-576-0003

Central Reservation Service
www.reservation-services.com   800-548-3311

Hotel Reservation Network
www.hoteldiscount.com   800-715-7666

San Francisco Convention & Visitors Bureau Leisure Reservation Service
www.sfvisitor.org   888-782-9673

San Francisco Reservations
www.hotelres.com   800-677-1500

SF Trips
www.sftrips.com   800-738-7477

(Toll-free numbers may not be accessible outside of North America.)

Bed and Breakfasts – Many privately owned historic homes outside the downtown area are operated as B&Bs ($80–$200/day). Continental breakfast is customarily included. Private baths are not always available, and smoking indoors is not usually allowed. The following reservation services represent properties in San Francisco and throughout the Bay Area: **Bed & Breakfast San Francisco,** *(PO Box 420009, San Francisco CA 94142;* ☎ *415-899-0060, 800-452-8249; www.bbsf.com);* **American Property Exchange,** *(2800 Van Ness Ave., San Francisco CA 94109;* ☎ *415-447-2000, 800-747-7784; www.we-rent-sanfran.com);* **The Independent Innkeepers Association,** *(PO Box 150, Marshall MI 49068;* ☎ *616-789-0393 or 800-344-5244; www.innbook.com).*

Hostels and apartments – A no-frills, economical option, **hostels** charge $14–$25 per night. Amenities include a community living room, showers, laundry facilities, full-service kitchen and dining room, dormitory-style and private rooms. (Guests must bring their own towels.) See budget lodging alternatives in the Address Book for specifics. Furnished apartment rentals *(starting at $100/day)* are available through **American Property Exchange** *(above).*

Index

S

Notes